MANAGEMENT ACCOUNTING

EDITION 2

W. STEVE ALBRECHT, PhD, CPA, CIA, CFE
Brigham Young University

JAMES D. STICE, PhD
Brigham Young University

EARL K. STICE, PhD
Brigham Young University

K. FRED SKOUSEN, PhD, CPA
Brigham Young University

MONTE R. SWAIN, PhD, CPA, CMA
(Consulting Editor)
Brigham Young University

SOUTH-WESTERN
THOMSON LEARNING™

Australia · Canada · Mexico · Singapore · Spain · United Kingdom · United States

Management Accounting, 2e, by W. Steve Albrecht, James D. Stice, Earl K. Stice, K. Fred Skousen, and Monte R. Swain (Consulting Editor)

Publisher: Dave Shaut
Acquisitions Editor: Sharon Oblinger
Developmental Editor: Leslie Kauffman, Litten Editing and Production, Inc.
Production Editor: Kara ZumBahlen
Manufacturing Coordinator: Doug Wilke
Marketing Manager: Dan Silverburg
Promotions Manager: Jon Schneider
Photo Research: Fred Middendorf
Photo Manager: Cary Benbow
Cover Design: Lamson Design/Cincinnati
Cover Photography: Greg Grosse Photography/Cincinnati
Internal Design: Michael H. Stratton
Production House: Peggy Shelton, Litten Editing and Production, Inc.
Compositor: GGS Information Services
Printer: R.R. Donnelley, Willard

Printed in the United States of America
1 2 3 4 5 04 03 02 01

For more information contact South-Western, 5101 Madison Road, Cincinnati, Ohio, 45227 or find us on the Internet at http://www.swcollege.com

For permission to use material from this text or product, contact us by
- **telephone: 1-800-730-2214**
- **fax: 1-800-730-2215**
- **web: http://www.thomsonrights.com**

ISBN: 0-324-06759-3 (text and CD)
ISBN: 0-324-11169-X (text only)
ISBN: 0-324-06760-7 (CD only)

Library of Congress Cataloging-in-Publication Data

Management accounting/W. Steve Albrecht ... [et al.] — 2nd ed.
p. cm.
Includes bibliographical references and indexes.
ISBN 0-324-06759-3
1. Managerial accounting I. Albrecht, W. Steve.

HF5657.4 .M3284 2001
658.15'11—dc21 00-067079

photo credits

Page 12	© Bettmann/CORBIS
Page 38	© Manfred Vollmer/CORBIS
Page 53	© 2001/PhotoDisc, Inc.
Page 104	© Bettmann/CORBIS
Page 111	© 2001/PhotoDisc, Inc.
Page 182	© George Hall/CORBIS
Page 193	© Michael S. Yamashita/CORBIS
Page 232	© 2001/PhotoDisc, Inc.
Page 248	© 2001/PhotoDisc, Inc.
Page 298	© Sergio Dorantes/CORBIS
Page 315	© 2001/PhotoDisc, Inc.
Page 344	© Bob Rowan; Progressive Image/CORBIS
Page 353	© Dave Bartruff/CORBIS
Page 406	© 2001/PhotoDisc, Inc.
Page 410	© Philip Gould/CORBIS
Page 456	© 2001/PhotoDisc, Inc.
Page 474	© 2001/PhotoDisc, Inc.
Page 522	© Premium Stock/CORBIS
Page 529	© 2001/PhotoDisc, Inc.

brief contents

contents

PART m3
Control 297

Appendices

Management Accounting Indexes

The Best Team

Authors **W. Steve Albrecht, James D. Stice, Earl K. Stice,** and **K. Fred Skousen,** and Consulting Editor **Monte R. Swain** are all key players in the curriculum change process at Brigham Young University. Individually and as a team, the authors feel passionately about making this the most relevant and useful book you will ever use.

W. Steve Albrecht is the Arthur Andersen & Co. Alumni Professor of Accountancy and the Director of the School of Accountancy & Information Systems at Brigham Young University. He received a bachelor's degree in accounting from Brigham Young University and MBA and Ph.D. degrees from the University of Wisconsin at Madison. Dr. Albrecht, a certified public accountant, certified internal auditor, and certified fraud examiner, came to BYU in 1977 after teaching at Stanford and at the University of Illinois. Earlier in his career, he worked as a staff accountant for Deloitte & Touche. Dr. Albrecht has received numerous awards and honors, including the BYU School of Management's Outstanding Faculty Award and the BYU Outstanding Researcher Award, and was recognized, as part of Utah's Centennial Celebration, as one of 131 Utahians who have made outstanding contributions or brought unusual recognition to the state. Dr. Albrecht has served as President of the American Accounting Association, the Administrators of Accounting Programs Group, and the Association of Certified Fraud Examiners and is currently president-elect of Beta Alpha Psi.

James D. Stice is the Distinguished Teaching Professor of Accounting at Brigham Young University. He is also the Associate Director of BYU's MBA program. He holds bachelor's and master's degrees from BYU and a Ph.D. from the University of Washington, all in accounting. He has been on the faculty at BYU since 1988. During that time, he has been selected by graduating accounting students as "Teacher of the Year" on numerous occasions, selected by his peers in the Marriott School of Management at BYU to receive the "Outstanding Teaching Award," and received the University's top award for teaching excellence, the Maeser Award, in 1999. Professor Stice has published articles in *The Accounting Review, Decision Sciences, Issues in Accounting Education, The CPA Journal,* and other academic and professional journals.

Earl K. Stice is the PricewaterhouseCoopers Professor of Accounting in the School of Accountancy & Information Systems at Brigham Young University. He holds bachelor's and master's degrees from Brigham Young University and a Ph.D. from Cornell University. Dr. Stice has taught at Rice University, the University of Arizona, Cornell University, and the Hong Kong University of Science and Technology (HKUST). He won the Phi Beta Kappa teaching award at Rice University and was twice selected at HKUST as one of the ten best lecturers on campus. Dr. Stice has also taught in a variety of executive education and corporate training programs in the United States, Hong Kong, and South Africa. He has published papers in the *Journal of Financial and Quantitative Analysis, The Accounting Review, Review of Accounting Studies,* and *Issues in Accounting Education*, and his research on stock splits has been cited in *Business Week, Money,* and *Forbes.*

K. Fred Skousen is Advancement Vice President at Brigham Young University. Previously, he was Dean of the Marriott School of Management and Director of the School of Accountancy at BYU. He earned a bachelor's degree from BYU and master's and Ph.D. degrees from the University of Illinois. Dr. Skousen taught at the University of Illinois and the University of Minnesota prior to joining the faculty at Brigham Young University. In 1983, Dr. Skousen was awarded the Peat Marwick Professorship at BYU. In 1984, Dr. Skousen was elected to the AICPA Council, and in 1985, he received the UACPA Outstanding Faculty Award.

Monte R. Swain is an Associate Professor of management accounting and information systems at Brigham Young University. He received his undergraduate degree in accounting and his master's degree in management accounting from BYU. In 1992, Dr. Swain received his Ph.D. in management accounting and information systems from Michigan State University, received a university-wide teaching award, and was honored with the department's Outstanding Doctoral Scholar Award. At BYU, he has received the college Teaching Excellence Award several times, was named the Marriott School of Management Outstanding Teacher in 1999, and is listed on the Outstanding Faculty List in *Business Week*'s "Guide to the Best Business Schools." Dr. Swain has published papers in a number of journals, including *Decision Sciences, Behavioral Research in Accounting,* the *Journal of Accounting Case Research,* the *Case Research Journal, Advances in Accounting Education,* and the *Journal of Accounting Education.*

How the Best got Better.

preface

edition 2

A Benchmark Text—Raising the Bar Even Higher

Management Accounting has come to be the text by which all others are judged. With the perfect blend of procedure and concepts, the text gives students an inside, realistic view of how accounting is done in leading companies across the nation and around the world. Now in its second successful edition, the book takes the bar up a notch by offering a combination of new and proven features that make the best even better:

- New! An enhanced integration of real company financial information and real-world examples gives students a clear picture of how to use accounting information
- New! A completely integrated learning system that includes elements for classroom learning, technology-assisted learning, and distance learning
- Unique Competency Enhancement Opportunities (CEO) included in the end-of-chapter material, which enhance students' skills in critical thinking, ethics, oral and written communications, electronic research, and teamwork
- Specialized customer service through trained and personal consultants

How the Best got Better

The Best Language for Business

In order for today's student to be the best, they must have a complete understanding of the numbers. Understanding what the numbers reveal, and what they do not reveal, allows business managers and investors to make every type of business decision: expand, merge, close, launch, subcontract, downsize, invest, reposition, lease, replace. As the basis for all these decisions, accounting is the universal language of business. This edition makes it even easier to understand what the numbers mean.

Take, for instance, the case of Wal-Mart, as examined in the opening vignette of **Chapter 6: Traditional Cost Management.** In just forty years, Wal-Mart has grown from a small five-and-dime store in rural Arkansas to become the world's #1 retailer. Much of Wal-Mart's success can be attributed to the effective management of accounting information and the evolution of its industry-leading cost control and distribution systems. Precise expense control allows Wal-Mart to maintain its consistent low-price structure. Its sophisticated distribution system drives timely, cost-efficient movement of inventory from suppliers to stores all around the world. Given that Wal-Mart operates over 4,000 stores, and that each store has over 70,000 items in stock at any one time, this is no small feat!

What does the Wal-Mart experience tell us? It tells us that to truly comprehend what is going on in a business, whether in the retail store or in the corporate boardroom, one must understand accounting data—both how it is prepared, and why it is meaningful.

Changing for the Better

The past few years have seen many calls for improving accounting education. This call for change drove the first edition of **Management Accounting** to be the best book on the market. The central themes in all these calls for change have been (1) that the business world and accounting professions are changing rapidly, (2) that accountants of the past must become the premier information professionals of the future, and (3) that accounting and business graduates need new skills and knowledge if they are to effectively meet tomorrow's professional demands. We answered those calls by creating a textbook that teaches students both how to interpret financial information and how to use that accounting information to make smart business decisions.

In creating this Second Edition, we crafted a textbook that does an even better job of addressing the needs of an ever-changing world of accounting education. **Management Accounting,** Second Edition is written and organized in a manner that allows students and instructors at all institutions to capitalize on our positive curriculum development experience and strive to make the best education even better.

The Best Business is Real Business

We are working hard to address a growing demand for an introductory textbook that places management accounting in a context of supporting the strategic and operating management processes. In addition, we recognize that students learn, and retain learning, better when the material is "hands on" and is placed in context. Hence, in this edition, we have divided the presentation into four parts.

In the **Foundations** section of the textbook, we establish the need for management accounting and distinguish that need from the impetus for financial accounting. We then introduce students to the management process of planning, controlling, and evaluating organizations. In this context, we introduce students to the classic terminology of management accounting. However, we avoid the typical "list approach" of terms. Instead, terms and concepts are introduced in the process of *using* accounting to support planning, controlling, and evaluating processes. With students oriented to using accounting to support the management process, we proceed directly to what is likely one of the most interesting and elegant user aspects of management accounting—cost–volume–profit (i.e., breakeven) analysis. We end the Foundations section by using product cost flows to compare and contrast the three types of classic business structure—manufacturing, merchandising, and service. The advent of e-business and its impact on these three business structures are also introduced.

In the **Planning** section of the textbook, we describe strategic planning and use that understanding as a lead-in to teach the tools of capital budgeting. The next chapter in this section describes the differences between strategic and operational management and presents operational budgeting. In contrast to many other introductory textbooks, this chapter presents some concrete material on revenue budgeting and analysis.

The first chapter in the **Controlling** section of the textbook describes traditional product costing issues specific to manufacturing, merchandising, and service organizations, and describes some impacts of e-business on product costing for these organizations. The next chapter introduces some of the groundbreaking cost and process management tools of the last 20 years, including ABC, TQM, and JIT.

Finally, the **Evaluating** section of the textbook leads off with a chapter that introduces students to classic management accounting evaluation tools for products and processes. The next chapter focuses on evaluation of personnel (managers) and divisions. Finally, the textbook concludes by introducing students to the fact that competitive world markets demand that management accounting continues to grow and expand to support new management needs. In this context, nonfinancial, strategy-focused measures (as currently captured in the Balanced Scorecard model) are presented, and students are encouraged to participate as users and providers of future changes and enhancements to the management accounting discipline.

Ahead of the Curve

With the Best Technology

Today's students learn in more visual and interactive ways than ever before. These are students that have grown up in a multimedia- and technology-enhanced world. In order to educate these students, technology must be employed as an efficient means for both teaching and learning accounting. Educators now have the opportunity to bring more information to students in more media than ever before. **Management Accounting** takes full advantage of these possibilities with the best technology package that fills a variety of needs.

The technology package consists of three distinct elements that can effectively be woven together. The three elements are *Product Web Site, Personal Trainer,* and the *Personal Web Tutor.* Some key facets to this package include:

- Lecture Replacement/Enhancement
- Concept Reinforcement
- Application
- Competency/Testing/Quizzing
- Remediation

Flexible Coverage

Brings out the Best in Instructors

Because the authors know that the best instructors continually try to make their classrooms better, we have preserved the text's innovation of dividing most chapters into two parts. This flexibility allows the instructor the chance to easily alter what they cover in class to fit the needs of their particular students. The first part includes material that needs to be covered to understand essential accounting concepts, while the second part features "expanded material" dealing with additional topics to be covered at the instructor's discretion.

This strategy of dividing chapters into basic and expanded material was universally applauded by users of our first edition. It allows significant flexibility in covering desired material, without the disruption of skipping to appendices for more advanced material. Also note that end-of-chapter materials are divided and labeled to coincide with the essential/expanded division in the chapters.

The Best of the Best

Outstanding Features

This edition makes the connection to real-life business even better with the use of many insightful pedagogical features and real-world examples. As real companies and current events are examined, the focus is not only on how business managers collect and record data, but also why the information is important as the basis for decisions. For example, Microsoft's annual report is provided at the end of the text and referenced throughout.

Special Margin Features

FYI
FYI features provide relevant information for students, drawing from real business events or situations.

STOP & THINK
Students are encouraged to take a step back occasionally to consider thought-provoking issues.

CAUTION
These reminders speak directly to students, helping them avoid common mistakes or misconceptions.

NET WORK
These exercises give students practice in seeking out information on the Internet.

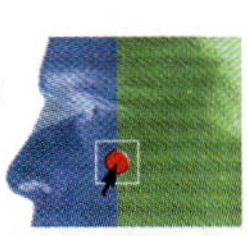

Other Pedagogy

LEARNING OBJECTIVES Each chapter begins with specific learning objectives to guide students in their study of the chapter. Where applicable, chapters include expanded learning objectives.

SETTING THE STAGE An interesting, real-life scenario sets the stage for each chapter. These scenarios tie directly to materials covered in the chapter and help students relate chapter topics to actual business happenings. For example, Chapter 4 begins with a discussion of FedEx.

BUSINESS ENVIRONMENT ESSAYS The text contains numerous real-world vignettes, adapted from financial newspapers and business publications, which illustrate important concepts being discussed. These examples enable students to see how the accounting topics they are studying are applied and interpreted in real-world situations.

More Outstanding Features

KEY TERMS Throughout each chapter, key terms are defined in the margins. A list of key terms (with page references) is presented at the end of each chapter, and all key terms are defined in a comprehensive glossary at the end of the book.

SUMMARIES Several concise summaries are presented within each chapter to help students remember the important points just discussed, and each chapter concludes with a comprehensive summary, organized by learning objectives.

REVIEW PROBLEMS A review problem is provided at the end of each chapter. These review problems (with solutions) demonstrate the application of the major concepts and procedures covered in the chapter.

COMPREHENSIVE PROBLEMS Two comprehensive problems, integrating multiple issues and methods, are found throughout the text.

FOCUS ON GLOBAL ECONOMY The focus in today's business world is on a global economy. To help students develop this global perspective, many international examples are provided throughout the Second Edition. In addition, there is at least one International Case provided at the end of each chapter.

International

FOCUS ON ETHICS Ethical considerations are increasingly important in all aspects of business. Each chapter contains an Ethics Case relating to the topics covered in the chapter. These cases present ethical dilemmas that require students to think about behavioral and moral issues in business and accounting. We believe these ethics cases will provide a basis for rich classroom discussions and more responsible business conduct by students exposed to them.

Practice Makes the Best Better

The old adage *"practice makes perfect"* holds true in accounting. This book has all the traditional end-of-chapter assignments which has rendered it the best. Before describing the traditional material, however, we want you to understand our excitement for what makes this book even better: the **Competency Enhancement Opportunities** (CEO) that are included in the end-of-chapter material. Responding to well-justified calls for changes in accounting education, this material is included to help students develop critical thinking, ethical perspectives, oral and written communication skills, experience with electronic research, and team skills.

In each chapter's assignments, the CEO section begins with *Analyzing Real Company Information* exercises, based on actual company annual reports and data. CEO also includes:

- *International cases*, focusing on businesses that operate across international borders
- *Ethics cases*, examining issues of personal and business responsibilities
- *Writing assignments*, to be completed individually or in groups
- *Debates*, requiring two teams to argue the opposing sides of an accounting issue
- *Internet search exercises*, requiring students to find specific information on the Net

We believe students will find these assignments very relevant, interesting, and beneficial in their business careers.

Users have responded favorably to the traditional end-of-chapter assignments in previous editions. The discussion questions are intended to refine students' understanding of specific accounting terms and concepts. Discussion cases encourage classroom discussion of real-world business situations. Exercises deal with single concepts, and each can be completed fairly quickly. Problems probe for a deeper level of understanding. Those problems identified as "Unifying Concepts" and those with "Interpretive Questions" require students to analyze or interpret the computed results.

The Best Support, the Best Service

Because we know how difficult management accounting can be to both teach and learn, we are not satisfied with merely offering the best textbook. We take it one step better by offering the most comprehensive and carefully prepared educational package available today.

The package accompanying **Management Accounting** consists of more than simple "supplements." Taken in whole, it is a comprehensive teaching and learning system that incorporates the Internet, powerful multimedia, and exceptional printed materials—all coming together to create an educational experience unlike any other. Using the text in combination with these well-designed ancillaries makes it simple—and smart—to integrate technology into your course and makes it easy to be the best that you can be.

For more information on any of these supplements, don't hesitate to contact your South-Western/Thomson Learning™ sales representative. They are committed to providing you with unparalleled service and support.

Ancillary Materials

Available to Instructors

Thomson Learning is committed to providing you, our educational partners, with the best educational resources available. Because we prepare our instructor resources with a variety of teaching environments in mind, it is likely that you will need only a portion of these for your course. Before you request an item, we ask that you please read thoroughly the description of each resource. If you still need more information about resources, we urge you to contact your local Thomson Learning sales representative or visit our Web site at http://albrecht.swcollege.com. Many teaching and learning resources can be downloaded directly from this site.

Instructor's Resource CD This CD contains all the resources listed below (except the videos) in an easily accessible format. No longer will you have to lug heavy print items from school to home back to school again. This CD is your one-stop resource for assistance in teaching your course.

Web Site This site, http://albrecht.swcollege.com, contains downloadable supplements, interactive quizzes, Internet exercises and related URLs, accounting career information, lecture enhancement slides, and numerous other teaching resources.

Solutions Manual (Prepared by W. Steve Albrecht, James D. Stice, Earl K. Stice, and Monte R. Swain) This manual contains independently verified answers to all end-of-chapter discussion questions, discussion cases, exercises, problems, and Competency Enhancement Opportunities (CEO). Suggested solutions to the Stop & Think questions are also included.

Instructor's Manual (Prepared by Michael Shapeero, Bloomsburg University) This manual contains learning objectives, chapter outlines, topical overviews of end-of-chapter materials, and assignment classifications with level of difficulty and estimated completion time. Transparency masters for each chapter are also provided.

Test Bank (Prepared by Peggy Hussey) The revised and expanded test bank contains a collection of more than 800 examination problems, multiple-choice questions, true-false questions, and matching exercises, all accompanied by solutions.

ExamView® Computerized Testing Software This supplement contains all of the questions in the printed test bank. This program is an easy-to-use test creation software compatible with Microsoft Windows®. Instructors can add or edit questions, instructions, and answers, and select questions (randomly or numerically) by previewing them on the screen. Instructors can also create and administer quizzes online, whether over the Internet, a local area network (LAN), or a wide area network (WAN).

Solutions Transparencies Acetate transparencies of solutions for all end-of-chapter exercises and problems are available to text adopters.

PowerPoint™ Slides (Prepared by Michael Blue, Bloomsburg University) Selected teaching transparency slides of key concepts and exhibits are available in PowerPoint presentation software, improving lecture organization and reducing preparation time.

Teaching Transparencies Acetate transparencies of key concepts and exhibits are available to text adopters.

BusinessLink™ Video A management accounting video features segments of actual companies illustrating key accounting concepts. An Instructor's Manual is available to assist in the use of the video and the optional student workbook.

Available to Students

Personal Trainer Online (Hints and Tips prepared by Suneel Maheshwari, Marshall University)
This Internet-based resource is designed to help students complete end-of-chapter assignments with helpful hints and interactive tips. By giving students this additional assistance in applying the concepts of the course you are ensuring their understanding of complex topics.

Study Guide (Prepared by W. Steve Albrecht, James D. Stice, Earl K. Stice, and Monte R. Swain)
The study guide provides a means for students to re-examine the concepts and procedures in each chapter from several different perspectives. This publication includes learning objectives; detailed chapter summaries; discussions of topics that typically cause problems for students and suggestions for overcoming those problems; and tests for student self-assessment.

Working Papers Forms for solving end-of-chapter problems are perforated for easy removal and use.

Spreadsheet Templates (Prepared by Michael Blue, Bloomsburg University)
Excel templates are provided for solving selected end-of-chapter exercises and problems, which are identified with the spreadsheet icon.

BusinessLink™ Video Workbook This workbook enriches understanding of the BusinessLink video through questions and related activities.

Personal Finance Resource CD-ROM This supplement helps students understand how the concepts they learn in the textbook can assist them in making better personal financial decisions. Topics have been chosen and ordered to correlate with the chapters in the textbook.

Acknowledgements

Throughout the textbook, relevant publications of standard-setting and professional organizations are discussed, quoted, or paraphrased. We are indebted to the American Accounting Association, the American Institute of Certified Public Accountants, and the Financial Accounting Standards Board for material from their publications.

The second edition of **Management Accounting** reflects many comments and suggestions from colleagues and students, all of which are deeply appreciated. In particular, we wish to thank the following accounting educators who have served as reviewers, diary keepers, and focus group participants:

Anwer Ahmed	Syracuse University
Matthew J. Anderson	Michigan State University
James W. Bannister	University of Hartford
Benjamin W. Bean	Utah Valley State College
Patricia A. Doherty	Boston University
Janice Glatt	North Dakota State University
Jeri Griego	Laramie County Community College
Gerald Lobo	Syracuse University
Robert L. Putman	University of Tennessee at Martin
Donald J. Raux	Sienna College
Lola Rhodes	Southern Methodist University
Frederic M. Stiner, Jr.	University of Delaware
Cynthia VanGelderen	Aquinas College

We would like to thank Cathy Xanthaky Larson, Middlesex Community College, for checking the accuracy of the text and solutions manual. Her meticulous review contributed to a more concise, higher-quality product. We would also like to thank James Emig, Villanova University, who served as verifier for the test bank and study guide.

Steve Albrecht
Jim Stice
Kay Stice
Fred Skousen
Monte Swain

part m1

Foundations

Introduction to Management Accounting

chapter **m1**

learning objectives

After studying this chapter, you should be able to:

1 Understand the essential differences between management accounting and financial accounting, as illustrated by managerial use of the ROI formula.

2 Understand that successfully managing a company requires good information that supports effective planning, controlling, and evaluating processes.

3 Know how the concepts of fixed and variable costs are used in C-V-P analysis in the management planning process.

4 Realize how the product cost classifications of direct materials, direct labor, and overhead are used in the management controlling process.

5 Be able to perform a simple segment analysis using the concepts of direct, indirect, and opportunity costs in the management evaluating process.

6 Understand that management accounting still continues to evolve.

setting the stage

You've probably never heard of **E. I. DU PONT DE NEMOURS AND COMPANY**, but you may be familiar with its more common name, **DUPONT**. Some of this company's best-known brands are Teflon® resins, SilverStone® nonstick finish, Lycra® spandex fiber, Stainmaster® stain-resistant carpet, Kevlar® fiber, Corian® solid surface material, Mylar® polyester films, Tyvek® spunbonded olefin fabric, and Coolmax® and Cordura® textile fibers. With revenues of nearly $28 billion and net income of nearly $8 billion in 1999, DuPont ranked number 42 in the Fortune 500 list. DuPont operates in approximately 70 countries worldwide with roughly 135 manufacturing and processing facilities. Working in these facilities are 94,000 employees; nearly one-third of them work outside the United States. In addition to its manufacturing and processing facilities, DuPont has more than 40 research and development and customer service labs in the United States and more than 35 labs in 11 other countries. This is a big company! So what does this company have to do with you (other than that you probably use many of its products)? In 1903, the owners of DuPont created for themselves a challenge that no one had ever before attempted. The way they handled this challenge profoundly affected the way American companies are managed today and permanently changed our approach to management accounting. So, if you want to understand the importance of management accounting in America (as well as in many other countries around the world), you need to put yourself in the shoes of three cousins, Alfred, Coleman, and Pierre du Pont.

One of the oldest continuously operating industrial enterprises in the world, the DuPont company was established in 1802 near Wilmington, Delaware, by a French immigrant, Eleuthére Irénée du Pont de Nemours, to produce black powder. Essentially, E. I. du Pont built a product that ignited when it was supposed to. Public enthusiasm for du Pont's product continued, and the company grew into a major family corporation. The start of the twentieth century brought increased competition from other companies, however, and DuPont fell on hard times. Seizing the opportunity created by the crisis, three of E. I. du Pont's great-grandsons, Alfred I. du Pont, Thomas Coleman du Pont, and Pierre Samuel du Pont, offered to purchase the firm's assets from the family in exchange for bonds and stock in a new corporation (a transaction known today as a leveraged buyout). The offer was accepted. In 1902, the company was restructured to look for new business and create new products through research and development.

Alfred, Coleman, and Pierre had some pretty innovative ideas about running a business. In 1903, the gunpowder industry looked much like any other industry in America. All of DuPont's competitors in the industry focused primarily on manufacturing. They purchased raw materials (such as charcoal, sodium nitrate, and crude glycerin) from suppliers and distributed their gunpowder products to customers using independent wholesalers and general merchants. For the du Pont cousins, the business they purchased looked a lot like the left side of Exhibit 1-1. After the purchase, they decided to expand the business beyond the manufacturing of high explosives, smokeless gunpowder, and black blasting powder. The DuPonts started "forward integrating" into the distribution business by creating their own network of branch sales offices scattered across the United States. They also "backward integrated" by buying out many (but not all) of their suppliers. When the dust finally settled, DuPont was America's first large-scale "vertically integrated" company (the right side of Exhibit 1-1). Most of the profits usually earned by outside companies (either selling DuPont products to customers or selling raw materials to DuPont) were now consolidated within DuPont. This type of organization is quite common today, but it was a strange-looking company at the turn of the twentieth century. Although Alfred, Coleman, and Pierre were confident that their new way of doing business was going to make them a lot of money (they were right!), they had created a serious challenge for themselves. They knew how to run a manufacturing business, but now they were in the purchasing and sales business as well. These were three very different businesses, each with its own way of communicating results and measuring success. The three cousins had a limited amount of time and resources to invest in developing their company. How were they going to be able to effectively plan schedules, control operations, and evaluate each division to determine additional investment needs?

exhibit 1-1 A Comparative Look at the DuPont Company before and after 1903

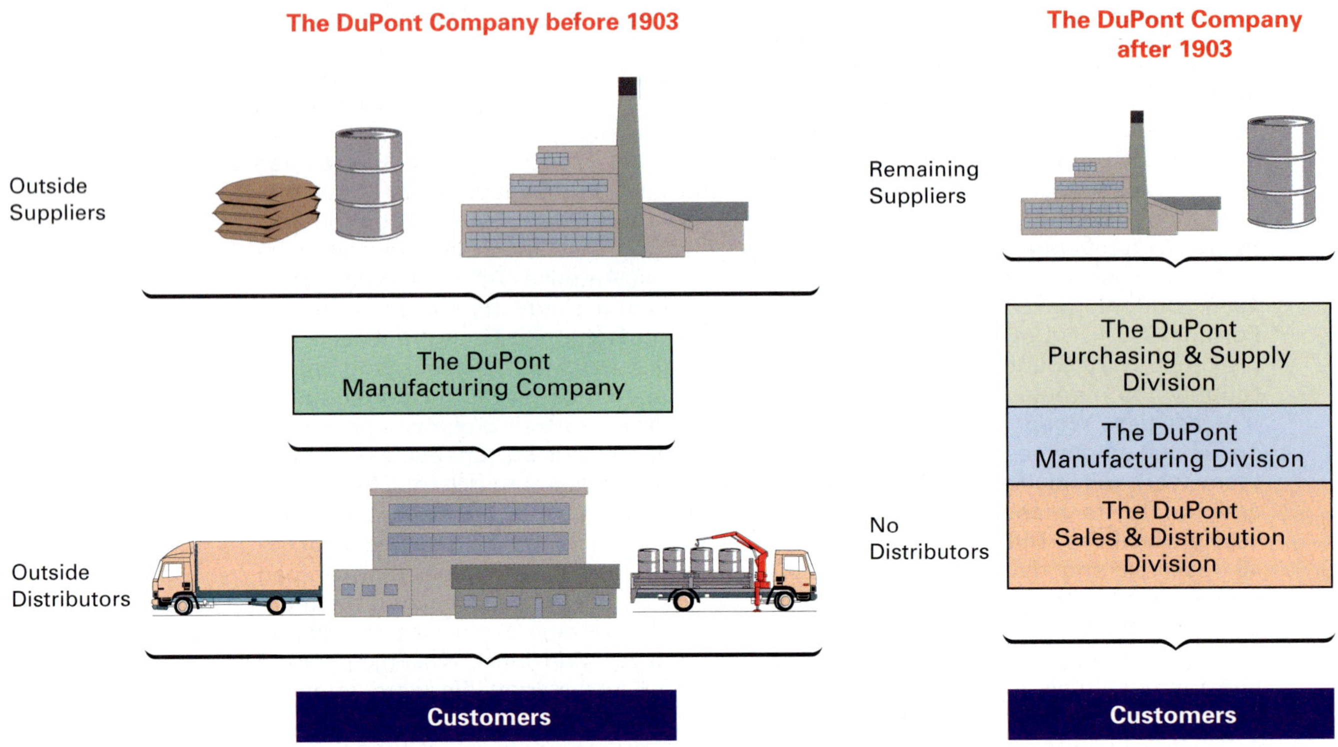

Essentially, Alfred, Coleman, and Pierre had an accounting problem. What would you have done if you were in their shoes in 1903? What the cousins did to handle the challenge was, to say the least, impressive.[1]

This chapter introduces management accounting and distinguishes it from financial accounting. We will use DuPont to introduce key management accounting concepts such as ROI. It is important to understand that the purpose of management accounting is to fulfill a competitive need. DuPont had a competitive need to manage a very large and diverse organization and so established ROI as an important management device. Accounting tools such as ROI are used to support the management process of planning, controlling, and evaluating. Every business organization uses a variety of accounting tools to support these important management processes. In this chapter we will use cost-volume-profit (C-V-P) analysis to introduce the planning process, product cost classifications to introduce the controlling process, and segment analysis to introduce the evaluating process. In working through a brief overview of these tools, you will be introduced to a variety of cost accounting terms. However, you also need to be aware that effective management in modern organizations requires management accountants to provide not only cost data, but also quality- and time-based information as well. Hence, this chapter has three purposes.

1. *To distinguish management accounting from financial accounting.*
2. *To outline the management process of planning, controlling, and evaluating, as well as the strategic issues of cost, quality, and time.*
3. *To introduce management accounting terminologies in the context of several key management tools.*

1 Historical sources: A. D. Chandler, *The Invisible Hand* (Boston: HBS Press, 1977); H. T. Johnson and R. S. Kaplan, *Relevance Lost* (Boston: HBS Press, 1987); the DuPont home page at **http://www.dupont.com/corp/gbl-company/history.html**; Microsoft Encarta 1994.

1

Understand the essential differences between management accounting and financial accounting, as illustrated by managerial use of the ROI formula.

MANAGEMENT ACCOUNTING VERSUS FINANCIAL ACCOUNTING

Knowing a little of the history of management accounting is very useful in understanding the differences between management accounting and financial accounting. Frankly, a lot of professionals have a difficult time separating the purposes of management accounting and financial accounting. Overall, the purpose of financial accounting, as determined by several regulatory groups, is to establish an objective and consistent format for all companies to use in reporting financial results to the public. In contrast, management accounting is established by individual companies that want to create proprietary information for internal use that has competitive value. The "rules" of management accounting are not governed by anything other than market forces.

The Return on Investment (ROI) Technique

By the time Alfred, Coleman, and Pierre du Pont had finished buying out suppliers and establishing sales offices throughout the country, they had created a giant organization. The fact that their company was big, however, is not what makes their situation interesting. Francis Cabot Lowell, Edward Henry Harriman, Andrew Carnegie, and Rowland H. Macy each had already created and successfully managed huge companies. Their companies, however, all focused on doing *one thing well*—making cloth, moving railway cars, producing steel, or selling goods. The du Ponts, on the other hand, were trying to combine within one company many different types of businesses: wholesale purchasing, raw materials and finished goods manufacturing, and retail distribution. They had a huge management hierarchy, complicated production processes, geographically dispersed business locations, and inventory that needed to turn over rapidly. Each of these divisions required constant attention and additional capital investments in order to grow and flourish. The du Ponts knew they could make or lose money in any part of this monstrous new company. Obviously, neither they nor their capital resources could be everywhere at once. They needed to make trade-off decisions. The problem was, with very diverse divisions, how could they decide which divisions should receive additional investments of time and money? They couldn't really compare the cost reports of retail stores in Denver with a black powder manufacturing factory in Delaware or with a sodium nitrate processing plant in Chile. Having all these unique business activities also made it quite difficult to relate various measures of efficiency directly to overall company profit. The first thing the new DUPONT management team did was develop extensive budgets to coordinate the flow of resources from raw materials to the final customer. But they still needed a measure for comparing performance in the firm's separate divisions with performance of the whole company. Enter the accountant. (Actually, he was an electrical engineer turned accountant. Nevertheless, if a management accountant hall of fame existed, the bust of F. Donaldson Brown would grace its entrance!)

Donaldson Brown, along with other executives at DuPont, realized that every division required an investment in capital (assets) in order to be in business. The overall goal of every business should be to effectively use its assets to make a profit. For example, an explosives plant earning $50,000 in profit with required capital investments of $1 million would not be performing as well as a major distributing division earning an equal $50,000 in profit with only $500,000 in required capital assets. If you had $1 million to invest, which division would receive your money? The distributing division is earning a 10% return ($50,000 ÷ $500,000) on the DuPont investment in inventory, equipment, and buildings. The explosives plant is earning only a 5% return on investment. Although this simple formula was not really new to American business in the first part of the twentieth century, Brown took the idea of **return on investment (ROI)** and turned it into a management technique that could be used to manage any kind of business operation at DuPont. Exhibit 1-2 illustrates how the DuPont ROI formula could be expanded into a comprehensive measurement system for performance. Study this exhibit for a moment. If any company division (or the company as a whole) is generating low ROI, the DuPont management team can immediately begin analyzing the problem. Is **asset turnover** too low? Perhaps the division needs to reduce its investment in assets or work to improve sales. Is the **profit margin** less than adequate? Maybe the division needs to concentrate on reducing selling expenses or manufacturing costs. The ROI tool allowed the du Pont cousins to be hugely successful in managing the country's first integrated

return on investment (ROI) A measure of operating performance and efficiency in utilizing assets; computed in its simplest form by dividing net income by average total assets.

asset turnover An overall measure of how effectively assets are used during a period; computed by dividing revenue by total assets.

profit margin An overall measure of the profitability of operations during a period; computed by dividing profit by revenue.

exhibit 1-2 An Illustration of the DuPont ROI Formula (simple and complex)

The DuPont ROI Formula (simple)

$$\text{Return on Investment (ROI)} = \frac{\text{Profit}}{\text{Revenue}} \times \frac{\text{Revenue}}{\text{Assets}}$$

Note: Later development of the DuPont formula expanded the model to include a measure of leverage (Assets/Equity). The effect of this modification is to create a return on equity (ROE) instead of ROI.

The DuPont ROI Formula (complex)*

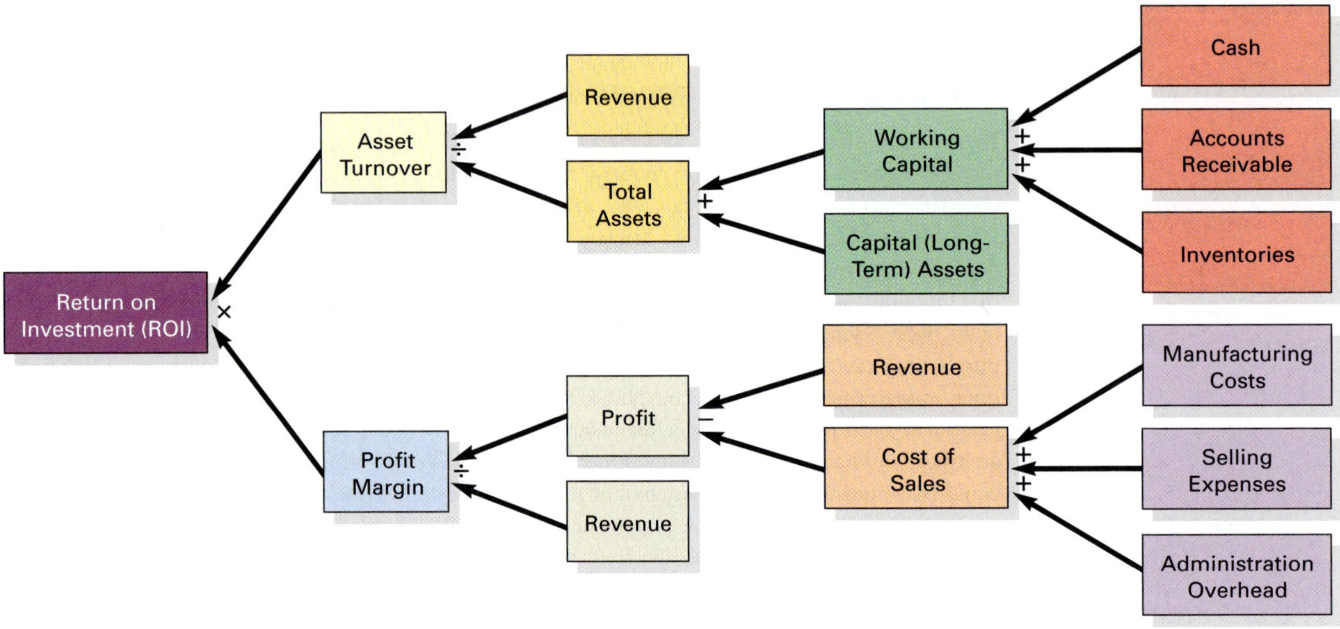

***Source:** T. C. Davis, "How the DuPont Organization Appraises Its Performance," in AMA *Financial Management Series No. 94* (New York: American Management Association, 1950), p. 7. Reprinted in Johnson and Kaplan, *Relevance Lost* (Boston: HBS Press, 1987), p. 85.

company by combining cost management with asset management and raising it to an art form! It's likely that no management accounting technique has had as great an impact on business management as the DuPont ROI formula. In fact, Donaldson Brown took the ROI approach with him when he followed Pierre du Pont to help rescue a little company in the midst of an inventory crisis in 1920. The name of the company was GENERAL MOTORS. The success of the DuPont technique at General Motors can be seen today in any parking lot in America.

Management Accounting and Financial Accounting

In addition to introducing the ROI formula, the DuPont story is an example of how management accounting evolves within organizations that have a particular need for good information. This development pattern has been playing out across companies for a long time. Since the first days of the Industrial Revolution, business owners and managers have generally adopted the best accounting ideas available from other companies and then created their own new accounting system that provided a competitive edge in terms of good management information. Over time, management accounting has, quite literally, evolved within and migrated between organizations and industries in the process of satisfying individual information needs in a competitive world. In fact, a company often regards a good management accounting system as *highly proprietary*—and rarely discloses its details to the public.

Conversely, primarily as a result of the Stock Market Crash of 1929, financial accounting has effectively developed in the United States to provide a *common reporting platform* to the public. In the rapidly rising stock market of the 1920s, many companies publicly issued shares for

caution

Don't think management accounting is not important just because it is not defined as precisely as financial accounting. As you study the story of ROI at DuPont, you will see that management accounting is critical to the success of businesses throughout the world.

the first time. These share issues were often accompanied by little or no financial disclosure. Thus, many stock traders were buying and selling shares based mainly on rumor, speculation, and deceit. In the aftermath of the crash, Congress established the Securities and Exchange Commission (SEC) to regulate the issuance and trading of securities in the United States. In addition to monitoring insider trading and stockbroker behavior, the SEC also ensures that companies issuing securities for purchase by U.S. investors provide full and fair disclosure of their financial status through the public release of financial statements prepared using a set of generally accepted accounting practices (GAAP). The SEC has the legal authority to prescribe accepted accounting standards, but has generally allowed the accounting profession in the United States to establish those rules. Currently, the Financial Accounting Standards Board (FASB), a nongovernmental body supported by the business community and the accounting profession, is the acknowledged source of authoritative accounting standards in the United States.

The important thing to remember is that the purpose of financial accounting, as defined by GAAP, is to comply with requests of outside investors, creditors, and regulators for fair and consistent reports of operations. Accordingly, all companies are required to apply the same general financial accounting rules so that outsiders can compare financial reports coming from many different companies. In contrast, no government regulator or auditor is going to insist that a company implement a good management accounting system; the choice of how to collect and use information within a company is part of a company's competitive strategy. For example, no one forced the du Pont cousins to use the ROI formula to better manage their business; however, because the ROI evaluation framework worked well for DuPont, it was subsequently mimicked by many (but not all) of DuPont's competitors. Remember, the only reason a company does management accounting is to satisfy a competitive need, and competitive need often dictates that one organization's management accounting system will not look like another's!

STOP & THINK We have described some differences in financial and management accounting. Why is it important for an accounting system to provide both types of accounting information?

to summarize

Among the successful innovators in management accounting were Donaldson Brown and the du Ponts who, at the beginning of the twentieth century, consolidated the previous work of others into the famous DuPont ROI management accounting model. The ROI story is typical of management accounting, which is the product of many years of business owners and managers experimenting with methods for capturing and using information about their organization that would give them a unique competitive edge. Organizations and managers are motivated to be innovative in developing and effective in deploying these new accounting tools by the need to compete in a growing economy. In contrast, financial accounting rules are established by an authoritative body in order to enhance company-to-company comparability of financial accounting reports.

2

Understand that successfully managing a company requires good information that supports effective planning, controlling, and evaluating processes.

THE MANAGEMENT PROCESS AND MANAGEMENT ACCOUNTING TERMINOLOGY

Critical to the success experienced by great companies like DUPONT is intelligent decision making by individuals supported by competitive management accounting information. Managers will always need to make choices. What should be produced? What should be sold? How should the service be delivered? What does this client need? Which supplier should be used? Who should be promoted? How should financing be obtained? Exhibit 1-3 illustrates the central role that decision making plays in the general management process.

Notice that the decision-making circle intersects three other circles, each representing a major management function. This intersection is meant to show that each of these functions re-

exhibit 1-3 The Management Process

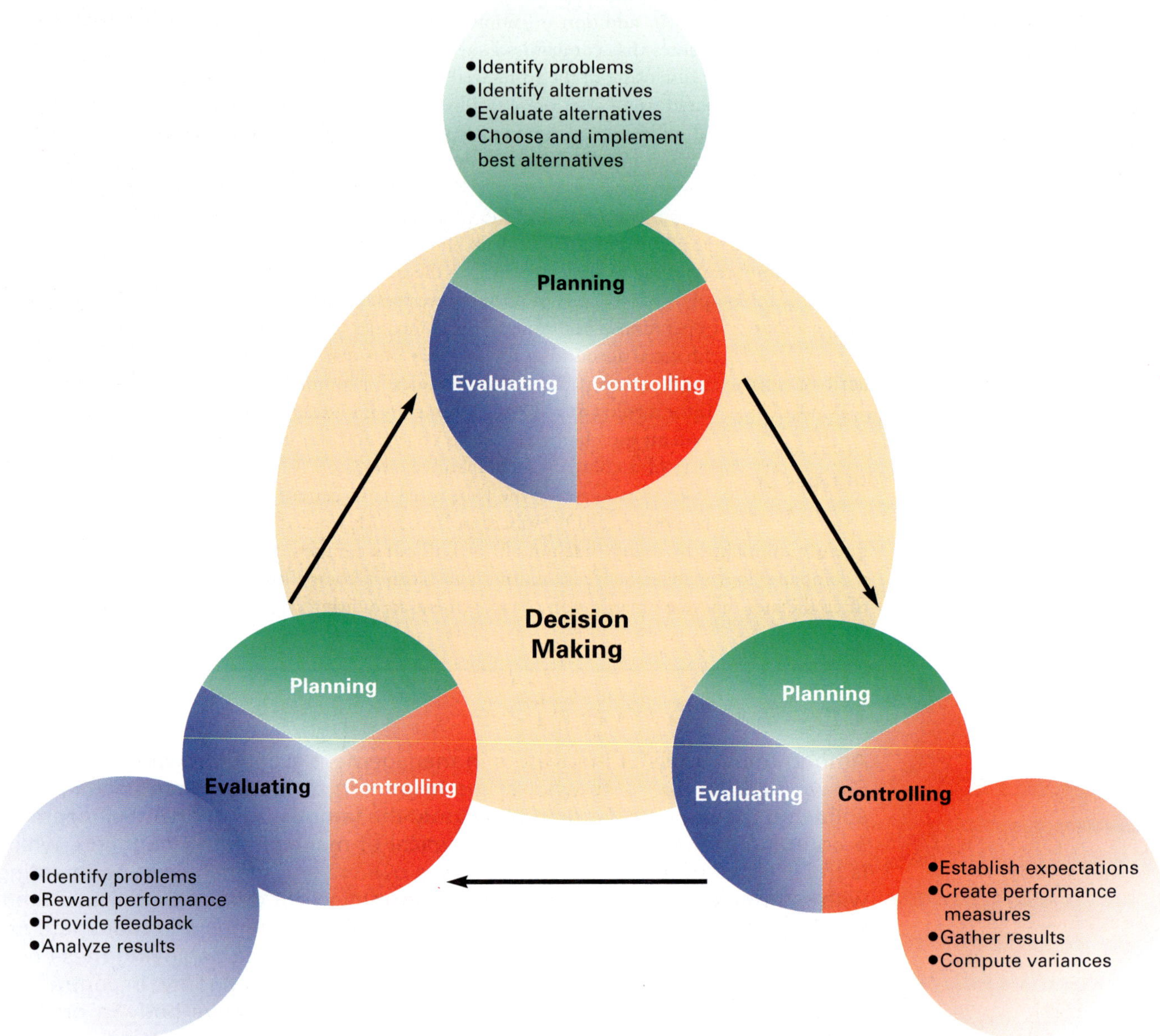

quires decision making. The three management functions of planning, controlling, and evaluating generally follow a natural order—at least in theory. In practice, managers and management accountants are often required to work with processes, customers, and employers requiring all three functions at once. Life can move pretty fast in business!

Planning

planning Outlining the activities that need to be performed for an organization to achieve its objectives.

Management **planning** involves a process of identifying problems or opportunities, identifying alternatives, evaluating alternatives, then choosing and implementing the best alternative(s). There are two basic types of planning:

1. Long-run planning, which includes:
   a. Strategic planning
   b. Capital budgeting

2. Short-run planning, which includes:
   a. Production and process prioritizing
   b. Operational budgeting (profit planning)

Long-run planning involves making decisions with effects that extend several years into the future—usually three to five years, but sometimes longer. This includes broad-based decisions about products, markets, productive facilities, and financial resources. Long-run planning is often called strategic planning. **Strategic planning**, likely the most critical decision-making process that takes place at the executive level in any organization today, usually involves identifying an organization's mission, the goals flowing from that mission, and strategies and action steps to accomplish those goals. Successful executives, such as Pierre du Pont or Andrew Carnegie, have always displayed great skill in studying the market, identifying customer needs, evaluating competitors' strengths and weaknesses, and defining the right investments and processes their organization needs for success. Good management accounting supports good strategic planning by providing the internal information needed by executives to evaluate and adjust their strategic plans. With strategic planning in place (or in process), the company can then plan for the purchase and use of major assets such as buildings or equipment to help the company meet its long-range goals. This type of long-run planning is called **capital budgeting**.

strategic planning Broad, long-range planning usually conducted by top management.

capital budgeting Systematic planning for long-term investments in operating assets.

Short-run planning is divided into two categories. Once the organization has made long-term resource commitments (e.g., land, buildings, equipment, management personnel, etc.), then managers need to determine how to best use those committed resources to maximize the return on their capital investments—a process often referred to as **production prioritizing**. Did you catch the phrase "return on capital investment" in the last sentence? Sound familiar? The DuPont ROI concept is one way to establish priorities on products, service processes, or divisions that make the largest contributions to the goals of the organization. In the next section, we'll introduce another popular method of prioritizing the production potential of an organization—cost-volume-profit (C-V-P) analysis. Once the organization has determined what to produce or otherwise provide to the marketplace in order to maximize its goals, then managers are ready to go on to the next phase of short-run planning—**operational budgeting**. Sometimes known as profit plans, operational budgets are used by managers to establish and communicate daily, weekly, and monthly goals (also known as "standards") for the organization. We will discuss operational budgets, along with production prioritizing, capital budgeting, and strategic planning, in subsequent chapters.

production prioritizing Management's continual evaluation of the profitability of the various product lines and divisions within an organization so that products or divisions that are performing below expectations can be analyzed to identify problems and potential solutions.

operational budgeting Managerial planning decisions regarding current operations and those of the immediate future (typically one year or less) that are characterized by regularity and frequency.

Controlling

Controlling involves a process of tracking actual performance in terms of costs, quality, and timeliness measures. These data are then used subsequently in the evaluating process to compare against the budgets previously prepared in the planning process to measure variances from the original goals or standards. The first management accounting systems focused on tracking costs within the organization. Today, sophisticated cost accounting systems carefully track prices paid for material, labor, overhead, and administrative costs. These systems often have built-in operational budgets so that they can simultaneously evaluate actual performance and compare it to expectations. These systems determine the desired amounts of labor, materials, and administrative support that should be used to efficiently achieve the right outputs of products and services. The foundation of management accounting is a carefully developed model of product and service costs. We'll explore this model later in this chapter.

controlling Implementing management plans and identifying how plans compare with actual performance.

Evaluating

Evaluating involves analyzing results, providing feedback to managers and other employees, rewarding performance, and identifying problems. Evaluating is typically a process of comparing actual performance against expected inputs of costs, expected outputs of quality, and expected timelines. This comparison typically results in information called *variances*, which tell management how well the organization is achieving its plans. If performance is in accordance with the plan, the variances signal that operations are in control and no unusual management action is

evaluating Analyzing results, rewarding performance, and identifying problems.

necessary. If performance is substantially different from the plan, management needs to decide how to alter operations in order to improve future performance.

One specific type of evaluation focuses on company personnel and their responsibilities within the organization. Upper-level management must evaluate how well lower-level managers have performed the activities assigned to them in the original planning stage. Feedback enables management to evaluate performance and provide direction for future improvements, an important aspect of growth in the organization. If performance is good, management needs to consider rewards; if performance is poor, corrective action must be taken. Too many companies fail to clearly link incentive compensation with management goals to ensure that everyone is focused on low cost, high quality, and timely delivery of goods and services expected by customers and clients.

Evaluating products and processes also takes place regularly. Managers need to assess the performance of their products or services, as well as the processes that have been put into place to create products and services. Such evaluation naturally leads to decisions that will affect future operations, including whether to enter or exit a market for a particular service or product, whether to make or buy a component, whether to sell a product before or after additional processing, and what prices to charge for services and products. This third function in the management process, evaluating, brings us back to the point where we started, planning. The information gained through the evaluating function is used in planning for the following period. Remember that as managers *evaluate* performance in the last period, they may also be making *planning* decisions to improve operations for the next period while gathering and receiving results to *control* the current period.

Introduction to Teflon® and Kevlar®

To better understand the nature of planning, controlling, and evaluating, we will work through some typical decisions that managers at DuPont may, in fact, be working on at the moment. We will focus on two product lines at DuPont—Teflon® resins and Kevlar® fiber. These are flagship products at DuPont so you may already be familiar with them. Teflon is considered the most slippery material in existence. It begins as a mixture of chemicals that are then manipulated by DuPont's engineers to produce a product that has become a familiar household name through its use as a nonstick liner for pots and pans and as a soil and stain repellant for fabrics and clothing. One of Teflon's many less known uses is as a coating for fiberglass fabrics used in permanent structures such as the Pontiac Silverdome in Detroit, Michigan, and the Carrier Dome at Syracuse University in Syracuse, New York. Currently, Teflon has an average wholesale price of approximately $145 per gallon.

Kevlar is an even more interesting product. It is a specialty fabric that is extremely strong and tough—so tough that ordinary scissors will not cut through a piece of the fabric! Kevlar starts in a liquid form, is then spun to the point where the Kevlar fibers come together, and finally is heated to complete the process. It is used for boat hulls, bullet-resistant vests, coats, dress shirts, cut-resistant gloves, fiber-optic cables, tennis rackets, and skis. For example, a bullet-resistant vest that is made of seven layers of Kevlar weighs only 2.5 pounds, but can deflect a knife blade and stop a .38-caliber bullet shot from only 10 feet away. The average wholesale price for Kevlar is approximately $45 per pound. This is expensive fabric! Usually, DuPont ships Kevlar as a staple fiber (cotton balls), continuous filament (yarn), and chopped fiber.

net work

We all love to hear a good story about how hard work and good luck can collide to create history. To read about such a story, go to the DuPont Company Web site at http://www.dupont.com, click on its search engine, and enter the phrase "history of Teflon" (be sure to put the phrase in quotation marks). When was Teflon discovered? What was the name of the now-famous scientist who invented it? What other DuPont product was he working on when he came upon the "white, waxy solid" that eventually became Teflon?

The Interrelation of Planning, Controlling, and Evaluating

The use of the ROI model in the case of DuPont is a good example of how planning, control, and evaluation interrelate. DuPont makes 2,000 different products. And, although this is a very large company, its production capabilities are not limitless. So trade-off decisions need to be made. The bottom-line question is, "What product lines provide the most value to DuPont?" The original DuPont ROI formula provides some useful insights here. Consider DuPont's Teflon and Kevlar products. Teflon is part of Dupont's Performance Coatings Segment, and Kevlar belongs to the Specialty Fibers Segment, both critical business divisions within the DuPont organization. How are these segments doing? There are a lot of ways to answer this question, including using the ROI formula. You could use DuPont's annual report to calculate the ROI numbers on these divisions. You would find out if one division's ROI was outperforming the other. More importantly, you could determine how division performance was related to the ability to generate profit margins and the ability to turn over the investment in assets (i.e., asset turnover). Perhaps most importantly, if you were a manager at DuPont, you could then ask some really good questions, such as *why* the profit margin is low for one division. Are costs too high? Is competition forcing prices down? Or, why isn't the asset turnover higher in the other division? Should DuPont consider reducing the amount of assets being purchased and maintained in this segment? Interesting questions—all the result of management accounting providing useful information to help manage the company to be a stronger competitor in the marketplace.

Now review Exhibit 1-3 and think for a moment about the DuPont management process and ROI. As we make ROI calculations on DuPont divisions and ask direct questions as managers, are we clearly using ROI only to *evaluate* the two segments, or could this discussion be part of *planning* for changes in management of and investments in the two segments for the future? It's even possible that ROI measures could be used as a mechanism for gathering data and providing effective *control* of the two divisions in the current operating period. Do you see how the planning, controlling, and evaluating processes interrelate? Although planning, controlling, and evaluating are not always clear and distinct procedures in the management process, we'll use these three critical management functions throughout the remainder of this book to organize the structure of management accounting and discuss where and how the management accounting information is being used to support competitive business management.

to summarize

The essential purpose of management accounting is to support decision making that adds value to the organization. Effective decision making is the key to the management process, and it is central to the management functions of planning, controlling, and evaluating. Planning is the process of making decisions about future products and services, operations, and investments. Controlling involves tracking actual costs, quality, and timing performance within the organization. Evaluating is a process of analyzing results, computing variances, and providing feedback to assess personnel, divisions, products, and processes. The natural end result of evaluating is the identification of problems and opportunities, and from there, the next stage of planning begins. As can be demonstrated by ROI calculations for two divisions at DuPont, however, the management process may (and often does) involve evaluation of the past operating period while simultaneously planning for the future and working to effectively control current business operations. (Note: We'll return to ROI calculations again in Chapter 9 of management accounting.)

3

Know how the concepts of fixed and variable costs are used in C-V-P analysis in the management planning process.

cost-volume-profit (C-V-P) analysis Techniques for determining how changes in revenues, costs, and level of activity affect the profitability of an organization.

variable costs Costs that change in total in direct proportion to changes in activity level.

COST-VOLUME-PROFIT ANALYSIS AT DUPONT

At this point, you have had a good introduction to the ROI management tool. We'll explore this tool further in later chapters. It's time now to introduce a management tool primarily used in the planning process. It is called **cost-volume-profit (C-V-P) analysis.** C-V-P analysis is a very traditional technique in management accounting and is primarily used to plan for the products and services the organization will focus on in the future. The basic concept is to determine the volume of products or services that will be required to generate a desired profit. To use C-V-P analysis successfully, the management accountant must categorize costs as either fixed or variable costs. The concept of fixed and variable costs is fairly simple. Total **variable costs** change in *direct proportion* to changes in some particular activity level, such as production or sales volumes. One example of a variable cost is the costs of materials (such as bolts of cloth in a clothing factory), which vary proportionately with the number of units produced. Sales commissions, which vary proportionately with sales volume, are another example of a

The cost of bolts of cloth used in a clothing factory is classified as a variable cost because it varies proportionately by the number of units produced. The more cloth used in production, the more the total amount of this cost.

fixed costs Costs that remain constant in total, regardless of activity level, at least over a certain range of activity.

variable cost. **Fixed costs** remain constant in total, regardless of activity level, at least over a certain range of activity. Examples of fixed costs related to administration are institutional advertising, insurance, and executives' salaries. Fixed costs related to the manufacturing process might include plant depreciation and supervisors' salaries. Regardless of changes in sales or production output, these costs typically remain constant.

caution

In theory, distinguishing between variable and fixed costs sounds simple. If the activity, such as production volume or sales volume, increases and the cost in question increases, then it must be a variable cost. Otherwise, it is a fixed cost. In reality, however, identifying and managing variable and fixed costs can involve many complexities. Subsequent chapters, particularly Chapter 2 of management accounting, will focus more on identifying and using variable and fixed costs in the planning process.

To demonstrate C-V-P analysis in the planning process, let's return to the two **DUPONT** products, Teflon and Kevlar. Let's assume that DuPont currently needs to work through which product line to prioritize for the next year. It's not simply a matter of which product line is more profitable or which is expected to return the higher ROI. The decision also involves an assessment of the risk of these two products—in this case, the risk that either or both of these products will generate a loss instead of a profit. C-V-P analysis is used to assess this risk. The fundamental question addressed by C-V-P analysis is as follows: At what sales volume will the company "break even" (i.e., profit is exactly zero) in the Kevlar product line and in the Teflon product line? Answering this question requires the use of the concept of fixed and variable costs. Assume the following estimated price and cost data for the Kevlar and Teflon product lines for the upcoming year:

	Kevlar Product Line	Teflon Product Line
Wholesale price	$45.00 per lb.	$145.00 per gallon
Variable cost	$17.90 per lb.	$60.30 per gallon
Total monthly fixed costs	$3,210,000	$9,630,000

Typical variable costs are the costs of the raw chemicals used to produce Kevlar and Teflon and the labor costs of the workers involved in the manufacturing process. These costs are variable because the more Kevlar or Teflon produced, the more the total amount of these costs. Typical fixed costs are the cost of insurance on a chemical plant, the cost of plant supervisors, and the property taxes paid on a chemical facility. These costs are fixed because, within limits, they are the same no matter how much Kevlar or Teflon is produced.

Examination of the assumed cost numbers for Kevlar indicates that DuPont sells a pound of Kevlar for $27.10 ($45.00 sales price per pound − $17.90 variable cost per pound) more than the variable costs associated with making the product. A basic objective of C-V-P analysis is to determine how many pounds of Kevlar must be sold each month to generate enough profit to pay the $3,210,000 in fixed costs associated with manufacturing that product. The computation of this "break-even" amount is as follows:

$3,210,000 fixed cost ÷ ($45.00 sales price per lb. − $17.90 variable cost per lb.)
= 118,451 lb. (rounded up)

fyi

C-V-P analysis is often referred to as break-even analysis.

This computation means that DuPont must sell 118,451 pounds of Kevlar each month, generating a surplus of $27.10 on each pound, in order to be able to pay its fixed costs of $3,210,000 per month. If DuPont sells fewer than 118,451 pounds in a month, then the fixed costs will not be covered, and the Kevlar product line will report a loss. And remember, by definition the fixed costs of $3,210,000 will be there no matter how many pounds of Kevlar are sold.

STOP & THINK Refer back to the fixed and variable cost data for the Teflon product line. For some C-V-P analysis practice, compute the number of gallons of Teflon that DuPont must sell each month in order to break even.

The information from this simple C-V-P analysis can be used as DuPont makes its production plans with respect to Kevlar. For example, if current production plans, in conjunction with an assessment of the market demand, indicate that DuPont will consistently sell fewer than 118,451 pounds of Kevlar per month, the manager of the Kevlar product line will almost certainly wish to change his or her plans. Costs must be squeezed, new markets need to be sought, perhaps prices should be raised—in short, something has to change because the C-V-P analysis suggests that sales of less than 118,451 pounds per month will not result in profits.

---

to summarize

By defining costs as either fixed or variable, management accountants can add cost-volume-profit (C-V-P) analysis to the set of tools available in the management process of planning. Management accountants define fixed costs as those costs that will not change in relationship to a particular activity level such as sales volume. Conversely, variable costs are those costs that change in direct proportion to sales volume. Organizations can use C-V-P analysis to determine the sales volume necessary to break even (i.e., profit equals zero). Insights gained from C-V-P computations are extremely useful in the process of planning how and which product lines to emphasize for the future. We'll spend significant time on the C-V-P tool in Chapter 2 of management accounting.

4

Realize how the product cost classifications of direct materials, direct labor, and overhead are used in the management controlling process.

PRODUCT AND PERIOD COSTS

product costs Costs associated with products or services offered.

The concept of managing operations by controlling costs is certainly not a new technique. The early innovations in cost control made by Andrew Carnegie and other successful businesspersons established management accounting practices that continue today. Basically, costs associated with the products or services offered are called **product costs**. In a manufacturing company such as DUPONT or CARNEGIE STEEL, for example, product costs (often referred to as manufacturing costs) are all costs necessary to create finished goods ready for sale. They include all costs related to production: the factory manager's salary, depreciation and taxes on the factory building, wages of the factory workers, and the materials that go into the product. In a merchandising company such as MACY'S or SEARS, product costs are the costs incurred to purchase goods and get them ready for resale to customers. In a service company such as the UNION PACIFIC RAILROAD or KELLY SERVICES (which provides temporary employees), product costs (sometimes called cost of services) involve labor, supplies, and other costs directly related to providing services to customers. At Kelly Services, labor costs for all personnel who provide part-time or temporary services for clients are classified as contract service costs and are subtracted from revenues to arrive at gross margin. In manufacturing and merchandising organizations, the product costs of units still

business environment essay

The Steely-Eyed Business Tycoon In the nineteenth century and much of the twentieth century, management accounting, known then as cost accounting, focused strictly on cost measurement and cost management. Business owners were making a great deal of money using this information to build and expand large companies. And no one understood cost information quite like Andrew Carnegie, who controlled about 25% of the American iron and steel production in 1899. Carnegie was obsessed with costs. One of his favorite sayings was "Watch the costs and the profits will take care of themselves." Was Carnegie's management accounting focus successful? In 1901 he sold his company, **CARNEGIE STEEL**, to the **UNITED STATES STEEL CORPORATION** for $250 million and retired. During his lifetime he gave more than $350 million to various educational, cultural, and peace institutions, many of which bear his name. Not bad for an immigrant with no formal education.

on hand at the end of the accounting period (e.g., the month or year being reported) clearly form the basis for the dollar amount of inventory carried on the balance sheet. The product costs of units sold during the accounting period are used to determine cost of goods sold, which is shown on the income statement as part of the calculation of gross margin for the period.

period costs Costs not directly related to a product, service, or asset that are charged as expenses to the income statement in the period in which they are incurred.

Period costs are all costs incurred that cannot be associated with or assigned to a product or service. These costs are usually not associated with inventory or any other kind of asset. The most common period costs are selling and administrative costs. Examples of selling costs are sales salaries, advertising, and delivery costs. Examples of administrative costs are salaries of the president and controller, depreciation or rent on office buildings, taxes on assets used in administration, and other office expenditures such as postage, supplies, and utilities. The accountant typically treats period costs very differently from product costs. Instead of using these costs to establish a value for inventory, period costs are usually recognized as an expense on the income statement in the period in which they are incurred. For example, if Sears, Roebuck & Company sells two-thirds of the inventory it purchased during November, only the cost of the inventory sold becomes an expense (Cost of Goods Sold) on that month's income statement. The other third of the inventory cost remains an asset (Inventory) on the balance sheet. Regardless of how many products are sold during the month, however, the president's entire salary for November is recognized as an expense on the monthly income statement. You can see that these costs are called period costs because they are always expensed in the period (e.g., month) in which they are incurred.

STOP & THINK A major difference between Kelly Services and manufacturers or merchandisers is inventory. Kelly sells services. Can we put service labor into inventory? Think about this question; we'll discuss it later in Chapter 3 of management accounting.

Types of Product Costs

Now let's examine how we measure and control product and period costs in a variety of organizations. How would one measure product costs for a merchandiser? Actually, that is a fairly easy question. The resources Macy's spends to acquire store inventory for resale to customers clearly are product costs. As products are sold, these inventory costs become an expense on the income statement. What about the wages and salaries of Macy's store clerks and managers? Macy's will likely categorize these costs as part of its selling and administrative expenses and treat them as a period cost on the income statement. That's not too difficult. Now consider the same question for **ARTHUR ANDERSEN LLP**, one of the largest certified public accounting (CPA) firms in the world. What are the products sold by this service firm? Arthur Andersen sells the time of its tax accountants, auditors, and consultants. The salaries of these professionals represent the costs of its "product." Arthur Andersen also employs many other people (such as clerks, secretaries, and office managers) to support the professionals and administer office needs. The wages and salaries of these clerks and office managers, along with costs of office rent, desk supplies, and computers, are likely treated as period costs and recognized as selling and administrative expenses on the income statement.

When identifying product costs for control purposes, the most challenging organization to analyze is a manufacturing business. Does DuPont purchase inventory for resale? Actually, it does purchase some inventory, such as basic chemicals. But it doesn't simply turn around and sell these basic chemicals to customers. Significant processing has to take place before these raw materials become a finished product ready for sale. DuPont must employ laborers to work with these chemicals. In addition, DuPont builds factory buildings and purchases manufacturing equipment. DuPont must also employ managers and other support personnel (such as engineers and custodians) to support the line workers' efforts to convert basic chemicals into salable products. These are all product costs. Basically, any cost required to get the product manufactured and ready for sale is a product cost.

direct materials Materials that become part of the product and are traceable to it.

indirect materials Materials that are necessary to a manufacturing or service business but are not directly included in or are not a significant part of the actual product.

direct labor Wages that are paid to those who physically work on direct materials to transform them into a finished product and are traceable to specific products.

indirect labor Labor that is necessary to a manufacturing or service business but is not directly related to the actual production of the manufactured or service product.

manufacturing overhead All costs incurred in the manufacturing process other than direct materials and direct labor.

To help management analyze the manufacturing cost of its products, product costs are divided into three components: (1) direct materials, (2) direct labor, and (3) manufacturing overhead. **Direct materials** are materials that become part of the product and are traceable to it. Some materials, however, such as the glue and nails in a finished piece of furniture, are so minor and their use so difficult to trace to a specific product that they are not considered direct materials, but rather **indirect materials. Direct labor** consists of the wages that are paid to those who physically work on the direct materials to transform them into a finished product. Conversely, wages and salaries paid to factory supervisors and management, maintenance staff, and factory security guards are treated as **indirect labor. Manufacturing overhead** includes all other costs incurred in the manufacturing process not specifically identified as direct materials or direct labor. Both indirect materials and indirect labor are included in manufacturing overhead. Exhibit 1-4 summarizes the relationship between product costs and period costs in various types of organizations.

Product Costing and Overhead Cost Allocation

Kevlar and Teflon are rather complex products. The manufacturing process to create these products is also necessarily complex. Controlling the costs, quality, and timely delivery of these processes is key to DuPont's profitability. In this work, DuPont's manufacturing managers need a constant flow of information from management accountants and other information technologists. This is a *lot* of information, particularly in light of the fact that these are not the only products at DuPont (remember that this company manufactures and sells approximately 2,000 products). To control the costs of Kevlar production, DuPont needs accurate information about how much it currently costs to produce Kevlar. This is where the traditional cost accounting systems come into play.

exhibit 1-4 Product Costs and Period Costs in Business Organizations

Type of Company	Product Costs	Period Costs
Service company	Costs of providing services	Selling costs Administrative costs
Merchandising company (wholesale or retail)	Costs incurred in purchasing goods from suppliers	Selling costs Administrative costs
Manufacturing company	All manufacturing costs including direct materials, direct labor, and manufacturing overhead	Selling costs Administrative costs

business environment essay

Watch Your Language in Management Accounting! As good business professionals and management accountants work to compete in the marketplace, a set of common management accounting terms has evolved. Remember, this is not financial accounting—it is important to understand that no official regulatory body of professionals has defined these terms. As you work in various organizations later in your career, you will likely find that these definitions can become ambiguous. Depending on the decision context, a particular cost can have several names. You need to understand this fact and recognize that allowing these definitions to "shift about" can be completely appropriate!

To illustrate, if you like playing card games such as bridge or canasta, you understand that it is often very important in the game to distinguish between cards of different suits—hearts, spades, clubs, or diamonds. On the other hand, for some decisions in the card game it may be more useful to concentrate on the value of the card—ace, 10, deuce, and so on. Thus, sometimes you care about the ace of hearts because of its "heartness," and at other times you are really more interested in its "aceness." Similarly, a product cost may also be a variable cost. Depending on the management setting, you may choose to categorize costs as fixed or variable versus product or period or direct or indirect.

So, in business conversations (discussions concerning costs, for example), never assume you are talking about the same concept as another individual. You always need to be sure that everyone is using the same definition of a management accounting term or concept before you let the conversation get too far.

As you now know, costs of manufacturing products can be broken down into three elements: (1) direct materials, (2) direct labor, and (3) manufacturing overhead. Although it is easy to assign direct materials and direct labor costs to specific products, it is extremely difficult to assign manufacturing overhead costs, such as rent or the custodian's salary, to specific manufactured products. Companies such as DuPont pay a great deal of attention to **overhead cost allocation** decisions. Unless all relevant costs are properly assigned, managers will not be able to effectively control costs and set prices. Lots of estimations must be made in allocating costs, however, and at some point, it simply isn't worth the effort to get the allocation exactly right (in other words, if management accountants aren't careful, they can start "spending dollars to manage dimes!"). Nevertheless, companies like DuPont are in a competitive market; they can't afford to not understand and manage their product and service costs. In that context, DuPont puts considerable effort into effective allocation of Kevlar and Teflon production costs.

overhead cost allocation A system of assigning the indirect costs of the manufacturing or service process to the actual product being created for the customer.

STOP & THINK One of the major reasons it is difficult to assign overhead costs is that these overhead costs are "lumpy" in nature and cannot be precisely matched to the production of specific goods and services. For example, assume that you are the sole driver in a car pool; all the other individuals in the car pool have agreed to reimburse you for their respective shares of the cost of the daily commute. In computing this cost, how would you factor in the costs of insurance, maintenance, and repairs on your car?

How Low Can You Go?

Imagine that another company has recently introduced a new product on the market that competes directly with DuPont's Kevlar. Soon the intense competition between DuPont and the other company for customer orders starts to force down the market price of Kevlar. Now DuPont has a problem. How low can DuPont let the price of Kevlar drop before the company starts losing money? Answering this question requires that DuPont do a good job of measuring the costs of creating Kevlar. Measuring the costs of direct materials and direct labor is not really a problem. The challenge is accurately measuring (i.e., allocating) the cost of overhead to this product.

Overhead Cost Allocation at DuPont

At this point, you can probably imagine that the DuPont accountants could take several approaches to allocate overhead costs to a product such as Kevlar.

Let's explore one possibility by picking up where we left off in our C-V-P analysis for Kevlar. You'll recall from our earlier discussion that monthly fixed costs for Kevlar are estimated to be \$3,210,000 and that variable costs are estimated at \$17.90 per pound. Remember that fixed and variable costs are *one* way to define costs. These same fixed and variable costs can also be categorized as direct materials, direct labor, and manufacturing overhead costs. Consider the following list of variable costs required to produce a 300-pound batch of Kevlar:

Standard Variable Costs to Produce 300 Pounds of Kevlar

	Average Cost per Pound	Average Pounds per Batch	Total Costs
Direct materials:			
Material 1	\$12	100	\$1,200
Material 2	18	200	3,600
	Average Rate per Hour	**Average Hours per Batch**	
Direct labor	\$18	10	180
Variable manufacturing overhead	39	10	390
Total variable costs*			**\$5,370**

*You can verify the number for total variable costs. Remember from the previous C-V-P example that variable costs for Kevlar are \$17.90 per pound. Divide the total variable costs of \$5,370 by 300 pounds to see that this works out to \$17.90 per pound.

Standard Monthly Fixed Costs Associated with the Kevlar Product Line

Manufacturing overhead	\$1,560,000
Sales and administrative costs	1,650,000
Total fixed costs	**\$3,210,000**

The variable manufacturing overhead costs might include some utility costs (e.g., power to run the equipment) and repairs and maintenance costs that change based on production volumes (similar to the way maintenance costs of your car increase the more you drive it).

Controlling these costs is a matter of continuously tracking what DuPont is spending on direct materials, direct labor, and variable manufacturing overhead and comparing those costs to what should be spent based on the actual volume of Kevlar being produced. Categorizing these costs provides both insight and the opportunity to make good management decisions on costs that are getting out of control; it also guides DuPont in making changes to Kevlar selling prices as costs change. This seems simple enough with one product like Kevlar. In a company as large and complex as DuPont, however, tracking these costs for Kevlar and 2,000 other products is a full-time job for a lot of people!

At this point, it should be clear that tracking the variable costs of producing Kevlar is insufficient to control total costs. A great deal of fixed costs must be managed as well. The Kevlar product generates approximately \$1,560,000 in fixed manufacturing overhead costs monthly. Managers somehow need to relate these fixed costs to the production volume in order to manage and control (1) the costs of producing Kevlar and (2) the pricing of the Kevlar product. How would you go about relating the manufacturing overhead costs to Kevlar production? Assuming that DuPont expects to produce 1,000 batches (300 pounds per batch) in the next month, the fixed manufacturing overhead cost per pound can be computed as follows:

$$\$1{,}560{,}000 \div 1{,}000 \text{ batches} = \$1{,}560 \text{ per batch} \div 300 \text{ lb. per batch} = \$5.20 \text{ per lb.}$$

Adding together the fixed and variable manufacturing costs per batch, the expected total manufacturing cost is \$23.10 (\$17.90 variable costs + \$5.20 fixed manufacturing overhead) per

> **caution**
>
> Remember that this section began by distinguishing between product and period costs. In our Kevlar cost example, we've focused on assigning only the product costs to pounds of Kevlar. Don't forget that there are also $1,650,000 in period costs, that is, selling and administrative costs, to consider. Although many companies typically do not *directly* allocate these costs to individual products (e.g., pounds of Kevlar), these costs must be effectively tracked and considered in the management process of controlling (as well as planning and evaluating) specific products and services.

pound of Kevlar. Assuming that this method of allocating manufacturing overhead costs to Kevlar is appropriate, DuPont accountants can use this measure as a benchmark to track actual production costs as they come in throughout the year. Thus, use of the classic product cost classification scheme described in this section allows managers and accountants to closely monitor and control the impacts of changes in direct material prices, direct labor rates, and other costs in the effort to profitably provide Kevlar to the market.

The allocation of fixed overhead to products and services may appear to you to be a simple and straightforward process. If you've ever walked through a large manufacturing plant or a large bank, however, you were likely impressed with the complexity of the operation. You may wonder how such complex organizations can effectively control costs and aggressively compete in the marketplace using a cost allocation system that seems almost simplistic. Actually, most cost accounting systems are more involved than what is described here. Nevertheless, the Kevlar product costing example that you've just worked through exhibits the basic pattern found in most cost accounting systems—identifying a meaningful allocation basis (sometimes called an "activity basis") and using it to relate costs to products and services (as well as other critical objects of manager focus). Keep this pattern in mind as we turn to more advanced cost accounting issues in subsequent chapters (particularly Chapters 3, 6, and 7 of management accounting).

to summarize

Costs are initially categorized as either product or period costs. Most period costs are classified as sales and administrative overhead and are, generally, quite difficult to associate with any of the particular products or services that the company provides to the marketplace. Examples of period costs include salaries of selling and advertising personnel and rent or depreciation costs on administrative office buildings. On the other hand, product costs are closely related to the actual process of providing specific goods and services to customers. These costs are typically assigned to specific products or services in an effort to effectively control production costs. Product costs for manufacturing companies such as DuPont are traditionally divided into costs of direct materials, direct labor, and manufacturing overhead. Direct materials are those items that become part of the final product and are easily traceable to it. Direct labor costs are the wages of workers who are "hands on" involved in the production of the final product. Manufacturing overhead costs are essentially defined as all costs essential to the production of goods or services that cannot be categorized as direct materials and direct labor. The management process of controlling costs involves the effort to classify and track costs of providing specific goods and services. Perhaps the most challenging aspect of controlling costs for accountants is the process of assigning (i.e., allocating) overhead costs to specific products using an allocation basis such as production volume.

5

Be able to perform a simple segment analysis using the concepts of direct, indirect, and opportunity costs in the management evaluating process.

SEGMENT ANALYSIS

Managers and executives are typically paid well to make hard decisions. Managers must constantly evaluate the performance of divisions, personnel, processes, and products as markets for particular products change based on developments in technology, new fads and trends in consumer taste, and increased pressure from new and existing competitors. Occasionally, the situation requires a serious look at the potential need to exit from a particular market or drop a specific product line. Sometimes these decisions are motivated by the opportunity to enter a new market or add a new product line. The decision to drop a product line is critical because subsequently reversing the decision can be difficult or impossible. Good management accounting can do much to facilitate the process of evaluating divisions, personnel, processes, and products. Conversely, a poor understanding of some critical management accounting concepts can lead to painful, if not potentially lethal, company problems. To illustrate how accounting supports this evaluation process, we need to extend our vocabulary of key management accounting terms.

Direct and Indirect Costs

So far we have identified fixed and variable costs as a method of cost classification that provides good support to the planning process. We've also defined product and period costs and used those classifications to demonstrate the management controlling process. Now we introduce some new ways to classify costs that are useful for evaluating performance. One of these classifications is direct costs and indirect costs. **Direct costs** are costs that can be obviously and physically traced to a business unit or segment being analyzed. The unit may be a sales territory, product line, division, plant, or any other subdivision for which information is accumulated for analysis. Direct costs are often described as those costs that would be saved if the segment were to be discontinued. Typically, many types of direct costs are variable, but some are fixed. For example, if the segment being considered is a branch sales office, the cost of inventory and labor to run the store would be direct costs that are variable, while the cost to rent the building would be a direct cost that is fixed.

direct costs Costs that are specifically traceable to a unit of business or segment being analyzed.

Indirect costs—sometimes referred to as common costs or joint costs—are costs that are normally incurred for the benefit of several segments. Indirect costs can also be either fixed or variable, although these costs are often fixed. Sometimes these costs are allocated in order to be assigned to a segment. For example, consider a sales manager's salary. If a segment is defined as a branch sales office and a sales manager supervises only one segment, the manager's salary is likely a direct cost of that sales office. If the manager is responsible for several segments, however, the company may choose to allocate the manager's salary to each sales office. In this case, the salary would be an indirect cost to any one of the sales offices. Total indirect costs, such as the manager's salary, normally do not change if one or more of the segments (in this case, the sales offices) are discontinued. Another example of an indirect cost may be manufacturing overhead. Many (but not all) types of manufacturing overhead costs are usually not directly identifiable with any product line and are, therefore, indirect costs to those product lines. These types of costs are incurred as a consequence of general or overall operating activities.

indirect costs Costs normally incurred for the benefit of several segments within the organization; sometimes called common costs or joint costs.

fyi

Activity-based costing (ABC) is a relatively new method of cost assignment that we will fully discuss in Chapter 7 of management accounting. A major emphasis of ABC is to connect costs directly with certain activities. One result of ABC is an increase in the number of costs that can be classified as direct costs.

Costs are designated as either direct or indirect so that a business segment such as a division or product line can be evaluated on the basis of only those costs directly traceable or chargeable to it. Although companies sometimes allocate indirect costs among segments, such allocations often confuse the analysis of the segment's operations. By focusing only on direct costs, management can both identify segments where performance needs to be improved and recognize segments where performance is outstanding and should be rewarded.

Differential Costs and Sunk Costs

The difference between direct costs and indirect costs is similar to the difference between another set of cost terms—differential costs and sunk costs. The **differential costs**—sometimes called avoidable costs, incremental costs, or relevant costs—of a decision are the future costs that change as a result of that decision. In the context of making a decision as to whether to drop a product line, there is likely little difference between the terms *differential cost* and *direct cost.* (The term *differential* is also commonly applied to future *revenues* that will be affected by the decision.) **Sunk costs**, on the other hand, are past costs that cannot be changed as the result of a future decision. You need to note that the definition of sunk costs is not quite the same as that of indirect costs. Indirect costs are those costs that are not affected by a *particular* decision. For example, whether DUPONT decides to continue or discontinue its Kevlar product line will likely not affect its general and administrative costs. These costs are indirect to the Kevlar prod-

differential costs Future costs that change as a result of a decision; also called incremental or relevant costs.

sunk costs Costs, such as depreciation, that are past costs and do not change as a result of a future decision.

uct line. This does not mean that management cannot change any of DuPont's general and administrative costs. It just means that a different management decision process is required to change these costs than the process used in evaluating the feasibility of the Kevlar product line. If this sounds as though a cost could be indirect to one evaluation situation or focus and direct to another, you're right! Defining a cost as direct or indirect depends on the object of the decision. On the other hand, sunk costs are not dependent at all on any decision object. A sunk cost is exactly what it sounds like—sunk! There is nothing a company can reasonably do to change a sunk cost.

As an example of sunk costs, the costs that DuPont may have spent last year upgrading its Teflon manufacturing facilities are not relevant to the decision this year as to whether it should continue to compete in the market for performance coatings. Yet many individuals and companies make poor decisions because they fail to correctly distinguish between differential costs and sunk costs. As a personal example, assume you have season tickets to a school's basketball games. On the night of a game, a friend asks you to go to a movie with her. You have wanted to see the movie for a long time. If you decline because you have already purchased the basketball tickets and believe you must therefore go to the game, you may have made the wrong decision. The cost of the basketball tickets is a sunk cost. The only costs that are relevant to your decision are the costs associated with going to the movie, such as the ticket price and popcorn and other goodies you might buy.

Out-of-Pocket Costs and Opportunity Costs

out-of-pocket costs Costs that require an outlay of cash or other resources.

At the most general level, costs can be separated into out-of-pocket costs and opportunity costs. **Out-of-pocket costs** require an outlay of cash or other resources. Many of the costs discussed thus far in this chapter could be called out-of-pocket costs (though sunk costs are *never* considered an out-of-pocket cost). If a company is deciding whether to accept a special order, the costs of materials needed to produce that order are out-of-pocket costs. If a fast-food restaurant is considering installing a drive-up window, the cost of construction is an out-of-pocket cost. Naïve individuals and organizations usually consider only out-of-pocket costs when making decisions. For example, an individual deciding whether to attend a movie might consider only the $7 cost

business environment essay

Accounting and the "Shaq Impact" Opportunity costs are important in all organizations but are especially critical in situations where there are defined limits on available resources. Professional basketball teams, for example, have league-imposed salary caps that dictate the maximum total amount of salaries they can pay to team members. In the 2000/2001 season, the salary cap is $35.5 million per team. When an exceptional player, such as Shaquille O'Neal (Shaq) of the **LOS ANGELES LAKERS**, comes up for salary negotiations, the team's management must consider both out-of-pocket and opportunity costs when deciding whether to pay the salary requested. For example, Shaq signed a seven-year contract in 1996 with the Los Angeles Lakers for $123 million; that works out to more than $17 million per year! Before agreeing to the contract, the Lakers management had to decide whether yearly ticket sales and TV revenues would be sufficient to meet the out-of-pocket cost of $17 million. Management also had to consider what other player(s) it could sign for $17 million per year and whether, based on the existence of the salary cap, it would be able to pay other current and prospective players enough. For example, the Lakers recently signed Kobe Bryant at approximately $9 million per year. Paying $26 million per year to Shaq and Kobe makes it nearly impossible for the Lakers to pay other players that much money and thus is a high opportunity cost for a professional basketball team. (Note: The Lakers' total team salary payout for 1999/2000 was a little over $54 million. The NBA penalizes teams going over the salary cap with a hefty salary "luxury tax.")

of the ticket required to gain admittance. On the other hand, opportunity costs do not require an outlay of resources. Nevertheless, they are as important as out-of-pocket costs to good management decision making. **Opportunity costs** are the benefits lost or forfeited as a result of selecting one alternative course of action over another. For example, choosing to go to a movie instead of working two hours at $6 per hour has an opportunity cost of $12, as well as an out-of-pocket cost of $7 for the ticket. Installing a drive-up window at a fast-food outlet may have several opportunity costs, such as lost seating or lost parking available to customers.

opportunity costs The benefits lost or forfeited as a result of selecting one alternative course of action over another.

STOP & THINK Which of the following costs are typically recorded in a traditional accounting system: product costs, fixed costs, indirect costs, out-of-pocket costs, sunk costs, opportunity costs?

Segment Analysis at DuPont

Let's return once more to DuPont and apply these new cost concepts to the management process of evaluating the Kevlar and Teflon product lines to determine if the company can continue to profitably offer both products to the public. Assume that the following data represent the results of operations this last month for these two products:

Operating Statements	Kevlar	Teflon	Total
Batches produced and sold	900	920	
Sales revenue	$12,150,000	$13,340,000	$25,490,000
Direct materials	(4,320,000)	(3,864,000)	(8,184,000)
Direct labor	(162,000)	(607,200)	(769,200)
Variable manufacturing overhead	(351,000)	(1,076,400)	(1,427,400)
Fixed manufacturing overhead	(1,560,000)	(4,680,000)	(6,240,000)
Sales and administrative costs	(1,650,000)	(4,950,000)	(6,600,000)
Operating profit	**$ 4,107,000**	**$ (1,837,600)**	**$ 2,269,400**

It looks as though DuPont had a tough month with the Teflon product. In fact, let's assume that the past several months show similar losses on the Teflon product line. In evaluating these results, perhaps management should consider the possibility of dropping this product line. Doing so would certainly improve overall profits for the organization, wouldn't it? Actually, we need to be careful with this analysis. The operating statements above categorize the costs in terms of product costs and period costs. Is that the right way to view these costs for this particular decision? What are the *direct* costs in this decision? Stated another way, what are the *differential* (or *avoidable*) costs of producing Teflon? If DuPont exited from the market for Teflon products, could it avoid all the related costs of direct materials in the future? Yes, certainly. What about the costs of direct labor? With some effort, yes. Variable manufacturing overhead? Again, eliminating these costs would not be automatic, but these costs (such as indirect supplies and equipment maintenance work) could be substantially reduced or removed from the system over time with management effort. How about fixed manufacturing overhead? These costs are going to be more difficult to handle. Fixed manufacturing overhead includes items such as supervisors' salaries and depreciation on equipment and plant facilities. Can these costs be avoided? Actually, perhaps some of these costs can be avoided, but most of these costs are likely unavoidable. For example, let's assume that both Kevlar and Teflon are manufactured in the same building. The depreciation on this building, a fixed manufacturing cost, is allocated to both product lines (a classic example of an indirect cost). If DuPont drops the Teflon product line, the cost related to building depreciation does not go away. It is simply reallocated to the remaining products still being produced in the facility. Sales and administrative costs assigned to the Teflon product line are even less likely to be avoided by a decision to exit this market. These costs often remain within the company and then end up being the responsibility of the remaining product lines.

To better support a decision process involving the possibility of dropping Teflon from DuPont's mix of products, we really need to redo the cost classifications in the operating statements for these two products. We'll classify the product and period costs above as either direct or indirect to the product line. In making this new classification, we'll assume in this example that approximately 30% of the fixed manufacturing overhead can be avoided if Teflon is dropped. Hence, 30% of the fixed manufacturing overhead is a direct cost to the segment.

Operating Statements	**Kevlar**	**Teflon**	**Total**
Batches produced and sold	900	920	
Sales revenue	$12,150,000	$13,340,000	$25,490,000
Direct costs:			
Direct materials	(4,320,000)	(3,864,000)	(8,184,000)
Direct labor	(162,000)	(607,200)	(769,200)
Variable manufacturing overhead	(351,000)	(1,076,400)	(1,427,400)
Fixed manufacturing overhead (30%)	(468,000)	(1,404,000)	(1,872,000)
Segment profit	**$ 6,849,000**	**$ 6,388,400**	**$13,237,400**
Indirect costs:			
Fixed manufacturing overhead (70%)	(1,092,000)	(3,276,000)	(4,368,000)
Sales and administrative costs	(1,650,000)	(4,950,000)	(6,600,000)
Operating profit	**$ 4,107,000**	**$ (1,837,600)**	**$ 2,269,400**

These new cost classifications are very insightful. To grasp the message of these numbers, you need to be very clear about the distinction between direct and indirect costs. By definition, those costs that can be removed from the system by discontinuing the Teflon business segment are direct costs to the segment. All other costs assigned by the accounting system to the Teflon segment are actually indirect costs; that is, these are the common costs that have been allocated to the segments. As you can see, $8,226,000 ($3,276,000 + $4,950,000) of indirect costs is assigned to the Teflon product line. Should DuPont choose to exit the market for Teflon products, these costs will remain in the company and will likely be reallocated to the remaining business segments. So what will be the financial impact of dropping the Teflon product line? The "true" performance of Teflon last month was not a loss, but a $6,388,400 contribution to overall company profits.

Interestingly, some costs that are relevant to the decision of whether to drop the Teflon product line may not be reported in the analysis above. The evaluating process also needs to consider the opportunity costs to DuPont of producing Teflon. Suppose that DuPont has alternative uses for its Teflon production resources (e.g., personnel, equipment, expertise, etc.). If DuPont leaves the Teflon business, what else might it be able to produce and sell? If DuPont chooses to not drop Teflon from its product mix, then it will miss out on the profits possible from an alternative use of these resources. Suppose that DuPont could alternatively use the Teflon resources to enter the business of providing a different polymer product. After consulting with the engineering and marketing departments, DuPont's accountants determine that this alternative product could generate approximately $7 million monthly in incremental segment profit. This information could certainly change the evaluation decision. If there is a $7 million opportunity for the Teflon resources, one could argue that perhaps DuPont should drop the Teflon business segment. When the (very relevant) opportunity costs of Teflon are considered, Teflon's "true" profit is actually an economic loss of $611,600.

Segment profit	**$ 6,388,400**
Opportunity cost (alternative product profit)	(7,000,000)
Economic profit (loss)	**$ (611,600)**

It is important to understand that opportunity costs are very important costs that are not formally tracked in the company's accounting system. Nevertheless, the opportunity costs of Teflon are very real and, as you can see, need to factor into the decision of whether DuPont should continue to produce and sell Teflon. We will spend more time on opportunity costs and segment analysis in Chapters 8 and 9 of management accounting.

to summarize

Different terms are used to describe costs depending on the aspect of the management process involved—planning, controlling, or evaluating. In the evaluation of segments such as product lines or business divisions, managers need to be clear about the difference between direct and indirect costs. Direct costs are costs that are specifically traceable to a segment. Sometimes direct costs are referred to as differential costs, avoidable costs, incremental costs, or relevant costs. The direct costs of a particular segment will change based on future decisions affecting the segment. On the other hand, indirect costs, or common costs, are costs that are normally incurred for the benefit of several segments. Although indirect costs can be changed by some high-level decisions, decisions affecting any one of the segments will not affect indirect costs that are common across all the segments. On the other hand, sunk costs are costs that cannot be changed based on *any* decisions made by management. These are costs that have already been spent (such as depreciation on a purchased building) or costs that cannot be realistically avoided (such as the property tax on the administration building). Finally, opportunity costs are measured as the benefits lost by choosing one alternative over another. Opportunity costs, though not recorded formally in most companies' accounting systems, are relevant to most decisions. These cost terms are particularly useful in the management process of evaluating the contribution of product lines.

6

Understand that management accounting still continues to evolve.

EXPANDING MANAGEMENT ACCOUNTING: COST, QUALITY, AND TIME

The **DUPONT** ROI formula is a terrific tool for managing most kinds of organizations. You realize, though, that ROI has been with us now for nearly a century. Most educated managers are fully aware of ROI and how to apply it within their particular organization. Remember that the development of management accounting is a function of the need for information and tools that provide a competitive edge. Would you expect then that the use of ROI provides managers a significant competitive edge in *today's* economy? The truth of the matter is that, in most industries, effective use of ROI and other traditional management accounting tools is still necessary, but using only these tools is probably not sufficient to successfully plan, control, and evaluate a business process. Today's managers need more and better information. In fact, beginning with the Japanese innovation of **just-in-time (JIT)** in the mid-twentieth century, accountants and other information providers have moved beyond just providing data on costs to include innovative methods of measuring the *quality* and the *timeliness* of products and production processes, as well as service and distribution systems. Businesses today create a competitive advantage by delivering more value to customers in less **cycle time** than competitors. As a firm creates and exploits a competitive advantage in cost, quality, and time, it creates increased shareholder value. In other words, if you make your customers happy, you create more profitable financial outcomes and, in the process, make the owners (shareholders) of the business happy! As a result, new performance measures related to cost, quality, and time are being accumulated, tracked, and monitored by firms in many modern industries and have become a hot topic for research among management accountants. Some examples of the new performance measures be-

just-in-time (JIT) A management philosophy that emphasizes removing all waste of effort, time, and inventory costs from the organization. One obvious result of JIT is the reduction or removal of needless inventory in a production process.

cycle time The total time a product spends moving through a particular process or cycle within the organization, such as the product design cycle, the production cycle, or the order and delivery cycle.

business environment essay

One Company's Experience with Cost, Quality, and Time Developing measures of cost, quality, and time is a highly proprietary strategic activity. Many organizations are very reluctant to disclose the specifics of their efforts to develop competitive information in these three areas. One company (a medium-sized aerospace corporation in the Pacific Northwest that chooses to remain anonymous) provides a good illustration of the process of creating cost, quality, and time strategic measures. In 1989, the executive team started work to develop new competitive information for this company. It first conducted a survey of key customers, asking about product design, quality, and reliability; the company's ability to meet delivery schedules and other commitments; pricing and perceived value; service and the capability to recover from mistakes; and the overall ease of doing business with the company.

The results were surprising. Contrary to expectations, customers weren't concerned with the company's technological innovations that management had been proud of for years. Instead, customers were concerned with cost, quality, and delivery performance. To their dismay, the executives discovered that customers were dissatisfied with the company's performance in these three areas. Some said they continued to buy from the company only because it was easy to do business with and resolved problems quickly. Clearly, the company was at risk of losing its customers to a competitor unless some changes were made!

To refocus the company on the needs of its customers, an executive staff team was formed to meet weekly to develop a new performance measurement system. The meetings turned into prolonged debates over the number and kind of measures to use. Hours of brainstorming eventually led to the following list:

ing tracked by management accountants in the strategic areas of cost, quality, and time are displayed in Exhibit 1-5. We'll discuss many of these performance measures in later chapters.

The idea of extending beyond cost to also compete on quality and time is having a major impact in industries across the world. These competitive developments present a real opportunity for today's management accountants to jump in and be a part of the process! Frankly, some accountants are not paying attention to this recent shift in management information needs. These accountants continue to focus on providing cost data only. Apparently, they haven't learned their history lesson. Success and profits flow to the business that creates new views of information it can use to gain a competitive edge in the marketplace. On the other hand, some far-sighted accountants see the trend and are currently bringing together "balanced scorecards" that combine cost, quality, and time data to support decision making that can literally redefine cus-

exhibit 1-5 New Measures of Cost, Quality, and Time

Cost Measures	Quality Measures	Time Measures
Engineering cost performance	Manufacturing first-pass yield	On-time delivery
Rework and scrap costs	Warranty returns	Master schedule stability
Cost versus features/benefits delivered	Vendor supply quality	New-product development cycle time
Costs of quality	Service and support events	Manufacturing cycle time
Life cycle costs	Successful availability events	Recovery-response time
Target costs	Alignment with customer expectations	Time to market
Learning costs	Six sigma error rate	Order fulfillment cycle time
Activity costs	Waste, scrap, and rework rates	Rework and other non-value-added time

Cost Measures

- Engineering cost performance
- Production efficiency
- Rework and scrap costs

Quality Measures

- Quality of supplier's products
- Manufacturing first-pass yield
- Warranty returns

Time Measures

- New-product development cycle time
- Master schedule stability
- Manufacturing cycle time
- On-time delivery

The executive team assigned the company's controller to collect performance data for each of these 10 measures and issue a monthly report. Graphs of the results were posted for employees and customers to see and became a critical part of any meeting in which management reviewed performance. Some adjustments to these measures were made based on feedback from employees and customers. Eventually, this new approach to performance measures played a crucial role in the company's overall efforts to increase its competitive position. By 1993, it achieved the following performance improvements:

- Customer-quoted delivery times were cut by 50%.
- On-time shipments rose 89%.
- Product-development cycle time fell 35%.
- Manufacturing costs as a percentage of manufacturing sales fell 10%.

Source: K. V. Ramanathan and D. S. Schaffer, "How Am I Doing?" *Journal of Accountancy,* May 1995, pp. 79–82.

fyi

In deciding how to make tradeoffs between costs, quality, and other factors, the lowest-cost alternative is not always best. Take major league baseball, for example. In 2000, the five teams with the highest player payrolls were the New York Yankees ($113.4 million), Atlanta Braves ($95.0 million), Los Angeles Dodgers ($94.2 million), Boston Red Sox ($93.9 million), and New York Mets ($89.7 million). Guess which teams were in the World Series in 2000? Hint: New Yorkers affectionately called it a "subway series." So, if winning the World Series is the most important measure of performance, then minimizing payroll costs is probably not a relevant goal.

tomer and client service. We'll talk more about balanced scorecards and other recent innovations in management accounting in Chapter 10 of management accounting.

to summarize

As we move into the twenty-first century, strategic performance measures of cost, quality, and time will continue to support and improve decisions that build organizations both in the profit and the not-for-profit sectors of our society. Management accountants, if they expect to have jobs as key decision-support professionals in the twenty-first century, must provide data that encompass all three of these strategic imperatives.

IN CONCLUSION—THE MANAGEMENT PROCESS

We have focused this chapter around **DUPONT** and the way this company uses management accounting to provide managers with information that has competitive value. To accomplish this, however, management accountants must understand the types of decisions being made and how these decisions affect management of a successful organization. In particular, we've introduced a number of important management accounting terms in the context of the management process of planning, controlling, and evaluating. Throughout the remainder of this text, we'll continue to organize management accounting topics around this management process.

review of learning objectives

1 Understand the essential differences between management accounting and financial accounting, as illustrated by managerial use of the ROI formula. Management accounting as we know it today is a product of managers and owners reacting to competitive forces. At the turn of the twentieth century, the DUPONT CORPORATION combined many management accounting innovations into a new performance evaluation model based on the return on investment (ROI) measure. Hence, the development trend of management accounting is in contrast to the legislative and regulatory forces that began defining financial accounting after the Stock Market Crash of 1929.

2 Understand that successfully managing a company requires good information that supports effective planning, controlling, and evaluating processes. Planning involves both long-term planning such as strategic planning and capital budgeting and short-term planning involving production and process prioritizing as well as operational budgeting. Effective control of costs in the organization requires good tracking of actual performance. Evaluating involves analyzing results, providing feedback to managers and other employees, rewarding performance, and identifying problems. Evaluating naturally leads management back to the planning process, illustrating the interrelationship of the management process.

3 Know how the concepts of fixed and variable costs are used in C-V-P analysis in the management planning process. It is important to understand how accounting terminology must change to support specific management settings. In the context of cost-volume-profit (C-V-P) analysis, costs are classified as variable costs or fixed costs. Using this classification, C-V-P analysis then follows a formula approach to determine the sales volumes necessary to achieve a specified profit level.

4 Realize how the product cost classifications of direct materials, direct labor, and overhead are used in the management controlling process. For manufacturing firms, product costs include direct materials, direct labor, and manufacturing overhead. In a merchandising company, product costs are costs incurred to purchase goods and get them ready for resale. For service firms, product costs are costs of providing a service to customers. These costs are used to determine both asset values on the balance sheet and costs of goods sold on the income statement. In contrast to product costs, period costs are used strictly to compute the selling and general administrative expenses on the income statement. The process of identifying, tracking, and controlling product costs requires an intelligent method of allocating overhead costs to goods and services.

5 Be able to perform a simple segment analysis using the concepts of direct, indirect, and opportunity costs in the management evaluating process. Costs can be distinguished as being direct or indirect depending on their relationship to a particular segment being evaluated. Essentially, all costs that would be eliminated if the business discontinued the segment are considered the direct costs of that particular segment. Other costs currently allocated to the segment being considered for removal that would essentially shift to other segments are indirect costs. Sunk costs are those costs in the organization that no reasonable decision of any kind can avoid. These costs are essentially irrelevant to any decisions in the organization. On the other hand, opportunity costs, which are rarely tracked in the formal accounting system, are nearly always relevant to decisions.

6 Understand that management accounting still continues to evolve. As competition has increased and markets have become more sophisticated, management accounting today is expanding beyond cost management to include performance measures of quality and timeliness.

key terms and concepts

opportunity costs 21
out-of-pocket costs 20
overhead cost allocation 16
period costs 14
planning 8
product costs 13
production prioritizing 9
profit margin 5
return on investment (ROI) 5
strategic planning 9
sunk costs 19
variable costs 11

discussion questions

1. DUPONT was America's first large-scale "vertically integrated" company. What does "vertically integrated" mean?
2. The chapter states that the focus of management accounting is to create information to fill a competitive need. Explain how management accounting can provide a competitive edge in business.
3. How can management accounting information help companies to be competitive and profitable?
4. What exactly did Donaldson Brown, the accountant for DuPont, develop, and why was it so revolutionary?
5. Management accounting and financial accounting provide different information for different purposes. Explain what this means and provide an example that illustrates the differences between management and financial accounting.
6. Managers need not be concerned about external financial statements. Do you agree or disagree with this statement? Explain.
7. Why is GAAP so important for external financial reporting but not for internal management reporting?
8. Identify the three management functions relating to the decision-making process. Briefly define each function.
9. How is strategic planning related to capital budgeting?
10. How do variable costs and fixed costs differ? Give an example of each.
11. Analyze your personal expenses on a variable and fixed basis. What are some of your personal fixed costs and variable costs? What would cause them to change?
12. What is C-V-P analysis used for?
13. Explain the difference between a product cost and a period cost.
14. What are the three components of manufacturing costs? Briefly describe them.
15. How do nonmanufacturing costs and indirect costs differ?
16. What classification determines whether materials used in the production of a product are direct materials or indirect materials? Is the classification always simple to determine? What are some examples of direct materials and indirect materials used in the production of a chair?
17. What are some of the major challenges in tracking and controlling manufacturing overhead costs?
18. Essentially, how are manufacturing overhead costs allocated to goods and services?
19. What is the difference between a direct cost and an indirect cost? Give an example of each in the context of teaching an accounting class at your school.
20. What is the difference between sunk costs and differential costs? Give an example of each.
21. How can out-of-pocket costs and opportunity costs be applied to your personal financial decisions?

discussion cases

CASE 1-1

DEVELOPING MANAGEMENT ACCOUNTING INFORMATION (DUPONT)

The story of E. I. DU PONT DE NEMOURS AND COMPANY detailed at the beginning of this chapter provides key insights into the development of management accounting. In particular, we see how the structure of a business affects the kinds of information required for planning, controlling, and evaluating purposes. Consider the decision to "vertically integrate" the company. What were the potential risks to DUPONT of this decision? What accounting information would have been required to determine if the decision to vertically integrate was successful? Does the traditional accounting system designed to produce external financial reports provide the required information in an easily obtainable fashion?

CASE 1-2

SUPPORTING THE MANAGEMENT PROCESS (IBM)

INTERNATIONAL BUSINESS MACHINES CORPORATION (IBM) has faced challenges this last decade due to increased competition in the home-consumer segment of the personal computer (PC) market. When IBM introduced the PC in the early 1980s, it was a huge success. Over time, however, the PC market grew immensely, and competition began to rise.

Although the PC was initially marketed toward businesses, a home-consumer market emerged as well. In 1995, IBM, under the direction of CEO Louis Gerstner, set up a home-consumer PC division to augment its business PC division. IBM hoped that with the two divisions, each employing its own design, manufacturing, and marketing personnel, it could better focus on the needs of its various customers and increase total sales.

IBM's consumer division quickly developed PCs that had high customer appeal. In early 1996, the division released its "Aptiva" PC in a sleek, dark gray color. The model was equipped with many high-tech features. Also, IBM's reputation for quality allowed the consumer division to charge a higher price for the PCs. (In December 1996, IBM PCs sold for an average of $1,880, whereas other companies charged as little as $1,300 to $1,400.)

Initially, the manufacturing department in IBM's consumer division could not keep up with consumer demand. Recently, however, IBM has been losing market share to companies such as **DELL**, **COMPAQ**, and **GATEWAY**. These companies are finding that consumers prefer low price to the extra "frills" that IBM offers in its computers. Furthermore, IBM is discovering that many consumers are no longer willing to pay higher prices for IBM's reputation. IBM, the company that once dominated the PC market, has plummeted in its market share and is currently at less than 5%.

1. Did IBM make a good decision in setting up its consumer division? How so?
2. Analyze IBM's decisions and actions involving the consumer division. Try to categorize these decisions and actions following the threefold management process of planning, controlling, and evaluating.
3. Based on the threefold management process of planning, controlling, and evaluating, where do you think IBM was weakest in its decision-making practice with respect to the consumer division? Where do you think it was strongest?
4. If you were Louis Gerstner, what information would you want from your management accountants in order to effectively plan, control, and evaluate the decision to either shut down or continue to operate the consumer division?

Source: Raju Narisetti, "IBM to Revamp Struggling Home-PC Business," *The Wall Street Journal,* October 14, 1997, p. B1.

exercises

EXERCISE 1-1

CHANGES IN BUSINESS AFFECTING MANAGEMENT ACCOUNTING

You are at the student union having lunch with a friend who is attending law school. In the course of your conversation, you tell your friend that, in contrast to financial accounting or tax accounting, management accounting has "competitive value" and is highly proprietary. Further, management accounting is more important in business today than ever before, and only those organizations that best control costs and improve quality are competitive. Your friend asks you two questions:

1. What do you mean by "competitive value"?
2. Why is it more important for management accountants to provide useful information to management today than it was before?

EXERCISE 1-2

CHARACTERISTICS OF ACCOUNTING REPORTS

Indicate whether each of the following is characteristic of financial accounting reports, management accounting reports, or both:

1. They are used primarily by creditors and investors.
2. They aid management in identifying problems.
3. They are based on generally accepted accounting principles.
4. They are standardized across companies.
5. They provide information for decision making by management.
6. They measure performance and isolate differences between planned and actual results.
7. They are created based on competitive needs that are unique to the organization.

EXERCISE 1-3

FINANCIAL AND MANAGEMENT ACCOUNTING

A friend who is thinking about majoring in accounting has asked you to distinguish between the work of a financial accountant and a management accountant. What is your response?

EXERCISE 1-4

PERIOD COSTS AND PRODUCT COSTS

Bright, Inc., a producer of educational toys for children, incurs the following types of costs:

a. Depreciation on the production plant
b. Depreciation on the corporate offices
c. Paper, toner, and miscellaneous supplies for the office copy machines
d. Wages of production-line employees
e. Raw materials used in the production of toys
f. Wages of the corporate headquarter's secretarial staff
g. Maintenance costs on the production equipment
h. Advertising costs
i. Shipping costs for products sold
j. Salaries of plant supervisors
k. Interest on bank loans
l. Property tax on the production plant
m. Property tax on the corporate offices
n. Commissions paid to sales personnel
o. Administrative salaries of corporate executives

Classify each cost as a period cost or a product cost. For each item classified as a product cost, indicate whether it would usually be included in direct materials, direct labor, or manufacturing overhead.

EXERCISE 1-5

MANUFACTURING COSTS

Jordan Industries is a manufacturing company that produces solid oak office furniture. During the year, the following costs were incurred. The building depreciation and the utilities are allocated three-fourths to production and one-fourth to administration. The cost of furniture parts can be traced to specific production runs.

Oak wood	$ 50,000
Miscellaneous supplies (glue, saw blades, varnish, etc.)	10,000
Furniture parts (wheels, locks, etc.)	5,500
Payroll—plant manager's salary	25,000
Payroll—administrative salaries	100,000
Payroll—production-line employees' wages	45,500
Building depreciation	28,000
Maintenance—plant and equipment	5,000
Utilities	16,000
Income taxes	8,500

1. Classify the costs into the following four categories: direct materials, direct labor, manufacturing overhead, and period costs.
2. Calculate the total amount of cost for each category.

EXERCISE 1-6

MANUFACTURING AND NONMANUFACTURING COSTS

The Benson Manufacturing Company produces rides for amusement parks. Parts for the rides are purchased from other suppliers. Rides are then assembled in various company plants.

Recently, Benson Manufacturing hired two new employees. One will be working in an assembly plant, and the other will be working in the marketing division of the corporate offices as a sales representative.

The assembly plant employee will be paid an annual salary of $25,000, or $12.50 per hour. Her time will be charged to the individual rides that she assembles. The marketing division employee will receive an annual salary of $20,000 plus commission. He will be responsible for both advertising and selling. His salary is for advertising responsibilities, and he will be paid a commission on sales of amusement rides.

1. Should the salary of the assembly plant employee be classified as a manufacturing or a nonmanufacturing cost? Should the salary of the marketing division employee be classified as a manufacturing or a nonmanufacturing cost? How is this classification made?
2. After classifying the salaries as manufacturing or nonmanufacturing costs, determine how the salary costs will affect the cost of assembling the amusement rides. Classify the employee costs as direct, indirect, fixed, variable, product, or period. (Each cost can be classified in more than one way.)

EXERCISE 1-7

PERFORMANCE MEASUREMENT

The president of Radkline Corporation, Karen Pinkus, has asked you, the company's controller, to advise her on whether Radkline should develop a new inventory management system. Is the decision facing Karen Pinkus an example of a strategic planning decision, a capital budgeting decision, a production prioritization decision, or an operational budgeting decision? Be sure to defend your answer.

EXERCISE 1-8

COST CLASSIFICATIONS

The following are costs associated with manufacturing firms, merchandising firms, or service firms:

a. Miscellaneous materials used in production
b. Salesperson's commission in a real estate firm
c. Administrators' salaries for a furniture wholesaler
d. Administrators' salaries for a furniture manufacturer
e. Freight costs associated with inventories of a grocery store
f. Office manager's salary in a doctor's office
g. Utilities for the corporate offices of a toy manufacturer
h. Line supervisor's salary for a clothing manufacturing firm
i. Training seminar for sales staff of a service firm
j. Fuel used in a trucking firm
k. Paper used at a printing business
l. Oil for machinery at a plastics manufacturing firm
m. Food used at a restaurant
n. Windshields used for a car manufacturer

Classify the costs as (1) product or period; (2) variable or fixed; and (3) for those that are product costs, as direct materials, direct labor, or manufacturing overhead. Write "not applicable (N/A)" if a category doesn't apply.

EXERCISE 1-9

COST CLASSIFICATIONS

The following are costs associated with manufacturing firms, merchandising firms, or service firms:

a. Legal services for an accounting firm
b. Car leases for company management

c. Oil used to service manufacturing equipment
d. Office supplies for a grocery store
e. Entertainment expense
f. Travel expenses for doctors in a medical firm
g. Plastic used in making computers
h. Collection costs of accounts receivable
i. Electricity to run saws at a lumber yard
j. Food for a company banquet
k. Advertising expense
l. Continuing education for a doctor
m. Commissions paid to salespersons
n. Depreciation on sports equipment by a professional football team
o. Calculators used by office employees
p. Earplugs used at an airport
q. Toll charges incurred because of business travel
r. Fuel used in manufacturing equipment

Classify the costs as (1) product or period; (2) variable or fixed; and (3) for those that are product costs, as direct materials, direct labor, or manufacturing overhead. Write "not applicable (N/A)" if a category doesn't apply.

EXERCISE 1-10

C-V-P ANALYSIS

Phelps, Inc., located in Irvine, California, manufactures high-end baby chairs. The firm's cost accountant, Amy, has been assigned by the CEO to determine how many baby chairs Phelps, Inc., needs to make to break even. She is given the following data:

Baby chair sales price	$ 16
Variable cost per baby chair	6
Production worker salary	1,000

Determine how many baby chairs Phelps, Inc., needs to make to break even.

EXERCISE 1-11

C-V-P ANALYSIS

The Los Angeles Lakers basketball team has hired you as its new accountant. On your first day on the job, Lakers Vice President of Basketball Operations, Magic Johnson, comes to you and asks, "How many tickets must we sell to pay for Shaq's salary?" He then hands you a sheet of paper with the following information:

Shaq's salary	$17,000,000
Average ticket price	75
Printing cost of one ticket	1

1. Prepare your response to Magic's question.
2. How many tickets would the Lakers have to sell to pay for the entire Lakers team if the total team salary (including Shaq) is $54,000,000?

EXERCISE 1-12

PRODUCT COSTING

BatsRUs, Inc., has created a unique line of aluminum baseball bats that, while illegal for league use, are designed to nearly double the average length of a batted ball. They are a great "hit" in the personal and family use market. Recently, a new competitor, Awesome Bats, Inc., has introduced a competing bat to the market. Suddenly, BatsRUs is experiencing severe market pressure to significantly lower its normal market price of $175. The problem is that management is not very confident about the actual production cost per bat. With some effort, the following data have been developed for management to use in setting a new market price and, more importantly, beginning an effort to better control costs.

Standard Variable Costs to Produce One Batch of 10 Bats (600 batches are typically produced each week)			
	Average Cost per Pound	**Average Pounds per Batch**	**Total Costs**
Direct Materials	$ 3	16	$ 48
	Average Rate per Hour	**Average Hours per Batch**	
Direct labor	$15	2	30
Variable manufacturing overhead	20	2	40
Total variable costs			$118

Standard Monthly Fixed Costs	
Manufacturing overhead	$240,000
Sales and administrative costs	180,000
Total fixed costs	$420,000

1. What appears to be the average cost for BatsRUs to manufacture a single baseball bat?
2. Do you have any questions or concerns about how the data are being used to determine the cost of manufacturing a baseball bat at BatsRUs?

EXERCISE 1-13

Spread-Sheet Software

PRODUCT COSTING AND C-V-P ANALYSIS

PrepNow, Inc., offers a CPA review course in cities throughout the eastern United States. PrepNow hires local CPAs to do the teaching. Each instructor is paid $110 an hour to teach the course; a course consists of 16 weeks of instruction with sessions taking place two evenings a week for three hours at each session. The other instruction costs to PrepNow are to pay for hotel conference rooms to host the course. Generally, PrepNow pays the hotel $500 per evening to rent a conference room. Also, tuition for the course includes all course materials, which cost the company $160 for each student.

1. What is the "product cost" of providing one evening of instruction for all students?
2. What is the "product cost" of training a student over the entire course (there are 50 students in this particular course)?
3. Assuming that PrepNow charges each student $1,100 for the course, how many students would be required to "break even" on this course?

EXERCISE 1-14

Spread-Sheet Software

SEGMENT ANALYSIS

You are the accountant for the largest manufacturer of aluminum cans. The company's hottest product is the X-96, which provides most of the firm's revenue. Management is considering dropping the W-96 product line, which hasn't turned a profit for two consecutive years. The CFO comes to you and asks what you would do given the following data:

Operating Statements	X-96	W-96	Total
Batches produced and sold	100	120	
Sales revenue	$15,000	$21,600	$36,600
Direct materials	(1,000)	(4,200)	(5,200)
Direct labor	(2,000)	(3,840)	(5,840)
Variable manufacturing overhead	(500)	(2,400)	(2,900)
Fixed manufacturing overhead	(1,000)	(8,700)	(9,700)
Sales and administrative costs	(1,000)	(3,000)	(4,000)
Operating profit	$ 9,500	$ (540)	$ 8,960

Note: Approximately 20% of the fixed manufacturing overhead is directly related to (i.e., created within) each segment.

1. Distinguish between direct and indirect costs and find the segment profit for each product.
2. Determine the gain or loss that the firm would incur if it dropped the W-96 product line. What figure would you provide the CFO?
3. Explain your recommendation to continue or discontinue product line W-96.

EXERCISE 1-15

OPPORTUNITY COSTS

Mike is employed by a company that currently pays him $80,000 per year. He owns a new car that he bought for cash of $35,000. Mike is thinking about returning to school to obtain a law degree. Tuition for the school he wants to attend is $25,000 per year, books average $1,000 per year, and room and board average $10,000 per year.

Determine the total sunk cost and the total opportunity cost for Mike if he decides to go back to law school for three years.

competency enhancement opportunities

- Analyzing Real Company Information
- International Case
- Ethics Case
- Writing Assignment
- The Debate
- Internet Search

The following additional assignments provide opportunities for students to develop critical thinking, ethical perspectives, oral and written communication skills, experience with electronic research, and teamwork through group and business activities.

ANALYZING REAL COMPANY INFORMATION

• *Analyzing 1-1 (Microsoft)*

1. Bill Gates wrote in his 1999 letter to **MICROSOFT** shareholders: "We are investing heavily in the future—from world-class customer support to the $3.8 billion we plan to spend in fiscal 2000 on research and development for the products of tomorrow." With the $2,970 billion that Microsoft spent on research and development (R&D) in 1999, it has increased its R&D spending by nearly 60% since 1997. R&D is more than 30% of its current operating expenses. Microsoft clearly spends a lot of its money on R&D. What are the potential advantages and disadvantages of this cost commitment to R&D?
2. A large part of Microsoft's R&D expenditures is for outside software developers who contract with Microsoft to work on specific projects. What factors does Microsoft need to consider in deciding to assign a research project to an outside contractor rather than to its internal software development staff?

• *Analyzing 1-2 (DuPont)*

As described in the chapter, the challenge facing **DUPONT** in the early twentieth century was how to manage the diverse set of businesses operating under the control of the DuPont management team. This diversity still exists today. In its 1999 annual report, DuPont notes that its strategic business units (operating segments) are organized by product line. For purposes of financial reporting, these have been aggregated into nine reportable segments: Agriculture & Nutrition, Nylon Enterprise, Performance Coatings & Polymers, Pharmaceuticals, Pigments & Chemicals, Pioneer, Polyester Enterprise, Specialty Fibers, and Specialty Polymers.

Summary segment results for 1999 for six of these nine segments are as follows (dollars in millions):

	Agriculture & Nutrition	Nylon Enterprise	Polymers	Pharmaceuticals	Pioneer	Polyester Enterprise
Total revenue	$2,598	$4,487	$6,111	$1,630	$ 422	$2,649
After-tax operating income.	358	63	582	230	(2,309)	(119)
Identifiable assets at December 31, 1999.	3,184	3,004	4,061	1,939	7,762	2,679

1. Which segment has the highest profit margin? The lowest?
2. Which segment has the highest asset turnover? The lowest?
3. Which segment has the highest return on investment? The lowest?
4. How could the segment with the lowest return on investment improve its financial performance?

INTERNATIONAL CASE

International

• *Toyota*

TOYOTA MOTOR CORPORATION was the company that originally defined and implemented the just-in-time (JIT) management technique mentioned in this chapter. Toyota was started in 1918 by Sakichi Toyoda as the **TOYOTA SPINNING AND WEAVING COMPANY**; in fact, a subsidiary of Toyota still makes spinning and weaving equipment today. In 1995, Toyota was the third-largest motor vehicle producer in the world, manufacturing 4,512,076 vehicles (behind **GENERAL MOTORS** at 7,997,794 and **FORD** at 6,401,495). In January 1997, Toyota made its 100 millionth vehicle.

In its 1997 annual report, Toyota said the following about its performance:

> Consolidated net income rose 50.2%, to 385.9 billion yen ($3,112 million), in the fiscal year ended March 31, 1997. That rise in earnings is attributable principally to the weakening of the yen, continuing cost savings, and growth in sales volume. The yen/dollar exchange rate averaged 112 yen during the past fiscal year, compared with 96 yen in the previous year. . . . The capacity for achieving cost savings on a continuing basis is integral to management at Toyota. New cost savings therefore will continue to contribute to earnings in the years ahead. . . . Our cost savings resulted from value-engineering improvements in designs and also from improvements in manufacturing processes and in logistics. Unending, systematic improvements in product designs and production processes will yield continuing cost savings.

1. Toyota attributes its 50% increase in net income to three factors: the weakening of the yen, cost savings, and growth in sales volume. Consider conducting a performance evaluation on the following people, and decide which of the three factors should be considered in the evaluation of:
   a. an assembly-line worker
   b. a factory manager
   c. a sales manager
   d. the company president
2. In relation to its cost savings, Toyota reports that the savings stem from improvements in engineering design, improvements in manufacturing processes, and improved logistics. Consider conducting a performance evaluation on the following people, and decide which (and why!) of the three cost savings factors should be considered in the evaluation of:
   a. an assembly-line worker
   b. a factory manager
   c. a purchasing manager
   d. the company president

ETHICS CASE

• Whom to Tell About Medicare Overbilling?

Professor Mary Allen is sitting in her office one day when Mark Sullivan, an accounting graduate from five years ago, knocks on her door. Mark had been an exceptionally good student and had started with the CPA firm Peat & Price on graduation. After three years with that firm, he joined MiniCare Health Company as the chief accountant and is now serving as its controller. Mark asks if he can talk with Professor Allen in confidence and then tells her that he has a problem: "Two years ago, I started working for MiniCare. Not long after I was promoted to controller, I noticed that the officers of the company were doing things that I didn't think were right. They have overbilled Medicare on several occasions, and senior management executives are misusing their positions by taking company perks that are against the company code of ethics. I have talked to my superior, the financial vice president, and he has, in essence, told me to mind my own business—that accountants are to report results and assist management, not question them."

Mark informs Professor Allen that he is making $100,000 a year, far more than he could earn in another company at this stage in his career. He asks her for advice. What should Professor Allen recommend that he do? Should Mark quit his job? Should he talk to someone else? If so, who? Should he go public with his information?

WRITING ASSIGNMENT

• Sunk Costs: They May Be Sunk, But They Aren't Forgotten.

You are the manager of the tire manufacturing subdivision of Uniyear Diversified Products. Last year, you were successful in convincing corporate executives that your division needed to purchase a new warehouse facility costing $40 million to house raw materials. You argued at the time that you could be much more productive if delays in getting materials from suppliers could be eliminated.

During the past 18 months, your company has worked hard to adopt JIT inventory and total quality control. You have successfully placed online terminals at key supplier locations, and the lag time in getting the raw materials you need has dropped from an average of four weeks to six hours.

Your problem now is that you no longer need the $40 million warehouse. It is a sunk cost. However, you are afraid that if you reveal that fact to the corporate executives, they will penalize or even fire you for being so shortsighted.

Draft a one-page memo to the president of Uniyear Diversified Products that explains why the $40 million warehouse is no longer needed. Remember that the memo has two purposes: to inform the president that the warehouse is no longer needed and to do so in a way that doesn't cost you your job.

THE DEBATE

• *When Should You Surrender?*

You are a partner in a CPA firm. For over 15 years, you conducted the audit of XYZ Corporation. Three years ago, however, the company went bankrupt. To your surprise, a class-action lawsuit was filed against your firm for $5 million, alleging that you failed to warn stockholders that the company was in financial difficulty. Your audit fee for XYZ Corporation was only $15,000 per year. Thus far you have spent $957,000 on legal fees and expert witness costs. Your attorney has worked out a settlement that would involve you paying the plaintiffs $750,000. You believe your defense is excellent, that the quality of your audits of XYZ Corporation was high, and that you will win the lawsuit. However, you also believe that it will cost another $800,000 in legal fees to successfully defend the case. Should you settle?

Divide your group into two teams.

- One team represents the "Fight to the Death" group. Prepare a two-minute oral presentation supporting the notion that you should not pay a penny to settle the lawsuit when you know that you did nothing wrong. You believe that the best long-run business strategy is to vigorously fight every lawsuit in order to discourage future suits.
- The other team represents the "Cut Our Losses" group. Prepare a two-minute oral presentation arguing that the past litigation costs are sunk and that the only reasonable comparison is between the cost of settling now and the cost of continuing the lawsuit.

INTERNET SEARCH

• *DuPont*

Access **DUPONT**'s Web site at **http://www.dupont.com**. Sometimes Web addresses change, so if this DuPont address doesn't work, access the Web site for this textbook (**http://albrecht.swcollege.com**) for an updated link to DuPont.

Once you've gained access to DuPont's Web site, answer the following questions:

1. Who is the current chief executive officer (CEO) of DuPont? How long has he or she been with the company? What is his or her background (e.g., legal, accounting, engineering, etc.)?
2. As mentioned in the chapter, the DuPont organization includes many diverse types of businesses. How many employees does DuPont have? In how many countries does DuPont operate? How many manufacturing facilities does DuPont operate? What fraction of DuPont's business is conducted outside the United States?

3. The history of DuPont, and some of its well-known products, is summarized in the chapter. DuPont's Web site offers further information. When did DuPont's polymer chemists invent nylon? What is Kevlar® used for?
4. DuPont reports a corporate commitment to moving toward zero emissions, zero employee injuries, and zero material waste. What progress does DuPont report in its effort to reduce air carcinogenic emissions?

Analyzing Cost-Volume-Profit Relationships

chapter m2

learning objectives After studying this chapter, you should be able to:

1 Understand the key factors involved in cost-volume-profit (C-V-P) analysis and why it is such an important tool in management decision making.

2 Explain and analyze the basic cost behavior patterns—variable, fixed, mixed, and stepped.

3 Analyze mixed costs using the scattergraph and high-low methods.

4 Perform C-V-P analyses, and describe the effects potential changes in C-V-P variables have on company profitability.

5 Visualize C-V-P relationships using graphs.

6 Identify the limiting assumptions of C-V-P analysis, and explain the issues of quality and time relative to C-V-P analysis decisions.

expanded material

7 Analyze mixed costs using the least squares method.

8 Explain the effects of sales mix on profitability.

9 Describe how fixed and variable costs differ in manufacturing, service, merchandising, and e-commerce organizations, and illustrate these differences with the operating leverage concept.

Recently, a profitable two-plant manufacturing company (that wishes to remain anonymous) built a new manufacturing facility less than one mile from its largest operating facility. This new facility provided no new features; it was built solely to provide additional manufacturing capacity. The company was expert in the design and manufacture of its products and, with the new facility coming on line, would have the capacity to make and sell more of its products.

As the firm's management considered the new facility, all involved parties got caught up in the excitement of the new plant. Executive management wanted to be "a bigger player in the industry" and believed that the new plant was its key to being one. Marketing said that the company could easily sell the "new capacity." Operations suggested that the new capacity would help the firm run more efficiently and facilitate manufacturing flow, thereby causing costs per unit to drop dramatically. And Finance approved capital appropriations based on the most favorable scenarios provided by everyone else.

What actually happened to this company was that fixed costs tripled while sales increased marginally, by about 30%. Profits turned quickly into losses, inventory increased, and over time the stock price fell to less than one-fourth of the pre-new facility level. In reality, the company had more than enough capacity in its pre-existing facility to manufacture 25 to 30% more product and, indeed, could have done so without incurring any additional fixed costs. As in so many cases, the data were available to all concerned, but the ability to analyze, interpret, and then act upon those data was missing or, worse, squandered.[1]

setting the stage

In Chapter 1 of management accounting, we discussed different ways to categorize costs. To review, some costs, such as direct materials and direct labor costs in a manufacturing firm, vary directly with the number of products or services produced. Other costs, such as some manufacturing overhead costs in a manufacturing firm, cannot be as easily traced to products. Costs that vary proportionately with the level of products produced or services offered are variable costs, while costs that do not vary in total with changes in the level of production are fixed costs. We used these definitions of variable costs and fixed costs to introduce you to ***cost-volume-profit (C-V-P) analysis****, a management accounting tool used to make planning decisions concerning appropriate levels of production and spending.*

In this chapter, you will further explore this important management tool to analyze relationships between variable costs, fixed costs, and revenues. You will learn that a key factor in making operating decisions is understanding ***cost behavior****—how costs change in relation to changes in activity levels, such as number of patients in a hospital or pounds of ore processed in a copper smelter. An understanding of how costs behave in relation to levels of activity helps managers predict the effects of their plans on future performance.*

You will also use the knowledge of cost behavior patterns to analyze the kinds of decisions facing companies like the one in the opening scenario. You will learn, for example, to make calculations that will determine how profits will change in relation to changes in sales volume, fixed costs, and variable costs. C-V-P analysis is critical in helping management plan future operations. Because the C-V-P analysis technique is applicable to all types of firms, we will also discuss the nature of costs in manufacturing, merchandising, service, and e-commerce firms. And while the focus will be primarily on examining the financial implications of cost-volume-profit analysis decisions, we will also pay attention to the effects these decisions have on quality and time issues as well.

cost-volume-profit (C-V-P) analysis Techniques for determining how changes in revenues, costs, and level of activity affect the profitability of an organization.

cost behavior The way a cost is affected by changes in activity levels.

1 John M. Brausch and Thomas C. Taylor, "Who Is Accounting for the Cost of Capacity?" *Management Accounting,* February 1997, p. 44.

1

Understand the key factors involved in cost-volume-profit (C-V-P) analysis and why it is such an important tool in management decision making.

UNDERSTANDING WHY C-V-P ANALYSIS IS IMPORTANT

Management must make many critical operating decisions that affect a firm's profitability. With respect to planning, management is often interested in the impact a particular action will have on profitability. C-V-P analysis can help managers assess that impact. The following are examples of questions that can be answered with C-V-P analysis:

- How will the profits of a bookstore be affected if the store raises its prices by 10%, resulting in a reduction of 2% in the number of books sold?
- How many customers must a scuba shop in the mall serve each month in order to break even and be able to pay the monthly rental fee?
- How many carpets must a fledgling entrepreneur clean in a month in order to generate a net profit of $3,000 each month?
- By how much will the profits of a discount computer store change if a $100,000 advertising campaign increases the number of units sold by 13%?
- How will the profits of a fast-food restaurant change if the restaurant stops selling milk shakes and instead focuses on raising the volume of soft drink sales by 25%?

It should be clear to you from these examples that C-V-P analysis involves studying the interrelationships among revenues, costs, levels of activity, and profits. However, quality of products and services and speed of production and delivery must also be considered as managers use C-V-P analysis to determine product prices, the mix of products, market strategy, appropriate sales commissions, advertising budgets, production schedules, and a host of other important planning decisions. Although C-V-P analysis is most useful for planning, it can also be used to assist with controlling decisions (e.g., are the costs too high for the level of sales?) and evaluating decisions (e.g., should we reward employees for holding costs down or be concerned that sales growth has slowed?). Indeed, the concept of C-V-P analysis is pervasive in management accounting. It offers tremendous potential for helping management increase the profitability and effectiveness of an organization. This chapter will help you learn the mechanics of C-V-P analysis as well as how to use this important concept. Before studying C-V-P analysis, however, you need to have a better understanding of basic cost behavior patterns. Once you understand these cost behavior patterns and how to determine them, you can use them to make the planning, controlling, and evaluating decisions discussed above.

to summarize

C-V-P analysis is a very important concept in management accounting. Key factors involved in C-V-P analysis include (1) the revenues derived from the sales prices charged for goods and services, (2) the fixed and variable costs, (3) the sales volume, (4) the mix of products, (5) the speed and quality of production, and (6) the resulting profits. Understanding the interrelationships of the key variables in C-V-P analysis can assist management in planning and in making critical controlling and evaluating decisions.

2

Explain and analyze the basic cost behavior patterns—variable, fixed, mixed, and stepped.

BASIC COST BEHAVIOR PATTERNS

The two basic cost behavior patterns—variable and fixed—were introduced in Chapter 1 of management accounting. Other cost behavior patterns, such as mixed costs, are variations of these two. Mixed costs exhibit characteristics of both variable and fixed costs. In this section, we will review both variable and fixed costs and examine the reality of how these costs often look in many organizations. We will also introduce mixed costs and stepped costs.

A cost is classified in one of the two basic categories by the way it reacts to changes in level of activity. The first task, then, is to define the activity involved and identify appropriate activity bases (often referred to as cost drivers). C-V-P analysis requires that we first determine what activity "drives" the costs. Once the activity is defined, measurements of changes in activity level can be used to determine cost behavior patterns.

Measuring Level of Activity

Level of activity is often measured in terms of output, input, or a combination of the two. Some of the most common activity bases used are number of units sold and number of units produced in manufacturing firms, number of units sold in merchandising firms, and number of contract hours paid for or billed in service firms. We will generally use production volume or sales volume as the activity basis in this chapter to demonstrate the use of C-V-P analysis. Note that just because a cost doesn't vary with a particular activity base (e.g., total units sold or units produced) does not mean it isn't a variable cost. For example, the total cost of wages for a convenience store may not vary with the amount of sales volume (the clerks get paid the same whether they serve a lot of customers or just a few), but total wages would vary based on the number of hours per week that the convenience store is open. So, if another type of activity other than sales volume is more relevant in determining changes in the variable costs being planned, the C-V-P analysis should be based on that activity. Managers must be careful to understand the various activity bases within their company so that they can properly plan for and control costs. We will discuss a number of alternative activity bases in Chapter 7 of management accounting.

Manufacturing and merchandising companies with a single product generally measure volume of activity in terms of output, for example, number of cars, television sets, or desks produced. However, many companies produce or sell several different products (refrigerators, toasters, and irons, for example), and a simple total of all the products manufactured or sold during a given period may not provide a good measure of activity. This is particularly true for manufacturing firms. For example, GENERAL ELECTRIC manufactures a wide variety of products, ranging from light bulbs to locomotives. It obviously takes more effort (and consequently costs more) to produce a locomotive than a light bulb; accordingly, it wouldn't make any sense to state that total production for a given day was 1,000,001—1,000,000 light bulbs and 1 locomotive. In multiproduct situations, these manufacturing firms usually use input measures, such as direct labor hours worked, machine time used, or the time needed to set up a job, as the activity base. Such measures are often better cost drivers than the more general output measures.

Variable Costs

variable costs Costs that change in total in direct proportion to changes in activity level.

Total **variable costs** change in direct proportion to changes in activity level. Examples are costs of direct materials, which vary proportionately with the number of units produced, and sales commissions, which vary proportionately with the sales volume. As an example, an automobile manufacturer might define the activity as the production of cars and the cost driver as the number of cars produced. If engines, tires, axles, and steering wheels are purchased from suppliers, the related costs would be variable because the total cost of steering wheels, for example, would vary proportionately with the number of cars produced. If no cars are produced, there are no steering wheel costs; if 1,000 cars are manufactured during a period, the total cost for steering wheels and other purchased parts is 1,000 times the unit cost of each item. As more cars are produced, the total cost of each item increases. The unit cost, however, remains constant. For example, if an auto company pays $150 per steering wheel, the total cost of steering wheels for 200 cars is $30,000; for 500 cars, it is $75,000. At both levels of activity, however, the unit cost is still $150. This relationship between variable costs and level of activity is shown graphically in Exhibit 2-1, which relates the number of cars produced to the total cost of the steering wheels used in production.

In addition to sales commissions and materials, many other costs (such as labor) have a variable cost behavior pattern. For example, if it takes four hours of labor to assemble a frame and

exhibit 2-1 An Example of Variable Costs

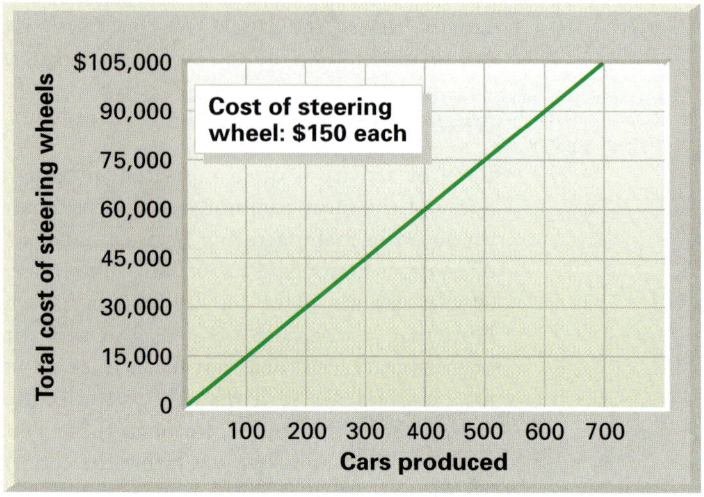

> **caution**
>
> Do not think that because a cost doesn't vary with production or sales, it cannot be a variable cost. For example, in a design engineering department, the activity base may be the number of changes to the architect's blueprints. Those costs that vary in total with the number of blueprint changes made would be classified as variable costs for that activity.

each hour costs $25, a unit labor cost of $100 per frame is a variable cost; the total labor cost would be $100 times the number of frames produced. As another example, if it generally requires $115 in materials and inspection time to do a quality check on a batch of chemicals being produced, then inspection costs of $115 per batch (regardless of the number of pounds of chemicals in the batch) is also a variable cost for batch-related activities. With respect to labor, however, a word of caution is in order. While the labor it takes to assemble a frame or perform quality checks varies proportionately with the number of frames assembled or quality checks performed, it isn't always easy to have exactly the right amount of labor on hand for various levels of production. When changes in production occur, it may take weeks or months to adjust labor costs to the amount that should be incurred. For example, automobile manufacturers understand (after years of negotiating with labor unions) that they cannot make sudden changes to their labor costs. If the market demand for cars goes down, rarely will manufacturers immediately lay off workers. Reductions in labor costs for these companies take time and must be handled appropriately. This does not necessarily mean that labor costs are fixed for a manufacturer. Given time, these costs can and will be adjusted.

curvilinear costs Variable costs that do not vary in direct proportion to changes in activity level but vary at decreasing or increasing rates due to economies of scale, productivity changes, and so on.

CURVILINEAR VARIABLE COSTS Our definition of the variable cost behavior pattern specifies that variable costs have a linear relationship to the level of activity; that is, when the level of activity increases, total variable costs rise at a directly proportional rate. For example, if the level of activity doubles, the total variable costs will also double; this is a called a linear relationship. The reality is that, in practice, a truly linear relationship usually does not exist. Overall, many variable costs are actually **curvilinear costs** when considered over many activity levels. That is, these curvilinear costs actually vary at increasing or decreasing rates with changes in activity level. To illustrate, assume that an ice cream manufacturer uses milk, sugar, and other ingredients purchased from suppliers to make ice cream. Assume that one gallon of milk is used to make one gallon of ice cream; so, if no ice cream is produced, there is no milk cost. If 1,000 gallons of ice cream are scheduled to be manufactured during the week, 1,000 gallons of milk will be purchased at a cost of $2.00 per gallon for a total of $2,000. As more ice cream is produced, the total cost of milk increases, but the price per gallon decreases because of quantity discounts. If 2,000 gallons of milk are purchased, the price is $1.85 per gallon; and if 3,000 gallons are purchased, the price is $1.70 per gallon. The price decreases $0.15 per gallon for each additional 1,000 gallons purchased until a price of $1.25 per gallon is reached. Thereafter, the price discounts start becoming smaller. Thus, this curvilinear cost increases at a decreasing rate, as depicted in the top graph in Exhibit 2-2.

exhibit 2-2 Curvilinear Variable Costs

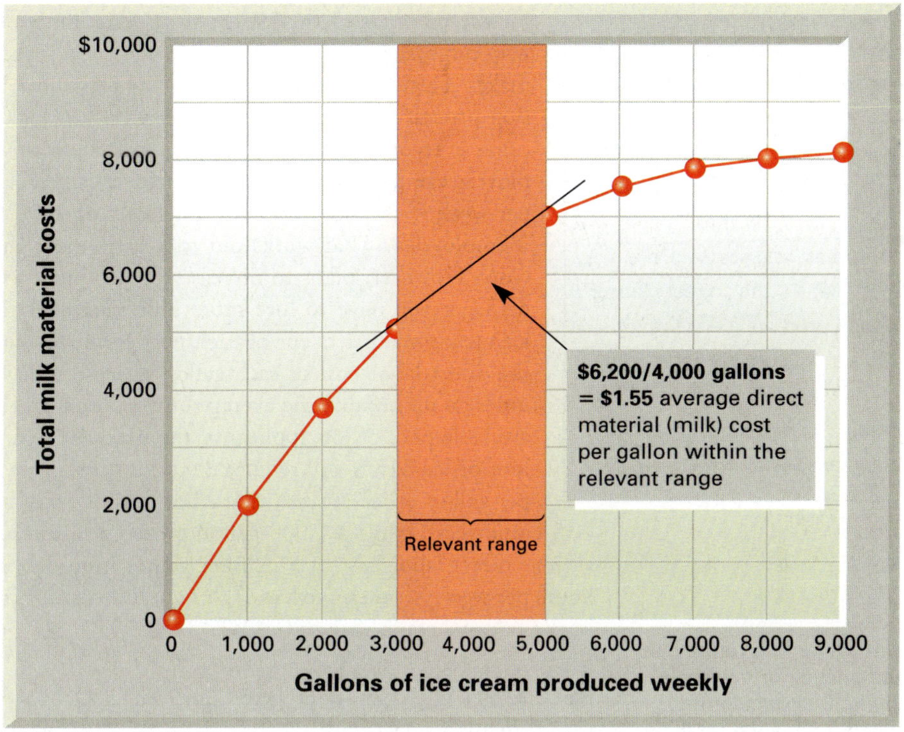

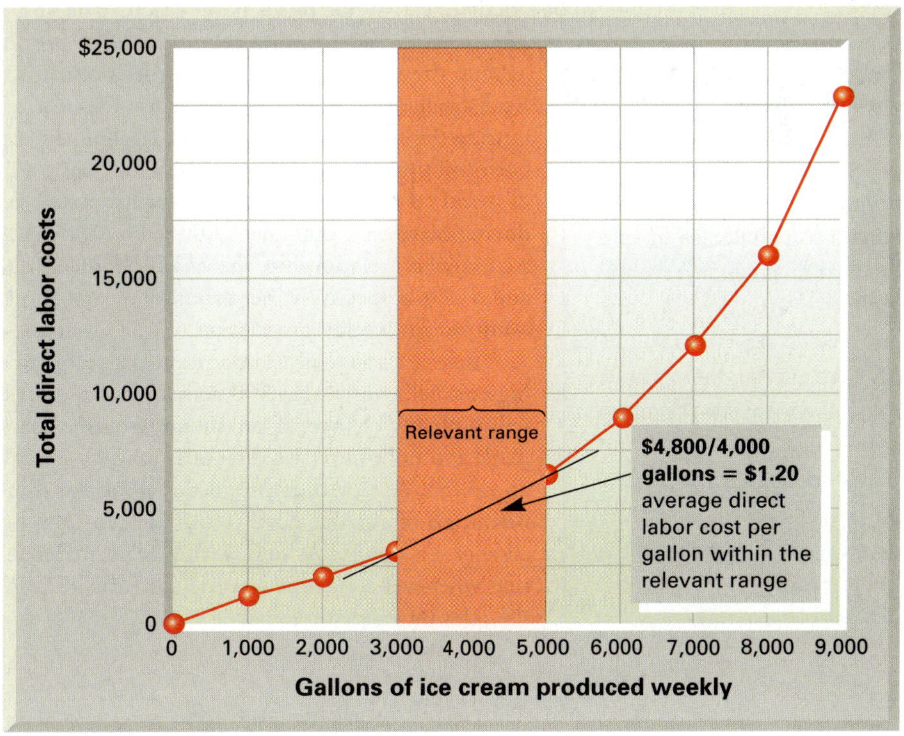

fyi

If you've had an introductory class in economics, you have likely been introduced to the term *economies of scale.* The cost of milk that becomes cheaper as production volume increases (top graph in Exhibit 2-2) is a cost that displays economies of scale. On the other hand, the direct labor costs to produce ice cream that become more costly as production increases (bottom graph in Exhibit 2-2) represent costs with *diseconomies* of scale.

To illustrate how curvilinear costs can increase at an increasing rate, let's assume that this particular ice cream manufacturer actually makes a very specialized "premium natural" ice cream that is handmade using a traditional preindustrial process. The problem for the manager of the ice cream production process is that it is difficult to find people who can make ice cream efficiently. Essentially, the production speed of an individual who makes ice cream can range from 4 to 12 gallons per hour. The manager of the production process has two top employees who can make 12 gallons of ice cream per hour. Because everyone on the ice cream production crew is paid $10 per hour, these two employees can produce 960 gallons of ice cream each week (12 gallons per hour × 40 hours per week × 2 employees) at a total cost of $800 ($10 per hour × 40 hours per week × 2 employees). That works out to a little more than 83 cents per gallon for direct labor costs. However, plans to increase the production volume of the operation mean that the manager will have to hire more individuals for the ice cream production crew, and the ice-cream-making talent of each new employee gets worse the more she hires! As a result, the direct labor cost of each gallon of ice cream will increase as planned production volumes go up because the average output per worker goes down. For example, based on the available pool of job applicants, the manager figures that weekly production of 3,000 gallons of ice cream will require 8 workers, resulting in an average direct labor cost of $1.07 per gallon of ice cream (total labor cost of $3,200 = $10 per hour × 40 hours per week × 8 employees), while a 5,000-gallon production week will require 16 workers, resulting in an average direct labor cost of $1.28 per gallon (total labor cost of $6,400 = $10 per hour × 40 hours per week × 16 employees). This curvilinear cost increases at an *increasing* rate, as depicted in the bottom graph in Exhibit 2-2.

relevant range The range of operating level, or volume of activity, over which the relationship between total costs (variable plus fixed) and activity level is approximately linear.

RELEVANT RANGE AND THE LINEARITY OF VARIABLE COSTS Curvilinear costs are very difficult to deal with when using C-V-P analysis to make planning decisions. In fact, as we'll discuss later, one of the limiting assumptions of C-V-P analysis is that all costs are assumed to be strictly linear! While this is never exactly true, it is usually safe to assume that variable costs are *approximately* linear within a certain range of production, called the **relevant range**. To illustrate the relevant range concept, let's return to our ice cream manufacturing business. Realistically, the production manager does not expect to vary weekly production volume outside the range of 3,000 to 5,000 gallons of ice cream. As displayed in Exhibit 2-2 for both milk material cost and direct labor cost, a linear segment within the relevant range of weekly production can effectively approximate the curvilinear cost relationship of producing between 3,000 and 5,000 gallons of ice cream. By assuming a linear (rather than a curvilinear) relationship, the variable costs of milk and direct labor are estimated at $1.55 and $1.20, respectively, per gallon of ice cream using the costs in the midpoint of the relevant range (weekly production of 4,000 gallons of ice cream).

caution

Remembering the concept of the relevant range is especially important when applying C-V-P analysis to companies in very high growth situations, such as high-tech start-ups. If a company's sales are increasing by 60% each quarter, for example, it is unlikely to remain in the same "relevant range" from quarter to quarter; so careful analysis of variable and fixed costs must be repeated on a regular basis.

Relevant range is an important concept and should be kept in mind when considering cost behavior patterns. If activity increases or decreases significantly, cost relationships will probably change. If production volume soars, for example, such factors as overtime work and bulk-purchase discounts may subject direct labor and materials costs to fluctuations that destroy their proportional relationship to volume. That is why we say that the definition of variable costs—costs that in total have a linear relationship with volume of activity—is applicable only within relevant ranges. The important point to remember is that whenever we define a particular variable cost, we are assuming that the cost is within the relevant range of activity.

Fixed Costs

fixed costs Costs that remain constant in total, regardless of activity level, at least over a certain range of activity.

Fixed costs remain constant in total, regardless of activity level, at least within the relevant range of activity. Examples include property taxes, insurance, executives' salaries, plant depreciation, and rent. Because total fixed costs remain constant as activity increases, the fixed cost per unit (total fixed cost ÷ level of activity) decreases. Similarly, as the level of activity decreases, the fixed cost per unit increases. This is in contrast to variable costs, where the costs

caution

While total variable costs increase as production increases, the per-unit variable cost is constant across activity levels within the relevant range. In contrast, while total fixed costs are constant over the relevant range, the per-unit fixed cost changes with increases or decreases in production.

fyi

Have you ever wondered why you always wait so long and why there are so many patients at one time in a dentist's office? Think about the nature of the dentist's costs. Most costs are fixed—dentists' salaries, rent or depreciation, and so forth. When costs are mostly fixed, seeing a high volume of patients is important to cover the fixed costs. Then, once fixed costs are covered, almost all additional patient revenue becomes profit. Thus, by seeing only a few additional patients, dentists can increase their profits substantially.

per unit are assumed to remain constant through changes in the level of activity within the relevant range.

Before we go any further, it would be a good idea to put all this concern about identifying fixed and variable costs in context. Remember that this chapter is about managing the relationships among costs, volume, and profit. In Chapter 1 of management accounting, we briefly introduced the concept of C-V-P and break-even analysis. In the C-V-P formula below that we used previously in Chapter 1, you can see that predicting (i.e., calculating) what a company needs to do to "break even" and start making a profit requires a clear measure of total fixed costs and variable costs per unit:

$$\frac{\text{Total fixed costs}}{(\text{Sales price per unit} - \text{Variable cost per unit})} = \text{Break-even sales (in units)}$$

In an actual company, these costs are very challenging to identify. That is why it is important that you understand the nature of cost behavior and how to (hopefully) classify costs as either fixed or variable. Once we've completed our discussion of cost behavior, we'll be ready to spend some time on this very useful C-V-P formula later in this chapter.

STEPPED FIXED COSTS The top graph in Exhibit 2-3 shows the relationship between the ice cream manufacturer's production line supervisor cost and the total number of gallons of ice cream produced. In this case, until weekly ice cream production reaches 1,000 gallons a week, the manufacturing manager is able to oversee all line workers. At 1,000 gallons a week production, however, the manager expects to hire a production line supervisor at $500 per week to provide more supervision of the workers. Further, the manager expects that she'll need to hire an additional supervisor each time weekly production is increased another 2,000 gallons. Yet, though the production line supervisor cost is changing as the scale of ice cream production changes, we still consider this cost to be fixed *within the relevant range.* Hence, as shown in the top graph in Exhibit 2-3, within a relevant range of activity of between 3,000 and 5,000 gallons of ice cream, the total fixed manufacturing supervisor cost of $1,000 does not change. On the other hand, the per-unit supervisor cost will drop considerably as production increases. For example, when the fixed supervisor cost is $1,000 and 3,000 gallons of ice cream are being produced, the supervisor cost per gallon of ice cream is $0.33 ($1,000 ÷ 3,000 gallons). With production of 4,000 gallons, however, the manufacturing supervisor cost is only $0.25 ($1,000 ÷ 4,000 gallons) per gallon.

stepped costs Costs that change in total in a stair-step fashion (in large amounts) with changes in volume of activity.

As you can see in the top graph of Exhibit 2-3, the fixed cost of production line supervision "steps up" as the volume of ice cream production increases. **Stepped costs** are costs that change in total in a stair-step fashion (that is, in large amounts) with changes in volume of activity. Another example of a stepped cost might be the labor charges for the maintenance of the tools and machinery in a small manufacturing plant. One maintenance worker can handle the upkeep of all the equipment during normal levels of activity. When there is a significant increase in activity, a second worker must be hired, and the maintenance cost approximately doubles.

RELEVANT RANGE AND THE LINEARITY OF FIXED COSTS How are stepped costs analyzed so that managers can make appropriate decisions? If the steps are wide compared to the relevant range (in other words, the costs essentially are unchanged within the relevant range), the costs are usually treated as fixed. This would be the case with the production line supervisor costs in Exhibit 2-3. If the steps are small and change throughout the relevant range, the costs are usually approximated with a variable cost line. Though this approximation is not perfect, it is better than making the more substantial error of ignoring the change in a stepped cost.

The bottom graph in Exhibit 2-3 illustrates a stepped cost that approximates a variable cost. This graph represents the depreciation and electricity costs required to operate a set of machines used to pack the ice cream in special cartons. Each machine can pack 10 half-gallon cartons per hour. The depreciation and electricity costs of each machine are approximately $50 per week.

exhibit 2-3 Stepped Fixed Costs

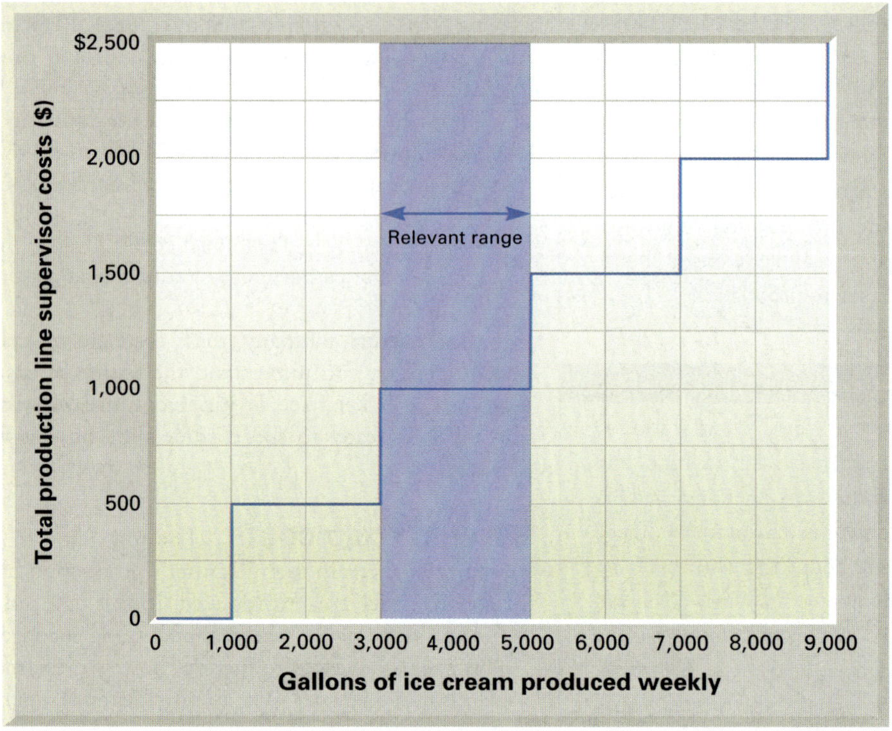

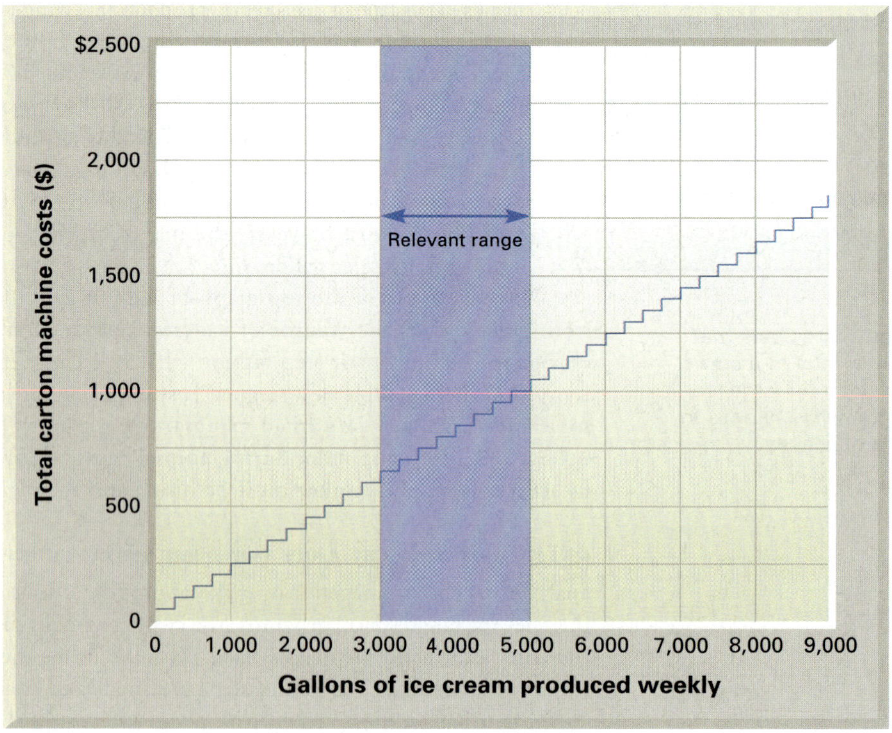

Each increase in planned weekly production of 200 gallons of ice cream will cause total carton machine costs to "step up" by $50. Therefore, at 1,000 gallons of production a week, total carton machine costs are $250; and at 3,000 gallons of production a week, total carton machine costs are $650. The management accounting question here is how to treat the behavior of carton machine costs in a C-V-P analysis. Clearly, the production line supervisor costs are fixed within the relevant range of between 3,000 and 5,000 gallons of production. But the carton machine costs are "stepping up" throughout the relevant range. Typically, though the carton machine costs are not actually linear variable costs with respect to incremental changes in each gallon of ice cream produced (as are the milk costs), accountants within the organization will treat these costs as if they were variable. In our example, the average carton machine cost per gallon of ice cream within the relevant range is $0.20.[2]

THE TREND TOWARD FIXED COSTS Over the past few decades, fixed costs have increased as a percentage of total costs for many manufacturing companies, primarily due to the increase in factory automation. As a machine replaces each manual job, costs change from variable labor costs to fixed depreciation or rental charges. It is important to note that many service companies have much higher ratios of fixed-to-variable costs than do manufacturing companies. The costs of providing services in companies such as banks, consulting agencies, and airlines typically do not vary much depending on the volume of banking transactions, consulting hours, or passengers carried. Perhaps more significantly, e-commerce organizations often have even fewer variable costs than service organizations do! Once the technology has been put in place to run an e-commerce business, there is typically very little additional cost of technology based on usage (within the relevant range). Personnel costs in e-commerce organizations, such as engineering personnel, marketing teams, and executive personnel, also do not change much based on customer use of the organization's technology.

As fixed costs in manufacturing organizations increase, and the economy continues to shift more and more to service and e-commerce organizations, this fixed cost emphasis has a significant effect on the decision-making process. When costs are fixed, management's ability to influence costs with activity-level decisions is limited. With variable costs, management has more flexibility to change activity levels and thereby increase or decrease total operating cost structures. This trend of replacing variable costs with fixed costs has an important impact on the cost structure of an organization that is captured in the concept of operating leverage, which is discussed in the expanded material section of this chapter.

Mixed Costs

mixed costs Costs that contain both variable and fixed cost components.

Mixed costs, like curvilinear costs and stepped costs, are variations of the basic fixed and variable cost behavior patterns. Specifically, mixed costs are costs that contain both variable and fixed components. An example is rent that is based on a fixed rental fee plus a percentage of total sales. Thus, the rental terms for an automobile dealer's showroom might include a flat payment of $4,000 per month plus 1% of each month's sales. The 1% of sales is the variable portion, and the $4,000 is the fixed cost. The total rent, therefore, would be considered a mixed cost and could be diagrammed as shown in Exhibit 2-4. As this exhibit shows, the cost of renting the showroom increases as sales increase. The total rent is $4,000 when there are no sales; $6,000 when sales are $200,000 [$4,000 + (0.01 × $200,000)]; and $8,000 when sales are $400,000 [$4,000 + (0.01 × $400,000)]. This increase is directly due to the variable cost element, which increases in total as activity level (car sales) increases.

One of the important challenges in using C-V-P analysis in the planning process is the need to effectively separate mixed costs into their fixed and variable cost components. Over the years several management accounting techniques have been developed by organizations for this purpose. We will explore these mixed cost analysis methods in the next section of this chapter.

2 This is calculated using the high-low method described later in this chapter.
($1,050 − $650)/(5,000 gallons − 3,000 gallons) = $0.20 per gallon

exhibit 2-4 An Example of a Mixed Cost

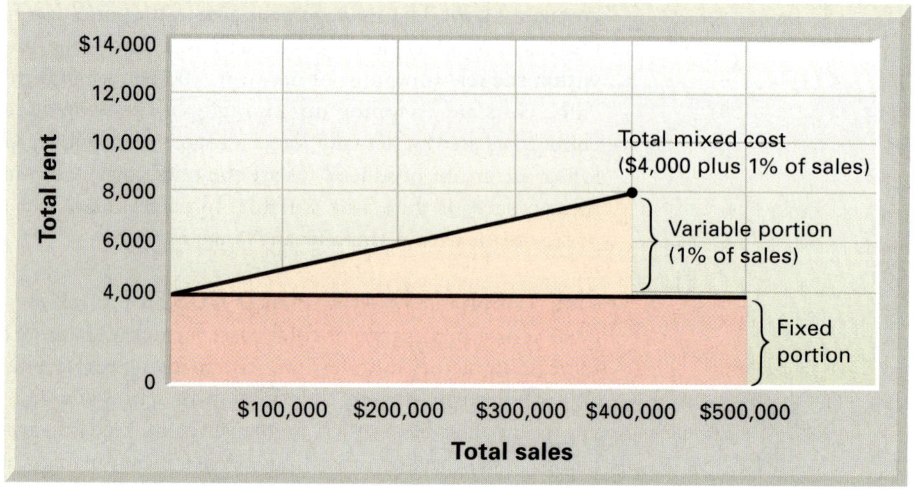

to summarize

Understanding cost behavior patterns is essential for the management process of effective planning. Cost behavior is the way a cost changes in response to changes in activity level. There are two basic cost behavior patterns, variable and fixed. Total variable costs change in direct proportion to changes in the level of activity over the relevant range; therefore, variable costs are constant per unit over this range. In analyzing variable costs, we generally assume a linear relationship between total costs and the level of activity within the relevant range; outside of this range, variable costs are usually curvilinear. Total fixed costs do not change over the relevant range; therefore, fixed costs decrease per unit as the level of activity increases within the relevant range. Stepped costs increase with the level of activity but not proportionately. If the steps are wide in relation to the relevant range, these costs can be treated as fixed; if the steps are narrow, they can be treated as variable. Because of such factors as technology and automation, many costs that were once variable now exhibit fixed cost behaviors. Mixed costs have both a variable and a fixed cost component. An increase in a mixed cost with a rising level of activity is due directly to the variable cost element.

3
Analyze mixed costs using the scattergraph and high-low methods.

ANALYSIS OF MIXED COSTS

So far in this chapter, we have introduced several types of behavior exhibited by costs. We will spend this section discussing and analyzing mixed costs for the purpose of making planning decisions using C-V-P analysis. Mixed costs are often difficult to separate into variable and fixed components. Usually, the fixed portion represents the cost necessary to maintain a service (such as a telephone) or a facility (such as a building), and the variable portion covers actual use. Recall the example of the automobile showroom's rental cost, part of which was a flat monthly fee and part a percentage of sales. Other common mixed costs are certain types of leases and such overhead costs as electricity, repairs, telephone, and maintenance.

The most accurate way to separate the actual fixed and variable components of mixed costs is to analyze each invoice. An electricity bill, for example, may include a flat monthly service charge that would be classified as a fixed cost. Additional variable costs are those based on the amount of electricity actually used during the month. This approach could be very time-consuming, however, and may not be cost-effective (that is, it would cost more than the detailed information is worth). A more useful approach would be to use, for each level of activity, the historical trend in past costs as the basis for classifying costs as fixed or variable. There are several methods of doing this. In this section we will concentrate on two: the scattergraph method and the high-low method. In the expanded material, we introduce least squares analysis, a more sophisticated method for analyzing mixed costs.

The Scattergraph, or Visual-Fit, Method

scattergraph (visual-fit) method A method of segregating the fixed and variable components of a mixed cost by plotting on a graph total costs at several activity levels and drawing a regression line through the points.

regression line On a scattergraph, the straight line that most closely expresses the relationship between the variables.

variable cost rate The change in cost divided by the change in activity; the slope of the regression line.

Probably the simplest method of segregating mixed costs into their variable and fixed components is the **scattergraph** (or **visual-fit**) **method**. The total mixed cost for each level of activity is plotted on a graph, and a straight line (called the **regression line**) is visually fitted through the points. The idea is to position the line through the set of plotted data points in a way that minimizes the average distance between all the data points and the fitted regression line. With the regression line inserted into the graph, the fixed portion of the mixed cost is estimated to be the amount on the cost (vertical) axis at the point where it is intercepted by the regression line. The variable cost per unit (referred to as the **variable cost rate**) is equal to the slope of the regression line, which is simply the change in cost divided by the change in activity.

To illustrate the scattergraph method, we will use the electricity costs for an automobile manufacturer. In the analysis and calculations that follow, all costs are assumed to fall within the relevant range of activity. In this example, we use direct labor hours as a measure of the activity level.

Exhibit 2-5 shows a scattergraph on which electricity costs and direct labor hours have been plotted. The regression line has been visually fitted to minimize the distance between data points. It appears that the total fixed portion of electricity cost is about $40,000 per month, which is where the regression line intersects the cost axis. The variable cost rate is approximately $4.29 per direct labor hour, which is the slope of the regression line. To calculate the slope, we use the following formula and the data points of zero and 7,000 direct labor hours, respectively.

$$\text{Variable cost rate} = \frac{\text{Change in (electricity) cost}}{\text{Change in activity (direct labor hours)}}$$

$$X = \frac{\$70{,}000 - \$40{,}000}{7{,}000 - 0}$$

$$X = \frac{\$30{,}000}{7{,}000}$$

$$X = \$4.29 \text{ (rounded)}$$

caution

Once the regression line has been fitted through the data points, the scattergraph method does not depend any longer on the *data points* to estimate fixed and variable costs. Cost estimations are entirely based on *points along the regression line.* For instance, notice that in this case we used the points 0 and 7,000 along the visually fitted regression line. However, we could have used any two points on the regression line to calculate the variable costs per direct labor hour.

Obviously, the scattergraph method has some limitations as a cost estimation tool. Perhaps the most critical limitation is that how the user fits the regression line through the data points is entirely subjective. Consider Exhibit 2-5 once more. If you were the one fitting the regression line to these data points, would you have set the line exactly where it is in this graph? Hopefully, your line would have been quite close to the current line. Still, it probably wouldn't have been exactly the same, resulting in some small differences in your own estimations of fixed and variable costs. Hence, the scattergraph method is a classic "quick and dirty" management accounting technique. Yet, although the scattergraph provides only subjective estimates of the fixed and variable portions of mixed costs, it can be an extremely useful tool to describe and discuss cost behavior in the planning process. It is also useful for controlling operating costs. For instance, it shows at a glance any trends and abrupt changes in cost behavior patterns. It is also a means of checking whether costs are rising at a directly

exhibit 2-5 Total Electricity Costs

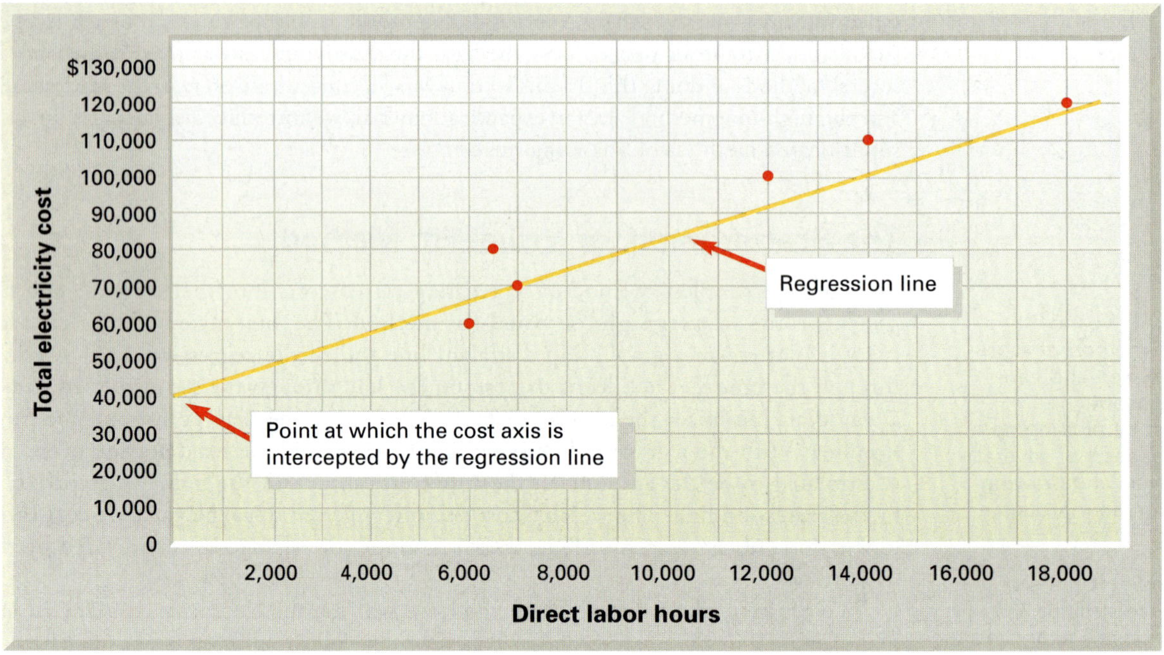

proportionate rate within the relevant range. As such, it can be used as a preliminary step before using more sophisticated methods of cost evaluation.

The High-Low Method

high-low method A method of segregating the fixed and variable components of a mixed cost by analyzing the costs at the highest and the lowest activity levels within a relevant range.

A second approach is the **high-low method**, which analyzes mixed costs on the basis of total costs incurred at both the highest and the lowest levels of activity. To illustrate this method, we refer again to the electricity costs of the automobile manufacturer. This time, however, we will focus on the following table of reported electricity costs and direct labor hours worked.

Month	Direct Labor Hours Worked	Total Electricity Cost
January	7,000	$ 70,000
February	6,000	60,000
March	12,000	100,000
April	6,600	80,000
May	18,000	120,000
June	14,000	110,000

Although these two columns of figures do not visually show trends as clearly as the scattergraph does, they do suggest that as the activity level (direct labor hours) increases, total electricity costs increase. Given this relationship, the high-low method can be used to determine the fixed and variable portions of the electricity cost as follows:

1. Identify the highest and lowest activity levels (18,000 hours in May and 6,000 hours in February). These two months also represent the highest and lowest levels of electricity costs, or $120,000 and $60,000, respectively (though this may not always be the case).
2. Determine the differences between the high and low points.

	Total Electricity Cost	Direct Labor Hours
High point (May)	$120,000	18,000
Low point (February)	60,000	6,000
Difference	$ 60,000	12,000

3. Calculate the variable cost rate (variable cost per unit). The formula is the same as the one used to compute the slope of the regression line in the scattergraph method. The results are different, of course, because the scattergraph method is based on a regression line that is plotted using all the data points, whereas the high-low method uses only the high and low data points.

$$\text{Variable cost rate} = \frac{\text{Change in costs}}{\text{Change in activity}}$$

$$= \frac{\$60{,}000}{12{,}000}$$

$$= \$5 \text{ per direct labor hour}$$

4. Determine fixed costs based on the variable cost rate ($5 in this case). The formula for this computation is:

Fixed costs = Total costs − Variable costs

At the high level of activity, the calculation would be:

$X = \$120{,}000 - (18{,}000 \times \$5)$
$X = \$120{,}000 - \$90{,}000$
$X = \$30{,}000$

You get the same results if you calculate fixed costs at the low level of activity:

$X = \$60{,}000 - (6{,}000 \times \$5)$
$X = \$60{,}000 - \$30{,}000$
$X = \$30{,}000$

In summary, using the high-low method of analyzing mixed costs, the variable portion of the total electricity cost is estimated to be $5 per direct labor hour, and the fixed portion is $30,000 per month. This means that $30,000 appears to be the amount the company pays each month just to have electricity available, and $5 is the average additional electricity cost for each hour of direct labor worked.

A Comparison of the Scattergraph and High-Low Methods

As we have illustrated, the scattergraph and high-low methods may produce different results.

Method	Variable Cost Rate	Fixed Cost
Scattergraph	$4.29	$40,000
High-low	5.00	30,000

Both methods are useful for a quick approximation. The scattergraph method takes all the data into account. Therefore, it tends to more accurate, although it is somewhat subjective (depending on how the line is drawn) and inconsistent because different people might draw the

business environment essay

From Bankruptcy to 23 Consecutive Profitable Quarters CONTINENTAL AIRLINES has increased profits each of the last six years, an amazing turnaround for a company that once was protected from many of its creditors under Chapter 11 bankruptcy. In 1995, when Continental's last failure, Continental Lite (an attempt to copy SOUTHWEST AIRLINES' cheap commuter flights), ended up costing the company $110 million, new management was brought in. Today, Continental Airlines is the fifth largest airline in the United States, offering more than 2,200 departures daily to 136 domestic and 92 international destinations. And for the third year in a row, Continental was ranked among the 100 Best Companies to work for by *Fortune* magazine.

What has changed? How has Continental's management team taken what airline creditors wanted to liquidate and turned it into a viable competitor in its industry? For one thing, Continental Airlines management carefully analyzed its costs, divided those

line through the points differently. On the other hand, anyone using the high-low method will consistently get the same results. However, because only two data points are used, the high-low method may not be representative of the costs incurred at all levels of activity. Essentially, the math used in the high-low method plots the regression line through the two most extreme points in a scattergraph. Check whether the high and low points in our example are representative by plotting the data on the scattergraph of Exhibit 2-5. You will notice that the low point lies below the scattergraph regression line and the high point lies above the scattergraph regression line, indicating that, in this case, a straight line drawn through the high and the low points would not necessarily represent all six data points plotted. Nevertheless, both methods can be used to predict future costs. If, for example, management wants to know how much electricity will cost next month with 10,000 direct labor hours budgeted, the following calculations would be made:

Method	Formula	Estimated Cost
Scattergraph	$40,000 + 10,000($4.29) =	$82,900
High-low	$30,000 + 10,000($5.00) =	$80,000

As you can see, the total estimated costs resulting from these two methods, in this case, are reasonably close to each other.

caution

Once you have selected the high and low activity levels to use in the high-low method, you must base all cost calculations on those two activity levels and related costs. Otherwise, if you use any other activity level or cost to perform the calculations, you will have erroneous results that could produce significantly different cost estimations.

to summarize

Two common techniques for analyzing mixed costs are the scattergraph and high-low methods. The scattergraph method involves visually fitting a straight line (the regression line) through data points plotted on a graph, then noting where the line intercepts the cost axis (the fixed cost) and calculating the slope of the line (the variable cost rate). With the high-low method, the high and the low levels of activity are used to calculate first the variable cost rate and then the fixed cost component.

costs into fixed and variable components, and made several decisions to reduce fixed costs. For example, Continental grounded 41 planes and slashed capacity roughly 9% to rebound from its disaster in 1995. The airline cut more than 4,900 jobs, or approximately 12% of its workforce to reach profitability.

With fixed costs under control, Continental Airlines became profitable. In fact, it is now one of the most profitable airlines. Because it cut costs, Continental Airlines passengers pay lower fares than on other airlines and receive better service. These lower fares and better service enable Continental to fill more seats than most of its competitors. Because its costs are low, it is highly profitable. Fixed costs are now a smaller percentage of total costs at Continental Airlines than at almost all other airlines.

Sources: Adapted from PR Newswire, "Continental Airlines Earnings Per Share Jump 45 Percent; Six Straight Years of Profit," http://www.datek.com, January 17, 2001, Copyright 2001, Datek Online; Wendy Zellner, "Back to 'Coffee, Tea, or Milk?'" *Business Week*, July 3, 1995.

4

Perform C-V-P analyses, and describe the effects potential changes in C-V-P variables have on company profitability.

METHODS OF C-V-P ANALYSIS

Now that you have a better understanding of cost behaviors and can separate both mixed and stepped costs into their fixed and variable cost elements, you are ready to use your knowledge of cost behaviors to make planning decisions. Chapter 1 of management accounting provided a quick introduction to C-V-P analysis in the process of planning and analyzing decisions to prioritize Kevlar versus Teflon product at DUPONT. We will further explore C-V-P analysis now and extend your ability to use this valuable management accounting tool. First, we need to spend some time working with the concept of contribution margin.

contribution margin The difference between total sales and variable costs; the portion of sales revenue available to cover fixed costs and provide a profit.

Contribution Margin

Contribution margin is equal to sales revenue less variable costs; it is the amount of revenue that remains to cover fixed costs and provide a profit for an organization. For example, the con-

The contribution margin generated by the sale of an order of french fries can be used to pay fixed costs such as rent, insurance, and salaries. Now you know why you often hear that ever popular question "Would you like fries with that?" at fast-food restaurants.

tribution margin from the sale of one order of french fries by a fast-food restaurant is the selling price less the variables costs (potatoes, salt, container, cooking oil, wages of the cook) of producing the fries. Any contribution margin generated by the sale of an order of french fries can be used to pay the fixed costs of the fast-foot outlet, such as the monthly rent, the insurance, the supervisor's salary, and so forth. Contribution margin is one of the most important management accounting concepts you will study because many operating decisions are made on the basis of how it will be affected. A company may decide, for example, to advertise one product more than others because it has a higher contribution margin.

THE CONTRIBUTION MARGIN INCOME STATEMENT To illustrate the concept of contribution margin, we will use the following format of a contribution margin income statement. The statement data for Jewels Corporation, a producer of high-quality baseball gloves, follow.[3]

Jewels Corporation
Contribution Margin Income Statement
For the Month Ended November 30, 2003

	Total	Per Unit
Sales revenue (1,000 gloves)	$200,000	$200
Less variable costs	110,000	110
Contribution margin	$ 90,000	$ 90
Less fixed costs	63,000	
Profit*	$ 27,000	

*In this chapter, "profit" means pretax income; the terms *income* and *profit* are interchangeable.

per-unit contribution margin The excess of the sales price of one unit over its variable costs.

As this income statement shows, for internal decision-making purposes, Jewels Corporation computes its contribution margin on a per-unit (glove) and total-dollar basis. During November, Jewels' **per-unit contribution margin** is $90; the total contribution margin at a sales volume of 1,000 baseball gloves is $90,000.

The per-unit contribution margin tells us that $90 is available from each glove sold to cover fixed costs and provide a profit. By showing the $63,000 of fixed costs separately, this income statement also indicates that Jewels must generate sufficient contribution margin to cover these costs before a profit can be earned. With $200,000 of sales revenue, the contribution margin ($90,000) is sufficient to cover the fixed costs and provide a profit of $27,000.

This type of contribution margin income statement is particularly useful as a planning tool. It enables a company to project profits at any level of activity within the relevant range. For example, if Jewels Corporation forecasts sales at 1,200 baseball gloves next month, it could prepare a forecasted (or pro-forma) income statement (in contribution margin format) as follows:

Jewels Corporation
Pro-Forma Contribution Margin Income Statement
For the Month Ended December 31, 2003

Sales revenue (1,200 gloves × $200)	$240,000
Less variable costs (1,200 gloves × $110)	132,000
Contribution margin	$108,000
Less fixed costs	63,000
Profit	$ 45,000

Notice that with an increase in sales of 200 baseball gloves, the contribution margin increases $18,000 ($108,000 − $90,000). This can be confirmed by multiplying the per-unit con-

3 In this example, we assume that there is only one model of baseball glove, which sells for $200.

tribution margin by the increase in volume ($90 per unit × 200 gloves = $18,000). Because we assume that the increase in volume is still within the relevant range of activity (which is *very* important!), the fixed costs remain at $63,000, and profit increases by the $18,000 change in contribution margin. The critical thing to see here is that once the fixed costs are covered, each subsequent dollar in contribution margin goes straight to profit! In other words, when Jewels Corporation hits its break-even point (i.e., all fixed costs are covered), each additional glove sold will generate $90 in profit.

Notice the importance of accurately determining cost behavior when forecasting profit levels. If one ignores cost behavior, then the $27,000 profit generated by November sales of 1,000 gloves leads to the conclusion that each glove creates $27 ($27,000 profit/1,000 gloves) in profit. With this *incorrect* information, the forecasted level of profit for December sales of 1,200 gloves is $32,400 ($27 per glove × 1,200 gloves). This forecast differs significantly from the $45,000 profit forecast above that stems from a *correct* consideration of the behavior of Jewels Corporation's costs.

contribution margin ratio The percentage of net sales revenue left after variable costs are deducted; the contribution margin divided by net sales revenue.

THE CONTRIBUTION MARGIN RATIO The contribution margin may be expressed as a percentage of sales revenue as well as on a per-unit or total-dollar basis. Knowing the **contribution margin ratio**, which is the percentage of sales revenue left after variable costs are deducted, management can compare the profitability of various products. For example, if product A has a 45% contribution margin ratio and the contribution margin ratio of product B is only 30%, the company should emphasize product A, assuming that other factors are equal.

To illustrate the calculation of contribution margin ratios, we refer again to the initial Jewels Corporation example. The ratio is computed as follows:

	Total	Per Unit	Ratio (Percentage)
Sales revenue (1,000 gloves)	$200,000	$200	100%
Less variable costs	110,000	110	55%
Contribution margin	$ 90,000	$ 90	45%
Less fixed costs	63,000		
Profit	$ 27,000		

The contribution margin ratio is 45% of sales revenue ($90 ÷ $200), which means that for every $1.00 increase in sales revenue, the contribution margin increases by $0.45 (45% of $1.00). If fixed costs are already covered, profit will also increase by $0.45 for every $1.00 increase in sales. Notice also that the variable cost ratio ($110 ÷ $200 = 55%) plus the contribution margin ratio (45%) must equal 100%.

STOP & THINK Consider your favorite hamburger fast-food outlet. Which food item do you think has a higher contribution margin ratio—hamburgers or french fries?

With contribution margin ratios, it is easy to analyze the impact of future changes in sales on the contribution margin. For example, if Jewels' management estimates that sales will increase by $20,000, it can apply the contribution margin ratio of 45% and estimate that the contribution margin will increase by $9,000 ($20,000 × 0.45). The higher the contribution margin ratio, the larger the share of each additional dollar of sales that goes toward covering fixed costs and increasing profit.

The C-V-P Equation

As you can see, contribution margin calculations are very useful for analyzing cost-volume-profit relationships in the management planning process. Doing C-V-P analysis using contribution margin calculations is a straightforward process of simple algebra. We began this chapter with the assumption that all costs can be described as either fixed or variable. To highlight the important idea that C-V-P analysis depends on dividing costs into fixed and variable behavior patterns, we will develop the C-V-P equation as follows:[4]

4 Granted, fixed and variable costs often get "mixed together" and can be difficult (and sometimes impossible) to separate. The fact that C-V-P analysis is based on an assumption that all costs can be divided clearly into fixed and variable is one of the limitations of this technique.

1. Because all costs can be classified as either variable or fixed, we can express the calculation of profit with the following basic formula:

$$\text{Revenues} - \text{Variable costs} - \text{Fixed costs} = \text{Profit}$$

2. We can specify the formula more precisely by expressing the equation in units:

$$(\text{Sales price} \times \text{Units}) - (\text{Variable cost} \times \text{Units}) - \text{Fixed costs} = \text{Profit}$$

3. Or, we can express the equation using ratios:

$$\text{Revenues} - (\text{Variable cost ratio} \times \text{Revenues}) - \text{Fixed costs} = \text{Profit}$$

These equations are quick and useful methods for examining the financial aspects of C-V-P analysis problems. To illustrate, we will use the data from the Jewels Corporation example and assume that sales of 1,200 baseball gloves are projected. What will Jewels' profit be using the equation based on units?

$$\begin{aligned} \textbf{(Sales price} \times \textbf{Units)} - \textbf{(Variable cost} \times \textbf{Units)} - \textbf{Fixed costs} &= \textbf{Profit} \\ (\$200 \times 1{,}200) - (\$110 \times 1{,}200) - \$63{,}000 &= \text{Profit} \\ \$240{,}000 - \$132{,}000 - \$63{,}000 &= \text{Profit} \\ \$45{,}000 &= \text{Profit} \end{aligned}$$

Alternatively, we could calculate Jewels' profits using the equation based on ratios.

$$\begin{aligned} \textbf{Revenues} - \textbf{(Variable cost ratio} \times \textbf{Revenues)} - \textbf{Fixed costs} &= \textbf{Profit} \\ \$240{,}000 - [(\$110 \div \$200) \times \$240{,}000] - \$63{,}000 &= \text{Profit} \\ \$240{,}000 - (0.55 \times \$240{,}000) - \$63{,}000 &= \text{Profit} \\ \$240{,}000 - \$132{,}000 - \$63{,}000 &= \text{Profit} \\ \$45{,}000 &= \text{Profit} \end{aligned}$$

Note that we obtained a profit of $45,000 using both formula approaches. This is no surprise because these are simply alternative routes to the same destination. Both methods are commonly used, depending on the data available for the analysis. So, although there may appear to be many alternative ways to write the C-V-P formula, there is really only one formula, and it is not hard to remember: Revenues − Variable costs − Fixed costs = Profit. Once you understand this fact, C-V-P analysis using the equation approach is basic math; you merely insert the known elements into the formula and solve for the one unknown element.

break-even point The amount of sales at which total costs of the number of units sold equal total revenues; the point at which there is no profit or loss.

BREAK-EVEN POINT Generally, management wants to know how many units need to be sold to break even, that is, to recover all costs. Thus, the **break-even point** is defined as the volume of activity at which total revenues equal total costs, or where profit is zero. The break-even point may also be thought of as the volume of activity at which the contribution margin equals the fixed costs.

Although the goal of business planning is to make a profit, not just to break even, knowing the break-even point can be useful in assessing the risk of selling a new product, setting sales goals and commission rates, deciding on marketing and advertising strategies, and other similar operating decisions. Because the break-even point is, by definition, that activity level at which no profit or loss is earned, the basic C-V-P equation can be modified to reflect a break-even point as follows:

$$\text{Revenues} - \text{Variable costs} - \text{Fixed costs} = \$0$$

As you can see, to compute the break-even point, we first set income equal to zero and then solve for the unknown—such as the number of units to be sold or the total revenues to be achieved.

Again using the Jewels Corporation example, how many units must Jewels sell to break even? (Note that we use X to represent the unknown element, in this case, the number of baseball gloves.)

$$\textbf{(Sales price} \times \textbf{Units)} - \textbf{(Variable cost} \times \textbf{Units)} - \textbf{Fixed costs} = \textbf{\$0}$$
$$[\text{Sales price} \times (X)] - [\text{Variable cost} \times (X)] - \text{Fixed costs} = \$0$$
$$\$200X - \$110X - \$63{,}000 = \$0$$
$$\$90X = \$63{,}000$$
$$X = \$63{,}000 \div \$90 = 700 \text{ units (baseball gloves)}$$

In this case, if Jewels sells 700 baseball gloves, it will generate enough revenues to cover its variable and fixed costs, earning zero profits [($200 × 700) − ($110 × 700) − $63,000 = $0]. Once you understand the basic C-V-P formula, you just set it up and solve for whatever unknown you're interested in planning. Think you've got it? Then try this one as a check on yourself: Assuming that Jewels can sell only 600 baseball gloves, what price per glove would the company have to use in order to break even?[5]

DETERMINING SALES VOLUME TO ACHIEVE TARGET INCOME Another way C-V-P analysis can be used in planning is to determine what level of activity is necessary to reach a target level of income. In this case, instead of setting profit at $0 to do a break-even analysis, we obviously set income in the formula at the targeted level and then use the formula to plan or predict what fixed costs, variable costs, sales prices, and sales volumes are needed to achieve the target level of income. **Target income** is usually defined as the amount of income that will enable management to reach its objectives—paying dividends, meeting analysts' predictions, purchasing a new plant and equipment, or paying off existing loans. Target income can be expressed as either a percentage of revenues or a fixed amount.

target income A profit level desired by management.

To illustrate target income, suppose the management of Jewels Corporation would like to know how many baseball gloves must be sold to achieve a target income of $36,000, assuming no changes in per-unit variable costs or total fixed costs. The calculation is as follows:

$$\textbf{(Sales price} \times \textbf{Units)} - \textbf{(Variable cost} \times \textbf{Units)} - \textbf{Fixed costs} = \textbf{Target income}$$
$$(\$200X - \$110X) - \$63{,}000 = \$36{,}000$$
$$\$90X = \$99{,}000$$
$$X = 1{,}100 \text{ units (baseball gloves)}$$

Thus, if Jewels could sell 1,100 baseball gloves at a contribution margin of $90 (assuming $63,000 of fixed costs), the company would earn a pretax profit of $36,000 [($90 × 1,100 units) − $63,000 = $36,000].

A fixed dollar amount of income, such as the $36,000 that would be earned by selling 1,100 baseball gloves, is probably the most typical way of expressing a target income goal for many companies. However, because investors often evaluate companies partially on the basis of the **return on sales revenue** (or simply "return on sales"), management may want to state its goal as a percentage return as opposed to a fixed amount of income. For example, if Jewels Corporation set a target income of a 20% return on sales, the computation would be:

return on sales revenue A measure of operating performance; computed by dividing net income by total sales revenue. Similar to profit margin.

$$\text{Sales revenue} - \text{Variable costs} - \text{Fixed costs} = 0.20 \text{ Sales revenue}$$
$$\$200X - \$110X - \$63{,}000 = 0.2(\$200X)$$
$$\$200X - \$110X - \$63{,}000 = \$40X$$
$$\$200X - \$110X - \$40X = \$63{,}000$$
$$\$50X = \$63{,}000$$
$$X = \$63{,}000 \div \$50 = 1{,}260 \text{ gloves}$$

5 $$\textbf{(Sales price} \times \textbf{Units)} - \textbf{(Variable cost} \times \textbf{Units)} - \textbf{Fixed costs} = \textbf{\$0}$$
$$[(X) \times \text{Units}] - (\text{Variable cost} \times \text{Units}) - \text{Fixed costs} = \$0$$
$$[(X) \times 600] - (\$110 \times 600) - \$63{,}000 = \$0$$
$$600X - \$66{,}000 - \$63{,}000 = \$0$$
$$600X = \$129{,}000$$
$$X = \$215 \text{ (new baseball glove price)}$$

business environment essay

Does Professional Soccer Have Any Real Future in the United States? Major League Soccer (MLS) had its fifth season in the United States in 2000. There have been many attempts to launch professional soccer as an American sport, but each attempt has failed. The last failure, that of the North American Soccer League (NASL)—which brought Pelé, Cruyff, Best, and Beckenbauer to the United States in the early 1970s—was especially painful because, with the big names, professional soccer looked so promising. One of the major reasons previous efforts failed is that player salaries and other fixed costs were too high for the small number of fans and meager TV revenues. Each attempt ended up with negative contribution margins and the team owners losing money.

Aware of past losses, this time the MLS has established itself in a different way. It has bet on an unusual single-entity structure, under which the league owns all the teams as well as all player contracts, and investors buy operating rights rather than setting up franchises. The MLS says the structure allows it to "eliminate the financial disparities between large and small markets, control player salaries and other fixed costs, and offer commercial affiliates an integrated sponsorship and licensing program." It also gives the

For Jewels Corporation, the 20% return on revenues would be earned by selling 1,260 baseball gloves.

SHORT-CUT FORMULAS FOR C-V-P ANALYSIS Notice that in the C-V-P analysis examples so far, the basic C-V-P equation has not changed. That's what makes this formula so powerful. Once you're comfortable with it, you can use it to manage any number of factors in planning for profits. However, you may remember from your brief introduction to C-V-P analysis in Chapter 1 of management accounting and from our C-V-P formula example on page 57 that we calculated break-even sales in units directly using the following formula.

$$\frac{\text{Total fixed costs}}{(\text{Sales price per unit} - \text{Variable cost per unit})} = \text{Break-even sales (in units)}$$

This formula is a "short-cut" version of the C-V-P formulas above. You can see that it is simply the last step in the C-V-P calculation above for Jewels' break-even point of 700 baseball gloves. So, if you understand the basic C-V-P equation, you can simply skip to the last step of the calculation. There are short cuts for computing the level of sales for both break-even volume and target income volume. The short-cut formula for both the break-even volume and the target income volume in units is:

$$\frac{\text{Fixed costs} + \text{Target income}}{\text{Contribution margin per unit}^{6}}$$

Note that if you use this formula to determine the break-even volume, then you will assume that target income is $0, giving you:

$$\frac{\text{Fixed costs}}{\text{Contribution margin per unit}}$$

Plugging in the numbers for Jewels Corporation, the results are the same as shown earlier. As you can see, the short-cut calculation for both the break-even volume and the target income volume is really the same formula. For target sales:

6 Remember that per-unit contribution margin is the sales price per unit less the variable cost per unit.

MLS significant economies of scale and allows it to allocate fixed costs across several teams.

Even though the fan base shrunk and TV ratings dropped during the first two years, financially the league is ahead of forecasts. The MLS lost $19 million in 1996, compared with anticipated losses of $22 million, and expected to lose $13 million more in 1997. The MLS is confident that the break-even point will come "by the end of the fourth year." That confidence may not be justified, however, as some report that the MLS has lost upwards of $100 million since its inception. The question is, does the MLS have the financial resources, the management expertise, and the fan and TV support to survive long term?

In the end, whether the MLS succeeds will depend on whether sufficient revenues can be generated to cover fixed and variable costs. While fixed costs, including player salaries, are low now, they may not always be. Already, 10 players, backed by the MLS Players Association, have filed a class action lawsuit arguing that the league's precious single-entity structure is designed expressly to hold down player salaries (fixed costs) and that, in doing so, it violates U.S. antitrust laws.

Sources: John McLaughlin, *Sky,* October 1997, pp. 27–32; and Willie Calderon, "Special to Soccer Times," March 28, 2000, http://www.soccertimes.com/mls/2000/mar28.htm.

net work

Bank of America has a tool for analyzing the decision to rent an apartment versus buy a home. Go to http://www.bofa.com/mortgage/ and select the "Toolbox" connection. Then choose the "Rent vs. Buy Analysis" option. Use the following data: price of home, $150,000; down payment percentage, 10%; interest rate, 8%, property taxes, $950; insurance, $700; term of loan, 30 years; property appreciation, 3%; monthly rent, $850; savings growth rate, 6%; tax bracket, 28%.

If the above data represented your current rent situation, should you consider buying a house? What appear to be the two most important issues about renting versus buying?

$$\frac{\$63{,}000 + \$36{,}000}{\$90} = 1{,}100 \text{ units}$$

For the break-even volume:

$$\frac{\$63{,}000 + \$0}{\$90} = 700 \text{ units}$$

Always remember, though, that short cuts are useful, but they should not be applied until you fully understand the basic C-V-P relationships. In addition, managing some aspects of the C-V-P relationships can be tricky when you use shorts cuts. So if you ever get confused in solving a C-V-P analysis problem, just put the problem back in the original C-V-P equation:

$$\text{Revenues} - \text{Variable costs} - \text{Fixed costs} = \text{Target income}$$

COMPUTATION IN DOLLAR AMOUNTS VERSUS UNITS Before leaving the equation approach, we should note that a variable cost ratio is sometimes used instead of a per-unit variable cost. In such cases, the basic C-V-P equation is modified as follows:

$$\text{Sales} - (\text{Variable cost ratio} \times \text{Sales}) - \text{Fixed costs} = \text{Profit}$$

Because the variable costs are stated as a percentage of sales dollars rather than on a per-unit basis, this approach expresses activity in terms of sales dollars, not units. This is still the same basic C-V-P equation, but setting up the equation using the variable cost ratio will result in a break-even point in dollars instead of units. For example, the break-even point for Jewels Corporation would then be expressed as $140,000 in sales revenue ($200 per unit × 700 units) instead of 700 units as previously illustrated. This may be verified using the preceding equation and a 55% variable cost ratio as follows:

$$\begin{aligned} \text{Sales} - (0.55)\text{Sales} - \$63{,}000 &= \$0 \\ (0.45)\text{Sales} &= \$63{,}000 \\ \text{Sales} &= \$140{,}000 \end{aligned}$$

> **caution**
>
> Remember, if you want to use C-V-P analysis to calculate the necessary sales volume in terms of *dollars,* the per-unit variable cost is *not* used. Rather, use the variable cost *ratio* times sales to determine total variable costs. Many students make the mistake of multiplying the per-unit variable cost times sales instead of the variable cost ratio times sales to get total variable costs.

The short-cut formula for break-even volume and target income volume in sales dollars is:

$$\frac{\text{Fixed costs} + \text{Target income}}{\text{Contribution margin ratio}}$$

Measuring the Effect of Potential Changes in C-V-P Variables

The basic techniques of C-V-P analysis that we have covered in this chapter are used almost daily by organizations in the management processes of planning, controlling, and evaluating. Managers must be adept at evaluating the effects on profitability of the following common changes in C-V-P variables: (1) the amount of fixed costs, (2) the variable cost rate, (3) the sales price, (4) the sales volume or the number of units sold, and (5) combinations of these variables.

CHANGES IN FIXED COSTS Many factors, such as an increase in property taxes or an increase in management's salaries, for example, will cause an increase in fixed costs. (Recall also from the opening scenario for this chapter that building a new manufacturing facility can also increase fixed costs.) If all other factors remain constant, an increase in fixed costs always increases the number of units needed to break even. Obviously, the number of units needed to reach a target income will also increase. To illustrate, we will assume that Jewels Corporation's fixed costs increase from $63,000 to $81,000. Because of the added fixed costs, Jewels must now sell 1,300 baseball gloves, instead of 1,100, to earn a target income of $36,000.

Target income of $36,000:

$$\begin{aligned}\text{Revenues} - \text{Variable costs} - \text{Fixed costs} &= \text{Target income}\\ \$200X - \$110X - \$81{,}000 &= \$36{,}000\\ \$90X &= \$117{,}000\\ X &= 1{,}300 \text{ gloves}\end{aligned}$$

The computations are quite simple. In fact, you may have found them unnecessary, realizing that if fixed costs increase by $18,000 ($81,000 − $63,000), and if the unit contribution margin remains $90 per glove, 200 additional gloves ($18,000 ÷ $90) will have to be sold in order to reach the $36,000 target income (1,100 + 200 = 1,300).

CHANGES IN THE VARIABLE COST RATE Like an increase in fixed costs, an increase in the variable cost rate also increases the number of units needed to break even or to reach target income levels, when all other factors remain constant. Suppose that the variable cost rate increased from $110 per baseball glove to $130 per glove because of higher wages for factory personnel, increased costs of direct materials, or other factors. With this increase, the number of units needed to reach the target income would be calculated as follows (assuming that fixed costs are again $63,000 and rounding up to the next unit):

Target income of $36,000:

$$\begin{aligned}\text{Revenues} - \text{Variable costs} - \text{Fixed costs} &= \text{Target income}\\ \$200X - \$130X - \$63{,}000 &= \$36{,}000\\ \$70X &= \$99{,}000\\ X &= 1{,}415 \text{ gloves*}\end{aligned}$$

*Technically, if the C-V-P analysis results in a fractional, you should always round the answer *up* to the next digit. In this case, if you round the calculated answer of 1,414.29 to 1,414 gloves, you won't quite achieve the target income of $36,000.

The increase in the variable cost rate reduces the unit contribution margin (from $90 to $70), which means that more gloves must be sold to maintain the same target income. With a unit contribution margin of $90, the company would make a $36,000 target income by selling 1,100 baseball gloves; with a unit contribution margin of only $70, an additional 315 (1,415 − 1,100) gloves must be sold to earn a $36,000 target income.

CHANGES IN SALES PRICE If all other variables remain constant, an increase in the sales price decreases the sales volume needed to reach a target income. This is because an increase in sales price increases the unit contribution margin per baseball glove, thereby decreasing the number of gloves that must be sold to earn the same amount of target income.

To illustrate, we will assume that the demand for baseball gloves is overwhelming and that Jewels cannot produce gloves fast enough. A decision is made to increase the price from $200 to $230 per glove. As a result of the price increase, the number of gloves that must be sold to reach the target income of $36,000 decreases:

Target income of $36,000:

$$\begin{aligned} \text{Revenues} - \text{Variable costs} - \text{Fixed costs} &= \text{Target income} \\ \$230X - \$110X - \$63{,}000 &= \$36{,}000 \\ \$120X &= \$99{,}000 \\ X &= 825 \text{ gloves} \end{aligned}$$

With the sales price increase of $30 per glove, the contribution margin also increased $30 per glove to $120; and with a $120 contribution margin per glove, only 825 gloves need to be sold to reach the $36,000 target income. Obviously, a decrease in the sales price would have the opposite effect; it would increase the number of units needed to reach the target income.

CHANGES IN SALES VOLUME As you have seen, the sales volume (the number of gloves to be sold) for the target income has varied with each change in one of the other variables. When other variables remain constant, an increase in the sales volume will result in an increase in income. Very simply, the more gloves sold, the higher the income (as long as the contribution margin is positive). The degree of change in profits resulting from volume change depends on the size of the unit contribution margin. To be specific, the change in income will be equal to the change in sales volume units multiplied by the contribution margin per unit. So, when the unit contribution margin is high, a slight change in volume results in a dramatic change in profit. With a lower unit contribution margin, the change in profit is less.

SIMULTANEOUS CHANGES IN SEVERAL VARIABLES Thus far, we have examined changes in only one variable at a time. Individual changes are quite rare, however; more often, a decision will affect several variables, all at the same time. For example, should Jewels Corporation increase fixed advertising costs by $20,000 and reduce the sales price by 10% if the result would be to increase sales volume by 500 units? The impact on the target income from these proposed changes is as follows:

Initial Data		Proposed Changes
Sales price per glove	$200	$180 ($200 × 90%)
Variable costs per glove	$110	$110
Fixed costs	$63,000	$83,000 ($63,000 + $20,000)
Target income	$36,000	*X*
Sales volume	1,100 gloves	1,600 gloves (1,100 + 500)

Computations and Result:

$$\begin{aligned} \text{Revenues} - \text{Variable costs} - \text{Fixed costs} &= \text{Target income} \\ (\$180 \times 1{,}600) - (\$110 \times 1{,}600) - \$83{,}000 &= X \\ \$288{,}000 - \$176{,}000 - \$83{,}000 &= X \\ \$29{,}000 &= X \text{ (target income)} \end{aligned}$$

The analysis shows that target income would drop by $7,000 ($36,000 − $29,000) as a result of these changes. So, the decision would be to not implement the proposed changes.

Consider another possible decision: Should Jewels automate part of its production, thereby reducing (by $10) variable costs to $100 per unit and increasing (by $5,000) fixed costs to $68,000? The computation would be:

business environment essay

Gathering Information for C-V-P Analysis Accurately determining fixed and variable costs and performing C-V-P analysis are not easy tasks, but the rewards of thorough work are well worth the effort. Through a detailed analysis of its costs, a manufacturing firm in the United Kingdom found that two of its three production processes were generating losses. Prices to its major customers had to be increased between 20 and 60%, yet only one customer stopped buying from the company as a result of the increase. To the company's surprise, that same customer returned not long after and confessed to being unable to find a better deal elsewhere. With inaccurate cost information, the company had simply been pricing its products too low.

Source: "Which Products Make a Profit?" *Management Accounting,* June 1993, pp. 34–36.

$$
\begin{aligned}
\text{Revenues} - \text{Variable costs} - \text{Fixed costs} &= \text{Target income} \\
(\$200 \times 1{,}100) - (\$100 \times 1{,}100) - \$68{,}000 &= X \\
\$220{,}000 - \$110{,}000 - \$68{,}000 &= X \\
\$42{,}000 &= X \text{ (target income)}
\end{aligned}
$$

caution

Remember, any change that affects the level of sales (such as a price decrease) also affects the total amount of variable costs. Some students change only the number of units of sales, and not the number of units multiplied by the variable cost per unit.

This analysis shows that management should implement these proposed changes because they would increase target income by $6,000 ($42,000 − $36,000). Obviously, this is true only if the assumptions can be relied on—that is, if fixed costs will rise by no more than $5,000 and unit variable costs will decrease by a full $10.

Consider another example. Suppose Jewels Corporation could use part of the excess capacity of its operating facilities to make baseball bats. These bats would sell for $90 per unit, increase fixed costs by $40,000, and have a variable cost per unit of $45. Jewels wants to add this new product line only if it can increase income by $25,000. How many baseball bats must Jewels sell to reach this target income? The computation follows:

$$
\begin{aligned}
\text{Revenues} - \text{Variable costs} - \text{Fixed costs} &= \text{Target income} \\
\$90X - \$45X - \$40{,}000 &= \$25{,}000 \\
\$45X &= \$65{,}000 \\
X &= 1{,}445 \text{ baseball bats (rounded up)}
\end{aligned}
$$

Management now must determine whether the company can produce and sell 1,445 baseball bats. If that sales goal seems attainable, the facilities should be used to make the bats.

to summarize

The contribution margin is sales revenue less variable costs. It is the amount of revenue left to cover fixed costs and provide a profit. The contribution margin can be expressed in total dollars, on a per-unit basis, or on a percentage basis. Because fixed costs remain constant within a relevant range, once fixed costs have been covered, income increases by the amount of the per-unit contribution margin for every additional unit sold. This relationship is used in C-V-P analysis. The basic C-V-P equation is:

$$\text{Revenues} - \text{Variable costs} - \text{Fixed costs} = \text{Target income}$$

Using this equation, management can plan, control, and evaluate the costs, prices, and sales output of the organization. The effects of changes in costs, prices, and volume on profitability may be determined by C-V-P analysis. Changes in individual variables or simultaneous changes in several variables can be analyzed with this technique.

5
Visualize C-V-P relationships using graphs.

USING GRAPHS TO "SEE" C-V-P RELATIONSHIPS

Cost-volume-profit relationships can also be expressed in graphic form. In fact, the graphic format may be the most effective way to communicate information to management. It allows managers to visualize and examine cost and revenue data over a range of activity rather than at a single volume. Reading precise information from a graph can be difficult, however, so management will typically use the C-V-P equation to analyze specific proposals.

On a C-V-P graph, volume or activity level usually is shown on the horizontal axis, and total dollars of sales and costs are shown on the vertical axis. Lines are then drawn to represent total fixed costs, total costs, and total revenues. Exhibit 2-6 shows a C-V-P graph for Jewels Corporation.

Fixed and variable cost relationships are valid only for the relevant range of activity (the screened area on the graph in Exhibit 2-6). In this case, fixed costs are $63,000, and variable costs are $110 per glove over the range of activity between 400 and 1,200 gloves sold. Total costs are $118,000 at 500 gloves [$63,000 + ($110 × 500 gloves)], $129,000 at 600 gloves [$63,000 + ($110 × 600 gloves)], and so on. Similarly, total revenues are $100,000 at 500 gloves

---

exhibit 2-6 A Cost-Volume-Profit Graph

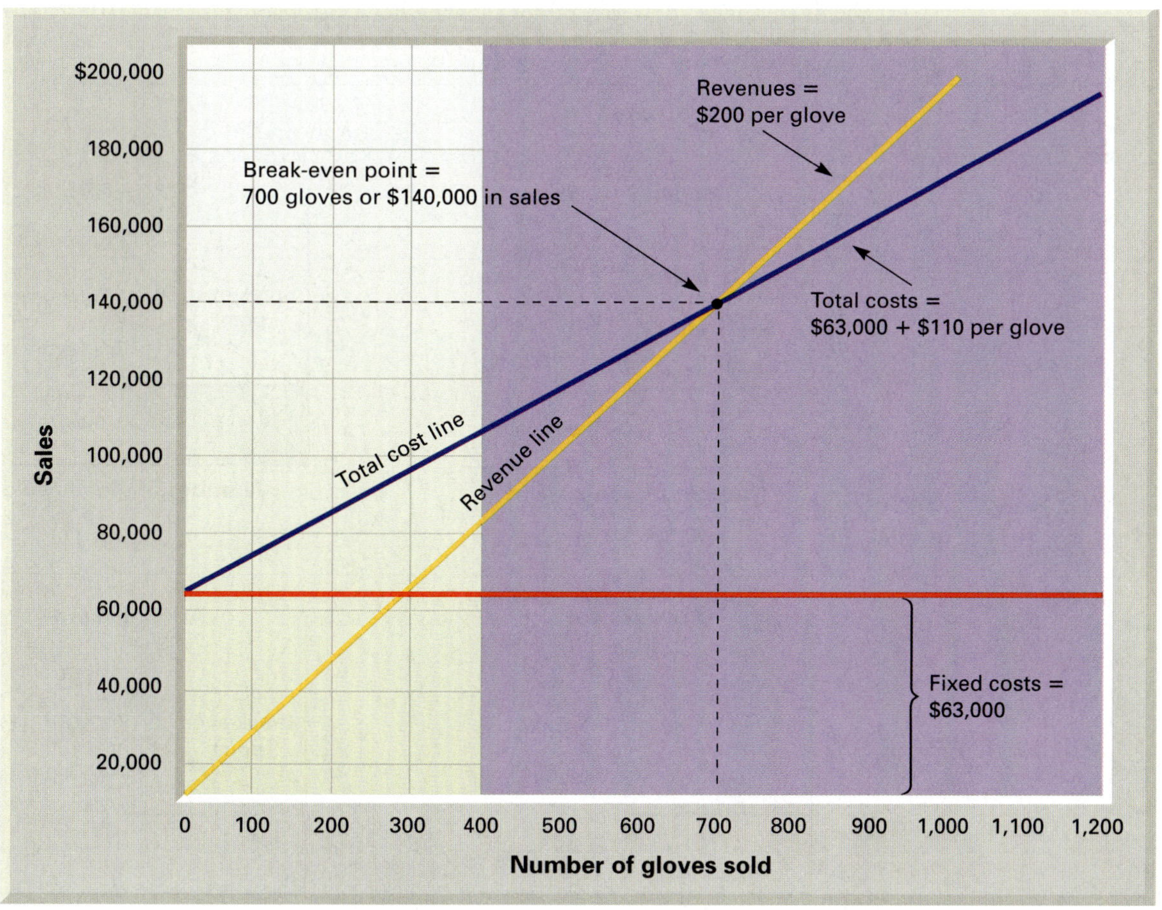

($200 × 500 gloves), $120,000 at 600 gloves, and so forth. The break-even point, the point at which total revenues equal total costs, is 700 gloves, or $140,000 in sales.

As shown in Exhibit 2-7, the graphic format can be used to isolate such items of interest as total variable costs, total fixed costs, the area in which losses occur, the area in which profits will be realized, and the break-even point. Because C-V-P graphs illustrate a wide range of activity, management can use them to quickly determine approximately how much profit or loss will be realized at various levels of sales.

The Profit Graph

profit graph A graph that shows how profits vary with changes in volume.

Some managers use another graphic approach, referred to as the **profit graph**, which plots only profits and losses and omits costs and revenues. Exhibit 2-8 shows a profit graph for Jewels Corporation.

Notice that, though the horizontal axis of the profit graph is the same as those of the previous graphs, the vertical axis represents only profits and losses. As long as the contribution margin is positive, the maximum amount of losses that can occur is at a zero level of sales. With no sales, total losses will be the amount of the fixed costs. With the axes properly labeled, the profit line is drawn as follows:

1. Locate the loss for zero sales volume on the vertical axis. This is the total fixed cost, or negative $63,000 in this case.
2. Locate the profit or loss at another sales volume. For example, at sales of 700 gloves, profits are zero [$140,000 − ($63,000 + $77,000)], or at sales of 1,000 gloves, profits are $27,000 [$200,000 − ($63,000 + $110,000)].
3. After the two profit or loss points have been identified, draw a line through them back to the vertical axis.

Because of its simplicity, the profit graph is widely used for comparing competing projects. It has the disadvantage, however, of not showing how costs vary with changes in sales volume.

exhibit 2-7 Cost-Volume-Profit Graphs

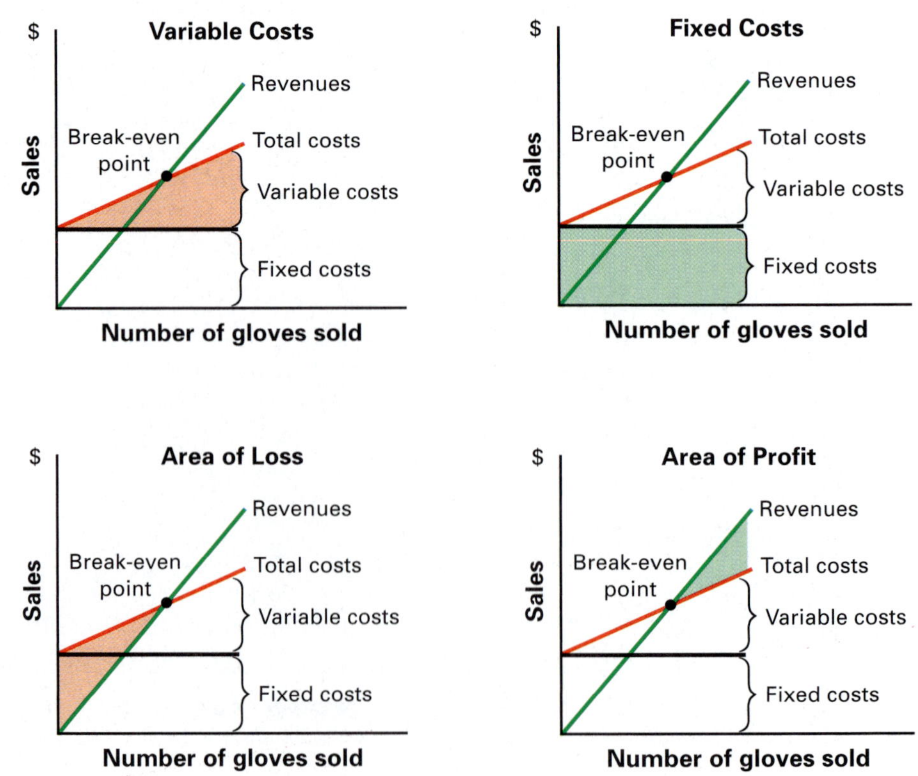

exhibit 2-8 Profit Graph for Jewels Corporation

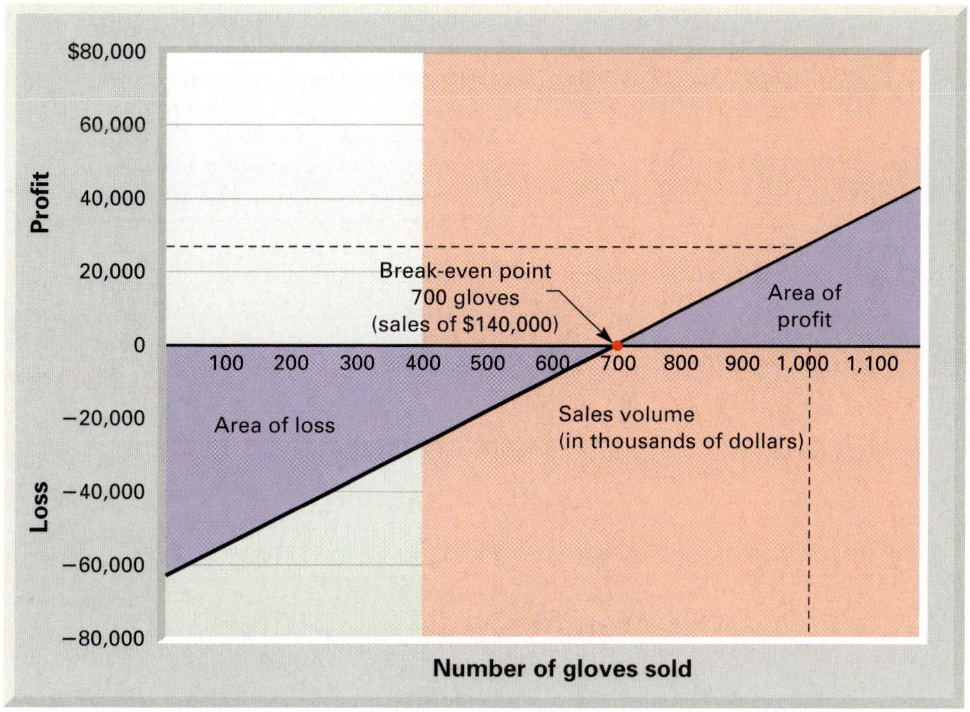

A Comparison of C-V-P Graphs with C-V-P Equations

C-V-P graphs are very useful for understanding the results of analyzing contribution margin statements with C-V-P equations. To illustrate this point, we will combine a C-V-P graph with a C-V-P equation to show you that both approaches are assessing the same contribution margin statement results. Again we'll explore the question of what volume of activity Jewels Corporation needs to reach a target income of $36,000. This was illustrated earlier with the equation approach, but it is repeated here to show that the graph approach will produce the same quantitative results. As shown in Exhibit 2-9, Jewels Corporation must sell 1,100 baseball gloves to reach a target income of $36,000.

STOP & THINK When analyzing costs, volume, and profit, do you think most managers would prefer to use graphs or equations?

to summarize

The financial effects on cost-volume-profit decisions can be examined by using either equations or graphs. These methods of analysis can be used to calculate the break-even point, which occurs at the point where total revenues equal total fixed costs plus total variable costs. These methods can also be used to project a target income level, with profit being equal to the excess of revenues over total costs. The graphic approaches can be useful because they highlight cost-volume-profit relationships over wide ranges of activity. The most common graphic approach involves plotting fixed costs as a horizontal line with variable costs above fixed costs. A profit graph, which shows only profit or loss and volume, is much simpler, but it does not show how costs vary with changes in sales volume. Regardless of the approach, C-V-P analysis is based on the same calculations and on the underlying concept of fixed and variable cost behavior patterns.

exhibit 2-9 Comparison of C-V-P Equation with C-V-P Graph

C-V-P Equation

(Sales price × Units) − (Variable costs × Units) − Fixed costs = Profit

$$\$200X - \$110X - \$63{,}000 = \$36{,}000$$
$$\$90X = \$99{,}000$$
$$X = 1{,}100 \text{ gloves}$$

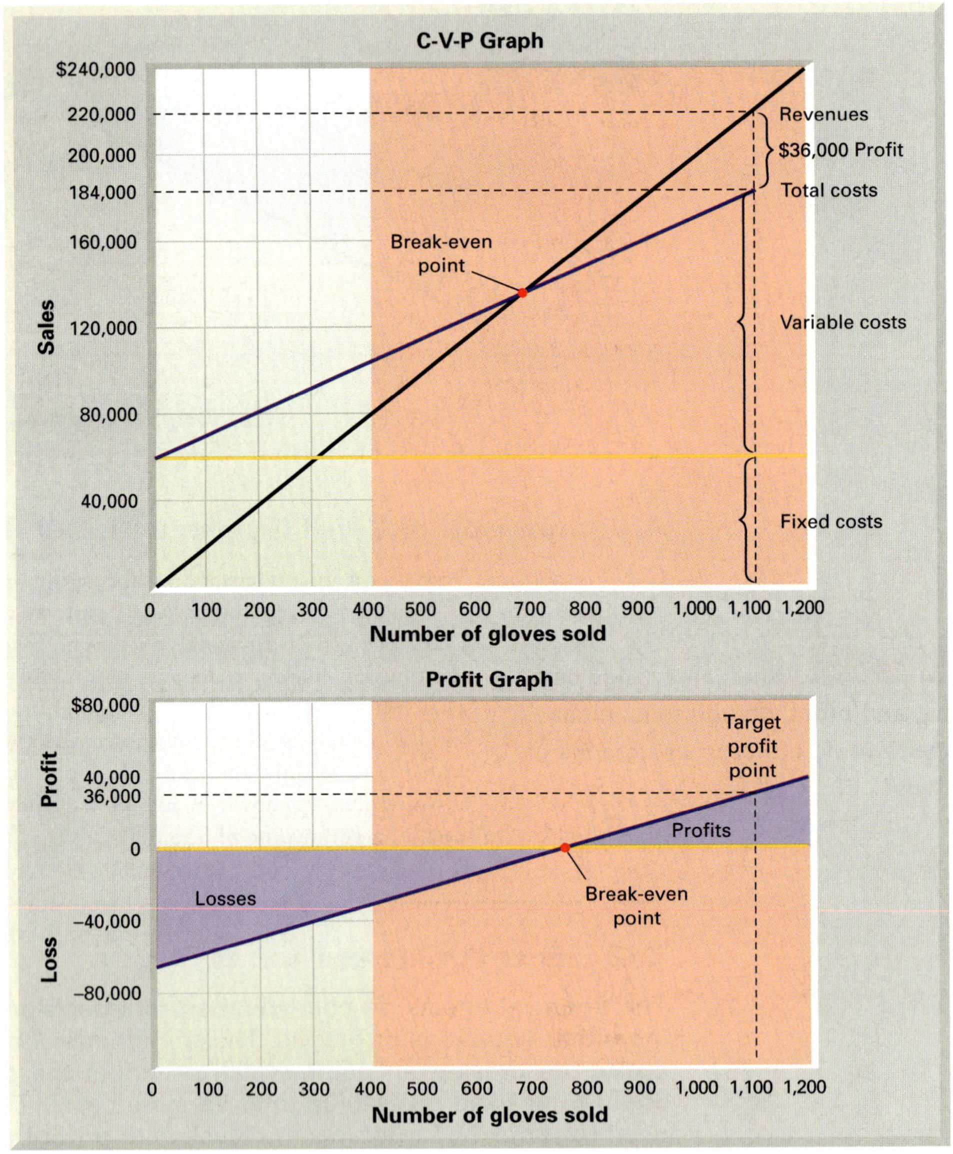

6 Identify the limiting assumptions of C-V-P analysis, and explain the issues of quality and time relative to C-V-P analysis decisions.

LIMITING ASSUMPTIONS OF C-V-P ANALYSIS

C-V-P analysis is an extremely useful tool for assisting management in making short-term operating decisions. However, C-V-P analysis has some limiting assumptions that must not be overlooked.

The key assumption is that the behavior of revenues and costs is linear throughout the relevant range. C-V-P analysis is valid only for a relevant range.

A second assumption is that all costs, including mixed costs, can be accurately divided into fixed and variable categories. As noted earlier in the chapter, some costs have characteristics of both fixed and variable costs. These costs sometimes are not easily classified into their fixed and variable components, which limits the accuracy of C-V-P analysis.

For companies with more than one product, a third major assumption in C-V-P analysis is required—that the mix of a company's products does not change over the relevant range. The sales mix is the proportion of the total units sold (or the total dollar sales) represented by each of a company's products. (Sales mix will be discussed in the expanded material section of this chapter.)

In addition to the three assumptions already identified, there are other limiting assumptions implicit in C-V-P analysis. For example, C-V-P analysis assumes that efficiency and productivity are held constant, that the prices of materials and other product components are constant, and that revenues and costs can be analyzed using a single activity base, such as volume. A related and very significant assumption, and one that clearly is not always valid, is that volume is the only, or even the primary, driver of costs.

Because of the limiting assumptions just described, the conclusions reached from C-V-P analysis must be considered with reasonable caution. Nevertheless, C-V-P analysis does provide a good model for predicting future operating results when specific relationships are defined and recognized.

Issues of Quality and Time

The emphasis in this chapter has been primarily on costs and profits and how they change when changes in variable costs, fixed costs, sales prices, and sales volume are made. Remember, however, that financial results are just one element of performance that management is interested in. Good managers are equally interested in how these changes will affect the quality of goods and services produced and sold and the speed at which products and services can be delivered to customers. If, for example, reducing fixed costs means that goods will be produced more slowly or that the quality of manufactured products will be reduced, the decision to reduce fixed costs may be a poor one. On the other hand, if management can automate a function using robotics instead of high-cost workers, for example, it may be possible to simultaneously reduce costs, increase quality and consistency, and improve speed of production. To determine whether quality and speed of production are good or bad, management may need to compare its results with those of other firms, a process called *benchmarking*, which will be introduced in Chapter 8 of management accounting.

to summarize

C-V-P analysis is based on three critical and limiting assumptions: (1) that the behavior of revenues and costs is linear throughout the relevant range, (2) that all costs can be categorized as either fixed or variable, and (3) that the sales mix does not change. When considering how changes in variable costs, fixed costs, sales prices, sales volume, and sales mix will affect profits, it is important to also consider how these changes will affect the quality of goods and services and the speed at which products and services can be delivered to customers. Changes that increase quality, reduce costs, and speed up production are good changes and should be made; changes that have a negative effect on one or more of these variables must be carefully analyzed and trade-offs considered.

expanded material

Thus far, we have covered various types of costs, simple methods of analyzing mixed costs, and the basics of C-V-P analysis. In this expanded section we cover an additional, more advanced method of analyzing mixed costs—least squares analysis. We also cover the effect of the sales mix on profitability and use the concept of operating leverage to explore differences in cost structures among manufacturing, merchandising, service, and e-commerce organizations.

7

Analyze mixed costs using the least squares method.

ANALYSIS OF MIXED COSTS—THE LEAST SQUARES METHOD

least squares method A method of segregating the fixed and variable portions of a mixed cost; the regression line, a line of averages, is statistically fitted through all cost points.

Earlier, we described two common methods for analyzing mixed costs: the scattergraph and high-low methods. These methods are relatively easy to use and provide useful estimates of the fixed and variable components of mixed costs. A more sophisticated method for analyzing mixed costs is the **least squares method**, which is the most accurate method of determining the fixed and variable portions of a mixed cost. Like the scattergraph, the least squares method fits a straight line through all points on a graph. However, instead of visually fitting the regression line through the cost points, it uses statistical analysis to guarantee that the line is the best possible fit for the applicable costs. (Note here that regression overcomes the subjectivity weakness of scattergraphs and the limited data use of the high-low method.)

The formula for the least squares method is based on the equation for a straight line:

$$Y = a + bX$$

In this equation, Y represents the total predicted cost; a represents the intercept and the fixed cost (if in the relevant range); b represents the variable cost rate or the slope of the line; and X represents the activity level. Using cost and activity level data, this method involves the use of simultaneous equations to find the values of a and b. Once computed, these values can be combined with the projected activity level X to predict total future cost Y. For example, if the values of a and b are computed to be \$200 and \$5, respectively, then for an estimated activity level of 100 direct labor hours, we find that:

$$Y \text{ (total predicted cost)} = \$200 + \$5(100 \text{ hours})$$
$$Y = \$200 + \$500$$
$$Y = \$700$$

Obviously, because the regression line is a line of averages, the actual total cost for 100 direct labor hours might be somewhat different from the predicted cost of \$700. The method of least squares, however, attempts to minimize the differences between predicted and actual costs. Once a regression line has been fitted to historical data, the fixed and variable costs represented by the line can be used to predict the level of future costs.

Calculating the estimates of a (the intercept, or the total fixed cost) and b (the slope, or variable cost rate) requires solving the following two simultaneous equations:

$$1.\ \Sigma XY = a\Sigma X + b\Sigma X^2$$
$$2.\ \Sigma Y = na + b\Sigma X$$

where

a = fixed cost
b = variable cost rate
n = number of observations
Σ = summation sign (which means the sum of all available historical data)
X = activity level, or independent variable
Y = total (predicted) mixed cost, or dependent variable

fyi

Use of the least squares equations results in the unique line that minimizes the sum of the squared distances between the actual observation points and the regression line. The equations are based on squared distances because the necessary derivation (based on differential calculus) is mathematically simple when squared quantities are included.

Solving these equations is easy with a calculator or computer, but difficult and tedious by hand. Because calculators and computers are so widely available and can analyze large amounts of data very quickly, we will focus on describing and interpreting the typical output from a computerized application of least squares analysis. We will leave it to math classes to illustrate the manual calculations of the least squares method.

To illustrate the concept of least squares, we return again to the electricity cost data used to describe the scattergraph and high-low methods. (Note that the data, e.g., 12 or 18 months of data, are given for only six months; thus, the resulting regression equation will be less accurate than it would be with more data.)

Month	Direct Labor Hours Worked	Total Electricity Cost
January	7,000	$ 70,000
February	6,000	60,000
March	12,000	100,000
April	6,600	80,000
May	18,000	120,000
June	14,000	110,000

Using these data, the following output, shown in Exhibit 2-10, was generated in just a matter of minutes using the "data analysis" tool in Excel®, a Microsoft database software program.[7] Comparing the least squares output with the results from our earlier examples of the scattergraph and high-low methods, we get the following:

	Fixed Costs	Variable Cost per Direct Labor Hour
Scattergraph method	$40,000 per month	$4.29 per direct labor hour
High-low method	30,000 per month	5.00 per direct labor hour
Least squares analysis	40,402 per month	4.68 per direct labor hour

exhibit 2-10 Output of Least Squares Analysis Application

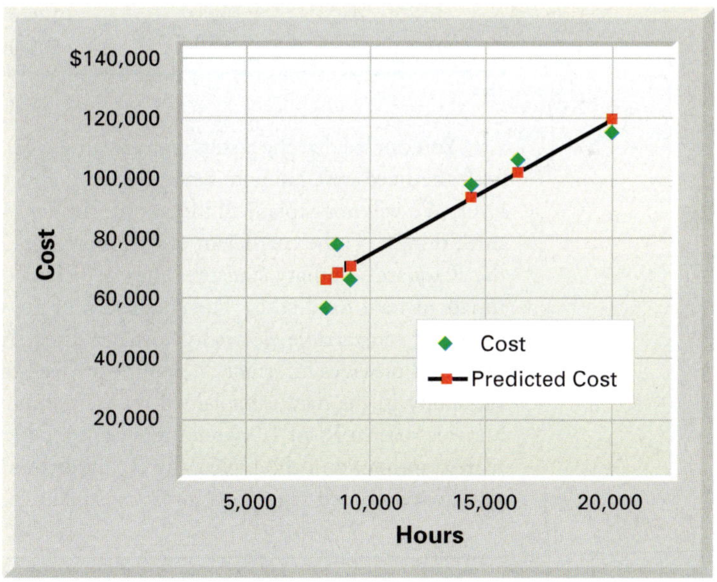

Month	Hours	Cost
January	7,000	$ 70,000
February	6,000	60,000
March	12,000	100,000
April	6,600	80,000
May	18,000	120,000
June	14,000	110,000

Summary Output	
Regression Statistics	
Multiple R	0.962
R square	0.926
Adjusted R square	0.907
Standard error	7207.705
Observations	6

(continued)

7 There are literally hundreds of software programs that can be used to run regressions or least squares analysis.

exhibit 2-10 (Concluded)

ANOVA					
	df	SS	MS	F	Significance F
Regression	1	2592195946	2.59E+09	49.89693	0.002118833
Residual	4	207804054.1	51951014		
Total	5	2800000000			

	Coefficients	Standard Error	t Stat	P-value	Lower 95%	Upper 95%
Intercept	$40,402.03	$7,613.10	$5.31	0.0061	$19,264.63	$61,539.43
Hours	$ 4.68	$ 0.66	$7.05	0.0021	$ 2.84	$ 6.52

Residual Output		
Observation	Predicted Cost	Residuals
1	$ 73,155.41	$(3,155.41)
2	68,476.35	(8,476.35)
3	96,550.68	3,449.32
4	71,283.78	8,716.22
5	124,625.00	(4,625.00)
6	105,908.78	4,091.22

You can see that the results are very similar for the least squares analysis and scattergraph method, with the fixed cost estimate being $40,402 and the variable cost rate being $4.68 per direct labor hour. We will not explain all the output shown in Exhibit 2-10; what is important is that you know three things: (1) the coefficient of the intercept, (2) the coefficient of the direct labor hours, and (3) the R square summary statistic. The coefficient of the intercept, or $40,402 in this case, is the estimate of total fixed costs. The coefficient of the direct labor hours, or $4.68 in this case, is the estimate of the variable electricity cost per direct labor hour. The R square (R^2) is a descriptive statistic that provides information about how well the regression line fits the data or how much of the variability in the data is explained by the computed regression statistics. For now, all you need to know is that an R^2 of 1.0 would represent a perfect fit (meaning all data points were exactly on the regression line) and the higher the R^2 the better. In this case, an R^2 of 0.926 is high and suggests that the computed regression statistics explain most of the variability in the data.[8]

to summarize

A more sophisticated technique for analyzing mixed costs is the least squares method. The least squares method is essentially equivalent to simple regression analysis, using the equation for a straight line ($Y = a + bX$) and simultaneous equations to calculate the fixed and variable portions of a mixed cost. Even though the least squares method is more mathematically correct than the scattergraph or high-low methods, it still should be used with caution in analyzing mixed costs. Least squares results can be quickly calculated using computer programs such as Microsoft's Excel®.

8 The adjusted R^2 of 0.907 is a more conservative estimate of the variance explained in the data and is preferred to the R^2 statistic in some circumstances.

8

Explain the effects of sales mix on profitability.

sales mix The relative proportion of total units sold (or total sales dollars) that is represented by each of a company's products.

SALES MIX

As we explained earlier in the chapter, **sales mix** is the proportion of the total units represented by each of a company's products. To keep our discussions simple, in previous sections of the chapter, we used examples of companies with only one product. Many companies have more than one product, however, so we need to illustrate how sales mix issues are resolved. To illustrate how a change in sales mix can affect a company's C-V-P relationships, we assume that Multi-Product, Inc., sells three different products. Following are the monthly revenues and costs for each type of product:

	Product A		Product B		Product C		Total	
	Amount	Percent	Amount	Percent	Amount	Percent	Amount	Percent
Sales revenue	$25,000	100%	$45,000	100.00%	$30,000	100%	$100,000	100%
Less variable costs	20,000	80	30,000	66.67	21,000	70	71,000	71
Contribution margin	$ 5,000	20%	$15,000	33.33%	$ 9,000	30%	$ 29,000	29%
Sales mix	25%		45%		30%		100%	

fyi

Obviously, a computer can make sales mix and other C-V-P analysis computations very easy. Using simulation or other programs, you can quickly calculate the financial effects of changes in the sales of one product or simultaneous changes in sales of several products.

Total sales are $100,000, which in this example includes $25,000 in sales of Product A, $45,000 of Product B, and $30,000 of Product C. Therefore, the sales mix is 25% Product A ($25,000 ÷ $100,000), 45% Product B ($45,000 ÷ $100,000), and 30% Product C ($30,000 ÷ $100,000). With this sales mix, the average contribution margin ratio is 29%, which is determined by subtracting total variable costs of $71,000 from total sales of $100,000, and dividing the result ($29,000) by $100,000. If Multi-Product, Inc., had fixed costs of $17,400 and desired a target income of $40,000, the necessary sales volume (in dollars) would be:

$$\begin{aligned} \text{Sales} - (0.71)\text{Sales} - \$17{,}400 &= \$40{,}000 \\ (0.29)\text{Sales} &= \$57{,}400 \\ \text{Sales} &= \$57{,}400 \div 0.29 \\ \text{Sales} &= \$197{,}932 \text{ (rounded up)} \end{aligned}$$

Alternatively, the company could divide the average contribution margin ratio (29%) into fixed costs plus target income ($17,400 + $40,000). As you can see, this revised, more compact formula is simply a restatement of the preceding equation.

$$\frac{\text{Fixed costs} + \text{Target income}}{\text{Average contribution margin ratio}} = \frac{\$57{,}400}{0.29} = \$197{,}932 \text{ (rounded up)}$$

Obviously, $197,932 in sales will make the target income only if the average contribution margin ratio, and therefore the sales mix, does not change. To illustrate the effect of a change in sales mix, assume that the total sales revenue and the sales price of each product remain the same but that the sales mix changes as follows:

	Product A		Product B		Product C		Total	
	Amount	Percent	Amount	Percent	Amount	Percent	Amount	Percent
Sales revenue	$50,000	100%	$30,000	100.00%	$20,000	100%	$100,000	100%
Less variable costs	40,000	80	20,000	66.67	14,000	70	74,000	74
Contribution margin	$10,000	20%	$10,000	33.33%	$ 6,000	30%	$ 26,000	26%
Sales mix	50%		30%		20%		100%	

In this example, the contribution margin ratio for each product remains the same, but the sales mix changes. Product A now comprises 50% of total sales instead of 25%. Because Product

A has a lower contribution margin ratio than Products B and C, the average contribution margin ratio decreases from 29 to 26%. Accordingly, the sales volume needed to generate $40,000 of target income increases to $220,770, computed as follows:

$$\frac{\text{Fixed costs} + \text{Target income}}{\text{Average contribution margin ratio}} = \frac{\$57{,}400}{0.26} = \$220{,}770 \text{ (rounded up)}$$

As you can see, a sensible profit-maximizing strategy for management would be to maintain as large a contribution margin as possible on all products and then to emphasize those products with the largest individual contribution margins. In the remaining chapters of this text we discuss procedures management can use to control costs and, hence, maintain high contribution margins. The second part of this strategy—emphasizing the products with the highest contribution margins—is a marketing function. Multi-Product, Inc., for example, should promote Product B more aggressively than Product A. With other factors being equal, a company should spend more advertising dollars and pay higher sales commissions on its higher contribution margin products. In fact, instead of paying commissions based on total sales, a good strategy would be to base sales commissions on the total contribution margin generated. This way, the mix of products that maximizes the sales staff's commissions will be the mix that provides the company with the greatest overall profit.

STOP & THINK Would maximizing the sales of the highest contribution margin products still be the best profit-maximizing strategy if the company experienced production constraints such that producing more of the highest contribution margin products severely limited the quality or production speed of other products?

to summarize

Sales mix is the proportion of the total units sold represented by each of a company's products. Changes in sales mix can affect profits because not all products have the same contribution margin. Other things being equal, to maximize profits, management should put greater emphasis on the sale of products with higher contribution margin ratios.

9

Describe how fixed and variable costs differ in manufacturing, service, merchandising, and e-commerce organizations, and illustrate these differences with the operating leverage concept.

COST STRUCTURE IN DIFFERENT TYPES OF ORGANIZATIONS

As noted earlier in the chapter, cost-volume-profit relationships and contribution margins, in particular, highlight the different effects that variable and fixed costs have on profitability. An important issue has to do with the amount of fixed costs a company has in its cost structure. The amount of fixed costs an organization commits itself to often has a lot to do with its type of business, e.g., merchandising, manufacturing, or service. In addition, a new type of organization has arrived in the economy—companies organized around the process of e-commerce. We'll talk more about differences between merchandising, manufacturing, service, and e-commerce companies throughout the remaining chapters in this textbook. For now, we'll simply illustrate the differences among these organizations using an example and then apply the concept of **operating leverage** to illustrate how a company can manage risk (in terms of profits) by the way it organizes its cost structure—in other words, how much the company is committed to using fixed costs versus variable costs to do business.

operating leverage The extent to which fixed costs are part of a company's cost structure; the higher the proportion of fixed costs to variable costs, the faster income increases or decreases with sales volume.

Imagine that three college students design a new computer software game that they would like to market to college campuses across the nation. They identify three ways that they can approach the market. First, they could take on the role of the merchant by contracting with a software manufacturing company to handle all the production of the packaged software. They would then concentrate on the sales and marketing of their new game. This approach won't require an expensive production facility, but the students know that they will have to pay a high price per unit to the company that handles the production of the packaged software. Second, they could take on the role of manufacturer by setting up their own production facilities. In this case, because all their effort would be dedicated to producing the game, they would need to wholesale their software product to another merchant company that would then resell the product to the actual customers. Finally, they could "virtually" sell their game to other college students by contracting with an e-commerce company that will host their software download site for a significant fixed fee per month. In any case, regardless of whether they will wholesale the game to another merchant or retail their game directly to the college student market, they determine that they will sell their game for $100. The costs of each of these methods of structuring their business are as follows:

Business Structure	Variable Cost per Unit to Manufacture or to Purchase from a Manufacturer	Fixed Cost per Year for the Merchandising, Manufacturing, or E-Commerce Facility
Traditional merchant	$80	$100,000
Manufacturer	25	375,000
E-commerce merchant	0	500,000

caution

Don't confuse the concept of operating leverage with the concept of financial leverage. While both concepts focus on risk and the sensitivity of profit to changes in sales volume, financial leverage has to do with the use of debt versus equity to provide financing for a company. In general, the financial leverage (and risk) of a company increases as management chooses to use debt, rather than equity, to raise funds for the company. Similarly, the operating leverage (and risk) of a company increases as management chooses to emphasize fixed cost, rather than variable cost, to create or obtain the product for sale to the marketplace.

As you can see, one of the issues that these students must decide when selecting their business structure is whether they want to commit to high fixed costs in order to have low variable costs, or vice versa. This trade-off of fixed versus variable costs is what we mean when we talk about operating leverage. As total fixed costs increase and variable costs per unit decrease, the operating leverage of the organization increases. In the example above, the operating leverage of the company will be very high if the students choose to structure their company as an e-commerce merchant. So, the question is, is it good or bad to have high operating leverage? The answer is, it depends on whether the company is operating above or below the break-even point.

Look at the C-V-P graphs in Exhibit 2-11 and you can see the impact of operating leverage for these three types of companies. The break-even point (which is the same for all three companies) is at a sales volume of 5,000 games sold each year. At this point, all three companies would generate the same level of profit—nothing. As sales move above or below the break-even point, however, there are significant differences in profit between the company structures. If sales are below the break-even point, then the e-commerce merchant structure will generate a lot of losses. If the three students can sell more than 5,000 games per year, however, then the e-commerce merchant structure will generate the most profit per year. Essentially, operating leverage is a measure of risk. With high levels of operating leverage, the company is at risk of losing a lot of money if sales go down. But business risk often has an upside. In the case of operating leverage, the risk of loss is balanced by the potential for large gains in income as sales go up. So the decision on how to structure a company partly depends on the impact on operating leverage and on how much risk the business owners are willing to accept.

STOP & THINK Think about the level of operating leverage you would expect to find in a service organization such as a consulting company or a law firm. Would these kinds of organizations typically have high or low levels of operating leverage?

to summarize

The relationship between fixed and variable costs differs across different types of organizations. Generally, traditional merchandising companies have relatively low levels of fixed costs and high levels of variable costs. On the other hand, manufacturing companies often have higher levels of fixed costs and lower levels of variable costs. The emergence of e-commerce in this economy has resulted in some companies that are even more extremely committed to fixed costs with little or no variable product

exhibit 2-11 "Seeing" Operating Leverages

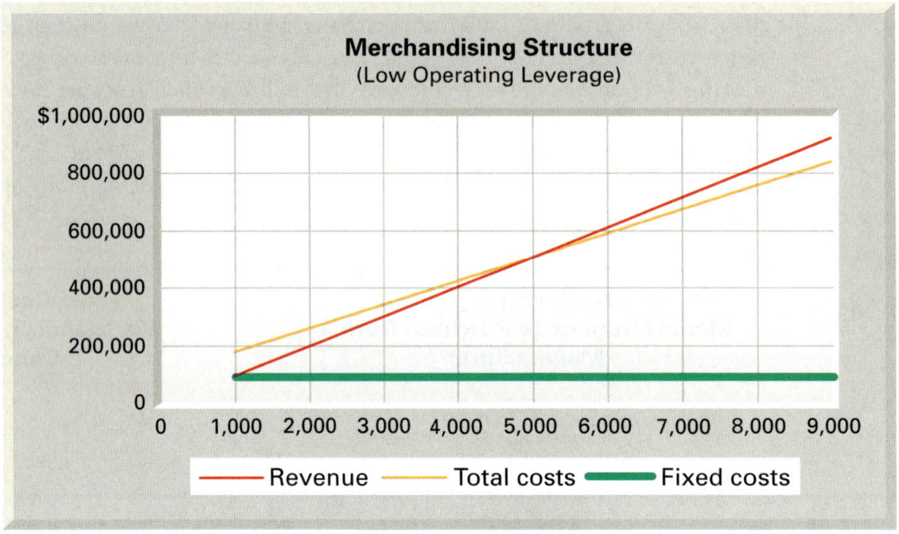

		Sales in Units	Revenue	Total Variable Costs	Contribution Margin	Total Fixed Costs	Operating Income
Price per unit	$ 100	3,000	$300,000	$(240,000)	$ 60,000	$(100,000)	$(40,000)
Variable cost per unit	80	5,000	500,000	(400,000)	100,000	(100,000)	—
Total fixed costs	100,000	7,000	700,000	(560,000)	140,000	(100,000)	40,000

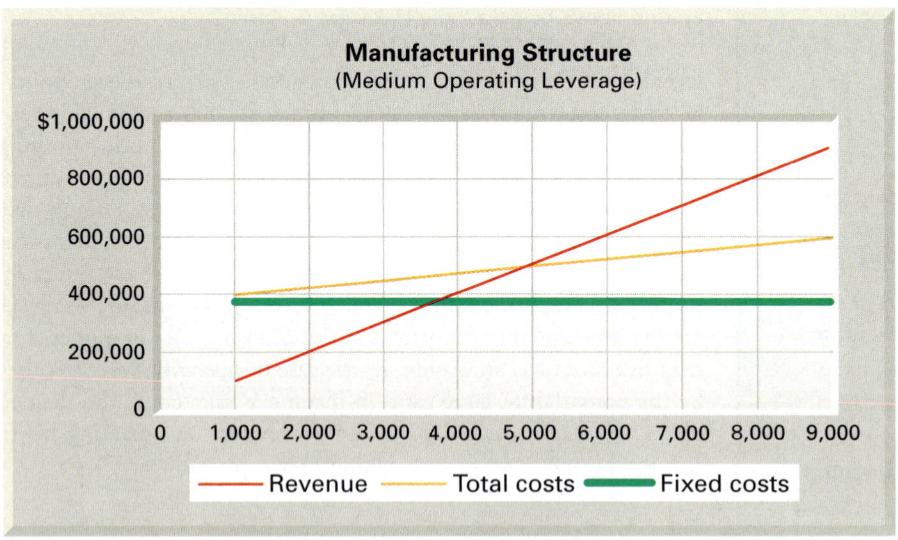

		Sales in Units	Revenue	Total Variable Costs	Contribution Margin	Total Fixed Costs	Operating Income
Price per unit	$ 100	3,000	$300,000	$ (75,000)	$225,000	$(375,000)	$(150,000)
Variable cost per unit	25	5,000	500,000	(125,000)	375,000	(375,000)	—
Total fixed costs	375,000	7,000	700,000	(175,000)	525,000	(375,000)	150,000

exhibit 2-11 (Concluded)

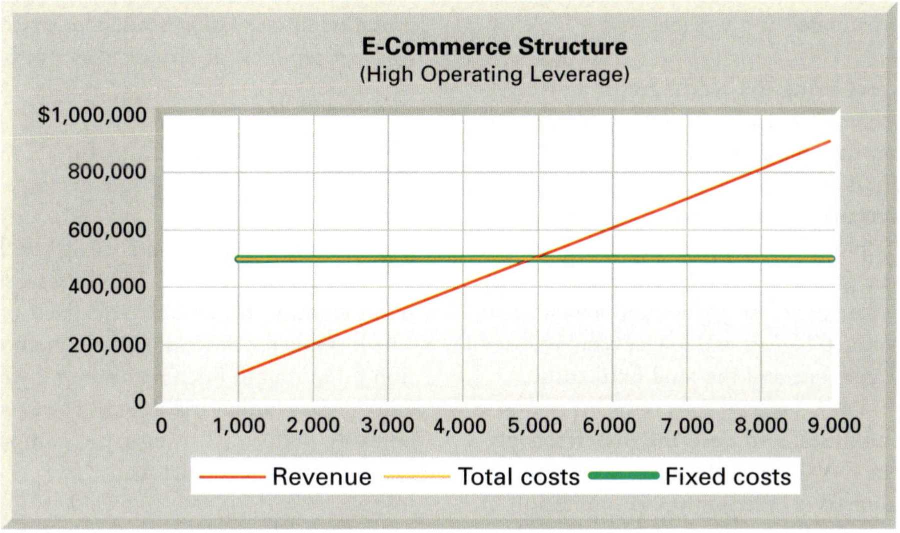

		Sales in Units	Revenue	Total Variable Costs	Contribution Margin	Total Fixed Costs	Operating Income
Price per unit	$ 100	3,000	$300,000	$ —	$300,000	$(500,000)	$(200,000)
Variable cost per unit	0	5,000	500,000	—	500,000	(500,000)	—
Total fixed costs	500,000	7,000	700,000	—	700,000	(500,000)	200,000

costs. These cost structure differences are important and are illustrated in the concept of operating leverage. Operating leverage relates to the amount of fixed costs a company has in its cost structure. When sales are expected to increase, high operating leverage results in higher income, and vice versa.

review of learning objectives

1 Understand the key factors involved in cost-volume-profit (C-V-P) analysis and why it is such an important tool in management decision making. C-V-P analysis is a very important management concept. It is a technique used by management to understand how profits may be expected to vary in relation to changes in key variables: sales price and volume, variable costs, fixed costs, and mix of products. C-V-P analysis is a particularly useful tool for planning and making operating decisions. It can provide data to stimulate increased sales efforts or cost reduction programs; assist in production scheduling or marketing strategy; and help establish company policies, for example, the appropriate product mix or the fixed cost structure of a company. Effective management requires a comprehensive understanding and use of C-V-P analysis.

2 Explain and analyze the basic cost behavior patterns—variable, fixed, mixed, and stepped. Understanding cost behavior patterns can assist management in making key operating decisions. The two basic cost behavior patterns are variable and fixed. Costs that vary in total in direct proportion to changes in the level of activity are variable costs. Therefore, per-unit variable costs remain constant. Generally, we assume a linear relationship between variable costs and level of activity within the relevant range; for other ranges, variable costs are curvilinear. Costs that do not change in total with changes in activity level, within the relevant range, are fixed costs; thus, per-unit fixed costs decrease as level of activity increases. Because of factors such as automation, fixed costs are becoming a greater percentage of total costs in most manufacturing companies. Costs that contain both fixed and variable components are mixed costs. Stepped costs increase in total in a stair-step fashion with the level of activity. If the steps are wide, the cost is treated as a fixed cost for analysis purposes; if the steps are narrow, the cost is approximated as a variable cost.

3 Analyze mixed costs using the scattergraph and high-low methods. Before mixed costs can be analyzed and used in decision making, they must be divided into their fixed and variable components. The scattergraph and high-low methods are commonly used to analyze mixed costs. The scattergraph method involves visually plotting a straight line (the regression line) through points on a graph of cost data at various activity levels. With the high-low method, the highest and lowest levels of activity and their associated highest and lowest costs are used to calculate the variable cost rate and the total fixed costs.

4 Perform C-V-P analyses, and describe the effects potential changes in C-V-P variables have on company profitability. C-V-P analysis is based on the computation of contribution margin, which is sales less variable costs. Contribution margin is the amount available to cover fixed costs and then provide a profit. C-V-P analysis is commonly used to assess break-even points (where contribution margin equals fixed costs) and to compute target income levels. The C-V-P equation is especially useful in assessing how profits can be expected to change when costs or revenues change. Increases in fixed or variable costs result in a larger number of sales being required to break even and reach target income levels. Increases in sales price result in a decreased number of sales being required to break even and reach target income levels.

5 Visualize C-V-P relationships using graphs. C-V-P graphs are an effective method for visualizing the effect of impacts on key variables in the C-V-P equation. In addition, the graphic approach effectively allows the simultaneous analysis of several different activity levels.

6 Identify the limiting assumptions of C-V-P analysis, and explain the issues of quality and time relative to C-V-P analysis decisions. C-V-P analysis has several limiting assumptions, including the following: (1) cost and revenue behavior patterns are linear and remain constant over the relevant range, (2) all costs can be categorized as either fixed or variable, and (3) the sales mix of products is constant over the relevant range. When making changes in costs, revenues, and volume, resulting changes in the quality of products or services and the speed at which those products and services can be delivered to customers must be considered. Changes that result in increased profits while decreasing product or service quality or slowing delivery of products or services may not be good decisions.

expanded material

7 Analyze mixed costs using the least squares method. The least squares method uses a simple regression analysis to identify the variable and fixed portions of mixed costs. The formula for the least squares method is based on the equation for a straight line, $Y = a + bX$, where a is total fixed cost and b is per-unit variable cost. Least square calculations can be easily performed using basic computer software programs or programmed calculators.

8 Explain the effects of sales mix on profitability. Sales mix is the proportion of total units sold represented by each of a company's products. Because all products do not have the same contribution margin ratios, changes in the sales mix of products sold can significantly affect total profits. The best profit-maximizing strategy is to maintain as large a contribution margin as possible on all products and then emphasize those products with the largest individual contribution margins.

9 Describe how fixed and variable costs differ in manufacturing, service, merchandising, and e-commerce organizations, and illustrate these differences with the operating leverage concept. The trade-off between fixed costs and variable costs is related to whether a company is structured as a manufacturing, merchandising, or service firm. The advent of e-commerce has created the potential for companies to have very high levels of fixed costs and very low levels of variable costs. The impact of the fixed cost/variable cost relationship on profits is captured in the concept of operating leverage. Operating leverage is a measure of the extent to which a company's costs are fixed rather than variable. Companies with higher fixed costs and lower per-unit variable costs will experience higher operating leverage and, therefore, a tendency for profits to increase at a faster rate when sales increase. A company with such a cost structure will be more profitable in good times but have higher losses in bad times.

key terms and concepts

break-even point 56
contribution margin 53
contribution margin ratio 55
cost behavior 39
cost-volume-profit (C-V-P) analysis 39
curvilinear costs 42
fixed costs 44
high-low method 50

mixed costs 47
per-unit contribution margin 54
profit graph 64
regression line 49
relevant range 44
return on sales revenue 57
scattergraph (visual-fit) method 49
stepped costs 45
target income 57
variable cost rate 49
variable costs 41

expanded material

least squares method 68
operating leverage 72
sales mix 71

review problems

1. Variable and Fixed Costs Analyses

Blade Corporation manufactures two types of inline skates—a basic model and a racing model. During the year 2003, Blade accumulated the following summary information about its two products:

	Racing Model	Basic Model
Selling price	$130	$65
Number of units manufactured and sold	14,000	9,000

	Racing Model		Basic Model	
	Units	Costs	Units	Costs
January	1,200	$ 112,000	800	$ 39,600
February	900	91,000	600	30,000
March	800	76,400	450	25,800
April	1,400	124,800	900	36,900
May	950	92,650	1,000	47,000
June	1,600	146,800	1,200	57,300
July	1,400	134,600	1,300	60,600
August	1,700	154,500	650	32,195
September	1,550	140,200	850	44,250
October	1,500	134,500	500	27,000
November	600	62,500	350	20,700
December	400	44,000	400	22,000
Totals	14,000	$1,313,950	9,000	$443,345

Required:

1. Use the high-low method to estimate the variable and fixed production costs of both the racing model and the basic model skates.
2. All selling costs are fixed, and they total $200,000 for the racing model and $80,000 for the basic model. Prepare a contribution margin income statement for each model at sales of 10,000 racing and 10,000 basic skates.

Solution

1. Variable and Fixed Costs

The high-low method involves finding the variable and fixed costs at the high and low levels of production. In this case:

	Racing Model	Basic Model
High-production month	1,700 (Aug.)	1,300 (July)
Low-production month	400 (Dec.)	350 (Nov.)
Difference	1,300	950
Total production costs of high month	$154,500	$60,600
Total production costs of low month	44,000	20,700
Difference	$110,500	$39,900

Once the differences are known, the change in units (production) is divided into the change in costs to determine the variable cost rate.

$$\frac{\text{Change in costs}}{\text{Change in units}} = \text{Variable cost rate}$$

$$\text{Racing model: } \frac{\$110{,}500}{1{,}300} = \$85$$

$$\text{Basic model: } \frac{\$39{,}900}{950} = \$42$$

Because total variable costs equal unit variable cost times number of units produced, and total costs equal total variable costs plus total fixed costs, fixed costs can now be calculated.

$$\text{Total costs} - (\text{Variable cost per unit} \times \text{Number of units}) = \text{Total fixed costs}$$

	Racing Model	Basic Model
High production level (X) =	\$154,500 − \$85(1,700) X = \$154,500 − \$144,500 X = \$10,000	\$60,600 − \$42(1,300) X = \$60,600 − \$54,600 X = \$6,000
Low production level (X) =	\$44,000 − \$85(400) X = \$44,000 − \$34,000 X = \$10,000	\$20,700 − \$42(350) X = \$20,700 − \$14,700 X = \$6,000

Thus, we have the following:

	Racing Model	Basic Model
Variable cost rate	$ 85	$ 42
Total fixed costs	10,000	6,000

2. Contribution Margin Income Statements

Blade Corporation
Contribution Margin Income Statements
For the Year Ended December 31, 2003

	Racing Model	Basic Model
Sales revenue (at 10,000 units)	$1,300,000	$650,000
Less variable cost of goods sold*	(850,000)	(420,000)
Contribution margin	$ 450,000	$230,000
Less fixed cost of goods sold	(10,000)	(6,000)
Less fixed selling costs	(200,000)	(80,000)
Income	$ 240,000	$144,000

*$85 per unit for racing model; $42 per unit for basic model.

2. Assessing the Effects of Changes in Costs, Prices, and Volume on Profitability

K&D Company plans the following for the coming year:

Sales volume	100,000 units
Sales price	$2.50 per unit
Variable costs	$1.30 per unit
Fixed costs	$60,000

Required:

1. Determine K&D's target income.
2. Compute what the target income would be under each of the following independent assumptions:
   a. The sales volume increases 20%.
   b. The sales price decreases 20%.
   c. Variable costs increase 20%.
   d. Fixed costs decrease 20%.

Solution

1. Target Income

Basic C-V-P equation: Revenues − Variable costs − Fixed costs = Target income

(Units sold × Sales price) − (Units sold × Variable unit cost) − Fixed costs = Target income
(100,000 × $2.50) − (100,000 × $1.30) − $60,000 = X
$250,000 − $130,000 − $60,000 = X
$60,000 = X

This answer can be validated by dividing fixed costs by the per-unit contribution margin to find the break-even point and then multiplying the excess units to be sold above the break-even point by the per-unit contribution margin of $1.20 ($2.50 − $1.30).

$$\frac{\text{Fixed costs}}{\text{Per-unit contribution margin}} = \text{Break-even point}$$

$$\frac{\$60{,}000}{\$1.20} = 50{,}000 \text{ units}$$

Units sold	100,000
Less break-even point (units)	50,000
Excess	50,000
Per-unit contribution margin	× $1.20
Target income	$60,000

2a. The sales volume increases 20%

(100,000 × 1.2 × $2.50) − (100,000 × 1.2 × $1.30) − $60,000 = X
$300,000 − $156,000 − $60,000 = X
$84,000 = X

In this case, the contribution margin does not change. Therefore, the answer can be validated by multiplying the units to be sold in excess of the break-even point by the per-unit contribution margin of $1.20 to find the target income.

Units sold	120,000
Less break-even point (units)	50,000
Excess	70,000
Per-unit contribution margin	× $1.20
Target income	$84,000

2b. The sales price decreases 20%

(100,000 × $2.50 × 0.8) − (100,000 × $1.30) − $60,000 = X
$200,000 − $130,000 − $60,000 = X
$10,000 = X

In this case, the contribution margin changes. Therefore, the answer can be validated by dividing fixed costs by the new per-unit contribution margin of \$0.70 (\$2.00 − \$1.30) to find the new break-even point and then multiplying the units to be sold in excess of the break-even point by the new per-unit contribution margin.

$$\frac{\$60{,}000 \text{ (fixed costs)}}{\$0.70 \text{ (new per-unit contribution margin)}} = 85{,}715 \text{ units (new break-even point, rounded up)}$$

Units sold	100,000
Less break-even point (units)	85,715
Excess	14,285
Per-unit contribution margin	× \$0.70
Target income	\$10,000 (rounded)

2c. Variable costs increase 20%

$$(100{,}000 \times \$2.50) - (100{,}000 \times \$1.30 \times 1.2) - \$60{,}000 = X$$
$$\$250{,}000 - \$156{,}000 - \$60{,}000 = X$$
$$\$34{,}000 = X$$

In this case, the contribution margin changes. Therefore, the answer can be validated by dividing fixed costs by the new per-unit contribution margin of \$0.94 (\$2.50 − \$1.56) to find the new break-even point and then multiplying the units to be sold in excess of the break-even point by the new per-unit contribution margin.

$$\frac{\$60{,}000 \text{ (fixed costs)}}{\$0.94 \text{ (new per-unit contribution margin)}} = 63{,}830 \text{ units (new break-even point, rounded up)}$$

Units sold	100,000
Less break-even point (units)	63,830
Excess	36,170
Per-unit contribution margin	× \$0.94
Target income	\$34,000 (rounded)

2d. Fixed costs decrease 20%

$$(100{,}000 \times \$2.50) - (100{,}000 \times \$1.30) - (\$60{,}000 \times 0.8) = X$$
$$\$250{,}000 - \$130{,}000 - \$48{,}000 = X$$
$$\$72{,}000 = X$$

In this case, the contribution margin does not change, but fixed costs, and hence the break-even point, do. Therefore, the answer can be validated by dividing the per-unit contribution margin of \$1.20 into the new fixed costs to find the break-even point and then multiplying the units to be sold in excess of the break-even point by the per-unit contribution margin.

$$\frac{\$48{,}000 \text{ (new fixed costs)}}{\$1.20 \text{ (per-unit contribution margin)}} = 40{,}000 \text{ units (new break-even point)}$$

Units sold	100,000
Less break-even point (units)	40,000
Excess	60,000
Per-unit contribution margin	× \$1.20
Target income	\$72,000

discussion questions

1. Explain how understanding cost behavior patterns can assist management.
2. Discuss how level of activity is measured in manufacturing, merchandising, and service firms.
3. What is meant by the linearity assumption, and why is it made? Relate this assumption to the relevant-range concept.
4. What factors seem to have caused the shift from variable to fixed cost patterns?
5. How should stepped costs be treated in the planning process?
6. Why must all mixed costs be segregated into their fixed and variable components?
7. What is the major weakness of the scattergraph, or visual-fit, method of analyzing mixed costs?
8. What is the major limitation of the high-low method of analyzing mixed costs?
9. What is the basic C-V-P equation?
10. What is the contribution margin, and why is it important for managers to know the contribution margins of their products?
11. How much will profits increase for every unit sold over the break-even point?
12. What is the major advantage of using C-V-P graphs?
13. When other factors are constant, what is the effect on profits of an increase in fixed costs? Of a decrease in variable costs?
14. What are the limiting assumptions of C-V-P analysis?
15. How do the issues of quality and time relate to C-V-P analysis decisions?

expanded material

16. How does the method of least squares differ from the scattergraph method?
17. What effect is a change in the sales mix likely to have on a firm's overall contribution margin ratio?

discussion cases

CASE 2-1

COLORADO OUTDOORS FEDERATION

The Colorado Outdoors Federation sponsors an annual banquet. This year the guest speaker is a noted wildlife photographer and lecturer. In planning for the event, the group's treasurer has determined the following costs:

Rental of meeting facility	$250
Honorarium for speaker	800
Tickets and advertising	300
Cost of dinner (per person)	20
Door prizes	500

Last year, tickets were sold at $20 per person, and 350 people attended the banquet. This year the planning committee is hoping for an attendance of 450 at a price of $25 each.

1. a. At $25 per person, how many people must attend the banquet for the Federation to break even?
   b. How much profit (loss) will occur if 450 people attend?
2. Should the Federation increase its advertising costs by $200 and its door prizes by $300 if it can expect another 100 people to attend the banquet?

3. If the Federation maintains its original expected costs but reduces the price per ticket from $25 to $22, it can expect 500 people to attend the banquet. Should the Federation reduce the price of its tickets to $22 per person?

CASE 2-2

ENTERTAINMENT ENTERPRISES

Entertainment Enterprises, a firm that sells magazine subscriptions, is experiencing increased competition from a number of companies. The president, Betty Kincher, has asked you, the controller, to prepare an income statement that will highlight the fixed and variable costs; this will provide more useful information for planning and control purposes. Sales revenues are $25 per subscription. An analysis of company costs for the past six months reveals the following:

Administrative salaries	$10,000 per month
Advertising expense	$2,000 per month
Cost of goods sold	$12.50 per subscription
Rent expense	$5,000 per month
Sales commissions	15% of sales

In addition, the company makes most sales contacts through an extensive telephone network. Consequently, the telephone expense is significant and has both fixed and variable components. Relevant data concerning the telephone expense for the past six months follow:

Month	Unit Sales	Telephone Expense
July	4,000	$10,200
August	5,000	12,300
September	3,500	9,150
October	4,500	11,250
November	5,200	12,720
December	5,500	13,350

Prepare a management report for the president that:

1. Computes the fixed and variable portions of the telephone expense using the high-low method. (*Note:* A scattergraph may be used to visually check your answer.)
2. Presents a budgeted (pro-forma) contribution margin income statement for Entertainment Enterprises for the next six months (January through June), assuming that it expects to sell 30,000 subscriptions at a price of $25 each.
3. Explains how the information provided in (3) might help the president make better management decisions.

exercises

EXERCISE 2-1

VARIABLE AND FIXED COSTS OVER THE RELEVANT RANGE

Cook Corporation manufactures plastic garbage cans. In a typical year, the firm produces between 40,000 and 50,000 cans. At this level of production, fixed costs are $10,000 and variable costs are $2 per can.

1. Graph the cost of producing cans, with cost as the vertical axis and production output as the horizontal axis.

2. Indicate on the graph the relevant range of the $10,000 in fixed costs, and explain the significance of the relevant range.
3. What would total production costs be if 46,000 cans were produced?

EXERCISE 2-2

FIXED COSTS—THE RELEVANT RANGE

Flying A Company manufactures airplanes. The following schedule shows total fixed costs at various levels of airplane production:

Units Produced	Total Fixed Costs
0–200	$200,000
201–500	300,000
501–800	400,000

1. What is the fixed cost per unit when 50 airplanes are produced?
2. What is the fixed cost per unit when 250 airplanes are produced?
3. What is the fixed cost per unit when 800 airplanes are produced?
4. Plot total fixed costs on a graph similar to that shown in Exhibit 2-3.

EXERCISE 2-3

SCATTERGRAPH METHOD OF ANALYZING MIXED COSTS

Wyoming Company makes windmills. The company has the following total costs at the given levels of windmill production:

Units Produced	Total Costs
20	$16,000
30	20,000
40	24,000
50	28,000

1. Use the scattergraph method to estimate the fixed and variable elements of Wyoming's total costs.
2. Compute the total cost of making 44 windmills, assuming that total fixed costs are $8,000 and that the variable cost rate computed in (1) does not change.

EXERCISE 2-4

SCATTERGRAPH METHOD OF ANALYZING MIXED COSTS

Given the following mixed costs at various levels of production, complete the requirements.

Month	Units Produced	Mixed Costs
January	2	$13.75
February	3	16.50
March	1	11.00
April	5	22.00
May	2	13.75

1. Plot the data on a scattergraph, and visually fit a straight line through the points.
2. Based on your graph, estimate the monthly fixed cost and the variable cost per unit produced.
3. Compute the total cost of producing eight units in a month, assuming that the same relevant range applies.
4. **Interpretive Question:** Why is it so important to be able to determine the components of a mixed cost?

EXERCISE 2-5

HIGH-LOW METHOD OF ANALYZING MIXED COSTS

Sailmaster makes boats and has the following costs at the given levels of production:

Units Produced	Total Costs
200	$200,000
250	225,000
300	250,000
350	275,000
400	300,000
450	325,000

1. Use the high-low method to compute the variable and fixed elements of Sailmaster's total costs.
2. Compute the total cost of making 500 boats, assuming that total fixed costs and the variable cost rate do not change.

EXERCISE 2-6

HIGH-LOW METHOD OF ANALYZING MIXED COSTS

The *San Fernando Herald* has determined that the annual printing of 600,000 newspapers costs 9 cents per copy. If production were to be increased to 900,000 copies per year, the per-unit cost would drop to 7 cents per copy.

1. Determine the total fixed and variable costs of printing 600,000 newspapers.
2. What would be the total cost of producing 800,000 copies?

EXERCISE 2-7

CONTRIBUTION MARGIN CALCULATIONS

Jerry Stone owns and operates a small beach shop in a mall on Sanibel Island, Florida. For the last six months, Jerry has had a display of sunglasses in the front window. Largely because of the display, Jerry has sold 100 pairs of sunglasses per month at an average cost of $26 and selling price of $50. The sales volume has doubled since the display was put in the window. One-fourth of Jerry's storage space is occupied by 190 ice coolers. The coolers have not been selling as well as Jerry hoped, but he is convinced that a front window display of coolers would increase sales by 50%. The coolers cost Jerry a total of $2,280 and have been selling at a rate of 100 per month at $28 each.

1. Assuming that cost of goods sold is the only variable cost, compute the contribution margin per unit for sunglasses and ice coolers.
2. Compute the total contribution margins for both sunglasses and ice coolers assuming window displays and no window displays for both items.
3. What are the economic costs associated with keeping the sunglass display in the store window?
4. What are the economic costs associated with replacing the sunglass display with an ice cooler display?

EXERCISE 2-8

CONTRIBUTION MARGIN INCOME STATEMENT

The following data apply to Gordon Company for 2003:

Sales revenue (10 units at $25 each)	$250
Variable selling expenses	45
Variable administrative expenses	25
Fixed selling expenses	30
Fixed administrative expenses	15
Direct labor	50
Direct materials	60
Fixed manufacturing overhead	5
Variable manufacturing overhead	3

1. Prepare a contribution margin income statement. Assume there were no beginning or ending inventories in 2003.
2. How much would Gordon Company have lost if only five units had been sold during 2003?

EXERCISE 2-9

ANALYSIS OF A CONTRIBUTION MARGIN INCOME STATEMENT

Fill in the missing amounts for the following three cases:

	Case I	Case II	Case III
Sales revenue	$100,000	$120,000	$ (7) ?
Variable cost of goods sold:			
Direct materials	$ 25,000	$ (4) ?	$10,000
Direct labor	(1) ?	30,000	10,000
Variable selling and administrative costs	7,000	(5) ?	5,000
Contribution margin	$ (2) ?	$ 40,000	$ (8) ?
Gross margin	40,000	60,000	20,000
Fixed selling and administrative costs*	11,000	20,000	(9) ?
Rent expense on office building	(3) ?	10,000	1,000
Depreciation expense on delivery trucks	10,000	5,000	4,000
Profit	$ 8,000	$ (6) ?	$ -0-

*Except rent and depreciation.

EXERCISE 2-10

ANALYSIS OF THE CONTRIBUTION MARGIN

Dr. Hughes and Dr. Hawkins, owners of the Spanish Fork Care Clinic, have $150,000 of fixed costs per year. They receive 20,000 patient visits in a year, charging each patient an average of $20 per visit; variable costs average $2 per visit (needles, medicines, and so on).

1. What is the contribution margin per patient visit?
2. What is the total contribution margin per year?
3. What is the total pretax profit for a year?
4. Drs. Hughes and Hawkins can bring in another doctor at a salary of $100,000 per year. If this new doctor can handle 5,000 patient visits per year, should the new doctor be hired? (Assume no additional fixed costs will be incurred.)

EXERCISE 2-11

CONTRIBUTION MARGIN ANALYSIS

Compute the missing amounts for the following independent cases. (Assume zero beginning and ending inventories.)

	Case I	Case II	Case III
Sales volume (units)	12,000	(5) ?	8,000
Sales price per unit	$5	$4	(9) ?
Variable costs (total)	(1) ?	$50,000	$25,000
Contribution margin (total)	(2) ?	(6) ?	$15,000
Contribution margin per unit (rounded)	$2	$1.50	(10) ?
Fixed costs (total)	(3) ?	(7) ?	(11) ?
Fixed costs per unit (rounded)	(4) ?	$1.00	(12) ?
Profit	$10,000	(8) ?	$10,000

EXERCISE 2-12

BREAK-EVEN POINT AND TARGET INCOME

Detienne Company manufactures and sells one product for $20 per unit. The unit contribution margin is 40% of the sales price, and fixed costs total $80,000.

1. Using the equation approach, compute:
   a. The break-even point in sales dollars and units.
   b. The sales volume (in units) needed to generate a profit of $40,000.
   c. The break-even point (in units) if variable costs increase to 80% of the sales price and fixed costs increase to $100,000.
2. Using the contribution margin approach in units, recalculate 1(a), 1(b), and 1(c).

EXERCISE 2-13

BREAK-EVEN POINT AND TARGET INCOME

Household Products, Inc., estimates 2003 costs to be as follows:

Direct materials	$4 per unit
Direct labor	$6 per unit
Variable manufacturing overhead	$2 per unit
Variable selling and administrative expenses	$1 per unit
Fixed expenses	$50,000

1. Assuming that Household will sell 40,000 units, what sales price per unit will be needed to achieve a $60,000 profit?
2. Assuming that Household decides to sell its product for $16 per unit, determine the break-even sales volume in dollars and units.
3. Assuming that Household decides to sell its product for $16 per unit, determine the number of units it must sell to generate a $50,000 profit.

EXERCISE 2-14

BREAK-EVEN POINT—GRAPHIC ANALYSIS

Using the graph below, answer the following questions:

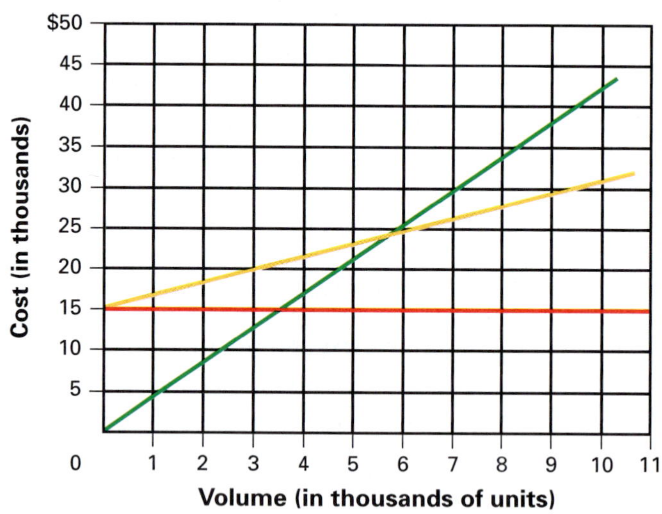

1. Copy the graph and identify (label) fixed costs, variable costs, total revenues, the total cost line, and the break-even point.
2. Determine the break-even point in both sales dollars and volume.
3. Suppose that as a manager you forecast sales volume at 7,000 units. At this level of sales, what would be your total fixed costs, approximate variable costs, and profit (or loss)?
4. At a sales volume of 3,000 units, what would be the level of fixed costs, variable costs, and approximate profit (or loss)?

EXERCISE 2-15

THE PROFIT GRAPH

Using the graph at the top of the next page, answer the following questions:

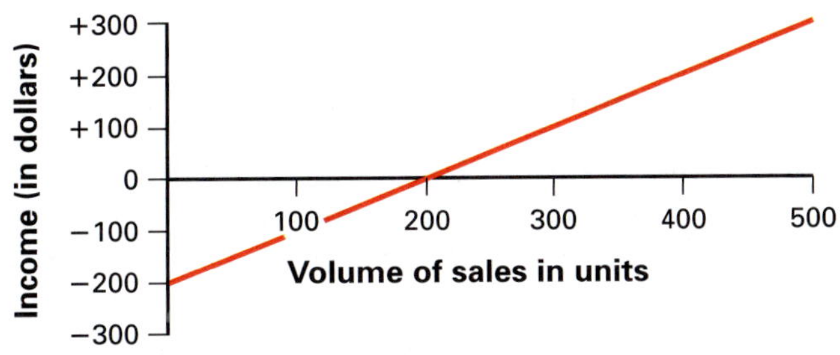

1. What is the break-even point in sales volume (in units)?
2. Approximately what volume of sales (in units) must this company have to generate an income of $300?
3. How much are the fixed costs?

EXERCISE 2-16

GRAPHING REVENUES AND COSTS

Montana Company manufactures chocolate candy. Its manufacturing costs are as follows:

Annual fixed costs	$15,000
Variable costs	$2 per box of candy

1. Plot variable costs, fixed costs, and total costs on a graph for activity levels of 0 to 30,000 boxes of candy.
2. Plot a revenue line on the graph, assuming that Montana sells the chocolates for $5 a box.

EXERCISE 2-17

C-V-P ANALYSIS

The Last Outpost is a tourist stop in a western resort community. Kerry Yost, the owner of the shop, sells hand-woven blankets for an average price of $30 per blanket. Kerry buys the blankets from Native Americans at an average cost of $21. In addition, he has selling expenses of $3 per blanket. Kerry rents the building for $300 per month and pays one employee a fixed salary of $500 per month.

1. Determine the number of blankets Kerry must sell to break even.
2. Determine the number of blankets Kerry must sell to generate a profit of $1,000 per month.
3. Assume that Kerry can produce and sell his own blankets at a total variable cost of $16 per blanket, but that he would need to hire one additional employee at a monthly salary of $600.
   a. Determine the number of blankets Kerry must sell to break even.
   b. Determine the number of blankets Kerry must sell to generate a profit of $1,000 per month.

EXERCISE 2-18

C-V-P ANALYSIS—CHANGES IN VARIABLES

Stop & Shop, Inc., estimates that next year's results will be:

Sales revenue (150,000 units)	$1,125,000
Less variable costs	(600,000)
Less fixed costs	(400,000)
Profit	$ 125,000

Recompute profit, assuming each of the following independent conditions:

1. A 10% increase in the contribution margin.
2. A 6% increase in the sales volume.
3. A 6% decrease in the sales volume.
4. A 6% increase in variable costs per unit.

5. A 7% decrease in fixed costs.
6. A 7% increase in fixed costs.
7. A 7% increase in the sales volume and a 5% increase in fixed costs.

EXERCISE 2-19

C-V-P ANALYSIS—CHANGES IN VARIABLES

Modern Fun Corporation sells electronic games. Its three salespersons are currently being paid fixed salaries of $30,000 each; however, the sales manager has suggested that it might be more profitable to pay the salespersons on a straight commission basis. He has suggested a commission of 15% of sales. Current data for Modern Fun Corporation are as follows:

Sales volume	15,000 units
Sales price	$40 per unit
Variable costs	$29 per unit
Fixed costs	$140,000

1. Assuming that Modern Fun Corporation has a target income of $50,000 for next year, which alternative is more attractive?
2. The sales manager believes that by switching to a commission basis, sales will increase 20%. If that is the case, which alternative is more attractive? (Assume that sales are expected to remain at 15,000 units under the fixed salary alternative.)

expanded material

EXERCISE 2-20

MIXED COSTS—LEAST SQUARES ANALYSIS

Given the following mixed costs at various levels of production, complete the requirements.

Month	Units Produced	Mixed Costs
January	2	$15
February	3	18
March	1	11
April	5	22
May	2	13

1. Using the least squares method (either the equation approach or a software package), calculate the monthly fixed and variable components of the mixed costs.
2. Using the estimates from (1), compute the total cost of producing four units in a month.
3. Describe a major advantage and a major disadvantage of the least squares method.

EXERCISE 2-21

SALES MIX

Klein Brothers sells products X and Y. Because of the nature of the products, Klein sells two units of product X for each unit of product Y. Relevant information about the products is as follows:

	X	Y
Sales price per unit	$20	$30
Variable cost per unit	16	24

1. Assuming that Klein's fixed costs total $140,000, compute Klein's break-even point in sales dollars and units of products X and Y.
2. Assuming that Klein sells two units of product Y for each unit of product X, and fixed costs remain at $140,000, compute Klein's break-even point in sales dollars and units of products X and Y.
3. Explain any differences in your answers to (1) and (2).

EXERCISE 2-22

C-V-P ANALYSIS

Mower Manufacturing's income statement for January 2003 is given below.

Sales (25,000 units × $25)	$625,000
Less variable costs	450,000
Contribution margin	$175,000
Less fixed costs	125,000
Profit	$ 50,000

1. Calculate the company's break-even point in sales dollars and units.
2. The company is contemplating the purchase of new production equipment that would reduce variable costs per unit to $16. However, fixed costs would increase to $175,000 per month. Assuming sales of 26,000 units next month, prepare an income statement for both the current and the proposed production methods. Calculate the break-even point (in dollars and units) for the new production method.

EXERCISE 2-23

OPERATING LEVERAGE

Relax Company and Recline Company both make rocking chairs. They have the same production capacity, but Relax is more automated than Recline. At an output of 1,000 chairs per year, the two companies have the following costs:

	Relax	Recline
Fixed costs	$40,000	$20,000
Variable costs at $10 per chair	10,000	
Variable costs at $30 per chair		30,000
Total cost	$50,000	$50,000
Unit cost (1,000 units)	$ 50	$ 50

Assuming that both companies sell chairs for $70 each and that there are no other costs or expenses for the two firms, complete the following:

1. Which company will lose the least money if production and sales fall to 500 chairs per year?
2. How much would each company lose at production and sales level of 500 chairs per year?
3. How much would each company make at production and sales levels of 2,000 chairs per year?

problems

PROBLEM 2-1

GRAPHING REVENUES AND COSTS

Cloward and Hawkins, CPAs, took in $350,000 of gross revenues this year. Besides themselves, they have two professional staff (one manager and one senior) and a full-time secretary. Fixed operating expenses for the office were $50,000 last year. This year the volume of activity is up 5%, and fixed operating expenses are still $50,000. Total variable operating costs, except for bonuses, average $5 per billable hour. The billable time for all professionals is as follows:

Partners:	3,000 hours at $75/hour
Manager:	1,800 hours at $40/hour
Senior:	2,120 hours at $25/hour

Salaries for the professional staff are \$40,000 and \$28,000, respectively; the secretary is paid \$18,000. The partners each draw salaries of \$60,000; plus they share a 5% bonus based on gross revenues. The manager is given a 2% bonus, also based on gross revenues.

Required:

1. Plot the data on a graph clearly showing (a) fixed costs, (b) variable costs, (c) total costs, and (d) total revenues.
2. How much profit did the CPA firm make this year (after partners' salaries)?

PROBLEM 2-2

HIGH-LOW AND SCATTERGRAPH METHODS OF ANALYSIS

Woodfield Company makes bed linens. During the first six months of 2003, Woodfield had the following production costs:

Month	Units Produced	Total Costs
January	10,000	\$ 68,000
February	20,000	100,000
March	15,000	90,000
April	8,000	52,000
May	17,000	94,000
June	12,000	74,000

Required:

1. Use the high-low method to compute the monthly fixed cost and the variable cost rate.
2. Plot the costs on a scattergraph.
3. **Interpretive Question:** Based on your scattergraph, do you think the fixed costs and the variable cost rate determined in (1) are accurate? Why?

PROBLEM 2-3

CONTRIBUTION MARGIN INCOME STATEMENT

Early in 2004, Delta Company (a retailing firm) sent the following income statement to its stockholders:

Delta Company
Income Statement
For the Year Ended December 31, 2003

Sales revenue (1,000 units)	\$60,000	
Less cost of goods sold (variable)	40,000	
Gross margin		\$20,000
Operating expenses:		
Selling	\$ 6,000	
Administrative	4,000	
Depreciation (fixed)	1,000	
Insurance (fixed)	50	
Utilities (\$20 fixed and \$30 variable)	50	11,100
Profit		\$ 8,900

Required:

1. Prepare a contribution margin income statement. (Assume that the fixed components of the selling and administrative expenses are \$3,000 and \$2,000, respectively.)
2. **Interpretive Question:** Why is a contribution margin income statement helpful to management?
3. **Interpretive Question:** How would the analysis in (1) be different if the depreciation expense was considered a stepped cost with wide steps compared to the relevant range?

PROBLEM 2-4

CONTRIBUTION MARGIN INCOME STATEMENT

Susan Young is an attorney for a small law firm in Arizona. She is also a part-time inventor and an avid golfer. One day Susan's golf foursome included a man named Henry Jones, a manufacturer of Christmas ornaments. Henry explained to Susan that he manufactures an ornament everyone loves, but stores will not carry the ornaments because they are very fragile and often break during shipping. Susan told Henry about a plastic box she had developed recently that would protect such fragile items during shipping. After crash testing the plastic box, Henry offered Susan a contract to purchase 100,000 of the boxes for $2.20 each. Susan is convinced that the box has many applications and that she can obtain future orders. Production of the plastic boxes will take one year. Estimated costs for the first year are as follows:

Lease payments on building	$800 per month
Lease payments on machine	$2,200 per month
Cost to retool machine	$10,000
Depreciation on machine	$9,600
Direct materials	$0.70 per box
Direct labor	$0.30 per box
Indirect materials and other manufacturing overhead	$10,000
Interest on loan	$2,500
Administrative salaries	$15,000

Required:

1. Using the information provided, determine Susan's contribution margin and projected profit at a sales level of 100,000 boxes.
2. If Susan's salary as an attorney is $44,500, determine how many boxes Susan must sell to earn profits equal to her salary.

PROBLEM 2-5

FUNCTIONAL AND CONTRIBUTION MARGIN INCOME STATEMENTS

Smooth Surface, Inc. (SSI) is a retail outlet for customized speedboats. The average cost of a boat to the company is $12,500. SSI includes a markup of 30% of cost in the sales price. In 2003, SSI sold 33 boats and finished the year with the same amount of inventory it had at the beginning of the year. Additional operating costs for the year were as follows:

Selling expenses:	
Advertising (fixed)	$ 500 per month
Commissions (mixed)	4,500 per month plus 2% of sales
Depreciation (fixed)	300 per month
Utilities (fixed)	150 per month
Freight on delivery (variable)	100 per boat
Administrative expenses:	
Salaries (fixed)	$4,000 per month
Depreciation (fixed)	300 per month
Utilities (fixed)	150 per month
Clerical (variable)	25 per sale

Required:

1. Prepare a traditional income statement using the functional approach.
2. Prepare an income statement using the contribution margin format.
3. **Interpretive Question:** Which statement is more useful for decision making? Why?

PROBLEM 2-6

CONTRIBUTION MARGIN AND FUNCTIONAL INCOME STATEMENTS

The following information is available for Dabney Company for 2003:

Sales revenue (at $20 per unit)	$151,200
Fixed manufacturing costs	24,000
Variable manufacturing costs (at $8 per unit)	60,480
Fixed selling expenses	70,000
Variable selling expenses (at $2 per unit)	15,120

Required:

1. Prepare a contribution margin income statement.
2. Prepare a functional income statement.
3. Calculate the number of units sold.
4. Calculate the contribution margin per unit.
5. Calculate markup as a percentage of manufacturing costs.
6. **Interpretive Question:** Why is a knowledge of the contribution margin more useful than a knowledge of the markup per unit when management has to make a decision about profitability?

PROBLEM 2-7

UNIFYING CONCEPTS: HIGH-LOW METHOD, CONTRIBUTION MARGINS, AND ANALYSIS

Press Publishing Corporation has two major magazines: *Star Life* and *Weekly News*. During 2003, *Star Life* sold 3 million copies at $1.00 each, and *Weekly News* sold 2.1 million copies at $1.10 each. Press Publishing accumulated the following cost information:

	Star Life		*Weekly News*	
Month	Copies Produced	Manufacturing Cost	Copies Produced	Manufacturing Cost
January	400,000	$170,000	300,000	$170,000
February	300,000	150,000	150,000	105,000
March	400,000	180,000	130,000	100,000
April	200,000	120,000	120,000	90,000
May	250,000	140,000	200,000	130,000
June	200,000	125,000	250,000	150,000
July	240,000	130,000	150,000	110,000
August	200,000	130,000	200,000	135,000
September	180,000	110,000	150,000	105,000
October	230,000	130,000	150,000	108,000
November	200,000	125,000	150,000	115,000
December	200,000	126,000	150,000	112,500

Required:

1. Use the high-low method to estimate the variable and fixed manufacturing costs of each magazine. (Round the variable cost rate to three decimal places.)
2. If all selling expenses are fixed and they total $500,000 for *Star Life* and $400,000 for *Weekly News*, prepare contribution margin income statements for the two magazines at sales of 3 million copies each.
3. Which magazine is more profitable at sales of 2 million copies?
4. **Interpretive Question:** If the same total dollar amount spent on either magazine will result in the same number of new subscriptions, which magazine should be advertised?

PROBLEM 2-8

CONTRIBUTION MARGIN ANALYSIS

Sunrise Company is a manufacturer of alarm clocks. The following information pertains to Sunrise's 2003 sales:

Sales price per unit	$ 15
Variable costs per unit	11
Total fixed costs	300,000

Required:

1. Determine Sunrise Company's unit contribution margin.
2. Using the contribution margin approach, compute:
   a. The break-even point in sales dollars and units.
   b. The sales volume (in dollars and units) needed to generate a target income of $50,000.
3. Using the equation approach of C-V-P analysis, compute:
   a. The break-even point in sales dollars and units.
   b. The sales volume (in dollars and units) needed to generate a 20 percent return on sales.

PROBLEM 2-9

CONTRIBUTION MARGIN ANALYSIS

Porter Company manufactures products X, Y, and Z. The following information relates to the three products:

	Product X	Product Y	Product Z
Sales volume (in units)	50,000	25,000	10,000
Sales revenue	$150,000	$125,000	$100,000
Variable costs	$100,000	$ 85,000	$ 70,000
Fixed costs	$ 30,000	$ 30,000	$ 30,000

Required:

1. At the current level of sales, which product provides the most profit?
2. With each additional unit of sales, which product provides the least contribution to profit?
3. If you could sell only 5,000 units, but all 5,000 must be either product X, Y, or Z, which would you sell?
4. If you could sell only 50,000 units, but all 50,000 must be either product X, Y, or Z, which would you sell?
5. **Interpretive Question:** If you had $5,000 for advertising and each dollar of advertising resulted in a one-unit increase in sales volume, which product would you advertise?

PROBLEM 2-10

BREAK-EVEN ANALYSIS

Trudy Sorensen paid $150 to rent a carnival booth for four days. She has to decide whether to sell donuts or popcorn. Donuts cost $1.20 per dozen and can be sold for $2.40 per dozen. Popcorn will require a $75 rental fee for the popcorn maker and $0.05 per bag of popcorn for the popcorn, butter, salt, and bags; a bag of popcorn could sell for $0.30.

Required:

1. Compute the break-even point in dozens of donuts if Trudy decides to sell donuts exclusively and the break-even point in bags of popcorn if she decides to sell popcorn exclusively.
2. Trudy estimates that she can sell either 50 donuts or 30 bags of popcorn every hour the carnival is open (10 hours a day for four days). Which product should she sell?
3. Trudy can sell back to the baker at half cost any donuts she fails to sell at the carnival. Unused popcorn must be thrown away. If Trudy sells only 80% of her original estimate, which product should she sell? (Assume that she bought or produced just enough to satisfy the demands she originally estimated.)

PROBLEM 2-11

C-V-P GRAPHIC ANALYSIS

Using the graph below, complete the requirements.

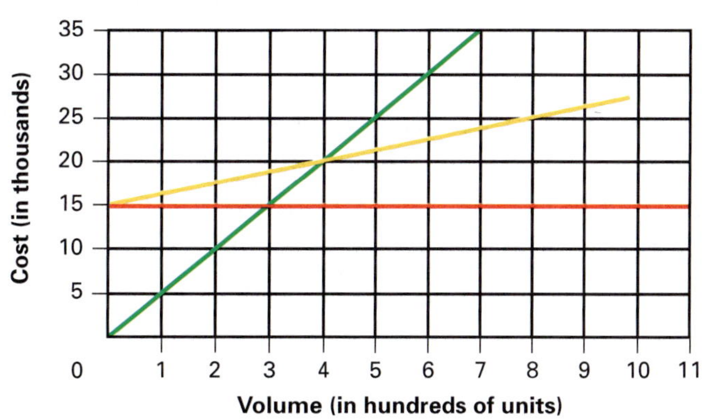

Required:

1. Determine the following:
   a. The break-even point in sales dollars and volume.
   b. The sales price per unit.

   c. Total fixed costs.
   d. Total variable costs at the break-even point.
   e. The variable cost per unit.
   f. The unit contribution margin.
2. What volume of sales must the company generate to reach a target income of $7,500?

PROBLEM 2-12

CONTRIBUTION MARGIN ANALYSIS—CHANGES IN VARIABLES

SMC, Inc., is a producer of hand-held electronic games. Its 2003 income statement was as follows:

SMC, Inc.
Contribution Margin Income Statement
For the Year Ended December 31, 2003

	Total	Per Unit
Sales revenue (150,000 games)	$5,250,000	$35
Less variable costs	3,750,000	25
Contribution margin	$1,500,000	$10
Less fixed costs	900,000	
Profit	$ 600,000	

In preparing its budget for 2004, SMC is evaluating the effects of changes in costs, prices, and volume on profit.

Required: Evaluate the following independent cases, and determine SMC's 2004 budgeted profit or loss in each case. (Assume that 2003 figures apply unless stated otherwise.)

1. Fixed costs increase $150,000.
2. Fixed costs decrease $100,000.
3. Variable costs increase $3 per unit.
4. Variable costs decrease $4 per unit.
5. Sales price increases $5 per unit.
6. Sales price decreases $5 per unit.
7. Sales volume increases 25,000 units.
8. Sales volume decreases 15,000 units.
9. Sales price decreases $4 per unit, sales volume increases 40,000 units, and variable costs decrease by $2.50 per unit.
10. Fixed costs decrease by $100,000, and variable costs increase $4 per unit.
11. Sales volume increases 30,000 units, with a decrease in sales price of $2 per unit. Variable costs drop $1.50 per unit, and fixed costs increase $50,000.

PROBLEM 2-13

INCOME STATEMENT AND BREAK-EVEN ANALYSIS

Zimmerman Company records the following costs associated with the production and sale of a steel slingshot:

Selling expenses:	
Fixed	$6,500
Variable	$0.50 per unit sold
Administrative expenses:	
Fixed	$4,500
Variable	$0.25 per unit sold
Manufacturing costs:	
Fixed	$15,500
Variable	$7.50 per unit produced

Required: Assume that in 2003 the beginning and ending inventories were the same. Also assume that 2003 sales were 11,000 units at $11.50 per slingshot.

1. Prepare a contribution margin income statement.
2. Determine the break-even point in sales dollars.
3. **Interpretive Question:** Zimmerman believes that sales volume could be improved 20% if an additional commission of $0.50 per unit were paid to the salespeople. Zimmerman also believes, however, that the same percentage increase could be achieved through an additional $3,000 investment in advertising. Which action, if either, should Zimmerman take? Why?

PROBLEM 2-14

C-V-P ANALYSIS—CHANGES IN VARIABLES

Rougely Manufacturing Company produces electric carving knives. The firm has not been as profitable as expected in the past three years. As a result, it has excess capacity that could be used to produce an additional 10,000 knives per year. However, any production above that amount would require a capital investment of $50,000. Operating results for the previous year are shown here. Assume that there is never any ending inventory.

Sales revenue (125,000 knives × $8)		$1,000,000
Variable costs (125,000 knives × $5)	$625,000	
Fixed costs	350,000	975,000
Profit		$ 25,000

Required: Respond to the following independent proposals, and support your recommendations:

1. The production manager believes that profits could be increased through the purchase of more automated production machinery, which would increase fixed costs by $100,000 and reduce the variable costs by $0.75 per knife. Is she correct if sales are to remain at 125,000 knives annually?
2. The sales manager believes that a 5% discount on the sales price would increase the sales volume to 135,000 units annually. If he is correct, would this action increase or decrease profits?
3. Would the implementation of both proposals be worthwhile?
4. The sales manager believes that an increase in sales commissions could improve the sales volume. In particular, he suggests that an increase of $0.50 per knife would increase the sales volume 30%. If he is correct, would this action increase profits?
5. The accountant suggests another alternative: Reduce administrative salaries by $10,000 so that prices can be reduced by $0.10 per unit. She believes that this action would increase the volume to 130,000 units annually. If she is correct, would this action increase profits?
6. The corporate executives finally decide to spend an additional $30,000 on advertising to bring the sales volume up to 135,000 units. If the increased advertising can bring in these extra sales, is this a good decision?

PROBLEM 2-15

C-V-P ANALYSIS—RETURN ON SALES

The federal government recently placed a ceiling on the selling price of sheet metal produced by MOB Company. In 2003, MOB was limited to charging a price that would earn a 20% return on gross sales. On the basis of this restriction, MOB had the following results for 2003:

Sales revenue (1,150,000 feet at $2.00 per foot)		$2,300,000
Variable costs (1,150,000 feet × $1.40)	$1,610,000	
Fixed costs	230,000	1,840,000
Profit		$ 460,000

In 2004, MOB predicted that the sales volume would decrease to 900,000 feet of sheet metal. With this level of sales, however, the company anticipated no changes in the levels of fixed and variable costs.

Required:

1. Determine MOB's profit for 2004 if all forecasts are realized. Compute both the dollar amount of profit and the percentage return on sales.

2. MOB plans to petition the government for a price increase so that the 2003 rate of return on sales (20%) can be maintained. What sales price should the company request, based on 2004 projections? (Round to the nearest cent.)
3. How much profit (in dollars) will MOB earn in 2004 if this sales price, as determined in (2), is approved?
4. **Interpretive Question:** What other factors must be considered by MOB and the government?

PROBLEM 2-16

UNIFYING CONCEPTS: C-V-P ANALYSIS AND CHANGES IN VARIABLES

The 2003 pro-forma income statement for Cedar Company is as follows (ignore taxes):

Cedar Company
Pro-Forma Income Statement
For the Year Ended December 31, 2003

Sales (60,000 units)		$660,000
Cost of goods sold:		
Direct materials	$40,000	
Direct labor	75,000	
Variable manufacturing overhead	18,000	
Fixed manufacturing overhead	11,000	
Total cost of goods sold		144,000
Gross margin		$516,000
Selling expenses:		
Variable	$45,000	
Fixed	98,000	
Administrative expenses:		
Variable	17,000	
Fixed	77,000	
Total selling and administrative expenses		237,000
Profit		$279,000

Required:

1. Compute how many units must be sold to break even.
2. Compute the increase (decrease) in profit under the following independent situations:
   a. Sales increase 30%.
   b. Fixed selling and administrative expenses decrease 10%.
   c. Contribution margin decreases 20%.
3. Compute sales in units and dollars at the break-even point if fixed costs increase from $186,000 to $260,400.
4. Compute the number of units that must be sold if expected profit is $1 million.

expanded material

PROBLEM 2-17

Spread-Sheet Software

UNIFYING CONCEPTS: HIGH-LOW, SCATTERGRAPH, AND LEAST SQUARES METHODS

You have been hired as a consultant for MediaPro Inc. The company manufactures high-density floppy disks and sells them to a wide variety of business clients. Management is eager to learn more about the company's cost behavior. You have been provided the following data. Assume all production falls within the relevant range.

Month	Machine Hours	Utility Costs
January	145	$5,350
February	140	5,200
March	160	5,800
April	170	6,050
May	175	6,200
June	145	5,375
July	150	5,400
August	150	5,450
September	155	5,600
October	170	6,100
November	145	5,300
December	155	5,500

Required:

1. Using the high-low method, compute the variable and fixed elements of MediaPro's utility costs.
2. Plot the information on a scattergraph. Based on your graph, determine the unit variable cost and monthly fixed costs.
3. Using the least squares method (either the equation approach or a software package), calculate the variable and fixed cost components. Determine the cost formula.
4. **Interpretive Question:** Why are the variable cost per unit and fixed costs different for each of these methods of analysis? Which method is the most accurate for determining variable and fixed cost components?

PROBLEM 2-18 SALES MIX

Mike's Ice Cream Company produces and sells ice cream in three sizes: quart, half-gallon, and gallon. Relevant information for each of the sizes is as follows:

	Quart	Half-Gallon	Gallon
Average sales price	$1.00	$1.85	$3.60
Less variable cost	0.80	1.40	2.40
Unit contribution margin	$0.20	$0.45	$1.20
Sales mix (% of sales)	15%	60%	25%

Mike anticipates sales of $500,000 and fixed costs of $120,000 in 2003.

Required:

1. Determine the break-even sales volume in units and dollars for 2003.
2. Determine Mike's 2003 projected profit.
3. Assume that Mike's sales mix changes to 10% quarts, 40% half-gallons, and 50% gallons. Determine Mike's break-even sales volume in units and dollars.

PROBLEM 2-19 UNIFYING CONCEPTS: BREAK-EVEN POINT AND OPERATING LEVERAGE

The following summary data are provided for Basalt Mercantile Corporation and Sunshine Service, Inc. (000's omitted):

	Basalt Mercantile Corp.		Sunshine Service, Inc.
Sales revenue (100,000 units)	$520	(200,000 units)	$1,050
Less variable costs	260		315
Contribution margin	$260		$ 735
Less fixed costs	100		300
Income	$160		$ 435

Required:

1. Determine the break-even point for Basalt and Sunshine in both sales dollars and units.
2. **Interpretive Question:** Which company has a higher operating leverage? Why?
3. **Interpretive Question:** Based on your analysis of the cost structures of Basalt and Sunshine, which company's cost structure is better? What factors are important to consider in answering such a question?

competency enhancement opportunities

- Analyzing Real Company Information
- International Case
- Ethics Case
- Writing Assignment
- The Debate
- Internet Search

The following additional assignments provide opportunities for students to develop critical thinking, ethical perspectives, oral and written communication skills, experience with electronic research, and teamwork through group and business activities.

ANALYZING REAL COMPANY INFORMATION

• ***Analyzing 2-1 (Microsoft)***

Annual revenues, as well as sales and marketing expenses, for the 1988-1999 years are provided below for **MICROSOFT CORPORATION**:

Microsoft Corporation (millions)

Year	Sales and Marketing Expenses	Annual Revenue
1988	$ 152	$ 591
1989	205	805
1990	300	1,186
1991	490	1,847
1992	758	2,777
1993	1,086	3,786
1994	1,135	4,714
1995	1,564	6,075
1996	2,185	9,050
1997	2,411	11,936
1998	2,887	15,262
1999	3,238	19,747

1. Operating output data, such as the number of computer products sold each year, are not provided in Microsoft's annual report. However, while it is a little odd to use revenues to predict marketing expense (instead of the other

way around), it seems sensible that changes in revenues should serve as an approximate measure of changes in the number of products sold by Microsoft. Use the high-low method to analyze the data above to determine if there is a relationship between revenues and sales and marketing expenses. (*Hint:* Don't round off the value you calculate for variable costs per revenue dollar.) What appears to be the amount of fixed costs in these expenses? Does this fixed cost amount make sense? (*Note:* Remember that the data are in millions of dollars!)

expanded material

2. Using your calculator (or some computer software program such as Microsoft Excel®), compute a regression analysis on the data above. What do you learn from the analysis? The Management's Discussion in Microsoft's 1999 Annual Report states: "The increase in the absolute dollar amount of sales and marketing expenses in the three-year period was due primarily to expanded product-specific marketing programs, such as Office 97 in 1997, Windows 98 in 1998, and Office 2000 in 1999. Sales and marketing costs as a percentage of revenue decreased primarily due to moderate headcount growth. Microsoft brand advertising expenses rose slightly in 1998, but declined in 1999." Does this statement provide any help in understanding the analysis?

• *Analyzing 2-2 (Star Video)*

It is likely that a number of grocery stores in your town have video rental departments. Generally, however, grocery stores do not focus much management attention on their small video rental businesses. The main purpose of having a video department is to encourage more customers to come into the store and purchase groceries! Nevertheless, a grocery store cannot simply buy a large selection of videotapes, corner off a section of floor space, and start renting tapes. Successfully managing a rental business requires being aware of an unimaginably large number of video titles. Obviously, new movies are constantly being released, while old movies gradually lose their appeal and are eventually scrapped. Further, large-scale video rental chains such as **BLOCKBUSTER** constantly track shifting consumer tastes for certain titles and movie categories. These consumer preferences differ based on demographic data like geographic location, average age, ethnicity, average income, etc. A grocery store really can't manage all these data without losing focus on its main business. Hence, most grocery stores contract out their video rental business to a large-scale video management company. These management companies can purchase huge quantities of tapes, maintain large distribution warehouses, and track demographic data that allow them to manage and move specific inventories to the appropriate grocery store locations. In 1992, one such video management company, Star Video (not its real name), was managing 86 stores representing three supermarket chains in five states—Arizona, California, Montana, Washington, and Wyoming. Total revenue in 1992 for Star Video was $3.6 million. Star Video made all the inventory investments and handled all management activities involved in providing video rentals at each of the 86 stores. Video rental revenue was then split between Star Video and each grocery store, with Star Video keeping the lion's share. Stores liked this arrangement because they made most of their money on grocery sales to customers who came to rent videotapes. Star Video needed to carefully manage revenue and costs at each store in order to stay profitable. Following are the data for six stores located in Washington:

Store Name	Monthly Revenue	Monthly Operating Expenses
Moses Lake	$ 6,408	$ 3,295
W. Kennewick	4,064	2,289
Pasco	4,038	2,270
S. Kennewick	3,692	2,142
E. Wenatchee	1,395	1,316
Richland	2,104	1,516
Total	$21,701	$12,828

Use the high-low method to analyze the operating expenses at these six stores. Determine if operating expenses are related to store revenue. What appear to be the fixed costs of operating each store? Create a graph and plot these costs using revenue on the horizontal axis and operating expenses on the vertical axis. Does the scattergraph agree or disagree with the results of your high-low analysis?

INTERNATIONAL CASE

• ***The Paper Company***

The **GHANATA GROUP OF COMPANIES** (GGC) is a locally owned and controlled company in Ghana, West Africa. One of its principal operating divisions, **THE PAPER COMPANY**, is one of Africa's most modern and largest manufacturers/distributors of paper products. For both operating and reporting purposes, The Paper Company is organized into product lines: scholastic, envelope, and stationery. During the 1980s, the economy in Ghana was stagnant. The country faced severe economic problems as a result of unfavorable trade terms with other countries. The official exchange rate of U.S. $1.00 to the local currency, the *cedi*, was about 39.00 as of the end of 1984. (The unofficial rate, e.g., the black market rate, was at least five times worse!) As a result of the economy, it became very difficult for GGC to secure direct materials for its divisions. If a division could secure direct materials, it could sell almost everything it produced. Hence, in terms of being able to predict sales volumes, there was a great deal of risk for GGC divisions. The 1985 budgeted operating data for the three departments in The Paper Company were as follows:

The Paper Company
1985 Budgeted Operations Data
(*Cedi* 000's)

	Scholastic	Envelope	Stationery
Budgeted sales	$1,785,000	$984,000	$3,334,050
Budgeted variable costs	(410,550)	(442,800)	(2,200,473)
Contribution margin	$1,374,450	$541,200	$1,133,577
Budgeted fixed costs	(1,267,350)	(482,160)	(933,534)
Income	$ 107,100	$ 59,040	$ 200,043

Using these operating data, create C-V-P graphs for each department. (Note: Since you don't have per-unit prices and costs, you may assume that the product sales price for each department is $1 per unit, and then plot your graphs at 0, 2 million, and 4 million units.) Given the high-risk business environment in Ghana at this time, which department presents the highest risk to GGC? The lowest risk? Be sure to explain your answer in terms of operating leverage. You may also want to consider each department's break-even point compared to budgeted (expected) operations.

Source: A. Oppong, "The Paper Company," *The Journal of Accounting Case Research,* Vol. 3, No. 2 (1996), pp. 80–88. Permission to use has been granted by Captus Press, Inc. and the Accounting Education Resource Centre of The University of Lethbridge. [Journal Subscription: Captus Press, Inc., York University Campus, 4700 Keele Street, North York, Ontario, M3J 1P3, by calling (416) 736-5537, or by fax at (416) 736-5793, E-mail: info@captus.com, Internet: http://www.captus.com]

ETHICS CASE

• *Pickmore International*

Joan Hildabrand is analyzing some cost data for her boss, Ross Cumings. The data relate to a special sales order that Pickmore International is considering from a large customer in Singapore. The following data are applicable to the product being ordered:

Normal unit sales price	$49.95
Variable unit manufacturing costs	10.50
Variable unit selling and administrative expenses	18.25

The customer is requesting that the sales order be accepted on the following terms:

a. The unit sales price would equal the unit contribution margin plus 10%.
b. Freight would be paid by the customer.
c. Pickmore International would pay a $5,000 "facilitating payment" to a "friend of the customer" to get the product through customs more quickly.

In considering the order, Ross has indicated to Joan that this is a very important customer. Furthermore, this work would help some employees earn a little extra Christmas money with overtime.

1. What are the accounting and ethical issues involved in this case?
2. Should Joan recommend acceptance of the sales terms proposed for this special order?

WRITING ASSIGNMENT

• *Issues of Quality and Time on C-V-P Analysis Decisions*

This chapter described how to analyze whether the difference between sales price and variable costs, as well as the volume of sales, is sufficient to pay for all fixed costs in an organization and provide a sufficient profit. A number of methods have been presented for analyzing these costs, volume, and price relationships. These methods all focus on *quantitative* issues that affect how a company manages its resources to maximize overall profits. However, there are a number of *qualitative* issues involving quality and time that should also affect decisions about what sales prices to set, how to manage fixed and variable costs, and which products should be emphasized within the organization. One way to trade off fixed costs for variable costs is to consider making large fixed cost investments in technology that result in automated production, merchandising, and service processes. These kinds of investments allow some variable costs, such as direct labor, to be reduced. Managing this cost trade-off often has strong implications on the quality of the product or service, as well as the timeliness with which it can be delivered. Both of these qualitative issues eventually affect the quantitative issues of costs, volume, and price. Go to your library and find an article describing one organization's effort to invest in automation or other technologies in order to reduce costs. Determine what quality and time issues are affected by the investment. Write a one- to two-page memo describing what you found.

THE DEBATE

• *Which Cost Analysis Method is Better?*

Many costs within an organization are mixed costs, combining elements of both fixed and variable costs. Separating these types of costs into their fixed and variable cost components is necessary before C-V-P analysis work can be done. Two potential cost analysis methods are the scattergraph (visual-fit) approach and the high-low approach. Each of these methods has both disadvantages and advantages compared to the other.

Divide your group into two teams and prepare a two-minute oral argument supporting your assigned position.

- One team represents "The scattergraph (visual-fit) method is superior!" Explain why this method should be used for determining the variable and fixed cost components in a mixed cost.
- The other team represents "High-low; the way to go!" Explain why this method should be used for determining the variable and fixed cost components in a mixed cost.

INTERNET SEARCH

• *Centre for Applied Ethics*

We have discussed ethical issues for accountants in this text and have included an ethics case at the end of each chapter. Obviously, ethical issues are of concern to accountants and all other business professionals. There are a number of good resources on the Internet for those interested in better exploring ethical issues in business (hopefully, we're all interested in this topic!). One of the better sites is the Centre for Applied Ethics at the University of British Columbia (**http://www.ethics.ubc.ca/resources/**). Sometimes Web addresses change, so if this address doesn't work, access the Web site for this textbook (**http://albrecht.swcollege.com**) for an updated link to the Centre for Applied Ethics.

Go to this site and explore the materials regarding applied ethics resources on the World Wide Web. Find an article that discusses either business or professional ethics. Write a short paragraph that describes exactly where you found the article and give a brief summary.

Product Cost Flows and Business Organizations

chapter

m3

learning objectives After studying this chapter, you should be able to:

1. Understand the difficulty, yet importance, of having accurate product cost information.
2. Explain the flow of goods and services in a manufacturing organization and follow the accumulation of product costs in its accounting system.
3. Understand the process of accounting for overhead.
4. Explain the flow of goods and services in a merchandising organization and follow the accumulation of product costs in its accounting system.
5. Explain the flow of goods and services in a service organization and follow the accumulation of product costs in its accounting system.
6. Understand the impact of e-business on product costing.

expanded material

7. Use the FIFO method to do process costing.

Before 1810, American business was basically made up of a loose bunch of independent contractors, each focused on doing one thing well.[1] As you can imagine, the wheels of commerce turned rather slowly. These small businesses were fairly easy to manage. They had few employees and simple processes. Cost accounting, if it existed at all, was not a difficult procedure. If the wainwright wanted to know how much it cost to build a wagon for a customer, he simply added up the costs of buying lumber products from the sawmill, leather products from the tanner, and iron products from the blacksmith. He then set the price of the wagon high enough to compensate him for his assembly labor.

When the Industrial Revolution came to America sometime after 1812, big business started appearing on the East Coast, beginning with the mechanized, integrated cotton textile factories of New England. In 1814, at a cotton mill established by the American industrialist Francis Cabot Lowell in Waltham, Massachusetts, all the steps of an industrial process were combined under one roof for the first time. Instead of contracting with a dozen different little family-owned businesses to card, spin, and sew raw material into cloth, Lowell brought raw cotton fiber into a heavily equipped factory staffed with workers who were organized by specialty and created a finished product ready for sale! This was "big business," and it really complicated the accounting process. (Actually, it is more likely that the development of management accounting did a great deal to facilitate the growth of these large-scale firms.) In order to run this textile mill, Lowell and his managers required a reporting system that would provide the information needed to plan, control, and evaluate work they were not actually doing themselves. History shows that these early textile mills developed a remarkably good accounting system that tracked inventory, payroll, and production work.

Shortly after the textile manufacturing industry was launched, the advent of railroads as a service industry probably presented some of the most complex administrative problems of the nineteenth century. By 1869, the **UNION PACIFIC RAILROAD** from the East and the **CENTRAL PACIFIC RAILROAD** from the West were joined at Promontory Point, Utah. Railroad companies soon grew to sizes that dwarfed the scale of the largest textile factories, and names like J. P. Morgan and Edward Henry Harriman became famous (or infamous, depending on your perspective). Managing these huge administrative entities required special record-keeping systems that recorded enormous numbers of daily transactions and summarized essential information for frequent internal reports to management. The challenge for railroads was that employees and processes were literally spread all over the map! Senior managers needed some means of assessing the performance of submanagers at terminals and yards across the country. Management accounting expanded as "costs per ton-mile" (the average cost to move a ton of material one mile) and "operating ratio" (a ratio of operating expenses to revenues that railroads studied constantly) began providing competitive information to indicate how the performance of various submanagers would affect the company's total financial performance. These performance measures were used to delegate responsibilities and to control and evaluate the business from a distance. As management accounting matured and added competitive value, companies were able to spread out geographically.

setting the stage

The last quarter of the nineteenth century brought an incredible outpouring of inexpensive, mass-produced goods and services for consumers, leading to the emergence of the mass merchandising industry composed of wholesalers and retailers. Besides making many diverse items available for purchase from one source, these wholesalers and retailers provided other critical services, including distribution, delivery, and credit service on account. Companies such as **R. H. MACY & COMPANY, INC.**, in New York City and **SEARS, ROEBUCK & COMPANY** in Chicago were achieving tremendous financial success by focusing on a very important idea: move the inventory! The success of the mass merchant hinged on **inventory turnover**, called "**stockturns**." By selling goods faster than smaller local merchants, large-scale wholesalers and retailers could charge lower prices and still realize tremendous profit. Up to this point, big business in

inventory turnover (stockturns) The number of times the inventory in an organization "turns over" during a period of time. It is often easier to think of inventory turnover as the number of times a dollar invested in inventory is sold during a period of time. Inventory turnover is computed as cost of goods sold divided by average inventory value.

1 Historical sources: A. D. Chandler, *The Invisible Hand* (Boston: HBS Press, 1977); H. T. Johnson and R. S. Kaplan, *Relevance Lost* (Boston: HBS Press, 1987).

America had focused almost exclusively on costs. But wholesalers and retailers introduced a new concept to management accounting. By controlling and evaluating the use of assets (in this case, inventory), merchandisers helped management accounting grow to include the process management technique of asset (or capital) management.

manufacturing organizations Organizations that focus on using labor and/or machinery to convert raw materials into marketable products.

merchandising organizations Organizations that focus on procuring tangible products, then distributing them to customers. These customers may include individuals or other business organizations such as manufacturing organizations.

service organizations Organizations that focus on delivery of marketable services, such as legal advice or education, to individuals or other organizations.

*As described in the opening scenario, management accounting has developed as a mature discipline to support the needs of business organizations. You understand at this point that management accounting is essentially the result of the efforts of many individuals and organizations to create information that has a competitive value in the marketplace. To really understand management accounting, you need to grasp how **manufacturing, merchandising** and **service organizations** do business. Management accounting historically began with a focus on planning, controlling, and evaluating costs. Cost accounting continues to be a central facet of management accounting. In fact, understanding cost flows is a useful way to understand how a business is structured or organized. And while accurately determining the costs of products and services is difficult, it is one of the most important aspects of management accounting and provides one of the most useful pieces of information for business decision makers. Without accurate cost information, it is difficult to set appropriate prices, evaluate performance, reward employees, or make production decisions. It is even difficult to know whether a company should be competing in a specific market.*

In this chapter, you will learn how goods and services flow in manufacturing, merchandising, and service companies and how product costs incurred in these organizations are tracked and accumulated. In subsequent chapters you will learn how to use product costs to manage and control manufacturing, merchandising, and service companies.

1

Understand the difficulty, yet importance, of having accurate product cost information.

WHY HAVING ACCURATE PRODUCT COSTS IS SO DIFFICULT, YET IMPORTANT

As discussed in Chapter 1 of management accounting, management is constantly making planning, controlling, and evaluating decisions. Managers need accurate product cost information to plan for the future, to control current operations, and to evaluate past performance. They also need accurate product cost information so that they can deliver high-quality products to customers at the lowest price and at the fastest speed.

Bad Product Cost Information Can "Hurt!"

net work

Access **HONDA**'s Web site at http://www.honda.com. The base price for this year's Accord LX V-6 is $22,400. How much does the price increase if keyless entry, a security system, and a CD player are added? How do these features affect Honda's manufacturing costs?

For most companies, accurately determining their product costs is a difficult challenge. Regardless of the difficulty, however, having accurate product cost information is critical for a business. Without knowledge of accurate product costs, managers could easily over- or underprice products and make other poor decisions. What if, for example, **HONDA** sells its 2002 Accord LX for $23,945 (its intended sales price), but the actual cost of producing the car is $26,000? How long could Honda stay in business losing $2,055 ($26,000 − $23,945) per car? In this case, buyers will probably rush to buy Accords because they will likely be priced much lower than other comparable cars (assuming Honda's competitors have more accurate cost information and have priced their cars to cover their total manufacturing costs). Not only will Honda lose money on every car it sells, but the more cars Honda sells, the greater its losses will be. What if Honda attempts to sell its Accord LX for $23,945, not realizing that its cost of making the car is actually only $18,000? If the accurate cost is only $18,000, other manufacturers, such as **FORD**, may sell their cars for much less than Honda (assuming Ford has a better cost accounting system); sales of Accords will dwindle. If Honda really believes its costs are higher than $18,000, say, $22,500, it will not lower prices to the point where the company can compete with Ford and other manufacturers. The competitors that better understand their own costs will probably reduce prices, leaving Honda behind in the market. With lower (maybe even zero) sales, Honda may again lose money because it can't sell enough cars to cover its operating expenses. As you can see, having accurate product cost information helps managers in many ways, including making planning, controlling, and evaluating decisions such as the following:

1. As part of the *planning* process, a company can determine whether it can or should compete in certain markets. It is possible that prices of competitors in some markets are already lower than the manufacturing costs would be for a new company trying to compete.
2. When *controlling* operations, a company can analyze the relationship between production levels and costs and determine whether to increase or decrease production levels of certain products. These control data will help the company in planning future operations because it can determine if the increased cost of additional production would be less than the revenue that would be derived from sales of those products.
3. In the *evaluation* process, a company can compare actual costs against budgeted costs (a management accounting process know as variance analysis that we'll discuss in Chapter 9 of management accounting) and identify both progress and problems for subsequent management action.

Having accurate product cost information also allows a company to identify and eliminate costly, complicated processes so that higher-quality, lower-priced products and services can be delivered to customers in increasingly shorter **cycle times**. Accurate cost information allows management to determine the appropriate level at which to operate, to assess the long-term profitability of various products, and to manage the costs of production activities.

cycle time The total time a product spends moving through a particular process or cycle within the organization, such as the product design cycle, the production cycle, or the order and delivery cycle.

Overhead: The Problem in Determining Accurate Product Costs

In Chapter 1 of management accounting, you learned that costs of manufacturing products can be broken down into three elements: (1) direct materials, (2) direct labor, and (3) manufacturing overhead. Direct materials include the cost of raw materials that are used directly in the manufacture of products. Direct materials are kept in the raw materials warehouse until used and include such things as rubber used in making tires, steel used to make cars, wood used to make tables, and plastic used to make eyeglasses. Direct labor includes the wages and other payroll-related expenses of factory employees who work directly on products. Direct labor includes the cost of wages and benefits for assembly-line workers, but it does not include the wages and benefits of the factory custodians or the factory controller because, even though they work in the factory, they don't work directly on making products. Manufacturing overhead includes all manufacturing costs that are not classified as direct materials or direct labor. This includes miscellaneous materials used in production, such as glue or nails; wages for the factory supervisor, controller, and custodians who work in the factory, but not directly on products; and other manufacturing costs such as utilities, depreciation of manufacturing facilities, insurance, and property taxes.

caution

Product costs are only one element management must consider when establishing prices for its products. Pricing is a complex issue, and management usually looks to its own strategy and to the market to set prices (also considering competitors' prices, market's ability to pay, and so forth). Assuming that management uses only its product cost information to set prices is a wrong assumption.

While it is easy to assign direct materials and direct labor costs to specific products, it is extremely difficult to assign manufacturing costs, such as rent or the custodian's salary, to specific manufactured products. One of the major reasons for this difficulty is that many of these overhead costs are "lumpy" in nature and do not match the production of goods. To be more specific, production output in a manufacturing plant tends to occur in an even flow throughout the year. Similarly, the costs of raw materials and direct labor used also follow a generally even pattern throughout the year. On the other hand, most manufacturing overhead costs are not related to the flow of production. For example, think about the nature of maintenance and repair costs on your car (if you have one). If you're a careful car owner, then you get an oil change for your car every 3,000 to 4,000 miles. Occasionally, you need to rotate or replace the tires. Sometimes an alternator or battery (or worse!) goes out and needs replacement. The car gets used every day, and each day's use eventually leads to costs for oil changes, tires, and alternators. Paying for these costs on an occasional basis makes it difficult to budget for and to apply these costs to daily use. As a result, most of us don't have a good idea of what it costs per mile to drive our car. Companies face the same problem. They have insurance and tax bills that

business environment essay

The Commercialization of the Internet Who invented the Internet? The Internet began at the U.S. Department of Defense in the late 1950s at the direction of President Dwight D. Eisenhower. At the time of the Cold War and the Soviet Union's successful launch of *Sputnik*, the Eisenhower administration felt the need for a network of computers between major U.S. cities so that the Department of Defense could easily connect with them. Soon major universities began to tap into the network. The timeline below shows the network's origins and growth.

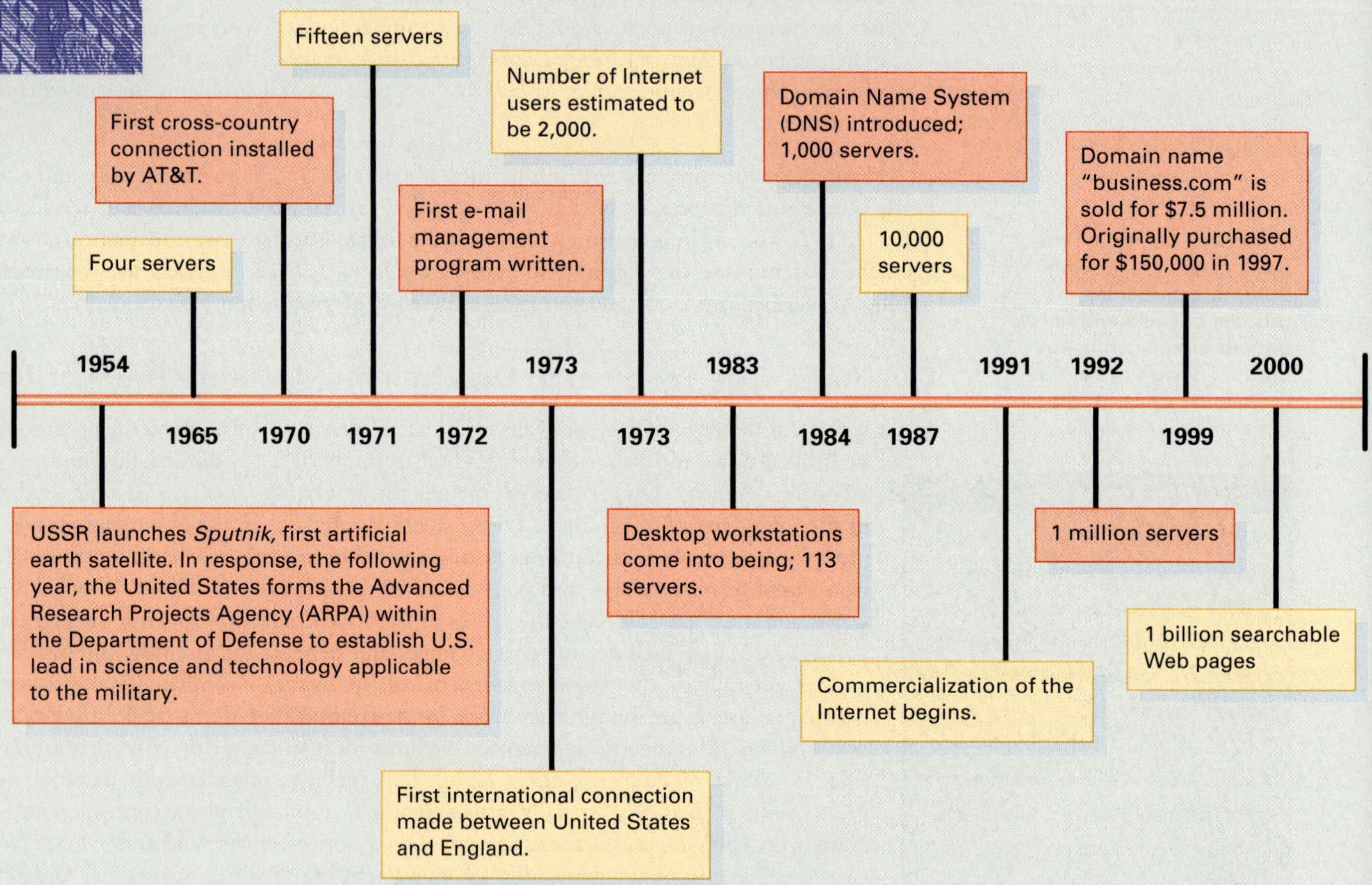

Source: Robert Hobbes, *Hobbes' Internet Timeline.* http:// www.zakon.org/robert/internet/timeline/.

are part of manufacturing overhead costs that must be paid only once or twice a year. Utility costs, like heating and air conditioning in the plant, vary from month to month, sometimes significantly! The occasional repairs and maintenance on equipment are difficult to predict and to budget for accurately. Nevertheless, most management accountants are required by their organizations to relate these "lumpy" costs back to the volume of production output. In addition, accurate product pricing is even more difficult because the actual amount of all manufacturing overhead costs isn't known until the end of the period, long after some products have been completed and even sold.

Exhibit 3-1 shows this product costing problem. While direct materials and direct labor are directly related or associated to the manufacture of certain products, the various expense items that

As early as 1988, pressure to commercialize the Internet began when businesses saw its potential as a means of communication and a way to create new marketplaces. Before the Internet could become commercial property, however, Congress had to enact new laws. A few years passed before the Internet was successfully commercialized. Then businesses jumped onto the "backbone" that the government had established and have since created a World Wide Web that enables businesses and consumers to enjoy the technology of the Internet that has been termed the "Technological Revolution" in business.

Like the Industrial Revolution, the Technological Revolution started with individuals who had a unique vision that eventually profited millions of people. For example, Barry Shein, a college dropout, created the first ISP (Internet service provider) in 1989. Barry's idea stemmed from the "withdrawal" he felt when he no longer had Internet access after leaving his university. Soon after, giants such as **AMERICA ONLINE (AOL)**, **PRODIGY**, and **COMPUSERVE** began reaping the benefits of Barry's "withdrawal" symptoms. E-commerce on the Internet as we know it today is the result of the vision and efforts of many individuals such as Barry Shein. Without them, the explosive growth in e-commerce shown in the following graph would not have occurred.

Source: John Thomson, Jr., *Privatization of the New Communication Channel: Computer Networks and the Internet*, © 2000. http://www.sit.wisc.edu/%7Ejcthomsonjr/j561/.

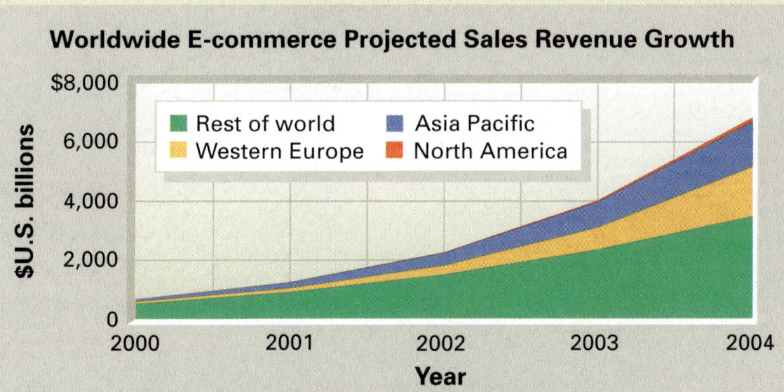

Source: Data from Forrester Research, Inc., 2000. Data are located at http://www.forrester.com/ER/Research/Brief/0,1317,9229,00.html.

comprise manufacturing overhead are not. Therefore, management accountants must find some artificial (but hopefully logical) and fair way to "allocate" or "assign" manufacturing overhead costs to products produced. This "artificial allocation" can result in inaccurate product costs and can lead to serious problems when making planning, controlling, and evaluating decisions.

Most product costing systems were initially designed for the purpose of assigning direct materials, direct labor, and manufacturing overhead costs to individual products. This would then determine which costs should flow to Cost of Goods Sold (as each product is sold) to be matched with revenues and which costs should be used to value the remaining inventory on the balance sheet. Because of the emphasis on financial and tax accounting, there sometimes wasn't much emphasis on accurately allocating manufacturing overhead to specific products. Product cost

exhibit 3-1 Production Flow and "Lumpy" Overhead Costs

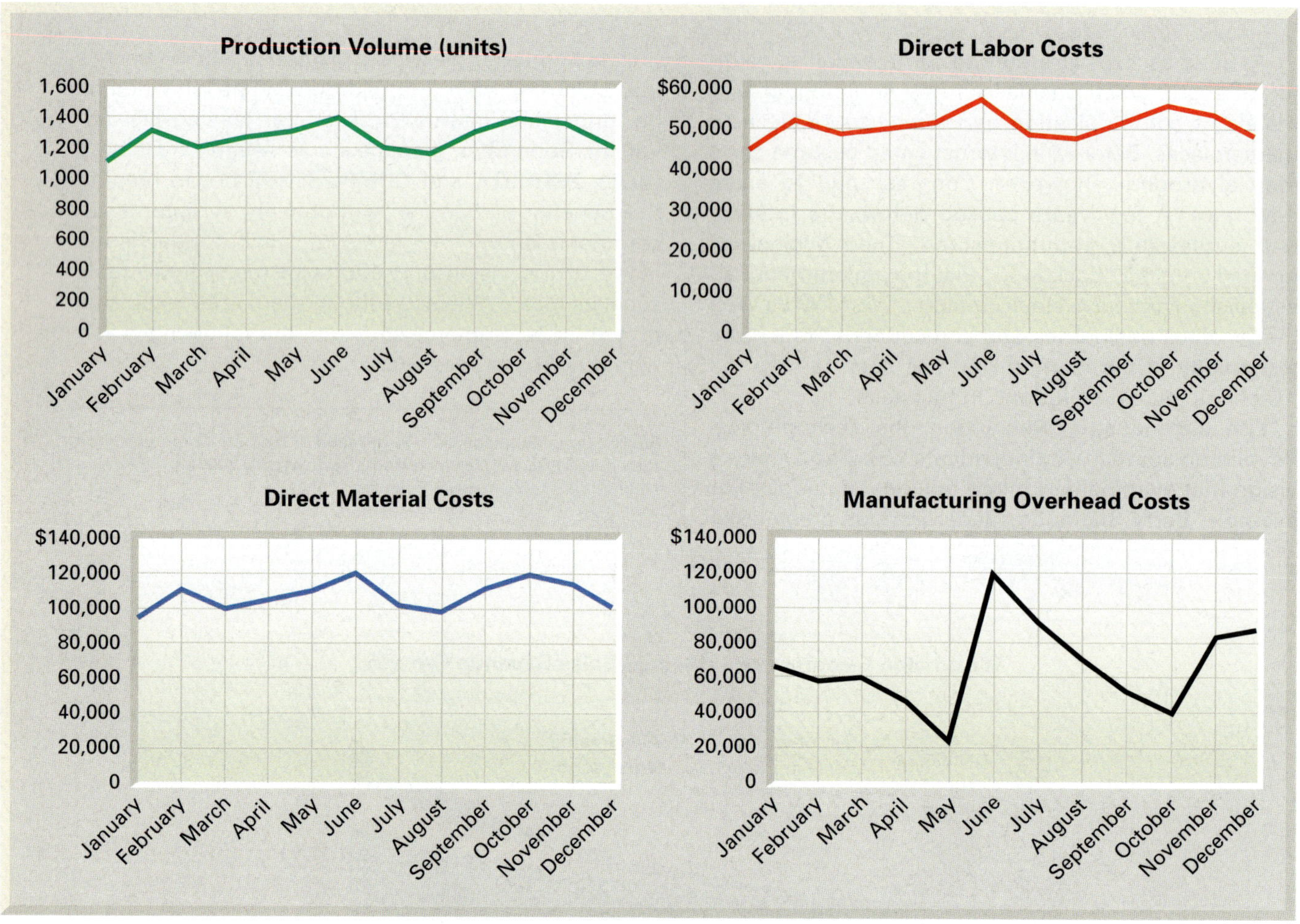

information was used primarily for external financial reporting (to measure the assets and income for an accounting period) and for income tax reporting (to measure taxable income). Because product costing systems were driven primarily by external reporting rules and needs, they did not necessarily provide the best information for management decision making. Only in recent years has emphasis been placed on developing good management accounting systems that provide cost information useful for decision making: planning (e.g., how much labor should we hire?); controlling (e.g., which products are costing more to produce than expected?); and evaluating (e.g., which processes are operating efficiently?).

New Methods of Cost Accumulation

As waves of modernization continue to sweep across the world, manufacturing, merchandising, and service companies are discovering that by integrating better technology into the process of creating and delivering goods and services, they can reduce overall costs, improve quality, and increase productivity. As investments in technology in the workplace continue, however, it can become virtually impossible for some companies to accurately measure costs of goods and services using traditional cost accounting systems. For example, as automation, robotics, and other innovations replace workers, significant changes are occurring in the types of costs that innovative companies must now manage. To provide accurate product costs, new and better ways of assigning costs to products have to be developed.

Management accountants are now working to develop radically different product costing systems. These new types of cost systems are providing information so different from that of

By integrating technology such as robotics into the production process, companies can reduce costs, improve quality, and increase productivity. However, technology also leads to significant changes in the types of costs companies must now manage.

conventional cost systems that many businesses have been able to refocus their manufacturing, merchandising, and service efforts and dramatically increase their profits while reducing prices. With better product cost information, some companies have been able to eliminate high-cost, low-productivity processes and replace them with lower-cost, less-complex processes. Researchers and manufacturers have spent more time trying to determine ways to provide accurate product cost information than they have spent on any other management accounting topic. The result has been the introduction of several new product costing methods including **activity-based costing (ABC)**. Because of these changes in management accounting and cost accumulation systems, many business organizations are currently in a state of transition. Companies such as DELUXE CORPORATION (the world's largest printer of bank checks as well as a provider of electronic products and services to financial institutions) have completely restructured strategies and operations based on new cost accounting systems.[2] Other companies have been slower to change and still use conventional cost accumulation systems. As a result, some companies struggle to compete effectively in their markets.

activity-based costing (ABC) A method of attributing costs to products based on first assigning costs of resources to activities and then costs of activities to products.

fyi

The very nature of the grocery business—selling perishable and dated products—makes inventory cost management crucial. One grocery food chain, HANNAFORD BROS., has implemented a new inventory management system that allows for quick and efficient communication between store managers and has saved several hundreds of thousands of dollars in paper reports, giving the company an important competitive advantage.

Source: Cisco Systems Customer Profiles at http://www.cisco.com/warp/public/cc/general/profile/hanna_cp.htm.

Most innovative companies have adopted costing approaches (such as ABC) that better track overhead costs and more accurately assign them to products. Advocates maintain that ABC can provide management with a more accurate assignment of overhead to products and, therefore, a better understanding of profitability. ABC systems use direct material and direct labor cost information in the same way as conventional systems. Where ABC systems differ is in their accounting for overhead costs. ABC advocates claim that traditional cost accounting distorts product costs by allocating overhead costs in irrelevant ways, which may lead to inaccurate and potentially damaging decisions. And despite the advances being made in new product costing systems, costs are only one of the strategic imperatives facing companies. Managers and accountants in companies that expect to remain competitive must always remember that the market demands high quality and timeliness, as well as low costs.

In view of the transitional state of accounting for product costs, we will cover both conventional product costing systems (in this chapter) and new cost accumulation systems (in later chapters). You need to understand both types of systems in order to facilitate organizational transitions to more competitive costing systems during your career. In the remainder of this chapter, we describe the conventional accumulation of product costs. The ABC concept will be defined and discussed in Chapter 7 of management accounting.

2 P. B. B. Turney, *Deluxe Corporation: A Strategic Need for Activity-Based Costing* (Charlottesville, Va.: University of Virginia Darden School Foundation, 1999).

business environment essay

Firestone Disaster Sometimes, a company's management will sacrifice the quality of its goods or services to obtain a cheaper product. Yet, in a world where consumers place absolute trust in the products they purchase, it is imperative that cost does not replace quality as the company's primary focus. This was not the case with **FIRESTONE** tires in 2000.

Lawsuits were brought against Firestone (whose parent company is **BRIDGESTONE**), claiming that its tires on sports utility vehicles, especially the **FORD** Explorer, were faulty and had caused accidents and even the deaths of numerous individuals (according to recent reports, 88 fatalities and 250 injuries have been blamed on Firestone tires). On further investigation, ex-employees of Firestone's plant in Decatur, Illinois, testified in court "that the facility was suffering from various quality-control problems. . . . [one] policy . . . shortened the time spent curing, or cooking, the tires—when the different layers are bonded together under intense heat—from 26 to 16 minutes." In an effort to cut down production time and costs, Firestone sacrificed the quality of its tires, which unfortunately led to unimaginable consequences for 88 individuals.

Needless to say, Firestone has lost most, if not all, consumer confidence. To date, Firestone has recalled approximately 6.5 million tires at an enormous cost, and some analysts doubt that the company will recover. As the graph on the next page shows, *Fortune* magazine ranked Bridgestone/Firestone as one of the worst companies in America. Management's decision to sacrifice quality for cost savings has left Firestone desperately hoping to survive.

to summarize

While it is difficult to determine true product costs, having accurate product cost information is extremely important. Without accurate costs, management can easily over- or underprice products and make bad business decisions. Although it is easy to allocate direct material and direct labor costs to specific products, manufacturing overhead costs make accurate product costing difficult. Traditionally, product cost information has been used primarily for financial reporting and tax purposes, and little emphasis has been placed on accurately assigning manufacturing overhead costs to manufacturing products. Recently, however, a number of innovative approaches to product costing have been developed. The new methods of cost accumulation, though challenging to implement, offer significant potential benefits to manufacturing, merchandising, and service companies. Management needs accurate product cost information to plan for the future, control current operations, and evaluate past performance.

2

Explain the flow of goods and services in a manufacturing organization and follow the accumulation of product costs in its accounting system.

THE FLOW OF GOODS AND COSTS IN A MANUFACTURING FIRM

It should be clear to you at this point that management accounting provides information with competitive value that supports management efforts to plan, control, and evaluate the organization's performance in providing goods and services to the world. In addition, you know that organizations compete on the basis of costs, quality, and timeliness, and that management ac-

Rank	Company	Rank	Company
526	TRANS WORLD AIRLINES	531	LTV
527	TRUMP RESORTS	532	US AIRWAYS GROUP
528	KMART	533	FEDERAL-MOGUL
529	BRIDGESTONE/FIRESTONE	534	WARNACO GROUP
530	AMERICA WEST HOLDINGS	535	CKE RESTAURANTS

The Bottom Ten of *Fortune*'s America's Most Admired Companies, 2001

Sources: D. Einsenberg, "Anatomy of a Recall," *Time*, September 11, 2000; and A. Diba and L. Munoz, "America's Most Admired Companies," *Fortune*, February 19, 2001.

counting needs to provide information regarding all three of these performance characteristics. As you read in the opening of this chapter, however, management accounting had its beginnings in tracking and reporting costs. Today, one of the best ways to understand how an organization works to provide goods and services is to "follow the money"; in other words, observe how costs flow through the organization. We'll use cost flows to introduce you to manufacturing, merchandising, and service organizations. For a long time, manufacturing was the basis of the U.S. economy. Today, relative to other industries, manufacturing is much smaller. Nevertheless, management accounting systems were originally built to support the manufacturing process, so we'll start there.

Consider the layout for a simple, hypothetical manufacturing company shown in Exhibit 3-2. This floor plan is for a manufacturer of furniture, Broyman Furniture Company. The floor plan shows a building that is partitioned into two sections. The administrative offices include office space for various vice presidents, the sales staff, the president, and the word-processing staff. The manufacturing facility encompasses the offices of the vice president of manufacturing, the plant manager, and the controller; the raw materials and finished goods warehouses; and the factory floor, where production takes place.

raw materials inventory The inventory of raw materials that have not yet begun the production process.

work-in-process inventory Inventory that is partly completed in the production process, but not yet ready for sale to customers.

finished goods inventory Inventory that has completed the production process and is ready for sale to customers.

The manufacturing process for Broyman is quite straightforward. When purchased, raw materials are delivered to the **raw materials inventory** warehouse where they are stored until requisitioned for production. When requisitioned, raw materials are moved out onto the factory floor for the actual manufacturing process; there all material is referred to as **work-in-process inventory** until the process is completed. The factory floor includes three different manufacturing departments: cutting, machining, and finishing. Whereas some furniture products require work in all three areas, others may require work in only one or two areas. On the factory floor, factory employees combine materials with their labor to produce finished products. The finished products are then moved into the **finished goods inventory** warehouse and stored until sold.

Although the movement of goods through this simple factory is straightforward, tracking the costs of goods manufactured (the product costs) is not always so simple. You remember from Chapter 1 of management accounting that product costs include all costs necessary to create the product: essentially, the costs of all people and processes within Broyman's manufacturing

exhibit 3-2 Broyman Furniture Company (A Manufacturing Firm's Layout)

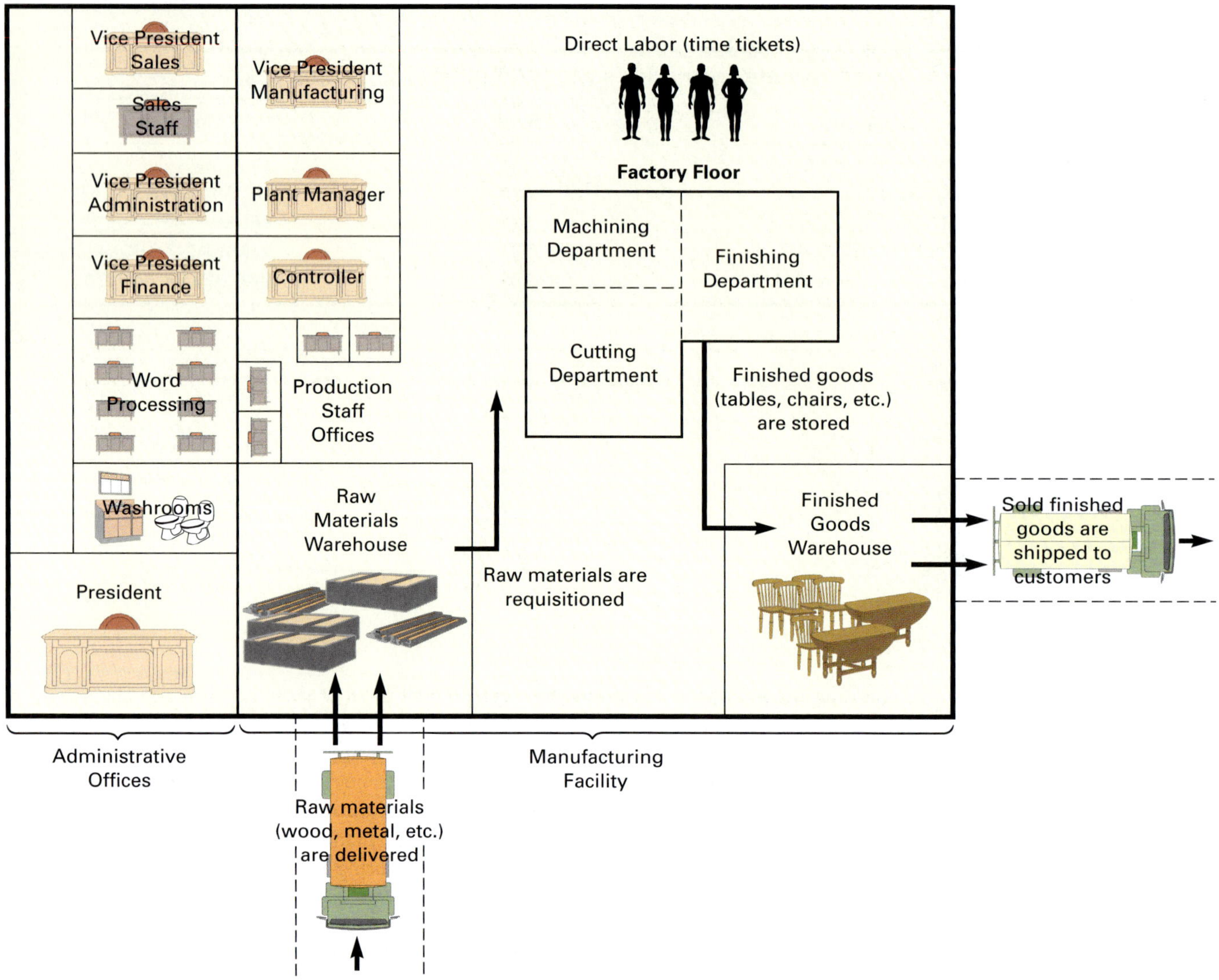

facility. On the other hand, the costs of people and processes in Broyman's administrative offices, which are not associated with the production of furniture, are period costs. The basic idea that defines product costs is that product costs can be associated with specific products. Certainly, the costs of the raw materials and the wages of factory employees who work on the factory floor are manufacturing costs that can be traced to specific products. But what about the salaries of the vice president of manufacturing, the plant manager, and the individuals working in the administrative offices? Should any part of their salaries be included in product costs? What about the utility bills to heat and light the building, the depreciation or rent on the building, the cost of the parking lot, the cost of paper towels for the washrooms, and other miscellaneous expenditures? Should any part of these expenses be included in manufacturing costs?

Because the individuals working in the administrative offices perform administrative and selling duties, rather than manufacturing functions, their salaries should probably not be classified as product costs. Likewise, the costs to pay for electricity, heat, and other expenses for the administrative offices are probably not manufacturing costs. However, the vice president of manufacturing and the plant manager perform functions related to manufacturing, so their salaries

fyi

In 1999, U.S corporations reported earnings of nearly $7.6 trillion. When we break this number down by industries, manufacturers earned $1.5 trillion, merchandisers earned another $1.5 trillion, and service companies (including transportation and finance companies) earned $4.6 trillion. Note, however, that nonprofit organizations do not report earnings. Therefore, service industries are even bigger than these numbers would indicate!

Source: U.S. Department of Commerce, Bureau of Economic Analysis, 1999.

should probably be included as product costs. Although these employees perform administrative functions within the manufacturing facility, the work they perform cannot easily be identified with or assigned to specific products, unlike the factory employees who work directly on the products. Similarly, the heat, power, and depreciation related to the manufacturing facility should be included as manufacturing costs but cannot be easily traced to specific products. What about the costs of delivering purchased raw materials to the plant or the delivery of finished goods to customers? Should these delivery costs be classified as manufacturing, administrative, or selling expenses?

As you can see, accurately determining the costs of manufactured products can be challenging, even in a simple firm with one product and one location. When the "real world" introduces the complexities of multiple products being produced in the same facility, changing prices and labor rates, multiple manufacturing locations (perhaps some international locations), and individuals performing multiple functions, it becomes very challenging to accurately determine product costs. Essentially, in order to accurately measure product costs, management accountants must be able to:

1. Determine which costs relate to manufacturing and which relate to administrative and selling functions.
2. Accurately identify and measure all costs associated with manufacturing.
3. Determine appropriate ways to assign costs incurred to products manufactured.

These issues are discussed in the following section.

The Product Costing System

Most accounting systems that track costs of producing and providing goods and services are based on a few key procedures.

- First, identify the product or project that needs cost measurement and track this project through the production process.[3]
- Second, specifically trace the direct costs (costs of direct materials and direct labor) to each product or project.
- Finally, allocate an appropriate amount of overhead costs to each product or project.

job order costing A method of product costing whereby each job, product, or batch of products is costed separately.

This accounting approach is traditionally called **job order costing**. As we discuss the mechanics of this product costing system, keep in the mind the overall procedure—identify the product or service (the "job"), trace the direct costs, and allocate the overhead. Also be sure to remember the big picture. In other words, why are we doing this? Product and service cost information is used to plan future operations (e.g., at what level of production should we operate?), to control current operations (e.g., are our costs too high?), and to evaluate performance (e.g., were our costs and performance last period good or bad?). This information is used by management to support continuous decisions about costs, quality, and time.

In our example, we will track product costs as we follow an order for a mahogany table that is manufactured by Broyman Furniture Company. The production of the table is a custom job requiring two operations: machining (preparing the mahogany) and finishing (assembling, staining, and packaging the table). (You will recall that there were three manufacturing areas in Exhibit 3-2. This table does not require work in the cutting department.)

Exhibit 3-3 shows that the mahogany table costs $393.50 to make. This amount includes $135 of direct materials, $134 of direct labor, and $124.50 of manufacturing overhead (which includes supervisor and production staff salaries, insurance, utilities, depreciation on plant and machinery, and so on). Looking at the cost summary in Exhibit 3-3, we can see that the hourly

3 In some organizations, it is not reasonable or possible to specifically track the product being produced. For example, a lumber mill that continuously processes timber into planks may not specifically track individual products. Instead, the mill would track the total production costs expended for a particular period of time (e.g., a day), then assign those costs to the total amount of timber processed during that same period of time. This management accounting approach is called process costing and will be discussed in the expanded material section of this chapter.

exhibit 3-3 Total Product Costs for One Mahogany Table

Machining Department Costs

Direct Materials	Direct Labor			Manufacturing Overhead (based on machine hours)		
Requisitioned	**Hours**	**Wage Rate**	**Amount**	**Hours**	**Overhead Rate**	**Amount**
$100	8	$10	$80	6	$11	$66

Finishing Department Costs

Direct Materials	Direct Labor			Manufacturing Overhead (based on direct labor hours)		
Requisitioned	**Hours**	**Wage Rate**	**Amount**	**Hours**	**Overhead Rate**	**Amount**
$30.00	3	$12.00	$36.00	3	$13.00	$39.00
5.00	1.5	$12.00	18.00	1.5	$13.00	19.50
$35.00			$54.00			$58.50

Final Product Cost for Mahogany Table

	Machining	Finishing	Total
Direct materials	$100.00	$ 35.00	$135.00
Direct labor	80.00	54.00	134.00
Manufacturing overhead	66.00	58.50	124.50
Total cost	$246.00	$147.50	$393.50

manufacturing overhead rate The rate at which manufacturing overhead is assigned to products; equals estimated manufacturing overhead for the period divided by the number of units of the activity base being used.

wage rate for direct labor is $10 per hour in machining and $12 per hour in finishing; the manufacturing overhead rate is $11 per machine hour in machining and $13 per direct labor hour in finishing. The **manufacturing overhead rate** is an estimate of the overhead that will be incurred for each unit (in this case, allocated on the basis of machine and direct labor hours). In this example, the company incurs an average of $11 of overhead for every hour the machine is run in the machining department. Thus, each table that requires the use of the machine is allocated a portion of the overhead costs. The use of different manufacturing overhead rates is common. Each department will allocate manufacturing overhead to products on the basis of the most meaningful activity in that department. (Remember the challenge discussed earlier of accurately estimating and allocating manufacturing overhead to products.) The machining department is more automated, so activity is tied more closely to machine hours; the finishing department requires more handwork, so activity is tied more closely to direct labor hours. With these "finished costs" in mind, let's talk about how Broyman Furniture Company actually created these data on the mahogany table. But first, take a brief look at Exhibit 3-4 on page 120. In this rather complicated-looking exhibit you can literally "see" how the costs follow the production process and flow through the accounting system. We'll work through the details of Exhibit 3-4 below. (Note: Don't worry if you are still a little confused about how Broyman creates and uses manufacturing overhead rates. We're going to discuss these concepts in detail later in this chapter.)

DIRECT MATERIALS COSTS To illustrate the accounting for direct materials costs, we will assume that Broyman purchased a supply of mahogany and placed it in a materials storeroom. The entry to record this purchase is:[4]

[4]In this chapter, we will use an *actual* cost accounting system. We will discuss standard cost accounting systems in Chapter 9.

business environment essay

Costs and the Medical Profession Have you ever gone to the doctor's office, spent 20 minutes in the waiting room, then another 20 minutes in the examination room before the doctor comes in? When she finally comes in, she examines you for 10 minutes and then sends you on your way, charging you $50 for the visit. No wonder medical doctors make so much money—or do they? Does the doctor put your $50 right in her pocket?

What costs must your $50 cover? Unfortunately, you must help the doctor pay for office medical supplies, rent on the office, utilities, salaries of nurses and office personnel, fees charged by hospitals to use their facilities, and costs of training seminars to remain current in her field. While these costs are expensive, perhaps the most rapidly rising cost is for malpractice insurance. As an example, in many communities in the United States, the cost of obstetrical malpractice insurance is so high that some doctors will no longer deliver babies.

Where does the doctor get the money to cover these costs? By charging you $50 for your visit. Medicine is a business. The doctor is pricing patient visits to cover all costs incurred in providing that service. Costs must be covered and we, the consumers, must pay for them. The next time you visit the doctor, take a look around the waiting room, enjoy those pictures, and read those magazines. After all, you paid for them!

Raw Materials Inventory	50,000	
Accounts Payable (or Cash)		50,000
Purchased 25,000 board feet of mahogany at $2 per foot.		

When raw materials are needed (such as for the manufacture of the table), the machining department sends a request (i.e., a requisition) to the storeroom (usually via computer) identifying the quantity and type of materials needed. When the raw materials warehouse fills the requisition, it records the transfer of goods to the factory floor by making an entry (usually by computer) that serves as the basis for the accounting records. The storeroom manager sends the requisition information to the accounting department, where the unit cost is entered and the total cost calculated. The accounting entry made to record the transfer of mahogany from storage to machining is:

Work-in-Process Inventory	100	
Raw Materials Inventory		100
Issued 50 board feet of mahogany to production at $2 per foot.		

Work-in-Process Inventory	35	
Raw Materials Inventory		35
Issued packaging material to production.		

The mahogany and packaging material were used directly in the production of the table ready to ship; the cost is assigned as direct materials for this particular job. Because the amount of direct materials used varies proportionately with the level of production, direct materials are almost always variable costs. Indirect materials and supplies used in production (classified as manufacturing overhead costs), such as glue, nails, and varnish, are ordered from the storeroom in the same manner. Although some inexpensive materials, such as glue, are used directly in the manufactured products and others are used to support production, it is generally not cost-beneficial to trace such miscellaneous items to a particular job. These miscellaneous items are treated as indirect materials costs and recorded in the manufacturing overhead account (explained later in the chapter). Manufacturing overhead consists of numerous expenditures such as indirect labor, indirect materials, utilities, rent, and the like. The sum of these various expenditures provides the balance in the manufacturing overhead account. The following entry records the sum of all the requisitions for indirect materials for the period:

Manufacturing Overhead (indirect materials)	15,000	
Raw Materials Inventory		15,000
Issued miscellaneous materials and supplies to the production floor.		

At the end of a period, the amount of materials and supplies that remain on hand in the raw materials warehouse is shown on the balance sheet as Raw Materials Inventory.

DIRECT LABOR COSTS The method of charging direct labor costs to production jobs is similar to that for direct materials costs. Most factories have a time clock where employees punch in and record their hourly activities. These time clocks often allow workers to identify specific jobs worked on. When the time clocks do not capture specific job information, the information is noted by making entries in the computer or on manual time tickets. The product costs, shown in Exhibit 3-3, reveal that machining employees worked on the mahogany table for 8 hours. Because the wage rate was $10 per hour in machining, the total direct labor cost in machining was $80 ($10 per hour × 8 hours). Similar calculations provide the entry to record the direct labor costs in the finishing department. The entries to record all the direct labor costs (ignoring payroll taxes and benefits) for the mahogany table are:

Work-in-Process Inventory	80	
Wages Payable		80
To record the machining department's direct labor costs.		

Work-in-Process Inventory	54	
Wages Payable		54
To record the finishing department's direct labor costs.		

Remember that within certain limits, direct labor costs vary proportionately with the number of products made and, thus, are typically considered variable costs.

Like materials, labor costs can be either direct or indirect. Indirect labor costs include the wages of employees who perform functions not related to a specific job, such as maintenance and custodial. Usually, these employees still punch time clocks, but their wages become part of the indirect labor costs that are included in manufacturing overhead, as discussed in the next section. The following entry records the sum of all indirect labor for the period:

Manufacturing Overhead (indirect labor)	20,000	
Wages Payable		20,000
To record indirect labor costs.		

STOP & THINK In our example, the company makes a mahogany table using two operations: machining and finishing. When making a real table, how many separate operations do you think would be necessary?

MANUFACTURING OVERHEAD COSTS In contrast to direct materials and direct labor, manufacturing overhead (the third type of product cost) involves more complex accounting procedures and estimation problems. As we've discussed earlier, while direct materials and direct labor can be readily assigned to specific jobs or products, manufacturing overhead costs are difficult to trace directly to the production of a single item and must often be estimated in advance of their incurrence. By definition, most manufacturing overhead costs benefit all products made in a department or a company during a period. The depreciation on equipment and the wages paid for maintenance in the machining department, for example, ensure the smooth operation of the entire department for the period; these cannot be traced directly to individual items produced during the period. Some manufacturing overhead costs, such as property taxes and repairs, are not known until the end of an accounting period. However, managers need current product cost information (for pricing similar jobs, estimating costs for next year, and so forth), so each job is assigned a share of *estimated* (i.e., budgeted) manufacturing overhead costs. In accounting terminology, manufacturing overhead costs are applied to (or absorbed by) jobs or products. Overall, knowing how to set up and handle the accounting for overhead costs at Broyman Company is a tricky business, which we'll talk further about later in this chapter.

For now, as *actual* manufacturing overhead costs for Broyman are incurred, the management accounting system needs to recognize and record the costs. During the current production period, these costs include $1,200 for repairs to equipment, $6,450 for monthly rent allocated to the production facility, $850 for liability insurance, and $2,900 in depreciation of manufacturing equipment. The total of these costs is debited of Manufacturing Overhead, and the individual amounts are credited to their respective accounts, as shown here.

caution

Many students will make the mistake of debiting manufacturing overhead costs to an expense account. Although these costs eventually do become an expense, first they are debited to Manufacturing Overhead, then allocated to Work-in-Process Inventory, then transferred to Finished Goods Inventory, and finally expensed in Cost of Goods Sold.

Manufacturing Overhead	11,400	
Accounts Payable		1,200
Rent Payable		6,450
Prepaid Insurance		850
Accumulated Depreciation		2,900
To record actual manufacturing overhead costs.		

In addition to recording the actual costs of manufacturing overhead, Broyman's accountants need to allocate overhead costs to the mahogany table in production. As you can see in Exhibit 3-3, the Broyman management accountants follow a traditional approach of assigning manufacturing overhead costs by taking the expected annual costs of overhead for each department and dividing this estimated amount by the selected activity base (in this case, machine hours for the machining department and direct labor hours for the finishing department). Estimated overhead costs typically come from the company's annual budgets. Selection of the activity base is the result of experience and analysis. The result is an allocation rate for each department that is used to uniformly assign a "fair share" of manufacturing overhead costs to production volume throughout the year. This allocation rate is called the **predetermined overhead rate**. In this case, Broyman's accountants allocate to the mahogany table $66 based on activity in the machining department ($11 predetermined overhead rate × 6 machine hours) and $58.50 based on activity in the finishing department ($13 rate × 4.5 direct labor hours). The entries to record these allocations are:

predetermined overhead rate A rate at which estimated manufacturing overhead costs are assigned to products throughout the year; equals total estimated manufacturing overhead costs divided by a suitable allocation base, such as number of units produced, direct labor hours, direct materials used, or direct labor costs.

Work-in-Process Inventory	66.00	
Manufacturing Overhead		66.00
To apply manufacturing overhead from the machining department.		

Work-in-Process Inventory	58.50	
Manufacturing Overhead		58.50
To apply manufacturing overhead from the finishing department.		

Notice in Exhibit 3-4 that as *actual* overhead costs are incurred (as with indirect materials and indirect labor), the manufacturing overhead account is debited. As overhead costs are *applied* to products, the manufacturing overhead account is credited. This relationship is better illustrated and discussed later in this chapter.

exhibit 3-4 Flow of Product Costs in Broyman Company Job Order Cost Accounting System

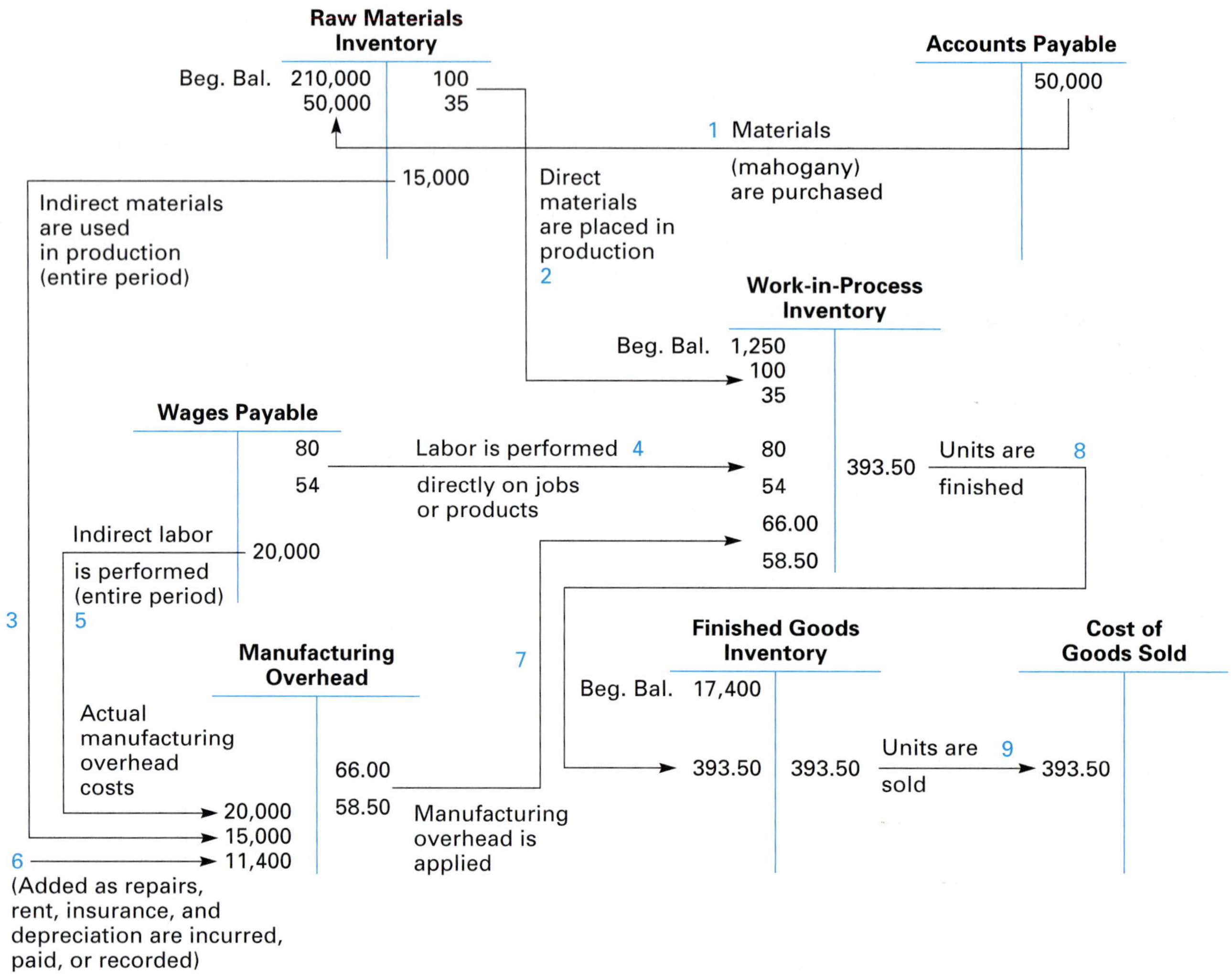

Journal Entries for Manufacturing Firms:

1	Raw Materials Inventory	50,000	
	Accounts Payable (or Cash)		50,000
	Purchased raw materials.		
2	Work-in-Process Inventory	100	
	Raw Materials Inventory		100
	Work-in-Process Inventory	35	
	Raw Materials Inventory		35
	Used direct materials in production (includes materials used in both the machining and finishing departments).		
3	Manufacturing Overhead	15,000	
	Raw Materials Inventory		15,000
	Used indirect materials in production (amount used during entire period).		
4	Work-in-Process Inventory	80	
	Wages Payable		80
	Work-in-Process Inventory	54	
	Wages Payable		54
	Incurred direct labor costs in the machining and finishing departments.		
5	Manufacturing Overhead	20,000	
	Wages Payable		20,000
	Incurred indirect labor costs (includes indirect labor costs for entire period).		

6	Manufacturing Overhead	11,400	
	Accounts Payable		1,200
	Rent Payable		6,450
	Prepaid Insurance		850
	Accumulated Depreciation		2,900
	Incurred manufacturing overhead costs (includes amounts for entire period).		
7	Work-in-Process Inventory	66.00	
	Manufacturing Overhead		66.00
	Work-in-Process Inventory	58.50	
	Manufacturing Overhead		58.50
	Applied manufacturing overhead from the machining and finishing departments to production.		
8	Finished Goods Inventory	393.50	
	Work-in-Process Inventory		393.50
	Completed production.		
9	Cost of Goods Sold	393.50	
	Finished Goods Inventory		393.50
	Sold finished goods.		

TRANSFERRING THE COSTS OF COMPLETED JOBS AND COMPUTING UNIT COSTS While a job is in process, the costs of direct materials, direct labor, and manufacturing overhead are accounted for separately. When the job is completed, however, these costs (in total) are transferred from Work-in-Process Inventory to Finished Goods Inventory. In the Broyman Furniture Company example, the total cost assigned to the mahogany table is $393.50, as illustrated in Exhibit 3-3. The entry to transfer the completed cost of the table to Finished Goods Inventory is:

Finished Goods Inventory	393.50	
Work-in-Process Inventory		393.50
To record the completion of the mahogany table.		

As you can see by comparing Exhibits 3-2 and 3-4, the product costs assigned to the table literally follow that table as it moves through the factory floor (and through the work-in-process inventory account) until the table is completed and moves into the finished goods warehouse (and into the finished goods inventory account). Once completed, cost data for the mahogany table are used in pricing similar jobs, estimating costs for the next year, and measuring income. Note that this process would be no different if, instead of a single table, Broyman were to identify and cost an entire batch of mahogany tables. In this case, at the completion of the job, the unit cost of each table is computed by adding the direct materials, direct labor, and manufacturing overhead costs for the batch and dividing the total by the number of tables produced in the batch (i.e., the job).

TRANSFERRING THE COSTS OF PRODUCTS THAT ARE SOLD When a product is sold, the costs assigned to it are transferred to Cost of Goods Sold. For example, when the mahogany table, which cost $393.50 to make, is shipped to a customer, the table is loaded from the warehouse onto the truck, and the cost of the table is transferred from Finished Goods Inventory to Cost of Goods Sold, using the following entry:

Cost of Goods Sold	393.50	
Finished Goods Inventory		393.50
To record the cost of goods sold for the mahogany table.		

With this entry, costs have been traced all the way through the production cycle and expensed onto the income statement. Once again, inspect Exhibit 3-4 and be sure that you can clearly see how all the costs flow through the manufacturing process for Broyman. Note that direct labor, when incurred, and raw materials, when used, are debited directly to Work-in-Process Inventory. Actual manufacturing overhead costs, on the other hand, are entered first as debits to Manufacturing Overhead and then are allocated to Work-in-Process Inventory by crediting Manufacturing Overhead. Be careful to note that in Exhibit 3-4, entry 1 is for mahogany that will be used on several jobs; entries 3, 5, and 6 are actual manufacturing costs incurred for the entire accounting period in which the table was manufactured. Entries 2, 4, 7, 8, and 9 are entries specifically associated with the mahogany table in our example. At the end of the period, the company will usually have three inventory balances: Raw Materials Inventory, Work-in-Process Inventory, and Finished Goods Inventory.

STOP & THINK Compare Exhibit 3-2 with Exhibit 3-4. Try to identify the physical location (from Exhibit 3-2) with each type of accounting cost in Exhibit 3-4.

to summarize

In traditional job order cost accounting systems for manufacturing organizations where a specific product can be identified, all direct labor, direct materials, and manufacturing overhead costs are accumulated for each unit or batch (generally referred to as a job). Because the exact amount of manufacturing overhead cannot be determined until the accounting period is completed, an estimated amount of manufacturing overhead is applied to jobs. To estimate the amount of manufacturing overhead to be applied to a job, a predetermined overhead rate is calculated for each department involved in production, using an appropriate measure of activity. This rate is multiplied by the actual quantity of the activity used to complete the job. Total costs for completed jobs are then transferred from Work-in-Process Inventory to Finished Goods Inventory. When manufactured goods are sold, costs are transferred from Finished Goods Inventory to Cost of Goods Sold.

3

Understand the process of accounting for overhead.

ACCOUNTING FOR OVERHEAD

In the Broyman Company example of producing a mahogany table and tracking its production costs, you can see that accounting for manufacturing overhead costs is not the same process as accounting for direct materials and direct labor costs. Because manufacturing overhead costs generally do not coincide with the flow of production (as was illustrated earlier in Exhibit 3-1), a few extra steps are required to handle the accounting. These steps are:

1. Before the year begins, budget the *estimated* manufacturing overhead, estimate the allocation activity, and establish the predetermined overhead rate.
2. During the year, as costs are incurred, record *actual* manufacturing overhead as debits to the manufacturing overhead account.
3. During the year, as activity takes place, record *applied* manufacturing overhead as credits to the manufacturing overhead account.
4. At the end of the year, compare *actual* and *applied* overhead balances and close out the difference in the manufacturing overhead account.

Estimated Manufacturing Overhead

estimated manufacturing overhead Budgeted manufacturing overhead costs that are used to establish the predetermined overhead rate.

As you can see, the list above includes three difference classifications of manufacturing overhead costs—estimated, actual, and applied. It is *critical* that you understand the differences among these numbers. **Estimated manufacturing overhead** is the amount of overhead costs that management has budgeted for the upcoming production period. The predetermined overhead rate is created by dividing estimated manufacturing overhead by the estimate of the expected level of activity (e.g., direct labor hours) to be used to allocate overhead during the year.

To illustrate the use of estimated manufacturing overhead to create the predetermined overhead rate for the machining department at Broyman Company, assume that at the beginning of the year the accountants and production personnel estimated that 24,500 machine hours would be used on the factory floor. Budgeted (estimated) overhead costs for the machining department are shown below. Note that these costs have been separated into fixed and variable components.

Variable manufacturing overhead:		
Indirect labor	$ 45,000	
Indirect materials	15,000	
Repairs	7,500	$ 67,500
Fixed manufacturing overhead:		
Rent	$105,000	
Depreciation	85,000	
Insurance	12,000	202,000
Total expected manufacturing overhead cost for the year (machining department)		$269,500

Using these data, the accountants then computed the predetermined overhead rate in the machining department to be $11 per machine hour, as follows:

$$\frac{\text{Total estimated manufacturing overhead cost for the year}}{\text{Total estimated machine hours}} = \frac{\$269{,}500}{24{,}500} = \$11 \text{ per machine hour in machining department}$$

> **fyi**
>
> One useful way to think about the manufacturing overhead account is to consider it to be simply a temporary holding tank for overhead costs that we don't immediately know how to assign to production. By the end of the period, however, we will have sorted out how much was actually spent on overhead and how much actual production took place. At that point, we can clear out the "holding tank" and start over the process of tracking and applying overhead costs.

Similar calculations were used to calculate the predetermined overhead rate of $13 per direct labor hour in the finishing department.

Actual Manufacturing Overhead

After studying financial accounting, some students have a difficult time with the accounting for actual manufacturing overhead. For example, in financial accounting, we accounted for salaries by debiting Salaries Expense and crediting Salaries Payable; the correct entry when the salaries are for sales or other nonmanufacturing personnel. However, as you saw in tracking production costs for Broyman's mahogany table, when the wages are related to manufacturing, the debit is to Work-in-Process Inventory for direct labor and to Manufacturing Overhead for indirect labor. Thus, in management accounting, it is important to determine first whether salaries are for manufacturing or for nonmanufacturing personnel. Then, for manufacturing personnel, it must be determined whether the individuals worked directly on the product (Work-in-Process Inventory) or indirectly on the product (Manufacturing Overhead). The same is true for other costs such as depreciation and rent. If these costs relate to manufacturing, they are debited to Manufacturing Overhead; costs not related to manufacturing are debited to Depreciation Expense, Rent Expense, and so forth. The manufacturing costs will eventually become expenses when the products are sold (Cost of Goods Sold).

Applied Manufacturing Overhead

It is important to understand that the debit side of the manufacturing overhead account is used to record actual overhead expenses. Conversely, the credit side of this account is used to record applied manufacturing overhead that is simultaneously debited to the work-in-process inventory account, as illustrated in Exhibit 3-5. In essence, this entry transfers the overhead cost from the temporary holding account called Manufacturing Overhead to the asset account called Work-in-Process Inventory.

Actual costs, including actual manufacturing overhead costs, are needed for accurate reporting of annual income and for computing a company's income tax liability at the end of the year. However, the management process of controlling and evaluating costs and setting prices cannot wait until the end of the year. Hence, while both actual and applied manufacturing overhead costs are accounted for constantly throughout the year, actual overhead costs are too sporadic (again, see Exhibit 3-1) to be effectively used for pricing and costing decisions that take place continuously. For this reason, predetermined overhead rates are used to apply overhead throughout the year.

exhibit 3-5 Recording Costs in the Manufacturing Overhead Account

Manufacturing Overhead	
Actual manufacturing overhead costs are entered as debits on a regular basis as they are incurred.	Applied overhead costs are entered as credits as production takes place; costs are applied to Work-in-Process on the basis of a predetermined overhead rate.

Disposition of Over- and Underapplied Manufacturing Overhead

If the beginning-of-the-year estimates of both manufacturing overhead costs *and* the activity basis (e.g., machine hours) are perfect, then at the end of the year the accountants at the Broyman Company will have applied as much overhead to Work-in-Process as was actually incurred, and the ending balance in the manufacturing overhead account will be $0 (this rarely happens). Typically, though, the ending balance in the manufacturing overhead account is not very large. Nevertheless, the manufacturing overhead account is a temporary account that must be closed out at the end of the year. Handling any balance left in Manufacturing Overhead is the process of disposing of over- and underapplied manufacturing overhead.

Note in Exhibit 3-4 that a total of $46,400 in actual costs have been debited to the manufacturing overhead account. To illustrate the accounting for the difference between actual and applied manufacturing overhead costs, we will assume that these costs represent the total actual manufacturing overhead for March 2003. Further, including the work done on the mahogany table in our example, the machining department at Broyman used a total of 1,600 machine hours and applied $17,600 to Work-in-Process Inventory, and the finishing department employed 1,250 direct labor hours and applied $16,250. Finally, the cutting department (using a similar overhead allocation procedure) applied $11,800. At the end of March, the manufacturing overhead account would appear as follows.

Manufacturing Overhead

(Actual costs)	(Applied costs)
20,000	17,600 applied in machining department
15,000	16,250 applied in finishing department
11,400	11,800 applied in cutting department
46,400	45,650
750 balance (underapplied)	

STOP & THINK What would it mean if the debit (actual overhead) and credit (applied overhead) amounts in the manufacturing overhead account were vastly different?

A comparison of the debit and credit sides of the manufacturing overhead account shows that actual manufacturing overhead costs incurred were $750 higher than applied costs. This difference is usually ignored until year-end because management is concerned with immediate decisions, for which current estimates are adequate. At year-end, however, this difference must be accounted for, not only to balance the books, but also to show actual costs in measuring income.

business environment essay

Simplifying Product Costing by Outsourcing One way to simplify operations and product costing is for a company to perform only the core, or strategic, functions inside the company and to outsource all support activities to a network of external companies that specialize in each function. These types of companies, sometimes referred to as virtual corporations, form functional alliances to manufacture products or provide services for customers. The goal of a virtual corporation is to position itself at the center of these relationships and serve as the catalyst that draws these cooperating companies together and organizes how the work will flow. Supposedly, this allows a company to maximize the return from these partnerships while making the minimum investment in permanent staff, fixed assets, and working capital. One such company is **SUPER BAKERY, INC.**, which was formed by former Pittsburgh Steelers' running back Franco Harris in 1983. Super Bakery, Inc., is a supplier of donuts and other

overapplied manufacturing overhead The excess of applied manufacturing overhead (based on a predetermined application rate) over the actual manufacturing overhead costs for a period.

underapplied manufacturing overhead The excess of actual manufacturing overhead costs over the applied overhead costs for a period (based on a predetermined application rate).

If, at the end of the year, total actual manufacturing overhead is less than the amount applied, the account will have a credit balance. This result is referred to as **overapplied manufacturing overhead.** Conversely, if applied manufacturing overhead is less than actual costs, the account will have a debit balance representing **underapplied manufacturing overhead.**

Which is better to have at the end of the year—under- or overapplied overhead? If overhead is underapplied, then the total cost of jobs will be understated. If a company were to price its products in the future based on this understated cost, the company could lose money because it might not cover its actual manufacturing overhead costs. On the other hand, overapplied manufacturing overhead indicates that jobs were overcharged for overhead and costs were overstated. If future pricing decisions were made based on these overstated costs, the company would soon find customers looking elsewhere for more reasonably priced products. Neither under- nor overapplied overhead is desirable. A company's objective is to attempt to anticipate overhead costs and accurately charge those costs to the various jobs.

There are two methods of treating over- and underapplied manufacturing overhead:

1. Close over- or underapplied manufacturing overhead directly to Cost of Goods Sold.
2. Allocate over- or underapplied manufacturing overhead to Work-in-Process Inventory, Finished Goods Inventory, and Costs of Goods Sold on the basis of the ending balances in these three accounts.

The first method is easier and more commonly used, especially if the over- or underapplied amount is small, because it requires only a single entry to correct the amount of manufacturing overhead applied. Let's assume that at year-end, when total actual and applied manufacturing overhead have been recorded, manufacturing overhead for Broyman was overapplied by $1,900. The entry to assign this overapplied manufacturing overhead to Cost of Goods Sold would be:

Manufacturing Overhead.	1,900	
Cost of Goods Sold		1,900
To recognize the excess of applied manufacturing overhead costs over actual manufacturing overhead.		

This entry will decrease the cost of goods sold account for the year by $1,900 and will close out the manufacturing overhead account. Companies that have very small or zero inventory balances would normally charge any over- or underapplied overhead to Cost of Goods Sold.

baked goods to the institutional food market. Since its inception, it has been gaining market share and establishing a firm foothold in the highly competitive institutional baked goods market. Instead of creating a large multifunctional organization to administer the business, the management of Super Bakery outsources selling activities to a network of independent brokers and contracts out manufacturing, warehousing, and shipping processes. Super Bakery handles inhouse the strategic planning, marketing, research and development, and finance/accounting processes. The company also purchases ingredients and formulates and produces its own dough. Super Bakery's product costing problem is significantly reduced by outsourcing so many functions. In essence, Franco Harris is letting other companies worry about many different aspects of product costing.

Source: Tim R.V. Davis and B. L. Darling, "ABC in a Virtual Corporation," *Management Accounting*, October 1996, pp. 18–26.

The second method is more accurate because, theoretically, any difference between applied and actual manufacturing overhead should be allocated proportionately to all items in production during the period. The items in production include those produced and sold (Cost of Goods Sold), those produced and not sold (Finished Goods Inventory), and those still being produced (Work-in-Process Inventory). If the estimate had been accurate, manufacturing overhead costs would have been allocated proportionately to all products. Therefore, those products actually sold should not be burdened with, or relieved of, the entire amount of the estimation error. This alternative is more complicated, however, and requires detailed calculations and several journal entries, so it will not be illustrated here. When differences between actual and applied overhead are small, this more accurate method is usually not worth the extra effort.

to summarize

Actual manufacturing overhead costs are accumulated and debited to Manufacturing Overhead throughout the year. Applied (or estimated) manufacturing overhead costs are assigned to jobs on the basis of a predetermined overhead rate. These costs are credited to Manufacturing Overhead and debited to Work-in-Process Inventory. Any difference between actual and applied manufacturing overhead at the end of the period must be accounted for in order to properly measure income. When total actual manufacturing overhead exceeds total applied overhead, the excess is referred to as underapplied manufacturing overhead. When total applied overhead exceeds total actual overhead, the excess is referred to as overapplied manufacturing overhead. The easiest and most commonly used method of eliminating over- or underapplied manufacturing overhead is to transfer it directly to Cost of Goods Sold. In some cases, the over- or underapplied manufacturing overhead is allocated among Work-in-Process Inventory, Finished Goods Inventory, and Cost of Goods Sold to arrive at a more accurate assignment of costs.

business environment essay

Wholesalers You Never Knew The distribution process that makes it possible for you to purchase a product, such as a car stereo, from a store is complex. The average customer does not give much thought beyond the local retail store. Consumers focus on the reputation of the retail store and the manufacturer instead of the wholesaler that distributes the product.

The Fortune 500 list of top ten wholesalers is shown on the next page. These large, powerful companies tap into numerous facets of the nation's economy.

Most people are familiar with grocery stores such as **ALBERTSON'S** and **SAVE-A-LOT**. But how many people have heard of the wholesaler for these retailers, **SUPERVALU**? SuperValu, one of the nation's top food service distributors, is a major player in the U.S. economy. Even though SuperValu ranks fifth on the list, this wholesaler achieves startling annual revenues of more than $17 billion. It employs over 67,000 people to assist numerous grocery stores with inventory. The company operates approximately 1,100 stores in 38 states. Perhaps a wholesaler like SuperValu should be better known considering its role of supplying grocery stores with the products consumers demand, enabling consumer purchases to take place.

4

Explain the flow of goods and services in a merchandising organization and follow the accumulation of product costs in its accounting system.

channel The distribution line that a product travels from the original manufacturer to the eventual end-user customer. The channel is typically composed of a manufacturer, a wholesaler, a retailer, and the end-user customer.

THE FLOW OF GOODS AND COSTS IN A MERCHANDISING FIRM

For most of us, retailing is the most visible component of a wonderful economic system that has provided great benefits to us for most of our lives. Nevertheless, we probably fail to appreciate that what happens over the last three feet of counter in the store is the culmination of the efforts of a great industrial machine and the related mass distribution system. Similar to the concept of an ecosystem in nature, manufacturers, wholesalers, and retailers are linked together in an economic system called a **channel**. If retailers cannot move goods and services the last three feet into the hands of those who will use them, the whole distribution system of manufacturing, wholesaling, and retailing falls apart.

The Distribution Channel

Exhibit 3-6 illustrates the channel system that typically interrelates manufacturers, wholesalers, and retailers. We've discussed manufacturing operations (the starting point of the channel) and the related management accounting systems. In order to understand the full cycle of business, we now discuss the process of distributing goods to customers. As you can see in Exhibit 3-6, the distribution channel does not prevent retailers from occasionally dealing directly with manufacturers. For example, WAL-MART is noted for its ability to use technology to make direct contact with manufacturers to obtain a significant number of its inventory items. Similarly, some manufacturers may handle some (or even all) of their distribution to retailers. For example, HONDA and FORD work directly with their car dealerships and bypass the wholesalers to distribute their products directly to retailers. Finally, a limited number of manufacturers, particularly small manufacturers, have direct relationships with the ultimate end-user customers of their products. They do this by setting up the well-known factory outlet store or by allowing customers to order directly from them. A good example of this particular distribution approach is DELL COMPUTER CORPORATION. Dell is one of several large personal computer manufacturers in the United States that take orders directly from end-user customers, build computers to customer specifications, then ship the finished computers directly to the customers. The management accounting issues do not change if one member of the distribution channel

Company	Revenues (millions)	Products
MCKESSON CORPORATION	$30,382	Health care products
INGRAMMICRO, INC.	28,069	Microcomputer products
CARDINAL HEALTH, INC.	25,034	Health and beauty care products
SYSCO CORPORATION	17,423	Food service provider
SUPERVALU	17,421	Food service provider
BERGEN BRUNSWIG	17,245	Pharmaceutical products
TECH DATA	16,992	IT products
FLEMING	14,646	Food
AMERISOURCE HEALTH	9,760	Health care products
CHS ELECTRONICS	9,737	Electronics

Source: Fortune 500 Industry List, 2000.

exhibit 3-6 A Typical Channel of Distribution

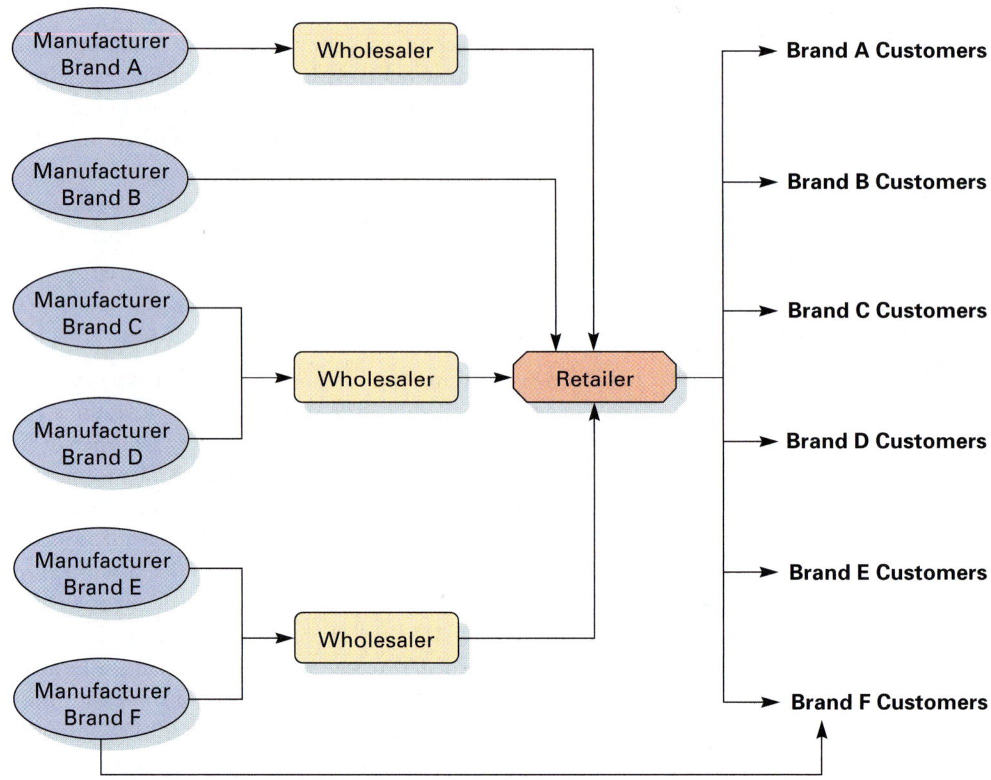

skips over another. Such "skipping" (or vertical integrating) in the chain simply means that the organization must handle a wider variety of management accounting issues. Exhibit 1-1 (page 4 of Chapter 1 of management accounting) shows the successful "skipping" accomplished by **DUPONT** owning nearly its entire distribution chain at the beginning of the twentieth century. Nevertheless, the process of manufacturers selling to wholesalers, wholesalers supplying retailers, and retailers selling to the final customers is the way most distribution works in the United States. We'll assume this to be the case for the rest of this textbook.

For many manufacturers, the only efficient way to get their products into the hands of the customer is through wholesalers and retailers. In a sense, these merchants are "middlemen." Some people argue that the presence of middlemen is economically inefficient and simply adds to the cost of getting products from manufacturers to consumers. In some cases, this is true. The furniture store probably adds to the consumer's cost of buying a rocking chair from our example manufacturer, the Broyman Furniture Company. But the reality is that most customers cannot buy directly from furniture manufacturers. Further, Broyman may not be interested in (nor equipped for) dealing directly with its many customers! Similarly, many retailers (such as your local grocery store) are not in a position to deal directly with the manufacturers of the items they sell to the public. On the other hand, some retailers can deal directly with manufacturers, but feel that dealing directly is more costly. A retailer may reap great benefits by using a wholesaler as a middleman between itself and the manufacturers. Wholesalers may be able to provide the retailer such things as next-day delivery, unlimited returns, expert advice on merchandise selection, and customized product mix. If the cost of using a wholesaler is less than the cost to the retailers of providing these services for themselves, then the use of a middleman makes good economic sense. Hence, in providing important options, services, and convenience, wholesalers and retailers can actually add to the efficiency of the distribution system and decrease costs for the ultimate consumer. In terms of costs, this is how merchants compete in the marketplace. Management accountants help merchandising companies carefully manage the costs of obtaining and distributing inventory. If costs become too high, then the merchant's customers may either go to a competitor to obtain the goods or skip over the middleman to negotiate directly with the supplier.

wholesalers Top-tier merchants who typically deal directly with the original manufacturers to distribute products to retailers.

logistics The management process involved in obtaining, managing, and transporting inventory and other assets in organizations.

Inventory Flow in the Distribution Channel

Spend a few minutes studying Exhibit 3-7. This exhibit shows the basic layout of a typical wholesaler's operation and a retailer's operation. Although the layouts of operations vary for both retailers and wholesalers, this exhibit will help us visualize the process of moving inventory from manufacturers into the hands of the ultimate end-user.

WHOLESALERS Let's begin with wholesalers. **Wholesalers** generally work within a particular industry (e.g., vegetable produce, running shoes, or calculators) to secure distribution contracts with a few key manufacturers. They receive goods in huge bulk shipments that they then break down for smaller shipments to retailers. This is a lot of inventory to manage, and a lot of money is at risk. Obviously, wholesalers will not make a profit unless there is a difference between the price at which they buy goods from manufacturers and the price at which they sell goods to retailers. However, the wholesaling process is much more involved than simply managing the cost of buying and selling goods. Quality and timelines are also important performance measures that are critical to successful wholesale management. Not only must wholesalers negotiate profitable contracts with manufacturers, but they must then handle the **logistics** of transporting those goods long distances to multiple retail locations. This requires wholesalers to work closely with large transportation companies to both receive and ship out goods as quickly and inexpensively as possible. To help control transportation costs and make the process as timely as possible, wholesalers often locate their distribution centers near large transit hubs such as train yards, shipping docks, airports, and major freeways. Usually, these distribution centers are very large buildings with little advertisement of their business to passersby. If you happen to live or travel near a large transit hub, see if you can spot these giant distribution warehouses, typically surrounded by lots of trucks, trains, or ships.

Managing the transportation of goods is not the only thing that wholesalers do. Manufacturers typically ship their goods in large bulk containers such as railway cars. Retailers, on the other hand, often require much smaller shipments. As a result, the logistics of the wholesale business will require many wholesalers to expand their distribution centers to include large areas where the manufacturers' shipping units can be opened and the goods repackaged for transportation to retail customers. Look at the wholesaler depicted in Exhibit 3-7. The large shipping crates received from manufacturers must be opened (or "broken down") and the goods designated for individual retailers (a process called "picking and packaging"). The process of repackaging goods for shipment to retailers often includes checks on both the quality of the goods and the accuracy of the packaged order. The key to success for wholesalers is to be sure that the right goods are received and shipped in the right manner to the right retailer for the right price at the right time.

fyi

Electronic Data Interchange (EDI) is a specialized computer link between companies that tremendously increases the efficiency with which companies can exchange the information necessary to handle supply transactions. WAL-MART, for example, requires all of its suppliers to use EDI links to tailor production and delivery of inventory to Wal-Mart stores based on customer demand. Recently, Wal-Mart has enabled its suppliers to monitor how each product is performing through real-time reports via the Internet. Using EDI, Wal-Mart has been able to reduce the time it takes to initiate a purchase, receive inventory, and pay the supplier from several weeks to just a few days. As a result of the collaborated effort, Wal-Mart is able to maintain an average level of inventory much lower than many of its competitors, resulting in increased return on investment (ROI).

Source: M. Cleary, "Wal-Mart Updates Supply System," *Interactive Week*, October 23, 2000. http://www.interactiveweek.com.

RETAILERS The business process for retailers is probably quite familiar to you. Most **retailers** place orders with and receive shipments from wholesalers. Because retailers need to provide a large variety of goods to their customers, they must often work with a large number of wholesalers (and, in some cases, manufacturers) to obtain their desired mix of inventory. As shown in the floor plan in Exhibit 3-7, many retailers have a receiving dock and a breakdown area used to prepare goods for display on their sales floor. Some retailers also keep a stock room for holding excess inventory. However, the cost of holding inventory in today's competitive environment is causing retailers to demand that wholesalers provide smaller and more frequent shipments. As a result, many retailers are able to avoid having a stock room. Inventory in these companies can then be moved directly from the breakdown area onto the sales floor.

retailers Second-tier merchants who typically purchase products from wholesalers to distribute to end-user customers. Many large retailers, however, often bypass wholesalers to purchase products directly from the original manufacturers.

Like wholesalers, retailers invest a lot of money in their inventory. Also similar to wholesalers, the big risk in the retailing business is having money tied up in inventory that is not selling. Obviously, having inventory is important to a retailer's business, but holding on to inventory for too long usually results in a significant opportunity cost. For example, as long as a shoe retailer has its money currently invested in a large inventory of running shoes, it is unable to use that money to purchase basketball shoes. These opportunity costs become particularly painful

exhibit 3-7 A Comparison of the Floor Plans for a Wholesaler and a Retailer

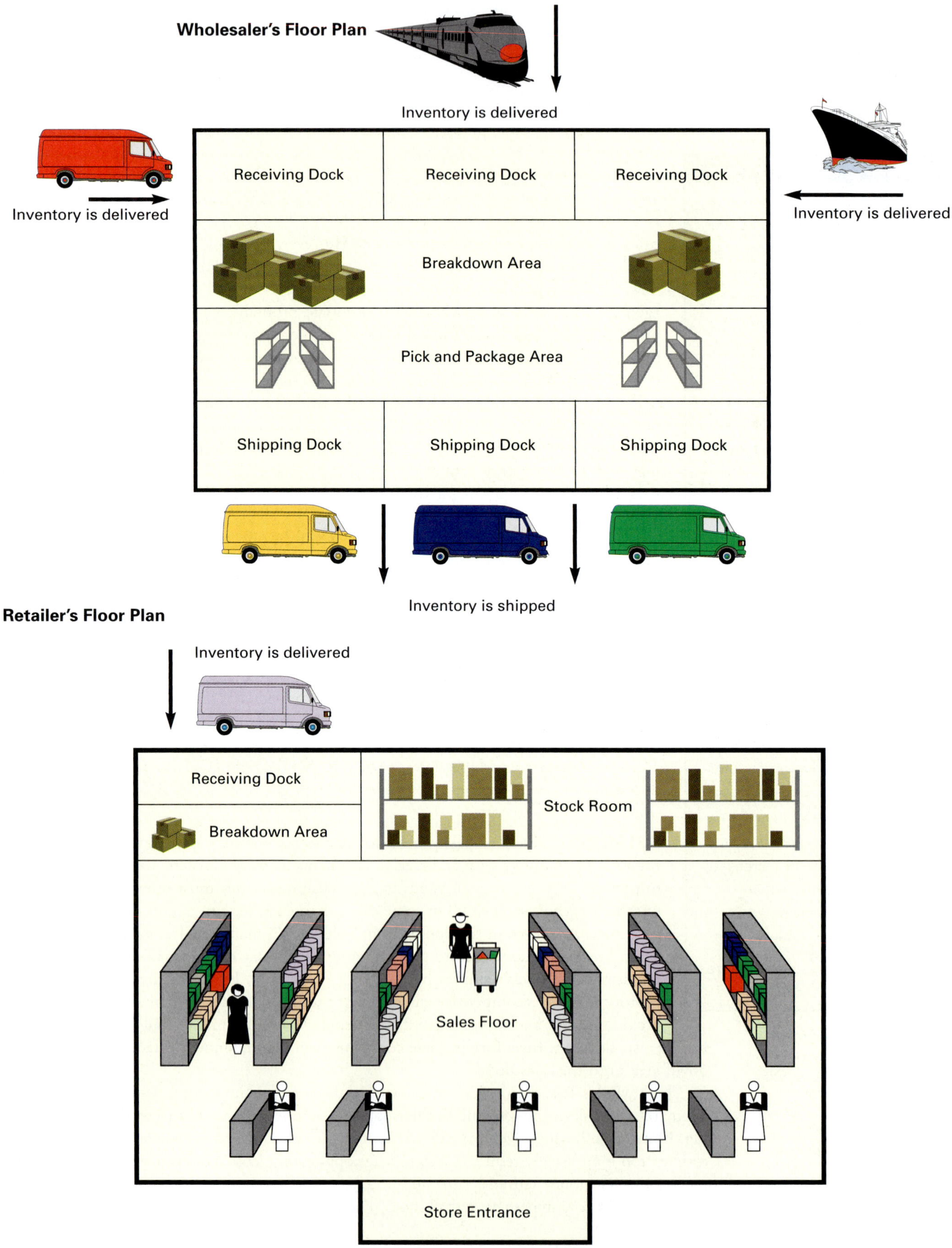

net work

Some retailers do not have a physical store location where customers come to shop. Instead, they have created a virtual store on the Internet. One of the most successful examples of a retailer that exists solely in the virtual economy is **AMAZON BOOKS**. A brief tour of its virtual bookstore is quite impressive. Access the Web site for Amazon Books at **http://www.amazon.com/books**. What is the "Amazon Top 100" list? What book currently sits atop this list?

when the retailer is unable to sell its inventory of running shoes during the running season and, as a result, lacks the money to purchase basketball shoe inventory in time for the basketball season. This is why management accountants in the merchandising business are so focused on measuring stockturns. The faster you can turn your stock (i.e., inventory), the sooner you have the money available to purchase more inventory to sell. Obviously, retailers are just as concerned as wholesalers with the cost and timeliness involved in managing inventory. Further, given the demanding nature of today's informed consumer, management accountants must also provide retail managers with information on inventory quality. We'll talk more about the opportunity costs of holding inventory too long in Chapter 6 of management accounting.

Product Cost Accumulation in Merchandising Organizations

The bulk of this chapter so far has focused on manufacturing companies and how management accountants accumulate costs for these organizations. Traditionally, accounting textbooks have not gone much beyond manufacturing to discuss how management accounting works in merchandising and service organizations. This may have been appropriate given that manufacturing used to dominate the U.S. economy. However, as we have discussed in previous chapters, manufacturing is no longer the dominant type of business today. Merchandising and service organizations continue to increase their prevalence in the world economy. Although both merchandising and service organizations borrow much of their management accounting from the manufacturing industry, there are some important differences. Many of these differences result from the need to support management decision processes in merchandising and service organizations that are very different from the decision processes required in the manufacturing business.

INVENTORY FLOW AND THE INCOME STATEMENT In contrast to accounting for manufacturing businesses, the flow of costs through the merchandising accounting system is relatively simple. Examine Exhibit 3-8 and compare it to Exhibit 3-4 on page 120. Notice how simple the flow of inventory costs is in Exhibit 3-8. Essentially, accounting for inventory in merchandising organizations is a fairly straightforward process. There are no raw materials inventory, manufacturing overhead, or work-in-process inventory accounts. Merchandise inventory, by definition, is essentially complete and ready for sale when purchased. Hence, the cost of purchased inventory is debited to Merchandise Inventory throughout the year as it is acquired.[5] Conceptually, the inventory costs for a merchant should also include all costs required to purchase the inventory, transport it to the merchant's place of business, and ready it for sale (unpacking, displaying, etc.). Hence, the inventory cost should include the purchase price, shipping costs (freight in), insurance while in transit, administrative costs incurred by the merchant related to purchasing and handling activities, and storage costs prior to sale. In practice, though, most of these overhead-related costs, other than freight in costs, are difficult to allocate to specific inventory items. As a result, overhead costs related to merchandise inventory are often expensed as a period cost and included in Selling and General Administrative Expenses.

As inventory is sold, the cost of inventory is credited from Merchandise Inventory and debited to Cost of Goods Sold. When customers return merchandise that can be resold, Cost of Goods Sold is credited and the inventory account is debited (if the returned merchandise cannot be resold, then nothing happens in either of these particular accounts).

Tracking inventory costs in a merchant's accounting system may appear to be a fairly easy conceptual process. However, developing useful information on merchandise inventory for managers who need to plan, control, and evaluate inventory and inventory costs is a bit more involved. As the successful merchants learned historically, the key to profits is stockturns. Managing merchandise inventory is a significant topic for Chapter 6 of management accounting.

5 Recall that this method of continuously debiting and crediting Merchandise Inventory as inventory is purchased and sold (and debiting Cost of Goods Sold as inventory is sold) is called the *perpetual* inventory method of accounting. The alternative to the perpetual method is the *periodic* inventory method. There are several more accounts involved with the periodic inventory method, including Purchases, Purchase Discounts, and Purchase Returns. A significant difference between the perpetual and periodic inventory methods is that the periodic inventory method adjusts Merchandise Inventory *only at the end* of each period when cost of goods sold is calculated for the income statement.

exhibit 3-8 Flow of Product Costs in a Merchant's Cost Accounting System

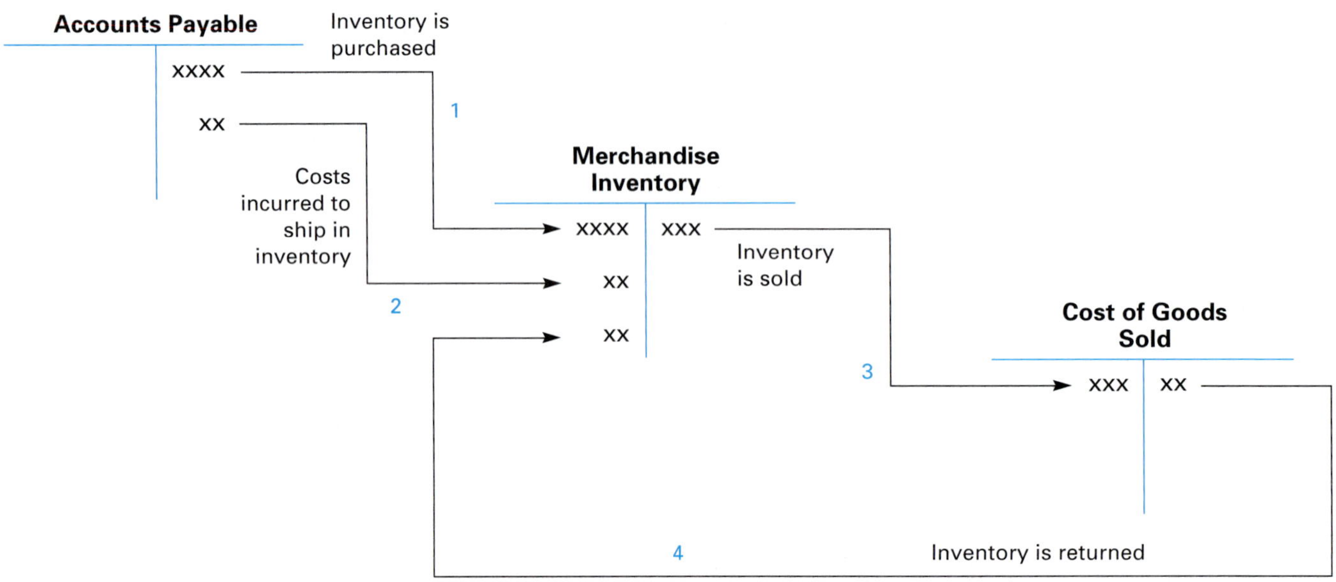

Journal entries:

1	Merchandise Inventory	XXXX		3	Cost of Goods Sold	XXX	
	Accounts Payable		XXXX		Merchandise Inventory		XXX
	Purchased inventory for sale.				*Sold inventory to customers.*		
2	Merchandise Inventory	XX		4	Merchandise Inventory	XX	
	Accounts Payable		XX		Cost of Goods Sold		XX
	*Incurred freight in costs on purchased inventory.**				*Inventory is returned by customers.*		

**Note:* Freight in is considered part of the purchase cost and should be added to inventory, eventually to be split between Cost of Goods Sold and the ending balance in Merchandise Inventory as goods are sold. In practice, the entire cost of freight in for a period is often simply debited directly to Cost of Goods Sold.

to summarize

Merchants are interconnected with manufacturers in a distribution channel that basically involves manufacturers selling to large-scale wholesalers, who then sell to retailers, who then sell to the end-user customer. Managing the movement (i.e., logistics) of inventory across the distribution channel is a critical business activity. Because wholesalers and retailers generally do not have to deal with raw materials or work in process, the process of accounting for inventory in a merchandising business is not nearly as complicated as it is in a manufacturing business. However, *managing* inventory costs (discussed in Chapter 6) is both complicated and critical for a merchant.

5
Explain the flow of goods and services in a service organization and follow the accumulation of product costs in its accounting system.

THE FLOW OF SERVICES AND COSTS IN SERVICE COMPANIES

So far in this chapter we have defined and discussed the nature of manufacturing and merchandising businesses and identified examples of companies in each type of business. The third type of business is service. What is a service business? Frankly, this is a rather difficult question. Simply stated, the service industry in the United States generally comprises all businesses that cannot be classified as merchandising or manufacturing (this assumes that we classify organizations that convert natural resources into useful products, such as farming or mining, as manufacturers). This is obviously a simple definition, but it is not very useful for us. It is important to more precisely define the service industry because nonmerchandising/nonmanufacturing businesses are the largest and fastest-growing sector in our economy. Hence, it is more likely that your career will involve working with service businesses than any other business type. For our purposes, we'll define a service business as follows:

> A service business is any organization whose main economic activity involves producing a nonphysical product that provides value to a customer.

The definition sounds pretty academic, but it needs to cover a lot of conceptual ground. As you'll see in the list in Exhibit 3-9, there is a lot of variety in the specific types of organizations that are neither merchandising nor manufacturing. As you study Exhibit 3-9, try to apply our definition of a service business to each of these categories and see if the definition fits.

Effects of Deregulation

Not very long ago, many service organizations were not nearly as concerned about cost management as they are today. Increasing global competition has put tremendous pressure on manufacturers and merchants to continuously improve their ability to compete on costs, quality, and time. In contrast, the nature of most service businesses means that they face little in the way of foreign-based competition. Nevertheless, it is becoming increasingly more important for service businesses to develop useful management accounting systems that support strategic imperatives of managing costs, quality, and timelines in creating and delivering a service product. The reason for this increased competition for service industries is really quite interesting. Prior to the 1980s, the communications, banking, health-care, utilities, and transportation industries were subject to tremendous government regulation. Even some professional services, such as accounting and legal services that have been essentially unregulated by government agencies, were more self-regulated than they are today. This self-regulation had the effect of discouraging competition by limiting the way these professionals could advertise their services. As a result of this regulation, most service-oriented companies were essentially sheltered. Government regulators restricted entry by low-cost suppliers and set prices in relationship to overall costs so that a minimum return on investment (ROI) could be earned. Essentially, prices were set to cover the least efficient producer. Self-regulation restricted information in the marketplace so that consumers were not well equipped to compare quality and price of services. **Deregulation** in the service sector has now changed the pricing and profitability picture for many industries. Now the most efficient producers establish

deregulation The term used to describe the process of removing restrictions on competition in the marketplace for a particular industry.

exhibit 3-9 Categories of Service Businesses

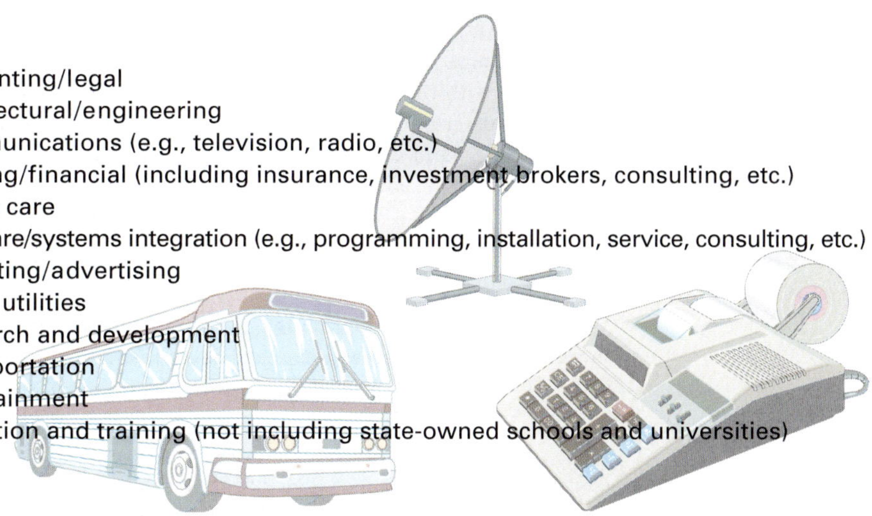

- Accounting/legal
- Architectural/engineering
- Communications (e.g., television, radio, etc.)
- Banking/financial (including insurance, investment brokers, consulting, etc.)
- Health care
- Software/systems integration (e.g., programming, installation, service, consulting, etc.)
- Marketing/advertising
- Public utilities
- Research and development
- Transportation
- Entertainment
- Education and training (not including state-owned schools and universities)

Source: Adapted from O. B. Martinson, *Cost Accounting in the Service Industry: A Critical Assessment* (Montvale, N.J.: Institute of Management Accountants, 1989).

business environment essay

Union Pacific Had a Tough Year in 1996 Ineffective management of a single prominent service company can have catastrophic effects on the rest of the nation. In 1996, **UNION PACIFIC**, the nation's largest railway company, purchased **SOUTHERN PACIFIC RAIL CORPORATION**. Combining the service operations of these two companies turned out to be a lot more difficult than Union Pacific had anticipated. The operational problems resulting from the merger caused financial and production distress for numerous companies that depended on the railway industry as a primary means of transportation.

Stalled cars that caused trains to sit in limbo, congested lines that limited train movement, and shortages of crew members and locomotives were just a few of the problems Union Pacific faced as it worked to merge the two railway services. Every day, thousands of railroad cars failed to arrive at their destinations. Shipments that used to be delivered by Union Pacific in one week were taking two or three weeks. The economic effects of the clogged 36,000-mile system included factory production slowdowns and depleted inventory stock in stores. As a result, manufacturers' and merchants' costs rose as they switched to more expensive forms of delivery or halted production to wait for deliveries. As a result of delayed deliveries to its Michigan assembly plant, **FORD MO-**

prices. Today, service providers who don't know their costs will not be able to aggressively set prices, be responsive to consumer demands, and make enough money to stay in business.

Comparing Service and Manufacturing Business Activities

Service companies actually share more similarities with manufacturing companies than with merchandising companies. In this section, we will discuss the similarities of and the differences between service and manufacturing firms.

SIMILARITIES BETWEEN SERVICE AND MANUFACTURING FIRMS As you now understand, merchants purchase goods from manufacturers in finished condition. As a result, inventory in merchandising companies requires little, if any, conversion cost before being sold to customers. Inventory costs used to determine cost of goods sold on the merchant's income statement are relatively easy to determine. On the other hand, like manufacturers, most service companies perform a significant number of activities to prepare their service products for sale and delivery to their customers. Typically, a lot of direct labor and overhead is involved in a service business. Hence, the management process in service organizations shares a number of similarities with the process of managing a manufacturing business. Consider the following fundamental description of a service company; think about the similarities between this management process and what you now understand about the management process in manufacturing.

> A service organization identifies a need in the economy for which customers are willing to pay. Satisfying this need profitably involves creating a high-quality product that must be delivered in a timely manner while keeping costs low. The creative process often requires that the organization make investments in highly paid skilled labor or expensive capital equipment and buildings (or both!). In addition, a sophisticated management structure is important in order to effectively plan, control, and evaluate labor or equipment activities. Determining the total cost of the service product will require that a large amount of overhead be allocated to the direct service provided to the customer.

TOR COMPANY shut down factory lines for two days, causing a loss in the production of 600 cars. Even farmers in Nebraska became concerned about running out of molasses to feed their cattle.

Faced with the enormous task of fixing the mess created by the merger with Southern Pacific, executives at Union Pacific set forth a plan that would incrementally improve customer service, systems and facilities, safety, and efficiency. For example, throughout 1998, Union Pacific vigorously worked on expanding its capacity. Building new rail lines alleviated the "traffic jams" its locomotives were facing; this directly improved customer service and helped Union Pacific regain the confidence of its customers. These improvements did not come without significant capital expenditures that hurt operating margins, however.

Has Union Pacific's incremental plan worked? The company improved its net income from a *negative* $633 million in 1998 to a *positive* $842 million in 2000. During the implementation of the plan, Union Pacific's executives saw the company's stock price rise from $34.25 a share to $53.20 in February 2001. After the messy merger, it appears that Union Pacific is back on track and chugging along!

Sources: "Union Pacific Tie-Ups Reach across Economy," *Wall Street Journal*, October 8, 1997, pp. B1, B16; "Union Pacific Claims over Delays," *Wall Street Journal*, October 10, 1997, pp. A3, A6; Union Pacific home page at http://www.up.com.

The description sounds quite familiar, doesn't it? Most service companies engage in a very real production activity. However, what they provide is not nearly as tangible as the product provided by manufacturers. Yes, an architect or engineer does provide a tangible set of drawings or blueprints. But what is really being sold is the knowledge and customized advice that is represented by drawings. Public utilities provide heating or lighting that can be considered tangible in terms of watts or BTUs. What they are really selling, though, is the service of lighting or heating your home or business.

Service companies essentially build a product (the service) and deliver it to the customer (versus a merchant that resells a product built by another company). Consider the organizational effort required for a CPA firm to provide an audit service to a client. This organization is depicted in Exhibit 3-10. As you can see, there is direct labor (the auditing staff) involved in this audit that is supported by a complex system of supervisors, supplies, equipment, capital assets, and so forth. This support system essentially forms the overhead costs of the audit product, and these overhead costs will need to be appropriately allocated as part of the product cost of the audit. You can see, then, that there are many similarities between the process of manufacturing and service companies.

caution

When trying to decide whether a company is in the service business, consider the following old joke:

A plumber is called out to fix a clogged pipe. The plumber examines the situation for a few seconds, then pulls out a hammer and taps on the offending pipe. The problem is solved. However, the customer is a bit upset upon receiving the bill for $100.17. "All you did was tap on the pipe. I demand an itemized bill!" the customer complains. So, the plumber sends the following itemized bill:

Tapping on pipe	$ 0.17
Knowing where to tap	100.00
Total	$100.17

Remember that expertise is a significant component of most service companies.

DIFFERENCES BETWEEN SERVICE AND MANUFACTURING FIRMS Some service organizations do sound as though they are really in the manufacturing business. Notwithstanding, there are some important differences between most service and manufacturing businesses that affect the information provided by management accountants. For example, the use of distribution channels is not nearly as prevalent in the service sector. Whereas manufacturers are dependent on merchants to distribute their products to the final customers, most service businesses deal directly with the end-user customer. Also, there is probably a lot more customization in the service process than in the manufacturing process. Hence, most service businesses use a job order approach rather than a process approach to cost accounting (with some exceptions, such as public utilities). Additionally, very little raw material is involved in the process of converting labor or capital equipment into a service product (again, some public utilities will be the exception here, e.g., coal-burning power plants). Note, though, that items such as paper and syringes are sometimes included as part of the delivered service, but these items are not the main focus of what the customer is paying to

exhibit 3-10 The Service Process at a CPA Firm

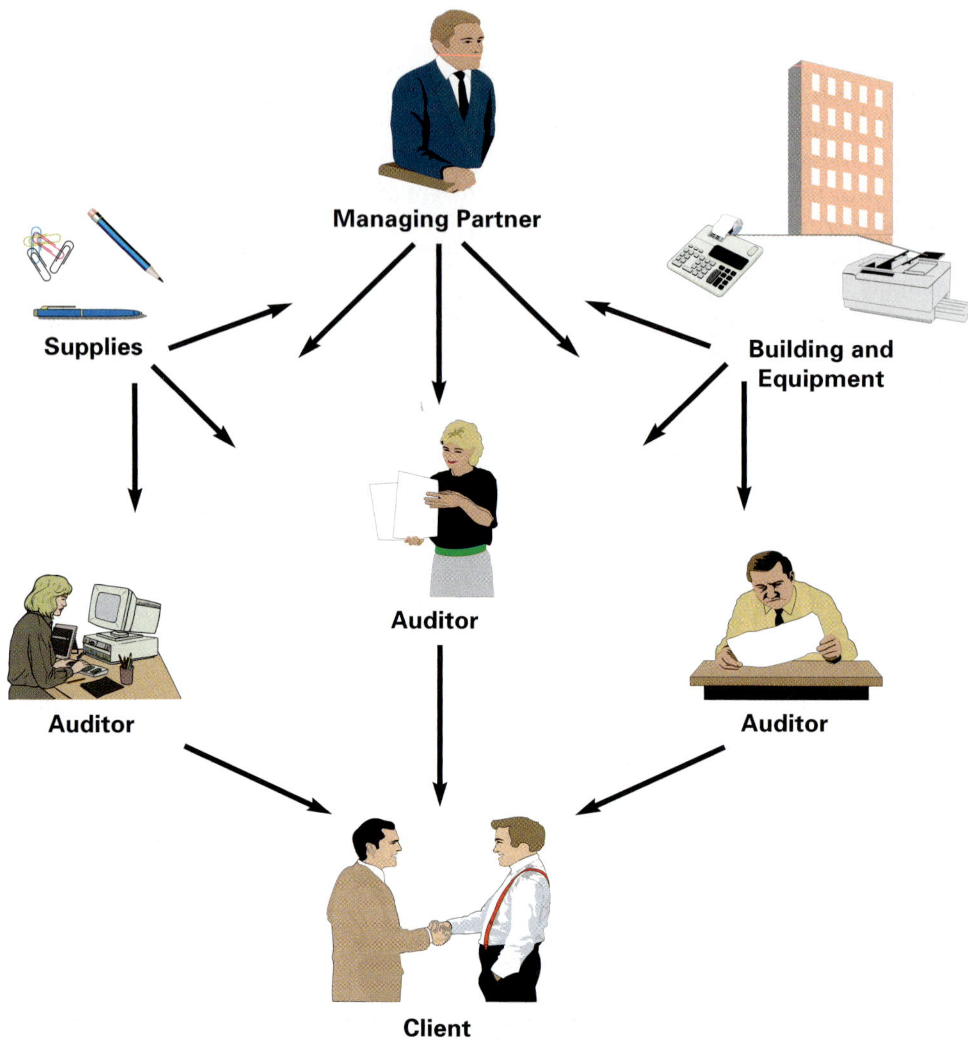

receive. As a result, raw material inventories are insignificant or nonexistent in a service business. Similarly, it is often difficult to store a finished service in anticipation of a later sale to customers, making finished goods inventories insignificant or nonexistent. At the close of a reporting period, however, most service companies will be in the process of completing a service for delivery to a customer. This suggests that work-in-process inventories exist and may be significant for many service organizations. (We will discuss work-in-process inventories further below.)

As you can see, defining a service business can be challenging. Don't worry too much about being able to perfectly identify every organization as either a manufacturer or a service business. An overall familiarity with the basic differences and similarities between service, manufacturing, and merchandising businesses will help in determining the relevant management accounting that adds competitive value as managers work to plan, control, and evaluate operations.

Product Cost Accumulation in Service Organizations

As you now understand, there are a number of accounting similarities between manufacturing and service organizations. The most important similarity is that both manufacturing and service organizations use a significant amount of direct labor in producing their products. In addition, large amounts of overhead costs typically are allocated to individual products. Similar to many manufacturers, service businesses often allocate overhead on the basis of direct labor hours. One

> **fyi**
>
> Over the past 100 years, costs for raw materials in manufacturing firms have averaged nearly 50% of total product costs.

important difference is that manufacturers must also manage large amounts of raw materials costs, while the materials included in the services sold by service companies are typically limited to insignificant amounts of supplies used in the service process.

"INVENTORY" FLOW AND THE INCOME STATEMENT IN SERVICE COMPANIES Exhibit 3-11 summarizes the flow of costs for a service company. Comparing Exhibit 3-11 to Exhibits 3-4 and 3-8 illustrates that accounting for service cost flows can be more complicated than accounting for merchandise inventory cost flows, but is quite similar to accounting for manufacturing cost flows. Materials (e.g., supplies), labor, and overhead costs are all involved in, and should be assigned to, the process of creating and delivering a service product to the customer.

The overhead for service firms can involve nearly any kind of management costs—service firms generally do not distinguish between manufacturing and administrative overhead costs. Allocating overhead to service activities generally involves factoring an overhead rate into the billing rate used to charge customers. Think about all the services you buy and use. Often some type

exhibit 3-11 Summary of Service Cost Flows

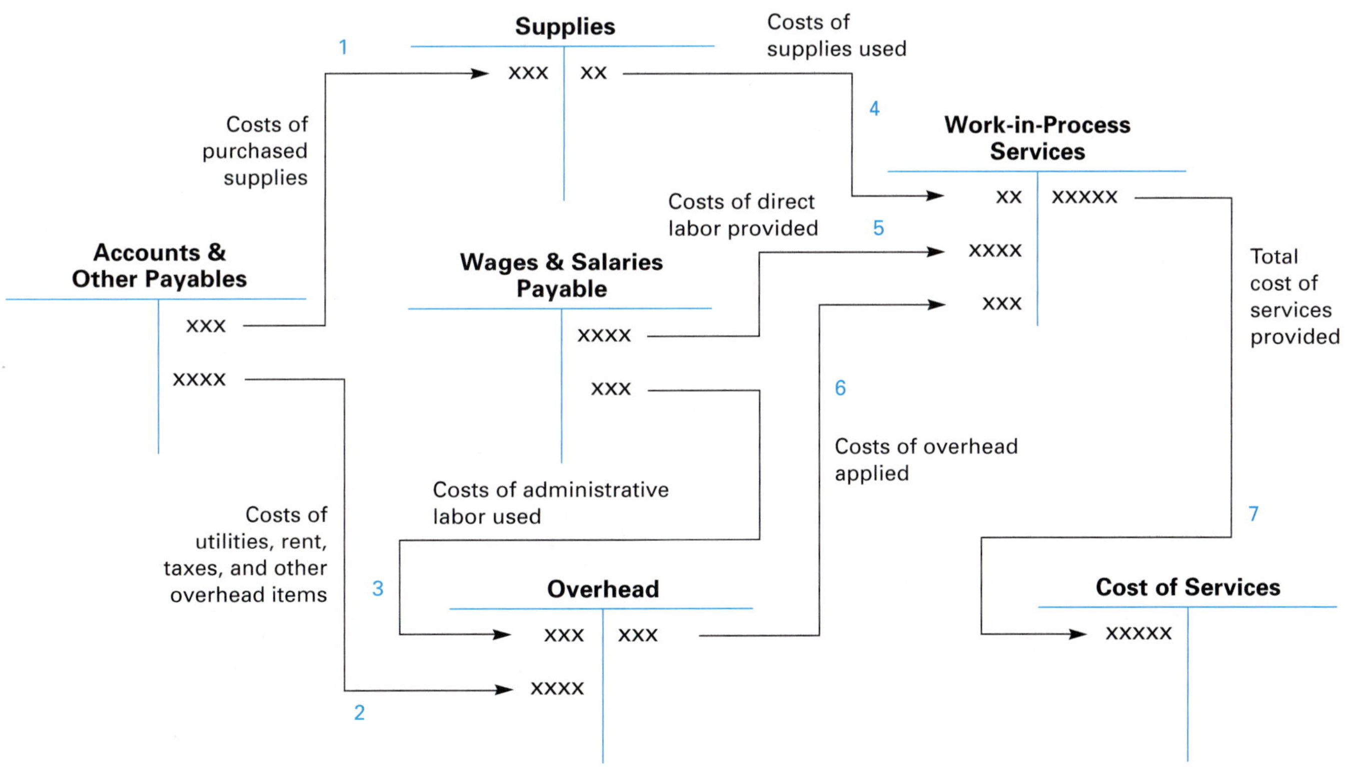

Journal entries:

1 Supplies	xxx	
Accounts & Other Payables		xxx
Supplies are purchased.		
2 Overhead	xxxx	
Accounts & Other Payables		xxxx
Overhead costs are recognized.		
3 Overhead	xxx	
Wages & Salaries Payable		xxx
Administrative labor costs are recognized.		
4 Work-in-Process Services	xx	
Supplies		xx
Supplies are used in service activities.		
5 Work-in-Process Services	xxxx	
Wages & Salaries Payable		xxxx
Direct labor is used in service activities.		
6 Work-in-Process Services	xxx	
Overhead		xxx
Overhead is applied to service activities.		
7 Cost of Services	xxxxx	
Work-in-Process Services		xxxxx
Services are completed and billed out.		

of a billing rate per hour or per event is used to determine the price you pay for the service. For example, accountants, lawyers, consultants, programmers, and repair shops often charge by the hour. When you get the bill, you understand that the huge rate per hour does not represent solely the wage or salary of the professional who provided a service to you. This rate has been enhanced (sometimes significantly!) in order to cover all the overhead and supplies costs necessary to support the work done by the service professional. Similarly, doctors, trainers, entertainers, and transportation companies usually charge by event. You understand that the doctor isn't paid the full $175 charge when he or she gives you a physical exam. Much of that amount goes to pay for the costs of staff, equipment, and building occupancy necessary to support the actual service provided by your doctor.

Assigning overhead costs to a service event follows a pattern very similar to that for manufacturing firms. Total overhead for the service organization is estimated for a period of time, generally a year. This estimated overhead is then divided by an appropriate activity measure. For an accountant, this activity measure may be billable hours. The measure for a bank could be the number of teller transactions or number of accounts. For a cable TV company, it could be the average number of accounts expected for the year. The activity measure for an electric company might be the expected number of kilowatts produced during the next year. Other examples of possible overhead rate calculations for several types of service companies are shown below.

STOP & THINK The selection of the activity base that is used to allocate overhead is a very important management decision because any particular activity base could have a significant impact on how much cost is assigned to one product versus another. For example, suppose that the academic advisement center at your college is trying to determine what it costs to provide advisement services to a specific student each semester. What are some possible activity bases this department might use to allocate the costs of the office equipment, supervisor salary, and other overhead items? Would your choice of a base have an effect on which students are then identified as "high-cost-to-serve" students?

With a predetermined overhead rate, service companies are able to allocate overhead costs to service events as they occur. This method of allocating overhead helps managers control overhead costs, establish prices for services provided, and measure profit on each service event or contract. The overhead account for a service company is used in much the same manner as in a manufacturing firm. As actual overhead costs are incurred, they are debited to the overhead account rather than being debited to an expense account. Then, as the appropriate overhead activities actually take place (e.g., consulting hours, teller transactions, and kilowatts), overhead costs are allocated to Work-in-Process Services (more about this account in the next section). As services are actually billed, these overhead costs are combined with the direct labor costs of the service professionals (if any) and any incidental costs of supplies and debited to Cost of Services (an account very similar to the cost of goods sold account used by manufacturers and merchants). At the end of the year (or any other time period relevant to the company), the total actual overhead costs are compared to the total allocated overhead costs to determine an over- or underapplied overhead amount. If overhead is overapplied, there will be a credit balance in the service company's overhead account. This balance means that too much overhead cost was allocated to the cost of service activities. The overapplied costs are removed (and the overhead account is closed) with the following entry:

Overhead	xxx	
Cost of Services		xxx

If overhead is underapplied, then there will be a debit balance in the overhead account, and Cost of Services is adjusted (increased) by closing the overhead account with the following entry:

Cost of Services	xxx	
Overhead		xxx

Similar to manufacturing firms, the service company may choose to apportion the over- or underapplied overhead amount between Cost of Services and Work-in-Process Services. The question you might be asking at this point is, "Why would a service organization have a work-in-process inventory account?" Good question! We'll talk about this account next.

WHO HAS WORK-IN-PROCESS INVENTORY? In manufacturing companies, accounting for work-in-process inventory is a significant part of the product cost accounting effort. Costs of resources used in the process of creating a product are attached to that product. Typically, at the end of an income period (e.g., a month, a quarter, or a year), a number of products are still in process. A significant amount of costs can be tied up in these in-process products. GAAP requires that these costs be capitalized (identified as assets) and assigned to the balance sheet until the products are actually sold. Only at the time that goods are sold and revenue is recognized can the related costs be charged to the income statement. The basic underlying accounting concept behind this approach is the all-important matching principle.

The logic for identifying work-in-process inventory as a balance sheet asset applies to both manufacturing and service businesses. Service companies typically earn revenue as the service is provided to the customer. At the end of an accounting period, however, significant effort and resources may have been invested in a service product that is not yet completed for the customer. As a result, revenue is not yet earned, and the costs invested at this point should not be recognized as expenses. In other words, until they actually complete the project and bill it to the client, service companies have work in process.

The following are some examples of work in process that are likely to exist at the end of an accounting period for various types of service companies:[6]

- Accounting/legal—An audit that will take three months to complete is in its initial stage.
- Architectural/engineering—The blueprints for a large construction project are only partially completed.
- Banking/financial—The fieldwork has been completed and the lending documents are being finalized for a large loan that will be closed next month.
- Marketing/advertising—Three weeks of effort have been expended on the development of a new advertising campaign that will not be ready for presentation to the client for another three weeks.
- Transportation—A large shipment of coal is being held in a midwestern freight yard en route to its shipping point on the East Coast.

In each of these examples, resources have been invested in creating a service that the customer has not yet received. As a result, work in process exists and should be recognized on the balance sheet. As you can see in Exhibit 3-11, as supplies and labor costs are directly invested in the process of creating a service for customers, these amounts are debited to Work-in-Process Services. As overhead costs such as utilities, rent, taxes, and support staff salaries are incurred, these costs are debited to the overhead account and are subsequently allocated to Work-in-Process Services using an overhead rate. When the service is completed and delivered to the customer, then the revenue earning process is complete and the service costs are transferred out of Work-in-Process Services and into Cost of Services.[7]

6 O. B. Martinson, *Cost Accounting in the Service Industry: A Critical Assessment* (Montvale, N.J.: Institute of Management Accountants, 1989), pp. 47–48.

7 Some fairly large long-term service contracts are sometimes designed to allow the provider to bill and receive partial payments as the contract is completed. In these cases, as the revenue process is partially completed, some service costs can be transferred out of Work-in-Process Services and into Cost of Services. Learning about this type of accounting is reserved for more advanced accounting courses.

business environment essay

The Birth of an e-Business Jeffrey P. Bezos quit his lucrative job with a New York investment firm and moved his family to Seattle, Washington, to start a new company in a new industry. A short time later, on July 16, 1995, **AMAZON.COM**, the largest e-tailer in the world in 2001, opened its Web doors. After having 300 of his friends and family members test the site, Jeff asked them to tell everyone they knew about Amazon.com. Within 30 days, with no press or traditional advertising, Amazon.com had sold books in all 50 states and 45 countries—an instant Web success! How did this all begin?

Amazon.com began as a bookseller over the Internet that offered competitive prices, accessibility, and extreme convenience. It was readily apparent to Bezos, as his book-selling Web site grew exceptionally fast, that Amazon.com could become the "Earth's Biggest Store." In 1998, Amazon.com offered its first product other than books—music CDs. From there, Amazon.com has expanded into videos, DVD movies, toys, hardware, greeting cards, electronics, software, home improvement products, auctions, and more. How does Amazon.com manage this huge distribution channel?

With more than 2 million unique visitors a month currently, Amazon.com has established a highly au-

to summarize

Essentially, a service business is any organization whose main economic activity involves producing a nonphysical product that provides value to a customer. As service industries have been deregulated in the last few decades, the increased competition has forced these companies to develop better cost management. Because service companies generally create the service they provide, they have some similarities with manufacturing companies in both the management and the accounting processes, including the need to manage and account for work in process. A major difference between service and manufacturing operations is that raw materials typically are not a significant component of a service company's product. Costs flow through a service firm in a manner very similar to a manufacturing firm. Costs of supplies (usually insignificant in size) and direct labor (usually significant in size) accumulate in an account called Work-in-Process Services. This account performs much the same function as a work-in-process inventory account in a manufacturing firm. In addition, overhead must often be applied to Work-in-Process Services as service activities take place. The process of applying overhead is typically done using a predetermined overhead application rate.

6
Understand the impact of e-business on product costing.

THE EFFECT OF E-BUSINESS

Before we conclude the main part of this chapter, we should say a little about the impact of e-business on business organizations and the product costing process.[8] First of all, it is important to understand that e-business is not a separate new industry like manufacturing, merchandising, or service. Rather, e-business provides new platforms for conducting business *within* the current industries in the economy.

8 Some of the material in this section is based on information presented in S. M. Glover, S. W. Liddle, and D. F. Prawitt, *eBusiness: Principles & Strategies for Accountants* (Upper Saddle River, N.J.: Prentice Hall, 2001).

tomated system that prides itself on discovering and satisfying customer needs. In addition, the Amazon system must maintain a critical relationship with manufacturers and suppliers. One glitch in the system could spell disaster for the company and its end-users (us!). The life of an order begins well before a customer hits the "Buy it" button on the site. Management must forecast consumer needs, arrange to be able to ship merchandise from suppliers on demand, maintain a precise calculation of inventory available from its suppliers, and meet customer demands quickly and effectively. One of the original strengths of Amazon's business model was that it rarely held inventory (recently, Amazon expanded its business operations significantly by building some large distribution warehouses that do hold inventory). Instead, in many cases Amazon has direct connections to its suppliers that allow customer orders to be shipped directly from supplier to customer. Computers track most of this complicated distribution channel, but it is the knowledge of management that ultimately provides the success that Amazon.com enjoys.

Source: J. C. Ramo, "1999 Person of the Year," *Time*, December 27, 1999.

fyi

Many people originally predicted that the Internet would open up new, previously untapped markets. The reality is that, in 1999, only 6% of consumer e-business revenue was new spending. In other words, sales on the Internet are not, by and large, *new* sales, but represent commerce that is *replacing* business previously done within traditional manufacturing, merchandising, or service settings.

Source: Jupiter Communications, 1999.

You have probably had some experience in shopping on the Internet. Most organizations today have an Internet site. Generally, all you have to do is open your Internet browser and add a ".com" to the end of the name of your favorite company, and you can be doing business with that company in no time. Obviously, a lot of business is being transacted on the Internet. However, the lion's share of Internet business is *not* taking place with individual consumers like most of us. To help you understand this point, we need to distinguish between two kinds of e-business. One kind is conducted between companies and consumers (or end-users). This sort of business is often referred to as business-to-consumer (or "B2C"). When you shop at WALMART.COM or NORDSTROMS.COM, you're engaged in B2C e-business. B2C e-business in the United States amounted to $33 billion in 2000 and is expected to grow to between $200 billion and $400 billion by 2003. In addition, business also takes place between businesses, such as the purchase of raw materials, consulting, outsourcing of services, and important partnerships or joint ventures where companies work together to provide goods and services to the public. When this work is managed with Internet-type technology, it is referred to as a business-to-business process (or "B2B"). This aspect of e-business is, frankly, huge. B2B e-business amounted to $251 billion in 2000 and is expected to grow to between $1.5 trillion and $2 trillion by 2003!

As manufacturers, merchants, and service providers move more and more of their business onto the Internet, they expect to enjoy a number of significant benefits, including expanded sales opportunities; improved communications, customer service, and loyalty; and better management of human resources and supply channels. Perhaps most relevant to this chapter is the fact that companies expect to lower their costs of business using Internet technology. For example, bank transactions involving a teller cost an average of $1.07 per transaction. When you log on to your bank at its ".com" Internet site, however, an online banking transaction costs only $0.01. As another example, IBM bought $13 billion worth of goods and services over the Internet in 1999, saving more than $270 million in procurement costs. E-billing, the delivery of routine bills online, can save as much as 60% per bill in handling costs. Hence, cost savings in running a billing process at a large utility could be as much as $50 million per year when an e-billing process is implemented. WAL-MART has achieved tremendous improvements in the costs, quality, and timing of goods purchased from wholesalers through the use of inventory management systems that have direct Internet-based connections to its suppliers. Even hiring costs can be reduced, as evidenced by the fact that IBM has installed Internet software that has cut the cost of hiring temporary workers by $3 million annually.

fyi

In a *Business Week* article, GENERAL ELECTRIC's CEO Jack Welch was asked how high the Internet was on his company's agenda. Welch responded, "Where does the Internet rank in priority? It's No. 1, 2, 3, and 4."

Source: N. Byrnes and P. C. Judge, "Internet Anxiety," *Business Week*, June 28, 1999.

E-business can have tremendous impacts on product costs. Specifically, costs of raw materials are reduced as organizations use the Internet to find and demand better pricing and save significant costs in the process of ordering and managing raw material inventories. Costs of direct labor can also be better managed by using the Internet to identify, hire, and train the organization's workforce. In some cases, direct service labor, such as bank tellers, are redeployed to new assignments in the organization as Internet technology becomes the means of interacting with clients and customers. Perhaps most significantly, companies are making significant changes in the structure of their organizations, which can greatly affect the costs of overhead. At many companies, overhead costs are much higher than the costs of raw materials/supplies and direct labor combined, so finding new ways to handle the management and logistics of a company can have immediate and important impacts on costs. The example of IBM using the Internet to change the way it obtains goods and services (and temporary employees) demonstrates the savings that can result.

to summarize

E-business and Internet technology are dramatically changing all types of business organizations, including manufacturing, merchandising, and service organizations. As these companies make adjustments in both their organizational structure and in the way they connect to and do business with suppliers and customers within their distribution channel, there have been (and will continue to be) significant changes and improvements in the costs, quality, and timeliness of goods and services. These changes are affecting the process of both business-to-consumer (B2C) and business-to-business (B2B) operations.

expanded material

In the first part of the chapter we illustrated product costing using the job order costing method. This method is commonly used in both manufacturing and service organizations. In this expanded material section, we discuss how companies, predominantly manufacturers, use process costing when it is difficult to specifically identify unique products or jobs during the manufacturing process.

7

Use the FIFO method to do process costing.

THE PROCESS COSTING SYSTEM

All the product costing methods described so far in this chapter assume that the accountant is able to specifically identify the job (i.e., the product or service) being produced for customers. By identifying each specific job, the accountant is then able to specifically track a job as it moves through the work-in-process inventory and into the finished goods inventory. While it is in the production process, the accountant assigns the actual direct materials and direct labor costs, as well as allocates a specific amount of overhead costs, that are required to produce to a particular job. This cost accounting method is often referred to as job order costing. Some manufacturing companies cannot use job order costing because they cannot specifically identify each job (product) being produced. Examples of such companies include manufacturers of bricks, lumber, paint, soft drinks, and newspapers and most food processing plants. These companies manufacture large volumes of product using a series of uniform processes. For these companies, **process costing** is the appropriate product cost accounting method. Because these companies can't focus on costing a particular job, they focus on costing the amount of work done for a particular *period of time*. We'll talk more about this concept of work done in a particular time period below. For now, remember that for process costing to be appropriate, two general conditions typically exist:

process costing A method of product costing whereby costs are accumulated by process or work centers and averaged over all products manufactured in a center or department during a particular production period. There are two methods of process costing: The FIFO method separately tracks the costs of beginning work-in-process units and the costs of units started in the current production period. The weighted-average method (not discussed in this text) averages together the costs of beginning work-in-process units and the costs of units started in the current production period.

1. The activities performed in each process center are identical for all units.
2. The units produced as a result of passing through the process centers are basically the same.

Steps in Process Costing

A firm whose products and processes meet the preceding conditions would employ process costing using five steps:

1. Identify units that went into the process and identify where those units are at the end of the processing time. Determine the amount of "work done" (equivalents units of production) during the processing time period.
2. Determine the amount of production costs that went into the process and compute the product costs per unit for the processing time period.
3. Compute the total cost of units completed and transferred out (costs of goods manufactured) during the processing time period.
4. Compute the total cost of units remaining in process (ending work-in-process inventory) at the end of the processing time period.
5. Prepare the production cost report.

equivalent units of production A method used in a process costing system to measure the production output during a period. Equivalent units of production essentially measures the "work done" by the center or department in terms of units of output.

STEP 1. COMPUTE EQUIVALENT UNITS OF PRODUCTION The first step in process costing is to track the flow of units and compute the **equivalent units of production**. The concept of equivalent units of production essentially means to calculate the amount of work actually done during any particular period of time in terms of units of output. It's really a very simple concept. For example, let's assume that you are being paid by the hour to hand paint porcelain figurines for a small local art shop. It's an arduous process, taking several hours to paint a single figurine. On average, you can do only three or four figurines per day. At the end of your first day on the job, you have painted three figurines and have another one nearly complete. If your boss were to ask you how much work you did for the day, are you going to reply that you painted only three figurines? Of course not! Instead, you'll likely tell her that you completely painted three figurines and that you have another one nearly done (let's say it is 90% done). So, did you paint four figurines? Not really. The amount of work done on your first day is 3.9 figurines (three whole units plus 90% of a fourth unit), right? In other words, you did 3.9 equivalent units of production. Also note that you have one unit in ending work-in-process inventory (the figurine that is 90% done).

The real measure of equivalent units of production is what happens on your second day on the job. When you come back to the shop the next day, the first thing you will do is work on that day's beginning work-in-process inventory, which is the figurine that is 90% done from the day before.[9] Let's assume that you then start and complete three more figurines. Before it's time to go home, you are able to start one more figurine and get it about 30% done. Now how do you answer the boss's question about how much work was done on your second day? You completed a total of four figurines (the figurine that was work-in-process when you came to work plus three more that were both started and completed this same day), but to say that you did the work of four figurines isn't quite accurate, is it? To be accurate, you completed 10% of one figurine, 100% of three figurines, and 30% of a final figurine that is still work-in-process. In other words, the work done for the day was 3.4 figurines, computed as follows:

9 This is the reason we call this particular method of process costing the FIFO (first in, first out) method. It is based on the assumption that all beginning work-in-process inventory is completed before any new units are started.

	Physical Units		Percent Completed (i.e., "work done")		Equivalent Units of Production
Beginning work-in-process	1	×	10%	=	0.1
Started and completed	3	×	100%	=	3.0
Ending work-in-process	1	×	30%	=	0.3
Total equivalent units of production					**3.4**

With this example of equivalent units of production in mind, let's now use an example that's more representative of manufacturers that follow the process costing approach to accounting for product costs. Exhibit 3-12 shows how products and costs move through the two process centers (mixing and bagging) of the Allied Cement Company. For now, we will focus on the process costing for the mixing center at Allied Cement. Production units at Allied are measured in pounds of finished cement. When the mixing machines are shut down at the end of a production period (let's assume a production period at Allied is one month), not all pounds of cement started the last day of the month in the mixing center will have been completed. In fact, as at most manufacturers, units are usually in process at both the beginning and the end of a period. Were it not for these beginning and ending work-in-process inventories, the number of units actually produced in the mixing center for the period could be determined merely by counting all pounds of cement that were transferred out of the mixing center and into the bagging center. However, as you saw in our earlier example of hand painting figurines, the amount of work actually done in the mixing center for the period is partly based on how much work was done in the beginning and ending work-in-process inventories.

With this in mind, look at the report below on equivalent units of production for the mixing center.

Step 1: Compute equivalent units of production.

		Direct Materials Costs		Conversion Costs	
	Physical Units (pounds)	Percent Done	Equivalent Units	Percent Done	Equivalent Units
Beginning work-in-process	4,000	0%	0	80%	3,200
Started and completed	44,000	100%	44,000	100%	44,000
Ending work-in-process	2,000	100%	2,000	60%	1,200
Equivalent units of production			**46,000**		**48,400**
Transferred out (to Bagging)	48,000				

The "Physical Units" column reports that the mixing center had 4,000 pounds of cement in beginning work-in-process when the month started. The department finished mixing these 4,000 pounds and mixed an additional 44,000 pounds before the end of the month, allowing the mixing center to transfer a total of 48,000 pounds to the bagging center. At the end of the month, 2,000 pounds of cement remained in ending work-in-process.

Now look at the "Equivalent Units" column for the Direct Materials Costs. In this case, all of the materials necessary to mix a pound of cement are put in place at the beginning of the mixing process. In other words, when the month began, the 4,000 pounds of cement in beginning work-in-process were already 100% complete in terms of materials. Similarly, at the end of the month, the 2,000 pounds of cement in ending work-in-process were 100% complete in terms of materials. As a result, the equivalent units of production (i.e., "work

exhibit 3-12 The Flow of Products and Costs through Process Centers

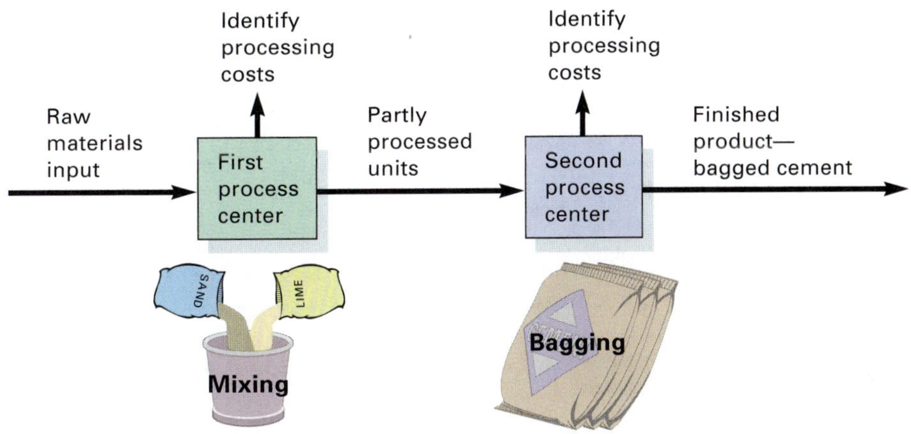

done") to be used when accounting for costs of direct materials for Allied is simply the number of pounds of cement *started* into production during the production period, or 100% of units started and completed plus 100% of units in ending work-in-process (and 0% of units in beginning work-in-process).[10]

conversion costs The costs of converting raw materials to finished products; include direct labor and manufacturing overhead costs.

Finally, look at the "Equivalent Units" column under "Conversion Costs." **Conversion costs** is the term we use to describe all product costs necessary to "convert" raw materials into finished goods. Hence, conversion costs include all costs of direct labor and manufacturing overhead.[11] In this example, at the beginning of the month, the beginning work-in-process inventory was 20% complete in terms of costs of direct labor and manufacturing overhead. As a result, the first work done in the mixing center for the current production period was to finish the remaining 80% of the effort required to complete these 4,000 pounds of cement. In other words, the mixing center did 3,200 equivalent units of production (4,000 × 80%) on beginning work-in-process. At the end of the month, there were 2,000 pounds in ending working-in-process that were 60% complete in terms of direct labor and manufacturing overhead costs, which means that the mixing center did 1,200 equivalent units of production (2,000 × 60%) on ending work-in-process. When combined with the work done on units started and completed, the mixing center's "work done" in terms of direct labor and manufacturing overhead was 48,400 equivalent units (3,200 + 44,000 + 1,200).

fyi

In the FIFO approach to process costing, the total physical units "started" always equal total units "started and completed" plus total units in "ending work-in-process." Similarly, the total physical units "transferred out" always equal total units "started and completed" plus total units in "beginning work-in-process."

STEP 2. COMPUTE THE PRODUCT COSTS PER UNIT With Step 1 completed, we know how much work was done in terms of production output for the mixing center. Now, to compute the product cost per unit, we need to determine how much was spent on production. For the mixing center, we will assume that the beginning work-in-process of 4,000 pounds includes $800 in direct materials and $1,200 in direct labor and manufacturing overhead (i.e., conversion costs). Further, Allied spent $9,660 for direct materials and $70,180 for conversion costs in the current production period. Computing the product costs per unit (pound) for the mixing department is then a simple matter of dividing the product costs by the appropriate equivalent units of production, reported as follows:

10 When computing equivalent units in this chapter, we will always assume that direct materials are all added at the beginning of the process. However, this assumption is not always the case in actual companies.

11 Because we assume in this example that costs of manufacturing overhead are being allocated on the basis of direct labor, we can combine the equivalent units calculation for direct labor and for manufacturing overhead costs into one calculation for conversion costs. This is the assumption that we will follow for all subsequent equivalent unit calculations in this chapter.

Step 2: Compute the product costs per unit.

	Total Costs	Equivalent Units	Cost per Unit
Beginning work-in-process			
Direct materials costs	$ 800	4,000	$0.20
Conversion costs	1,200	800	1.50
Total	$ 2,000		**$1.70**
Current period			
Direct materials costs	$ 9,660	46,000	$0.21
Conversion costs	70,180	48,400	1.45
Total	$79,840		**$1.66**

caution

When using beginning work-in-process in the calculation of equivalent units of production for the current production period, remember to use the percentage *yet to be done.* In other words, the "work done" in the current period on *beginning* work-in-process is:

Number of physical units in inventory × (1 − Percent done)

The "work done" on *ending* work-in-process for the current period is:

Number of physical units in inventory × Percent done

As you can see in the report above on product costs per unit, Allied spent $0.21 per pound for direct materials in the mixing center in the current production period. This cost is based on dividing the total equivalent units of 46,000 for work done on direct materials into the total direct materials costs of $9,660. Bearing in mind that beginning work-in-process came from the previous production period, Allied can compare the current direct materials cost to the direct materials cost in the previous production period, which was $0.20 per pound. This cost is obtained by dividing the costs of direct materials in beginning work-in-process by the equivalent units in beginning work-in-process (remember that when the day begins, all 4,000 pounds in inventory are 100% done with respect to direct materials). The current-period conversion cost per unit is $1.45, based on dividing the total equivalent units of 48,400 for work done in terms of direct labor and manufacturing overhead into the total conversion costs of $70,180. Again, Allied's management can check their efforts to control conversion costs by comparing the current-period costs with the previous period's cost of $1.50 per pound, which is calculated by dividing conversion costs in beginning work-in-process by the work already done in beginning work-in-process when the month begins (800 equivalent pounds = 4,000 physical pounds × 20% "work done").

STEP 3. COMPUTE THE COSTS TRANSFERRED OUT Allied has spent a total of $79,840 in the current production period in the mixing center. In addition, when the production period began, there was work-in-process inventory in the mixing center that had a total value of $2,000. Hence, as you can see in the report above on product costs per unit, the mixing center needs to account for $81,840. Assuming that there has been no waste or pilferage in the mixing process, at the end of the production period all costs have either been transferred out to the bagging center or remain in ending work-in-process. To compute the costs transferred out to the bagging center, the mixing center needs to account for the costs of completing the cement in beginning work-in-process, as well as the cement that was started and completed in the current period. The following report shows the costs transferred out:

Step 3: Compute the costs transferred out.

	Cost per Unit	Equivalent Units	
Beginning work-in-process			
Initial direct materials costs			$ 800
Initial conversion costs			1,200
Costs to complete materials	$0.21	0	0
Costs to complete conversion	$1.45	3,200	4,640
Total			$ 6,640
Started and completed	$1.66	44,000	73,040
Total costs transferred out			**$79,680**

As you can see in the above report, the mixing center did not need to add any more direct materials costs to complete the beginning work-in-process. However, there were 3,200 equivalent units of work in terms of direct labor and manufacturing overhead that needed to be completed in the current period before the 4,000 pounds of cement in beginning work-in-process could be transferred out to the bagging center. Hence, the mixing department spent $4,640 in conversion costs ($1.45 per unit × 3,200 equivalent units) to complete the mixing on beginning work-in-process. When added to the initial beginning work-in-process costs of $2,000 ($800 + $1,200), the first 4,000 pounds of cement transferred to the bagging center carried total production costs of $6,640.

Of the total 48,000 pounds transferred to the bagging center, 44,000 pounds were started and completed in the current production period. At a total cost per unit of $1.66 ($0.21 per unit for direct materials + $1.45 per unit for direct labor and manufacturing overhead), the mixing department spent $73,040 to mix the remaining units transferred out of its operations in the current production period.

STEP 4. COMPUTE COSTS OF ENDING WORK-IN-PROCESS INVENTORY The fourth step in the mixing center's process costing effort is to determine the costs of the 2,000 pounds of cement remaining in work-in-process inventory at the end of the current production period. These calculations are reported below.

Step 4: Compute costs of ending work-in-process inventory.

	Cost per Unit	Equivalent Units	
Costs for direct materials.	$0.21	2,000	$ 420
Conversion costs	$1.45	1,200	1,740
Cost of ending work-in-process.			**$2,160**

Because all 2,000 pounds are 100% complete in terms of direct materials, this inventory represents $420 ($0.21 per unit × 2,000 pounds × 100%) in direct materials costs. On the other hand, because these 2,000 pounds are only 60% complete in terms of direct labor and manufacturing overhead, there are $1,740 ($1.45 per unit × 2,000 pounds × 60%) in conversion costs residing in ending work-in-process inventory. In total, ending work-in-process contains $2,160 ($420 + $1,740) in product costs.

production cost report A document that compiles all the costs of a manufacturing center for a particular production period. The information on this report is used to control and evaluate production costs, as well as transfer costs and units of output from one manufacturing center to another.

STEP 5. PREPARE THE PRODUCTION COST REPORT All the data calculated so far are combined into the **production cost report** for the mixing center. This report is shown in Exhibit 3-13. As you can see, this report includes a large number of calculations. However, we've carefully worked through all the calculations in this report together, so you should feel fairly comfortable understanding how it all fits together. (You'll feel more comfortable once you've worked through the review problem at the end of this chapter and a few homework problems!) Remember that the report is composed of four overall steps, each of which should make sense to you.

When a lot of calculations are involved, as in the production cost report in Exhibit 3-13, a good check figure can be a wonderful tool! Notice in Exhibit 3-13 that the arrows point to a very good check figure—$81,840. This amount represents the total dollars that have gone into the mixing center in the current period ($2,000 in beginning work-in-process + $79,840 in current production costs), as well as the total dollars that have come out of the mixing process ($79,680 transferred out + $2,160 in ending work-in-process). If the production cost report can balance out to this check figure, you have good (though not perfect) assurance that the calculations have been done correctly.

to summarize

Process costing involves five steps: (1) determine the amount of "work done" (equivalents units of production) during the processing time period, (2) compute the product costs per unit by dividing total costs by "work done," (3)

exhibit 3-13 A Production Cost Report

Allied Cement Company
Mixing Center
Production Cost Report
For the Month of October 2003

Equivalent Units of Production

	Physical Units (pounds)	Direct Materials Costs Percent Done	Direct Materials Costs Equivalent Units	Conversion Costs Percent Done	Conversion Costs Equivalent Units
Beginning work-in-process	4,000	0%	0	80%	3,200
Started and completed	44,000	100%	44,000	100%	44,000
Ending work-in-process	2,000	100%	2,000	60%	1,200
Equivalent units of production			**46,000**		**48,400**
Transferred out	48,000				

Product Costs Per Unit

	Total Costs	Equivalent Units	Cost per Unit
Beginning work-in-process			
Direct materials costs	$ 800	4,000	$0.20
Conversion costs	1,200	800	1.50
Total	$ 2,000		**$1.70**
Current period			
Direct materials costs	$ 9,660	46,000	$0.21
Conversion costs	70,180	48,400	1.45
Total	$79,840		**$1.66**
TOTAL DOLLARS IN	**$81,840**		

Costs Transferred Out

	Cost per Unit	Equivalent Units	
Beginning work-in-process			
Initial direct materials costs			$ 800
Initial conversion costs			1,200
Costs to complete materials	$0.21	0	0
Costs to complete conversion	$1.45	3,200	4,640
Total			$ 6,640
Started and completed	$1.66	44,000	73,040
Total costs transferred out			**$79,680**

Costs of Ending Work-in-Process

	Cost per Unit	Equivalent Units	
Costs for direct materials	$0.21	2,000	$ 420
Conversion costs	$1.45	1,200	1,740
Cost of ending work-in-process			**$ 2,160**
TOTAL DOLLARS OUT			**$81,840**

compute the total cost of units completed and transferred out, (4) compute the total cost of units in ending work-in-process inventory, and (5) prepare the production cost report. With process costing, both units and costs must be transferred from one process center to the next until the final unit cost is accumulated at the end of the total production process. The production cost report provides a method of accounting for the flow of units and costs between process centers.

review of learning objectives

1 **Understand the difficulty, yet importance, of having accurate product cost information.** It is relatively easy to associate direct materials and direct labor costs with specific products. However, it is very difficult, and often even arbitrary, to assign overhead costs to specific products. Hence, it is difficult to accurately determine the cost of products because overhead costs have to be estimated before being incurred; they often cannot be easily assigned to units produced; and they are often "lumpy"—that is, overhead costs typically do not follow the same even flow pattern of production and service output as followed by direct materials and direct labor. Regardless of the difficulty, however, having accurate product cost information is critical for management to make good planning, controlling, and evaluation decisions.

2 **Explain the flow of goods and services in a manufacturing organization and follow the accumulation of product costs in its accounting system.** In a manufacturing firm, employees work with raw materials to make finished goods to be sold to customers. When purchased, raw materials are stored in a raw materials warehouse as raw materials inventory; as they are manufactured, goods move through the factory floor as work-in-process inventory; when completed, goods are stored in a finished goods warehouse as finished goods inventory. The costs of direct materials and direct labor (factory employees who work directly in production) are combined with manufacturing overhead costs as goods are being produced to make up the cost of finished goods. The process of tracing manufacturing costs to specific goods typically follows an accounting method traditionally known as job order costing. When a manufacturing firm purchases materials, the costs are recorded in a raw materials inventory account. As direct materials are used, costs are removed from this account and debited to Work-in-Process Inventory. Direct labor and manufacturing overhead costs are also debited to Work-in-Process Inventory. As units are completed, the costs in Work-in-Process Inventory are transferred to Finished Goods Inventory. When the units are sold, the costs are transferred to Cost of Goods Sold. Whereas direct materials and direct labor costs assigned to products are actual costs, manufacturing overhead is transferred to Work-in-Process Inventory and assigned to products on the basis of some predetermined overhead rate.

3 **Understand the process of accounting for overhead.** *Estimated* manufacturing overhead costs for a period are determined at the beginning of the period and combined with an estimated level of activity (such as direct labor hours) to create the predetermined overhead rate that is used to allocate overhead costs to products as they are produced. As *actual* manufacturing overhead costs are incurred, they are debited to Manufacturing Overhead. This account is credited (and Work-in-Process Inventory is debited) as overhead costs are applied to specific jobs on the basis of the predetermined rate. At the end of the period, if total *applied* manufacturing overhead costs are larger (smaller) than total *actual* manufacturing overhead costs, the manufacturing overhead account will have a credit (debit) balance, indicating that manufacturing overhead costs were overapplied (underapplied). The debit or credit balance in the manufacturing overhead account is either closed directly to Cost of Goods Sold or allocated among Cost of Goods Sold, Finished Goods Inventory, and Work-in-Process Inventory.

4 **Explain the flow of goods and services in a merchandising organization and follow the accumulation of product costs in its accounting system.** Manufacturers sell to large-scale wholesalers, who then sell to retailers, who then sell to the end-user customer. These interconnected business relationships are called a distribution channel. Within this system, wholesalers and retailers are the merchants who are most concerned with effectively managing the costs involved in the inventory movement along the distribution channel. Because merchants basically purchase inventory in a finished state, the process of accounting for inventory in a merchandising business is not nearly as complicated as it is in a manufacturing business.

5 **Explain the flow of goods and services in a service organization and follow the accumulation of product costs in its accounting system.** Essentially, a service business is any organization whose main economic activity involves producing a nonphysical product that provides value to a customer. As service industries have deregulated in the last few decades, increased competition has forced these companies to develop better cost management systems. There are a number

of similarities between accounting for service organizations and accounting for manufacturing organizations. Although most service firms do not need to manage large investments in raw materials, some firms do have large investments in partially completed service projects and contracts. Partially completed service jobs require management accounting that is very similar to the process of accounting for work-in-process in manufacturing firms. Supplies, direct labor, and overhead costs accumulate in an account called Work-in-Process Services. This account performs much the same function as Work-in-Process Inventory in a manufacturing firm. In addition, as service activities take place, overhead is applied to Work-in-Process Services using a predetermined overhead application rate. When the firm has completed and delivered the contracted service, the relevant costs are transferred from Work-in-Process Services to Cost of Services (an account similar to the cost of goods sold account used by manufacturing and merchandising firms).

6 **Understand the impact of e-business on product costing.** As a result of the growth of e-business being conducted on the Internet, accountants and managers are experiencing tremendous change in the way business is conducted across all types of organizations (manufacturing, merchandising, and service). These changes in business processes are also dramatically changing the size of (and the process of managing) all three types of product costs, i.e., direct materials, direct labor, and overhead.

expanded material

7 **Use the FIFO method to do process costing.** Process costing involves five steps: (1) Identify units that went into the process and identify where those units are at the end of the processing time. Determine the amount of "work done" (equivalents units of production) during the processing time period. (2) Determine the amount of production costs that went into the process and compute the product costs per unit for the processing time period. (3) Compute the total cost of units completed and transferred out (costs of goods manufactured) during the processing time period. (4) Compute the total cost of units that remain in process (ending work-in-process inventory) at the end of the processing time period. (5) Prepare the production cost report. The production cost report provides unit cost data that are used to cost inventory as it transfers from one process center to the next and to cost the ending work-in-process inventory of each process center.

key terms and concepts

activity-based costing (ABC) 111
channel 127
cycle times 107
deregulation 133
estimated manufacturing overhead 122
finished goods inventory 113
inventory turnover (stockturns) 105
job cost sheet 116
job order costing 115
logistics 129
manufacturing organizations 106
manufacturing overhead rate 116
merchandising organizations 106
overapplied manufacturing overhead 125
predetermined overhead rate 119
raw materials inventory 113
retailers 129
service organizations 106
underapplied manufacturing overhead 125
wholesalers 129
work-in-process inventory 113

expanded material

conversion costs 145
equivalent units of production 143
process costing 143
production cost report 147

review problems

Job Order Costing

Salem Manufacturing Company applies manufacturing overhead costs on the basis of direct materials costs. The year 2003 estimates are:

Direct materials costs	$300,000
Manufacturing overhead	180,000

For every dollar of direct materials costs, 60 cents of overhead is applied ($180,000 ÷ $300,000 = $0.60).

Following are the Salem Manufacturing Company transactions for 2003 (entries rounded to the nearest dollar):

a. Purchased materials for cash, $500,000.
b. Issued $400,000 of materials to production (80% direct, 20% indirect).
c. Incurred direct labor costs of $250,000.
d. Incurred indirect labor costs of $70,000.
e. Incurred costs for administrative and sales salaries of $70,000 and $60,000, respectively.
f. Incurred manufacturing overhead costs: property taxes on manufacturing plant, $6,000; plant utilities, $14,000; insurance on plant and equipment, $3,000. (Assume these expenses have not yet been paid.)
g. Recorded depreciation on manufacturing plant and equipment of $18,000 and $6,000, respectively.
h. Applied manufacturing overhead.
i. Transferred 65% of Work-in-Process Inventory to Finished Goods Inventory. Beginning Work-in-Process Inventory was $13,000.
j. Sold 90% of finished goods on account at a markup of 60% of cost. There was no beginning inventory of finished goods.
k. Closed the balance in Manufacturing Overhead to Cost of Goods Sold.

Required: Prepare a journal entry for each transaction.

Solution

	Debit	Credit
a. Raw Materials Inventory	500,000	
Cash		500,000
Purchased raw materials.		
b. Manufacturing Overhead	80,000	
Work-in-Process Inventory	320,000	
Raw Materials Inventory		400,000
Issued materials to production.		
c. Work-in-Process Inventory	250,000	
Wages Payable (or Cash)		250,000
Incurred direct labor costs.		
d. Manufacturing Overhead	70,000	
Wages Payable (or Cash)		70,000
Incurred indirect labor costs.		
e. Salaries Expense, Administrative	70,000	
Salaries Expense, Sales	60,000	
Salaries Payable (or Cash)		130,000
Incurred sales and administrative salaries expense.		
f. Manufacturing Overhead	23,000	
Property Taxes Payable		6,000
Utilities Payable		14,000
Insurance Payable		3,000
Incurred manufacturing overhead costs.		
g. Manufacturing Overhead	24,000	
Accumulated Depreciation—Plant		18,000
Accumulated Depreciation—Equipment		6,000
Recorded depreciation on plant and equipment.		
h. Work-in-Process Inventory	192,000	
Manufacturing Overhead		192,000*
Applied manufacturing overhead to Work-in-Process Inventory.		

*The predetermined overhead rate is equal to estimated total manufacturing overhead divided by estimated direct materials costs ($180,000 ÷ $300,000), or 60% of direct materials costs. In this case, $192,000 ($320,000 × 0.60) is applied because direct materials costs were $320,000 ($400,000 × 0.80).

i. Finished Goods Inventory	503,750	
Work-in-Process Inventory		503,750*
Transferred Work-in-Process Inventory to Finished Goods Inventory (0.65 × $775,000).		

*The amount transferred is determined as follows:

Work-in-Process Inventory

Beginning Balance	13,000		
(b)	320,000		
(c)	250,000		
(h)	192,000		
	775,000	(i)	503,750
Ending Balance	271,250		

j. Accounts Receivable	725,400	
Sales		725,400*
Cost of Goods Sold	453,375*	
Finished Goods Inventory		453,375
Sold 90% of Finished Goods Inventory.		

*Because Finished Goods Inventory is $503,750 (i), Cost of Goods Sold is $453,375 ($503,750 × 0.90). Because Finished Goods Inventory is marked up 60%, Sales is $725,400 ($453,375 × 1.6).

k. Cost of Goods Sold	5,000	
Manufacturing Overhead		5,000*
Closed underapplied manufacturing overhead.		

*The amount of underapplied manufacturing overhead is determined as follows:

Manufacturing Overhead

Actual Overhead	(b)	80,000	(h)	192,000	Applied Overhead
	(d)	70,000			
	(f)	23,000			
	(g)	24,000			
	Balance	5,000			

Accounting for Overhead in a Service Business

Columbus & Hercules, a public accounting firm, is computing the overhead rates to use when billing customers and bidding on jobs. Columbus & Hercules provides the following estimates relating to overhead costs for the year 2003:

Utilities	$ 12,000
Rent	30,000
Equipment depreciation	22,000
Office supplies	20,000
Support staff salaries	120,000
Total estimated overhead costs	$204,000

In addition, Columbus & Hercules offers the following annual estimates (based on a 50-week work year) regarding the salaries and estimated hours associated with the professionals employed by the firm:

Position	Total Estimated Salaries	Total Estimated Billable Hours
Partners (2 × $100,000)	$200,000	4,400
Managers (3 × $70,000)	210,000	6,600
Seniors (6 × $50,000)	300,000	13,200
Staff auditors (10 × $25,000)	250,000	22,000

Columbus & Hercules computes a chargeable hourly rate for each position that is the sum of the following: (1) each position's hourly rate (based on salary), (2) an overhead rate, and (3) a markup of 20% of (1) and (2). The overhead rate allocates estimated overhead costs to each position, then relates the allocated costs to the hours expected to be worked by each position. Travel and materials costs are directly traceable and billed to each job.

Columbus & Hercules has no client projects in process on January 1, 2003. During January of 2003, Columbus & Hercules worked on several auditing and accounting jobs and incurred the following costs:

Jan. 1 Paid rent for January, $2,500.
4 Purchased office supplies on account, $1,200.
9 Paid $4,500 for payables from last year.
15 Paid office support salaries, $5,000.
15 Paid biweekly salaries of professionals: partners, $8,000; managers, $8,400; seniors, $12,000; staff, $10,000.
15 Applied overhead costs based on billable hours: partners, 170 hours; managers, 270 hours; seniors, 500 hours; staff, 900 hours.
18 Used office supplies totaling $800 to prepare client materials.
21 Purchased office supplies on account, $1,100.
25 Received and paid invoice from office supply store for purchase on January 4.
27 Billed clients for the following jobs using the computed hourly rate for each position:

	Job #1	Job #2
Partner	90 hours	80 hours
Manager	150 hours	140 hours
Senior	320 hours	200 hours
Staff	560 hours	400 hours

27 Transferred costs from Work-in-Process Services to Cost of Services based on information from January 27.
31 Estimated utility costs for the month of January to be $1,000.
31 Paid office support salaries, $5,400.
31 Recognized depreciation of office equipment, $1,900.
31 Paid biweekly salaries of professionals: partners, $8,000; managers, $8,400; seniors, $12,000; staff, $10,000.
31 Applied overhead costs based on billable hours: partners, 180 hours; managers, 280 hours; seniors, 525 hours; staff, 950 hours.

Required:

1. Compute the billing rate to be used for each position.
2. Provide the journal entries made by Columbus & Hercules for January.
3. Compute the ending balance in Work-in-Process Services.
4. Compute the ending balance in Overhead.

Solution

1. Billing rate

Overhead allocation rate: $204,000 ÷ $960,000 = $0.2125 per dollar of salary.

Position	Estimated Salaries	Preliminary Rate	Allocated Overhead	Billable Hours	Overhead Rate per Hour
Partner	$200,000	$0.2125	$ 42,500	4,400	$9.66
Manager	210,000	0.2125	44,625	6,600	6.76
Senior	300,000	0.2125	63,750	13,200	4.83
Staff	250,000	0.2125	53,125	22,000	2.41
Total	$960,000		$204,000		

Billable Rate for Each Position

Position	Hourly Rate (1)	Overhead Rate (2)	Markup [(1) + (2)] × 0.20 = (3)	Billable Rate (1) + (2) + (3)
Partner	$45.45[1]	$9.66	$11.02	$66.13
Manager	31.82[2]	6.76	7.72	46.30
Senior	22.73[3]	4.83	5.51	33.07
Staff	11.36[4]	2.41	2.75	16.52

[1]$200,000 ÷ 4,400 hours = $45.45 per hour
[2]$210,000 ÷ 6,600 hours = $31.82 per hour
[3]$300,000 ÷ 13,200 hours = $22.73 per hour
[4]$250,000 ÷ 22,000 hours = $11.36 per hour

2. Journal entries

Date	Account	Debit	Credit
Jan. 1	Overhead	2,500	
	Cash		2,500
	Paid rent for the month of January.		
4	Office Supplies	1,200	
	Accounts Payable		1,200
	Purchased office supplies on account.		
9	Accounts Payable	4,500	
	Cash		4,500
	Paid accounts payable from prior period.		
15	Overhead	5,000	
	Cash		5,000
	Paid office support salaries.		
15	Work-in-Process Services	38,400	
	Cash		38,400
	Paid salaries of professionals.		

Partners	$ 8,000
Managers	8,400
Seniors	12,000
Staff	10,000
Total	$38,400

Date	Account	Debit	Credit
15	Work-in-Process Services	8,051	
	Overhead		8,051
	Allocated overhead based on billable hours.		

Partners—170 hours × $9.66	$1,642
Managers—270 hours × $6.76	1,825
Seniors—500 hours × $4.83	2,415
Staff—900 hours × $2.41	2,169
Total	$8,051

Date	Account	Debit	Credit
18	Work-in-Process Services	800	
	Office Supplies		800
	Used office supplies on behalf of clients.		
21	Office Supplies	1,100	
	Accounts Payable		1,100
	Purchased office supplies on account.		
25	Accounts Payable	1,200	
	Cash		1,200
	Paid for supplies purchased on January 4.		

		Debit	Credit
27	Accounts Receivable	57,724	
	Service Revenue		57,724
	Billed clients for Jobs #1 and #2.		

Partners—170 hours × $66.13	$11,242
Managers—290 hours × $46.30	13,427
Seniors—520 hours × $33.07	17,196
Staff—960 hours × $16.52	15,859
Total	$57,724

		Debit	Credit
27	Cost of Services	48,107	
	Work-in-Process Services		48,107
	Transferred completed work in process to cost of services; comprised of each position's hourly rate and overhead rate.		

Partners—170 hours × ($45.45 + $9.66)	$ 9,369
Managers—290 hours × ($31.82 + $6.76)	11,188
Seniors—520 hours × ($22.73 + $4.83)	14,331
Staff—960 hours × ($11.36 + $2.41)	13,219
Total	$48,107

		Debit	Credit
31	Overhead	1,000	
	Utilities Payable		1,000
	To record estimated utilities expense for the month.		
31	Overhead	5,400	
	Cash		5,400
	Paid office support salaries.		
31	Overhead	1,900	
	Accumulated Depreciation—Office Equipment		1,900
	To record depreciation expense for the month.		
31	Work-in-Process Services	38,400	
	Cash		38,400
	Paid salaries of professionals.		

Partners	$ 8,000
Managers	8,400
Seniors	12,000
Staff	10,000
Total	$38,400

		Debit	Credit
31	Work-in-Process Services	8,458	
	Overhead		8,458
	Allocated overhead based on billable hours.		

Partners—180 hours × $9.66	$1,739
Managers—280 hours × $6.76	1,893
Seniors—525 hours × $4.83	2,536
Staff—950 hours × $2.41	2,290
Total	$8,458

3. Ending balance in Work-in-Process Services

Work-in-Process Services

1/15	38,400	1/27	48,107
1/15	8,051		
1/18	800		
1/31	38,400		
1/31	8,458		
End. bal.	46,002		

4. Ending balance in Overhead

Overhead			
1/1	2,500	1/15	8,051
1/15	5,000	1/31	8,458
1/31	1,000		
1/31	5,400		
1/31	1,900		
		End. bal. (overapplied)	709

expanded material

Process Costing

Cleveland Enterprises produces flour in a continuous manufacturing process. The flour is mixed in one step and transferred to the finished goods department. At the beginning of September, Cleveland had 1,600 bags of flour in process (100% complete as to materials and 20% complete as to processing) that held $2,800 in costs of direct materials and $800 in conversion costs. During September, 20,000 bags of flour were placed into production, and by the end of the month, only 2,000 bags of flour remained in process (100% complete as to materials and 30% complete as to processing). Production costs for September are as follows:

Direct materials	$36,000
Conversion costs	47,712

Required:

1. Prepare the production cost report for September.
2. Prepare the journal entries required to record the production of flour and the transfer of the finished bags to finished goods inventory. Assume that the processing costs are 75% direct labor and 25% manufacturing overhead.

Solution 1. Production cost report

Cleveland Enterprises
Production Cost Report
For the Month of September

EQUIVALENT UNITS OF PRODUCTION

		Direct Materials Costs		Conversion Costs	
	Physical Units	**Percent Done**	**Equivalent Units**	**Percent Done**	**Equivalent Units**
Beginning work-in-process	1,600	0%	0	80%	1,280
Started and completed	18,000	100%	18,000	100%	18,000
Ending work-in-process	2,000	100%	2,000	30%	600
Equivalent units of production			**20,000**		**19,880**
Transferred out	19,600				

PRODUCT COSTS PER UNIT

	Total Costs	**Equivalent Units**	**Cost per Unit**
Beginning work-in-process			
Direct materials costs	$ 2,800	1,600	$1.75
Conversion costs	800	320	2.50
Total	$ 3,600		**$4.25**
Current period			
Direct materials costs	$36,000	20,000	$1.80
Conversion costs	47,712	19,880	2.40
Total	$83,712		**$4.20**
TOTAL DOLLARS IN	**$87,312**		

COSTS TRANSFERRED OUT

	Cost per Unit	Equivalent Units	
Beginning work-in-process			
Initial direct materials costs			$ 2,800
Initial conversion costs			800
Costs to complete materials	$1.80	0	0
Costs to complete conversion	$2.40	1,280	3,072
Total			$ 6,672
Started and completed	$4.20	18,000	75,600
Total costs transferred out			**$82,272**

COSTS OF ENDING WORK-IN-PROCESS

	Cost per Unit	Equivalent Units	
Costs for direct materials	$1.80	2,000	$ 3,600
Conversion costs	$2.40	600	1,440
Cost of ending work-in-process			**$ 5,040**
TOTAL DOLLARS OUT			**$87,312**

2. Journal entries

Work-in-Process Inventory	36,000	
Direct Materials Inventory		36,000
Transferred direct materials to work-in-process inventory.		
Work-in-Process Inventory	47,712	
Wages Payable		35,784
Manufacturing Overhead		11,928
To record the department's payroll costs and applied manufacturing overhead ($47,712 × 75% = $35,784; $47,712 × 25% = $11,928).		
Finished Goods Inventory	82,272	
Work-in-Process Inventory		82,272
Transferred finished goods to the finished goods inventory.		

discussion questions

1. Why do managers need accurate product cost information?
2. For financial reporting, which costs are usually included as product costs in a manufacturing company?
3. Why should a firm know how much it costs to produce its goods and services?
4. How can companies improve quality while also reducing product costs?
5. Why is it difficult to track the costs of manufactured products?
6. What is the difference in the accounting treatment for direct materials and indirect materials?
7. Why are actual manufacturing overhead costs not assigned directly to products as they are incurred?
8. What is the normal flow of costs in a job order costing system?
9. What are some common bases for applying manufacturing overhead costs to products?
10. Why might Manufacturing Overhead be referred to as a "clearing account"?
11. How does a firm dispose of over- or underapplied overhead costs?
12. What is the difference between a manufacturing company and a merchandising company? Between a merchandising company and a service company?
13. What does a distribution channel consist of?
14. What is a service organization?
15. What effect does deregulation have on the service industry?

16. Name three ways in which the service industry differs from the manufacturing industry.
17. What is the principal "product cost" for a service company?
18. Which three costs go into the work-in-process services account for a service company? How does this account differ between service and manufacturing firms?
19. What similarities and differences exist among the costs of merchandising, manufacturing, and service firms?
20. Should managers concentrate only on the costs of production (e.g., the cost of goods sold), or should they also consider other costs and factors?

expanded material

21. What is the major difference between job order costing and process costing?
22. What two conditions generally exist for process costing to be appropriate?
23. What are the five steps involved in employing process costing?
24. What is meant by the term "equivalent units of production"?

discussion cases

CASE 3-1

PACKARD, INC.

Packard, Inc., produces and sells mousetraps. The cost of a mousetrap can be broken down as follows:

Direct materials	$0.23
Direct labor	0.09
Manufacturing overhead	0.12
Cost per trap	$0.44

The traps are then sold for 120% of cost, or $0.53 each. The manufacturing overhead is applied based on direct labor costs and was computed at the beginning of the year using the following estimates:

Estimated manufacturing overhead for the period	$540,000
Estimated direct labor costs	405,000
Predetermined overhead rate (per direct labor dollar)	1.33

During the year, several changes in the production process were made. As a result, expected manufacturing overhead costs have been significantly reduced below the original estimate of $540,000. For the first six months of the year, overhead costs of $272,000 were actually incurred. For that same time period, actual direct labor costs were $204,000. For the last six months of the year, overhead costs are expected to be $225,000, and direct labor costs are expected to be $202,500.

1. What changes (if any) should be made in the predetermined manufacturing overhead rate for Packard, Inc.?
2. Assuming that direct materials and direct labor costs will remain the same for the last six months of the year, determine the new cost of a single mousetrap.
3. Because the cost of producing mousetraps dropped during the second half of the year, Packard can reduce the price of its traps and still earn its 20% markup on cost. Should the company reduce the price of its mousetraps? What factors would affect your decision?

CASE 3-2

US MACDONALD CORPORATION

You work for US MacDonald Corporation (USMC), an airplane manufacturer. USMC makes airplanes for commercial airlines, such as UNITED, AMERICAN, and DELTA, and for the U.S. AIR FORCE. Many parts are common to all planes made by USMC. The market for commercial planes is extremely competitive with GENERAL DYNAMICS, LOCKHEED, and European manufacturer AIRBUS often bidding lower than USMC. However, USMC's contract with the Air Force allows it to bill them at cost plus a 9% profit.

Times have been tough lately for USMC. In fact, if you can't find a way to increase profits, the company may have to lay off 5,000 employees.

A colleague has just presented you with an idea that he believes will increase profits. He suggests that instead of using direct labor hours to allocate overhead costs among airplanes, you should allocate costs on the basis of the number of each type of airplane made. Because you make far more, smaller, less expensive planes for the Air Force, more of the overhead costs will be allocated to those planes. This action will not only decrease your cost per unit on commercial planes (allowing you to be competitive in that market), but will also increase your profits on Air Force planes because the cost per plane will be higher.

You are not sure about your colleague's suggested action. You do know that your allocation base of direct labor hours is quite arbitrary and probably does not correspond well to the way overhead costs are consumed.

1. What is an appropriate allocation basis? Would adopting the suggestion be ethical?
2. Would you change your mind if you learned that competitors were allocating overhead on the basis of number of each type of plane made?
3. Is your action appropriate, from both a business and an ethical point of view, if direct labor hours is not an accurate allocation base?

CASE 3-3

THE DISTRIBUTION CHANNEL

You have just been hired as a branch manager for Perkins Retailers, a chain of office-supply stores in the Midwest. Perkins often purchases inventory items from Walker Wholesalers, a local distributor. However, Perkins also has the option of purchasing directly from various manufacturers, all of whom ensure prompt delivery. A comparative price list is as follows:

Lined paper:	
Gates Paper Manufacturers	$ 0.25
Walker Wholesalers	0.35
Steno chairs:	
Sturdychairs Manufacturers	$27.80
Walker Wholesalers	30.00
Desk lamps:	
Illumination Manufacturers	$ 7.60
Walker Wholesalers	11.25
Day planners:	
Olsen Manufacturers	$12.50
Walker Wholesalers	15.40

While examining past purchase invoices, you are perplexed to discover that despite the significantly higher prices, the previous branch manager had made most of his purchases from Walker Wholesalers.

1. Why might the previous branch manager have purchased from Walker Wholesalers when purchasing directly from the manufacturers is less expensive?
2. Why do wholesalers need to charge higher prices than manufacturers? Are they justified from the customers' point of view?
3. Will you, the new branch manager, always purchase from the manufacturers? Why or why not?

CASE 3-4

SERVICE COST FLOWS

The CPA firm you work for has just been hired by Phillips Attorneys at Law to perform an audit. In the process of the audit, you notice that Phillips' accountant has been inconsistent in accounting for the company president's salary. You notice that sometimes he has accounted for the company president's salary as follows:

Overhead	20,000	
Salaries and Wages Payable		20,000
To record the company president's salary.		

Other times, the accountant has debited Salaries and Wages Expense instead of Overhead. When you confront the accountant about the inconsistency, he gets somewhat defensive and says that it doesn't matter which method is used because both methods result in an expense; net income will be the same either way.

1. Assuming that the company president's tasks are exclusively administrative, do you agree with the accountant? Why or why not?
2. Which journal entry is correct? Why?

exercises

EXERCISE 3-1

MANUFACTURING COSTS

Springville Manufacturing Company uses a job order costing system. For Job #151, the production manager requisitioned $1,200 of direct materials and used 40 hours of direct labor at $18 per hour. Manufacturing overhead is applied on the basis of direct labor hours, using a predetermined overhead rate. At the beginning of the year, $800,000 of manufacturing overhead costs were estimated based on a forecast of 200,000 direct labor hours. Prepare a summary of the costs for Job #151. (*Note:* You have to calculate the predetermined overhead rate.)

EXERCISE 3-2

MANUFACTURING COSTS

The Make-It-Right Company manufactures special wheelchairs for handicapped athletes. The company uses a job order costing system. Partial data for a particular job include:

Direct materials	$450
Direct labor	375
Manufacturing overhead	?
Total cost	$?

The company allocates manufacturing overhead on the basis of direct labor hours. The estimated total manufacturing costs for the year are $750,000, and the total estimated direct labor hours are 150,000. Factory workers are paid $15 per hour.

1. Compute the predetermined manufacturing overhead rate.
2. What is the allocated manufacturing overhead cost and the total cost of the above referenced job?

EXERCISE 3-3

PREDETERMINED MANUFACTURING OVERHEAD RATES

Memphis Corporation uses a job order costing system. Thus, management must establish a predetermined overhead rate for applying manufacturing overhead. During the past three years, the following data have been accumulated:

	2001	2002	2003
Direct labor hours	40,000	52,000	65,000
Machine hours	80,000	65,000	45,000
Direct materials costs	$400,000	$250,000	$390,000
Total budgeted manufacturing overhead	$80,000	$65,000	$45,000

1. What would the predetermined overhead rate be for each of the three years, if based on (a) direct labor hours, (b) machine hours, (c) direct materials costs?
2. **Interpretive Question:** Which allocation basis would you recommend be used in the future for applying manufacturing overhead? Why?

EXERCISE 3-4

PREDETERMINED MANUFACTURING OVERHEAD RATES

East Lake Corporation uses a job order costing system and applies manufacturing overhead using a predetermined overhead rate. The following data are available for the past two years.

	2002	2003
Direct labor hours	104,000	130,000
Direct materials costs	$500,000	$780,000
Machine hours	100,000	70,000
Total budgeted manufacturing overhead	$130,000	$90,000

1. Compute the predetermined overhead rate for each of the two years, based on (a) direct labor hours, (b) direct materials costs, and (c) machine hours.
2. **Interpretive Question:** Which allocation basis would you recommend for applying manufacturing overhead? Why?

EXERCISE 3-5

WORK-IN-PROCESS ANALYSIS IN A MANUFACTURING ORGANIZATION

Matt Jones, a recently hired internal auditor, is currently auditing the work-in-process inventory account. Matt has forgotten some basic cost accounting concepts and asks for your assistance. Identify the four types of transactions or events that affect the work-in-process inventory account in a manufacturing organization. Prepare and explain a sample journal entry for each type of transaction.

EXERCISE 3-6

FLOW OF MANUFACTURING COSTS

Post the following cost data to the appropriate T-accounts to trace the flow of costs from the time they are incurred until the product is completed and sold. (Assume that purchases and expenses are credited to Cash or Accounts Payable.)

a.	Direct materials purchased	$ 60,000
b.	Direct materials used	50,000
c.	Indirect materials purchased	9,000
d.	Indirect materials used	7,000
e.	Wages payable, direct	60,000
f.	Wages payable, indirect	12,000
g.	Selling and administrative expenses	32,000
h.	Actual manufacturing overhead costs other than indirect materials and indirect labor	25,000
i.	Manufacturing overhead applied	40,000
j.	Work-in-process completed	120,000
k.	Finished goods sold	135,000

Raw Materials Inventory

Beg. Bal.	9,000	

Manufacturing Overhead

Work-in-Process Inventory

Beg. Bal.	30,000	

Finished Goods Inventory

Beg. Bal.	20,000	

Cash (Accounts Payable)

Wages Payable

Cost of Goods Sold

Selling and Administrative Expenses

EXERCISE 3-7

APPLYING MANUFACTURING OVERHEAD

Newstar Company has four manufacturing subsidiaries: A, B, C, and D. Each subsidiary keeps a separate set of accounting records. Manufacturing cost forecasts for 2003 for each subsidiary are:

	Subsidiaries			
	A	**B**	**C**	**D**
Materials to be used (lb.)	80,000	80,000	60,000	52,500
Direct labor hours	30,000	40,000	25,000	40,000
Direct labor costs	$12,000	$10,000	$3,750	$7,000
Machine hours	25,000	15,000	9,500	40,000
Manufacturing overhead	$30,000	$45,000	$20,000	$50,000

The predetermined overhead rates for each subsidiary are based on the following:

Subsidiary A: Machine hours
Subsidiary B: Direct labor costs
Subsidiary C: Materials to be used
Subsidiary D: Direct labor hours

1. Compute the predetermined overhead rate to be used in 2003 by each subsidiary.
2. If Subsidiary B actually had $8,000 of direct labor costs and $37,500 of manufacturing overhead, will overhead be over- or underapplied and by how much?
3. If Subsidiary C used 66,000 pounds of materials in 2003, what will be the applied manufacturing overhead?
4. **Interpretive Question:** Identify the two most commonly used methods to dispose of under- or overapplied manufacturing overhead. What is the major advantage of each method?

EXERCISE 3-8

APPLYING MANUFACTURING OVERHEAD

Valtec Company has three manufacturing divisions: A, B, and C. Each division has its own job order costing system and forecasts the following manufacturing costs for the year 2003:

	Division		
	A	**B**	**C**
Materials to be used (lb.)	120,000	100,000	80,000
Direct labor hours	45,000	60,000	25,000
Machine hours	40,000	25,000	15,000
Total budgeted manufacturing overhead	$50,000	$70,000	$45,000

The predetermined overhead rates for each division are based on the following:

Division A: Machine hours
Division B: Materials to be used
Division C: Direct labor hours

1. Compute the predetermined overhead rate to be used in 2003 by each division.
2. If Division A actually had 37,000 machine hours and $49,000 of manufacturing overhead, will overhead be over- or underapplied and by how much?
3. If Division B used 95,000 pounds of materials in 2003, what will be the applied manufacturing overhead?
4. **Interpretive Question:** Of the two commonly used methods to dispose of over- or underapplied manufacturing overhead, which method would you recommend and why?

EXERCISE 3-9

ASSIGNING MANUFACTURING COSTS TO JOBS

Noah Manufacturing Company uses a job order costing system. All relevant information for Jobs #609 and #610, which were completed during June, is provided here. No other jobs were in process during the month of June.

	Job #609	Job #610
Direct materials cost	$5,000	$6,500
Direct labor cost	$3,900	$5,400
Direct labor hours on job	400	700
Units produced	500	875

A predetermined overhead rate of $6 per direct labor hour is used to apply manufacturing overhead costs to jobs. Actual manufacturing overhead for the month of June totaled $9,000. All completed products are delivered to customers immediately after completion, so costs are transferred directly to Cost of Goods Sold without going through Finished Goods Inventory.

1. How much manufacturing overhead will be assigned to each job completed during June?
2. Compute the total cost of each job.
3. Compute the unit cost for each job.
4. Compute the over- or underapplied manufacturing overhead for June.
5. Prepare the journal entries to transfer the cost of direct materials, direct labor, and manufacturing overhead to Work-in-Process Inventory and to transfer the cost of completed jobs to Cost of Goods Sold. (Omit explanations.)
6. **Interpretive Question:** How would the company have computed its predetermined overhead rate of $6 per direct labor hour? Explain.

EXERCISE 3-10

ASSIGNING MANUFACTURING COSTS TO JOBS

Remington Company uses predetermined overhead rates in assigning manufacturing overhead costs to jobs. The rates are based on machine hours in the Machining Department and on direct labor hours in the Assembly Department. Estimated costs, machine hours, and direct labor hours for the year in each department are:

	Machining	Assembly
Direct labor cost	$64,000	$100,000
Manufacturing overhead	$90,000	$50,000
Direct labor hours	12,000	32,000
Machine hours	18,000	2,500

During the month of April, Job #402X had the following data for 50 completed units of product:

	Machining	Assembly
Direct materials cost	$400	$700
Direct labor cost	$650	$2,300
Direct labor hours	120	740
Machine hours	900	80

1. What predetermined overhead rates would be used by the company in assigning manufacturing overhead costs to Job #402X in machining and in assembly? (*Note:* You should round all rates you calculate to two decimal places.)
2. Using the overhead rates you calculated in (1), how much manufacturing overhead is applied to Job #402X?
3. What is the unit cost for Job #402X? (Round the unit cost to two decimal places.)

EXERCISE 3-11

ANALYZING MANUFACTURING COSTS

The following T-accounts represent inventory costs as of December 31, 2003:

Raw Materials Inventory

Debit		Credit
Bal. 12/31/02	140,000	400,000
	350,000	
Bal. 12/31/03	90,000	

Finished Goods Inventory

Debit		Credit
Bal. 12/31/02	79,000	673,000
	700,000	
Bal. 12/31/03	106,000	

Work-in-Process Inventory

Debit		Credit
Bal. 12/31/02	25,000	700,000
	400,000	
	249,000	
	172,000	
Bal. 12/31/03	146,000	

Manufacturing Overhead

Debit	Credit
49,000	249,000
52,000	
60,000	
72,000	

1. Determine the direct labor costs for 2003.
2. Determine the cost of goods manufactured for 2003.
3. Determine the cost of goods sold for 2003.
4. Compute over- or underapplied manufacturing overhead for 2003.
5. Determine actual indirect manufacturing costs for 2003.

EXERCISE 3-12

SERVICE COST FLOWS

Xavier & Associates Law Firm estimated its total overhead costs for 2003 to be $1.8 million. It allocates overhead based on direct labor hours. Xavier employs a total of 11 attorneys, each working an average of 2,000 hours per year. The average annual salary for Xavier attorneys is $140,000, or approximately $70 per hour. Xavier attorneys worked a total of 23 hours and used $150 of supplies in doing work for Mr. Bailey, one of Xavier's clients.

1. What is Xavier's overhead rate?
2. Prepare the journal entry to record the overhead for the Bailey job.
3. Prepare the journal entry to record the cost of supplies for the Bailey job.
4. Prepare the journal entry to record the cost of labor for the Bailey job.

EXERCISE 3-13

SERVICE COST FLOWS

Pierce Engineers incurred the following costs in 2003:

Use of supplies for clients	$ 3,500
Utilities	8,000
Property taxes	12,000
Engineers' salaries	100,000
Support staff salaries	35,000
Applied overhead	50,000

Prepare the journal entries to account for the costs given. Close the overhead account to Cost of Services.

EXERCISE 3-14

PREDETERMINED SERVICE OVERHEAD RATES

The following data are available for Haul-It-Away Truckers:

	2002	2003
Budgeted direct labor hours	135,000	140,000
Planned number of moving jobs	300	310
Total miles to be driven	450,000	597,000
Total budgeted overhead	$900,000	$1,200,000

1. Compute the predetermined overhead rate for each of the two years, if based on (a) direct labor hours, (b) number of moving jobs, and (c) total miles driven.
2. **Interpretive Question:** Which allocation basis would you recommend for applying overhead? Why?

EXERCISE 3-15

APPLYING OVERHEAD

Lemon Schools teaches private drivers' education courses. It applies overhead based on instructor hours, i.e., direct labor hours. The following information was forecasted for 2003:

Direct labor	$360,000
Property tax on cars	$3,600
Supplies	$12,000
Rent	$24,000
Support staff salaries	$160,000
Instructor hours	24,000

1. Calculate the predetermined overhead rate for 2003.
2. If Lemon actually had 23,000 instructor hours and spent $170,000 on overhead, will overhead be under- or overapplied for 2003? By how much?

EXERCISE 3-16

SERVICE COSTS

The following information is available for a particular job performed by Newland Business Consultants in 2003:

Direct labor	$4,000
Supplies	500
Overhead	?
Total cost	$?

Newland applies overhead on the basis of consulting hours, i.e., direct labor hours. The estimated total overhead costs for 2003 are $6.2 million, and the estimated total consulting hours are 150,000. Newland pays its consultants $40 per hour.

1. Compute the predetermined overhead rate.
2. What are the allocated overhead cost and the total cost of this particular job?

expanded material

EXERCISE 3-17

EQUIVALENT UNITS—PROCESS COSTING

Assume that you are the owner and sole employee of a bicycle service business that you run out of your home. Currently, you are running a spring special on a "super maintenance service" on bikes. The maintenance service you offer is quite comprehensive and includes (among other things) adjusting gears and brakes, cleaning and greasing all moving parts, "trueing" both wheels, and touching up the paint. It takes about 45 minutes to an hour to complete a bike. With the great price you're offering on this service, you immediately find yourself with about five days of customer order backlog. To catch up, you decide to spend the next week working solely on the "super maintenance service." Further, you want to track your output to see if you can improve the amount of maintenance work you do each of the next five days.

When you come to work the following Monday, you have one bike that is about 70% complete. At the end of the week, the results are as follows:

	Total Bikes Completed Each Day	End-of-Day Bike in Process
Monday	8	60% complete
Tuesday	8	90% complete
Wednesday	10	20% complete
Thursday	9	90% complete
Friday	10	10% complete

How much work did you get done each day? In other words, how many equivalent units of production did you have each day?

EXERCISE 3-18

EQUIVALENT UNITS AND UNIT COSTS—PROCESS COSTING

A large factory that manufactures wooden furniture has several assembly lines. One of the assembly lines is dedicated to assembly of wooden kitchen chairs. All raw materials necessary to complete each chair are requisitioned from the raw materials warehouse at the time each chair starts production on the assembly line. The following data relate to one week of production:

Beginning Work-in-Process

40 chairs; 80% complete; $350 in direct materials costs; $320 in conversion costs

Ending Work-in-Process

60 chairs; 40% complete

Current Week

550 chairs started and completed; $4,880 requisitioned from raw materials warehouse, $5,820 incurred in conversion costs

1. Compute the equivalent units of production for both direct materials and conversion costs for the week.
2. Compute the total production cost per chair for the week on the assembly line.
3. How does this week's production cost on the assembly line compare to last week's production cost?

EXERCISE 3-19

Spread-Sheet Software

EQUIVALENT UNITS AND UNIT COSTS—PROCESS COSTING

Savana Corporation began producing "quick-stick glue" in April 2003 (i.e., there was no beginning work-in-process inventory on April 1). The manufacturing process involves only one step. In April, the costs were $8,000 for direct materials and $6,216 for conversion costs. During the month, 6,400 pounds of direct materials were placed in production. At the end of April, 1,200 pounds of direct materials were still being processed and were 60% complete. Assume that all direct materials are added at the beginning of production.

1. Compute the number of equivalent units of output in terms of materials costs and labor and overhead (conversion) costs for April, assuming FIFO cost flow.
2. Determine the total cost of goods transferred to Finished Goods Inventory and the total cost of Work-in-Process Inventory at the end of April.

problems

PROBLEM 3-1

JOB ORDER COSTING IN A MANUFACTURING ORGANIZATION—JOURNAL ENTRIES

Following are transactions for Montigo Manufacturing Company. Assume that the company has no beginning work-in-process inventory.

1. Montigo purchased $600,000 of raw materials, paying 10% down, with the remainder to be paid in 10 days.
2. The production manager requisitioned $260,000 of materials (90% for direct use and the remainder for indirect purposes).
3. The liability incurred in (1) was paid in full.
4. 24,000 hours of direct labor and 2,000 hours of indirect labor were incurred. (Assume an average hourly wage rate of $9 for both direct and indirect labor.)
5. The following salaries were paid:

Factory supervisor (a product cost)	$80,000
Administrative executives	70,000
Sales personnel	90,000

6. Rent and utilities for the building of $30,000 and $7,000, respectively, were paid. Three-fourths of these expenses are applicable to manufacturing and the remainder to administration.
7. Depreciation on factory equipment was $15,000.
8. Advertising costs for the year totaled $15,000.
9. Manufacturing overhead is applied at a rate of $6.90 per direct labor hour.
10. All but $35,000 of Work-in-Process Inventory was completed and transferred to Finished Goods Inventory.
11. The sales price of finished goods that were sold was 130% of manufacturing costs. Assume a perpetual inventory system and that all finished goods were sold.
12. Close over- or underapplied overhead directly to cost of goods sold.

Required: Prepare journal entries for the transactions.

PROBLEM 3-2

ACCOUNTING FOR MANUFACTURING TRANSACTIONS—JOURNAL ENTRIES

Payson Company uses a job order costing system. The following is a partial list of the company's accounts. (*Note:* Additional accounts may be needed.)

Cash
Manufacturing Overhead
Sales
Cost of Goods Sold
Sales Commissions Expense
Administrative Expenses
Accounts Receivable
Commissions Payable

Required:

1. Prepare journal entries for each of the following transactions (omit explanations).
2. Prepare T-accounts and post the journal entries to the T-accounts. Transaction (a) has been completed as an example.

a. Raw materials previously purchased on account were paid for in cash, $700.

Cash (Debit)	Cash (Credit)	Accounts Payable (Debit)	Accounts Payable (Credit)
	(a) 700	(a) 700	

b. Raw materials were purchased for $1,500 on account.
c. Direct labor costs of $3,000 were recorded.
d. Direct materials costing $1,100 were issued directly to production.
e. Depreciation of $1,500 on manufacturing equipment was recorded. (Assume this is a product cost.)
f. Property taxes payable of $2,600 were recorded, half to manufacturing and half to administration.
g. Manufacturing overhead costs of $400 were applied to a job in process.
h. Materials previously purchased on account were paid for in cash, $1,500.
i. Sales commissions of $240 were recorded.
j. Goods costing $2,700 were transferred from Work-in-Process Inventory to Finished Goods Inventory.
k. Finished goods costing $2,300 were sold for $3,200 on credit, and the cost of goods sold was recorded.

PROBLEM 3-3

MANUFACTURING COST FLOWS

Tremonton Corporation uses a job order costing system in its manufacturing operation. For the year 2003, Tremonton's predetermined overhead rate was 90% of direct labor costs. For September 2003, the company incurred the following costs:

Purchased raw materials on account	$140,000
Issued raw materials to manufacturing process	130,000
Incurred direct labor costs ($10 per hour × 15,000 hr)	150,000
Actual manufacturing overhead costs	128,500
Cost of goods completed and sold	483,000

The company's inventories at the beginning of September 2003 were as follows:

Raw materials	$ 24,000
Work-in-process	115,000

The costs of all completed orders are transferred directly from Work-in-Process Inventory to Cost of Goods Sold.

Required:

1. Compute the following amounts.
   a. Work-in-Process Inventory balance at the end of September 2003.
   b. Over- or underapplied manufacturing overhead for the month of September.
2. Prepare journal entries to reflect the flow of costs into and out of Work-in-Process Inventory during September (omit explanations).

PROBLEM 3-4

USING T-ACCOUNTS: COST FLOWS IN A JOB ORDER MANUFACTURING ORGANIZATION

High Country Furniture Company manufactures custom furniture only and uses a job order costing system to accumulate costs. Actual direct materials and direct labor costs are accumulated for each job, but a predetermined overhead rate is used to apply manufacturing overhead costs to individual jobs. Manufacturing overhead is applied on the basis of direct labor hours. In computing a predetermined overhead rate, the controller estimated that manufacturing overhead costs for 2003 would be $80,000 and direct labor hours would be 20,000. The following information is available for the year 2003:

a. Direct materials purchased, $22,000.
b. Direct materials used in production, $19,500.
c. Wages and salaries paid for the year: direct labor (18,000 hours), $117,000; indirect labor, $12,000; sales and administrative salaries, $21,000.
d. Depreciation on machinery and equipment, $9,000.
e. Rent and utilities for building (75% factory), $16,000.
f. Miscellaneous manufacturing overhead, $51,500.
g. Advertising costs, $12,000.
h. Manufacturing overhead is applied to Work-in-Process Inventory.
i. Eighty percent of Work-in-Process Inventory was completed and transferred to Finished Goods Inventory.

Required:

1. Compute the predetermined overhead rate at which manufacturing overhead costs will be applied to jobs.
2. Set up T-accounts and post the transactions.
3. Compute the under- or overapplied manufacturing overhead. Prepare a journal entry to close Manufacturing Overhead and transfer the balance to Cost of Goods Sold.

PROBLEM 3-5

APPLYING MANUFACTURING OVERHEAD

Pinegor Corporation has four independent manufacturing divisions. The following data apply to the divisions for the year ended December 31, 2003:

	A	B	C	D
Direct materials costs	$120,000	$140,000	$80,000	$65,000
Direct labor hours	40,000	30,000	24,000	14,000
Direct labor costs	$110,000	$65,000	$70,000	$42,000

(continued)

	A	B	C	D
Actual manufacturing overhead	$120,000	$60,000	$70,000	$16,500
Machine hours worked	20,000	6,000	14,000	8,000
Number of units produced	100,000	2,000	15,000	5,000
Predetermined overhead rate	90% of direct labor costs	57% of direct materials costs	$1.25 per direct labor hour	$2 per machine hour

Required:

1. For each of the four divisions, calculate:
   a. Applied manufacturing overhead.
   b. Over- or underapplied manufacturing overhead.
   c. Cost of goods manufactured, assuming no work-in-process inventories.
   d. Average cost per unit produced.
2. **Interpretive Question:** How would you recommend that the over- or underapplied manufacturing overhead be disposed of in each division? Why?

PROBLEM 3-6

APPLYING MANUFACTURING OVERHEAD

Openshaw Manufacturing Company made the following estimates at the beginning of the year:

	Department G	Department H
Direct labor costs	$219,000	$166,980
Manufacturing overhead	$86,700	$153,340
Machine hours	17,000	12,500
Direct labor hours	30,000	22,000

Manufacturing overhead is applied on the basis of machine hours in Department G, and on the basis of direct labor hours in Department H. During the year, the following two jobs were completed:

Job #29

	Department G	Department H
Direct materials used	$16,000	$9,200
Direct labor costs	$18,250	$14,420
Direct labor hours	2,500	1,900
Machine hours	1,410	1,080

Job #30

	Department G	Department H
Direct materials used	$17,500	$8,100
Direct labor costs	$19,710	$13,920
Direct labor hours	2,700	1,800
Machine hours	1,530	1,020

Required:

1. Compute the predetermined overhead rate for each department.
2. Determine the amount of manufacturing overhead to be applied to each job.
3. Determine the total cost of each job.
4. Given that the actual manufacturing overhead costs for the year in Departments G and H were $88,200 and $152,500, respectively; that the actual machine hours in Depart-

ment G were 18,100; and that the direct labor hours in Department H were 21,600; compute the amount of over- or underapplied manufacturing overhead.

5. **Interpretive Question:** Why is the predetermined overhead rate based on estimated rather than actual information?

PROBLEM 3-7

UNIFYING CONCEPTS: JOB ORDER COSTING, COST FLOWS, JOURNAL ENTRIES, AND PREDETERMINED OVERHEAD RATES

Itsu Manufacturing Company applies manufacturing overhead on the basis of direct materials costs. The estimates for 2003 were:

Direct materials costs	$500,000
Manufacturing overhead.	150,000

Following are the transactions of Itsu Manufacturing Company for 2003:

a. Raw materials purchased on account, $550,000.
b. Raw materials issued to production, 90% for direct use and 10% for indirect use, for a total of $350,000.
c. Direct labor costs, $500,000.
d. Indirect labor costs, $50,000.
e. Administrative and sales salaries, $140,000 and $90,000, respectively.
f. Utilities, $21,000; plant depreciation, $40,000; maintenance, $15,000; miscellaneous administrative expenses, $4,000. (These costs are allocated on the basis of plant floor space—administrative facilities, 500 square feet; manufacturing, 2,500 square feet; sales facilities, 1,000 square feet.)
g. Manufacturing equipment depreciation, $12,000.
h. Additional raw materials issued to production for direct use, $250,000.
i. Manufacturing overhead is applied.
j. Recorded factory foreman's salary, $54,000.
k. Ninety percent of existing Work-in-Process Inventory is transferred to Finished Goods Inventory. (Work-in-Process beginning inventory was $30,000.)
l. All finished goods are sold. (Assume no beginning or ending inventories. Sales are marked up 50% of cost.)
m. Over- or underapplied manufacturing overhead is closed to Cost of Goods Sold.

Required:

1. Prepare a journal entry for each of the transactions and show the T-accounts for Manufacturing Overhead and Work-in-Process Inventory. (Assume that all manufacturing overhead is a product cost.)
2. What is the ending balance in the cost of goods sold account?
3. **Interpretive Question:** Comparing actual manufacturing overhead with estimates for 2003, what would you recommend that Itsu Manufacturing Company estimate for manufacturing overhead costs in 2004?

PROBLEM 3-8

UNIFYING CONCEPTS: JOB ORDER COSTING

Jones Custom Furniture Manufacturing, Inc., made the following estimates at the beginning of the year, 2003:

Budgeted direct labor costs	$300,000
Budgeted direct labor hours	20,000
Budgeted manufacturing overhead	$520,000

Jones applies manufacturing overhead to specific job orders on the basis of direct labor hours.

During the month of January, the following transactions occurred for Job #345, an order for 10 custom oak chairs, manufactured in the first week of January 2003:

Jan. 3 Requisitioned direct materials (lumber, fabric, paint), $876; put into production on Job #345.

3 Requisitioned indirect materials (glue, staples, sandpaper, and equipment grease), $154, for use in manufacturing the 10 chairs for Job #345, as well as other subsequent jobs.

7 Processed time card for Employee #214; 25 direct labor hours attributed to Job #345 at wage rate of $15 per hour.

7 Applied manufacturing overhead at the predetermined rate to Job #345, based on the actual direct labor hours.

7 Processed the manufacturing supervisor's weekly salary of $1,000. (This salary is considered indirect labor because the supervisor oversees all jobs in process and does not account for her time on a job-by-job basis.)

7 Job #345 was completed and transferred to the finished goods warehouse to await shipment to the customer.

9 The 10 oak chairs (Job #345) were shipped to the customer. The sales invoice reflects a sales price of $3,000 on account.

In addition to Job #345, Jones completed 47 other job orders in January and had 7 others in process at month-end. The following information summarizes additional manufacturing transactions for Jones for the month of January (not relating to Job #345):

a. Raw materials purchased on account, $102,675.
b. Requisitioned raw materials to specific job orders, $90,430; 80% direct materials, and the remainder indirect materials not directly attributable to any one specific job.
c. Incurred and paid direct labor wages totaled, $24,600; an average of $15 per hour for 1,640 total direct labor hours for January.
d. Applied manufacturing overhead at the predetermined rate to all jobs in progress on the basis of the actual direct labor hours incurred by job.
e. Incurred and paid supervisor salaries and other indirect manufacturing labor (e.g., maintenance labor) totaled, $7,000.
f. Incurred and paid the following costs associated with the manufacturing process and facility:

Factory rent	$ 7,600
Factory utilities	2,700
Insurance	1,200
Miscellaneous	1,900
	$13,400

g. Recorded depreciation of manufacturing equipment for the month, $5,500.
h. The cost of the 47 jobs completed during the month totaled $125,446.
i. Shipped all completed jobs to customers by month-end at a total sales price of $200,714 on account.
j. Incurred and paid selling and administrative costs (e.g., administrative salaries, sales commissions, office supplies, office rent, etc.), $46,514.

Required:

1. a. Calculate Jones' predetermined overhead rate for the year 2003.
   b. Prepare journal entries for the first seven transactions (relating to Job #345). Omit explanations.
   c. Determine the total cost of manufacturing each of the 10 oak chairs.
   d. Determine the total gross margin earned on all 10 oak chairs.
2. Prepare the journal entries for transactions (a)–(j). Omit explanations.
3. Close Manufacturing Overhead to Cost of Goods Sold (include all transactions noted for Job #345).
4. Calculate Jones' total gross margin for January, including Job #345.
5. Calculate Jones' total operating income for January.

6. Determine the ending January balances in Raw Materials Inventory, Work-in-Process Inventory, and Finished Goods Inventory (assume no beginning balances).

PROBLEM 3-9

COMPUTING OVERHEAD RATES AND CLIENT BILLING IN A SERVICE FIRM

Morgan Engineering Company employs three professional engineers, each having a different specialty. Don Corbin specializes in structural engineering; Bob Rouse, electrical engineering; and Bill Phillips, mechanical engineering. The firm expects to incur the following operating costs for 2003; travel and materials costs are billed separately to clients.

Office salaries and wages	$ 36,000
Office supplies	20,000
Utilities and telephone	15,400
Depreciation	16,200
Taxes and insurance	10,300
Miscellaneous expenses	2,100
Total estimated costs for 2003	$100,000

The salaries and billable hours of the three engineers are expected to be as follows:

	Expected Salary	Expected Hours
Corbin	$ 60,000	2,000
Rouse	48,000	1,760
Phillips	42,000	1,925
Total	$150,000	5,685

Required:

1. Compute the overhead cost rate that should be used for each of the engineers (based on the expected hours to be billed, with overhead cost rates varying in proportion to each engineer's compensation) to ensure that the total expected operating costs for 2003 will be recovered from clients. (*Hint:* Allocate total estimated overhead costs to each engineer based on relative salaries, then relate the allocated costs to the hours expected to be worked by each.)
2. Using the overhead cost rates determined in (1), determine the costs associated with the firm's work for Seaside Company with the following engineering services and related costs: Corbin, 100 hours; Rouse, 40 hours; Phillips, 10 hours; transportation and supplies costs, $1,600.

PROBLEM 3-10

SERVICE COSTING—JOURNAL ENTRIES

Following are transactions for Andersen Custodial, Inc. Assume the company's beginning work-in-process services account balance is zero.

1. Purchased supplies costing $5,000 for cash.
2. Received and immediately paid a utility bill, $800.
3. Used supplies costing $3,000 in doing work for a customer.
4. 3,000 hours of direct labor and 1,500 hours of indirect labor were incurred and paid. The average hourly wage rate for both direct and indirect labor is $7.
5. Monthly rent payment was made, $2,000.
6. Applied overhead at $4.50 per direct labor hour.
7. Andersen bills its customers at a rate of $20 per direct labor hour. All work in process was moved to Cost of Services.
8. All under- or overapplied overhead is closed to Cost of Services.

Required: Prepare the journal entries for the above transactions.

PROBLEM 3-11

SERVICE COSTING—JOURNAL ENTRIES

Blake Accounting Services has the following transactions. Its beginning work-in-process services account balance is zero.

a. Purchased supplies costing $11,000 on account.
b. Paid property tax, $20,000.
c. Paid rent, $2,000; and utilities, $700.
d. Paid support staff salaries, $35,000.
e. Used supplies costing $9,000.
f. Paid direct labor salaries, $50,000. Average rate was $10 per hour.
g. Applied overhead at $11.50 per direct labor hour.
h. Transferred $100,000 from Work-in-Process to Cost of Services and billed customers for 4,500 hours of work. Blake bills its customers $40 per direct labor hour.
i. Closed under- or overapplied overhead to Cost of Services.

Required:

1. Prepare the journal entries for the above transactions.
2. Determine the ending balance in the work-in-process services account.

PROBLEM 3-12

SERVICE COST FLOWS

Tolman Company had the following balances at the beginning of 2003:

	Debit	Credit
Accounts receivable	$22,000	
Supplies	5,000	
Work-in-process services	15,000	
Accounts payable (related to supplies)		$ 3,500
Salaries and wages payable		35,000
Utilities payable		1,200
Rent payable		1,500

Tolman estimates that its total 2003 overhead will amount to $200,000. It allocates overhead based on direct labor hours. Tolman estimates that its total 2003 direct labor hours will be 50,000 hours. Because it produces monthly financial statements, Tolman makes adjusting entries at the end of each month. However, over- or underapplied overhead is not closed to Cost of Services until the end of the year.

During January 2003, Tolman had the following transactions:

Jan. 1 Paid rent. Tolman has a two-year, $72,000 lease. Rent is payable on the 1st of each month.
4 Paid all utilities payable from 2002.
5 Paid all salaries and wages payable from 2002. $23,000 was for direct labor; $12,000 was for indirect labor.
8 Paid for all supplies purchased in 2002.
10 Used supplies, $450.
19 Collected $15,000 from a customer for services performed and billed in December 2002.
23 Purchased supplies, $600.
25 Used supplies, $1,300.
31 Paid all employees for January labor. Total direct labor costs for the month of January were $25,000, direct labor hours, 4,000. Indirect labor costs were $15,000.
31 Tolman estimates its January utility expenses to be $1,000.
31 Tolman completed and billed jobs costing $40,000. The company billed customers $55,000.

Required:

1. Prepare all journal entries necessary for the month of January.
2. What is the balance in the work-in-process services account at the end of January?
3. Compute the balance in the overhead account on January 31.

expanded material

PROBLEM 3-13

FIFO COST FLOW—PROCESS COSTING

The cleaning division of Sunshine Grain Company had the following data for January 2003:

	Tons	Percentage Completed	Direct Materials Costs	Conversion Costs
Beginning work-in-process inventory	400	65%	$ 8,500	$ 1,200
Units started in production	26,600	—		
Costs added this month			598,500	126,192
Ending work-in-process inventory	600	25%		
Units completed during month and transferred to packing	26,400	—		

Required:

1. Compute the per-ton cost of grain processed by the cleaning division in this period.
2. Using the FIFO cost flow method, compute the cost of the 26,000 tons of grain that were started and completed during January.
3. Compute the cost of the ending work-in-process inventory.

PROBLEM 3-14

FIFO COST FLOW—PROCESS COSTING

Western Oil Company has three process centers: drilling, processing, and distributing. During September 2003, the processing department had the following operating data:

	Barrels	Percentage Completed	Direct Materials Costs	Conversion Costs
Beginning work-in-process inventory	4,000	60%	$ 2,200	$ 4,200
Units started and completed this month	36,000	—		
Costs added this month			33,150	88,410
Ending work-in-process inventory	15,000	30%		
Units completed during month and transferred to distributing	40,000	—		

Required:

Assuming a FIFO flow of costs, compute:

1. The "work done" for September (in equivalent units of production) for direct materials and for conversion costs.
2. The September cost per barrel of oil in the processing department.
3. The cost of all oil transferred to distributing.
4. The cost of ending work-in-process inventory in the processing department.

PROBLEM 3-15

FIFO COST FLOW—PROCESS COSTING

The Assembly Department of Southeastern Electronics Company reported the following data for the month of June 2003:

	Units	Costs
Beginning inventory (60% complete)	4,000	
Units transferred from prior department	30,000	
Ending inventory (50% complete)	6,000	
Cost of beginning inventory (materials $15,000, conversion $15,000)		$ 30,000
Cost of materials used in assembly department		90,000
Conversion costs for June in assembly department		157,300
Total cost		$277,300

(*Note:* Materials used in the assembly department are added at the beginning of the assembly process.)

Required: Prepare the production cost report for the assembly department. (Note: For purposes of this problem, prior department's manufacturing costs are not included in this department's production cost report.)

PROBLEM 3-16

Spread-Sheet Software

EQUIVALENT UNITS AND FIFO COST FLOW—PROCESS COSTING

Midtown Manufacturing Company has two process centers—manufacturing and assembly. The data that follow show the production and cost results for the manufacturing center for the month of July 2003:

Production data:	
Units in process, July 1 (materials 50% complete, conversion 40% complete)	500
Units started in production	2,500
Units in process, July 31 (materials 100% complete, conversion 60% complete)	700
Cost data:	
Units in process, July 1:	
Direct materials	$ 3,000
Conversion costs	6,400
Direct materials used in July	27,500
Conversion costs for July	73,080
Total	$109,980

(*Note:* In this problem, materials are *not* added at the beginning of the manufacturing process.)

Required: Prepare the production cost report for the manufacturing center.

competency enhancement opportunities

- Analyzing Real Company Information
- International Case
- Ethics Case
- Writing Assignment
- The Debate
- Internet Search

The following additional assignments provide opportunities for students to develop critical thinking, ethical perspectives, oral and written communication skills, experience with electronic research, and teamwork through group and business activities.

ANALYZING REAL COMPANY INFORMATION

- ***Analyzing 3-1 (Microsoft)***

1. Is **MICROSOFT** a service business, a manufacturing business, or a merchandising business? Explain.
2. Microsoft's 1999 income statement (Appendix A) lists research and development expense of $2,970 billion for the year. The notes to the financial statements say that "research and development costs are expensed as incurred" in accordance with generally accepted accounting principles. Do you think that Microsoft treats R&D costs any differently in its internal accounting reports? Explain.
3. In its management's discussion and analysis (Appendix A), Microsoft describes its three primary sales channels. What are they?

- ***Analyzing 3-2 (Pump, Inc.)***

Acquiring management accounting data on real companies can be a challenge because this information is generally highly proprietary and of significant competitive value. The cost data below are for a medium-size family-owned pump manufacturing business located in the Midwest. (This business chooses to remain anonymous in order to keep its competitors from using these data to compete against it.) We'll refer to this company simply as Pump, Inc.

Pump, Inc., had reorganized much of its production into manufacturing "cells": self-supervising work centers that produce complete products. The cell program was initiated because of a strategic decision (with no management accounting data to support it) to improve customer service. The financial impact of the program was unclear; the operational causes and the financial effects were murky. As a result, the management team at Pump, Inc., was having a difficult time evaluating the effects of its strategic decision to change *most* of the company to manufacturing cells. (Some of the production process continued to be organized as a typical production line, similar to what is demonstrated in the chapter.) The current year's cost data are presented below in the standard format typically used by the management accountant for Pump, Inc.

Typical Cost Data Format

Cost Category	Cost	Percent of Cost
Direct materials	$433,966	54.55%
Direct labor	96,990	12.19
Manufacturing overhead	264,583	33.26
Total costs	$795,539	100.00%

The management team, however, had a difficult time using the cost data in the typical format to effectively control and evaluate its reorganization decision. The management accountant was asked to reformat the data to make them more useful for the management team. After some analysis, the accountant decided to provide more detail by breaking down Manufacturing Overhead into subcategories organized by function: Indirect Materials, Indirect Labor, Factory Support, Occupancy Costs, and Non-Factory Support. The accountant also realized that she could divide all costs into two additional categories: People Costs (represent costs for wages and salaries) and Purchased Costs (represent costs for materials, supplies, and services acquired from outside agencies). The new report format is presented below.

New Cost Data Format

Cost Category	People Costs	Purchased Costs	Total Cost
Direct materials		$433,966	$433,966
Indirect materials		9,460	9,460
Direct labor	$ 96,990		96,990
Indirect labor (production line supervision)	29,100		29,100
Factory support (material handling, equipment depreciation, utilities, expediting, engineering, etc.)	80,953	71,310	152,263
Occupancy costs (rents, taxes, maintenance, etc.)	15,180	32,550	47,730
Non-factory support (cost accounting, personnel, etc.)	23,390	2,640	26,030
Total costs	$245,613	$549,926	$795,539

Source: Adapted from J. S. McGroarty and C. T. Horngren, "Functional Costing for Better Teamwork and Decision Support," *Journal of Cost Management*, Winter 1993, pp. 24–36. Reprinted with permission.

Consider the two reports on cost data for Pump, Inc.

1. Do you think the new report format provides any additional information value for controlling and evaluating the decision to change most of the production process into manufacturing cells?
2. What costs do you think the management team at Pump, Inc., should pay careful attention to in its effort to better control costs in the production plant?
3. Most importantly, if you were on the management team at Pump, Inc., what *additional* data would you like to see the management accountant provide?

INTERNATIONAL CASE

• *Management Accounting in France*

France has a well-developed set of financial accounting rules, as embodied in the *Plan Comptable Général (PCG)*. The French PCG is comparable to U.S. GAAP. You may not have realized it, but the cost accounting for manufacturers we have studied in this chapter has a very clear connection to the way financial accounting is reported. Exhibit 3-2 in the text visibly demonstrates the difference between the production process and the administration process in a manufacturing organization. U.S. cost accounting makes a clear functional distinction between costs related to the production process (e.g., direct materials, direct labor, and manufacturing overhead) versus the administration process (e.g., selling costs and general administration costs). Further, Exhibit 3-4 demonstrates that the flow of direct materials costs and direct labor costs through the accounting system, as well as the allocation of manufacturing overhead costs, allows U.S. companies to determine product costs and easily compute cost of goods sold for financial reporting purposes. However, cost accounting (*comptabilité analytique*) in France is explicitly decoupled from financial accounting, as defined by the PCG. What this means is that the chart of accounts French companies use for cost accounting is completely different from the chart of accounts used for financial accounting. The reason is not necessarily because French companies perform cost accounting differently from U.S. companies, but that the nature of French financial accounting is quite different from financial accounting in the United States. The PCG requires financial accounting reports in France to organize and report costs by their inherent nature (materials, labor, depreciation, etc.). Costs are not assigned to products or to departments. Hence, one wouldn't expect to see a French company report Costs of Goods Sold or Selling and General Administrative Expense.

Think about this for a moment. If costs are not being assigned to products, departments, or operations within the organization, how does the organization perform the management processes of planning, controlling, and evaluating? Actually, French companies do not have a tradition of using costs to manage their companies. In fact, the traditional phrase used in France to describe the techniques and practices of planning, control, and evaluation has been *contróle de gestion*, literally, "management control." The absence of the word *comptabilité* (accounting) in this phrase is significant: it indicates that accounting numbers play a limited role in managerial reporting systems in France. Only very recently has the phrase *comptabilité de gestion* become more common. French business has had a long tradition of being led by engineers, not by accountants and financiers. Even today some 50% of managing directors in France are engineers by profession or training.

Costs are not being used as the main tool for managing companies in France. Given that a large number of the management executives of French companies have engineering backgrounds, how do French companies handle the management processes of planning, controlling, and evaluating (e.g., what kinds of numbers and reports might you expect to find in a French company)? Would you expect that French companies reconcile their *comptabilité analytique* systems with their financial accounting systems, as U.S. companies typically do?

Source: Reprinted from A. Roberts, "Management Accounting in France," *Management Accounting (UK)*, March 1995, pp. 44–46, by permission of the publisher Academic Press Limited, London.

ETHICS CASE

• *State Home Builders Inc.*

You have recently been hired as an accountant for the largest residential construction company in the state. Your primary responsibility is to track costs for each home being constructed. Tracking the costs for direct materials and direct labor is relatively straightforward. Materials requisitioned for each home site are carefully tracked, and the construction workers are very careful about assigning their time to the homes they work on.

Accounting for manufacturing overhead costs, on the other hand, presents quite a problem. In the past, overhead has been allocated on the basis of direct labor hours. As a result, because larger houses require more workers, those houses have been allocated a larger share of the overhead.

Your company was recently selected by the state to build a number of low-income housing complexes. The state has agreed to an arrangement whereby it will pay your costs plus a 10% profit. Construction of these low-income housing units will be relatively simple and will not require a great deal of materials or labor, compared to the average house the company builds.

At a meeting following the granting of the construction contract by the state, the production foreman proposes the following idea:

> Since the state has agreed to pay our costs plus 10%, the higher the costs on the project, the more money we make. What we need to do is to funnel as much of our costs as possible to this low-income housing project. Now I don't want anyone to think I am proposing something unethical. I am not saying that we should charge the state for fictitious costs. What I am saying is that we should allocate as much overhead as possible to the low-income project. Therefore, I propose that we allocate overhead on a per-house basis with each house, regardless of size, being allocated the same amount of overhead.

You have analyzed the activities that drive overhead costs and have found that bigger houses, in addition to requiring more direct materials and direct labor, require more inspections, more supervision, etc. You can see that most in attendance at the meeting are being persuaded by the production foreman's idea. You slowly raise your hand. It takes about 10 seconds before all the voices quiet. You look around the table and see 10 of your colleagues staring at you. You open your mouth and . . .

1. What would you do in this situation? Is the overhead allocation method being proposed by the production foreman illegal? Is it unethical?
2. Suppose you argue that overhead should continue to be allocated on the basis of direct labor hours. After hearing your points, the group votes to go with the production foreman and allocate the overhead on a per-house basis. What would you do next?

WRITING ASSIGNMENT

• *Trends in Product Cost Relationships*

The ratios among the three types of product costs have changed quite a bit over the last 150 years of business. Generally, costs of direct materials have consistently formed approximately 50% of total product costs for manufacturing firms. However, the ratio of direct labor costs has been decreasing with an offsetting increase in the ratio of manufacturing overhead costs. What kinds of costing challenges does this shift from direct costs to manufacturing overhead costs pose for a manufacturing company? What factors do you think have contributed to this trend? Do you think that the advent of e-business will significantly affect the amount or ratio of direct labor costs in manufacturing products? If so, how? Write a one- to two-page paper on this topic.

THE DEBATE

• *When Does a Direct Materials Cost Turn Into an Indirect Cost (e.g., Manufacturing Overhead)?*

Consider your automobile. What costs would be considered direct materials? What costs would be considered indirect materials? Are the fender panels direct or indirect materials? Are the rivets that connect the fender to the frame direct or indirect materials? Are the headlights direct or indirect materials? Are the screws that hold the headlights in place direct or indirect materials? In light of the intense price competition that takes place in the automobile industry, these are important cost questions: direct materials are assigned to a specific automobile (or automobile model), while indirect materials are gathered together in the pool of manufacturing overhead costs and generally allocated across all types of automobiles in the manufacturing plant.

Divide your group into two teams.

- One team represents: "Rivets and screws should be treated as direct costs." Prepare a two-minute oral argument supporting this view. Be careful that you don't make too many quick assumptions. Tracking direct materials costs to specific product units or product lines can be a very expensive process in a complex manufacturing organization.
- The other team represents: "Rivets and screws should be treated as indirect costs." Prepare a two-minute oral argument supporting this view. You must be careful that you don't make too many quick assumptions. Before you say that rivets and screws are indirect because their costs are small, consider that the bigger automakers spend tens of millions of dollars each year on rivets and screws.

INTERNET SEARCH

• ***Wal-Mart***

Access **WAL-MART**'s customer web site at **http://www.walmart.com**. Sometimes Web addresses change, so if this address doesn't work, access the Web site for this textbook (**http://albrecht.swcollege.com**) for an updated link.

Once you've gained access to the site, answer the following questions.

1. Use Wal-Mart's Store Finder to find the store nearest you.
2. What is the current price on a paperback version of J. K. Rowling's *Harry Potter and the Sorcerer's Stone* (a popular children's book)?

Now access Wal-Mart's corporate Web site at **http://www.walmartstores.com** (you could also click on the "Wal-Mart Stores, Inc." link at the bottom of the customer Web site). Again, if this Web address should change, access the Web site for this textbook (**http://albrecht.swcollege.com**) for an updated link.

Once you've gained access to this site, answer the following questions:

3. In order to be a Wal-Mart supplier you would need to adhere to certain "Supplier Standards." Although these standards are very detailed, what are the nine basic categories of supplier standards?
4. Wal-Mart's first non-U.S. store opened in December 1991. Where? How many Wal-Mart stores are located in China?

part 2

Planning

Capital Investment Decisions

chapter

m4

learning objectives

After studying this chapter, you should be able to:

1 Understand the importance of capital budgeting and the concepts underlying strategic and capital investment decisions.

2 Describe and use two nondiscounted capital budgeting techniques: the payback method and the unadjusted rate of return method.

3 Describe and use two discounted capital budgeting techniques: the net present value method and the internal rate of return method.

4 Understand the need for evaluating qualitative factors in strategic and capital investment decisions.

expanded material

5 Use sensitivity analysis to assess the potential effects of uncertainty in capital budgeting.

6 Explain how to use capital budgeting techniques in ranking capital investment projects.

7 Explain how income taxes affect capital budgeting decisions.

FEDERAL EXPRESS CORPORATION (FEDEX) is the largest air-freight company in the world. Fred Smith, founder of Federal Express, came up with his initial overnight-delivery idea as he was writing a term paper in 1965 as a Yale undergraduate. Smith's Yale professor was unimpressed with the idea and gave the paper a "C" grade. After serving two tours of duty in Vietnam as a Marine, Smith returned to the United States and began assembling the pieces to implement his idea. In 1971, Smith was optimistic about obtaining the contract to ship canceled checks around the country; he named his company "Federal Express" because the contract would have been with the Federal Reserve System. That contract never came to be, and Smith focused his attention on shipping small, time-sensitive packages through his hub-and-spoke air system centered in Memphis, Tennessee. The inaugural night of service was March 12, 1973, but only six packages arrived at the 10,000-per-hour package handling system in Memphis. After further marketing in an expanded set of cities, a second start was attempted on April 17, 1973. That night, Federal Express handled 186 packages, and daily volume has climbed steadily ever since. In 2000, FedEx Corporation delivered nearly 5 million shipments per day.

For FedEx and other firms in the air-freight industry, their most important investment is the airplanes that haul the freight. Indeed, making good airplane acquisition decisions is critical to the success of FedEx and its competitors. Though FedEx is profitable and expanding, questions have been raised about whether the company has made the right kind of airplane investment decisions. In early 1998, the Federal Aviation Administration (FAA) began public hearings to question the structural safety of scores of FedEx's aircraft. The FAA contended that the maximum allowed weight limit of these 727s should be cut from 8,000 pounds per modular cargo container to 3,000 pounds, which would significantly increase the per-pound cost of shipping cargo and reduce FedEx's profitability.

For years, the air-freight industry has relied heavily on the practice of converting retired passenger planes into cargo freighters. The safety questions raised by the FAA involve how cargo doors were installed and other structural changes made when the aircraft were modified. Safety concerns range from the stability of cargo doors to the ability of aircraft to survive a strong downward gust. FAA research has shown that under combinations of certain extreme conditions, the floor beams of 727s might fail, causing the aircraft to suddenly break apart in a massive midair convulsion. [Those who have seen the Tom Hanks movie *Cast Away* are familiar with this scenario.]

FedEx countered that the probability of the combination of conditions that would cause such an accident is highly remote. The FAA said it didn't want to wait until after an accident had occurred to raise safety issues about the 727s. In the end, the FAA compromised and only required FedEx to reduce its modular cargo container weights to 4,800 pounds in the 120 FedEx **BOEING** 727s in question. While FedEx was fighting the FAA claims and allegations, the company must have wondered if it made the right kind of investment decision by acquiring and converting the 727s. At a minimum, the questions raised about the safety of FedEx's operations represented a public relations nightmare for FedEx.

Sources: Douglas A. Blackmon, "FedEx Faults Claims by FAA Over Aircraft," *The Wall Street Journal*, Wednesday, February 18, 1998, p. A3; Paul Richfield, "FAA Issues Final Ruling on 727 Freighters," *The Wall Street Journal*, January 11, 1999, p. B2; Robert A. Sigafoos, *Absolutely Positively Overnight!: The Unofficial History of Federal Express* (Memphis: St. Lukes Press, 1988).

setting the stage

How do FedEx and other companies decide which types of equipment to buy and what other capital investments to make? In this chapter, we examine that part of planning called ***capital budgeting,*** *the systematic planning for long-term investments in operating assets (primarily property, plant, equipment, intangible assets, and natural resources). Capital budgeting techniques are also important in planning for a company's investments in people and information. For example, the most important*

capital budgeting Systematic planning for long-term investments in operating assets.

decisions a university makes are not about where or when to build buildings but instead are about whom to hire for the university's faculty.

Capital budgeting differs from the types of planning already discussed in that it is more permanent and less retractable. A decision to increase inventory levels, for example, can be reversed within a relatively short time by cutting back on future purchases or by lowering prices to increase sales. Even a nonroutine decision to purchase, rather than make or deliver internally, a component or service can generally be changed without too much disruption to operations. On the other hand, a capital investment decision to purchase 120 Model 727 freight aircraft at several million dollars each requires a long-term commitment of resources, a commitment that will probably be difficult and very expensive to change at a later date. Because of its long-term consequences, capital budgeting is an important part of a company's strategic plan. Strategic planning involves establishing the overall direction of a company's activities. Strategic planning is discussed in Chapter 5 of management accounting.

Because capital budgeting involves long-range planning, the time value of money must be considered. But before we begin to explain how capital budgeting provides management with information for evaluating long-term investments in operating assets, we must introduce some basic concepts.

1

Understand the importance of capital budgeting and the concepts underlying strategic and capital investment decisions.

CONCEPTUAL BASIS OF CAPITAL BUDGETING

The primary objective of a business is to generate a profit for its owners. Profitable businesses can be based on a low-cost strategy (such as WAL-MART), a customer service strategy (such as FEDEX), a product-branding strategy (such as COCA-COLA), and a variety of other business strategies. No matter what a company's underlying strategy, it must make long-term investment decisions in buildings, equipment, information technology, personnel, and so forth. Capital budgeting is the process of determining whether the future sales, cost savings, quality improvements, and other future benefits stemming from these strategic investment decisions are sufficient to justify the significant up-front costs associated with those decisions. In short, capital budgeting involves a comparison of the magnitude of up-front costs to the magnitude of estimated future multiyear benefits.

capital The total amount of money or other resources owned or used to acquire future income or benefits.

The term **capital** may be defined broadly as any form of material wealth. As used in business, it is more specifically defined as the total amount of money or other resources owned or used by an individual or a company to acquire future income or benefits.

Thus, capital is something to be invested with the expectation that it will be recovered along with a profit, and capital budgeting is the planning for that investment. From a quantitative viewpoint, the success of an investment depends on the amount of net future cash inflows (or future cash savings) in relation to the cost (current cash outlays) of the investment. Ignoring the time value of money for the moment, if a company invests $10,000 and receives only $10,000 in the future, there has been only a return of the investment but no profit. However, if $15,000 is received in the future, there is not only a return of the original investment but also an additional return, or profit, of $5,000. Other things being equal, investors obviously wish to receive the greatest future benefits for the least investment cost.

Importance of Capital Investment Decisions in Planning

Three aspects of capital investment decisions are critical to long-run profitability:

1. *Large initial outlay.* Decisions to invest in assets such as land, buildings, and equipment usually require large outlays of capital. Unless a reasonable return is received on such significant investments, the overall profitability of a firm will suffer.
2. *Potential long-term impact on earnings.* Long-term investments, by definition, extend over several years. Thus, poor capital budgeting, resulting in bad investment decisions, is likely to have an adverse effect on earnings over a long period.
3. *Difficult to reverse course.* Long-term investments in land, buildings, and specialized equipment are much less liquid than other investments. Investments in stocks and bonds, for example, can usually be terminated by sale through regularly established markets at almost any time; operating assets may not be so readily disposed of.

Each of these three factors can be seen in the FedEx scenario described at the beginning of the chapter. FedEx had expended millions of dollars on the 120 BOEING 727s that the FAA was concerned about. The efficient, or inefficient, use of this portion of FedEx's fleet would have implications for FedEx's reported earnings for many years; many 727s have now been in use for over 30 years. Finally, once FedEx had committed itself to using these converted 727 freighters, it was extremely costly to overhaul or retire the planes in response to the FAA concerns.

net work

The Web site for the U.S. President's Office of Management and Budget is http://www.whitehouse.gov/omb. This Web site can be used to find a copy of the most recent Federal budget. Associated with the budget itself is an analysis of different budget categories; this document is called Analytical Perspectives. In this Analytical Perspectives is an analysis of the "Federal Investment Spending and Capital Budgeting." For the most recent Federal budget year, determine how most of the direct Federal capital investment funds were spent.

Uses of Capital Budgeting: Screening and Ranking

Clearly, all long-term investment decisions are important. The larger the investment, however, the more critical is the need to budget for that expenditure. And the longer the time period, the more difficult it is to assess future outcomes and to plan accordingly. Following are some typical business situations that lend themselves to analysis with capital budgeting techniques:

1. A machine breaks down. Should the manager have the machine repaired or replaced?
2. Should a pharmaceutical company hire a renowned research scientist and commit to supporting this scientist and her staff for the next 10 years?
3. Should a company add to its manufacturing facility or build a new, larger factory?
4. Should a professional sports team sign a long-term guaranteed contract for $252 million with a key player?
5. Should Company A purchase Company B and, if so, on what terms?

Situations such as these require careful consideration of all factors, qualitative as well as quantitative, and it is just as important for nonprofit organizations to make sound strategic and capital investment decisions as for-profit organizations. Thus, the concepts and techniques discussed in this chapter are applicable to all types of organizations—companies, governmental agencies, school districts, hospitals, city governments, and so forth.

Capital budgeting analysis can help by answering two basic questions. First, does the investment make sense? That is, does it meet a minimum standard of financial acceptability? This is the **screening** function of capital budgeting. Second, is an investment the best among available acceptable alternatives? We determine this by **ranking** the alternatives. Before we discuss the screening and ranking of investment alternatives, we will briefly review the time value of money concept.

screening Determining whether a capital investment meets a minimum standard of financial acceptability.

ranking The ordering of acceptable investment alternatives from most to least desirable.

interest The payment (cost) for the use of money.

The Time Value of Money

Like other commodities, money has value because it is a scarce resource. Therefore, a payment is generally required for its use. This payment is called **interest**. Because the time value of money is widely recognized, few people would consider hiding money under a mattress or otherwise keeping large amounts of idle cash; they realize that there is a significant opportunity cost in doing so. Money left idle will not earn interest, nor will it earn the potentially higher returns that can be obtained from investments in corporate stocks and bonds or real estate, for example.

Because money has value over time, the timing of expected cash flows is important in investment decisions. This is the essence of capital budgeting—comparing the cost of an investment with the expected future net cash inflows to decide whether, given the risks and available alternatives, the project should be undertaken. An investment made today will not generate cash inflows until the future, either periodically over a number of years or in a lump sum several years hence. Thus, for the comparison of cash flows to be accurate, all amounts should be stated at their value at one point in time, generally the present; this means that all future cash flows should be stated in terms of their present values. This mathematical process of adjusting future cash flows to their present values is called discounting.

The choice of the correct interest rate, or discount rate, to use in doing time value of money computations is extremely important. In fact, this is one of the topics emphasized in the field of finance. Generally speaking, managers use relatively high discount rates when evaluating projects or investments that involve a high degree of risk; an expectation of a high rate of return is necessary to entice a rational manager into undertaking a very risky project. In addition, a manager must consider what it will cost to obtain the funds to finance the project. We will return later to the problem of selecting a discount rate for making capital investment decisions.

In the remainder of this chapter and in the end-of-chapter exercises and problems, we will assume that you understand the concepts of present value and the underlying notion of the time value of money. If you do not, or if you want to refresh your memory, you might want to review the appendix to this chapter.

Discounting Cash Flows

Because of the time value of money, a difference in the timing of cash flows can make one investment more attractive than another, even if both involve the same total amount of money. To illustrate, we assume that project A will produce $100,000 at the end of one year and that project B will return $50,000 at the end of each year for two years. Both projects will generate a total of $100,000. However, by using present value computations (reviewed in the chapter appendix) and assuming a discount (interest) rate of 10 percent per year, you will see that the discounted cash flows from project A are $90,910 and from project B are $86,775. In other words, if the appropriate discount rate is 10 percent, receiving $90,910 right now is the same as receiving $100,000 one year from now. Similarly, receiving $86,775 right now is the same as receiving $50,000 at the end of each year for the next two years. The difference in the present values of these two projects with the same total cash flows arises because with project A, the cash is received sooner. Cash received sooner is worth more because it can be put to productive use—invested, used to pay off loans, and so forth. If all other factors—that is, any qualitative considerations—are the same, an investor would be $4,135 (in today's dollars) better off by investing in project A.

Project A

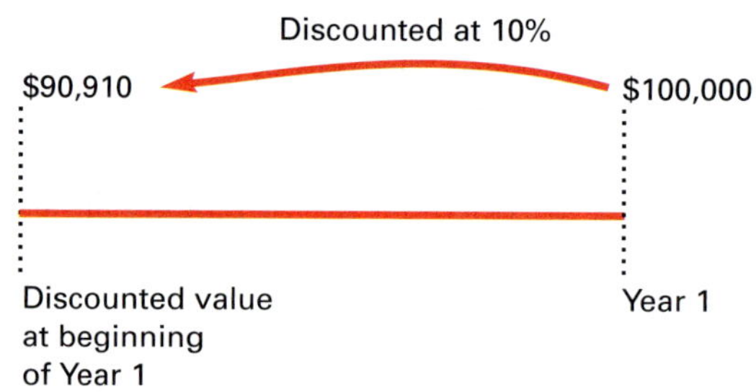

Project B

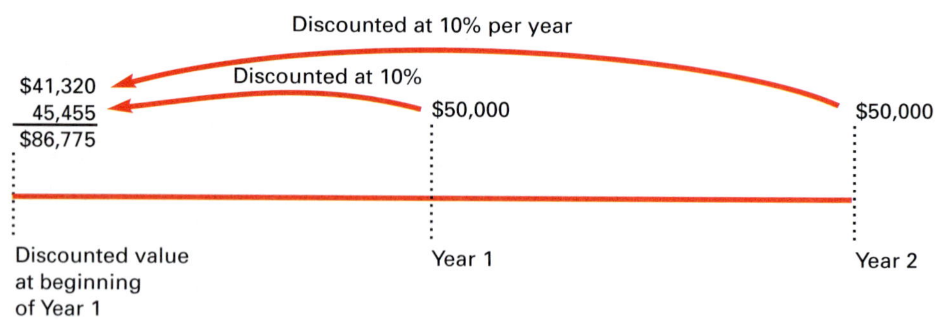

As this analysis shows, discounted cash flows reflect the time value of money and should be considered in capital budgeting. The determination of net income in accordance with GAAP is based, as you know, on accrual concepts that recognize income when it is earned, not when cash is actually received. Thus, accounting net income doesn't necessarily coincide with cash flows. For short-term investments, this approach does not significantly affect the results. Ignoring the time value of money can be misleading, however, for evaluating long-term projects.

To be able to compare cash outflows and inflows, you need a solid understanding of the discounting of cash flows. In the following paragraphs, we provide some definitions and examples.

cash outflows The initial cost and other expected outlays associated with an investment.

CASH OUTFLOWS **Cash outflows** include the initial cost of an investment plus any other expected future cash outlays associated with the investment. For example, suppose that a company purchases a drill press for $8,000 cash less a trade-in allowance of $500 for its old press. With maintenance expenses of $400 at the end of each year for the 5-year life of the press, and assuming a 12 percent discount rate, the present value of the cash outflows for the investment is:

	Time Period	Cash Outflows	Present Value Factor	Present Value of Cash Outflows
Initial cash outlay	Today	$7,500	1.0000	$7,500
Future cash outlays	Years 1–5	400	3.6048*	1,442
Total present value of cash outflows				$8,942

*From Table II, 5 years at 12 percent.

caution

In the examples used in this chapter, we provide the amounts of the future cash flows that are discounted. With real capital budgeting decisions, however, it is often very difficult to determine what the amounts of future cash inflows and outflows will be. With capital budgeting, we are dealing with future outcomes that are often difficult to project. It is this uncertainty about the future that makes capital budgeting so complex in the real world.

The $7,500 is invested immediately, so it is already stated at its present value. The $400 series of equal payments (an annuity) is to be extended over five years, so it must be discounted to its present value equivalent.

Maintenance expense is only one category of future cash outflows. Another is manufacturing overhead costs, such as heat, electricity, and rent, that may be incurred as a consequence of an investment. In addition, income taxes are expenses that must be considered in almost all capital budgeting decisions made by businesses. For simplicity, income taxes are ignored in the first part of this chapter; the impact of income taxes on capital budgeting decisions is explained in the expanded material section of the chapter. In brief, all current or expected cash outlays (expressed in terms of present values) should be considered as cash outflows in evaluating investments.

Note that some expenses, although deducted from revenues in arriving at accounting net income, do not involve actual cash disbursements and so should not be considered outflows in capital budgeting. It would obviously be wrong, for example, to include depreciation expense as an outflow, since no cash flow is directly involved.

cash inflows Any current or expected revenues or savings directly associated with an investment.

CASH INFLOWS **Cash inflows** include all current and expected future revenues or savings directly associated with an investment. For example, rent receipts, installment payments, and other revenues represent cash inflows. Returning to our earlier example, we now assume that the drill press is expected to generate annual revenues of $2,500 for five years, after which it can be sold as scrap for $750. The present value of the cash inflows for the investment is:

	Time Period	Cash Inflows	Present Value Factor	Present Value of Cash Inflows
Revenues	Years 1–5	$2,500	3.6048*	$9,012
Salvage value	Year 5	750	0.5674**	426
Total present value of cash inflows				$9,438

*From Table II, 5 years at 12 percent.
**From Table I, 5 years at 12 percent.

These revenues may be shown "net"—that is, reduced by any direct expenses, such as those for maintenance or materials and supplies. Thus, the net annual cash inflows from the drill press would be $2,100 per year ($2,500 − $400 maintenance expense).

Less obvious cash inflows are represented by the present value of the savings to be derived from an investment that reduces costs. In brief, the present value of all cash that is likely to be received or saved as a result of an investment should be included as cash inflows.

---

to summarize

Certain long-term investment decisions require significant capital outlays. Proper planning for these decisions is critical to long-run profitability. Capital budgeting techniques are designed to help in analyzing the quantitative factors relating to these decisions. Essentially, capital budgeting involves a comparison of the current and expected cash outflows and inflows in order to decide whether, given the risks and available alternatives, an investment should be made. To make comparisons more meaningful, all future cash flows should be discounted to the present.

2

Describe and use two nondiscounted capital budgeting techniques: the payback method and the unadjusted rate of return method.

NONDISCOUNTED CAPITAL BUDGETING TECHNIQUES

The four most commonly used capital budgeting techniques are (1) the payback method, (2) the unadjusted rate of return method, (3) the net present value method, and (4) the internal rate of return method. We will discuss the first two methods in this section and the latter two in the next section.

We have chosen the sequence of our discussion to parallel the pattern of most companies as they grow larger and become more sophisticated in the way that they make investment decisions. That is, companies generally first use the payback method or the unadjusted rate of return method because these techniques are relatively simple. Both of these techniques have a serious weakness, however, in that they ignore the time value of money. As a result, most companies eventually turn to either the net present value method or the internal rate of return method, both of which are more theoretically correct approaches to capital budgeting. The last two techniques are referred to as **discounted cash flow methods** because they use a discount rate in comparing the cash flows of investments.

discounted cash flow methods Capital budgeting techniques that take into account the time value of money by comparing discounted cash flows.

payback method A capital budgeting technique that determines the amount of time it takes the net cash inflows of an investment to repay the investment cost.

Payback Method

The **payback method** is widely used in business because it is simple to apply and it provides a preliminary screening of investment opportunities. It can also be used as a crude measure of a project's risk. Basically, this method is used to determine the length of time it will take the net cash inflows of an investment to equal the cash outlay. The payback period may be a particularly important consideration for companies in a tight credit position. Assuming that the payback period is to be computed in years (any time frame can be applied) and that equal cash flows are generated for each period, the formula for a project's payback period is:

$$\frac{\text{Investment cost}}{\text{Annual net cash inflows}} = \text{Payback period}$$

To illustrate the payback method, we will consider Kristi Felt's decision to purchase a personal computer, printer, and software for typing and printing essays and term papers for other students. A reasonably good PC, printer, and appropriate software will cost Kristi a total of \$1,500. She can borrow the \$1,500 from her parents, who require no interest but need to be repaid at the end of 18 months. Kristi expects to make $100 per month after paying for supplies and other related expenses. The payback period (in months) may be computed as follows:

$$\frac{\$1{,}500}{\$100} = 15 \text{ months}$$

Since Kristi would generate sufficient cash to recover the investment in 15 months, she could repay her parents within the agreed period of time (assuming she spends none of the money).

This is one of the strengths of the payback method: It can be used to determine whether an investment fits within an acceptable period for the use of funds. For example, a company's cash position may lead it to establish a rule of thumb that no investment with a payback period exceeding three years will be accepted. In such a situation, a manager may be obliged to select an investment alternative with a slightly lower rate of return but a shorter payback period.

The payback method has several weaknesses, however. One is that it measures the time needed to recover the initial outlay but does not consider the investment's profitability. Investments obviously are made in order to earn an acceptable return, not just to recover their costs. In our example, Kristi is not solely interested in recovering the $1,500 in the shortest time possible. Her purpose in buying the equipment is to earn some extra money. Assuming that the equipment will last for more than 15 months, Kristi not only will recover her initial investment, but will also generate subsequent earnings (at least $100 per month). Although the payback method may provide some clues about the advisability of investments, it does not directly measure profitability.

To clarify this last point and show why the payback method must be used with care, consider a manager's decision to purchase one of two machines. Machine A costs $5,500 and is expected to generate $1,000 of net cash inflows annually. Machine B costs $3,500 and will produce $800 of net cash inflows annually. The payback period for machine A is 5.5 years ($5,500 ÷ $1,000); for machine B, the payback period is 4.4 years ($3,500 ÷ $800). Other things being equal, the payback method would indicate that the manager should purchase machine B because it would result in a shorter payback period. That is, its original cost would be recovered in a shorter time. However, if machine B were expected to last less than 4.4 years, such an investment would be unwise. The machine would not last long enough to recover its original cost, let alone generate any earnings.

Now suppose that both machines were estimated to have a 7-year life. Which machine would be the better investment? What if the estimated lifetimes of both machines were more than 10 years? To answer these questions, we would have to use one of the discounted cash flow methods (to be discussed later) in conjunction with the payback period.

This example highlights the other major weakness of the payback method: It does not take into account the time value of money. As a result, incorrect investment decisions may result unless the payback period is relatively short.

Unadjusted Rate of Return Method

unadjusted rate of return method A capital budgeting technique in which a rate of return is calculated by dividing the increase in the average annual net income a project will generate by the initial investment cost.

Another commonly used capital budgeting technique is the **unadjusted rate of return method**. Also referred to as the simple rate of return method or the accounting rate of return method, it is computed as follows:

$$\frac{\text{Increase in future average annual net income}}{\text{Initial investment cost}} = \text{Unadjusted rate of return}$$

To illustrate the unadjusted rate of return method, consider the following situation. Seal Right Company manufactures cans for fruits, vegetables, and other farm produce. Management wants to add a new, larger can size to the product line in order to take advantage of a potential demand for food storage items in the western states. This new can is expected to increase the company's annual net income by an average of $30,000 a year for 10 years. The additional

fyi

While the payback and unadjusted rate of return methods do not consider the time value of money, they are widely used in practice because they involve simple computations and are so easy to use. In fact, smaller, unsophisticated companies rarely use the more complex discounted methods.

machinery needed to manufacture the can will cost \$215,000. The expected return on the investment is \$30,000 ÷ \$215,000 = 14% (rounded).

Unlike the payback method, the unadjusted rate of return method attempts to measure the profitability of an investment. A company compares the unadjusted rate of return with a preselected rate that it considers acceptable. Management invests only in projects with rates of return that are equal to or greater than the established standard. Thus, if Seal Right's standard acceptance rate is less than or equal to 14 percent, the project would be acceptable.

The main weakness of the unadjusted rate of return method is that, like the payback method, it does not consider the time value of money. The computation uses average future net income rather than expected future earnings discounted to the present. A second problem is that this method counts the initial investment cost twice. This occurs because depreciation is a component in the computation of the average net income added by a project.

The problem of double counting can be eliminated by using refined models of the unadjusted rate of return method. The more serious problem—the omission of the time value of money—cannot be corrected. And since this omission can produce misleading results and incorrect long-term investment decisions, the unadjusted rate of return method must be used with extreme care.

to summarize

The payback method measures the time required to recover the initial cost of an investment from future net cash inflows (investment cost divided by annual net cash inflows). It may be useful as a preliminary screen of investment projects. The unadjusted rate of return method provides a measure of the profitability of an investment (increases in future average annual net income divided by the cost of the investment). If the resulting return is greater than the company's minimum standard of acceptability, the project is acceptable quantitatively. Because the payback and the unadjusted rate of return methods do not consider the time value of money, they should be used only in conjunction with one of the discounted cash flow methods.

3

Describe and use two discounted capital budgeting techniques: the net present value method and the internal rate of return method.

DISCOUNTED CAPITAL BUDGETING TECHNIQUES

Two widely used capital budgeting techniques recognize the time value of money—the net present value method and the internal rate of return method. Both methods apply discounted cash flow principles in determining the acceptability of an investment. The net present value method uses a standard discount rate to restate all cash flows in terms of present values and then makes comparisons. The internal rate of return method calculates the investment's "true" discounted rate of return and compares it with the firm's "hurdle" rate. Thus, an appropriate discount rate is extremely important in capital budgeting. Before explaining each of the two methods, we first discuss how to select an appropriate discount rate.

Selecting a Discount Rate

cost of capital The average cost of a firm's debt and equity capital; equals the rate of return that a company must earn in order to satisfy the demands of its owners and creditors.

An excellent starting point for computing the correct discount rate is a company's cost of capital. The **cost of capital** is basically an average cost of a firm's debt (primarily bank loans and bonds) and its equity (primarily common and preferred stock and retained earnings). These costs are measured in terms of effective interest rates on bank loans and bonds and the rate of return expected to be earned by the company's stockholders. In essence, then, the cost of capital is the rate a company must earn in order to satisfy its owners and creditors.

The computation of the cost of capital is complex and beyond the scope of this book. However, the following example should help you understand the concept. Assume that 30 percent of a company's total capital is debt, 20 percent is equity from the issuance of stock, and 50 percent is equity from retained earnings. Upon analysis, the company has determined that the cost of its debt capital is 10 percent, and the cost of its equity capital is 22 percent from stock and 16 percent from retained earnings. (Note: The cost of equity capital from the issuance of new shares is considered to be higher because of the commissions, registration fees, and so forth associated with the issuance of new shares.) The firm's cost of capital would be determined as follows:

Type	Cost of Capital	×	Weight	=	Average Cost of Capital
Debt (bonds)	10%	×	30%	=	3.0%
Equity (stocks)	22	×	20	=	4.4
Equity (retained earnings)	16	×	50	=	8.0
Total cost of capital			100%		15.4%

STOP & THINK Assume you were trying to decide whether to purchase or lease an automobile and you wanted to use the net present value method to determine which alternative to choose. What factors would you consider in determining the rate at which to discount the future cash outflows (i.e., what factors would determine your personal cost of capital)?

The weighting procedure may seem fairly simple. As you will learn in more advanced courses, however, it is not always easy to calculate the costs of the different types of capital. This is because the necessary information is often not readily available or absolutely verifiable. For example, debt costs must be adjusted to an after-tax basis, and equity costs include some subjective elements, such as the opportunity cost of retained earnings. Although you now have a general understanding of the cost of capital, you will need further study to use this concept.

As mentioned above, the cost of capital is a starting point in identifying an appropriate discount rate. The riskiness of a project should also be considered in choosing the appropriate discount rate. For example, the cost of capital computed earlier is 15.4 percent. If the company were considering a very risky project, a higher discount rate would be used because high-risk projects must yield higher-than-average returns in order to compensate for the increased probability of no returns at all. The techniques of correctly computing risk-adjusted discount rates are beyond the scope of this text; however, remember that the selection of the right discount rate is critical in the execution of a useful capital budgeting analysis.

Net Present Value Method

net present value method A capital budgeting technique that uses discounted cash flows to compare the present values of an investment's expected cash inflows and outflows.

The **net present value method** compares all expected cash inflows associated with an investment with the current and future cash outflows. All cash flows are discounted to their present values, giving recognition to the time value of money. For this reason, the net present value method is superior to both the payback method and the unadjusted rate of return method.

In general, the net present value method involves the following three steps:

1. *Compute.* Using a predetermined interest rate or discount factor, compute the present values of all the expected cash inflows and outflows of an investment. (Note that most present value tables assume end-of-year inflows and outflows.)
2. *Subtract.* Subtract the total present value of the cash outflows from the total present value of the cash inflows. The difference is the investment's net present value.
3. *Evaluate.* If the net present value of the investment is positive, or at least zero, the project is acceptable from a financial standpoint.

The following case illustrates the net present value method. The fleet manager of MBK Company is thinking of replacing an old truck before it begins to need major repairs. Because the company has limited funds and cannot spend more than $18,000, the manager is considering a small, fuel-efficient pickup truck that is presently selling for that amount. The truck would save the company $5,625 a year in gas and other expenses. The truck's estimated useful life is four years, and the expected salvage value is $1,800. The company uses a 10 percent discount rate. What is this investment's net present value? Should the truck be purchased?

Step 1 of the net present value method is to use the predetermined discount rate to state all cash flows at their present values (rounded to the nearest dollar in this example).

Cash inflows:

Annual cash savings	×	Discount factor	=	Present value
$5,625	×	3.1699*	=	$17,831
Salvage value	×	Discount factor	=	Present value
$1,800	×	0.6830**	=	$1,229

Cash outflows:

Initial cost	×	Discount factor	=	Present value
$18,000	×	1.0000	=	$18,000

*From Table II, 4 years at 10 percent.
**From Table I, 4 years at 10 percent.

net present value The difference between the present values of an investment's expected cash inflows and outflows.

Step 2 is to compute the **net present value**, that is, the difference between the present values of cash inflows and outflows.

Present value of inflows:	
Cash savings	$17,831
Salvage value	1,229
Total	$19,060
Less present value of outflows:	
Cost of truck	18,000
Net present value	$ 1,060

The analysis in Step 2 shows that investing in the truck would produce a positive net present value. In other words, after adjusting for the time value of money, purchasing the truck is like paying $18,000 in exchange for a stream of cash flows that is worth $19,060. Clearly, this is something that you would want to do. Thus, from a quantitative standpoint, it seems that the truck should be purchased. Exhibit 4-1 illustrates the process just described.

exhibit 4-1 Computing Net Present Value

	Present Time	Year 1	Year 2	Year 3	Year 4
Cost	$18,000				
Savings		$5,625	$5,625	$5,625	$5,625
Salvage value					1,800

	Time Period	Cash Flows	Present Value Factor	Present Value of Cash Flows
Present value of cash inflows:				
Savings	Years 1–4	$ 5,625	3.1699*	$17,831
Salvage value	Year 4	1,800	0.6830**	1,229
				$19,060
Present value of cash outflows:				
Cost	Today	(18,000)	1.0000	18,000
Net present value				$ 1,060

*From Table II, 4 years at 10 percent.
**From Table I, 4 years at 10 percent.

A common misinterpretation of the $1,060 net present value is that the acquisition of the truck will generate a net profit of just $1,060. Actually, because a 10 percent discount rate was used in evaluating the truck, the $1,060 net present value means that the investment in the truck will yield a net value gain of $1,060 OVER AND ABOVE the 10 percent minimum required rate of return. Similarly, a computed net present value of $0 does not mean that an investment just barely breaks even; instead, a $0 net present value means that the investment yields a return exactly equal to the discount rate used in evaluating the investment.

Before the company decides whether to purchase the truck, however, management must consider other factors. For example, a policy of support for U.S. car manufacturers or a lack of certain safety features on the pickup might dictate a particular course of action. Qualitative factors are discussed in greater detail later in the chapter.

LEAST-COST DECISIONS The net present value method generally assumes that an investment must be justified by cash savings or increased revenues. Sometimes, however, funds must be used to purchase assets regardless of whether they can be justified financially. Such situations arise, for example, when (1) government regulations require a firm to purchase safety or pollution-control equipment, (2) personnel contracts stipulate the establishment of retirement funds, or (3) a company is required to invest in cafeteria or recreational facilities, either to comply with a labor union contract or because management is persuaded that morale considerations warrant it.

Such situations may seem to be beyond help from capital budgeting. However, the net present value method may assist managers in making a **least-cost decision**—a decision that satisfies certain requirements at the lowest possible cost to the firm. The two major differences between least-cost decisions and all other capital budgeting decisions are:

least-cost decision A decision to undertake the project with the smallest negative net present value.

1. Least-cost decisions are limited to alternatives that fulfill certain imposed requirements.
2. None of the alternatives may produce a positive net present value.

To illustrate, we will assume that New England Steel Company has been told by the Environmental Protection Agency to install a pollution-control device. One alternative would cost $1,000,000 immediately but would not add to operating costs. It would last for 10 years. A second alternative is a device that costs $200,000 immediately but would add $125,000 to annual operating costs. Like the first device, it would last 10 years. Which device should be purchased? The firm uses a 12 percent discount rate.

The first alternative involves no future cash inflows or outflows. Its outlay cost in net present value terms is its initial cash outlay of $1,000,000. The second alternative has an initial cost

Managers must sometimes make least-cost decisions to fulfill certain imposed requirements at the lowest possible cost. For example, a company may be required to invest in a cafeteria to comply with a labor union contract.

business environment essay

Investing for a Cleaner World Businesses have traditionally used capital budgeting to guide them on making wise investments in property, plant, and equipment that will earn a return. However, in recent years, investments in environmental cleanup activities have become extremely common. Companies today face a climate with increasingly significant environmental concerns. Environmental costs have soared, in some cases to billion of dollars each year. Fines and penalties for violation of environmental regulations are substantial. And, due to new sentencing guidelines, strict liability for environmental losses has been imposed on directors and officers of companies. There is currently a myriad of environmental laws forcing companies to spend huge amounts of money to comply with these laws and to clean up environmental damage. Some of the most costly laws are the Clean Air Act, the Clean Water Act, the Resource Conservation and Recovery Act of 1976, the Comprehensive Environmental Response, the Compensation and Liability Act of 1980 (known as Superfund), and the Superfund Amendments Reauthorization Act of 1986 (SARA). The impact of these laws on capital in-

of $200,000 plus future cash outflows of $125,000 per year for the next 10 years. Therefore, its outlay cost in net present value terms would be:

Annual cash outflows	×	Discount factor	=	Present value
$125,000	×	5.6502*	=	$706,275
Initial cost				200,000
Outlay cost at net present value				$906,275

*From Table II, 10 years at 12 percent.

STOP & THINK Over your lifetime, you will make many personal, long-term investments such as buying automobiles and buying a home. Are the capital budgeting techniques we have discussed in this chapter relevant to these personal decisions? Since you probably won't be earning a return on your automobile and home investments, what type of capital budgeting decisions are these?

If the company had a choice between installing and not installing, neither alternative would be acceptable because both net present values are negative. However, one of the alternatives must be accepted. Because a cost of $906,275 is less than a cost of $1,000,000, the second alternative should be chosen to minimize costs.

Internal Rate of Return Method

internal rate of return method A capital budgeting technique that uses discounted cash flows to find the "true" discount rate of an investment; this true rate produces a net present value of zero.

internal rate of return The "true" discount rate that will produce a net present value of zero when applied to the cash flows of investment inventory goods held for resale.

The **internal rate of return method**, also known as the time-adjusted rate of return method or the discounted rate of return method, is similar to the net present value approach in that it emphasizes the profitability of investments and takes into account the time value of money. As a discounted cash flow method, it is superior to either the payback method or the unadjusted rate of return method. Some managers consider the internal rate of return method more tedious than the net present value method because, in the absence of a business calculator, the computations can be difficult. Some managers, however, prefer to analyze investment alternatives in terms of comparative rates of return rather than net present values.

The **internal rate of return** is defined as the "true" discount rate that an investment yields. For example, assume that your parents have $100,000 that they are considering investing in one of two ways—in a mutual fund containing the stocks of large U.S. companies or in your collegiate education. They learn that the mutual fund investment will yield an average return of 12 percent. They estimate the increased value of your lifetime annual output stemming from your college education and calculate that, after adjusting for the time value of money, the investment in your college education will yield an average return of, say, 20 percent per year. The 20 percent number is the internal rate of return generated by an investment in your education; be-

vestment decisions can be substantial. For example, under SARA, purchasers of real property are usually financially liable for environmental cleanup costs even if the property was contaminated before it was purchased.

Environmental concerns impact several stages of the capital budgeting decision. First, capital budgeting decision makers must expand traditional company boundaries to consider all entities affected by environmental degradation. Even though a project may be profitable from the firm's perspective, if it pollutes the environment, cleanup liability may make the investment a real loser. Second, environmental laws, current conditions, and trends can significantly affect the feasibility of an investment. Third, in deciding whether an investment is profitable, environmental costs and benefits, as well as environmental risk, must be considered. Finally, once an investment in a capital asset is made, attention must be given to environmental events such as accidents or increased regulation, which might affect the continued viability of the investment.

Source: Devaun Kite, "Capital Budgeting: Integrating Environmental Impact," *Journal of Cost Management*, Summer 1995, Vol. 9, No. 2, pp. 11–14.

caution

Of course, as mentioned earlier, there may be QUALITATIVE considerations that would cause your parents to invest in your education even if the MONETARY return were expected to be lower than what they could earn in the stock market.

cause this return is higher than the return your parents can earn on a mutual fund, they would naturally invest the $100,000 in your future.

Mathematically, the internal rate of return is the discount rate that yields a net present value of zero when applied to the cash flows of an investment—both inflows and outflows.

When using present value tables, the internal rate of return method involves three steps.

1. Calculate the present value factor by dividing the investment cost by the annual net cash inflows.
2. Using applicable present value tables and the life of the investment, find the present value factor closest to the number derived in step 1.
3. Using interpolation, if necessary, find the exact internal rate of return represented by the present value factor in step 1.

To help you understand this concept, we will again refer to MBK Company's plan to purchase a new truck. For the purpose of this explanation, however, we will ignore the truck's salvage value; later, we will show how to incorporate salvage value into the calculation. The calculations for the MBK example are as follows:

1. Calculate the present value factor with the following formula:

$$\frac{\text{Investment cost}}{\text{Annual net cash inflows}} = \text{Present value factor}$$

$$\frac{\$18{,}000}{\$5{,}625} = 3.2000$$

(Note that this is also the formula for calculating the payback period.)

2. In Present Value Table II, find the applicable row for the life of the investment. By moving across the table, you can find the present value factor closest to the number derived in step 1. In our example, the investment's life is known to be 4 years, so find row 4 and move across the row until you come to the factor 3.2397. This is the factor for 9 percent. The next factor, 3.1699, represents 10 percent. Since the factor is between these two numbers, the truck purchase yields between a 9 and 10 percent return.
3. If necessary, use **interpolation** to find the exact internal rate of return. Interpolation is most easily visualized by setting up a table as follows:

interpolation A method of determining the internal rate of return when the factor for that rate lies between the factors given in the present value table.

	Rate of Return (Discount Rate)	Present Value Factors: High and True Factors	Present Value Factors: High and Low Factors
High factor*	9%	3.2397	3.2397
True factor		3.2000	
Low factor	10		3.1699
Differences	1%	0.0397	0.0698

*Note that the high factor is associated with the low rate and that the low factor is associated with the high rate.

The number 0.0397 is the difference between the high factor and the true factor determined in step 1. The number 0.0698 is the difference between the high factor and the low factor. One percent is the difference between the discount rates for the high and the low factors. To find the exact rate of return in this example, you would make the following calculation:

$$\text{Internal rate of return} = 0.09 + \left(0.01 \times \frac{0.0397}{0.0698}\right) = 0.0957 \text{ or 9.6 percent (rounded)}$$

caution

Although the internal rate of return and net present value capital budgeting methods provide answers that appear to be very precise, they should be used with caution. There are many assumptions made when using these methods. Some of these assumptions are (1) that the discount rate (cost of capital) is accurate and (2) that the future cash flows, useful lives of the assets, and salvage values are known. It is often easy in accounting to assume that precise calculations are accurate without giving due consideration to the assumptions underlying the calculations.

What we are doing is adding the proportion 0.0397 ÷ 0.0698 of the 1 percent difference to the low rate to get the true rate. The result, 9.6 percent, means that if the annual savings of $5,625 were discounted at 9.6 percent, the net present value of the investment would be zero. (Note that there may be slight differences due to rounding.)

The purpose of interpolation is to determine the "true" rate of interest indicated by the present value factor. Although the factor's true rate of interest is fairly easy to roughly estimate, interpolation produces a more precise estimate.

Computation of internal rates of return is one area in which knowledge of how to use a standard business calculator really pays off. For example, the internal rate of return in the MBK example could be computed using the following keystrokes with a Hewlett-Packard business calculator:

Hewlett-Packard Keystrokes:

1. −18,000: Press **PV** (you must enter the cash outflow as a NEGATIVE number)
2. 5,625: Press **PMT** (this is the annual cash inflow)
3. 4: Press **N** (number of years)
4. Press **I/YR** for the answer = 9.5642274%

USING THE INTERNAL RATE OF RETURN To determine the value of an investment, management must compare the project's internal rate of return with the company's usual discount rate, often called the **hurdle rate**, or the rate that must be cleared for a project to be acceptable. If the internal rate is higher than or equal to the company's hurdle rate, the project is acceptable. If the internal rate is lower than the hurdle rate, the project is usually rejected. As with any of the capital budgeting techniques, even if the investment is acceptable from an internal rate of return standpoint, qualitative factors must still be considered before a final decision can be made.

hurdle rate The minimum rate of return that an investment must provide in order to be acceptable.

fyi

A calculator actually computes the internal rate of return using a repeated interpolation process; most business calculators take a couple of seconds to come up with the final answer.

THE PROBLEM OF UNEVEN CASH FLOWS In the truck example, annual cash flows were the same because salvage value was ignored. However, when salvage value is considered, the investment will have uneven cash flows. When this occurs, an annuity table cannot be used. Each cash flow has to be discounted back at an assumed discount rate until the net present value of all the cash flows discounted at this rate approximates zero. The rate that results after a trial-and-error process or a computer simulation is the internal rate of return. A simplified example of this method is shown on page 199. Although this can be a tedious procedure, it is facilitated by using computers or calculators. For example, computing the internal rate of return of the MBK truck purchase, including consideration of the $1,800 salvage value cash inflow at the end of four years, would be done as follows using a Hewlett-Packard business calculator:

Hewlett-Packard Keystrokes:

1. −18,000: Press **PV**
2. 5,625: Press **PMT**
3. 4: Press **N** (number of years)
4. 1,800: Press **FV** (this is a single amount occurring at the end of the period of time indicated in step 3)
5. Press **I/YR** for the answer = 12.5774719%

Note that the internal rate of return is higher (12.6% vs. 9.6%) when the additional cash inflow from the salvage value is considered.

to summarize

The net present value method is a capital budgeting technique that takes into consideration the time value of money by discounting future cash flows to their present values. By comparing the discounted net cash inflows and outflows, this method derives a net present value figure. If the net present value is zero or positive, the project is acceptable from a quantitative standpoint. The discount rate used is the minimum rate of interest that a company will accept. The net present value method also may be used in making least-cost decisions. The internal rate of return is a capital budgeting technique that utilizes discounted cash flows. It derives the "true" rate of return for an investment by comparing the cost of the project with the amounts to be returned. This produces a present value factor that is associated with the internal rate of return for the project. Often, the rate must be derived by interpolation and, if uneven cash flows are involved, by trial and error, computer simulation, or business calculator.

COMPARATIVE EXAMPLE OF CAPITAL BUDGETING TECHNIQUES

To solidify your understanding of the capital budgeting techniques introduced thus far in this chapter, we present the example of Will's Pit Stop, a small service station that sells gasoline on a self-service basis as its only source of revenue. Because one wall of the enclosed station area is vacant, the manager has decided to install one or two food vending machines. A sales representative has suggested that a freezer for ice cream and other dairy items would do well. The freezer would cost $42,045. It has an estimated useful life of 10 years, with an expected salvage value of $4,000. The sales representative is confident that the freezer will generate revenues of $15,000 a year on goods that cost $7,600. The freezer will need $8,000 of servicing during its fifth year of operation. The increase in Will's average yearly net income if the freezer is purchased is estimated to be $3,500. Note that the difference between annual net cash inflows of $7,400 ($15,000 − $7,600) and the estimated average net income of $3,500 is due to noncash expenses, such as depreciation, which are deducted on the income statement.

The manager of the station has come to you for advice, indicating that the firm's hurdle rate is 12 percent—Will's estimated cost of capital. Compute the payback period, the unadjusted

business environment essay

McDonald's Probably the most successful fast-food restaurant of all time is MCDONALD'S. However, as of early 1997, things weren't going so well for McDonald's. Jokes about McDonald's food were rampant. Ronald McDonald had become a symbol for botched marketing schemes. McDonald's sales were off target. McDonald's image was off kilter. And, McDonald's solutions to problems were off the mark.

By 1997 McDonald's had realized that it needed to take drastic action to correct these problems and lift the company back above its competitors. So what was McDonald's solution? In 1997 and 1998, it started investing $500 million in a new cooking and food delivery system that would allow the company to serve hot food to every customer, made to order, faster than ever before. For the first time in decades, McDonald's planned to serve hotter, fresher food, in less than three-and-a-half minutes per customer.

rate of return, the net present value, and the internal rate of return of the project. Then give your recommendations. Note that companies generally do not analyze an investment with all these techniques. They are all used here for illustrative purposes.

1. *Payback period:*

$$\frac{\$50{,}045 \text{ (investment cost)*}}{\$7{,}400 \text{ (annual net cash inflows)}} = 6.76 \text{ years}$$

*$42,045 initial investment + $8,000 servicing cost after 5 years.

Note that the salvage value is not considered here because it is received in the tenth year.

2. *Unadjusted rate of return:*

$$\frac{\$3{,}500 \text{ (increase in future average annual net income)}}{\$42{,}045 \text{ (initial investment cost)}} = 8.3 \text{ percent}$$

3. *Net present value:*

	Time Period	Cash Flows	Present Value Factor	Present Value of Cash Flows
Present value of cash inflows:				
Net revenues				
($15,000 − $7,600)	Years 1–10	$ 7,400	5.6502*	$41,811
Salvage value	Year 10	4,000	0.3220**	1,288
Total cash inflows				$43,099
Present value of cash outflows:				
Initial cost	Today	$42,045	1.0000	$42,045
Servicing cost	Year 5	8,000	0.5674***	4,539
Total cash outflows				$46,584
Net present value				$ (3,485)

*From Table II, 10 years at 12 percent.
**From Table I, 10 years at 12 percent.
***From Table I, 5 years at 12 percent.

The new ad campaign was called "made for you." In two test stores, sales were up 20 percent, even without advertising. One thing was certain, however. Investing $500 million in new equipment and technology was a lot more risky than McDonald's earlier attempted solutions to resurrect its image. These involved offering new products such as the Arch Deluxe and McRib Sandwich. By early 1998, McDonald's was convinced that the investment would result in increased sales, higher profits, and an improved reputation. Franchise owners, who were being asked to pay $300 million of the $500 million total cost, weren't so sure. To some of them, the charge seemed like an awfully big and risky capital investment gamble. However, the market seemed to like the bold move—from January 1997 through January 1999, McDonald's stock price almost doubled, from $44 per share to $80 per share.

Source: Bruce Horovitz, "Fast-Food Giant's New Plan: Hot, Juicy, Made to Order," *USA Today,* February 20, 1998, p. B1.

4. *Internal rate of return:*

Since the cash flows are uneven due to the servicing cost and the salvage value, a trial-and-error process is required in computing the internal rate of return. From the net present value method, we can see that the 12 percent rate is too high. A 10 percent rate is selected for trial, and the net present value at that rate is calculated.

	Time Period	Cash Flows	Present Value Factor	Present Value of Cash Flows
Present value of cash inflows:				
Net revenues				
($15,000 − $7,600)	Years 1–10	$ 7,400	6.1446*	$45,470
Salvage value	Year 10	4,000	0.3855**	1,542
Total cash inflows				$47,012
Present value of cash outflows:				
Initial cost	Today	$42,045	1.0000	$42,045
Servicing cost	Year 5	8,000	0.6209***	4,967
Total cash outflows				$47,012
Net present value				$ 0

*From Table II, 10 years at 10 percent.
**From Table I, 10 years at 10 percent.
***From Table I, 5 years at 10 percent.

At 10 percent, the net present value is zero. Therefore, 10 percent is the internal rate of return.

On the basis of the foregoing information, you should recommend rejection. The payback period is well within the life of the investment; however, it is not short enough to warrant any special consideration. The unadjusted rate of return is only 8.3 percent, and the internal, or adjusted, rate of return of 10 percent is well under Will's hurdle rate, which means that the project's net present value is negative. Therefore, on the basis of the quantitative results, the manager should look for an opportunity that is more attractive financially. However, if the 10 percent rate is close enough to the 12 percent hurdle rate, perhaps qualitative factors, such as the probability that the additional customers attracted by the freezer items will also buy gas, might make the project acceptable.

4

Understand the need for evaluating qualitative factors in strategic and capital investment decisions.

QUALITATIVE FACTORS IN STRATEGIC AND CAPITAL INVESTMENT DECISIONS

In explaining the fundamental concepts of capital budgeting, we have focused on the financial (quantitative) aspects of analyzing investment alternatives. However, a discussion of capital budgeting is incomplete without mentioning factors that cannot be reduced to numbers. These qualitative factors are often of overriding importance in strategic and capital investment decisions. Here, we consider three types of qualitative factors: (1) an investment's effect on the *quality* of products and services offered, (2) an investment's effect on the *time* with which products and services can be produced and delivered to customers, and (3) other qualitative factors. Thus far in the chapter, we have made the determination of whether a capital investment decision is a good one solely on the basis of its financial return, computed using one of four methods. If the financial return was positive, our conclusion was to invest; if the financial return was negative, we recommended that the project not be undertaken. However, throughout the management accounting chapters of this book, we have focused on three aspects of decision making: cost, quality, and time.

fyi

In today's world economy, most companies have to be competitive on a cost basis. What makes good companies even better is their attention to quality and time (speed of delivery of products and services) considerations—the same factors that are important in capital investment decisions.

Quality and time considerations can sometimes dictate that a capital investment should be made even if the financial returns don't justify the expenditure. For example, if buying a new machine will help the company produce higher quality products or deliver those products to its customers faster, the machine may be a good investment. Companies know that their competitors are doing everything possible to speed up delivery and increase quality. Thus, even if a company has a cost of capital of 12 percent, and an investment will return only 8 percent, if buying a machine will allow the company to deliver products or services faster than competitors, the purchase may be a good one. Likewise, if buying a machine will mean fewer defects, higher quality, and more satisfied customers, the purchase may be a good one. Companies must always be continuously improving in order to keep up with or surpass their competition. Unfortunately, capital investments often are long-term decisions that make continuous improvement difficult. Thus, even if a company has not completely recovered its investment in a capital project, recognizing that competitors have better or more efficient equipment may motivate a company to abandon an investment (a machine that works fine, for example) and make a costlier new investment that will allow the company to remain competi-

business environment essay

Ethics in Capital Investment Decisions

In 1990, after making substantial investments in two plants in Thailand and one in China, **HUNTSMAN CHEMICAL CORPORATION (HCC)** abruptly sold out its business interests when unethical practices were encountered. After winning a major bid in competition with worldwide firms, HCC was virtually guaranteed a significant profit on a $40 million investment. It became clear, however, that business practices involving bribes, payoffs, inflated invoices, and the like were going to be a part of the deal. As soon as Jon Huntsman, founder, chairman, and CEO of HCC, became aware of these unethical practices, he called his managers home and refused to participate further in the projects. HCC sold all its interests and walked away from the deal. When asked about this situation, Mr. Huntsman was quoted as saying, "We simply refuse to carry out negotiations based on factors other than competitiveness, quality, and productivity."

Although the quantitative factors led HCC to become involved in a major capital investment project, other factors caused the company to withdraw. As noted in the text, qualitative factors often override purely quantitative results.

Source: Adapted from "The Heart of the Deal," *Wharton Alumni Magazine* (Summer 1991), pp. 8–14.

tive. The impact of quality and time on capital budgeting decisions cannot be underestimated. In fact, because of the need to continuously improve, companies are always looking for shorter and shorter capital investment opportunities so that they are more flexible, such as leasing or renting equipment and other operating assets where possible.

In addition to quality and time, there are a number of other qualitative factors that must be considered when making capital budgeting decisions. Consider, for example, consumer safety. In one lawsuit, a major U.S. automobile manufacturer was cited for producing cars that were not as safe as they should have been. The company was essentially accused of comparing the present value of the legal and other costs that might result from the unsafe condition of the cars with the cash savings from manufacturing the cars more cheaply, and of choosing the less expensive route. The question was then posed: What is the value of a life? This situation provides a dramatic illustration of the need to include qualitative factors in capital investment decisions.

Other qualitative factors include such matters as (1) government regulations, (2) pollution control and environmental protection, (3) worker safety, (4) company image and prestige, (5) preferences of owners and management, and (6) the general welfare of the community in which the company operates. The business environment essay (on page 200) provides a specific example of one company that combined strategic objectives with humanitarian motives in making a major capital investment decision. Many more examples could be mentioned, but the point is that numbers alone do not control the investment decisions of a good manager. Quality, time, and other qualitative, as well as quantitative, factors should all be considered in reaching long-term investment decisions.

to summarize

In making capital budgeting decisions, the effects of a decision on the quality of and the time with which products can be delivered to customers must be considered. In addition, other qualitative factors such as litigation effects, government regulations, environmental impact, worker safety, company image, preferences of owners, and welfare of community must also be considered.

expanded material

In the previous sections of the chapter, we have explained the importance of capital budgeting and the concepts underlying strategic and capital investment decisions, including the time value of money. We have also described and illustrated the four most commonly used capital budgeting techniques. Finally, we have discussed briefly the need for evaluating qualitative factors in any investment decision. In the expanded material, we explain how to use sensitivity analysis in dealing with uncertainty in capital budgeting decisions and the concept of "capital rationing," i.e., the process of ranking capital investment projects. We also discuss the impact of taxes on capital budgeting decisions.

5

Use sensitivity analysis to assess the potential effects of uncertainty in capital budgeting.

DEALING WITH UNCERTAINTY IN STRATEGIC AND CAPITAL INVESTMENT DECISIONS

sensitivity analysis A method of assessing the reasonableness of a decision that was based upon estimates; involves calculating how far reality can differ from an estimate without invalidating the decision.

Throughout this chapter, we have applied capital budgeting techniques as though the future were certain. That is, we have assumed perfect knowledge of expected cash flows, the useful lives of assets, salvage values, and so forth. Actually, the future is almost always uncertain, and the applicable numbers are estimates. By using "sensitivity analysis," we can evaluate, at least to some extent, the degree to which an error in a particular estimate is likely to invalidate the decision reached. Essentially, **sensitivity analysis** is a method of examining the effect of changes in an estimate on the results of the calculations. We use sensitivity analysis to determine whether the conclusions still seem reasonable under modified circumstances.

To illustrate this approach, we will consider the following situation. An asset can be purchased for $100,000; it is expected to provide $20,000 of annual net cash inflows. It has a 10-year life and an expected salvage value of $10,000. The hurdle rate is 8 percent. We can use either of the discounted cash flow techniques to assess this investment opportunity. For illustrative purposes, we use both.

Net present value method:

Discounted expected cash inflows ($20,000 × 6.7101*)	$134,202
Discounted disposal value ($10,000 × 0.4632**)	4,632
Net cash inflows	$138,834
Net cash outflows	100,000
Net present value	$ 38,834

*From Table II, 10 years at 8 percent.
**From Table I, 10 years at 8 percent.

Internal rate of return method:

$$\frac{\text{Investment cost (\$100,000} - \text{\$4,632)}}{\text{Annual net cash inflows}} = \frac{\$95,368}{\$20,000} = 4.7684 \text{ present value factor}$$

For 10 years, the internal rate of return is between 16 and 18 percent.

The net present value is greater than zero, and the internal rate of return is considerably more than the minimum acceptable rate of 8 percent. Therefore, from a quantitative standpoint, we should accept this investment opportunity. But what about the uncertainties? What if $20,000 is not received each year? What if the asset does not last 10 years? What if the disposal value is less than $10,000? Sensitivity analysis enables us to evaluate the potential effect of each of these uncertainties.

If Expected Cash Flows Are Uncertain

To assess the amount of error we can tolerate in expected cash flows, we need to determine the break-even amount of net cash flow—that is, the annual cash flow that would earn the minimum rate of 8 percent. We accomplish this by determining the discounted net cost of the investment and dividing that amount by the present value factor for the minimum acceptable interest rate (8 percent) for 10 years.

Computations:

Initial cost	$100,000
Discounted disposal value	4,632
Net cost of investment	$ 95,368

$95,368 ÷ 6.7101 (present value factor of 8 percent) = $14,213 cash flow return in order to break even.

We could then assess how likely it is that this project will generate annual cash flows of at least $14,213. Any amount above that, of course, would be acceptable with an 8 percent hurdle rate.

If Useful Life Is Uncertain

To assess the amount of error we can tolerate in the estimate that the asset will have a useful life of 10 years, we take the discounted net cost of the investment and divide it by the expected cash flows. This produces a present value factor of 4.7684. Looking under 8 percent interest in Table II, we find that this factor falls between 6 and 7 years. Thus, assuming that the $20,000 estimate of cash inflows is reliable, the asset does not have to last a full 10 years for the investment to be acceptable. In fact, only 7 years are necessary.

Computations:

$$\frac{\text{Net cost of investment}}{\text{Annual net cash inflows}} = \frac{\$95{,}368}{\$20{,}000} = 4.7684 \text{ at 8 percent}$$

$$= \text{Between 6 and 7 years of useful life in order to break even}$$

If Disposal Value Is Uncertain

Usually, the disposal value is an insignificant factor in the investment decision. However, to see if it would make a difference in the acceptability of a project, we can assume it is zero. In our example, if the asset has a zero disposal value, the investment cost of $100,000 divided by $20,000 annual net cash inflows equals a 5.0 present value factor. For an assumed 10-year life, the return is between 15 and 16 percent, which is clearly acceptable according to our 8 percent hurdle rate.[1]

Computations:

$$\frac{\text{Initial investment cost}}{\text{Annual net cash inflows}} = \frac{\$100{,}000}{\$20{,}000} = 5.0 \text{ for 10 years}$$

$$= \text{15 to 16 percent return}$$

---

to summarize

Capital budgeting decisions always involve estimates of future amounts, and estimates involve uncertainty. To evaluate the potential effect of this uncertainty, we can use sensitivity analysis, which shows how far reality can deviate from the estimate without invalidating an investment decision.

6

Explain how to use capital budgeting techniques in ranking capital investment projects.

CAPITAL RATIONING

Thus far, we have dealt exclusively with the screening function of capital budgeting—that is, determining whether an investment meets a minimum standard of acceptability. In many cases, however, a company has not one but several investment opportunities, all of which offer returns in excess of the company's hurdle rate. Since a company's resources are limited, some projects should be given priority. The ranking function of capital budgeting enables management to select the most profitable investments first. Projects should not be ranked, however, until the screening process is completed.

1 In this example, we looked at the uncertainty of each variable separately. Using computer simulation, uncertainty in all variables could have been examined simultaneously.

Another factor to consider in ranking projects is whether particular projects are compatible, complementary, or mutually exclusive. We assume mutually exclusive projects in this section on ranking, that is, that each project is independent and adds neither an advantage nor a disadvantage to other projects. Certainly, there are situations where the acceptance of one project adds value, directly or indirectly, to another project and might therefore alter a ranking consideration. These factors, like the qualitative factors that we discussed earlier, may significantly influence the strategy involved in a capital investment decision.

The objective of ranking is to help a company use limited resources to the best advantage by investing only in the projects that offer the highest return. The process of allocating limited resources based on the ranking of projects is called **capital rationing**. Either the internal rate of return method or the net present value method may be used in ranking investments.

capital rationing Allocating limited resources among ranked acceptable investments.

Ranking by the Internal Rate of Return Method

If the internal rate of return method is used, investments that pass the screening test are ranked in the order of their internal rate of return, from highest to lowest. This method is simple, requires no additional computations, and is widely used.

To illustrate the process, we will assume the following situation. Sundance Enterprises is considering six capital investment projects. Management requires a minimum return of 15 percent on its investments. The six projects are first screened, then ranked by their internal rates of return, as shown below.

Project	Expected Rate of Return	Screening Decision	Ranking Decision
A	10%	Reject	—
B	18	Accept	3
C	12	Reject	—
D	22	Accept	1
E	20	Accept	2
F	16	Accept	4

From a quantitative standpoint, Sundance should invest in all four of the projects that passed the screening test. If resources are limited, however, capital must be rationed. In this situation, the ranking process indicates that limited resources would be allocated to project D first, then to projects E, B, and F, respectively. This conclusion ignores the additional complications of the investments having different lives. It also does not consider differences in the size of the initial investment.

Ranking by the Net Present Value Method

If the net present value method is used for ranking investments, additional computations are necessary because the net present value of one investment usually cannot be directly compared with that of another. Only projects that require the same amount of investment are comparable. For example, you cannot readily compare an investment of $10,000 that produces a $2,000 net present value (project A) with a $20,000 investment that also results in a $2,000 net present value (project B), although project A certainly seems more desirable. To rank such projects, we need to compute a **profitability index**.

profitability index The present value of net cash inflows divided by the cost of an investment.

$$\frac{\text{Present value of net cash inflows}}{\text{Investment cost}} = \text{Profitability index}$$

Projects can then be ranked from highest to lowest in terms of their respective profitability indexes. The project with the highest profitability index should obviously be undertaken first; other projects will be undertaken according to the amount of resources available for investment.

To illustrate the ranking of projects using the net present value method, we will use the example in the preceding paragraph. The amount of the investment and its net present value are added to arrive at the present value of net cash inflows. Then, present value is divided by the investment cost to calculate a profitability index and respective ranking.

	Project A	Project B
Present value of net cash inflows	$12,000 (a)	$22,000 (a)
Investment cost	10,000 (b)	20,000 (b)
Net present value	$ 2,000	$ 2,000
Profitability index (a ÷ b)	1.20	1.10
Rank	1	2

Note that the profitability index must be 1.0 or greater for a project to be acceptable; this means that the net present value is at least zero.

Exhibit 4-2 summarizes the rules for making screening and ranking decisions using the net present value (with a profitability index) and the internal rate of return methods. Note that each technique leads management to the same screening decision. However, the methods may produce different rankings. In selecting between the two for the purposes of ranking, the profitability index is preferred because it considers directly the amount invested in each project, which results in the selection of the most profitable alternative.

to summarize

The screening function determines if projects are acceptable; the ranking function enables management to select the most profitable investment first and thus use limited resources to the best advantage. Ranking may be accomplished by the internal rate of return or by the net present value method.

7

Explain how income taxes affect capital budgeting decisions.

INCOME TAX CONSIDERATIONS IN CAPITAL BUDGETING DECISIONS

To keep the concepts simple, when considering capital budgeting decisions thus far in the chapter, we ignored the effects of income taxes on capital budgeting decisions. Unfortunately, ignoring

exhibit 4-2 Capital Budgeting Decision Rules

Selected Capital Budgeting Techniques	Decision Rules: Screening	Decision Rules: Ranking
Net present value method (NPV) using the profitability index (PI)	If PI > 1, invest If PI = 1, indifferent If PI < 1, don't invest	For two projects, a and b; If $PI_a > PI_b$, pick a, etc.
Internal rate of return (IRR)	If IRR > CC*, invest If IRR = CC, indifferent If IRR < CC, don't invest	For two projects, a and b; If $IRR_a > IRR_b$, pick a, etc.

*CC = cost of capital, or hurdle rate.

tax effects is not very realistic because capital budgeting decisions can be significantly affected by tax considerations. You will remember that an investment is acceptable financially if the net present value of the cash flows is zero or positive, given a desired rate of return. The discount rate used to compute the net present value is generally based on the company's cost of capital, which is usually the minimum rate of return a company must earn to satisfy its owners and creditors.

As an example of the income tax effects, a capital investment may allow a company to take an expense deduction for the cost of the asset and expense deductions for repairs and depreciation. Similarly, the resulting income from operations and any gain on the eventual sale of an asset are affected by taxes. Such tax effects can be so significant that the net present value of the cash flows changes from positive to negative, or vice versa.

To illustrate these income tax effects, we will use the Will's Pit Stop example discussed earlier. Recall that the gas station owner was considering installing a freezer for ice cream and other dairy products. The cost of the freezer was $42,045. It was expected to have a salvage value of $4,000 at the end of its 10-year useful life and to generate revenues of $15,000 per year on goods that cost $7,600. Thus, the cash flow was expected to be $7,400 ($15,000 − $7,600). At the end of the fifth year, the freezer would need $8,000 of repairs and servicing. Based on this information, the management of Will's Pit Stop decided not to buy the freezer because, at a hurdle rate of 12 percent, the net present value was negative. Furthermore, the internal rate of return was only 10 percent.

In making this decision, management neglected to consider the income tax effects. Here, we will incorporate the tax effects of the investment, based on the following initial assumptions: (1) Will's Pit Stop is a corporation with an effective tax rate of 25 percent, and (2) the hurdle rate of 12 percent is an after-tax rate. Assumption (2) means that the calculation of the cost of capital reflects the after-tax cost of interest expense, which is a deduction in computing a corporation's tax liability.

To compute the present values of the cash inflows and outflows, we must first convert them to after-tax amounts. This conversion is accomplished as follows:

1. Income on the freezer before taxes was $7,400 ($15,000 revenues − $7,600 cost of goods sold). At a 25 percent tax rate, net income is $5,550 ($7,400 × 0.25 = $1,850; $7,400 − $1,850 = $5,550). In other words, the company keeps 75 percent of the net revenues from the freezer ($7,400 × 0.75 = $5,550).
2. The U.S. income tax regulations allow a company to reduce its income tax liability by expensing some of the cost of tangible personal property immediately in the year of acquisition. If Will's Pit Stop elects to expense $10,000 of the cost of the freezer, this amount is deducted from the original cost in computing the depreciation base. The tax savings from taking this deduction in the year of acquisition is $2,500 ($10,000 × 0.25 tax rate).
3. Although the freezer has an estimated useful life of 10 years, the accelerated cost recovery system would allow Will's Pit Stop to write the freezer off over a 7-year period on an accelerated basis (using the double-declining-balance method) or over 10 or more years on a straight-line basis. We will assume that Will's Pit Stop elects to use the 7-year period to write off the remaining $32,045 ($42,045 − $10,000). The cost recovery for each year will be as follows:

Year	Pretax Cost Recovery
1	$ 4,578 ($32,045 on a double-declining-balance basis for ½ year)
2	7,848 [($32,045 − $4,578) ÷ 7 × 2]
3	5,605 [($27,467 − $7,848) ÷ 7 × 2]
4	4,004 [($19,619 − $5,605) ÷ 7 × 2]
5	2,860 [($14,014 − $4,004) ÷ 7 × 2]
6	2,860 [straight-line: ($10,010 − $2,860) ÷ 2½ years]
7	2,860 (straight-line)
8	1,430 (straight-line for ½ year)
	$32,045

Note that the company shifts to the straight-line method in year 6 in order to deduct as much depreciation as possible in that year and thereafter. As shown in Exhibit 4-3, at a 25 percent tax rate, the accelerated cost recovery deduction will save the company $1,145 in the first year in addition to the $2,500 saved by expensing the first $10,000 of the freezer's cost.

4. Under the IRS depreciation method known as the modified accelerated cost recovery system (MACRS), the entire cost of the freezer will have been written off in the first 8 years of its life. If the freezer is sold at the end of 10 years at its $4,000 estimated salvage value, there will be a $4,000 gain on the sale. This gain will be taxable as ordinary income at 25 percent (assuming no change in tax rates), so the after-tax cash inflow will be only $3,000 ($4,000 × 0.75).
5. The estimated repairs and servicing cost of $8,000 at the end of Year 5 is an expense deduction from the company's income for that year. Therefore, the net cost of this expense to the company is only $6,000 ($8,000 × 0.75).

These adjusted cash flows can now be used to compute the net present value of the cash inflows and outflows that would result if the freezer were purchased. The present values of these cash flows are presented in Exhibit 4-3 at three different hurdle rates: 8, 10, and 12 percent.

Three different rates are used to illustrate that the net present value decreases as the hurdle rate increases from 8 to 12 percent. In other words, as the rate of return increases, the present value of the cash inflows decreases in relation to the present value of the cash outflows, eventually changing the net present value from positive to negative. The point at which the present values of the inflows and outflows are equal reflects the expected internal rate of return. If the expected return is less than the company's hurdle rate, it is unlikely that the company will acquire the asset unless there are compensating qualitative factors.

Exhibit 4-3 shows that the tax effects on cash inflows and outflows, given a tax rate of 25 percent, reduce the rate of return on Will's Pit Stop's proposed freezer from a pretax 10 percent calculated earlier in the chapter to just over 8 percent. This occurs because taxes reduce the present value of the cash inflows more than they reduce the present value of the cash outflows. (Remember the initial cost is already at its present value.) If the tax rate were at the maximum corporate rate of 34 percent (when taxable income is in the $75,000 to $100,000 range), a likely event for many corporations, the internal rate of return would decrease even further. This is because the negative effect of the increased tax expense on gross margin is greater than the positive effect of the increased tax savings from expensing the first $10,000 of the freezer's cost and from the tax effects of the annual depreciation deduction and the deduction for repairs. In general, income taxes reduce the internal rate of return—and the higher the tax rate, the greater the reduction.

For the company to justify purchasing the freezer in the face of a 12 percent hurdle rate, the company would have to increase its gross margin significantly (increase sales volume with the same freezer capacity). You should also keep in mind that when the net present value at a selected hurdle rate is at or near zero, important qualitative factors not incorporated into the calculations of net present value will be the primary determinants of whether the asset is acquired.

to summarize

The cash inflows and outflows of capital budgeting decisions must be converted to after-tax amounts before the present values are computed in order to obtain a realistic measure of net present value. Cash inflows and outflows are converted to after-tax amounts by including such factors as the expense deduction, the modified accelerated cost recovery system (MACRS), any gain or loss on disposal, and the cash operating revenues and expenses.

exhibit 4-3 Income Tax Effects of Capital Budgeting

Will's Pit Stop
Net Present Value of Cash Inflows and Outflows (25% Tax Rate)

Type of Cash Flow	Period	After-Tax Cash Flow	8% Present Value	8% Amount*	10% Present Value	10% Amount*	12% Present Value	12% Amount*
Inflows:								
Revenue less cost of goods sold								
(net of tax): ($15,000 − $7,600) × 0.75 . .	Years 1–10	$ 5,550	6.7101	$37,241	6.1446	$34,103	5.6502	$31,359
MACRS expensing ($10,000 × 0.25)	Year 1	2,500	0.9259**	2,315	0.9091	2,273	0.8929	2,232
MACRS [($42,045 − $10,000): $32,045								
at 7-year, 200%]:								
$4,578 × 0.25	Year 1	$ 1,145	0.9259	$ 1,060	0.9091	$ 1,041	0.8929	$ 1,022
7,848 × 0.25	2	1,962	0.8573	1,682	0.8264	1,621	0.7972	1,564
5,605 × 0.25	3	1,401	0.7938	1,112	0.7513	1,053	0.7118	997
4,004 × 0.25	4	1,001	0.7350	736	0.6830	684	0.6355	636
2,860 × 0.25	5	715	0.6806	487	0.6209	444	0.5674	406
2,860 × 0.25	6	715	0.6302	451	0.5645	404	0.5066	362
2,860 × 0.25	7	715	0.5835	417	0.5132	367	0.4523	323
1,430 × 0.25	8	357	0.5403	193	0.4665	167	0.4039	144
				$ 6,138		$ 5,781		$ 5,454
Salvage value ($4,000 × 0.75).	End of Year 10	3,000	0.4632	$ 1,390	0.3855	$ 1,157	0.3220	$ 966
Total cash inflows				$47,084		$43,314		$40,011
Outflows:								
Initial freezer cost	Today	42,045	1.0000	$42,045	1.0000	$42,045	1.0000	$42,045
Repairs and servicing cost ($8,000 × 0.75) .	End of Year 5	6,000	0.6806	4,084	0.6209	3,725	0.5674	3,404
Total cash outflows				$46,129		$45,770		$45,449
Excess cash inflow (outflow).				$ 955		$ (2,456)		$ (5,438)

*After-tax cash flow × present value.
**Note that this is the present value of the cash flow discounted for 1 year.

APPENDIX: THE TIME VALUE OF MONEY

Present Value and Future Value Concepts

The concepts of present value and future value are used to measure the effect of time on the value of money. To illustrate, if you are to receive $100 one year from today, is it worth $100 today? Obviously not, because if you had the $100 today you could either use it now or invest it and earn interest. If the $100 isn't to be received for one year, those options are not available. The present value of $1 is the value today of $1 to be received or paid in the future, given a specified interest rate. To determine the value today of money to be received or paid in the future, we must "discount" the future amount (reduce the amount to its present value) by an appropriate interest rate. For example, if money can earn 10 percent per year, $100 to be received one year from now is approximately equal to $90.91 received today.

Putting it another way, if $90.91 is invested today in an account that earns 10 percent interest for one year, the interest earned will be $9.09 ($90.91 × 10% × 1 year = $9.09). The sum of the $90.91 principal plus $9.09 interest would equal $100 at the end of one year. Thus, the present value of $100 to be received (or paid) in one year with 10 percent interest is $90.91. This present value relationship can be diagramed as follows:

Present Value (Computed) $90.91	(One Year Period @ 10%)	Future Amount (Known) $100

$90.91 is the present value of the $100 future amount.

The relationships in this diagram can be described in two ways. We have just looked at the relationship by recognizing that the $90.91 is the present value of $100 to be received one year from now when interest is 10 percent. In this example, the $100 to be received one year from now is known, and the present value of $90.91 must be computed. We are computing a present value amount from a known future value amount.

Another way to look at the relationship is on a future value basis. Future values apply when the amount today ($90.91) is known, and the future amount must be calculated. Future values are exactly the opposite of present values. Thinking in terms of future values, $100 is the future amount we can expect to receive in one year, given a present known amount of $90.91 when the interest rate is 10 percent. We can diagram this relationship as follows:

Present Value (Known) $90.91	(One Year Period @ 10%)	Future Amount (Computed) $100

$100 is the future value of the $90.91 present value.

Present and future values can be calculated using formulas. However, if more than one period is involved, the calculations become rather complicated. Therefore, it is more convenient to use either a present value table or a calculator that gives the present value of $1 for various numbers of periods and interest rates (see Table I, page 212) or a future value table that gives the future value of $1 for various numbers of periods and interest rates (see Table III, page 214). We will illustrate the use of both a present value table and a future value table.

PRESENT VALUE TABLE To use a present value table, you simply locate the appropriate number of periods in the leftmost column and the interest rate in the row at the top of the table. The intersection of the row and column is the factor representing the present value of $1 for the number of periods and the relevant interest rate. To find the present value of an amount other than $1, multiply the factor in the table by that amount.

To illustrate the use of a present value table (Table I) to find the present value of a known future amount, assume that $10,000 is to be paid four years from today when the interest rate is 10 percent. What is the present value of the $10,000 payment?

Amount of payment	$10,000
Present value factor of $1 to be paid in 4 periods at 10% interest (from Table I)	×0.6830
Present value of payment	$ 6,830

This present value amount, $6,830, is the amount that could be paid today to satisfy the obligation that is due four years from now. As indicated, this procedure is sometimes referred to as "discounting." Thus, we say that $10,000 discounted for four years at 10 percent is $6,830. Stated another way, if $6,830 is invested today in an account that pays 10 percent interest, in four years the balance in that account would be $10,000.

FUTURE VALUE TABLE To find the future value of an amount that is known today, you use a future value table. When using a future value table, you simply locate the appropriate number of periods in the leftmost column and the interest rate in the row at the top of the table. The intersection of the row and column is the factor representing the future value of $1 for the number of periods and the relevant interest rate. To find the future value of an amount other than $1, multiply the factor in the table by that amount.

To illustrate the use of a future value table (Table III), we will use the same information that was presented before, except that we will now assume that the present value of $6,830 is known, not the future amount of $10,000. Assume that we have a savings account with a current balance of $6,830 that earns interest of 10 percent. What will be the balance in that account in four years?

Present value in savings account	$ 6,830
Future value factor of $1 in 4 periods at 10% interest (from Table III)	×1.4641
Future value	$10,000*

*Rounded

When computing future values, we often use the term *compounding* to mean the frequency with which interest is added to the principal. Thus, we say that interest of 10 percent has been compounded once a year (annually) to arrive at a future value at the end of four years of $10,000. If the interest is added more or less frequently than once a year, the future amount will be different.

The preceding example assumed an annual compounding period for interest. If the 10 percent interest had been compounded semiannually (twice a year) for four years, the calculation would have involved using a 5 percent (one-half of the 10 percent) rate for 8 periods (4 years × 2 periods per year) instead of 10 percent for 4 periods. To illustrate, what is the present value of $10,000 to be paid in four years if interest of 10 percent is compounded semiannually?

Amount of payment	$10,000
Present value factor of $1 to be paid in 8 periods at 5% interest (from Table I)	×0.6768
Present value of payment	$ 6,768

Thus, the present value of $10,000 to be paid in four years is $6,768 if interest is compounded semiannually. Likewise, if semiannual compounding is used to determine the future value of $6,768 in four years at 10 percent compounded semiannually, the result is as follows:

Present value in savings account	$ 6,768
Future value factor of $1 in 8 periods at 5% interest (from Table III)	×1.4775
Future value	$10,000*

*Rounded

Note that the present value ($6,768) is lower with semiannual compounding than with annual compounding ($6,830). The more frequently interest is compounded, the greater the total amount of interest deducted (in computing present values) or added (in computing future values).

Since interest may also be compounded quarterly, monthly, daily, or for some other period, you should learn the relationship of interest to the compounding period. Semiannual interest means that you double the interest periods and halve the annual interest rate; with quarterly interest you quadruple the periods and take one-fourth of the annual interest rate. The formula for interest rate is:

$$\frac{\text{Yearly interest rate}}{\text{Compounding periods per year}} = \text{Interest rate per compounding period}$$

The number of interest periods is simply the number of periods per year times the number of years. That formula is:

$$\text{Compounding periods per year} \times \text{Number of years} = \text{Number of interest periods}$$

The Present Value of an Annuity

In discussing present values and future values, we have assumed only a single present value or future value with one of the amounts known and the other to be computed. With liabilities, we generally know the future amount that must be paid and would like to compute the present value of that future payment.

Many long-term liabilities involve a series of payments rather than one lump-sum payment. For example, a company might purchase equipment under an installment agreement requiring payments of $5,000 each year for five years. Determining the value today (present value) of a series of equally spaced, equal amount payments (called annuities) is more complicated than determining the present value of a single future payment. If you were to try to calculate the present value of an annuity by hand, you would have to discount the first payment for one period, the second payment for two periods, and so on, and then add all the present values together. Because such calculations are time-consuming, a table is generally used (see Table II, page 213). The factors in the table are the sums of the individual present values of all future payments. Based on the present value of an annuity of $1, the table provides factors for various interest rates and payments.

To illustrate the use of a present value of an annuity table (Table II), we will assume that $10,000 is to be paid at the end of each of the next 10 years. If the interest rate is 12 percent compounded annually, Table II shows a present value factor of 5.6502. This factor means that the present value of $1 paid each year for 10 years discounted at 12 percent is approximately $5.65. Applying this factor to payments of $10,000 results in the following:

Amount of the annual payment.	$10,000
Present value factor of an annuity of $1	
discounted for 10 payments at 12%	×5.6502
Present value	$56,502

This amount, $56,502, is the amount (present value) that could be paid today to satisfy the obligation if interest is 12 percent.

table I The Present Value of $1 Due in *n* Periods*

Period	1%	2%	3%	4%	5%	6%	7%	8%	9%	10%	12%	14%	15%	16%	18%	20%
1	.9901	.9804	.9709	.9615	.9524	.9434	.9346	.9259	.9174	.9091	.8929	.8772	.8696	.8621	.8475	.8333
2	.9803	.9612	.9426	.9246	.9070	.8900	.8734	.8573	.8417	.8264	.7972	.7695	.7561	.7432	.7182	.6944
3	.9706	.9423	.9151	.8890	.8638	.8396	.8163	.7938	.7722	.7513	.7118	.6750	.6575	.6407	.6086	.5787
4	.9610	.9238	.8885	.8548	.8227	.7921	.7629	.7350	.7084	.6830	.6355	.5921	.5718	.5523	.5158	.4823
5	.9515	.9057	.8626	.8219	.7835	.7473	.7130	.6806	.6499	.6209	.5674	.5194	.4972	.4761	.4371	.4019
6	.9420	.8880	.8375	.7903	.7462	.7050	.6663	.6302	.5963	.5645	.5066	.4556	.4323	.4104	.3704	.3349
7	.9327	.8706	.8131	.7599	.7107	.6651	.6227	.5835	.5470	.5132	.4523	.3996	.3759	.3538	.3139	.2791
8	.9235	.8535	.7894	.7307	.6768	.6274	.5820	.5403	.5019	.4665	.4039	.3506	.3269	.3050	.2660	.2326
9	.9143	.8368	.7664	.7026	.6446	.5919	.5439	.5002	.4604	.4241	.3606	.3075	.2843	.2630	.2255	.1938
10	.9053	.8203	.7441	.6756	.6139	.5584	.5083	.4632	.4224	.3855	.3220	.2697	.2472	.2267	.1911	.1615
11	.8963	.8043	.7224	.6496	.5847	.5268	.4751	.4289	.3875	.3503	.2875	.2366	.2149	.1954	.1619	.1346
12	.8874	.7885	.7014	.6246	.5568	.4970	.4440	.3971	.3555	.3186	.2567	.2076	.1869	.1685	.1372	.1122
13	.8787	.7730	.6810	.6006	.5303	.4688	.4150	.3677	.3262	.2897	.2292	.1821	.1625	.1452	.1163	.0935
14	.8700	.7579	.6611	.5775	.5051	.4423	.3878	.3405	.2992	.2633	.2046	.1597	.1413	.1252	.0985	.0779
15	.8613	.7430	.6419	.5553	.4810	.4173	.3624	.3152	.2745	.2394	.1827	.1401	.1229	.1079	.0835	.0649
16	.8528	.7284	.6232	.5339	.4581	.3936	.3387	.2919	.2519	.2176	.1631	.1229	.1069	.0930	.0708	.0541
17	.8444	.7142	.6050	.5134	.4363	.3714	.3166	.2703	.2311	.1978	.1456	.1078	.0929	.0802	.0600	.0451
18	.8360	.7002	.5874	.4936	.4155	.3503	.2959	.2502	.2120	.1799	.1300	.0946	.0808	.0691	.0508	.0376
19	.8277	.6864	.5703	.4746	.3957	.3305	.2765	.2317	.1945	.1635	.1161	.0829	.0703	.0596	.0431	.0313
20	.8195	.6730	.5537	.4564	.3769	.3118	.2584	.2145	.1784	.1486	.1037	.0728	.0611	.0514	.0365	.0261
25	.7798	.6095	.4476	.3751	.2953	.2330	.1842	.1460	.1160	.0923	.0588	.0378	.0304	.0245	.0160	.0105
30	.7419	.5521	.4120	.3083	.2314	.1741	.1314	.0994	.0754	.0573	.0334	.0196	.0151	.0116	.0070	.0042
40	.6717	.4529	.3066	.2083	.1420	.0972	.0668	.0460	.0318	.0221	.0107	.0053	.0037	.0026	.0013	.0007
50	.6080	.3715	.2281	.1407	.0872	.0543	.0339	.0213	.0134	.0085	.0035	.0014	.0009	.0006	.0003	.0001
60	.5504	.3048	.1697	.0951	.0535	.0303	.0173	.0099	.0057	.0033	.0011	.0004	.0002	.0001	†	†

*The formula used to derive the values in this table was $PV = F \frac{1}{(1+i)^n}$ where PV = present value, F = future amount to be discounted, i = interest rate, and n = number of periods.
†The value of 0 to four decimal places.

table II The Present Value of an Annuity of $1 per Number of Payments*

Number of Payments	1%	2%	3%	4%	5%	6%	7%	8%	9%	10%	12%	14%	15%	16%	18%	20%
1	0.9901	0.9804	0.9709	0.9615	0.9524	0.9434	0.9346	0.9259	0.9174	0.9091	0.8929	0.8772	0.8596	0.8621	0.8475	0.8333
2	1.9704	1.9416	1.9135	1.8861	1.8594	1.8334	1.8080	1.7833	1.7591	1.7355	1.6901	1.6467	1.6257	1.6052	1.5656	1.5278
3	2.9410	2.8839	2.8286	2.7751	2.7232	2.6730	2.6243	2.5771	2.5313	2.4869	2.4018	2.3216	2.2832	2.2459	2.1743	2.1065
4	3.9820	3.8077	3.7171	3.6299	3.5460	3.4651	3.3872	3.3121	3.2397	3.1699	3.0373	2.9137	2.8550	2.7982	2.6901	2.5887
5	4.8884	4.7135	4.5797	4.4518	4.3295	4.2124	4.1002	3.9927	3.8897	3.7908	3.6048	3.4331	3.3522	3.2743	3.1272	2.9906
6	5.7985	5.6014	5.4172	5.2421	5.0757	4.9173	4.7665	4.6229	4.4859	4.3553	4.1114	3.8887	3.7845	3.6847	3.4976	3.3255
7	6.7282	6.4720	6.2303	6.0021	5.7864	5.5824	5.3893	5.2064	5.0330	4.8684	4.5638	4.2883	4.1604	4.0386	3.8115	3.6046
8	7.6517	7.3255	7.0197	6.7327	6.4632	6.2098	5.9713	5.7466	5.5348	5.3349	4.9676	4.6389	4.4873	4.3436	4.0776	3.8372
9	8.5660	8.1622	7.7861	7.4353	7.1078	6.8017	6.5152	6.2469	5.9952	5.7590	5.3282	4.9464	4.7716	4.6065	4.3030	4.0310
10	9.4713	8.9826	8.5302	8.1109	7.7217	7.3601	7.0236	6.7101	6.4177	6.1446	5.6502	5.2161	5.0188	4.8332	4.4941	4.1925
11	10.3676	9.7868	9.2526	8.7605	8.3064	7.8869	7.4987	7.1390	6.8052	6.4951	5.9377	5.4527	5.2337	5.0286	4.6560	4.3271
12	11.2551	10.5733	9.9540	9.3851	8.8633	8.3838	7.9427	7.5361	7.1607	6.8137	6.1944	5.6603	5.4206	5.1971	4.7932	4.4392
13	12.1337	11.3484	10.6350	9.9856	9.3936	8.8527	8.3577	7.9038	7.4869	7.1034	6.4235	5.8424	5.5831	5.3423	4.9095	4.5327
14	13.0037	12.1062	11.2961	10.5631	9.8986	9.2950	8.7455	8.2442	7.7862	7.3667	6.6282	6.0021	5.7245	5.4675	5.0081	4.6106
15	13.8651	12.8493	11.9379	11.1184	10.3797	9.7122	9.1079	8.5595	8.0607	7.6061	6.8109	6.1422	5.8474	5.5755	5.0916	4.6755
16	14.7179	13.5777	12.5611	11.6523	10.8378	10.1059	9.4466	8.8514	8.3126	7.8237	6.9740	6.2651	5.9542	5.6685	5.1624	4.7296
17	15.5623	14.2919	13.1661	12.1657	11.2741	10.4773	9.7632	9.1216	8.5436	8.0216	7.1196	6.3729	6.0472	5.7487	5.2223	4.7746
18	16.3983	14.9920	13.7535	12.6593	11.6896	10.8276	10.0591	9.3719	8.7556	8.2014	7.2497	6.4674	6.1280	5.8178	5.2732	4.8122
19	17.2260	15.6785	14.3238	13.1339	12.0853	11.1581	10.3356	9.6036	8.9501	8.3649	7.3658	6.5504	6.1982	5.8775	5.3162	4.8435
20	18.0456	16.3514	14.8775	13.5903	12.4622	11.4699	10.5940	9.8181	9.1285	8.5136	7.4694	6.6231	6.2593	5.9288	5.3527	4.8696
25	22.0232	19.5235	17.4131	15.6221	14.0939	12.7834	11.6536	10.6748	9.8226	9.0770	7.8431	6.8729	6.4641	6.0971	5.4669	4.9476
30	25.8077	22.3965	19.6004	17.2920	15.3725	13.7648	12.4090	11.2578	10.2737	9.4269	8.0552	7.0027	6.5660	6.1772	5.5168	4.9789
40	32.8347	27.3555	23.1148	19.7928	17.1591	15.0463	13.3317	11.9246	10.7574	9.7791	8.2438	7.1050	6.6418	6.2335	5.5482	4.9966
50	39.1961	31.4236	25.7298	21.4822	18.2559	15.7619	13.8007	12.2335	10.9617	9.9148	8.3045	7.1327	6.6605	6.2463	5.5641	4.9995
60	44.9550	34.7609	27.6756	22.6235	18.9293	16.1614	14.0392	12.3766	11.0480	9.9672	8.3240	7.1401	6.6651	6.2482	5.5553	4.9999

*The formula used to derive the values in this table was $PV = F\left(\frac{1 - \frac{1}{(1+i)^n}}{i}\right)$ where PV = present value, F = periodic payment to be discounted, i = interest rate, and n = number of payments.

table III Amount of $1 Due in *n* Periods

Period	1%	2%	3%	4%	5%	6%	7%	8%	9%	10%	12%	14%	15%	16%	18%	20%
1	1.0100	1.0200	1.0300	1.0400	1.0500	1.0600	1.0700	1.0800	1.0900	1.1000	1.1200	1.1400	1.1500	1.1600	1.1800	1.2000
2	1.0201	1.0404	1.0609	1.0816	1.1025	1.1236	1.1449	1.1664	1.1881	1.2100	1.2544	1.2996	1.3225	1.3456	1.3924	1.4400
3	1.0303	1.0612	1.0927	1.1249	1.1576	1.1910	1.2250	1.2597	1.2950	1.3310	1.4049	1.4815	1.5209	1.5609	1.6430	1.7280
4	1.0406	1.0824	1.1255	1.1699	1.2155	1.2625	1.3108	1.3605	1.4116	1.4641	1.5735	1.6890	1.7490	1.8106	1.9388	2.0736
5	1.0510	1.1041	1.1593	1.2167	1.2763	1.3382	1.4026	1.4693	1.5386	1.6105	1.7623	1.9254	2.0114	2.1003	2.2878	2.4883
6	1.0615	1.1262	1.1941	1.2653	1.3401	1.4185	1.5007	1.5869	1.6771	1.7716	1.9738	2.1950	2.3131	2.4364	2.6996	2.9860
7	1.0721	1.1487	1.2299	1.3159	1.4071	1.5036	1.6058	1.7138	1.8280	1.9487	2.2107	2.5023	2.6600	2.8262	3.1855	3.5832
8	1.0829	1.1717	1.2668	1.3686	1.4775	1.5938	1.7182	1.8509	1.9926	2.1436	2.4760	2.8526	3.0590	3.2784	3.7589	4.2998
9	1.0937	1.1951	1.3048	1.4233	1.5513	1.6895	1.8385	1.9990	2.1719	2.3579	2.7731	3.2519	3.5179	3.8030	4.4355	5.1598
10	1.1046	1.2190	1.3439	1.4802	1.6289	1.7908	1.9672	2.1589	2.3674	2.5937	3.1058	3.7072	4.0456	4.4114	5.2338	6.1917
11	1.1157	1.2434	1.3842	1.5395	1.7103	1.8983	2.1049	2.3316	2.5804	2.8531	3.4785	4.2262	4.6524	5.1173	6.1759	7.4031
12	1.1268	1.2682	1.4258	1.6010	1.7959	2.0122	2.2522	2.5182	2.8127	3.1384	3.8960	4.8179	5.3502	5.9360	7.2876	8.9161
13	1.1381	1.2936	1.4685	1.6651	1.8856	2.1329	2.4098	2.7196	3.0658	3.4523	4.3635	5.4924	6.1528	6.8858	8.5994	10.699
14	1.1495	1.3195	1.5126	1.7317	1.9799	2.2609	2.5785	2.9372	3.3417	3.7975	4.8871	6.2613	7.0757	7.9875	10.147	12.839
15	1.1610	1.3459	1.5580	1.8009	2.0789	2.3966	2.7590	3.1722	3.6425	4.1772	5.4736	7.1379	8.1371	9.2655	11.973	15.407
16	1.1726	1.3728	1.6047	1.8730	2.1829	2.5404	2.9522	3.4259	3.9703	4.5950	6.1304	8.1372	9.3576	10.748	14.129	18.488
17	1.1843	1.4002	1.6528	1.9479	2.2920	2.6928	3.1588	3.7000	4.3276	5.0545	6.8660	9.2765	10.761	12.467	16.672	22.186
18	1.1961	1.4282	1.7024	2.0258	2.4066	2.8543	3.3799	3.9960	4.7171	5.5599	7.6900	10.575	12.375	14.462	19.673	26.623
19	1.2081	1.4568	1.7535	2.1068	2.5270	3.0256	3.6165	4.3157	5.1417	6.1159	8.6128	12.055	14.231	16.776	23.214	31.948
20	1.2202	1.4859	1.8061	2.1911	2.6533	3.2071	3.8697	4.6610	5.6044	6.7275	9.6463	13.743	16.366	19.460	27.393	38.337
30	1.3478	1.8114	2.4273	3.2434	4.3219	5.7435	7.6123	10.062	13.267	17.449	29.959	50.950	66.211	85.849	143.37	237.37
40	1.4889	2.2080	3.2620	4.8010	7.0400	10.285	14.974	21.724	31.409	45.259	93.050	188.88	267.86	378.72	750.37	1469.7
50	1.6446	2.6916	4.3839	7.1067	11.467	18.420	29.457	46.901	74.357	117.39	289.00	700.23	1083.6	1670.7	3927.3	9100.4
60	1.8167	3.2810	5.8916	10.519	18.679	32.987	57.946	101.25	176.03	304.48	897.59	2595.9	4383.9	7370.1	20555.	56347.

table IV Amount of an Annuity of $1 per Number of Payments

Number of Payments	1%	2%	3%	4%	5%	6%	7%	8%	9%	10%	12%	14%	15%	16%	18%	20%
1	1.0000	1.0000	1.0000	1.0000	1.0000	1.0000	1.0000	1.0000	1.0000	1.0000	1.0000	1.0000	1.0000	1.0000	1.0000	1.0000
2	2.0100	2.0200	2.0300	2.0400	2.0500	2.0600	2.0700	2.0800	2.0900	2.1000	2.1200	2.1400	2.1500	2.1600	2.1800	2.2000
3	3.0301	3.0604	3.0909	3.1216	3.1525	3.1836	3.2149	3.2464	3.2781	3.3100	3.3744	3.4396	3.4725	3.5056	3.5724	3.6400
4	4.0604	4.1216	4.1836	4.2465	4.3101	4.3746	4.4399	4.5061	4.5731	4.6410	4.7793	4.9211	4.9934	5.0665	5.2154	5.3680
5	5.1010	5.2040	5.3091	5.4163	5.5256	5.6371	5.7507	5.8666	5.9847	6.1051	6.3528	6.6101	6.7424	6.8771	7.1542	7.4416
6	6.1520	6.3081	6.4684	6.6330	6.8019	6.9753	7.1533	7.3359	7.5233	7.7156	8.1152	8.5355	8.7537	8.9775	9.4420	9.9299
7	7.2135	7.4343	7.6625	7.8983	8.1420	8.3938	8.6540	8.9228	9.2004	9.4872	10.8090	10.7305	11.0668	11.4139	12.1415	12.9159
8	8.2857	8.5830	8.8923	9.2142	9.5491	9.8975	10.2598	10.6366	11.0285	11.4359	12.2997	13.2328	13.7268	14.2401	15.3270	16.4991
9	9.3685	9.7546	10.1591	10.5828	11.0266	11.4913	11.9780	12.4876	13.0210	13.5795	14.7757	16.0853	16.7858	17.5185	19.0859	20.7989
10	10.4622	10.9497	11.4639	12.0061	12.5779	13.1808	13.8164	14.4866	15.1929	15.9374	17.5487	19.3373	20.3037	21.3215	23.5213	25.9587
11	11.5668	12.1687	12.8078	13.4864	14.2068	14.9716	15.7836	16.6455	17.5603	18.5312	20.6546	23.0445	24.3493	25.7329	28.7551	32.1504
12	12.6825	13.4121	14.1920	15.0258	15.9171	16.8699	17.8885	18.9771	20.1407	21.3843	24.1331	27.2707	29.0017	30.8502	34.9311	39.5805
13	13.8093	14.6803	15.6178	16.6268	17.7130	18.8821	20.1406	21.4953	22.9534	24.5227	28.0291	32.0887	34.3519	36.7862	42.2187	48.4966
14	14.9474	15.9739	17.0863	18.2919	19.5986	21.0151	22.5505	24.2149	26.0192	27.9750	32.3926	37.5811	40.5047	43.6720	50.8180	59.1959
15	16.0969	17.2934	18.5989	20.0236	21.5786	23.2760	25.1290	27.1521	29.3609	31.7725	37.2797	43.8424	47.5804	51.6595	60.9653	72.0351
16	17.2579	18.6393	20.1569	21.8245	23.6575	25.6725	27.8881	30.3243	33.0034	35.9497	42.7535	50.9804	55.7178	60.9250	72.9390	87.4421
17	18.4304	20.0121	21.7616	23.6975	25.8404	28.2129	30.8402	33.7502	36.9737	40.5447	48.8837	59.1176	65.0751	71.6730	87.0680	105.9306
18	19.6147	21.4123	23.4144	25.6454	28.1324	30.9057	33.9990	37.4502	41.3013	45.5992	55.7497	68.3941	75.8364	84.1407	103.7403	128.1167
19	20.8190	22.8406	25.1169	27.6712	30.5390	33.7600	37.3790	41.4463	46.0185	51.1591	63.4397	78.9692	88.2118	98.6032	123.4135	154.7400
20	22.0190	24.2974	26.8704	29.7781	33.0660	36.7856	40.9955	45.7620	51.1601	57.2750	72.0524	91.0249	102.4436	115.3797	146.6280	186.6880
30	34.7849	40.5681	47.5754	56.0849	66.4388	79.0582	94.4608	113.2832	136.3075	164.4940	241.3327	356.7868	434.7451	530.3117	790.9480	1181.8816
40	48.8864	60.4020	75.4013	95.0255	120.7998	154.7620	199.6351	259.0565	337.8824	442.5926	767.0914	1342.0251	1779.0903	2360.7572	4163.2130	7343.8578
50	64.4632	84.5794	112.7969	152.6671	209.3480	290.3359	406.5289	573.7702	815.0836	1163.9085	2400.0182	4994.5213	7217.7163	10435.6488	21813.0937	45497.1908
60	81.6697	114.0515	163.0534	237.9907	353.5837	533.1282	813.5204	1253.2133	1944.7921	3034.8164	7471.6411	18535.1333	29219.9916	46057.5085	114189.6665	281732.5718

review of learning objectives

1 Understand the importance of capital budgeting and the concepts underlying strategic and capital investment decisions. Strategic planning, especially as related to capital investment decisions, is critical to the success of organizations. The systematic planning for long-term investments in operating assets is known as capital budgeting. Long-term investments are usually large and represent commitments that are difficult to change, so capital budgeting is crucial to the long-run profitability of a company.

2 Describe and use two nondiscounted capital budgeting techniques: the payback method and the unadjusted rate of return method. Several capital budgeting techniques have been developed to assist in the decision-making process. The payback and unadjusted rate of return methods are commonly used in business because they are simple to apply. However, they generally should be used together with the discounted cash flow methods—net present value and internal rate of return—which are theoretically more correct because they consider the time value of money.

3 Describe and use two discounted capital budgeting techniques: the net present value method and the internal rate of return method. The net present value method uses a predetermined discount rate to state all the cash flows of an investment in present value terms. This rate is a company's cost of capital. The discounted cash inflows and outflows are then compared, and if the result is positive, or at least zero, the project is acceptable from a quantitative standpoint.

The internal rate of return method determines the "true" rate of return on an investment. This is the discount rate at which a project would have a net present value of zero. The internal rate is compared with the company's hurdle rate. If the internal rate is higher than or equal to the hurdle rate, the project is acceptable from a quantitative standpoint.

4 Understand the need for evaluating qualitative factors in strategic and capital investment decisions. Qualitative factors—such as the effect of an investment on quality and time, consumer and worker safety, and environmental and civic responsibility—are important considerations in capital investment decisions and may override the conclusions suggested by quantitative data.

expanded material

5 Use sensitivity analysis to assess the potential effects of uncertainty in capital budgeting. Sensitivity analysis is used to assess the potential effect of uncertainty with regard to capital budgeting. It enables management to examine how the results of the calculations would vary if certain estimates were to change and thereby to gauge how reasonable the decision is.

6 Explain how to use capital budgeting techniques in ranking capital investment projects. Capital budgeting deals with both the screening and the ranking of projects. Investments must first be screened to determine which are acceptable. They must then be ranked to ensure that a company's limited funds are invested in the projects that will earn the greatest rate of return and otherwise accomplish the company's overall objectives.

7 Explain how income taxes affect capital budgeting decisions. The cash inflows and outflows of capital budgeting decisions must be converted to after-tax amounts before the present values are computed in order to obtain realistic measures of net present values. Cash inflows and outflows are converted to after-tax amounts by taking into account such tax provisions as expense deductions for repairs and depreciation, the estimated gain on disposal of the asset at the end of its useful life, and annual operating revenues and expenses.

key terms and concepts

internal rate of return method 194
interpolation 195
least-cost decision 193
net present value 192
net present value method 191
payback method 188
ranking 185
screening 185
unadjusted rate of return method 189

expanded material

capital rationing 204
profitability index 204
sensitivity analysis 202

review problem

Capital Budgeting

High Flying Company has an opportunity to make an investment that will yield $1,000 net cash inflow per year for the next 10 years. The investment will cost $6,000 and will have no salvage value. After cost reductions and depreciation related to the new investment, the future average annual net income will increase $800.

Required: Compute the following:

1. The payback period.
2. The unadjusted rate of return.
3. The net present value. (Use a 10 percent discount rate.)
4. The internal rate of return. (The hurdle rate is 10 percent.)

Solution

1. The Payback Period

To compute the payback period, divide the investment cost by the annual net cash inflows.

$$\frac{\text{Investment cost}}{\text{Annual net cash inflows}} = \frac{\$6{,}000}{\$1{,}000} = 6 \text{ years}$$

2. The Unadjusted Rate of Return

To compute the unadjusted rate of return, divide the increase in future average annual net income by the initial investment cost.

$$\frac{\text{Increase in future average annual net income}}{\text{Initial investment cost}} = \frac{\$800}{\$6{,}000} = 13.3 \text{ percent}$$

3. The Net Present Value

To compute the net present value, first state in present value terms all expected cash outflows and inflows.

Present value of 10 annual payments of $1,000 discounted at 10 percent	$6,145
Present value of payment of $6,000 now	6,000
Net present value of project (present value of cash inflows minus present value of cash outflow)	$ 145

Since this investment's net present value is greater than zero, it is acceptable from a quantitative standpoint.

4. The Internal Rate of Return

To compute the internal rate of return, first compute the present value factor, as follows:

$$\frac{\text{Investment cost}}{\text{Annual net cash inflows}} = \frac{\$6{,}000}{\$1{,}000} = 6.0000$$

Next, use this present value factor to find the investment's internal rate of return in a present value table. Using Table II, find the row for 10 years, the life of the investment. Move across the row until you find the present value factor closest to 6.0000, which is 6.1446. This is the factor for 10 percent. Since 6.0000 is between 6.1446 and 5.6502, the investment's internal rate of return is between 10 and 12 percent. Next, use interpolation to find a more exact internal rate of return.

	Rate of Return	Present Value Factors	
High factor	10%	6.1446	6.1446
True factor		6.0000	0.0000
Low factor	12		5.6502
Differences	2%	0.1446	0.4944

The number 0.1446 is the difference between the high factor and the true factor. The number 0.4944 is the difference between the high factor and the low factor. The difference between the high rate and the low rate is 2 percent. The proportion 0.1446 ÷ 0.4944 of this 2 percent difference must be added to the low rate to give the true internal rate of return.

$$\text{True internal rate of return} = 0.10 + \left(0.02 \times \frac{0.1446}{0.4944}\right) = 10.58 \text{ percent}$$

The internal rate of return could also be computed using the following keystrokes with a Hewlett-Packard business calculator:

Hewlett-Packard Keystrokes:

1. −6,000: Press **PV** (you must enter the cash outflow as a NEGATIVE number)
2. 1,000: Press **PMT** (this is the annual cash inflow)
3. 10: Press **N** (number of years)
4. Press **I/YR** for the answer = 10.56%

Note that the answer obtained using table interpolation (10.58 percent) is very close to the actual internal rate of return of 10.56 percent.

Next, this internal rate of return is compared with the hurdle rate. Since it is greater, the investment is acceptable quantitatively. Note that this is the same decision reached by calculating the net present value.

discussion questions

1. Define capital budgeting. Give two examples of long-term investment decisions that require capital budgeting.
2. Why do long-term capital investment decisions often have a significant effect on a company's profitability?
3. Why is the time value of money so important in capital budgeting decisions?
4. If the time value of money is so important, why isn't the timing of cash flows emphasized in the accounting cycle?
5. How is depreciation expense treated when the discounted cash flow methods are used? Why?
6. How are cost savings and increased revenues related in capital budgeting?
7. Identify four capital budgeting methods, and explain why some are considered better than others.
8. Why is the payback method inferior to the discounted cash flow methods? When is the payback method helpful?

9. What is the major weakness of the unadjusted rate of return method?
10. Does a net present value of zero indicate that a project should be rejected? Explain.
11. As the desired rate of return increases, does the net present value of a project increase? Explain.
12. Under what circumstances might a project with a negative net present value be accepted?
13. What discount rate yields a net present value of zero? How is it determined?
14. What is a company's hurdle rate? How is it used?
15. How do quality and time considerations affect capital budgeting decisions?
16. Identify several qualitative factors, other than quality and time considerations, that may affect strategic and capital investment decisions. Why are qualitative factors important?

expanded material

17. How can we deal with uncertainties involved in capital budgeting?
18. Distinguish between the screening and ranking functions of capital budgeting.
19. Of what value is a profitability index in capital budgeting?
20. How do income taxes influence capital budgeting decisions?

discussion cases

CASE 4-1

SHOULD WE PURCHASE THAT NEW COPIER?

Campus Print Shop is thinking of purchasing a new, modern copier that automatically collates pages. The machine would cost $22,000 cash. A service contract on the machine, considered a must because of its complexity, would be an additional $200 per month. The machine is expected to last eight years and have a resale value of $4,000. By purchasing the new machine, Campus would save $450 per month in labor costs and $100 per month in materials costs due to increased efficiency. Other operating costs are expected to remain the same. The old copier would be sold for its scrap value of $1,000. Campus requires a return of 14 percent on its capital investments.

1. As a consultant to Campus, compute:
   a. The payback period.
   b. The unadjusted rate of return.
   c. The net present value.
   d. The internal rate of return.
2. On the basis of these computations and any qualitative considerations, would you recommend that Campus purchase the new copier?

CASE 4-2

COST AND QUALITATIVE FACTORS IN CAPITAL INVESTMENT DECISIONS

Yoshika Landscaping is contemplating purchasing a new ditch-digging machine that promises savings of $5,600 per year for 10 years. The machine costs $21,970, and no salvage value is expected. The company's cost of capital is 12 percent. You have been asked to advise Yoshika relative to this capital investment decision. As part of your analysis, compute:

1. The payback period.
2. The unadjusted rate of return.
3. The net present value.
4. The internal rate of return.

What factors besides your quantitative analysis should be considered in making this decision?

exercises

Note: Unless otherwise indicated, the exercises and problems assume that all payments are made or received at the end of the year.

EXERCISE 4-1 PRESENT VALUES

Consider each part independently.

1. Super-Fix Company would like to move its auto repair shop to a downtown location in order to attract more customers. What is the maximum Super-Fix should pay to purchase a building at the new location, assuming that the company needs to earn 12 percent? The new building will last 40 years. Super-Fix estimates that moving to the new location will result in a $10,000 increase in annual income.
2. If Audrey Ostler buys a new small automobile that costs $14,000 and provides annual gasoline savings of $1,200, how long must she own the car before the savings justify its cost? Assume an 8 percent cost of capital.

EXERCISE 4-2 TIME VALUE OF MONEY

Your late, rich uncle left you $250,000. The executor of the estate has asked if you would rather receive the full amount now or $30,000 a year for the next 40 years.

Which of these options would you take, assuming that your desired rate of return is:

1. 10 percent?
2. 12 percent?

EXERCISE 4-3 PAYBACK METHOD

The manager of Simple Company must choose between two investments. Project A costs $50,000 and promises cash savings of $10,000 a year over a useful life of 10 years. Project B costs $60,000, and the estimated cash savings are $11,000 per year over a useful life of 11 years. Using the payback method, determine which project the manager should choose.

EXERCISE 4-4 UNADJUSTED RATE OF RETURN METHOD

Um Good, Inc., a candy maker, is thinking of purchasing a new machine. A marketing firm has estimated that the new machine could increase revenues by $30,000 a year for the next 5 years. The expenses directly relating to the machine total $60,000 ($12,000 × 5 years). The initial purchase cost would be $80,000. What is the unadjusted rate of return?

EXERCISE 4-5 NET PRESENT VALUE METHOD

The Carroll Broom Company is thinking of purchasing a new automatic straw-binding machine. The company president, Joan Carroll, has determined that such a machine would save the company $10,000 per year in labor costs. The machine would cost $46,500 and would have a useful life of 10 years and a scrap value of $500. The machine would require servicing after 5 years at a cost of $1,000. Carroll uses a discount rate of 16 percent. Compute the net present value. From a quantitative standpoint, should the machine be purchased?

EXERCISE 4-6 LEAST-COST DECISION

The local fire department has determined the Sleep-Eazy Mattress Company is not in full compliance with local fire regulations. To comply, Sleep-Eazy has two alternatives: It may install an automatic sprinkler system, or it may hire a fire safety expert to make weekly fire safety checks. The automatic sprinkler system will cost $125,000, including installation charges, and will last for 10 years. It will have no salvage value. The entire system is virtually maintenance-free. The fire safety expert's fee is $14,000 per year. The cost of capital is 10 percent. Which alternative should Sleep-Eazy Mattress Company choose? Why?

EXERCISE 4-7

INTERNAL RATE OF RETURN

Juan Gonzales, the president of Nogalis Corporation, is trying to decide whether he should buy a new machine that will improve production efficiency. The machine will increase cash inflows $5,000 a year for 5 years. It will cost $18,000, and there will be no salvage value. What is the internal rate of return?

EXERCISE 4-8

COST OF CAPITAL

Daphney Corporation has raised $200,000 in equity financing through the issuance of shares. Stockholders expect to earn an average of 20 percent per year on their equity investment in Daphney. In addition, the corporation has issued $100,000 of 10 percent bonds. The corporation has also accumulated $25,000 in earnings that have been retained in the company. Investors expect to earn about 16 percent on the earnings that are retained in the company. Using the weighting procedure discussed in the chapter, calculate Daphney Corporation's cost of capital. (Ignore taxes in calculating the cost of debt.)

EXERCISE 4-9

NET PRESENT VALUE AND INTERNAL RATE OF RETURN

A real estate investment requires an initial outlay of $150,000 in cash. The investment will return a single sum cash payment of $606,796 after 10 years. The rate of return required on projects as risky as this one is 18 percent.

1. What is the net present value of this real estate investment?
2. What is the internal rate of return of this real estate investment?
3. Is this an attractive investment?

EXERCISE 4-10

NET PRESENT VALUE AND INTERNAL RATE OF RETURN

A retired person has $700,000 in a retirement account. An insurance company is offering to give the retired person an annuity of $61,029 at the end of each year for the next 20 years in exchange for the $700,000. The retired person requires a rate of return of 8 percent on investments; this is the rate currently being earned in the retirement account.

1. What is the net present value of this exchange?
2. What is the internal rate of return implied in this exchange?
3. Should the retired person accept the exchange offered by the insurance company?

EXERCISE 4-11

QUALITY AND TIME FACTORS

Tucker Yard Service Company is contemplating purchasing a new riding lawnmower for its business. One particular model has special features that enhance the cutting and the collecting of the mowed grass, but that mower is quite expensive. Another model is more basic and costs $1,000 less. The payback period on the more expensive model is estimated to be 3.5 years and on the less expensive model 2.5 years. The "bumper-to-bumper" warranties are two years and one year, respectively. From these limited data, what factors should Tucker consider in making this decision?

EXERCISE 4-12

QUALITATIVE CONSIDERATIONS

The Upscale Department Store has been plagued with shoplifting. The president, Hector Conrad, has suggested that the store hire a security force to "frisk" all customers as they leave the store. It is estimated that annual shoplifting losses are $100,000. Expenses associated with the security force are estimated to be $50,000 annually. Before Mr. Conrad makes his final decision, what other factors might he consider?

expanded material

EXERCISE 4-13

SENSITIVITY ANALYSIS

You have accumulated $10,500 in a savings account that pays 10 percent interest. You are offered the opportunity to buy 30 ounces of gold at $350 per ounce. The price of gold is expected to rise to $700 per ounce by the end of 10 years. You realize, however, that this is only an estimate.

To what price would gold have to rise in order to earn a 10 percent return? (Note that the future value factor for $10,500 at 10 percent at the end of 10 years is 2.5937.)

EXERCISE 4-14 SCREENING FUNCTION

Your company's cost of capital was determined to be 12 percent. Several investment alternatives are being considered, and the discounted cash flows have given the following results:

Net present value:

1. A new machine was analyzed, and a net present value of zero resulted.
2. A new product line was analyzed, and a negative net present value of $60 resulted.
3. An investment was being considered. The analysis yielded a net present value of $250.

Internal rate of return:

1. A plant expansion project promised a yield of 12 percent.
2. An investment in additional transport trucks would yield an internal rate of return of 10 percent.
3. The addition of another assembly line would add cash flows that would give an internal rate of return of 16 percent.

Determine which projects should be accepted as investment opportunities and which should be rejected.

EXERCISE 4-15 RANKING PROJECTS

Using net present value (NPV) analysis, a manager can select those projects that will maximize the present value of future cash flows. NPV analysis is a powerful tool; however, surveys of current practice indicate that the internal rate of return (IRR) method enjoys considerable popularity among decision makers. What would account for IRR's appeal? What are the drawbacks to using only the IRR method to rank projects?

EXERCISE 4-16 PROFITABILITY INDEX

California Company is trying to determine the relative profitability of two alternative investments. Investment A requires an initial cash outlay of $10,000 and has a net present value of $500. Investment B requires an initial cash outlay of $2,000 and has a net present value of $150. Compute the profitability index of each investment. Which alternative is more profitable?

EXERCISE 4-17 INCOME TAX EFFECTS

Kade Corporation is considering purchasing a new piece of equipment. The equipment will cost $135,000 and is expected to have a useful life of five years. The gross cash flow savings is estimated to be $50,000 per year. The company elects not to take the expense deduction and will depreciate the full cost of the asset for tax purposes under MACRS using a 5-year recovery period and the straight-line method. The company is in the 40 percent tax bracket (including federal, state, and local taxes).

1. Compute the after-tax cash flow savings on the asset.
2. Compute the after-tax internal rate of return that will equate the present value of the savings with the net outlay cost.

problems

PROBLEM 4-1 NET PRESENT VALUE METHOD

A fast-food establishment is thinking of buying a new cooking grill and refrigeration unit. The cost of these new machines is $12,500 and $9,000, respectively. The installation costs of the new equipment will run about $800. It is estimated that 10 percent more customers can be served with the new equipment, which would mean an additional annual net cash flow of approximately $4,500. The salvage value of the old grill and refrigeration unit is estimated to be $1,000.

The firm's cost of capital is 12 percent. The equipment should last 10 years, at a minimum.

Spread-Sheet Software

Required: Using the net present value method, should the company purchase the new equipment? (Ignore income tax effects.)

PROBLEM 4-2

NET PRESENT VALUE METHOD—UNEVEN CASH FLOWS

Southside Junk Yard needs to buy a car smasher. The machine would add the following revenues to the business over the next three years:

Year 1 Cash savings = $30,000
Year 2 Cash savings plus additional scrap sales = $40,000
Year 3 Cash savings plus additional scrap sales = $55,000

The initial cost of the machine is $100,000. At the end of three years, its salvage value is estimated at $20,000. The firm has a cost of capital of 12 percent.

Required: Using the net present value method, determine whether the company should purchase the machine. (Ignore income tax effects.)

PROBLEM 4-3

INTERNAL RATE OF RETURN

You have been offered the opportunity to purchase a franchise of Sunshine Juice Stores. You will have to pay $155,625 for the initial investment in the store and its equipment, plus $30,000 per year for the lease payments and the franchise fee. The franchise contract obligates you for 10 years. Operating costs for each year will be $125,000, and the expected revenue is $180,000 a year. Your hurdle rate is 10 percent. Ignore income taxes.

Required:

1. Does this investment yield a satisfactory rate of return?
2. What qualitative factors might be considered?

PROBLEM 4-4

INTERNAL RATE OF RETURN AND HURDLE RATE

Nina Roberts has the opportunity to invest in a timber forest. She would have to invest $100,000. Revenues of $20,000 per year are projected for 20 years. However, these revenues will not begin coming in for five years because the timber must be seasoned before cutting and selling can begin. Ms. Roberts's hurdle rate is 10 percent. Ignore income taxes.

Required:

1. Calculate the internal rate of return, and determine whether or not Ms. Roberts should make the investment.
2. If Ms. Roberts has to borrow the $100,000 necessary for the investment from her bank at 12 percent interest, should she make the investment?
3. **Interpretive Question:** Why is it important for Ms. Roberts to determine her cost of capital before making this investment decision?

PROBLEM 4-5

PAYBACK, NET PRESENT VALUE, AND INTERNAL RATE OF RETURN METHODS

Nucore Company is thinking of purchasing a new candy-wrapping machine at a cost of $370,000. The machine should save the company approximately $70,000 in operating costs per year over its estimated useful life of 10 years. The salvage value at the end of 10 years is expected to be $15,000. (Ignore income tax effects.)

Spread-Sheet Software

Required:

1. What is the machine's payback period?
2. Compute the net present value of the machine if the cost of capital is 12 percent.
3. What is the expected internal rate of return for this machine?

PROBLEM 4-6

INTERNAL RATE OF RETURN

The manager of Soft & Creamy Ice Cream is thinking of buying a new soft ice cream machine. The machine will cost $13,500 and will last 10 years. Soft ice cream sales are expected to generate $3,000 in income per year.

Required: What is the internal rate of return on this project?

PROBLEM 4-7

CHOOSING AMONG ALTERNATIVES

Tom Thurlow wants to buy a boat but is short of cash. Two alternatives are available: Tom can accept $2,000 per year from his brother for partial ownership in the boat, or he can earn money by renting the boat to others. Rental income would be $2,500 per year. Under either alternative, the boat will last eight years. If Tom rents the boat out, he will have to pay $3,000 to overhaul the engine at the end of the fourth year.

Required: Which alternative should Tom select, assuming that the cost of capital is 12 percent and that only quantitative considerations are involved?

PROBLEM 4-8

LEASE-OR-BUY DECISION

A small sales company is committed to supplying three sales representatives with new cars. The company has two alternatives. It can either buy the three cars and sell them after two years, or it can lease the cars for two years. The company uses a 16 percent discount rate. The information for each alternative is as follows:

Alternative 1: Buy

Cost	$36,000
Annual service costs	3,000
Anticipated repairs during the 1st year	700
Anticipated repairs during the 2nd year	1,500
Salvage value at the end of 2 years	10,000

Alternative 2: Lease

To lease the cars, the company would simply pay $20,000 a year for the two years.

Required: Assuming the lease is paid at the end of each year, determine the better alternative.

PROBLEM 4-9

RENT-OR-PURCHASE DECISION

As one aspect of its business, New Lawn Company currently rents a ditch-digging machine for an average of $48 per job. A used machine is available for $995 but would cost $498 to repair. The machine, if purchased, would cost $800 a year to maintain and in two years would need a new chain costing $394. The used digger has a useful life of four years with no salvage value.

Required: If the company averages 30 jobs a year and has a cost of capital of 10 percent, which alternative is more profitable?

PROBLEM 4-10

SELL-OR-RENT DECISION

Clarence Gleason has inherited an apartment complex. He is now faced with the decision of whether to sell or to rent the property. A real estate adviser believes that Clarence should rent the property, because he could receive $65,000 per year for 10 years and then could sell the property for $400,000. A development company has offered Clarence $300,000 down and promises to pay $50,000 per year for the next 15 years. The land has a remaining mortgage of $130,000. If Clarence sells the complex, he will have to pay that sum now. If he rents the property, he will have to pay $20,000 per year for 10 years. The cost of capital is 16 percent.

Required:

1. Calculate the net present value of each alternative.
2. **Interpretive Question:** Discuss the qualitative factors that might affect the decision to sell or rent.

PROBLEM 4-11

UNIFYING CONCEPTS: NET PRESENT VALUE AND INTERNAL RATE OF RETURN METHODS

Julie Kowalis, an investment analyst, wants to know if her investments during the past four years have earned at least a 12 percent return. Four years ago, she had the following investments:

a. She purchased a small building for $50,000 and rented space in it. She received rental income of $8,000 for each of the four years and then sold the building this year for $55,000.
b. She purchased a small refreshment stand near the city park for $25,000. Annual income from the stand was $5,000 for each of the four years. She sold the stand for $20,000 this year.

c. She purchased an antique car for $5,000 four years ago. She sold it this year to a collector for $7,000.

Required:

1. Using the net present value method, determine whether or not each investment earned at least 12 percent.
2. Did the investments as a whole earn at least 12 percent? Explain.

expanded material

PROBLEM 4-12 SENSITIVITY ANALYSIS

Falcon Manufacturing is a leading manufacturer of airframe components for small aircraft. Heidi Saxton, Falcon's operations manager, has submitted a request for a new piece of production equipment. Using the new machine, the company will be able to reduce expenses for both maintenance and labor. Data on the project are as follows:

Initial investment	$80,000
Useful life	10 years
Salvage value of old machine	$1,500
Annual cash savings	$15,000
Salvage value of new machine	$10,000
Maintenance overhaul (Year 5)	$7,600
Cost of capital	12%

Assume all cash flows occur at the end of each year. (Ignore income tax effects.)

Required:

1. Using the above data, calculate the net present value of the investment. From a strictly quantitative standpoint, should the machine be purchased?
2. Suppose that Heidi receives another analysis that increases the cost of capital estimate to 14 percent and the new machine's salvage value to $17,000. Would the purchase still make sense?
3. Falcon's CEO, Kevin Davis, is responsible for approving all capital investment projects. Having spent his entire career dealing with one estimate after another, Davis has asked you to consider two specific changes:
   a. Reduce annual cash inflows by 10 percent.
   b. Cut in half the estimated salvage value of new equipment.

   Using the original problem data, calculate the net present value using the CEO's two changes.

PROBLEM 4-13 NET PRESENT VALUE USED TO RANK ALTERNATIVES

Taglioni's Pizza Company has to choose a new delivery car from among three alternatives. Assume that gasoline costs $1.30 per gallon and that the firm's cost of capital is 12 percent. The car will be driven 12,000 miles per year.

	Car 1	Car 2	Car 3
Cost	$12,000	$4,000	$8,000
Mileage per gallon	40	8	12
Useful life	5 years	5 years	5 years
Salvage value	$2,000	$500	$1,000

Required:

1. Which car should the company purchase?
2. How would your answer change if the price of gasoline increased to $2 per gallon?

PROBLEM 4-14 SCREENING AND RANKING ALTERNATIVES

Sunshine Corporation is considering several long-term investments. Management wants to accept the two best projects, given the following data:

	A	B	C	D	E
Present value of net cash inflows	$24,000	$44,000	$15,000	$30,000	$50,000
Investment cost	20,000	40,000	16,000	24,000	41,000

Required:

1. Determine the net present value and the profitability index for each project.
2. Which projects are acceptable using the profitability index as a screening tool?
3. What would be the ranking of the acceptable projects according to the profitability indexes?
4. **Interpretive Question:** What additional information would be needed to screen and rank the projects using the internal rate of return method? What are the decision rules using the IRR method for screening and ranking capital budgeting projects?

PROBLEM 4-15

UNIFYING CONCEPTS: COMPARING THE INTERNAL RATE OF RETURN AND THE NET PRESENT VALUE METHODS

Get Rich Corporation has to choose between two investment opportunities. Investment A requires an immediate cash outlay of $100,000 and provides after-tax income of $20,000 per year for 10 years. Investment B requires an immediate cash outlay of $1,000 and generates after-tax income of $350 per year for 5 years.

Required:

1. Using a cost of capital of 12 percent, calculate the net present value of each investment, and determine which one Get Rich should select.
2. Calculate the internal rate of return of each investment. On the basis of this method, which investment should Get Rich select?
3. **Interpretive Question:** How do you account for the difference in rankings? Under the circumstances, which method would you rely on for your decision?

PROBLEM 4-16

UNIFYING CONCEPTS: PAYBACK AND INTERNAL RATE OF RETURN

The management of Kitchen Shop is thinking of buying a new drill press to aid in adapting parts for different machines. The press is expected to save Kitchen Shop $8,000 per year in costs. However, Kitchen Shop has an old punch machine that isn't worth anything on the market and that will probably last indefinitely. The new press will last 12 years and will cost $41,595. (Ignore income tax effects.)

Required:

1. Compute the payback period of the new machine.
2. Compute the internal rate of return.
3. **Interpretive Question:** What uncertainties are involved in this decision? Discuss how they might be dealt with.

PROBLEM 4-17

UNIFYING CONCEPTS: CAPITAL RATIONING USING THE PAYBACK AND NET PRESENT VALUE METHODS

Dino Corporation is trying to decide which of five investment opportunities it should undertake. The company's cost of capital is 16 percent. Owing to a cash shortage, the company has a policy that it will not undertake any investment unless it has a payback period of less than three years. The company is unwilling to undertake more than two investment projects. The following data apply to the alternatives:

Investment	Initial Cost	Expected Returns
A	$100,000	$30,000 per year for 5 years
B	50,000	25,000 per year for 6 years
C	30,000	8,000 per year for 10 years
D	20,000	7,000 per year for 6 years
E	10,000	3,500 per year for 3 years

Required:

1. Using the payback method, screen out any investment project that fails to meet the company's payback period requirement.
2. Using the net present value method, determine which of the remaining projects the company should undertake, keeping in mind the capital rationing constraint.
3. **Interpretive Question:** What advantages do you see in using the payback method together with other capital budgeting methods?

PROBLEM 4-18 INCOME TAX EFFECTS

Sylvania Manufacturing Company is considering the purchase of new equipment to perform operations currently being performed on less efficient equipment. The purchase price is $142,000 delivered and installed. The company elects to expense $10,000 of the purchase price in the first year. A company engineer estimates that the new equipment will save $28,000 in labor and other direct costs annually. The new equipment will have an estimated life of 10 years and zero salvage value at the end of the 10 years. The equipment will be depreciated over 10 years on the optional straight-line basis for income tax purposes, after taking the $10,000 expense election in the first year. The existing equipment has a book value of $4,000, a remaining economic life of five years, and can be disposed of now for $4,000. The company's average tax rate is 40 percent (including federal, state, and local taxes), and its after-tax cost of capital is 12 percent.

Required:

1. Should the new equipment be purchased?
2. What would the decision be if the cost of capital were 10 percent?
3. **Interpretive Question:** Assuming that the net present value of an investment in new equipment is so small that you are indifferent about whether to make the purchase or keep the old equipment, what other factors would you consider in making the decision?

competency enhancement opportunities

- Analyzing Real Company Information
- International Case
- Ethics Case
- Writing Assignment
- The Debate
- Internet Search

The following additional assignments provide opportunities for students to develop critical thinking, ethical perspectives, oral and written communication skills, experience with electronic research, and teamwork through group and business activities.

ANALYZING REAL COMPANY INFORMATION

• *Analyzing 4-1 (Microsoft)*

The 1999 annual report for MICROSOFT is included in Appendix A. The section of the annual report relating to management's discussion and analysis provides detail as to factors that might affect Microsoft's future and, as a result, the company's long-term decisions. Review the financial statements and the "Management Discussion and Analysis" section, and answer the following questions:

1. Microsoft has no long-term debt. Does that mean its cost of capital is zero? Explain.

2. Microsoft specifically states that the company "does not provide forecasts of future financial performance." If that is the case, how can it make any capital budgeting decisions?
3. In Bill Gates's letter to shareholders, he makes the following comment:

   > We are investing heavily in the future—from world-class customer support to the $3.8 billion we plan to spend in fiscal 2000 on research and development for the products of tomorrow. There is, however, no guarantee of success. Competition continues to intensify, and regulatory pressures are unlikely to ease. Although global PC sales have proved remarkably robust, some slowdown is likely in the coming year. And as Microsoft's business becomes more complex, the strategic challenges and risks we face grow exponentially.

   Microsoft is committed to making heavy investments in the future. However, Bill notes that "there is no guarantee of success." How would such factors as competition, regulation, and a changing computer world affect the company's capital budgeting process? What specific inputs into the capital budgeting models would be affected by these factors?

• ***Analyzing 4-2 (The Boeing Company)***

As you probably know, **BOEING** builds airplanes. While most famous for the big 747, Boeing is continually developing newer models. Over the past several years, Boeing has been developing the 737 and 777 families of airplanes. In 1996, Boeing formed a joint venture with **GENERAL ELECTRIC** to develop planes that can fly over 6,000 miles without refueling.

1. What factors must Boeing consider when making the decision to produce a new family of airplanes like the 777? What would be the expected cash inflows, and what would be the expected cash outflows? Categorize the outflows into two types: one-time outflows and annual outflows.
2. The costs of developing a new family of airplanes are enormous. Why would Boeing agree to incur these costs when it is able to continue producing older model planes like the 747 and the 767? Frame this discussion in terms of a capital budgeting decision. That is, evaluate the opportunities in terms of cash inflows and cash outflows.

INTERNATIONAL CASE

International

• ***DaimlerChrysler***

DAIMLERCHRYSLER discloses the following information relating to its long-term debt in its 1999 annual report:

- 6.9 percent notes/bonds
- 5.6 percent commercial paper
- 4.7 percent liabilities to financial institutions

FORD MOTOR COMPANY also provides information relating to its debt in the notes to its annual report. That information is given below.

- Secured indebtedness, 8.3 percent
- Unsecured senior indebtedness—notes and bank debt, 6.4 percent
- Unsecured senior indebtedness—debentures, 3.2 percent
- Unsecured subordinated indebtedness—notes, 6.6 percent

1. Assume that each company's debt is distributed equally across the various categories. Compute an average cost interest rate for each company.
2. If your answer from (1) represented each firm's cost of capital, what would it tell you about the kinds of projects that DaimlerChrysler can undertake as compared to Ford?

ETHICS CASE

• ***Wheeler, Nevada***

The city council of Wheeler, Nevada, is faced with an important decision: whether or not to rezone a parcel of property and allow ChemStor, Inc., to purchase the land and build a chemical waste storage facility on the property. Several factors enter into the decision.

a. The property is currently zoned for agricultural use and is surrounded by ranching operations in a rural community.
b. Several ranchers have joined together and offered to buy the property from the city over a 40-year period. In return for an agreed-upon interest rate of one point below prime, they will donate 20 acres of the land for a city park.
c. ChemStor has offered to pay cash for the land. Company management also points out that the facility will create about 25 new jobs for local residents and generate close to $100,000 a year in increased property taxes for the city.
d. ChemStor, a New Jersey-based company, learned of this property from its controller, who is a brother-in-law to one of the Wheeler City council members. ChemStor has offered a "finder's fee" for locating a waste storage site. The finder's fee would be split between the controller and the brother-in-law.

Identify the ethical and other issues involved in this capital investment decision.

WRITING ASSIGNMENT

• ***Lease versus Buy***

You are fresh out of college, have your first real job, and just received your first big paycheck. You decide you need some wheels. Off you go to the car dealer. You carefully review the various makes and models of cars, determine the price range you can afford, and select "YOUR FIRST CAR." You thought that was the hard part. Now you need to decide on financing. The salesperson says you can either borrow money to purchase the vehicle or you can lease the car.

What factors should you consider in making this capital budgeting decision? Identify those factors that should enter into the lease versus buy decision. Prepare a short memo discussing the pros and cons of leasing versus buying and identifying the cash inflows and outflows associated with each option.

THE DEBATE

• ***The Time Value of Money***

The text discusses two general types of capital budgeting techniques: nondiscounted and discounted. The nondiscounted methods involve comparing the outflows of cash to the inflows. These methods do not take into account the time value of money. The discounted capital budgeting techniques factor into the evaluation the time value of money.

Divide your group into two teams.

- Team 1 is to take the position that the nondiscounted methods provide the best means of evaluating capital budgeting alternatives. Prepare a short presentation that identifies the advantages of using the nondiscounted methods and discusses the disadvantages of the discounted capital budgeting techniques.
- Team 2 is to take the position that the discounted methods are preferred. Prepare a short presentation in support of the various methods that incorporate into their analysis the time value of money.

INTERNET SEARCH

• *Federal Express*

We began this chapter with a look at **FEDERAL EXPRESS**. Let's continue our examination of this company using its Internet site. Access Federal Express's site at **http://www.fedex.com**. Sometimes Web addresses change, so if this address doesn't work, access the Web site for this book at **http://albrecht.swcollege.com** for an updated link to Federal Express.

Once you have gained access to the company's Web site, answer the following questions:

1. Find the portion of the Web site containing information about the early history of FedEx Express. Why was Memphis, Tennessee, chosen as the company headquarters?
2. Find the portion of the Web site containing "FedEx Express Facts." How many aircraft does FedEx have in its worldwide fleet?
3. Find FedEx's most recent annual report. Does the company lease any of its aircraft or equipment? [Hint: Look in the notes to the financial statements.] What factors would the company have considered when determining whether to lease or buy its aircraft and equipment?

comprehensive problem 1–4

Imagine that one of your parents has traveled across the country to visit you at college. As the two of you have dinner together at one of your favorite restaurants, the discussion turns to your accounting class. You begin describing some of the new ideas and techniques you have been learning lately. Suddenly, your parent wants to talk about the family business. As the discussion goes on, it becomes clear that your parent is expecting you to provide some specific ideas about how to improve the management process in the family business using current accounting methods. You certainly want to impress your parent with all the detailed knowledge that you have gained since beginning your course work in accounting. However, you are also concerned that you may describe something incorrectly or say something misleading. One day you expect to inherit the family business, and you would hate to say anything during dinner that might later cause problems in the company!

Required: You need to respond to your parent using insights gained from the last four chapters (1–4 of management accounting) of this textbook. Further, answering your parent's questions will require you to carefully construct your remarks in light of the exact nature of the family business. Hence, we will assume three separate types of businesses for your family:

1. Computer manufacturing plant
2. Neighborhood grocery store
3. Large architectural firm

For each of these businesses, divide your comments into two parts:

- Return on investment

Discuss the nature of the family business in terms of the DuPont formulation of return on investment (Profit margin × Asset turnover = Return on investment). What aspects of this formula are most important for the type of strategy that the family business may choose to follow?

- Relevant topics

Listed below are a number of topics from Chapters 1–4 of management accounting. Briefly describe (three sentences or less) how each topic may relate to the family business.

1. Direct materials costs
2. Direct labor costs
3. Overhead costs
4. Direct materials inventory
5. Work-in-process inventory
6. Finished goods inventory
7. Job order costing
8. Process costing*
9. Cost behavior
10. Break-even analysis
11. Capital budgeting
12. Net present value
13. Internal rate of return

*Relates to expanded material.

Operating Budgets

chapter

m5

learning objectives

After studying this chapter, you should be able to:

1. Describe different types of budgeting and identify the purposes of budgeting.
2. Describe the budgeting process and its behavioral implications.
3. Explain the master budget and its components for manufacturing firms, merchandising firms, and service firms.

expanded material

4. Prepare pro-forma financial statements.
5. Distinguish between static and flexible budgets.

setting the stage

Every organization needs to budget. Budgets help allocate resources effectively so that the organization can accomplish its mission. Consider how the federal government budgets, for example. The arrival of the president's budget on Capitol Hill signals the beginning of the annual budget process in Congress—a process that can last more than eight months and require the passage of scores of bills and resolutions.[1] Congress drafts a budget resolution—a spending plan that defines in broad terms how much the government will take in through taxes and other receipts and spend on all government accounts during the coming fiscal year. The House and Senate Budget Committees each draft their own version, bring the drafts to their respective chambers for approval, iron out differences in conference, and return the resulting version to their chambers for adoption. Because the president's signature is not required, the resolution does not carry the force of law—although Congress is forced to abide by the limits it sets for itself. Discretionary spending is allocated to the Appropriations Committees in both chambers. Throughout the budget process, Congress passes authorization bills that set the maximum amounts that may be spent in specific fiscal years for individual discretionary programs, as well as goals for those programs. The budget resolution serves as a blueprint for congressional spending decisions. It sets the total levels for budget authority, outlays, incoming revenues, direct-loan obligations, and loan guarantee commitments, as well as the public debt ceiling for the upcoming fiscal year.

In 1999, for example, the federal budget was broken down as follows:

Spending Category	Amount	Percentage of Total
Social Security	$387 billion	22.5%
Other discretionary spending	300 billion	17.5%
Defense	275 billion	16.0%
Interest on debt	231 billion	13.5%
Medicare	220 billion	12.8%
Other entitlements	196 billion	11.4%
Medicaid	108 billion	6.3%

As you can see, a significant portion of the budget goes to pay interest on the national debt. However, given that revenues are anticipated to be $1.75 trillion in fiscal year 2000 and grow to $2 trillion by 2004, large budget surpluses are expected. If Congress and the president can resist the urge to spend the excesses, the national debt can be reduced or even eliminated.

Budgeting probably consumes more congressional time than any other single activity. Even though you may argue that Congress and the president have not been as fiscally responsible as they could have been, the budgeting process has instilled some discipline in their spending habits and provided a sense of order for governmental expenditures and management of programs.

On a more local level, consider how budgeting can resolve problems at your university. The administration probably wants to hold down spending and keep tuition competitive and affordable. At the same time, however, the department chairs and deans probably want to spend more money to enhance the education of the students.

Shouldn't the arts and humanities departments get more money this year to help emphasize the importance of a liberal arts education? Already, salaries of faculty in those areas are near poverty levels. What about the business school? Shouldn't business and accounting receive more operating funds because their classes have the highest demand and are the largest on campus? Wait a minute, shouldn't more money be put into program diversity to help students become more aware of the differences between cultures, races, and sexes and enhance understanding? How about the buildings and grounds—the roofs need

1 Information on the federal budget process was obtained from http://hillsource.house.gov/LegislativeDigest/Digest/DigestArchives/D99/Wk8pt2.htm.

replacing and the sidewalks are cracking. Don't we need to make repairs? What's more, how can we have a winning basketball team without a new basketball arena?

The poor administration. How would you like to be responsible for resolving these questions and allocating the limited funds? Each department within the university has its own sense of mission, priorities, goals, objectives, and agendas. Furthermore, some departmental priorities may not be consistent with university goals. Prioritizing the funding requests may be difficult if the university has no clear, agreed-upon criteria to use in evaluating them. The difficulty of measuring the benefits of each program makes the process even more challenging. The budgeting process that we will discuss in this chapter can help the university resolve these conflicting objectives and facilitate order in its spending. Without budgeting, no matter how difficult, the university will never be able to accomplish its objectives.[2]

budget A quantitative expression of a plan of action that shows how a firm or an organization will acquire and use resources over some specified period of time.

A ***budget*** *is a quantitative expression of a plan of action that shows how a firm, an organization (such as the government or a university in the opening scenario), or an individual will acquire and use resources over a specified period of time. For a firm, implicit in most budgets is management's expectation of earning sufficient profit to provide a reasonable return on investment. The budget identifies and allocates resources necessary to effectively and efficiently carry out the mission of the organization. Although budgeting may sound to you like an unappealing activity (maybe you have tried budgeting your personal expenditures), successful budgeting is absolutely critical to the success of a business. In this chapter, we will briefly touch on personal budgeting and then cover budgeting for manufacturing, merchandising, and service firms.*

1

Describe different types of budgeting and identify the purposes of budgeting.

TYPES AND PURPOSES OF BUDGETING

As you learned in Chapter 1 of management accounting, budgeting is part of the management planning process, a process that involves identifying problems or opportunities, identifying alternative solutions, evaluating those alternatives, then choosing and implementing the best alternatives. As you learned in Chapter 1 of management accounting, there are two basic types of planning: (1) long-run planning, which includes strategic planning and capital budgeting, and (2) short-run planning, which includes production and process prioritizing and operational budgeting or profit planning. Long-run planning involves making decisions where the effects will extend several years into the future. Long-run planning includes broad-based decisions about products, markets, productive facilities, and financial resources. This type of planning is often referred to as strategic planning. Strategic planning takes place at the executive level in an organization and involves identifying the organization's mission, the goals flowing from that mission, and the strategies and actions that will be taken to accomplish those goals. With strategic planning in place, the company can then plan for the purchase and use of major assets such as buildings or equipment to help the company meet its long-range goals. This type of planning is called capital budgeting.

As you also learned in Chapter 1 of management accounting, short-run planning is divided into two categories. Once the organization has made long-term commitments to capital structure (land, buildings, equipment, management personnel, etc.), then managers need to determine how to best use those committed resources to maximize the return on their capital investments—a process often referred to as production prioritizing. Once the organization has determined what to produce or otherwise provide to the marketplace in order to maximize its goals, managers are ready to go to the next phase of short-run planning—operational budgeting. Sometimes known as profit plans, operational budgets are used by managers to establish and communicate daily, weekly, and monthly goals for the organization. Failure to carefully perform strategic planning, capital budgeting, or budgeting for operations can have adverse conse-

2 James C. Horsch, "Redesigning the Resource Allocation Process," *Management Accounting*, July 1995, pp. 55–59.

quences for organizations, even to the point of causing bankruptcy. The list of companies that have failed in recent years as a result of poor planning and execution is getting longer each day. Casualties of poor planning include such common names as EASTERN AIRLINES, MANVILLE CORPORATION, ATARI COMPUTERS, and CIRCLE K. In Chapter 4 of management accounting, we discussed strategic planning and capital budgeting elements of planning. In this chapter, our focus is on budgeting for operations.

operating (master) budget A network of many separate schedules and budgets that together constitute the overall operating and financing plan for the coming period.

The **operating (master) budget** is the most detailed and most heavily used budget in an organization. As the name implies, this budget details the immediate goals for revenues, production, expenses, and cash for the next period. Before we can examine the operating budget in detail, we need to identify its purposes, describe its evolution, and discuss the major issues involved in budget preparation. This will give us a framework for preparing an operating budget.

Purposes of Budgeting

The overall purpose of an operating budget is to quantify a general plan so that performance in relation to a goal can be carefully monitored. Thus, budgeting has a twofold purpose. The first purpose is to allow individuals or companies to develop a plan to meet a specified goal. The second purpose is to allow ongoing comparison between actual results and the plan in order to control operations or activities. To illustrate, let us assume that Dick Cotton earns $3,000 a month (and takes home only $2,000 after taxes) and has prepared a budget of his income and expenses.

disposable income Income left after withholdings and fixed expenses have been subtracted from gross salary; the amount left to cover variable expenditures.

The budget in Exhibit 5-1 contains an important warning that spending is exceeding earnings. The commitment of $1,300 to fixed expenses leaves only $680 to cover all of Dick's necessary expenditures for utilities, food, clothing, and the like. Because Dick cannot cover these expenditures using his **disposable income** of $680 a month, he must revise his plans; perhaps he could ask for a raise, get a second job or a new job that pays more, obtain a loan, or decrease his spending. This simple illustration shows that budgeting is extremely important. Unless Dick takes corrective action, he will soon join the growing number of individuals declaring bankruptcy. To learn more about personal budgeting, study the budgeting chapter of the personal financial planning supplement that accompanies this book.

exhibit 5-1 Monthly Budget for Dick Cotton

Gross salary		$ 3,000
Withholdings:		
Federal income taxes	$500	
State income taxes	150	
FICA taxes	230	
Other withholdings	140	(1,020)
Net take-home pay		$ 1,980
Fixed expenses:		
House mortgage expense	$750	
Car payment expense	350	
Insurance expense	200	(1,300)
Disposable income		$ 680
Utilities expense	$200	
Food expense	400	
Clothing expense	100	
Entertainment expense	100	
Miscellaneous expenses	200	(1,000)
Net surplus (deficit)		$ (320)

business environment essay

Budgeting Woes The budgeting process can be frustrating if the prepared budgets are not realistic. For example, if a married couple determine that they will spend only $100 per month on food when in reality food will cost at least $400 per month, communication and other problems will usually occur. The following list highlights some warning signs that the budgeting process needs revamping:

1. Decision makers who must comply with the budget become frustrated.
2. There is a lack of agreement on amounts budgeted.
3. Prioritizing expenditures or agreeing on the allocation of funds is difficult.
4. There is confusion about who is accountable for funding decisions.
5. Budgeting is not integrated across various segments of the firm.
6. The "squeaky wheel gets the grease" rule is used to allocate resources.
7. The budgeting process requires more effort than it is worth.
8. Managers are held responsible for budgets that include elements over which they have no control.
9. Long-term budgeting and strategic planning are absent.
10. The budgeting process is "political."

Source: Adapted from James C. Horsch, "Redesigning the Resource Allocation Process," *Management Accounting,* July 1995, pp. 55–59.

fyi

A study conducted several years ago revealed that only 4 of every 100 employees who join the workforce at age 25 have sufficient funds to retire at age 65. The other 96 must either keep working or depend on someone else for help.

In addition, someday Dick will want to retire. Currently, Dick's budget does not provide for any savings or investments. With all the planning tools available today, such as tax-sheltered retirement plans, investments, annuities, and so forth, an individual who plans and budgets well can prepare adequately for the future. Unfortunately, at his present rate, Dick will not be one of these individuals.

Indeed, the penalty for not budgeting is severe. Individuals who budget successfully have found that they can spend just as much if they budget as they can if they don't. The only difference is that those who budget spend money how, where, and when they want to.

The previous example was of a personal budget. The same advantages that budgeting provides on a personal level exist for organizations. Specifically, there are seven major reasons why budgeting is important to an organization's success:

1. *Planning and setting objectives.* The preparation of a budget forces managers to consider explicitly where the firm is going and how it is going to get there. Budgeting forces managers to quantify objectives for the organization and the means of achieving those objectives. The federal government, as described in the opening scenario, uses the budgeting process to plan its expenditures for the upcoming year. Similarly, by budgeting, an organization, such as the university described in the opening scenario, will be better prepared to decide where its scarce resources will be spent.
2. *Communication.* Budgets improve communication between the various management levels of a business, helping managers plan activities that enhance the smooth functioning of the enterprise. In general, budgets relay top management's expectations and show each segment how it fits into the overall plan. Budgets establish a benchmark to which actual performance will be compared. In both families and business organizations, it is usually not the lack of money that causes problems but the lack of communication about money. Couples and organizations that budget adequately find that their budgets are a great communication tool. For example, once the budget is established for the university in the opening scenario, the budget communicates to various departments and groups how university money will be spent.

3. *Coordination.* Budgets help management coordinate activities of business segments. By coordinating and integrating the goals of each segment, management ensures that its efforts to meet the overall objectives of the firm will be realized. In addition, budgeting helps to identify potential bottlenecks and allows management to develop plans to alleviate them. For example, the budgeting process may reveal that a resource, critical to the production process, is in short supply. Management can then take action to address this shortage. Budgets help guarantee that the combined expenditures of the various segments do not exceed the total budgeted expenditures for the organization.
4. *Authorization.* Once budgets are approved by top management, they provide authorization for investing, spending, ordering, producing, and borrowing by lower-level managers and employees. At most major companies, IBM for example, the budget becomes the law. If something is budgeted, it can be purchased. If not budgeted, the purchase cannot be made. This is one area where many personal budgets fail. Many individuals use their budget as a guide instead of as authorization to spend; as a result, they often "exceed" their budget.
5. *Motivation.* Budgets help motivate people. By providing a clear set of quantified objectives, budgets guide people to perform the activities that need to be accomplished. The motivational aspect of budgets can be quite strong. Care must be exercised in budgeting to ensure that budgets do not create a "success at any cost" attitude.
6. *Conflict resolution.* In most organizations, everyone usually wants additional resources. Budgeting forces up-front planning, which helps resolve conflicts over how limited resources will be allocated among an organization's various parts. (Remember the conflicting objectives of the university in the opening scenario?) Consider, for example, a family that will have \$1,000 of disposable income next year. How shall they spend the money? Suppose the wife wants to spend \$500 on clothes for the children because they are quickly outgrowing their wardrobes. In addition, she would like to spend the other \$500 on piano lessons for the children. On the other hand, the husband would like to spend \$500 to replace the garage door, which is falling down, and another \$500 to fix the transmission on the car (it's starting to slip). A budget, prepared by the husband and wife together, could help them resolve these conflicting priorities.
7. *Performance measurement (evaluation).* Budgets provide quantitative measures of expectations and objectives. These objectives later serve as benchmarks against which the performance of managers and others in a firm can be evaluated. Employees and managers who meet or exceed budgets are often rewarded. When productivity is inadequate, as measured against budgeted performance, employees may be penalized or even terminated.

In recent years, a number of concerns have been expressed about operational budgeting and the way firms budget. As you will see with even a simple example in this chapter, the budgeting process can be a very time-consuming, "number-crunching" exercise. Even worse, some companies have found that their business environment is changing so rapidly that once the process is finally finished, the budget has little to do with the realities they face. In some companies, budgets analyze minute spending without recognizing the bigger picture, such as the fact that the company is losing customers or that a new product is selling far below expectations. In some cases, traditional budgets have undermined the growth potential of companies by forcing managers to focus exclusively on short-term financial numbers. The following are some of the problems with traditional budgeting that have led to revisions in the way companies budget:

- Departments and business units have tended to create budgets based on how much they spent in previous years.
- Once budgets are set, resource allocations have been inflexible and unable to adapt to change.
- In many companies, managers who have been evaluated and compensated according to how well they met their numbers have been powerless to step outside the budget and act on opportunities.
- Often budgeting time lines (e.g., calendar years) have not matched new product schedules.
- Frequently, because of fast-paced business changes, a budget is outdated before it is completed.

business environment essay

The Principles of Warfare: "The Art of War" Twenty-five hundred years ago, Sun Wu, general to the Chinese state of Wu, wrote a treatise entitled "The Art of War." It is one of those rare works that transcends time. It is the first text on budgeting and strategy, and some would argue that it is still the most important text on strategy ever written. Little did Sun Wu realize that his work would be absorbed by others of influence throughout history—from the fearless samurai of the sixteenth century to the shrewd business leaders of the twenty-first century. The following are a few quotations from the treatise. Although Sun Wu is talking about war and battle, see if you can determine which comments relate to short-term planning (budgeting) and which relate more to strategy.

- Calculate advantages by means of what was heard, then create force in order to assist outside missions (in other words, gather information before you proceed).
- The best warfare strategy is to attack the enemy's plans, next is to attack alliances, next is to attack the army, and the worst is to attack a walled city.
- Generally in warfare: If ten times the enemy's strength, surround them; if five times, attack them; if double, divide them; if equal, be able to fight them; if fewer, be able to evade them; if weaker, be able to avoid them.
- There are three ways the ruler can bring difficulty to the army: (1) To order an advance when not realizing the army is in no position to advance, or to order a withdrawal when not realizing the army is in no position to withdraw. This is called entangling the army. (2) By not knowing the army's matters,

fyi

While budgeting is very helpful for decision making, organizations are often required to prepare detailed budgets before bankers will loan money or before a company can issue stock or debt for sale to the public. When companies declare bankruptcy and are taken over by court-ordered trustees, one of the trustee's first steps is to prepare detailed budgets. These budgets help to determine whether the company should cease operations, or whether the trustee should ask the court to give the company time to work through its financial problems so that it can fully or partially repay its debts.

A high-level manager of a large company summed up the shortcomings of traditional budgets with this comment: "Trying to figure out how much fax paper you will need next November and what that will cost is like forecasting the weather."

Recognizing such concerns but also realizing that a well-conceived strategy and supporting budgets are essential to effective growth, in recent years some organizations have spent large sums of money to make their budgeting more relevant and timely to what they do. With developments in technology, companies can now measure results almost instantly. CISCO and DELL COMPUTER, for example, now receive immediate information about how they are doing (compared to processes that used to take several months) and can use these data to make real-time decisions on resource allocations and forecasts about profit margins and growth rates of different products. With such timely information, organizations can now both predict revenues and costs and measure them on a timely basis. Because companies can make real-time changes in their budgets, projections are much more accurate, and the budgeting process is much more meaningful. FUJITSU, for example, now uses a monthly, rolling forecast, which is part of its enterprise planning software, that allows financial managers to make corrective budget changes on a timely basis. Instead of the usual multi-iterative planning and budgeting process, where unsupported assumptions are repeated up and down the management ladder, Fujitsu's process now takes only about 10 to 15 days compared with six to eight weeks under the previous system.

Effective and timely budgets, aided by developments in technology, can help companies overcome the weaknesses in traditional budgeting. The right budgeting system provides financial managers with a map that can guide their company to competitive advantages. Effective budgets tie all the pieces together, providing goals and benchmarks against which performance can be measured as defined by a company's strategic plan. As noted earlier, however, the faster an industry moves, and the faster a company shifts its priorities, the more often plans must be adjusted and budgets changed. E-businesses, for example, need to plan and re-plan quickly. Fast, efficient budgeting, rolling forecasts, and effective management reporting and analysis are keys to success in these types of companies.

and administering the army the same as administering civil matters, the officers and troops will be confused. (3) By not knowing the army's calculations, and taking command of the army, the officers and troops will be hesitant. When the army is confused and hesitant, the neighboring rulers will take advantage.

- One who knows how to unite upper and lower ranks in purpose will be victorious.
- One who knows the enemy and knows himself will not be in danger in a hundred battles. One who does not know the enemy but knows himself will sometimes win, sometimes lose. One who does not know the enemy and does not know himself will be in danger in every battle.
- A victorious army first obtains conditions for victory, then seeks to do battle. A defeated army first seeks to do battle, then obtains conditions for victory.
- Generally, commanding of many is like commanding of a few. It is a matter of dividing them into groups.
- Generally, the principles of warfare are: The general receives his commands from the ruler, assembles the troops, mobilizes the army, and sets up camp.
- If the general is weak and not disciplined, his instructions not clear, the officers and troops lack discipline and their formation is in disarray. This is called chaos.
- The wise general thinks about it, and the good general executes it. If it is not advantageous, do not move; if there is no gain, do not use troops; if there is no danger, do not do battle.

Source: http://www.sonshi.com/suntintro.html.

net work

The best-known budget in the United States is the budget of the federal government. The Congressional Budget Office offers a monthly update on the level of government receipts and outlays relative to budgeted levels. Go to the CBO's Web site at http://www.cbo.gov to get a budget review for the most recent month.

to summarize

Budgeting in most organizations is based on that organization's strategic plan. Using the strategic plan to guide decisions, organizations perform two types of budgeting: capital budgeting and operations budgeting. The operating budget has several purposes: (1) assist in planning and setting objectives, (2) facilitate communication, (3) coordinate activities, (4) authorize expenditures and actions, (5) motivate employees, (6) assist in resolving conflicts, and (7) provide a vehicle for performance measurement.

2

Describe the budgeting process and its behavioral implications.

budget committee A management group responsible for establishing budgeting policy and for coordinating the preparation of budgets.

THE BUDGETING PROCESS

Budgeting is such an important activity that the top executives of most companies coordinate and participate in the process. Large firms usually establish a **budget committee**, which includes among its members the vice presidents for sales, production, purchasing, and finance and the controller or chief financial officer. These executives coordinate the preparation of a detailed budget in their areas of responsibility and then together oversee the preparation of a comprehensive budget for the firm. As noted previously, recent developments in software have made the budgeting process much more useful and relevant. Using enterprise-wide software, such as that developed by ORACLE, SAP, BONN, and PEOPLESOFT, companies can now integrate

business environment essay

Losing Focus on Budgeting Goals XYZ was a sleepy little firm, barely making a profit, when it got a new CEO. He said, "I'm going to make this a go-go company. And pretty soon, instead of a price-earnings ratio (stock price divided by earnings per share) of 10:1, it's going to be 40:1. We're all going to get rich." In trying to make the company more profitable, he hired a group of high-powered executives, and the company as a whole, not just the CEO, adopted a new budgeting policy. Essentially, the CEO and division managers decided together on next year's earnings budgets for their respective divisions, and the managers were responsible for meeting these goals. Implied in the budgets was the idea that the budget represented a fair goal. However, as it turned out, the CEO leaned on managers at the start of the year. To one manager, for example, he said, "Look, this company is going to have an earnings per share of $1.90 next year. Your division's share of that is $0.42." As the year progressed, periodic meetings were held with the manager. If the division was not on target to earn $0.42 a

their budgeting process into their accounting systems, get immediate feedback about how they are doing, and use the feedback to make timely changes in their budgeting process. Two important issues faced by executives in the budgeting process are:

1. Behavioral considerations, and
2. Delegation of responsibility for preparing the budget—the top-down versus bottom-up issue.

Behavioral Considerations

Research has shown that several behavioral factors determine how successful the budgeting process will be. First, the process must have the support of top management. Without a clear indication from top management that the budgeting process is important to the organization, managers will not be motivated to devote the time necessary to formulate an effective and efficient budget.

Second, all managers, and as many employees as possible, should participate in the budgeting process. Managers will be more motivated to achieve budget goals that they understand and help design. For this process to work, managers must feel that their opinions are respected and given full consideration. In addition, this communication and participation process must remain open throughout the year. If internal or external circumstances change, all parties must meet to discuss the necessary budget adjustments. The most efficient and effective companies are those that involve employees in the decision-making process.

Third, deviations from the budget must be addressed by managers in a positive and constructive manner. Identifying deviations from the plan is simply a way to focus management's attention on areas needing improvement. Unfortunately, some managers treat these deviations as an opportunity to find fault and assign blame to lower-level managers. The result is usually a loss of motivation, accompanied by such dysfunctional behavior as interdepartmental bickering, defensive attitudes, and attempts to "build slack" into the budget. ("Building slack" is the process of inflating a department's budget request so that the department manager can more easily achieve the budget.) Obviously, all these behaviors waste an organization's resources and do not contribute to solving its problems. A more useful reaction to deviations is to focus on the action to be taken. As one CEO stated, "I never made a dime for the company by assessing blame or firing a manager. If I can provide help to a manager to solve a problem, though, we can see the benefit." In administering the budget process, it is extremely important that top management not use the budget as a "club" or "whipping stick." To illustrate the negative effects of using budgets inappropriately, consider what happened at XYZ Company, as described in the Business Environment Essay above.

share, the manager would be told by the CEO, "If you can't find a way to make your budget, we'll hire someone else who can."

One of the ways division managers met their budgets was to recognize sales before they occurred. "Who cares when you close the books at the end of the period? A sale is a sale, right? Does it really matter whether we reach a little into next week and take some of the sales we ship next week and include them with this week's sales? After all, the sales were all made in the same month." Soon, one week stretched into two weeks, then three, until eventually it wasn't too hard for managers to rationalize, "We know that a customer is going to buy our product eventually; let's record it as a sale now." Consequently, the company's managers were driven by their budgets rather than using budgets as goals, until finally they were so far beyond reality that the company was committing massive fraud, eventually causing it to collapse.

Source: Adapted from Robert J. Sack, "Ethical Issues in the Practice of Accounting." In W. Steve Albrecht, ed., *Ethical Issues in the Practice of Accounting* (Cincinnati: South-Western Publishing Co., 1992), pp. 24–25.

Who Prepares the Budget: Top-Down versus Bottom-Up

A firm-wide operating budget could be prepared by top management, apportioned to the major segments of the firm, and then distributed to each lower-level segment manager. This is the top-down approach. Its proponents argue that only top management knows the strategic direction of the firm and is aware of all the external factors influencing its operations. Further, since top management involves only a few people who have risen to positions where they should no longer have special interests to protect, they are in the best position to efficiently coordinate the competing needs of the segments.

The alternative approach is bottom-up, whereby each division manager prepares a budget request for his or her segment. These requests are combined and reviewed as they move up the organization hierarchy, with adjustments being made to coordinate the needs and goals of individual units. Proponents of this approach contend that segment managers have the best information on the products or services they provide, the customers they serve, and the technology that is emerging; they are therefore in the best position to identify segment needs and to weigh alternative courses of action. More importantly, as mentioned earlier, managers who have a role in setting segment goals are more motivated to achieve these goals. It is also good training for managers to develop their planning skills in preparation for promotions to positions of greater authority. Naturally, the organization also benefits when its managers are proficient in planning.

Because these are both legitimate approaches, most organizations use some combination of the two. Top managers know the strategic direction of the firm and the important external factors that affect it, so they prepare a set of planning guidelines that are communicated to lower-level managers. These guidelines include such things as a forecast of key economic variables and their potential impact on the firm, plans for introducing and advertising new products, and some broad sales targets and resource allocations. With these guidelines in mind, lower-level managers prepare their individual budgets. Although these budgets are always reviewed to be sure they are consistent with the objectives of other segments and of the company as a whole, from a behavioral point of view, any changes to a manager's budget should be made with great care. This is not to suggest that changes should not be made, only that reasons for those changes should be substantial and should be discussed with the managers involved.

The blending of these two approaches will vary among organizations. A smaller organization with few management levels will rely more on the top-down approach than a larger organization. Top management in smaller organizations tends to be more knowledgeable about and more involved in the operating details.

to summarize

The behavioral factors that contribute to the success of the budgeting process include the support of top management, the participation of all managers in the budgeting process, and the need to address deviations from the budget in a positive and constructive manner. With the top-down approach, top management prepares the entire budget. With bottom-up budgeting, each segment manager makes budget requests. Most firms use a combination of the two approaches.

3

Explain the master budget and its components for manufacturing firms, merchandising firms, and service firms.

THE MASTER BUDGET

The operating budget is called the *master budget*; it is an integrated group of detailed budgets that together constitute the overall operating and financing plans for a specific time period. In a manufacturing firm, the master budget begins with a forecast of sales; is followed by detailed budgets for the production, selling, administrative, and financial activities; and culminates in a set of pro-forma (or budgeted) financial statements. The flow of the preparation of the individual budgets within this master network is shown in Exhibit 5-2. (Notice that the final items are the budgeted or "pro-forma" financial statements. Preparing these pro-forma statements is discussed in the expanded material.) Review this exhibit carefully because we will follow these schedules in sequence in the next sections of this chapter.

exhibit 5-2 The Master Budget for a Manufacturing Firm

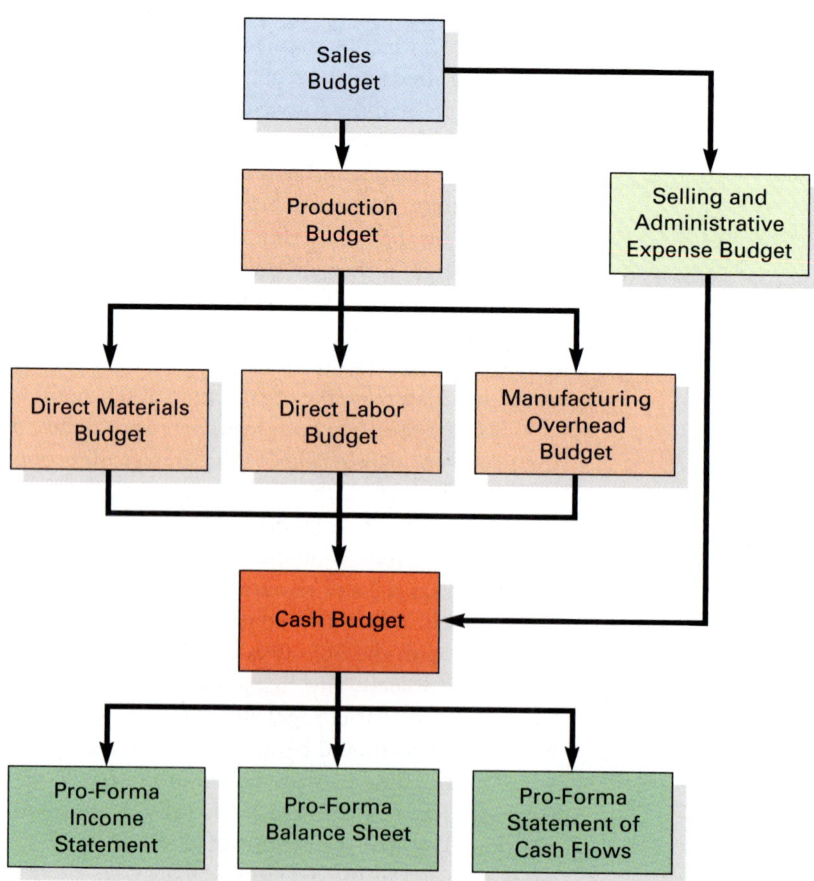

To help explain these steps, we will illustrate budgeting for three different kinds of companies. First, we will illustrate the budgeting process in a manufacturing firm using an integrated example of budgets for the Sunbird Boat Company, a manufacturer of small fishing boats. Second, we will illustrate budgeting in merchandising firms (retail and wholesale) for Wind River Boat Company, a company that buys its boats for resale from other manufacturers rather than making the boats itself. Third, we will illustrate budgeting in service firms by illustrating the budgeting process for a small motel, the Boulder View Inn. We thought seriously about including the budgeting process for an Internet or e-business company as well. In reality, however, these businesses represent either manufacturing, wholesale, retail, or service businesses. DELL COMPUTER, for example, makes and sells computers over the Internet and so is a manufacturing and retail company. AMAZON.COM sells books and other products and is also a retail company. PRICELINE.COM is a service company in that it matches buyers of airline tickets and other products with vendors selling those products and receives a commission for its matchmaking activities. Although the types of revenues these firms generate and even their cost structures often differ from those of traditional firms, their business models usually represent traditional types of firms.

As we examine our three companies, you will see similarities in the budgeting process for all three types of businesses. Basically, the budgeting process involves budgeting (or forecasting) revenues and cash that will be generated by those revenues, and budgeting costs that will be incurred and cash that will be expended. Budgeters—whether individuals, companies, or other entities—are always interested in how much revenues (inflows) and expenditures (outflows) they will have during each budgeted period, and how much cash and assets they will have at the end of each budgeted period. The budgeting discussions that follow may seem mechanical, but you should keep in mind that this formalized budgeting activity forces management to make many important decisions that guide a company toward its goals. For example, decisions regarding production scheduling, pricing, borrowing, investing, and research and development need to be made before the budget can be completed.

In most companies today, the actual preparation of the master budget is usually done on computerized spreadsheets and other software packages. Although automation takes care of much of the drudgery or tedious work, it is important that you understand the budgeting process and what is being done by the computer.

Another factor you should recognize is that many of the recent developments in management accounting, such as ABC and just-in-time (JIT) inventory systems, have a significant impact on the budgeting process. As we discuss the various elements of the master budget, we will explain how budgeting is affected by these developments.

Budgeting for Operations in a Manufacturing Firm

Our first illustration of the budgeting process is for Sunbird Boat Company, a manufacturing company that makes fishing boats. The boats are made of fiberglass and wood and come in 15-foot and 18-foot sizes. Because preparing actual budgets can be tedious and is usually done by computers, we will focus on the budgeting for only one product—the 15-foot boat—in this chapter. Our goal is to help you understand the budgeting process, not to force you to spend significant time following numbers through a complicated budgeting process. The budgeting process for the 18-foot boat would be similar to that illustated for the 15-foot boat. In explaining the budgeting for Sunbird Boat Company, we will begin with the sales budget and then discuss each budget identified in Exhibit 5-2.

sales budget A schedule of projected sales over the budget period.

SALES BUDGET The first step in developing a master budget is to prepare a **sales budget**. As shown in Exhibit 5-2, all the other budgets are developed from this budget. Projecting accurate sales is very difficult, however, because sales are a function of both external variables (customer tastes and economic conditions, for example) and internal variables (such as price, sales effort, and advertising expenditures). In fact, in preparing a sales budget, internal variables (such as how much production capacity do we have?) and external variables must first be analyzed separately.

Analysis of external variables is accomplished through sales-forecasting techniques. These techniques may be as simple as having the sales staff ask major customers about their buying plans for the next year or as sophisticated as statistical market research techniques. Some firms use quantitative forecasting models: these range from simple growth rate trends derived from the past year's sales (e.g., regression analysis) to complex forecasting models that attempt to measure the influence of many economic and industry variables.

Data on which to base sales forecasts are abundant. For example, economic data about the United States and many other countries are available from private vendors and from trade associations and sector specialists. Data about regions, cities, or markets are provided by vendors and trade groups, as well as by university business departments and forecasting centers.

Demographic data such as population projections, household spending patterns, and lifestyles (nationally and locally—down to city blocks) are available from vendors. These vendors use various statistical methods to project data from the national 10-year census to the current year. In their updating processes, they use other data sources such as the Current Population Survey (CPS) conducted annually by the Census Bureau, payroll taxes, home sales, apartment occupancy rates, state driver's licenses applications, school enrollments, and births and deaths. Government data often report economic conditions with some delay. The Consumer Price Index (CPI), a measure of inflation, is reported monthly at the national and regional levels with specific cities reported either monthly or semiannually. The CPI is a good indicator of a business's ability to pass along cost increases to its customers. The Producer Price Index (PPI), another measure of inflation, reports changes in business costs and is subject to larger fluctuations than the CPI. The Gross Domestic Product (GDP) Implicit Price Deflator measures inflation in the consumer and business sectors simultaneously.

Consumer spending patterns by region and income level are reported from the annual Consumer Expenditure Survey, conducted by the Census Bureau since 1980. Because consumer spending represents more than 65% of GDP, an understanding of how households allocate their expenditures can be very helpful in business planning. For example, if your business expects to sell home entertainment systems to middle-income consumers, it is helpful to know whether they are changing the share of income they spend on in-home entertainment. Production, capacity utilization, and shipment data by sector are estimated in the course of developing GDP estimates. This information also is valuable in forecasting the availability and cost of materials.

Business environment data include the regulatory climate and changes in regulations, product liability issues, competitive structure, technological changes, foreign markets, trends in consumer attitudes and behavior, and demographic trends. Government regulatory information is available on the Internet (for a price), and is available through many agency publications and reference sources such as the Commerce Clearing House. Business trends are tracked and reported by trade associations and magazines, as well as by consultants who specialize in various types of businesses.[3]

In analyzing the influence of internal variables, sales budgeting is viewed as an active process (what factors can we change to meet our sales targets?), not as a passive process (let us predict what customers will buy from us). Cost-volume-profit analysis (the subject of Chapter 2 of management accounting) is frequently used for analyzing the influence of internal variables.

Firms generally do not rely on a single approach to sales budgeting. Instead, they develop several tentative sales budgets, using different combinations of various forecasting and budgeting techniques. These budgets are then reconciled through discussions between the planning and marketing staffs and top management, and a final sales budget is agreed upon. Recent developments in management accounting that have focused on quality and continuous improvement have enabled many organizations to significantly reduce delivery times by using JIT inventory, electronic data interchange (EDI), and other techniques. **MOTOROLA CORPORATION**, for example, reduced the time needed from taking orders to delivery from four weeks to six hours. The effect of shorter lead times for production has significantly reduced the time horizons of sales and other budgets. Also, instead of the sales budget being fixed for an entire year (or period), there is flexibility to continuously revise the sales and other budgets. With full-time computer hookups to

3 Dianne Wilner Green, "Using Economic Data in Your Strategic Plan," *Management Accounting*, January 1997, p. 32.

suppliers and customers, and with automated budget preparation tools, the sales budget, as well as the entire budget process, is much more dynamic than ever before. With shorter lead times, management can more quickly adapt to increases, decreases, and other trends in revising budgets.

For purposes of this illustration, we will not go into the details about the development of data for the sales budget. Rather, assume that Sunbird Boat Company has projected the year 2003 sales to be 100 15-foot boats. The anticipated sales price for a 15-foot boat is $14,000.

Most organizations divide their yearly sales budget into monthly, weekly, or even daily budgets in order to plan production schedules and cash flows more precisely. Because this involves too much detail for our illustration, we will assume that Sunbird Boat Company projects its boat sales on a quarterly basis, as shown in Schedule 1. Note that we are using Microsoft Excel® as a tool for our budgeting examples.

Schedule 1

Microsoft Excel - sch-m0501.xls

Schedule 1
Sales Budget—2003

	Quarter				
	1	2	3	4	Total
15-foot boats:					
Selling price per unit	$ 14,000	$ 14,000	$ 14,000	$ 14,000	$ 14,000
Expected sales (units)	x 24	x 28	x 30	x 18	x 100
Expected revenues	$ 336,000	$ 392,000	$ 420,000	$ 252,000	$ 1,400,000

production budget A schedule of production requirements for the budget period.

PRODUCTION BUDGET The second detailed budget covers production, the number of units to be produced during the period. Factors to be considered in preparing this **production budget** are projected sales for the period, the desired amount of ending inventory, and the amount of time needed to obtain materials and then to make a unit of product.

Ending inventory is an important figure because management wants enough units on hand to meet customer demands, but not so many that unnecessary costs will be incurred because of excessive inventory. Usually, the desired ending inventory for any period is expressed as a percentage of the following period's expected sales volume. Sunbird Boat Company has determined that its desired ending inventory for each quarter should be approximately 80% of projected sales for the next quarter. The fourth quarter's ending inventory is 20 15-foot boats, which is 80% of the next quarter's (first quarter of 2004) expected sales.

The production budget (Schedule 2) supplies information needed for all manufacturing cost budgets. Only after production quantities are known can management determine the amount of direct materials, direct labor, and manufacturing overhead needed during the period.

Schedule 2

Microsoft Excel - sch-m0502.xls

Schedule 2
Production Budget—2003

	Quarter				
	1	2	3	4	Total
15-foot boats:					
Expected sales (Schedule 1)	24	28	30	18	100
Add desired ending inventory of finished boats	22	24	15	20	20
Total number of boats needed	46	52	45	38	120
Less beginning inventory of finished boats	18*	22	24	15	18
Total number of boats to be produced	28	30	21	23	102

*These numbers represent ending inventory in 2002; the 2002 ending inventory cost $150,000.

Although we are using quarterly production budgets in our example, the production budget has probably been most affected by recent developments in product costing and inventories. As was discussed in Chapter 7 of management accounting, JIT inventory is a "pull-through" rather than a "push" system. This means that raw materials arrive just in time for production and that finished goods arrive just in time for sale. With short production times, the sales order pulls production and procurement. In organizations where JIT inventory systems work well, there is less need for a production budget with desirable levels of ending inventory. Indeed, the optimum level of inventory in these organizations is zero. Most companies, however, do not have perfect JIT inventory systems; even those few companies that do often keep a minimal level of inventory on hand for unexpected or "walk-in" sales.

direct materials budget A schedule of direct materials to be used during the budget period and direct materials to be purchased during that period.

DIRECT MATERIALS BUDGET The next detailed budget to be prepared is the **direct materials budget** (Schedule 3). Based on the engineering department's estimates of the materials required to make a boat, this budget helps management schedule purchases from suppliers. Sunbird's engineers estimate that the amounts of wood and fiberglass needed per boat are as follows:

	15-Foot Boat
Direct materials requirements:	
Wood	70 board feet
Fiberglass	50 square feet

Based on these requirements for materials, the direct materials budget for Sunbird Boat Company for 2003 is shown in Schedule 3. The usage requirements are based not only on expected quarterly sales, but also on desired quarterly boat ending inventories. The materials purchase requirements are, in turn, based on the quarterly production requirements and the amount of raw materials inventory desired at the end of each quarter. Because raw materials can be obtained fairly soon after an order is placed, Sunbird has decided to maintain a supply of about 30% of the next quarter's production requirements for wood and fiberglass.

Like the production budget, the direct materials budget depends on the desired level of ending inventory. If management does not maintain sufficient materials inventory levels, costly work stoppages can occur; if inventories are excessive, inventory investment and storage costs may be unduly high.

As with the production budget, JIT inventory systems have decreased the time horizon, the amount of inventory needed, and, in some cases, even the need for the direct materials budget. When materials can be secured immediately on demand, the need for direct materials budgets is decreased. As stated before, however, relatively few companies have perfect JIT inventory systems.

direct labor budget A schedule of direct labor requirements for the budget period.

DIRECT LABOR BUDGET The fourth detailed budget is the **direct labor budget** (Schedule 4). The direct labor budget for Sunbird Boat Company is based on an hourly rate of $15 per hour for production workers and 80 labor hours to make a 15-foot boat.

Because labor is costly, the direct labor budget is often revised on a monthly or even weekly basis. Management must plan so that sufficient (but not excessive) labor is always available.[4] Otherwise, the company is likely to suffer the high cost of frequent hirings, firings, layoffs, and overtime work. Probably even more important than the high cost of employee turnover, however, is the feeling of demoralization among employees that such events

4 Just how variable labor costs are has aroused significant controversy in the management accounting literature. Some researchers argue that employees cannot easily be hired or terminated and, therefore, labor should be a fixed cost. Other researchers argue that labor can be easily hired and terminated—just read business newspapers where announcements of employee layoffs are printed every day. One thing is certain, though—management strives to be able to control labor costs.

Schedule 3

Schedule 3
Direct Materials Budget—2003

	Quarter 1	Quarter 2	Quarter 3	Quarter 4	Total	Unit Cost of Materials[1]	Cost of Materials Used
Direct materials usage per quarter:							
Wood (board feet):[2]							
15-foot boats (70 board feet per boat)	1,960	2,100	1,470	1,610	7,140	$10/bd. ft.	$71,400
Fiberglass (square feet):[3]							
15-foot boats (50 square feet per boat)	1,400	1,500	1,050	1,150	5,100	$5/sq. ft.	$25,500
Total materials cost							$96,900
Direct materials purchase requirements:							
Wood (board feet):							
Desired direct materials ending inventory	630	441	483	525[4]	525		
Direct materials needed for production	1,960	2,100	1,470	1,610	7,140		
Total direct materials needed	2,590	2,541	1,953	2,135	7,665		
Less beginning direct materials inventory	(588)[5]	(630)	(441)	(483)	(588)		
Direct materials to be purchased	2,002	1,911	1,512	1,652	7,077		
Unit cost	x $10	x $10	x $10	x $10	x $10		
Cost of wood purchases	$20,020	$19,110	$15,120	$16,520	$70,770		
Fiberglass (square feet):							
Desired direct materials ending inventory	450	315	345	375[4]	375		
Direct materials needed for production	1,400	1,500	1,050	1,150	5,100		
Total direct materials needed	1,850	1,815	1,395	1,525	5,475		
Less beginning direct materials inventory	(420)[5]	(450)	(315)	(345)	(420)		
Direct materials to be purchased	1,430	1,365	1,080	1,180	5,055		
Unit cost	x $5	x $5	x $5	x $5	x $5		
Cost of fiberglass purchases	$ 7,150	$ 6.825	$ 5,400	$ 5,900	$25,275		
Total direct materials to be purchased	$27,170	$25,935	$20,520	$22,420	$96,045		

[1]Supplier price quotations.
[2]Budgeted production in Schedule 2 multiplied by 70 board feet.
[3]Budgeted production in Schedule 2 multiplied by 50 square feet.
[4]Expected direct materials usage for the first quarter of 2004 is 1,750 board feet of wood (25 boats × 70 bd. ft.) and 1,250 square feet of fiberglass (25 boats × 50 sq. ft.).
[5]Ending direct materials figure from 2002.

Schedule 4

Schedule 4
Direct Labor Budget—2003

	Quarter 1	Quarter 2	Quarter 3	Quarter 4	Total
15-foot boats:					
Production units	28	30	21	23	102
Direct labor hours per unit	x 80	x 80	x 80	x 80	x 80
Total direct labor hours per quarter	2,240	2,400	1,680	1,840	8,160
Rate per direct labor hour	x $15	x $15	x $15	x $15	x $15
Direct labor cost	$33,600	$36,000	$25,200	$27,600	$122,400

Banks have replaced many of their full-time customer representatives with part-time employees. From management's perspective, the use of part-time workers makes direct labor budgeting easier.

can cause. If employees lack security, they usually behave in ways that maximize their own personal short-run benefits (e.g., they may slow down production, thus creating the need for overtime work).

The recent trend in many companies has been to keep a relatively small full-time staff and hire an increasing number of part-time employees. Not only are part-time employees much easier to hire and terminate, but the company does not have to pay retirement and other benefits for them. Banks, for example, have replaced many of their full-time customer representatives with part-time employees. As a result of the smaller full-time workforce, companies that provide temporary workers are increasing in both size and number. From management's perspective, both part-time and temporary workers increase workforce flexibility and make direct labor budgeting easier. Unfortunately, these same trends probably mean less stable and secure careers for more and more workers.

manufacturing overhead budget A schedule of production costs other than those for direct labor and direct materials.

MANUFACTURING OVERHEAD BUDGET The **manufacturing overhead budget** (Schedule 5) includes all production costs other than those for direct materials and direct labor. As noted in earlier chapters, manufacturing overhead is now a major element of total manufacturing costs in many organizations. As manufacturing overhead increases in size and complexity, it becomes much more important to use ABC and appropriate cost drivers.

In preparing this budget, Sunbird's accounting department first estimates the annual variable and fixed manufacturing overhead costs, as shown in the first column of Schedule 5. Total fixed costs are simply allocated evenly among the four quarters. The total variable cost of each item is allocated among the four quarters on the basis of some appropriate activity or cost driver. To keep the example simple, we will use direct labor hours to allocate manufacturing overhead to boats.[5] Schedule 4 showed that 8,160 direct labor hours are projected for the year 2003. By dividing 8,160 projected hours into the total estimated cost of each item of variable manufacturing overhead, we get the variable manufacturing overhead rate per hour for that item. This rate is then multiplied by the number of direct labor hours estimated for each quarter (also from Schedule 4) to figure that item's budgeted variable manufacturing overhead cost for that quarter.

5 Remember (from our discussions of ABC in Chapter 7 in management accounting), however, that direct labor hours is often not the relevant basis to allocate overhead in practice. We use direct labor hours here because using various cost drivers would unnecessarily complicate our examples.

Schedule 5

Schedule 5					
Manufacturing Overhead Budget—2003					
	Total Estimated Annual Manufacturing Overhead Costs	Manufacturing Overhead Costs Assigned to Each Quarter			
		1	2	3	4
Variable costs:					
Indirect materials costs ($1.50 rate)	$ 12,240	$ 3,360	$ 3,600	$ 2,520	$ 2,760
Indirect labor costs ($3.50 rate)	28,560	7,840	8,400	5,880	6,440
Other payroll costs ($2.00 rate)	16,320	4,480	4,800	3,360	3,680
Utilities expense ($1.00 rate)	8,160	2,240	2,400	1,680	1,840
Total variable costs	$ 65,280	$17,920	$19,200	$13,440	$14,720
Fixed costs:					
Property taxes expense	$ 3,000	$ 750	$ 750	$ 750	$ 750
Insurance expense	2,400	600	600	600	600
Depreciation expense—plant	10,000	2,500	2,500	2,500	2,500
Supervisors' salaries	33,560	8,390	8,390	8,390	8,390
Total fixed costs	$ 48,960	$12,240	$12,240	$12,240	$12,240
Total manufacturing overhead	$114,240	$30,160	$31,440	$25,680	$26,960

caution

Remember that the budgets being discussed in this chapter are for only one level of expected sales. If the level of sales changes, the variable cost and expense amounts budgeted will change also. This means that all the direct materials and direct labor budgets will change, as will some of the manufacturing overhead and selling and administrative expense budgets. This issue of changing levels of sales or operations is covered in the expanded material section of the chapter under the topic of flexible budgeting.

To illustrate, estimated total indirect materials costs are $12,240. Dividing that number by 8,160 direct labor hours yields a rate of $1.50 per hour. Multiplying the $1.50 rate by 2,240 direct labor hours produces $3,360 to be assigned to the first quarter as the budgeted cost of indirect materials. With 2,400 direct labor hours in the second quarter, the cost for that quarter is $3,600. The calculation is the same for the remaining quarters, as well as for other variable overhead items.

The manufacturing overhead budget serves two important purposes. First, when compared with actual manufacturing overhead costs, the data on this budget provide management with a basis for controlling costs and evaluating the performance of the managers responsible for those costs. Second, it is used in product costing. As you will recall from Chapter 2 in management accounting, the manufacturing overhead costs that flow through Work-in-Process Inventory to Finished Goods Inventory (and eventually to Cost of Goods Sold) are applied costs, based on one or more predetermined overhead rates. In our example, this rate is calculated by dividing estimated annual direct labor hours into estimated annual manufacturing overhead ($114,240/8,160 = $14).

When ABC is used, accurate measures of costs, identification of activities, and appropriate selection of cost drivers are important. As discussed in Chapter 7 of management accounting, properly budgeting and assigning overhead costs to products is often difficult and is an area where exciting advances are being made.

Now that we have discussed direct materials, direct labor, and manufacturing overhead (the three elements of a product's cost), we can compute the cost of making the 15-foot boats. Using information from the previous sections, the manufacturing costs are calculated as shown in Schedule 6 at the top of page 250.

selling and administrative expense budget A schedule of all nonproduction spending expected to occur during the budget period.

SELLING AND ADMINISTRATIVE EXPENSE BUDGET The **selling and administrative expense budget** (Schedule 7) includes planned expenditures for all areas other than production. The costs of supplies used by the office staff, the salaries of the sales manager and company president, and the depreciation of office buildings all belong in this category. Because this budget covers several areas, it is usually quite large and may be supported by individual budgets for specific departments within the selling and administrative functions.

The selling and administrative expense budget for Sunbird is prepared in a manner similar to the manufacturing overhead budget. Total selling and administrative expenses are estimated for the year, with each expense then being distributed among the four quarters. As shown in Schedule 7, fixed expenses are assigned equally to each quarter, whereas variable expenses

Schedule 6

Schedule 6 Boat Manufacturing Costs—2003	15-Foot Boat
Wood (Schedule 3):	
70 board feet x $10 per board foot	$ 700
Fiberglass (Schedule 3):	
50 square feet x $5 per square foot	250
Direct labor (Schedule 4):	
80 hours x $15 per hour	1,200
Manufacturing overhead (Schedule 5):	
80 hours x $14 per hour	1,120
Total cost per boat	$3,270

are allocated according to the number of boats to be sold. Variable delivery expenses, for example, are allocated to quarters by first determining the delivery expense rate ($50,000 estimated delivery expenses ÷ 100 boats expected to be sold during the year [from Schedule 1] = $500 per boat). This rate is multiplied by the number of boats sold in a quarter to determine the delivery expenses allocated to that quarter. Because Sunbird expects to sell 24 boats in the first quarter at a rate of $500 per boat, the amount of delivery expense budgeted for that quarter would be $12,000 ($500 × 24 boats). Sales commissions are allocated to each quarter in the same way.

Schedule 7

Schedule 7 Selling and Administrative Expense Budget—2003	Estimated Annual Costs	Quarter 1	Quarter 2	Quarter 3	Quarter 4
Variable expenses:					
Delivery expenses ($500 rate)	$ 50,000	$ 12,000	$ 14,000	$ 15,000	$ 9,000
Sales commissions ($1,600 rate)	160,000	38,400	44,800	48,000	28,800
Total variable expenses	$210,000	$ 50,400	$ 58,800	$ 63,000	$ 37,800
Fixed expenses:					
Executives' salaries	$220,000	$ 55,000	$ 55,000	$ 55,000	$ 55,000
Depreciation expense	40,000	10,000	10,000	10,000	10,000
Advertising expense	80,000	20,000	20,000	20,000	20,000
Miscellaneous expenses	10,000	2,500	2,500	2,500	2,500
Total fixed expenses	$350,000	$ 87,500	$ 87,500	$ 87,500	$ 87,500
Total selling and administrative expenses	$560,000	$137,900	$146,300	$150,500	$125,300

cash budget A schedule of expected cash receipts and disbursements during the budget period.

CASH BUDGET The **cash budget**, which shows expected cash receipts and disbursements during a period, summarizes much of the information discussed thus far. A detailed cash budget will point out when a company has excess cash to invest and when it has to borrow funds. This allows a firm to earn maximum interest on excess funds and to avoid the costs of unnecessary borrowing. Most firms prepare a month-by-month, or even week-by-week, cash budget. Because of space limitations, however, we will continue to show Sunbird's budget on a quarterly basis.

Typically, a cash budget is divided into four sections:

1. Cash receipts
2. Cash disbursements

3. Cash excess or deficiency
4. Financing

The cash receipts section summarizes all cash expected to flow into the business during the budget period. Because companies generally extend credit to their customers, most of their sales are originally recorded as accounts receivable. The collection of accounts receivable is thus a major source of cash, and its timing is an important consideration in preparing a cash budget.

To illustrate how the collection of accounts receivable is budgeted, we will assume that all sales are on credit; that Sunbird's sales during the last quarter of 2002 were $280,000, and that expected sales for each quarter of 2003 (Schedule 1) are $336,000, $392,000, $420,000, and $252,000, respectively. On the basis of experience, Sunbird's accountants estimate that 80% of credit sales are collected during the quarter of sale and the remaining 20% are collected in the next quarter. Expected quarterly collections for the year 2003 would therefore be:

Collection of Accounts Receivable—2003

Sales Quarter	Sales Revenue	Collection Quarter 1	2	3	4	2003 Total
2002:						
Fourth	$ 280,000	$ 56,000 (20%)				$ 56,000
2003:						
First	336,000	268,800 (80%)	$ 67,200 (20%)			336,000
Second	392,000		313,600 (80%)	$ 78,400 (20%)		392,000
Third	420,000			336,000 (80%)	$ 84,000 (20%)	420,000
Fourth	252,000				201,600 (80%)	201,600
Total	$1,680,000	$324,800	$380,800	$414,400	$285,600	$1,405,600

This analysis shows that total collections during 2003 are budgeted to be $1,405,600. In this example, we have assumed that all proceeds from credit sales are eventually collected. Usually, however, some customers never pay, and these uncollectible accounts must be considered when analyzing estimated cash collections from accounts receivable. You should recognize that economic factors play a significant role in the timing of collections of accounts receivable. During recessionary periods, customers often drag out their payments much longer than in prosperous times.

caution

When preparing a cash budget, be careful not to include expenditures that do not require cash (e.g., depreciation expense from the manufacturing overhead and selling and administrative expense budgets).

The cash disbursements section of Schedule 8 summarizes all expected cash outlays by a firm during the budget period. These include payments of accounts payable, payroll, other costs and expenses, capital improvements, and dividends. Note that to compute cash disbursements for "other costs and expenses," depreciation and other noncash items must not be included.

The section related to cash excess or deficiency merely reports the difference between budgeted cash receipts and disbursements. With a prospective excess of cash, management should look for the most attractive short-term investments. A deficiency obviously means that additional short-term funds will be needed.

The financing section analyzes the timing and amounts of all projected borrowings and repayments during the period. It also estimates the amount of interest to be paid on borrowed funds. By accurately projecting these amounts and events, firms can give banks and other lending institutions advance notice of their needs. Banks appreciate, and sometimes insist, that companies plan their cash needs in advance. Because money has a time value, management always walks a tightrope between having too much or too little cash on hand.

Exhibit 5-3 shows how a typical company's cash balance and requirements fluctuate constantly. Most of this fluctuation is due to the varying amounts of raw materials and finished

business environment essay

Budgeting at Budget Not only do companies forecast their revenues and earnings, but analysts and various investment institutions forecast companies' earnings as well. And, when a company's actual earnings fall short of analysts' expectations, the company's stock price usually falls. Take the case of **BUDGET RENTAL CAR**, for example. Both analysts and the company had forecast that the company's third quarter, 2000 earnings would be approximately $1 per share. However, because of losses in the international portion of its car rental business, Budget reported actual earnings of only $.30 per share, down from $.86 per share a year earlier. Having revenues and income that were 70% lower than expected significantly hurt Budget's stock price. After the announcement, the company's stock hit a 52-week low of $2.31 per share, down from a high of $10.44 per share the previous January. Trying to forecast earnings and predict earnings in the highly volatile car and truck rental business is no easy task. But, when a company is as far off as Budget was in the third quarter of 2000, stock prices, which are based on investors' expectations, usually take a substantial hit.

Source: Anne Marie Chaker, *The Wall Street Journal*, October 30, 2000, p. A8.

goods that are needed in the different seasons of the year. A prosperous firm could, if it desired, maintain enough cash on hand so that short-term borrowing would never be necessary, but such a policy might not be cost-beneficial. Long-term investments in productive assets usually earn considerably more than short-term cash investments; firms are generally better off maintaining lower cash balances, keeping as much capital as possible "at work" in the company's productive assets, and borrowing from time to time for short periods. For this reason, most companies obtain a line of credit from banks. A **line of credit** is a prearranged agreement whereby an organization or individual can borrow money on demand, up to a specific amount at specific rates.

line of credit An arrangement whereby a bank agrees to loan an amount of money (up to a certain limit) on demand for short periods of time, usually less than a year.

Schedule 8 gives the quarterly cash budget for Sunbird Boat Company for 2003. This cash budget assumes that when the company's cash balance at the end of a quarter is less than the desired minimum balance, cash is borrowed (in multiples of $10,000) and repaid at the end of a subsequent period when funds are available. It also assumes that loans are repaid on a first-in,

exhibit 5-3 A Typical Relationship between Cash Balance and Cash Needs

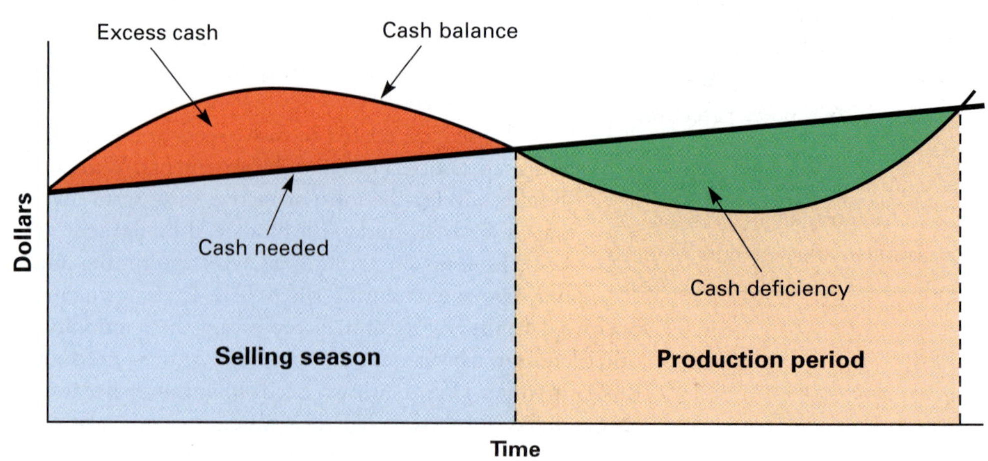

first-out basis and that interest is paid only when the principal is repaid. The $20,000 scheduled to be repaid in the third quarter has been outstanding for one quarter. Furthermore, note that the entries in the Total column do not always equal the sum of the four quarters; the beginning cash balance and the minimum cash balance desired are the same for the year as they are for the first quarter.

With the cash budget, the company is now able to make planning decisions regarding financing. For example, Sunbird is now aware that although the cash balance will be sufficient at the end of the year, there will probably be a cash shortage in the second quarter of 2003. With this knowledge, the company can take steps to deal with the situation. One solution would be to negotiate with a bank to obtain a loan. The company might also obtain money by attempting to get customers to pay sooner, trying to negotiate with creditors for a longer repayment period, or simply reducing the desired ending cash balance (currently at $140,000). The point is, with a knowledge of the coming cash shortfall, Sunbird is able to formulate a method of dealing with the problem now, rather than waiting until the company actually finds itself short of cash.

Schedule 8

Microsoft Excel - sch-m0508.xls

Schedule 8
Cash Budget—2003

	Quarter 1	Quarter 2	Quarter 3	Quarter 4	Total
Cash balance, beginning	$135,000[1]	$147,470	$141,095	$325,595	$ 135,000
Add collections from customers	324,800	380,800	414,400	285,600	1,405,600
(1) Total cash available before disbursement and financing	$459,800	$528,270	$555,495	$611,195	$1,540,600
Less disbursement for:					
Direct materials (Schedule 3)	$ 27,170	$ 25,935	$ 20,520	$ 22,420	$ 96,045
Direct labor (Schedule 4)	33,600	36,000	25,200	27,600	122,400
Manufacturing overhead (Schedule 5)[2]	27,660	28,940	23,180	24,460	104,240
Income tax expense	96,000[3]				96,000
Equipment purchase		150,000[4]			150,000
Selling and administrative expenses (Schedule 7)	127,900[5]	136,300	140,500	115,300	520,000
Dividends		30,000[6]			30,000
(2) Total disbursements	$312,330	$407,175	$209,400	$189,780	$1,118,685
Minimum cash balance desired	140,000	140,000	140,000	140,000	140,000[7]
Total cash needed	$452,330	$547,175	$349,400	$329,780	$1,258,685
Excess (or deficiency) of cash available before financing	$ 7,470	$(18,905)	$206,095	$281,415	$ 281,915
Financing:					
Borrowings	$ 0	$ 20,000			$ 20,000
Repayments			$ (20,000)		(20,000)
Interest (at 10%)			(500)		(500)[8]
(3) Total effect of financing	$ 0	$ 20,000	$ (20,500)		$ (500)
(4) Ending cash balance [(1)−(2)+(3)]	$147,470	$141,095	$325,595	$421,415	$ 421,415

[1]Estimated 12/31/02 balance.
[2]Does not include depreciation expense.
[3]Income taxes owed at 12/31/02 are assumed to be $96,000.
[4]Equipment costing $150,000 is assumed to be purchased for cash during the second quarter.
[5]Does not include depreciation expense.
[6]The company pays dividends of $30,000 during the second quarter of each year.
[7]Not a total of the four quarters—management's policy or plan.
[8]Computed as follows: $20,000 × 0.10 × ¼ = $500.

to summarize

The master budget consists of detailed budgets for sales, production, selling and administrative expenses, and financing activities. Both the sales forecasting process and the development of the master budget may need to be repeated until the results are consistent with the company's strategic plan. The detailed budgets that make up the master budget are prepared in a logical sequence, as shown in Exhibit 5-2. The budgets related to sales, production, and other expenses allow the company to prepare a detailed cash budget. The cash budget shows expected cash receipts and disbursements; it also signals when the company can expect a cash shortage requiring outside financing, or a cash overage, which should be temporarily invested in income-producing assets.

Budgeting for Operations in a Merchandising Firm

The approach illustrated thus far in the chapter is the budgeting process used by most manufacturing companies. Many organizations, however, do not manufacture products; they either purchase products to resell or are organizations that sell services instead of "products."

As discussed previously in this text, organizations that purchase the products they resell are often referred to as merchandising companies; these include retailers that sell directly to consumers and wholesale distributors that buy products from manufacturers or other suppliers and sell to retailers. Well-known retail companies include WAL-MART, SEARS, and KMART. Although retail companies such as Wal-Mart buy many of the products they sell directly from manufacturers (e.g., COCA-COLA, NABISCO, WRIGLEY, etc.), they also buy from wholesalers who either buy from domestic manufacturers or import their products from other countries.

STOP & THINK In this chapter, the emphasis is on budgeting costs and revenues, only one of the three elements management is interested in managing. Do you think management performs any budgeting related to quality or delivery time of products or services to customers?

Because merchandising companies buy products (rather than make them), their budgeting process is less complicated than the budgeting done by manufacturing companies. For example, if Sunbird Boat Company were a merchandising firm rather than a manufacturing firm, the company would prepare a purchases budget rather than a production budget. The result of the purchases budget would be the number of units to be purchased rather than the number of units to be produced. The format of the purchases budget would be similar to the production budget, combining expected sales and desired ending inventory to arrive at needs for the period. Inventory on hand at the start of the period would then be subtracted to arrive at the amount to be purchased during the period.

Exhibit 5-4 compares the master budgeting process for a merchandising firm with that for manufacturing firms (from Exhibit 5-2).

Looking at Exhibit 5-4, you can see that in merchandising companies, one purchases budget replaces four budgets (production budget, direct materials budget, direct labor budget, and manufacturing overhead budget) used by manufacturing firms.

Because the sales budget, the selling and administrative expense budget, and the cash budget are similar to those prepared for manufacturing firms, we will not discuss them again. To illustrate budgeting in a merchandising company, we will assume that Wind River Boat Company is a retail company that buys boats from manufacturers and sells them to consumers.

purchases budget A schedule of projected purchases over the budget period.

PURCHASES BUDGET Assuming the same level of sales as we did for Sunbird, the **purchases budget** for Wind River Boat Company is shown in Schedule 9.

You can see from Schedule 9 that Wind River Boat Company pays its suppliers $8,000 for each 15-foot boat. (If you compare this cost with the total manufacturing cost for Sunbird Boat Company, you will see that it is higher. This is because manufacturing companies also need to make a profit.) In Schedule 9, we have assumed the same beginning and ending inventory numbers we used in Schedule 2 for Sunbird, the manufacturing company. Total purchases in this schedule replaces the direct materials, direct labor, and manufacturing overhead lines in the cash budget for a manufacturing firm.

exhibit 5-4 A Comparison of the Master Budgets for a Manufacturing and a Merchandising Firm

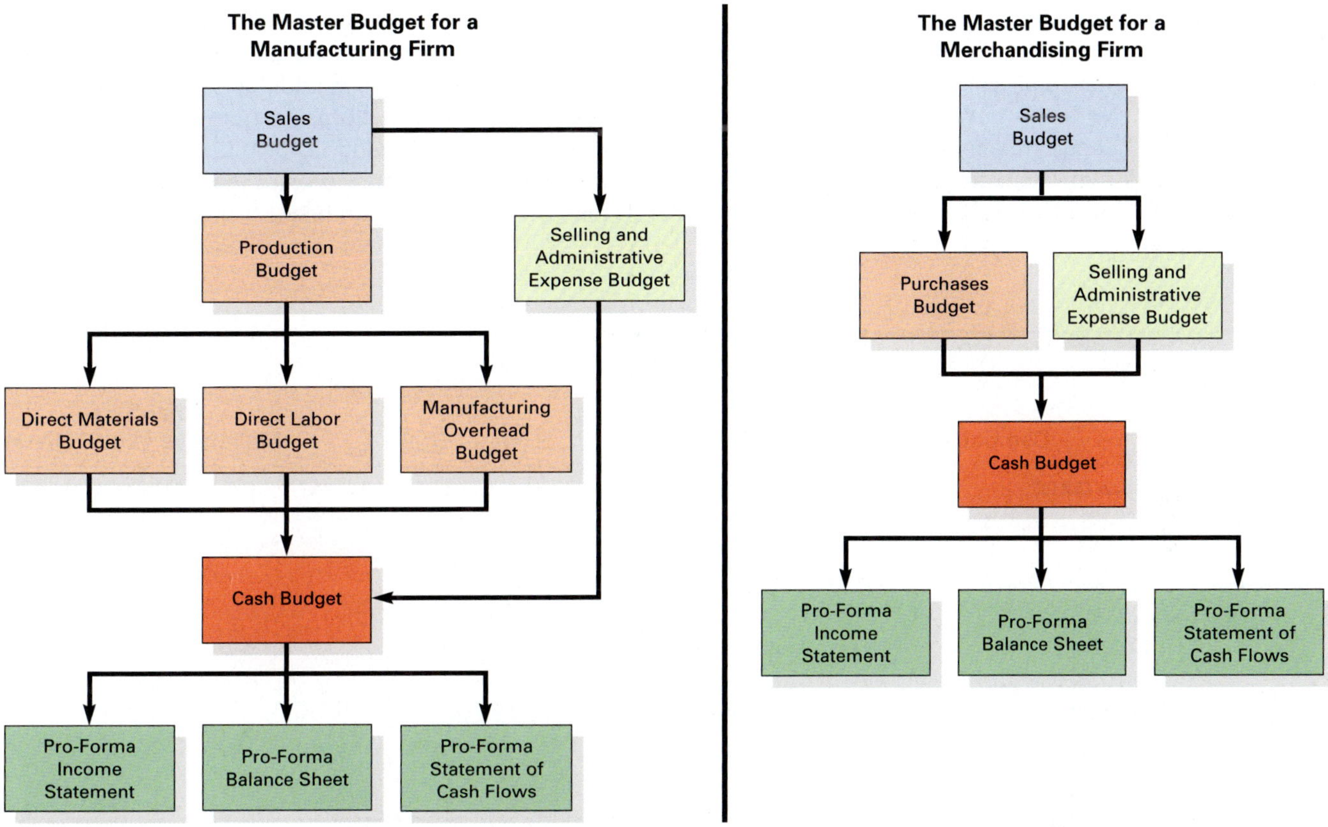

Schedule 9

Schedule 9
Purchases Budget—2003

	Quarter 1 15 ft.	Quarter 2 15 ft.	Quarter 3 15 ft.	Quarter 4 15 ft.	Total 15 ft.
Expected sales	24	28	30	18	100
Desired ending inventory	22	24	15	20	20
Boats needed	46	52	45	38	120
Less beginning inventory	(18)	(22)	(24)	(15)	(18)
Boats to be purchased	28	30	21	23	102
Cost per boat	x $8,000	x $8,000	x $8,000	x $8,000	x $8,000
Total purchases	$224,000	$240,000	$168,000	$184,000	$816,000

to summarize

The budgeting process for merchandising organizations (retail and wholesale companies) is similar, but easier, than that for manufacturing firms. The major difference is that a merchandising firm's purchases budget replaces four of a manufacturing firm's budgets—the production, direct materials, direct labor, and manufacturing overhead budgets. On the cash budget for a merchandis-

business environment essay

World's Largest Retailers In many industrialized countries, the growth rate for retail sales is barely keeping pace with the population growth rate. As a result, retailers are expanding into foreign markets to increase sales. Have you ever wondered which company is the largest retailer in the world? As of January 1, 2000, the largest retailer was WAL-MART, with 1999 sales of almost $167 billion. In addition to the United States, Wal-Mart operates stores in numerous other countries, including Argentina, Brazil, Canada, China, Indonesia, and Mexico. Here are the top nine global retailers as of December 1999.

Top Nine Global Retailers

Rank	Company	Country	Type of Store	1999 Sales (Millions of U.S. Dollars)*
1	WAL-MART	United States	Discount, warehouse	$166,809
2	SEARS, ROEBUCK	United States	Department, specialty	41,071
3	KMART	United States	Discount, warehouse	35,925
4	TARGET	United States	Discount	33,702
5	J.C. PENNEY	United States	Department	32,510
6	DAIEI	Japan	Department	25,320
7	GROUP PINAULT-PRINTEMPS	Europe	Department	20,144
8	FEDERATED DEPT. STORE	United States	Department	17,716
9	FONCIERE EURIS	Europe	Department	17,475

*Currency converted using average 1999 exchange rates.

Sources: http://Fortune500.com. Sales figures are from various sources.

ing company, total purchases replace cash expended for direct materials, direct labor, and manufacturing overhead. Otherwise, the entire master budgeting process is the same.

Budgeting for Operations in a Service Firm

Each year a larger and larger percentage of businesses in the United States are service entities. Service entities differ from manufacturing and merchandising companies in that they provide services to customers instead of products. Examples of service organizations are law, accounting, and engineering firms; doctors and dentists; hotels and motels; hunting and fishing guide services; automotive, home, and appliance repair services; and Internet providers. Budgeting for service firms is similar to budgeting for manufacturing firms. As was the case with both manufacturing and merchandising companies, the budgeting process for service firms begins with a sales budget. (For a service firm, this is usually called a revenue budget.) Expected revenues then drive the production budget, which is the number of billable hours in a CPA or law firm, the number of rooms to rent in a hotel, or the number of hours of service for an Internet provider. The production budget drives the separate budgets for supplies, wages and salaries, and overhead. These three budgets are similar to the direct materials, direct labor, and manufacturing overhead budgets for a manufacturing firm. These budgets, together with the revenue and selling and administrative expense budgets, provide the data needed for the cash budget. Once the cash budget is completed, pro-forma financial statements can be prepared. Exhibit 5-5 contrasts the budgeting process for a manufacturing and a service firm.

REVENUE BUDGET It is difficult to use either the Sunbird or Wind River examples discussed thus far to illustrate budgeting in service firms; both companies sold products—fishing boats. Therefore, to illustrate the budgeting process in service firms, we will use the example of the Boulder View Inn, a small motel that has 12 rooms to rent each night. The Boulder View Inn is located adjacent to a national park in southern Utah, and its business is highly seasonal, with April through December being busy (peak period) and January through March being very slow. The Boulder View Inn rents its rooms for an average rate of $55 per night during the peak period and $35 per night during the slow period. Guests who stay at the hotel either pay cash or use credit cards, such as VISA, MasterCard, American Express, or Discover. The motel has a direct link with its bank that immediately deposits credit card receipts in Boulder View Inn's bank account after charging a 4 to 5% discount fee, which covers the bank's costs as well as fees charged by the credit card companies. Historically, the Boulder View Inn has found that because most customers use credit cards to pay for their rooms, it pays an average of $2 per room per night to the credit card companies to cover the discount fee. After the discount fee, the net amount of revenues per room per night is $53 during peak periods and $33 during slow periods. Based on past experience, occupancy rates for the coming year are expected to be as follows:

January–March	25%
April–June	90%
July–September	80%
October–December	60%

exhibit 5-5 A Comparison of the Master Budgets for a Manufacturing and a Service Firm

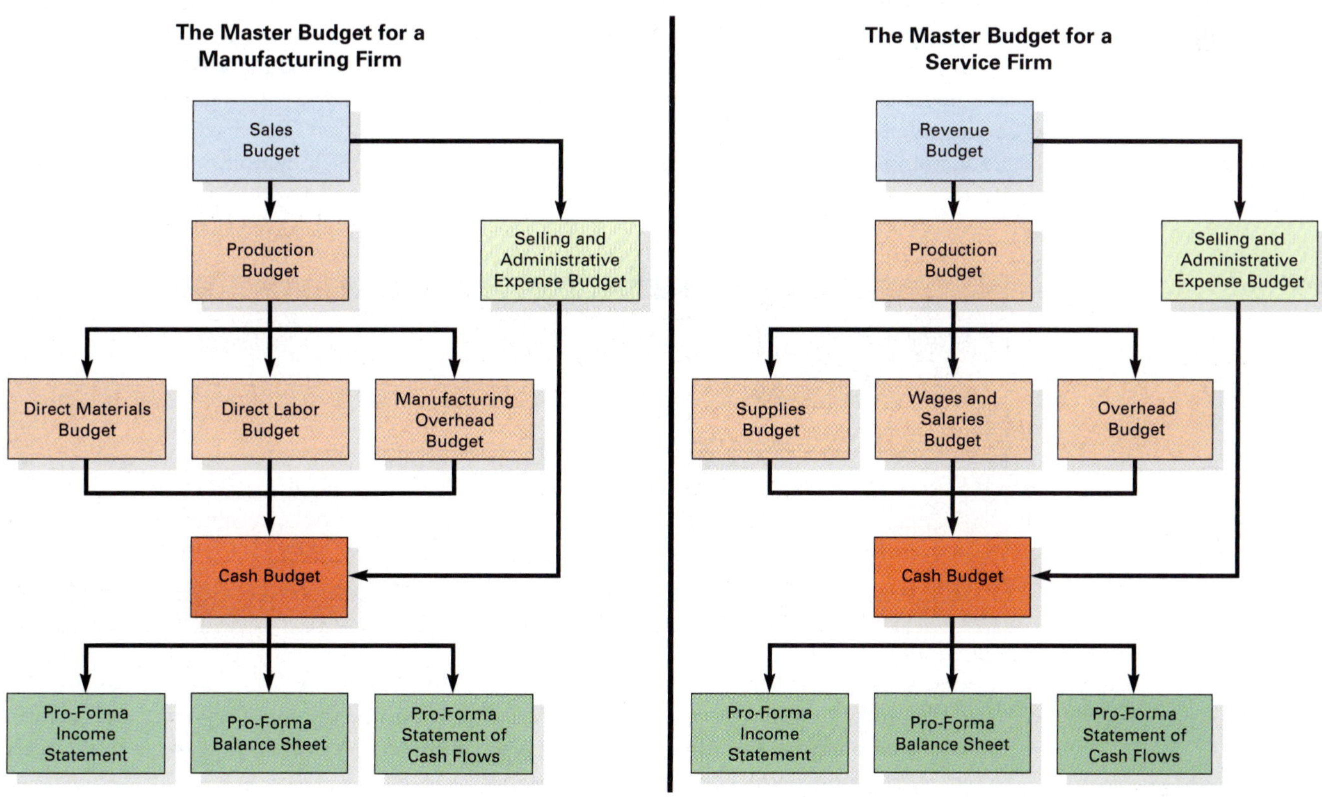

revenue budget A service entity's budget that identifies how much revenue (and often cash) will be generated during a period.

Using these data, the **revenue budget** for the Boulder View Inn would be as shown in Schedule 10.

This budget shows that the Boulder View Inn will generate gross revenues of $148,512 during the next year. Since the Boulder View Inn collects cash or its equivalent (credit cards) from each guest, there is no need to prepare a collection of accounts receivable budget as was done for the Sunbird Boat Company.

The revenue budget would be similar for other types of service firms, except that instead of a per-room revenue, the revenue would be based on per patient visit (for doctors and dentists), per service performed (for engineers, accountants, and lawyers), or per subscription (for Internet providers). Service companies that do not collect cash, but rather bill clients on a periodic basis (such as lawyers and accountants), would also prepare cash collection schedules to determine when the cash generated from revenues would be collected.

Schedule 10

Microsoft Excel - sch-m0510.xls

Schedule 10
Revenue Budget—2003

	January–March	April–June	July–September	October–December	Total
Gross revenue per room	$ 35	$ 55	$ 55	$ 55	
Number of days in quarter	x 90	x 91	x 92	x 92	
Total quarterly revenue per room	$ 3,150	$ 5,005	$ 5,060	$ 5,060	
Number of rooms to rent	x 12	x 12	x 12	x 12	
Possible revenues (at 100% occupancy)	$37,800	$60,060	$60,720	$60,720	
Occupancy rate	x 25%	x 90%	x 80%	x 60%	
Budgeted gross revenues	$ 9,450	$54,054	$48,576	$36,432	$148,512

PRODUCTION BUDGET The production budget for a service firm determines the total amount of services (the number of units of service) that will be used to earn the revenues budgeted. For a law firm, for example, the production budget would be the total number of billable hours at each billing rate used to generate the revenues. For a hunting and fishing guide service, the production budget would be the number of guide days. For Boulder View Inn, the production budget is the number of rooms that will be rented each quarter, as shown in Schedule 11.

Schedule 11

Microsoft Excel - sch-m0511.xls

Schedule 11
Production Budget—2003

	January–March	April–June	July–September	October–December	Total
Gross revenues	$9,450	$54,054	$48,576	$36,432	$148,512
Room rental rate	÷$35	÷$55	÷$55	÷$55	
Rooms rented (rounded)	270	983	883	662	2,798

This production budget is necessary in order to determine the supplies, wages and salaries, and overhead budgets. You can see from this production budget that Boulder View Inn expects to rent 2,798 rooms next year.

supplies budget The budget, prepared by service entities, that identifies projected supplies expenses over the budget period.

SUPPLIES BUDGET Most service businesses need supplies to operate their business. For a restaurant, supplies include the food used in preparing meals, napkins, afterdinner mints, and toothpicks. For a medical doctor, supplies might include needles, tape, bandages, and thread for stitching cuts. For Boulder View Inn, supplies include soap and shampoo for the guest rooms, as well as donuts, cereal, juice, and coffee for the continental breakfast. The **supplies budget** for the Boulder View Inn is shown in Schedule 12.

Schedule 12

Schedule 12
Supplies Budget—2003

Supplies Needed Per Room	January–March	April–June	July–September	October–December	Total
Soap	$ 0.40	$ 0.40	$ 0.40	$ 0.40	$ 0.40
Shampoo	0.60	0.60	0.60	0.60	0.60
Coffee	0.30	0.30	0.30	0.30	0.30
Juice	0.60	0.60	0.60	0.60	0.60
Cereal	0.40	0.40	0.40	0.40	0.40
Donuts	0.70	0.70	0.70	0.70	0.70
Total supplies per room	$ 3.00	$ 3.00	$ 3.00	$ 3.00	$ 3.00
Rooms rented	x 270	x 983	x 883	x 662	x 2,798
Total supplies cost	$ 810	$ 2,949	$ 2,649	$ 1,986	$ 8,394

wages and salaries budget The budget, prepared by service entities, that identifies projected labor costs involved directly in providing the service over the budget period.

WAGES AND SALARIES BUDGET The **wages and salaries budget** is reserved for labor costs involved directly in providing the service (similar to direct labor in a manufacturing firm). Administrative labor costs are not included in this budget; they are part of the selling and administrative expense budget. For a law firm, the wages and salaries budget would include salaries of lawyers (but not of paralegals), photocopy personnel, or computer specialists. For the Boulder View Inn, the only labor cost included in this budget is the $3 per room that is paid for cleaning the rooms. Schedule 13 is the wages and salaries budget for Boulder View Inn.

Schedule 13

Schedule 13
Wages and Salaries Budget—2003

	January–March	April–June	July–September	October–December	Total
Rooms rented	270	983	883	662	2,798
Cleaning fee	x $3	x $3	x $3	x $3	x $3
Total wages and salaries	$810	$2,949	$2,649	$1,986	$8,394

service overhead budget The budget, prepared by service entities, that identifies projected costs associated with providing the service.

OVERHEAD BUDGET As was the case with manufacturing firms, the **service overhead budget** includes all the costs associated with providing the product, or service in this case. The overhead budget does not include selling and administrative costs not directly associated with providing the service. For the Boulder View Inn, overhead includes utilities, depreciation, TV and telephone service, and miscellaneous expenses. Schedule 14 is the overhead budget for the Boulder View Inn.

The depreciation is calculated by dividing the motel cost of $300,000 by its 30-year life to arrive at $10,000 per year. The utilities include heat, lights, sewer, and garbage removal. Because the Boulder View Inn expects to rent 2,798 rooms during the year, the overhead assigned to each room rented is $9.29 ($26,000 ÷ 2,798 rooms).

Schedule 14

	January–March	April–June	July–September	October–December	Total
Schedule 14					
Overhead Budget—2003					
Utilities	$2,000	$2,000	$2,000	$2,000	$ 8,000
Depreciation expense	2,500	2,500	2,500	2,500	10,000
TV and telephone	800	800	800	800	3,200
Miscellaneous expenses	1,200	1,200	1,200	1,200	4,800
Total overhead	$6,500	$6,500	$6,500	$6,500	$26,000

Based on the three production-related budgets (supplies, wages and salaries, and overhead), we know it costs the Boulder View Inn approximately $15.29 to provide the services needed to rent one room for one night. The calculation of this cost is shown in Schedule 15.

Schedule 15

Schedule 15	
Per Room Rental Cost—2003	
Supplies cost	$ 3.00
Wages and salaries cost	3.00
Overhead	9.29
Total cost to provide motel rooms	$15.29

SELLING AND ADMINISTRATIVE EXPENSE BUDGET As was the case for Sunbird Boat Company, the selling and administrative expense budget includes planned expenditures for all selling and administrative expenses. As in manufacturing companies, the selling and administrative expense budget for a service firm can be quite large and is sometimes supported by individual budgets for specific elements included in this budget. The selling and administrative expense budget for the Boulder View Inn would be as shown in Schedule 16.

This selling and administration expense budget shows that the Boulder View Inn's total selling and administrative expense for the year is $29,596. The selling and administrative expenses include credit card charges, the manager's salary, and advertising expense, which includes yellow page directory advertisement and Internet listings.

Schedule 16

	Quarter 1	Quarter 2	Quarter 3	Quarter 4	Estimated Annual Cost
Schedule 16					
Selling and Administrative Expense Budget—2003					
Credit card fees*	$ 540	$1,966	$1,766	$1,324	$ 5,596
Manager's salary	5,000	5,000	5,000	5,000	20,000
Advertising expense	1,000	1,000	1,000	1,000	4,000
Total selling and administrative expenses	$6,540	$7,966	$7,766	$7,324	$29,596

*At $2 per room.

CASH BUDGET The cash budget, which shows expected cash receipts and disbursements during a period, summarizes information contained in both the revenue and the selling and administrative expense budgets. For the Boulder View Inn, and for most service organizations, once the individual budgets are prepared, preparing the cash budget is quite simple. As is the case with all cash budgets, the Boulder View Inn's cash budget allows the motel to determine when it will have excess cash and when it will have to borrow cash. The cash budget for the Boulder View Inn is shown in Schedule 17.

This cash budget makes several assumptions. First, the Boulder View Inn is a partnership, so there is no income tax. Instead, as in all partnerships, the income is allocated among the partners and claimed as income on their personal tax returns. Many service organizations are partnerships, so this assumption is not unusual (many are also corporations). Second, it is assumed that all expenditures are paid in the quarter incurred. If the Boulder View Inn paid some of its expenses in the quarters following their incurrence, a cash payments schedule would need to be prepared.

This cash budget shows that the Boulder View Inn generates excess cash in quarters two, three, and four, but has a net cash outflow of $2,710 in the first quarter. The Boulder View Inn can solve its cash flow shortage in the first quarter either by keeping enough cash in its bank account to cover the shortage or by borrowing money in the first quarter and repaying it in the second quarter.

Schedule 17

Microsoft Excel - sch-m0517.xls

Schedule 17

Cash Budget—2003

	January–March	**April–June**	**July–September**	**October–December**	**Total**
Cash receipts	$ 9,450	$54,054	$48,576	$36,432	$148,512
Cash outflows:					
Supplies	$ (810)	$ (2,949)	$ (2,649)	$ (1,986)	$ (8,394)
Wages and salaries	(810)	(2,949)	(2,649)	(1,986)	(8,394)
Overhead*	(4,000)	(4,000)	(4,000)	(4,000)	(16,000)
Selling and administrative expenses	(6,540)	(7,966)	(7,766)	(7,324)	(29,596)
Total cash expenditures	$ 12,160	$17,864	$17,064	$15,296	$ 62,384
Net cash inflow (outflow)	$ (2,710)	$36,190	$31,512	$21,136	$ 86,128

*Depreciation expense is not included because it is not a cash expenditure.

to summarize

The master budget for a service company is similar to budgeting in a manufacturing company. As a result, in addition to the pro-forma financial statements (covered in the expanded material section of the chapter), seven budgets are prepared: the revenue budget, the production budget, the supplies budget, the wages and salaries budget, the overhead budget, the selling and administrative expense budget, and the cash budget. The revenue budget is usually based on whatever the service performed is (e.g., per room, per service performed, per patient, or per subscription basis). The production budget identifies the number of units of the service that will be performed so that supplies, wages and salaries, and overhead budgets can be prepared. The selling and administrative expense budget includes all costs not directly related to providing the service. The cash budget is net revenues received less cash spent for supplies, wages, overhead (not including depreciation expense), and selling and administrative expenses. As was the case with manufacturing and merchandising companies, the budgeting process allows a service company to determine when it will have excess cash and when it will experience cash shortages.

expanded material

The budgeting process discussed to this point allows management to plan various activities within the firm, such as purchasing and borrowing. Armed with these budgets, management is now prepared to monitor the firm's performance and compare actual results to budgeted results. If corrective action is needed, management can identify deviations from the budget early and take the appropriate steps to remedy problems. In addition to preparing the detailed budgets, management can combine the various budgets to arrive at pro-forma, or budgeted, financial statements. In this section, we use the budgets from the Sunbird Boat Company to prepare a pro-forma income statement, balance sheet, and statement of cash flows. The section concludes with a discussion of static and flexible budgeting and illustrates the advantages of flexible budgeting.

4
Prepare pro-forma financial statements.

PRO-FORMA FINANCIAL STATEMENTS

The pro-forma income statement (often called a budgeted income statement) projects income for the coming period and, therefore, is valuable to management in making key decisions. Such questions as how high a dividend to pay, whether to invest in a new plant, and how strenuously to bargain with unions are usually decided on the basis of projected and actual profits. Because budgeting for manufacturing firms is the most complicated, we will illustrate pro-forma financial statements using the Sunbird Boat Company example illustrated earlier in the chapter. Sunbird's pro-forma income statement is shown in Schedule 18. In the income statement, we assume an income tax rate of 27% for Sunbird.

STOP & THINK How would the three financial statements be different if we assumed Sunbird was a merchandising company instead of a manufacturing company?

The final two items to be projected are the balance sheet and the statement of cash flows. These statements are presented in Schedules 19 and 20.

The master budget is now complete. It is ready for use to communicate information, coordinate and authorize activities, motivate employees, and measure performance. The decisions to be made on the basis of this budget depend on the answers to such questions as:

1. Is the net income of approximately $307,593 adequate? If not, how can it be increased?
2. How does the expected financial position at the end of the year fit with long-range objectives and goals?
3. Is the projected increase in cash sufficient to meet the firm's goals?
4. Are there sufficient liquid assets to purchase needed assets?
5. How should management be rewarded if these budgets are met?
6. Who should be responsible for meeting the goals set for sales, production, and costs?

These are only a few of the questions that management needs to answer. However, they should give you a sense of the master budget's usefulness. In fact, it is hard to imagine how a company could be profitable in the long run without such planning.

Schedule 18

Microsoft Excel - sch-m0518.xls

	A	C	E	G
1	**Schedule 18**			
2	**Pro-Forma Income Statement**			
3	**For the Year Ended December 31, 2003**			
4	Sales revenue (Schedule 1)			$1,400,000
5	Cost of goods sold:			
6	Beginning finished goods inventory (Schedule 2)		$150,000	
7	Manufacturing costs:			
8	Direct materials used (Schedule 3)	$ 96,900		
9	Direct labor (Schedule 4)	122,400		
10	Manufacturing overhead (Schedule 5)	114,240	333,540	
11	Total cost of goods available for sale		$483,540	
12	Less ending finished goods inventory*		(65,400)	
13	Cost of goods sold			(418,140)
14	Gross margin			$ 981,860
15	Selling and administrative expenses (Schedule 7)			(560,000)
16	Operating income			$ 421,860
17	Interest expense (Schedule 8)			(500)
18	Income before income taxes			$ 421,360
19	Income taxes (approximate 27% rate)			(113,767)
20	Net income			$ 307,593

*Calculation of ending Finished Goods Inventory. (Schedule 2 states that the desired ending inventory is 20 15-foot boats.) Per Schedule 6: Cost of 15-foot boat: $3,270 × 20 boats = $65,400.

Schedule 19

Microsoft Excel - sch-m0519.xls

	A	C	E
1	**Schedule 19**		
2	**Pro-Forma Balance Sheet**		
3	**December 31, 2003**		
4	**Assets**		
5	*Current assets:*		
6	Cash (Schedule 8)	$ 421,415	
7	Accounts receivable[1]	50,400	
8	Direct materials[2]	7,125	
9	Finished goods (Schedule 18)	65,400	$ 544,340
10	*Long-term operating assets:*		
11	Land (assumed)	$ 234,305	
12	Building and equipment[3]	1,650,000	
13	Less accumulated depreciation[4]	(170,000)	1,714,305
14	Total assets		$2,258,645
15	**Liabilities and Stockholders' Equity**		
16	*Current liabilities:*		
17	Accounts payable[5]	$ 90,000	
18	Income taxes payable[6]	113,767	$ 203,767
19	*Stockholders' equity:*		
20	Common stock, $5 par, 20,000 shares outstanding (assumed)	$1,000,000	
21	Paid-in capital in excess of par, common stock (assumed)	250,000	
22	Retained earnings[7]	804,878	2,054,878
23	Total liabilities and stockholders' equity		$2,258,645

[1]Accounts receivable:
beginning balance + sales (Schedule 1) − collections (Schedule 8) = ending balance
(assumed) $56,000 + $1,400,000 − $1,405,600 = $50,400

[2]Direct materials:
Wood $5,250 (525 × $10 per board foot) + fiberglass $1,875 (375 × $5) = $7,125

[3]Building and equipment:
beginning balance + equipment purchase (Schedule 8) = ending balance
(assumed) $1,500,000 + $150,000 = $1,650,000

(continued)

[4]Accumulated depreciation:
beginning balance + plant overhead (Schedule 5) + selling and administrative expenses (Schedule 7) = ending balance
(assumed) $120,000 + $10,000 + $40,000 = $170,000

[5]Accounts payable:
beginning balance + direct materials purchased (Schedule 3) + direct labor (Schedule 4) + manufacturing overhead (less depreciation) (Schedule 5)
(assumed) $90,000 + $96,045 + $122,400 + $104,240 ($114,240 − $10,000)
+ selling and administrative expenses (less depreciation) (Schedule 7) + income tax expense (Schedule 8) + dividends (Schedule 8) + equipment (Schedule 8) − amount paid for cash payments (Schedule 8) = ending balance
+ $520,000 ($560,000 − $40,000) + $96,000 + $30,000 + $150,000 − $1,118,685 = $90,000

[6]Income taxes payable:
beginning balance + estimated taxes − payment = ending balance
(assumed) $96,000 + $113,767 − $96,000 = $113,767

[7]Retained earnings:
beginning balance + net income − dividends = ending balance
(assumed) $527,285 + $307,593 − $30,000 = $804,878

Schedule 20

Microsoft Excel - sch-m0520.xls

Schedule 20
Pro-Forma Statement of Cash Flows
For the Year Ended December 31, 2003

Cash flows from operating activities:		
Net income (Schedule 18)		$307,593
Add (subtract) adjustments:		
Depreciation (Schedules 5 and 7)	$ 50,000	
Decrease in direct materials*	855	
Decrease in finished goods*	84,600	
Decrease in accounts receivable*	5,600	
Increase in income taxes payable*	17,767	
		158,822
Net cash provided by operating activities		$466,415
Cash flows from investing activities:		
Purchase of equipment (Schedule 8)	$(150,000)	
Net cash used in investing activities		(150,000)
Cash flows from financing activities:		
Cash obtained from borrowing (Schedule 8)	$ 20,000	
Repayment of borrowed funds (Schedule 8)	(20,000)	
Payment of dividends (Schedule 8)	(30,000)	
Net cash used in financing activities		(30,000)
Net increase in cash		$286,415

*2002 year-end balances are assumed to be $7,980 for direct materials, $150,000 for finished goods, $56,000 for accounts receivable, and $96,000 for income taxes payable.

to summarize

Following the preparation of the cash budget, which provides an indication of the financing activities of the business, pro-forma financial statements can be prepared. The pro-forma income statement, balance sheet, and statement of cash flows follow directly from the components of the master budget. The pro-forma balance sheet also relies heavily on beginning account balances. Once these pro-forma financial statements have been prepared, management can then determine if budgeted sales and production levels will allow the company to achieve its strategic goals. These pro-forma financial statements serve as a basis for key management decisions.

5

Distinguish between static and flexible budgets.

static budget A quantified plan that projects revenues and costs for only one level of activity.

flexible budget A quantified plan that projects revenues and costs for varying levels of activity.

STATIC VERSUS FLEXIBLE BUDGETING

The budgets discussed thus far were **static budgets**; that is, they were geared to only one level of activity. Actual results were compared to budgeted costs at the budgeted activity level. Although such budgets help in planning, they are not very useful for controlling costs and measuring performance because the actual level of activity may have differed significantly from the planned level.

A **flexible budget** is much more useful for control and performance evaluation because it is not confined to one level of activity. Flexible budgets are dynamic; that is, they can be tailored to any level of activity within the relevant range. Using flexible budgeting, a manager can look at the actual level of activity attained and then determine what costs should have been at that level.

Weaknesses in Static Budgeting

To illustrate why a static budget is inadequate for controlling operations, we will use an example for Kemper Manufacturing Company and assume only variable costs. We use this different example so as not to complicate the Sunbird Boat Company example used throughout the chapter. Here we are interested only in illustrating the concept of flexible budgets.

Using information from various sources, Kemper developed the following budgeted per-unit manufacturing costs for its product:

Direct materials	$0.90
Direct labor	0.74
Manufacturing overhead	1.36
Total	$3.00

Extending these per-unit costs to establish a total budgeted amount for the month of August, the company might prepare a static budget as follows:

Kemper Manufacturing Company
Budgeted Manufacturing Costs
For the Month of August 2003

Budgeted production (units)	4,000
Budgeted manufacturing costs:	
Direct materials ($0.90 × 4,000)	$ 3,600
Direct labor ($0.74 × 4,000)	2,960
Manufacturing overhead ($1.36 × 4,000)	5,440
Total manufacturing costs	$12,000

Now, let's assume that Kemper produced only 3,800 units in August and that actual costs incurred were $3,370 for direct materials, $2,900 for direct labor, and $5,400 for manufacturing overhead. Comparing actual results with the static budget information, the performance report for the month would be as follows:

Kemper Manufacturing Company
Static Budget Performance Report
For the Month of August 2003

	Actual	Budgeted	Difference
Production (units)	3,800	4,000	(200)
Manufacturing costs:			
Direct materials	$ 3,370	$ 3,600	$(230)
Direct labor	2,900	2,960	(60)
Manufacturing overhead	5,400	5,440	(40)
Total actual and budgeted manufacturing costs	$11,670	$12,000	$(330)

Obviously, something is wrong with this performance report. Producing fewer units than budgeted (3,800 actual units versus 4,000 budgeted units) has led to actual costs that are $330 less than budgeted costs. Should management be rewarded for keeping costs down or penalized for producing fewer units than budgeted? The deficiencies of this static budget performance report can be explained as follows: A production manager is responsible for controlling two things—production (output) and costs; that is, he or she must try to meet budgeted production volume and control costs in the process. To measure a manager's performance, the production and cost control functions must be separated. It makes no sense to note that the actual cost of producing 3,800 units is less than the budgeted cost of producing 4,000 units. It obviously should be. The manager in our example clearly has not met budgeted production volume, but to determine whether he or she has controlled costs adequately, we must be able to compare actual costs to budgeted costs at the same number of units of production.

Using the Flexible Budget

Instead of providing budgeted costs for only one level of activity, the flexible budget covers a range of activity levels so that managers can easily determine what costs should have been at the actual activity level. Because it is possible to prepare budgeted costs at every possible activity level, per-unit costs that can be applied to any activity level within the relevant range are developed. The actual steps in preparing a flexible budget are:

1. Determine a relevant range over which production is expected to vary during the coming period.
2. Analyze the projected manufacturing costs for the coming period.
3. Using the per-unit costs for each element, prepare a budget showing what costs are expected to be incurred at several points within the relevant range.

To illustrate the preparation of a flexible budget, let us assume that Kemper's relevant range of activity per month is between 3,600 and 4,200 units. As noted earlier, the per-unit costs are:

business environment essay

Budgeting at Theme Parks Although the rides are idle at many theme parks during the winter, theme park accountants are not without work. When the gates close for the last time each fall, accountants at **SIX FLAGS GREAT AMERICA** in Illinois use the off-period to prepare the annual operating budget for the coming season.

The process begins with the development of the park's anticipated attendance levels and the daily operating schedule. Attendance levels from the preceding season are used to make projections for the next year. Attendance is computed by summing the number of tickets sold at the entrance, the number of pre-sold tickets redeemed, and the number of season pass admissions. In addition, turnstiles are used at entrances and exits to count admissions and the number of guests riding each ride. Turnstile meters are "read" on an hourly basis to enable management to monitor varying attendance throughout the day. This information is used to anticipate and budget staffing needs.

Based on past performance and other information (such as planned improvements), revenues and expenses are projected for each area of the park. For example, gift shops, food outlets, movable carts, and support areas are budgeted individually. The master budget, then, is a consolidation of the several hundred budgets of individual activity centers.

Theme parks are an established cultural phenomenon in America. Those parks that budget and then execute their budgets most effectively are the most financially successful.

Source: Adapted from Kevin A. Roth, "Theme Park Accounting: What Do We Really Do All Winter?" *Management Accounting*, February 1994, pp. 48–51.

Direct materials	$0.90
Direct labor	0.74
Manufacturing overhead	1.36
Total	$3.00

These per-unit costs can now be used to prepare a flexible budget showing expected costs for several levels of production.

Kemper Manufacturing Company
Manufacturing Cost Flexible Budget
For the Month of August 2003

		Range of Production (units)			
	Manufacturing Costs per Unit	**3,600**	**3,800**	**4,000**	**4,200**
Direct materials	$0.90	$ 3,240	$ 3,420	$ 3,600	$ 3,780
Direct labor	0.74	2,664	2,812	2,960	3,108
Manufacturing overhead	1.36	4,896	5,168	5,440	5,712
Total	$3.00	$10,800	$11,400	$12,000	$12,600

With the flexible budget prepared, Kemper can compare actual amounts against budgeted amounts for the production level attained. In this case, 3,800 units were actually produced, so the actual costs for the period can be compared with the budget for 3,800 units. If actual production had been 3,700 units, a number not included in the budget, Kemper could simply multiply the per-unit cost of each item (direct materials, direct labor, and manufacturing overhead) by the actual activity level in order to judge performance. The performance report based on flexible budgeting for the 3,800 units actually produced now makes much more sense.

Kemper Manufacturing Company
Flexible Budget Performance Report
For the Month of August 2003

Actual production (units)	3,800
Budgeted production (units)	4,000
Difference	(200)

	Cost per Unit	**Actual Costs Incurred at 3,800 Units**	**Budgeted Costs for 3,800 Units**	**Difference**
Direct materials	$0.90	$ 3,370	$ 3,420	$ (50)
Direct labor	0.74	2,900	2,812	88
Manufacturing overhead	1.36	5,400	5,168	232
Total costs	$3.00	$11,670	$11,400	$270

Notice that the actual costs for both direct labor and manufacturing overhead exceeded budgeted costs for the actual level of activity. We are now comparing apples with apples, or actual costs of producing 3,800 units with budgeted costs of producing 3,800 units. Using the same activity level has revealed that total manufacturing costs exceeded budget by $270 during the month and that the most significant difference was in the cost of manufacturing overhead.

Flexible budgets provide management with useful information for investigating problem areas. This flexible budget performance report shows that not only was planned production not achieved, but also that the costs incurred exceeded those budgeted at the attained level of activity. Apparently, the manager is having problems with both production and cost control. Having meaningful cost comparisons is very useful for evaluating performance and overcoming breakdowns in cost control.

to summarize

The master budget described in this chapter was a static budget. A static budget is a budget that is prepared for only one level of activity. Static budgets are useful for planning purposes, but flexible budgets are much more useful for control and performance evaluation. A flexible budget is a budget prepared over a range of activity. Flexible budgets allow budgeted and actual costs to be compared at the same level of activity, thereby revealing cost and production effectiveness.

review of learning objectives

1 Describe different types of budgeting and identify the purposes of budgeting. A budget is a quantitative expression of a plan of action. The budget identifies and allocates resources necessary to carry out the mission of the organization. Based on the strategic plan, the organization prepares a capital budget and a budget for operations. The operating budget provides quantitative estimates of sales and expected costs for each activity to be performed during a specified period of time (usually, one year). The budgeting process has several purposes. Budgeting encourages planning, enhances communications, helps management at all levels coordinate activities, provides authorization for actions (investing, spending, borrowing, producing), helps motivate employees to perform, assists in reducing conflicts, and provides quantitative measures of expectations and objectives.

2 Describe the budgeting process and its behavioral implications. Most organizations establish a budget committee composed of several vice presidents who coordinate the preparation of detailed budgets in their areas of responsibility and oversee the preparation of the overall budget. There are significant behavioral ramifications to consider in preparing an operating budget. For the process to be successful, top management must give its full support, all members of management must actively participate in the process, and deviations from the budget must be addressed in a constructive manner. If only the top management is involved in budget preparation, it is referred to as top-down budgeting. When each segment manager prepares a budget for that segment's operations, it is called bottom-up budgeting. Most budgeting processes incorporate both approaches to some degree.

3 Explain the master budget and its components for manufacturing firms, merchandising firms, and service firms. The operating budget, also called a master budget, is an integrated group of detailed budgets that together provide overall operating and financing plans for a specific time period. The master budget for a manufacturing firm starts with a sales forecast, which serves as the basis for the sales budget. The sales budget is followed in sequence with detailed budgets for production, direct materials usage and purchases, direct labor, manufacturing overhead, selling and administrative expenses, and cash. These detailed budgets are usually prepared on a monthly or quarterly basis. For operations budgeting in merchandising companies, a purchases budget replaces the production, direct materials, direct labor, and manufacturing overhead budgets used in manufacturing companies. Operations budgeting in service firms includes preparing revenue, production, selling and administrative expense, and cash budgets. Together these budgets provide management with a master plan of action for the coming year.

expanded material

4 Prepare pro-forma financial statements. Once a cash budget is prepared to project the firm's ending cash balances and borrowing and investing activities, pro-forma financial statements can be prepared. The pro-forma balance sheet relies heavily on the balances at the beginning of the period, along with components of the master budget. The pro-forma income statement and statement of cash flows are prepared primarily from the detailed budgets included in the master budget. With these pro-forma financial statements, management is able to determine if budgeted results are consistent with the firm's master plan.

5 Distinguish between static and flexible budgets. Static budgets project expected results at only one activity level. When the actual production level differs significantly from the budgeted level, it is difficult to know what costs should have been for the actual production level. Flexible budgets estimate costs for various activity levels and allow actual costs to be compared to budgeted costs for the actual production level. Flexible budgets allow management to focus on both the production and cost control elements of budgeting.

key terms and concepts

budget 234
budget committee 239
cash budget 250
direct labor budget 246
direct materials budget 246
disposable income 235
line of credit 252
manufacturing overhead budget 248
operating (master) budget 235
production budget 245
purchases budget 254
revenue budget 258
sales budget 243
selling and administrative expense budget 249
service overhead budget 259
supplies budget 259
wages and salaries budget 259

expanded material

flexible budget 265
static budget 265

review problem

Budgeting in a Manufacturing Firm

The following information is available for the Call Company:

Expected sales (units):	
June	840
July	980
August	1,400
Selling price per unit	$15
Accounts receivable balance, June 1	$6,300
Desired finished goods inventory, August 31 (units)	250
Beginning finished goods inventory, June 1 (units)	270
Direct materials needed per unit	11 feet
Desired direct materials inventory, August 31	2,800 feet
Beginning direct materials inventory, June 1	2,700 feet
Total direct labor time per finished unit	3 hours
Direct materials cost per foot	$0.60
Direct labor cost per hour	$8

Additional information:

a. Seventy-five percent of a month's sales is collected by the month's end; the remaining 25% is collected in the following month.
b. The desired ending finished goods inventory every month is 25% of the next month's sales.
c. The desired ending direct materials inventory every month is 20% of the next month's production needs.

Required:

1. Prepare sales budgets for June, July, and August (in dollars).
2. Prepare cash collection budgets for June, July, and August (in dollars).
3. Prepare production budgets for June, July, and August (in units).
4. Prepare direct materials budgets for June, July, and August (in dollars).
5. Prepare direct labor budgets for June, July, and August (in dollars).

Solution

1. Sales Budgets

	June	July	August
Expected sales (units)	840	980	1,400
Selling price per unit	× $15	× $15	× $15
Expected revenues	$12,600	$14,700	$21,000

2. Cash Collection Budgets

	June	July	August
From accounts receivable	$ 6,300		
From June's sales (75%/25%)	9,450	$ 3,150	
From July's sales (75%/25%)		11,025	$ 3,675
From August's sales (75%/25%)			15,750
Total	$15,750	$14,175	$19,425

3. Production Budgets

	June	July	August
Expected sales (units)	840	980	1,400
Add desired ending inventory			
(25% of next month's sales)	245	350	250*
Total needed	1,085	1,330	1,650
Less beginning inventory	(270)*	(245)	(350)
Budgeted production (units)	815	1,085	1,300

*Given.

4. Direct Materials Budgets

	June	July	August
Units to be produced	815	1,085	1,300
Direct materials needed per unit	× 11 feet	× 11 feet	× 11 feet
Total production needs	8,965 feet	11,935 feet	14,300 feet
Desired ending direct materials inventory (20% of next month's production needs)	2,387	2,860	2,800*
Total feet needed	11,352	14,795	17,100
Less beginning inventory	(2,700)*	(2,387)	(2,860)
Direct materials to be purchased	8,652	12,408	14,240
Cost per foot	× $0.60	× $0.60	× $0.60
Total direct materials cost (rounded)	$ 5,191	$ 7,445	$ 8,544

*Given.

5. Direct Labor Budgets

	June	July	August
Units to be produced	815	1,085	1,300
Direct labor hours per unit (given)	× 3	× 3	× 3
Total hours needed	2,445	3,255	3,900
Cost per hour	× $8	× $8	× $8
Direct labor cost	$19,560	$26,040	$31,200

discussion questions

1. How are strategic planning, capital budgeting, and operations budgeting different?
2. What are the advantages of budgeting?
3. How does management use the operating budget?
4. Describe the advantages of the top-down approach and the bottom-up approach to budgeting.
5. Why are budgets usually prepared for one year?
6. Why does the accuracy of the entire master budget depend on a reliable sales forecast?
7. Identify the sequence of schedules used in preparing a master budget for a manufacturing firm.
8. Describe the four sections of a cash budget.
9. How is the budgeting process for a merchandising firm different from the budgeting process for a manufacturing firm?
10. How is the budgeting process for a service firm similar to the budgeting process for a manufacturing firm? What are any differences?

expanded material

11. How does a cash budget differ from a pro-forma income statement?
12. How are flexible budgets useful in controlling costs?

discussion cases

CASE 5-1

WEST MOUNTAIN CANNING COMPANY

West Mountain Canning Company produces several food items, including certain tomato-based products. For about nine months during the year, the company is able to purchase tomatoes from various parts of the country. The tomatoes are then processed and canned for sale in grocery stores.

The processing department employs three highly skilled workers, who are paid an average of $15 per hour. Between January and March, tomatoes are not available, and the processing and canning departments are shut down. Rather than lay off these three specialists, who have excellent alternative job opportunities, the company transfers them to the shipping department, at the same $15 pay rate. The shipping department manager is not happy, however, because his five regular employees are paid only $9 per hour. His unhappiness has become particularly acute since he was told he was $9,000 over budget for wages during the January-to-March quarter (budget was $36,000; actual was $45,000). Note that the actual amount includes 1,500 hours (3 employees × 500 hours) at $15 per hour, and that each employee works 2,000 hours in a year.

The shipping department manager feels that he is being unduly penalized for two reasons: (1) $15 is too much to pay even a good shipping clerk, and (2) the three skilled workers do not work as hard as his regular employees because they know they are needed for tomato processing and will not be fired. Therefore, he has suggested to his boss that the wages in excess of the $9 he normally pays be assigned elsewhere or that he be allowed to hire his own temporary employees during this busy period.

Answer the following questions:

1. Does the shipping department manager have a legitimate complaint? Explain.
2. Explain how management arrived at the budgeted figure for shipping wages.
3. How might the quarterly figures be reported to satisfy the shipping department manager?
4. How would you recommend that the problem be solved?

CASE 5-2

TIP TOP COMPANY

Tip Top Company recently hired a new hot-shot CEO. Traditionally, the budgeting process at Tip Top has been pretty relaxed, with the executive vice president for sales providing "best-guess" sales projections and the controller providing "ballpark" cost estimates. Although the budget has been due each year 30 days prior to the new fiscal year, it generally is not finalized until two or three months into the new fiscal year. One of the first actions of the new CEO is to institute a formalized top-down budgeting process, complete with fairly sophisticated sales projections and cost data based on benchmark statistics from industry competitors.

Discuss the issues involved in the new budgeting process for Tip Top Company.

CASE 5-3

NEW AGE BUDGETING

Manes.com is an Internet company that searches out job listings on corporate home pages, organizes them by type of job, and lists them so that individuals seeking jobs can see the kinds of jobs that are available. The Internet site is free to all users. Manes.com hopes that by providing a job-matching service, its site will attract substantial traffic, and advertisers will be willing to pay large sums of money to advertise. The company has a $20 million investment from a venture capitalist to get started but must provide budget projections to secure additional funding. Assume you are the controller for the company. How would you go about forecasting revenues and preparing budgets and profit projections to show potential investors?

CASE 5-4

DISAGREEMENTS OVER THE VALUE OF BUDGETS

Tueller Enterprises is a large manufacturer of airplane parts for commercial and military aircraft. In addition to making parts, it also serves as a distributor for other, smaller manufacturers. Traditionally, the company has spent large amounts of time preparing operational budgets, only to find that they are rarely useful and often outdated. Some managers have even argued that because they are evaluated on the basis of how well they meet the budget, they have been unable to react to changing markets and take advantage of new opportunities that have become available. The managers argue that the entire budgeting process is too constraining and should be scrapped. The new controller agrees that the traditional budgeting process has been flawed but argues that with the new enterprise-wide information systems and the availability of up-to-date performance information, budgets can now be revised more frequently and will be much more useful than in the past. The company is trying to decide what to do. Should it scrap the entire budgeting process? Or, should it work to make the budgeting process more relevant and useful?

exercises

EXERCISE 5-1

Spread-Sheet Software

PERSONAL BUDGETING

Jennifer Swartz works as an interior decorator for Modern Fashion Corporation. Her annual salary is $36,500. Of that amount, 20% is withheld for federal income taxes, 7.15% for state taxes, 7.65% for FICA taxes, and 2% as a contribution to the United Way. Another 5% is deposited directly into a company credit union for savings. Jennifer has four monthly payments: $225 for her car, $80 for furniture, $410 for rent, and $100 to repay college loans. Jennifer's other monthly expenses are approximately:

Food expense	$250
Clothing expense	100
Entertainment expense	125
Utilities expense	80
Insurance expense	30
Gas and maintenance expenses on car	180
Miscellaneous expenses	200
Total	$965

Prepare both a monthly budget and an annual budget for Jennifer that identifies gross salary, net take-home pay, net disposable income, and net surplus or deficit.

EXERCISE 5-2

PERSONAL BUDGETING

Trent Jones, a recent college graduate, has been hired by Midwest Corporation at a salary of $36,000 per year. In anticipation of his salary, Trent purchased a $14,000 automobile and will pay for it at a rate of $350 per month, including interest, for four years. He also rented a townhouse for $475 a month and bought some furniture on account for $230 a month. In addition, Trent figures that his other monthly expenses will be:

Food expense	$200
Clothing expense	100
Entertainment expense	175
Insurance expense	100
Gas and other car expenses	170
Utilities expense	100

1. On the assumption that Trent also pays income and FICA taxes of 20 and 7.65%, respectively, prepare his monthly budget.
2. Trent plans to get married soon and have a family, so he intends to save enough money for a down payment on a house. If a $15,000 down payment is needed, how long will it take him to save the needed amount? (Ignore interest on savings, and assume that Trent does not have any savings at the present time.)

EXERCISE 5-3

PRODUCTION BUDGETING

Daytona Electric makes and sells two kinds of portable radios—an AM-FM radio with CD player and an AM-FM radio. The sales forecasts for these radios for the next four quarters are as follows:

	AM-FM with CD Player	AM-FM Radio
1st quarter	170	130
2nd quarter	178	139
3rd quarter	166	127
4th quarter	190	145
Totals	704	541

At the beginning of the first quarter, Daytona has 140 AM-FM radios with CD players and 120 AM-FM radios in stock. Experience has shown that Daytona must maintain an inventory equal to two-thirds of the next quarter's sales.

How many radios of each type must be produced during each of the first three quarters to meet sales and inventory demands?

EXERCISE 5-4

PRODUCTION BUDGETING

James Seigel is the CEO of Seigel Monitor Company, a manufacturer of computer monitors. Seigel manufactures three types of computer monitors: SVGA, VGA, and EGA. The sales projections (in units) for 2003 and the first quarter of 2004 are:

	SVGA	VGA	EGA
1st quarter, 2003	3,000	5,000	2,000
2nd quarter, 2003	2,500	4,750	2,150
3rd quarter, 2003	2,850	4,900	1,800
4th quarter, 2003	3,200	4,876	2,150
1st quarter, 2004	2,900	5,100	2,200

Beginning inventory for SVGA, VGA, and EGA are 1,350, 1,500, and 1,275, respectively. Seigel requires that half of the next quarter's sales be maintained in inventory.

How many monitors must be manufactured for each quarter of 2003 to meet sales and inventory demand?

EXERCISE 5-5

DIRECT MATERIALS BUDGETING

Shaver Bicycle Shop assembles and sells tricycles and bicycles. The frames are purchased from one supplier and the wheels from another. The following materials are required:

Bicycles	Tricycles
One 22-inch frame, $35	One 12-inch frame, $15
Two 22-inch wheels, $10 each	Two 4-inch wheels, $10 each
	One 12-inch wheel, $7.50

Management anticipates that 150 bicycles and 160 tricycles will be assembled during the first quarter of 2003. On December 31, 2002, the following assembly parts are on hand:

22-inch frames	12
22-inch wheels	20
12-inch frames	8
4-inch wheels	24
12-inch wheels	10

Management also decides that, beginning in January, the inventory of parts on hand at the end of each month should be sufficient to make 10 bicycles and 10 tricycles.

Prepare a direct materials budget for the first quarter of 2003.

EXERCISE 5-6

DIRECT MATERIALS BUDGETING

Shanahan Corporation produces three types of videocassettes: VHS, S-VHS, and 8 millimeter. Shanahan purchases tape for the videocassettes from a firm in Mexico and purchases the cases from another supplier in Brazil. The following materials are required for production.

	VHS	S-VHS	8MM
Tape	$1.75	$2.30	$3.05
Cases	2.50	2.50	2.00

Beginning inventory for Shanahan Corporation is 5,000, 7,000, and 3,500 tapes for VHS, S-VHS, and 8 MM, respectively. Management wants to have 5,000 VHS and 8MM tapes and 2,500 S-VHS tapes in ending inventory. Projected sales for the first half of 2003 are 40,000 VHS tapes, 14,000 S-VHS tapes, and 21,000 8 MM tapes.

Prepare a direct materials budget for the first half of 2003.

EXERCISE 5-7

DIRECT LABOR BUDGETING

Super Good Chocolate Company makes and sells two kinds of candy: chocolate peanut bars and caramel bars. The production budget for the next three months for each of the bars is as follows:

	Boxes of Chocolate Peanut Bars	Boxes of Caramel Bars
January	640	700
February	870	450
March	920	630

From experience, Super Good's management knows that it takes approximately 20 minutes to make a box of chocolate peanut bars and 30 minutes to make a box of caramel bars. Super Good pays its direct labor employees $8 per hour.

Prepare a direct labor budget for each of the two products in both hours and costs for January, February, and March.

EXERCISE 5-8

DIRECT LABOR BUDGETING

Sanford Shoe Company makes three shoe styles: loafers, work boots, and tennis shoes. The production budget for the next three months for each type of shoe is:

	Loafers	Work Boots	Tennis Shoes
January	2,900	5,400	3,160
February	3,100	6,000	5,400
March	2,750	6,600	4,300

From experience, Sanford's management knows that it takes 15 minutes of direct labor to make a pair of loafers, 20 minutes to make a pair of work boots, and 12 minutes to make a pair of tennis shoes. At Sanford, direct labor employees are paid $5 per hour.

Prepare a direct labor budget in both hours and costs for each of the three months.

EXERCISE 5-9

COMPUTATION OF UNIT COSTS

High Lift Garage Door Company makes two types of garage doors: aluminum and wood. During the past several years, management has kept accurate records of costs and resource requirements and has determined that the following is needed to make the garage doors:

Wood Door	Production Requirements	Unit Cost
Wood	200 board feet	$1.70
Paint	2 gallons	7.50
Direct labor	6 hours	9.00
Manufacturing overhead	6 hours	5.50
Aluminum Door		
Aluminum	40 pounds	$3.50
Paint	1½ gallons	7.50
Direct labor	12 hours	9.00
Manufacturing overhead	12 hours	5.50

Compute the total unit costs of both the wood and aluminum garage doors.

EXERCISE 5-10

CASH BUDGETING—HOSPITAL

The management of West Valley Memorial Hospital needs to prepare a cash budget for July 2003. The following information is available:

a. The cash balance on July 1, 2003, is $236,000.
b. Actual services performed during May and June and projected services for July are:

	May	June	July
Cash services (bills paid by individuals as they leave the hospital)	$110,000	$ 90,000	$120,000
Credit services (bills paid by insurance companies and Medicare)	900,000	1,000,000	875,000

Credit sales are collected over a two-month period, with 60% collected during the month the service is performed and 40% in the following month.

c. Hospital personnel plan to purchase $80,000 of supplies during July on account. Accounts payable are usually paid one-half in the month of purchase and one-half in the following month. The accounts payable balance on July 1, 2003, is $35,000.
d. Salaries and wages paid during July will be approximately $600,000. (Ignore income and other tax withholdings.)
e. Depreciation on the hospital and equipment for July will be $100,000.
f. A short-term bank loan of $80,000 (including interest) will be repaid in July.
g. All other cash expenses for July will total $56,000.

Prepare the hospital's July cash budget.

EXERCISE 5-11

CASH BUDGETING

Medical Supplies, Inc., purchases first-aid items from large wholesalers. Medical Supplies then assembles and sells first-aid kits to businesses and contracts to maintain the first-aid kits. You have been asked to prepare a cash budget for January. The following information is provided:

a. Cash in the bank on January 1 is $33,000.
b. Actual sales for October, November, December, and projected sales for January are as follows:

	October	November	December	January
Cash	$12,000	$11,500	$ 8,200	$12,500
Credit	31,000	29,400	32,000	28,000

Payments on credit sales are received 50% in the month of sale, 31% in the month following the sale, and 15% and 4% in the second and third months, respectively, following the sale.

c. Total administrative and selling expenses (all cash) are $25,000.
d. Purchases are always paid 30 days after delivery. Purchases for October, November, and December were $28,000, $39,000, and $29,500, respectively.
e. Cash dividends of $22,000 are paid.
f. Any cash excess is used to purchase 30-day government securities, and any cash deficiency is compensated by short-term borrowing.
g. Management desires a minimum balance of $9,000 in the bank.

Prepare a cash budget for the month of January.

EXERCISE 5-12

CASH BUDGETING (MERCHANDISING COMPANY)

Whitlock, Inc., buys hardware parts from various manufacturers and sells them to retail stores. Management is currently trying to prepare a cash budget for August and has the following information available:

a. The cash balance on August 1 is $25,000.
b. Actual sales for June and July and projected sales for August are as follows:

	June	July	August
Cash sales	$ 30,000	$ 45,000	$ 50,000
Credit sales	100,000	120,000	130,000

Credit sales are collected 63% during the month of sale, 26% during the month following the sale, and 11% during the second month following the sale.

c. Whitlock's actual purchases for June and July and its projected purchases for August are as follows:

	June	July	August
Cash purchases	$10,000	$20,000	$25,000
Credit purchases	40,000	50,000	60,000

All accounts payable are paid in the month following the purchase.

d. Total administrative and selling expenses (including $14,000 depreciation) for August are expected to be $105,000.

e. Whitlock expects to pay a $26,000 dividend to stockholders and to purchase, for cash, a $25,000 piece of land during August.

f. Cash on hand should never drop below $25,000.

1. Prepare Whitlock's August cash budget, assuming that the company borrows any amounts needed to meet its minimum desired balance.
2. **Interpretive Question:** What types of expenses other than depreciation would be excluded from a cash budget?

EXERCISE 5-13

BUDGETING FOR A SERVICE COMPANY

Dr. Dawn Gifford is a new dentist specializing in treating children under the age of 18. Dr. Gifford has two primary sources of revenues: (1) fees from regular dental work (checkups, cleanings, fillings, etc.) and (2) fees from specialized dental reconstructive surgery. Last year, Gifford earned an average of $75 per patient visit from regular customers and $800 per surgery. The following operating expenses were incurred last year in running the office:

Variable operating expenses:	
Dental supplies (per patient)	$ 10
Hospital surgery room rental (per surgery)	200
Annual fixed operating expenses:	
Office manager's salary	$18,000
Dental hygienist's salary	26,000
Utilities	3,600
Rental of office space	12,000
Depreciation expense on office equipment*	20,000
Liability insurance	48,000
Other expenses	9,600

*Total equipment cost, $200,000; depreciated over 10 years on a straight-line basis.

Last year Dr. Gifford treated an average of 200 patients per month and performed an average of eight surgeries per month. She expects to increase the number of patients serviced by 10% this coming year and increase the number of surgeries by two per month. She also expects the average patient fee to be $80 and the average surgical fee to be $850. Gifford expects the variable expenses to remain constant this year, but is expecting to raise the manager's salary by 5% and the hygienist's by 15%. She thinks the other expenses will stay about the same.

Based on these data (and ignoring payroll and income taxes):

1. What was the operating profit (loss) for last year?
2. Prepare a revenue budget, operating expense budget, and cash budget for this coming year.

expanded material

EXERCISE 5-14

PRO-FORMA INCOME STATEMENT

Gold Manufacturing, Inc., is a manufacturer of electric pencil sharpeners. The following is information regarding Gold Manufacturing for the fiscal year-end, May 31, 2003:

Beginning finished goods inventory	$ 55,000
Ending finished goods inventory	42,000
Interest expense	28,000
Selling and administrative expenses	72,000
Sales revenue	425,000
Direct materials used	52,000
Direct labor	63,000
Manufacturing overhead	32,000

Assume a tax rate of 33%. Prepare a pro-forma income statement for the year ended May 31, 2003, for Gold Manufacturing, Inc.

EXERCISE 5-15

PRO-FORMA INCOME STATEMENT

Silver Company has asked you to prepare a pro-forma income statement for the coming year. The following information is available:

Expected sales revenue	$1,240,000
Manufacturing costs:	
Variable cost of goods sold	625,000
Fixed overhead	125,000
Selling expenses:	
Variable expenses	140,000
Fixed expenses	45,000
Administrative expenses:	
Variable expenses	45,000
Fixed expenses	160,000
Other:	
Interest expense	28,000
Income tax rate	35%

Prepare a pro-forma contribution margin income statement for Silver Company.

EXERCISE 5-16

PRO-FORMA STATEMENT OF CASH FLOWS

The accountants at Bryant Hardware Company are currently preparing the pro-forma statement of cash flows for August. In getting ready to prepare the statement, they have the following information available:

Dividends to be paid in August	$ 7,500
Bonds to be issued in August	44,000
Equipment to be sold in August	27,000
Repayment of short-term loans in August	24,000
Depreciation expense during August	6,000
Expected August net income	15,000
Expected changes in current assets and liabilities during August:	
Accounts receivable increase	3,500
Accounts payable decrease	2,750
Increase in inventory	4,200
Decrease in income taxes payable	8,400

Prepare Bryant's pro-forma statement of cash flows.

EXERCISE 5-17

PRO-FORMA INCOME STATEMENT AND BALANCE SHEET (SERVICE INDUSTRY)

Horrock's, Inc., is a small engineering corporation that surveys land for development. The company has grown rapidly over the past few years, and management has to decide whether to hire new engineers and open new offices. To assess future growth, the company's accountant has gathered budgeted information for the coming year, 2003:

Ending common stock balance	$ 48,000
Beginning retained earnings balance	34,000
Ending accounts payable balance	6,000
Ending equipment balance	159,000
Ending accumulated depreciation balance	24,000
Ending accounts receivable balance	19,500
Ending cash balance	18,000
Interest expense	3,000
Salary expense	105,000
Other expenses (including depreciation)	37,500
Service revenue	300,000
Income tax rate	33%

Income taxes due on the coming year's net income will be paid during 2004. Dividends of $70,000 are to be declared and paid during 2003.

1. Prepare a pro-forma income statement and balance sheet for 2003 from which the company president can make expansion decisions.
2. **Interpretive Question:** On the basis of this information, is the company very profitable? How should this level of profits affect its expansion plans?

EXERCISE 5-18

STATIC VERSUS FLEXIBLE BUDGETING—PERFORMANCE REPORTS (SERVICE FIRM)

Flannery Muffler Shop has budgeted to repair 10,000 mufflers during 2003. Each repair job takes 1½ hours, and employees are paid $12 per hour. During 2003, Flannery actually repaired 9,425 mufflers, and the salary expense amounted to $179,000.

1. Assuming a static budget, use the information to prepare a performance report for Flannery Muffler Shop for 2003.
2. Assuming a flexible budget, use the information to prepare a performance report for Flannery Muffler Shop for 2003.
3. **Interpretive Question:** The manager of the muffler shop believes he deserves a bonus because the actual salary expense ($179,000) was less than budgeted. Do you agree? Explain.

EXERCISE 5-19

FLEXIBLE BUDGETS (SERVICE FIRM)

Outdoors Unlimited operates a fishing lodge in northern Canada. The following cost information has been developed by the company's accountant:

Fixed costs:	
Salaries	$68,000
Mortgage payments	24,000
Taxes	4,000
Other	3,000
Variable costs (per guest):	
Fishing tackle	$20
Food	80
Other	16

1. In planning for its 2003 summer season, Outdoors Unlimited does not know exactly how many guests to expect and, hence, how much to charge per guest. Prepare a flexible budget showing expected total costs at 200, 300, 400, and 500 guests.
2. Assume that Outdoors Unlimited conservatively estimates 300 guests for the year. If it wants to earn profits of $100,000 for the 300 guests, how much should it charge per guest?

problems

PROBLEM 5-1

PERSONAL BUDGETING

Ben Fleming has just received a job offer of $35,000 salary per year plus overtime pay, which will amount to 10% of his salary. Ben estimates his living costs as follows:

Federal, state, and FICA taxes amount to	35% of income
Rent	$550/month
Car payment	$210/month
IRA	$1,500/year
Other savings	4% of net take-home pay
Utilities	$90/month
Gas and maintenance—automobile	$130/month
Insurance	$75/month
Food	$240/month
Entertainment	$170/month
Clothing	$80/month

Required:

1. Prepare a budget for the year. Assume Ben starts his job on January 1.
2. Is Ben's offer sufficient to meet his projected expenses?
3. Ben has always dreamed of going to Africa to photograph wildlife. The trip will cost $5,000. How long will it take Ben to save for the trip? (Ignore interest earnings, and assume that he has no savings at the present time.)

PROBLEM 5-2

PERSONAL BUDGETING

Carol Baum is an advertising specialist for Success Advertising, Inc. Her annual salary is $37,500, of which 20% is withheld for federal income taxes, 7% for state income taxes, 7.65% for FICA taxes, and 5% for a tax-sheltered annuity. She estimates that her monthly expenses are approximately as follows:

Rent	$ 475
Automobile payment	250
Food	240
Automobile gasoline and maintenance	120
Utilities	70
Clothing	100
Entertainment	150
Miscellaneous	130
Total monthly expenses	$1,535

Required:

1. Prepare Carol's monthly budget, assuming that the car payments will continue for about three years.
2. Assume that Carol would like to accumulate savings of $12,000 in order to take an extended leave from her job. This will allow her to travel and take courses as a way of generating some fresh ideas she can use in creating new approaches to advertising. How long will it take her to save the needed amount? (Ignore interest earnings, and assume that she has no savings at the present time.)
3. **Interpretive Question:** If Carol asked you for advice on how she might reduce her expenses, what would you suggest?

PROBLEM 5-3

PRODUCTION BUDGETING

Rockville Cabinet Company makes and sells two products: two-drawer and four-drawer cabinets. The sales forecasts for these cabinets for the next four quarters are as follows:

	Two-Drawer Cabinets	Four-Drawer Cabinets
1st quarter	30	30
2nd quarter	50	60
3rd quarter	90	76
4th quarter	96	48
Total	266	214

On January 1, Rockville has a stock of 40 completed two-drawer cabinets and 30 four-drawer cabinets. Experience indicates that Rockville must maintain an inventory equal to one-half of the next quarter's sales.

Required:

1. How many two-drawer and four-drawer cabinets must be produced during each of the first three quarters to meet sales and inventory demands?
2. **Interpretive Question:** Assume Rockville is a wholesale merchandising company instead of a manufacturing company. How would the budget information provided in (1) change?

PROBLEM 5-4

PRODUCTION AND DIRECT MATERIALS BUDGET

Chandler Manufacturing Company makes two products: widgets and gidgets. The following information is available on May 1:

a. Direct materials needed to make a widget: six units of X, three units of Y. Direct materials needed to make a gidget: two units of X, six units of Y.

b. Number of units available at beginning of May:

Direct material X	72 units
Direct material Y	43 units
Finished widgets	12
Finished gidgets	15

c. Expected sales during May:

Widgets	100
Gidgets	95

d. Desired levels of ending inventory:

Direct material X	70 units
Direct material Y	35 units
Widgets	11
Gidgets	13

e. Cost of direct materials:

Direct material X	$3 per unit
Direct material Y	$2 per unit

Required: Prepare a production budget and a direct materials budget for Chandler Company for the month of May.

PROBLEM 5-5

COMPUTATION OF UNIT COSTS

Jersey Candy Company makes and sells two kinds of candy bars: chocolate almond and coconut. During the past several years, the company has kept accurate records of costs and resource requirements and has determined that the following are needed to make the candy bars:

One Box of 24 Chocolate Almond Bars	Cost
Chocolate (1½ pounds)	$3.00/pound
Almonds (1 pound)	$5.00/pound
Sugar (2 pounds)	$0.50/pound
Direct labor (20 minutes)	$9.00/hour
Manufacturing overhead (20 minutes)	$7.00/direct labor hour

One Box of 24 Coconut Bars	Cost
Chocolate (1 pound)	$3.00/pound
Coconut (1¼ pounds)	$2.00/pound
Sugar (1¾ pounds)	$0.50/pound
Direct labor (30 minutes)	$9.00/hour
Manufacturing overhead (30 minutes)	$7.00/direct labor hour

Required:

1. Compute the unit cost of making a box of each type of candy bar.
2. If management wants to mark up each box of candy 30% to cover other costs and earn a profit, how much should be charged for a box of each type of candy bar?

PROBLEM 5-6

UNIFYING CONCEPTS: PRODUCTION AND DIRECT MATERIALS BUDGETS AND COST OF GOODS SOLD COMPUTATIONS

San Antonio Furniture Company makes two products: bookshelves and rocking chairs. The following information is available for September:

a. Production requirements:

	Bookshelves	Rocking Chairs
Materials needed:		
Wood	100 board feet at $0.90/ft.	90 board feet at $0.90/ft.
Stain	2 gallons at $9/gallon	3 gallons at $9/gallon
Bolts, nuts, etc.	1 dozen at $1.50/dozen	1½ dozen at $1.50/dozen
Direct labor	12 hours at $8.50/hour	10 hours at $8.50/hour
Variable manufacturing overhead	12 hours at $4/ direct labor hour	10 hours at $4/ direct labor hour
Fixed manufacturing overhead	$16 per unit	$15 per unit

b. Levels of inventories:

	Actual Beginning Inventory	Desired Ending Inventory
Wood	1,100 board feet	1,000 board feet
Stain	11 gallons	12 gallons
Bolts, nuts, etc.	15 dozen	9 dozen
Finished bookshelves	3	5
Finished rocking chairs	6	7

c. Total actual resources used in production during September:

Direct materials	$4,259
Direct labor	3,850
Variable manufacturing overhead	1,500
Fixed manufacturing overhead	700

Required:

1. Prepare the production budget, assuming that the company expects to sell 40 bookshelves and 50 rocking chairs in September.
2. Based on the production budget and the desired ending inventory level, prepare the direct materials usage and purchases budget for September.
3. If the company actually sold the number of bookshelves and rocking chairs projected, how much would the cost of goods sold be for September?

PROBLEM 5-7

UNIFYING CONCEPTS: SALES, CASH COLLECTIONS, PRODUCTION, DIRECT MATERIALS, AND DIRECT LABOR BUDGETS

The following information is available for Raleigh Company:

Expected sales volume:	
April	1,600 units
May	1,500 units
June	1,750 units
Selling price per unit	$12
Accounts receivable balance, April 1	$6,000
Desired finished goods inventory, June 30	200 units
Beginning finished goods inventory, April 1	210 units
Direct materials needed per unit	5 pounds
Desired direct materials inventory, June 30	550 pounds
Beginning direct materials inventory, April 1	420 pounds
Total direct labor time per finished product	2 hours
Direct materials cost per pound	$0.50
Direct labor cost per hour	$8

Additional information:

a. Each month 70% of sales is collected by month-end; the remaining 30% is collected in the following month.
b. The desired finished goods inventory every month is 20% of the next month's sales.
c. The desired direct materials inventory every month is 10% of the next month's production needs.

Required:

1. Prepare sales budgets for April, May, and June (in dollars).
2. Prepare cash collection budgets for April, May, and June (in dollars). Assume that all sales are on credit.
3. Prepare production budgets for April, May, and June (in units).
4. Prepare direct materials budgets for April, May, and June (in dollars).
5. Prepare direct labor budgets for April, May, and June (in dollars).

PROBLEM 5-8

Spread-Sheet Software

UNIFYING CONCEPTS: SALES, CASH COLLECTIONS, AND PURCHASES BUDGETS

The following information is available for Durham Company, a merchandising retail company:

Expected sales volume:	
April	3,200 units
May	3,000 units
June	3,500 units
Selling price per unit	$25
Accounts receivable balance, April 1	$12,000
Desired ending inventory, June 30	650 units
Beginning inventory, April 1	420 units

Additional information:

a. Each month 70% of sales is collected by month-end; the remaining 30% is collected in the following month.
b. The desired inventory every month is 20% of the next month's sales.

Required:

1. Prepare sales budgets for April, May, and June (in dollars).
2. Prepare cash collection budgets for April, May, and June (in dollars). Assume that all sales are on credit.
3. Prepare purchases budgets for April, May, and June (in units).

PROBLEM 5-9

CASH BUDGETING (MANUFACTURING COMPANY)

Hare Manufacturing Company makes wax for automobiles. As part of overall planning, a cash budget is prepared quarterly each year. You have been asked to assist in preparing the cash budget for the fourth quarter of the company's fiscal year. The following information is available:

a. Sales:

Third quarter (actual)	$180,000
Fourth quarter (expected)	175,000

All sales are made on account, with 70% collected in the quarter in which the sales are made and 30% collected during the following quarter.

b. Materials purchases are scheduled as follows:

Third quarter (actual)	$90,000
Fourth quarter (expected)	80,000

Materials are purchased on account and paid for at the rate of 80% in the quarter of purchase and 20% in the following quarter.

c. Direct labor and manufacturing overhead costs (including $6,000 of depreciation) are expected to be $45,000 and $21,000, respectively, during the fourth quarter.
d. Selling and administrative expenses are expected to total $27,000 during the fourth quarter, including $2,000 of depreciation.
e. Plans have been made to purchase, for cash, $15,000 of equipment during the fourth quarter.
f. The cash balance at the beginning of the quarter is $16,000. The company can borrow money in $1,000 multiples at 12% interest from a local bank. The bank assesses interest for a full quarter, both for the quarter in which the money is borrowed and for the quarter in which it is repaid. All interest is paid at the time of note repayment. Hare ran short of cash during the third quarter and had to borrow $8,000 from the bank. Hare wishes to maintain a minimum cash balance of $16,000.

Required: Prepare a schedule showing the cash budget and financing needs of Hare Manufacturing Company for the fourth quarter.

PROBLEM 5-10

CASH BUDGETING (MERCHANDISING COMPANY)

Keven Johnson, owner of Meyers Department Store, is negotiating a $50,000, 15%, four-month loan from the Lee County National Bank, effective October 1, 2003. The bank loan officer has requested that Meyers prepare a cash budget for each of the next four months as evidence of its ability to repay the loan. The following information is available as of September 30, 2003:

Cash on hand	$ 4,500
Accounts receivable	48,750
Inventory	32,000
Accounts payable	72,250

a. The accounts payable are for September merchandise purchases and operating expenses and will all be paid in October. Sales forecasts for the next few months are October, $110,000; November, $150,000; December, $200,000; January, $100,000; February, $70,000.

b. Collections on sales are usually made at the rate of 20% during the month of the sale, 60% during the month following the sale, and 16% during the second month after the sale. Four percent of accounts receivable are written off as uncollectible. Of the $48,750 of accounts receivable at September 30, $32,500 will be collected in October, and $16,250 will be collected in November. Cost of goods sold is 60% of sales, with all purchases paid for in the month following purchase. Ending inventory should always equal the cost of the goods that will be sold during the next month. Operating expenses are $12,000 a month plus 5% of sales, all paid in the month following their incurrence.

Required: Prepare a cash budget showing receipts and disbursements for October, November, December, and January. Also prepare supporting schedules for cash collections, purchases, and operating expenses. Assume that the loan plus interest will be paid on January 31.

PROBLEM 5-11 CASH BUDGETING

Athlete World is a sporting goods store. The following data are for use in preparing its forecast of cash needs for June:

a. Current assets (May 31):

Cash	$22,000
Inventory	17,500
Accounts receivable	29,400
Property, plant, and equipment	90,000
Accounts payable (merchandise purchases only)	13,100
Recent and estimated future sales:	
May	49,000
June	57,000
July	52,000

b. Sales are made 60% on credit and 40% for cash. All credit sales are collected in the month following the sale.

c. Athlete World's June expenses are estimated to be:

Salaries and wages expense	20% of sales
Rent expense	4% of sales
All other cash expenses	6% of sales
Depreciation expense	$600
Gross margin	40% of sales

d. Athlete World buys all its inventory from companies on the West Coast and wants to maintain an inventory level equal to one-half of the next month's sales. Payments for merchandise are made 50% during the month of purchase and 50% in the next month.

e. Other cash expenditures planned for June are:
   1. The purchase of $8,000 of furniture.
   2. The payment of $5,000 of dividends.

f. Athlete World desires to maintain a minimum cash balance of $10,000. The store has an arrangement with a local bank whereby it can borrow money in multiples of $1,000. Interest is charged on all loans at an annual rate of 10% and is assessed for a full quarter both in the quarter in which the money is borrowed and in the quarter in which the money is repaid. Interest is paid when the loan is repaid.

Required: Prepare Athlete World's cash budget for June.

PROBLEM 5-12 BUDGETING FOR A SERVICE COMPANY

Riverside Country Club has approximately 435 members. Each member has paid a $10,000 initiation fee and pays $100 a month in dues to remain an active member of the club. The club offers golf, tennis, and food and beverage services. The club is essentially run on a cash basis. Operating data for 2002 are as follows:

Riverside Country Club
Operating Data
For the Year 2002

Revenues:		
Dues[1]	$742,000	
Guest fees[2]	6,500	
Golf revenues	455,000	
Tennis revenues	145,000	
Food and beverage	325,000	
Miscellaneous	2,500	$1,676,000
Expenses:		
Golf course	$395,000	
Tennis courts	170,000	
Food and bar	272,000	
Administration and maintenance[3]	515,000	
Interest on debt[4]	50,000	
Miscellaneous	27,000	(1,429,000)
Net operating profit		$ 247,000

[1]Dues (410 × $1,200 = $492,000; 25 new members × $10,000 = $250,000).
[2]Guest fees (130 × $50 = $6,500).
[3]Maintenance includes $125,000 depreciation on facilities.
[4]Interest ($500,000 × 0.10 × 1 year).

Assume the following additional facts for the year 2003:

a. There are 425 members paying dues, as well as 10 additional new members.
b. Guest fees are 110% of 2002 fees.
c. Golf revenues are 125% of 2002 revenues.
d. Tennis revenues are 90% of 2002 revenues (due to courts being closed for one month).
e. Food and beverage revenues are the same as 2002.
f. Operating expenses (golf, tennis, and food and beverage) are up 5%.
g. Administration and maintenance will increase $40,000 due to expected repairs.
h. Principal payment of $50,000 during 2003 will reduce interest expense by 10% for 2003.
i. Miscellaneous revenues will stay the same; miscellaneous expenses are expected to be $25,000.

Required:

1. Prepare an annual budget for Riverside for the year 2003.
2. What is the expected cash flow for Riverside for the year 2003?
3. **Interpretive Question:** Is Riverside in better shape financially in 2003 as compared to 2002? What areas of concern do you see?

expanded material

PROBLEM 5-13

UNIFYING CONCEPTS: THE PRO-FORMA INCOME STATEMENT, BALANCE SHEET, AND STATEMENT OF CASH FLOWS

Alex Corporation makes trailers for trucks. During the past few days, the company's accountants have been preparing the master budget for 2003. To date, they have gathered the following projected data:

For the Year Ended December 31, 2003:

Sales revenue	$10,127,200
Variable selling expenses	448,000
Variable administrative expenses	672,000
Interest expense	67,200
Cost of goods sold (variable costs only)	5,600,000
Fixed manufacturing expenses	784,000
Fixed administrative expenses	492,000
Fixed selling expenses	336,000

Account Balances at December 31, 2003:

Cash	$448,000
Accounts receivable	168,000
Land	417,200
Buildings	504,000
Equipment	358,400
Accumulated depreciation—equipment	89,600
Accumulated depreciation—buildings	80,000
Direct materials inventory	106,400
Finished goods inventory	117,600
Accounts payable	45,240
Common stock	700,000
Retained earnings	?
Paid-in capital in excess of par	40,000
Income taxes payable	200,000

Other Information:

Dividends to be declared and paid during 2003	$600,000
Income tax rate	33%

In addition, last year's balance sheet was as follows:

Alex Corporation
Balance Sheet
December 31, 2002

Assets		
Cash		$ 189,600
Accounts receivable		45,400
Direct materials inventory		90,000
Finished goods inventory		123,200
Land		336,000
Buildings	$448,000	
Less accumulated depreciation	(50,000)	398,000
Equipment	$324,800	
Less accumulated depreciation	(60,000)	264,800
Total assets		$1,447,000
Liabilities and Stockholders' Equity		
Liabilities:		
Accounts payable	$ 75,000	
Income taxes payable	225,000	
Total liabilities		$ 300,000
Stockholders' Equity:		
Common stock	$700,000	
Paid-in capital in excess of par, common stock	40,000	
Retained earnings	407,000	
Total stockholders' equity		1,147,000
Total liabilities and stockholders' equity		$1,447,000

Required:

1. Prepare a pro-forma income statement for 2003 (contribution margin approach).
2. Prepare a pro-forma balance sheet as of December 31, 2003.
3. Prepare a pro-forma statement of cash flows for 2003.

PROBLEM 5-14

PRO-FORMA INCOME STATEMENT AND BALANCE SHEET

Style Right Company makes hair dryers. During the past few days, its accountants have been preparing the master budget for the coming year, 2003. To date, they have gathered the following projected data:

Sales revenue (at $20 per unit)	$281,750
Variable selling expenses	17,250
Variable administrative expenses	40,250
Interest expense (not included in selling and administrative expenses)	1,725
Cost of goods sold (includes only variable costs)	103,500
Ending cash balance	30,475
Ending accounts receivable balance	47,150
Ending land balance	24,150
Ending buildings balance	71,300
Ending equipment balance	24,150
Ending accumulated depreciation—buildings balance	47,150
Ending accumulated depreciation—equipment balance	9,200
Ending direct materials inventory balance	16,100
Ending finished goods inventory balance	25,300
Ending accounts payable balance	6,900
Ending common stock balance	32,200
Retained earnings balance, January 1	64,050
Balance in paid-in capital in excess of par account	23,000
Fixed selling expenses	23,000
Fixed administrative expenses	28,750
Fixed manufacturing overhead	11,150
Income tax rate	35%

Required:

1. Prepare a pro-forma income statement (contribution margin approach) and balance sheet for the coming year. Any income taxes owed on the coming year's net income will be paid the following year.
2. By approximately how much would Style Right's profits increase if another 3,000 units were produced and sold for $20 each?

PROBLEM 5-15

PRO-FORMA STATEMENT OF CASH FLOWS

The accountants at Toledo Department Store are preparing the pro-forma statement of cash flows for 2003. The following information is available:

Expected net income	$70,000
Dividends to be paid	22,000
Equipment to be purchased	34,000
Expected short-term borrowing	8,000
Expected long-term borrowing	24,000
Expected depreciation expense for 2003	15,000
Expected issuance of common stock	80,000
Expected purchase of a new plant	71,000
Expected changes in current assets and liabilities during 2003:	
Increase in accounts receivable	$ 900
Increase in accounts payable	1,000
Increase in inventory	1,000
Decrease in income taxes payable	1,800

Required: Prepare the pro-forma statement of cash flows for Toledo Department Store.

PROBLEM 5-16

STATIC VERSUS FLEXIBLE BUDGETING (SERVICE FIRM)

Wasatch Medical Clinic has three doctors on staff. The clinic's budget for 2003 is as follows:

Wasatch Medical Clinic
Budget for the Year Ended December 31, 2003

Expected number of patient visits		26,000
Average charge per patient		× $25
Total revenues		$650,000
Budgeted costs:		
Variable costs:		
Supplies for each patient ($2 × 26,000)		$ 52,000
Fixed costs:		
Utilities	$ 2,400	
Rent	9,600	
Nurses' salaries	90,000	
Malpractice insurance	150,000	
Equipment leases	25,000	
Other	30,000	
Total fixed costs		307,000
Total budgeted costs		$359,000
Expected income		$291,000
Number of doctors on staff		÷ 3
Expected income per doctor		$ 97,000

Required:

1. Is this a static or flexible budget?
2. Prepare a flexible budget showing expected income per doctor at 22,000, 26,000, 30,000, and 34,000 total patient visits.
3. **Interpretive Question:** Why does the expected income per doctor increase so dramatically as the number of patient visits increases?

PROBLEM 5-17

STATIC VERSUS FLEXIBLE BUDGETING (SERVICE FIRM)

Peterson Management, Inc., is a small firm that sponsors time-management seminars in hotels throughout the country. It sponsors 20 two-day seminars during the year for a tuition fee of $200 per student. The following is a budget for a single seminar:

Peterson Management, Inc.
Budget Per Seminar

Expected enrollment	40
Tuition per person	× $200
Revenue per seminar	$8,000
Variable costs:	
Catering ($25 per person)	$1,000
Books and handouts ($10 per person)	400
Fixed costs:	
Airfare	425
Hotel rental fee	600
Advertising	1,000
Other	300
Total costs	$3,725
Expected income	$4,275

Required:

1. Bruce Peterson, owner of the company and the speaker at the seminars, would be pleased with an income of $4,275 per seminar. With 20 seminars per year, the company's annual

income would be $85,500. He is concerned, however, that every seminar may not have 40 participants. Prepare a flexible budget, showing what annual income would be if 10, 20, 40, or 50 people enroll in each seminar.

2. What is the break-even point per seminar in number of participants?

competency enhancement opportunities

- Analyzing Real Company Information
- International Case
- Ethics Case
- Writing Assignment
- The Debate
- Internet Search

The following additional assignments provide opportunities for students to develop critical thinking, ethical perspectives, oral and written communication skills, experience with electronic research, and teamwork through group and business activities.

ANALYZING REAL COMPANY INFORMATION

• *Analyzing 5-1 (Microsoft)*

Auditors are extremely reluctant to publish any projections of future financial performance for the companies they are auditing. **DELOITTE & TOUCHE LLP** obviously has made no such predictions in its audit of **MICROSOFT**'s 1999 financial performance (the annual report in Appendix A). However, the Management's Discussion of the Income Statement results, in the section titled "Outlook: Issues and Uncertainties," provide some hints about what executives may expect to affect future revenues. Elsewhere in the management discussion are insights useful in predicting future operating expenses, interest income, and income taxes. These discussions can be extremely useful to investors who are trying to understand what Microsoft plans to do in 2000. Essentially, these investors need to put together their own pro-forma financial statements on Microsoft for use in planning, controlling, and evaluating their investment decisions in this company.

Consider the 1999 income statement on the following page and use the information provided in Microsoft's Management Discussion of "Outlook: Issues and Uncertainties" to prepare your own pro-forma 2000 income statement for Microsoft. Be sure to read and consider each item in the management discussion relating to Microsoft's income statement in the annual report in Appendix A. You may also want to consider the 1997 and 1998 revenue and cost trends from the income statement published in this same annual report. For each line item (i.e., for each revenue and cost category), briefly defend the budget number you chose to use.

	1999
Revenue	$19,747
Operating expenses:	
Cost of revenue	$ 2,814
Research and development	2,970
Sales and marketing	3,231
General and administrative	689
Other expenses	115
Total operating expenses	$ 9,819
Operating income	$ 9,928
Investment income	1,803
Gains on sale of Softimage Inc.	160
Income before income taxes	$11,891
Provision for income taxes	4,106
Net income	$ 7,785

• *Analyzing 5-2 (Participative Living, Inc.)*

Participative Living, Inc. (a fictitious name) is an actual charitable organization in a medium-size community in Canada. It was organized by parents of disabled adults to provide accommodation and training for severely disabled adults in the community. With the help of the Ministry of Community and Social Services, the parents eventually organized six different homes, each with two to four residents. In addition to the six homes, Participative Living also had an employment and education program that provided training and assistance for residents seeking employment or educational opportunities. Overall, the organization had eight divisions composed of six homes, the employment and education program, and an administrative program. A supervisor who reports to the Participative Living executive team staffs each division. The executive team, in turn, reports to a volunteer board of directors composed of 12 people from the community.

Participative Living is a not-for-profit organization. Hence, while surpluses and deficits are occasionally expected, each division is expected to break even each operating period. Seven of the eight divisions are established as break-even operations, with responsibility for both revenues and expenses. The main revenue source is the Ontario government, through the Ministry of Community and Social Services, which provides all funding necessary to support each home as well as the employment and education program. All costs of Participative Living's administrative division in excess of any donations from the community are allocated to its other seven divisions. The Ministry follows a procedure of disbursing operating funds for all social service agencies under its direction based on annual operating budgets submitted to the Ministry. Generally, the Ministry is not concerned about whether an individual budget item was overspent as long as the overall spending is within the approved budget. As a result, it became a common practice among agencies to transfer expenses from one budget line to another and, in the case of Participative Living, to transfer expenses from one division to another depending on which division had excess budgeted funds. As with most government organizations, the Ministry's administrative process of reviewing and approving a new home for Participative Living is often quite slow. As long as the Ministry is holding up the establishment of a proposed new home, it provides significant interest payments to Participative Living. The Ministry was making large interest payments during the first few months of Participative Living's 2000 fiscal year (which ended on March 31, 2000) while the organization waited for government approval and funding of the sixth group home.

In November 1999, Mr. Brad Dunford, the executive director of Participative Living, Inc., was reviewing the financial statements for the first seven months of the 2000 fiscal year. He was puzzled about how the agency could suddenly be $50,000 over budget in salaries and benefits when just last month the statements indicated that spending was slightly under budget.

1. As you review operating results for the last seven months at Participative Living, Inc., what problems do you foresee?
2. Consider the style of management and management accounting for this not-for-profit organization, as well as its relationship with the Ministry of Community and Social Services. What aspects of the way business is conducted here do you think have led to the current situation?

Participative Living, Inc.
Operating Results
For the Seven Months Ended October 31, 1999

YTD	Admin. Costs	Admin. Budget	Employ. and Edu. Costs	Employ. and Edu. Budget	Group Homes Costs	Group Homes Budget	Total Actual	Total Budget*	% of Budget
Revenues:									
Ministry**	$ —	$ —	$206,315	$297,675	$521,841	$476,714	$728,156	$774,389	94.0%
Interest	20,943	—	—	—	—	—	20,943	—	0%
Donations	1,567	—	—	—	—	—	1,567	—	0%
Total revenues	$ 22,510	$ —	$206,315	$297,675	$521,841	$476,714	$750,666	$774,389	96.9%
Expenses:									
Salaries	$ 59,029	$ 61,754	$141,034	$197,386	$434,014	$327,789	$634,077	$586,929	108.0%
Occupancy costs	10,392	12,264	39	2,205	61,598	68,761	72,029	83,230	86.5%
Services, supplies, and food	4,375	7,000	3,643	14,147	16,812	35,301	24,830	56,448	44.0%
Personal needs	—	—	3,077	—	35	26,327	3,112	26,327	11.8%
New furnishing and equip.	5	350	60	2,765	6,548	19,236	6,613	22,351	29.6%
Other expenses	1,176	4,669	197	7,707	15,681	7,868	17,054	20,244	84.2%
Travel and training	436	875	1,972	8,792	1,992	4,900	4,400	14,567	30.2%
Specific reimbursements	—	—	—	—	(32,119)	(35,707)	(32,119)	(35,707)	90.0%
Allocated admin. costs	(75,417)	(86,912)	56,293	64,673	19,123	22,239	(1)	—	0.0%
Total expenses	$ (4)	$ —	$206,315	$297,675	$523,684	$476,714	$729,995	$774,389	94.3%
Net surplus (deficit)	$ 22,514	$ —	$ —	$ —	$ (1,843)	$ —	$ 20,671	$ —	N/A

*Budget columns represent 7/12ths of the total annual budget (e.g., Participative Living is now seven months into its fiscal year).
**Ministry revenues are based on actual payments made by the Ministry. Total payments limited to maximum of total annual budget approved.

Source: Adapted from M. Heisz, "Participative Living, Inc.," *Journal of Accounting Case Research* 2(3), 1995, pp. 87–91. Permission to use has been granted by Captus Press, Inc. and the Accounting Education Resource Centre of The University of Lethbridge. [Journal Subscription: Captus Press Inc., York University Campus, 4700 Keele Street, North York, Ontario, M3J1P3, by calling (416) 736-5537, or by fax at (416) 736-5793, E-mail: info@captus.com, Internet: http://www.captus.com]

INTERNATIONAL CASE

• *It's Not Easy Being an Accountant in Poland*

The late 1980s and early 1990s were a very significant time for Eastern Europe. Several national boundaries and political ideologies, as well as the names of a few countries, changed during this period. Poland, like its neighbors, experienced tremendous upheaval in its political and economic climate during this time. In 1989, Poland changed to a non-Communist government and a free market economy. Since the end of World War II in 1945, Poland had been a centrally planned economy with government-enforced economic rules based on Marxism-Leninism. A Polish accountant's professional life during the 1945–1989 period was not very exciting. Most university-trained accountants worked in a state-owned enterprise, earning a reasonable salary. The work was not complicated, generally entailing only basic bookkeeping. Performing the accounting work essentially required simple mathematical operations. In addition, the nature of Poland's history since the fifteenth century had generally created disdain for business and profiteering in general. These traditions, coupled with the social environment engendered by a Marxist government, resulted in a serious lack of respect (sometimes bordering on distrust) for accountants, economists, and business managers from 1945 to 1989.

The failure of the Communist system in 1989 was the beginning of a new career stage for most accountants in Poland. The accounting profession suddenly became prestigious. It also became very challenging. Past accounting knowledge and skills were simply inadequate for the new economic situation, particularly for accountants moving out of state-owned enterprises and into the private sector. Business terminology, performance measures, and goals changed. Before 1989, the Communist regime promoted a view that everything a "capitalist" did was wrong and everything a Communist did was right. After the change in the political system, a lot of people began to see things in an opposite way; they expected that life in a capitalist country would be completely just and everyone would be employed with plenty of money. Obviously, life in a capitalist country is not perfect. There are problems, including injustice and unemployment. Complicating this reality, many people also carried over into the 1990s some of the prevailing pre-1989 attitudes that accountants and for-profit businesses were not trustworthy. Today Poland is making steady progress, but the accounting profession continues to face a number of challenges as attitudes and business processes are still in transition.

Assume that you have just been transferred by your U.S.-based company to an accounting or management position in the company's Poland division. Your assignment is to implement a traditional budgeting system (similar to the budget systems described in this chapter) in a large-scale manufacturing plant. Based on your understanding of Polish history and attitudes, what specific challenges would you expect to encounter in this new assignment? Do you have any ideas on how to handle these challenges?

Source: Adapted from P. Stec, "Mr. Kowalski: A Man Against All Odds," *Journal of Accounting Case Research* 2(3), 1995, pp. 52–54. Permission to use has been granted by Captus Press, Inc. and the Accounting Education Resource Centre of The University of Lethbridge. [Journal Subscription: Captus Press Inc., York University Campus, 4700 Keele Street, North York, Ontario, M3J1P3, by calling (416) 736-5537, or by fax at (416) 736-5793, E-mail: info@captus.com, Internet: http://www.captus.com]

ETHICS CASE

• *Skipper Enterprises*

You are the management accountant for Skipper Enterprises, a manufacturer of screen doors. Recently, one of the commissioned salespersons (your close personal friend) confided in you that a problem with the budgets is hurting the company's profitability.

Your friend explained that salespersons are paid a straight commission of $15 for every screen door they sell. If a salesperson meets the budgeted sales of 3,000 screen doors per year, he or she is paid an annual bonus of $5,000. Your friend stated that it is actually quite easy to reach budgeted sales of 3,000 doors by October or early November. Because there is no financial incentive to sell additional doors once the 3,000 sales level is met and the $5,000 bonus is earned, salespersons only "line up" sales for next year during the last couple of months of each year. In other words, instead of selling additional doors during November and December, they commit customers to buy during January of next year. This way, the doors count as next year's sales, ensuring that the commissioned salespersons are well on their way to meeting the sales budget for next year.

You realize the current bonus plan is causing two problems. First, valuable sales are being deferred each year because there is less incentive to sell near the end of the year. Second, customers are receiving less than optimum service because it can take as long as two months for customers to get their desired doors.

You don't know what to do with your new information.

1. Should you inform management that the sales plan is hurting company profits, or should you keep the information confidential as your friend requested?
2. If it becomes known that you had this information and didn't come forward, you could lose your job. On the other hand, you hate to lose a good friend. What should you do?

WRITING ASSIGNMENT

• *Preparing a Personal Budget*

Most people have the ability to spend more than they make. As a student, you probably fit in that category. This writing assignment requires you to prepare a personal budget for a one-month period. Forecast your income and expenses to determine what your cash position will be at the end of the month. If you forecast a cash shortage, what actions can you take to address the problem (e.g., increase income, reduce expenses, borrow money, etc.)? If you forecast a cash surplus, what are your options for the surplus?

THE DEBATE

• *The Hatchet Has Arrived!*

Assume that your local hospital has just hired a new COO (chief operating officer). Everyone in the hospital understands that the new COO was essentially hired to save the hospital. During the last five years, cost overruns have created tremendous spending deficits in the organization. The hospital is clearly headed for insolvency within three to five years if something isn't done. The new COO has a reputation as a focused manager, who is able to make difficult decisions. She doesn't waste any time proving her reputation in the new job. At the first meeting with the chief medical staff and administrators, the COO rolls out the new budget goals with the following statement:

> Everyone here knows that this hospital is in serious financial trouble, and it's not hard to understand why. After carefully reviewing cost reports for the last several years, it's obvious that there has been very little discipline in controlling costs. There are no improvement goals for cost savings, and no one is required to take responsibility when cost overruns occur. Looking at next quarter's operating budget doesn't give me much hope for improvement in this mess. Well, folks, that party is over! It's time to get to work saving this hospital. We will reconvene in one week; I expect each department head to provide a new departmental operating budget that demonstrates a reduction in costs that is equal to 5% of department revenues. Thereafter, until we turn this situation around, each new quarterly budget will reflect an *additional* decrease in operating costs equal to 2% of department revenues. Any questions?

There were no questions. Everyone filed out of the meeting in shocked silence. Five percent of revenues is a big number!

Divide your group into two teams and prepare a two-minute defense of your team's assigned position.

- One team represents "Support the COO!" A difficult situation requires a tough response. Defend the COO's new budget proposal. What should be the positive results in the hospital if the COO's budget instructions are fully implemented?
- The other team represents "Out with the new budget proposal!" Overreacting to a difficult situation only worsens the problem. Criticize the COO's new budget proposal. What could be the negative results in the hospital if the COO's budget instructions are fully implemented?

INTERNET SEARCH

• Using the Internet to Budget Personal Finances

There are a number of terrific tools on the Internet that can be very useful to you in managing your finances. For one example, go to http://www.financenter.com. Sometimes Web addresses change, so if this address does not work, access the Web site for this textbook (http://albrecht.swcollege.com) for an updated link. Once there, select the "Budgeting" link, then select "How much am I spending?" from the SmartCalcs™ menu. You will see here that FinanCenter provides a form on which you can enter your current income and budgeted expenditures, as well as your desired expenditures.

1. Complete the information on the input form, then hit the "Calculate" button. You should now learn whether your income is sufficient to handle your expenditures (actually, you probably already knew the answer to this question). Print out your budget.
2. Now go back to the input form and change the numbers in order to assess what might need to change in your future personal "operations." Put to-

gether a realistic budget. Try to create a little "extra" that can be used for investment. Note how the difference affects your long-term savings. When you're satisfied, print out your new budget.

3. Now that you have a better understanding of your cash budget, work through FinanCenter's tools to identify and answer another important personal finance and budgeting question for yourself. Go back to the SmartCalcs™ page and select an additional budgeting function to perform. When completed, list two important insights you learned about your personal budgeting process.

m3
part

Control

Traditional Cost Management

chapter

m6

learning objectives

After studying this chapter, you should be able to:

1 Outline the different cost flow patterns in manufacturing, merchandising, and service organizations and understand how these costs are reflected in the income statement and balance sheet.

2 Interpret a cost of goods manufactured schedule and analyze the levels of raw materials, work-in-process, and finished goods inventories in a manufacturing organization.

3 Understand how merchants manage cost information in their organizations.

4 Measure profitability and personnel utilization in a service organization.

expanded material

5 Calculate and interpret holding costs in merchandising and service businesses.

6 Use classic quantitative tools in inventory management (economic order quantity, reorder point, and safety stock).

Sam Walton didn't invent discount retailing, but the company he founded, **WAL-MART**, is now the undisputed giant in the field.[1] Sam Walton started his career in retailing at a **J.C. PENNEY** store in Des Moines, Iowa. Sam was a good salesperson, though he disliked the bookkeeping that went along with the job: "[I] couldn't stand to leave a new customer waiting while I fiddled with paperwork on a sale I'd already made."

After World War II, Sam borrowed $20,000 from his father-in-law and bought a variety store in Newport, Arkansas. By 1962, Sam Walton had built a chain of 16 variety stores located in Missouri, Arkansas, and Kansas. By this time, however, Walton had become convinced that there were big opportunities in opening discount retail locations in the smaller U.S. towns and cities that were being overlooked by the traditional retailers such as **SEARS**. Walton pitched his idea to a couple of retail chains, but he couldn't generate any interest. He finally had to fund the start-up of his first discount store with his own money, putting up 95% of the financing, with another 3% coming from his skeptical brother Bud and 2% from the person he hired to manage the store. On July 2, 1962, this first Wal-Mart opened its doors—the first of what has now grown into an international network of 2,985 stores (as of January 31, 2000).

fyi

Two other well-known discount retailers also began operations in 1962: **KMART** and **TARGET**.

The crucial idea behind discount retailing is that lower prices will lead to a large enough increase in sales volume to make up for the fact that a smaller profit is made on each sale. As the discount retailing industry has expanded and become more competitive, Wal-Mart has had to be ever more aggressive in cutting its profit margins in order to keep its prices low. For example, in 1980 Wal-Mart's gross profit percentage was 27%; by 1989, it had dropped to 23%, and by 2000, to 21%. For a company wrestling with tightening margins, inventory control is a crucial part of operations. Wal-Mart leased its first computer, an IBM 360, in 1969 in order to track the inventory flow at its new distribution center in Bentonville, Arkansas. Ever since, Wal-Mart has been a leader in using information technology to monitor and manage its inventory. In the late 1980s, Wal-Mart was a leader in implementing Electronic Data Interchange (EDI), which involves the electronic transfer of invoices, purchase orders, and shipping notices, thus speeding up the communication between Wal-Mart and its suppliers. Beyond this, Wal-Mart's "Retail Link" system now gives vendors access to Wal-Mart's own store-by-store sales information in real time, so that the vendors themselves can know when to make additional product shipments to specific Wal-Mart locations. The information partnership between Wal-Mart and **PROCTER & GAMBLE**, dating back to 1987, is legendary as an example of a buyer and a seller exchanging detailed transaction data in order to improve the operating efficiency of both companies.

fyi

In its 2000 financial statements, Procter & Gamble (P&G) disclosed that Wal-Mart is its single largest customer, accounting for 14% of P&G's sales in 2000.

Other elements contributing to Wal-Mart's success include a steadfast dedication to customer service, company policies designed to engender loyalty from employees, and sophisticated mechanisms for keeping overhead costs low. It is precisely because Wal-Mart carefully controls expenses that the company is able to consistently maintain its low price structure. Backing up Wal-Mart's cost control is the industry's most efficient and sophisticated distribution system, as well as significant cost-control relationships with the manufacturers and wholesalers it does business with.

setting the stage

Today, Wal-Mart employs over 1,140,000 people worldwide and has annual sales in excess of $165 billion. In addition, like many other merchandisers, Wal-Mart is experimenting with the retail distribution potential of the Internet (**http://www.walmart.com**). Providing the management accounting information necessary to effectively control this massive merchandising organization is no easy task. Providing merchandise at the right time, to the right place, and at the right price is how a retailer "wins" customers. However, winning the merchandising game also requires

1 Information from Sandra S. Vance and Roy V. Scott, *Wal-Mart: A History of Sam Walton's Retail Phenomenon* (New York: Twayne Publishers, 1994); Sam Walton and John Huey, *Sam Walton: Made in America* (New York: Doubleday, 1992).

that the merchandiser be able to provide these items at a cost that provides a reasonable profit to the organization. Sound simple? Consider that at any given moment, a typical Wal-Mart discount store has more than 70,000 different items of inventory in stock. Every one of these items must be identified, ordered, inventoried, and replenished—all the while keeping an eye on costs. (Inventory costs at a typical Supercenter are even tougher to manage because these stores also carry more than 20,000 grocery items, many of them perishable.) So how does Wal-Mart do it? With the wave of a magic wand! These "magic wands" are actually small handheld computers that link by radio frequency to in-store terminals. The next time you're in a Wal-Mart store, watch to see if you can spot an employee using these magic wands to manage inventory on the shelves. These small computers provide the critical link between Wal-Mart's suppliers and customers. With this technology, Wal-Mart management is able to get faster and more accurate information to plan, control, and evaluate every aspect of inventory management. This leads to better cost control and better merchandise and service. As a result of its leadership in technology, Wal-Mart is able to generate management accounting information that provides truly competitive cost, quality, and time information.

Some companies, such as COCA-COLA and NIKE, have become successful through convincing potential customers that their soft drinks or sports shoes are superior to all others. We talk of the marketing genius of Coca-Cola and Nike, not their cost management techniques. In contrast, WAL-MART does not offer unique products; to a large extent, Wal-Mart sells the same products sold by every other discount retailer in the world. Wal-Mart attracts us with its low prices, and consistent low prices are possible only in an organization that meticulously and relentlessly controls its costs. In this chapter, we will introduce techniques used to manage costs in manufacturing organizations, service organizations, and merchandising organizations (like Wal-Mart).

1

Outline the different cost flow patterns in manufacturing, merchandising, and service organizations and understand how these costs are reflected in the income statement and balance sheet.

COST FLOWS IN ORGANIZATIONS

In Chapter 3 of management accounting, we discussed the ways in which costs flow from one activity to the next in manufacturing, merchandising, and service organizations. These cost flow patterns are summarized in Exhibit 6-1. Recall that the extended production process characteristic of both manufacturing and service firms means that those organizations have significant levels of work-in-process inventory—goods or services that have not yet been completed but have already resulted in work being done and costs being incurred. In addition, note that both manufacturing and merchandising firms maintain significant inventories of goods that are ready for sale (finished goods or merchandise inventory); the nature of the service business means that once a service has been completed, typically it is delivered to the final customer and does not remain in inventory.

Exhibit 6-2 compares the income statements for three fictitious firms. The exhibit also presents selected balance sheet accounts. Carefully examine this exhibit to be sure you understand how the activities of manufacturing, service, and merchandising organizations are reflected in the financial statements.

As you can see, each income statement in Exhibit 6-2 follows a typical income statement format:

Sales revenue	$XXX,XXX
Costs of goods sold	(XX,XXX)
Gross margin	$XXX,XXX
Selling and administrative expenses	(X,XXX)
Operating income	$XXX,XXX

exhibit 6-1 Cost Flows in Manufacturing, Merchandising, and Service Organizations

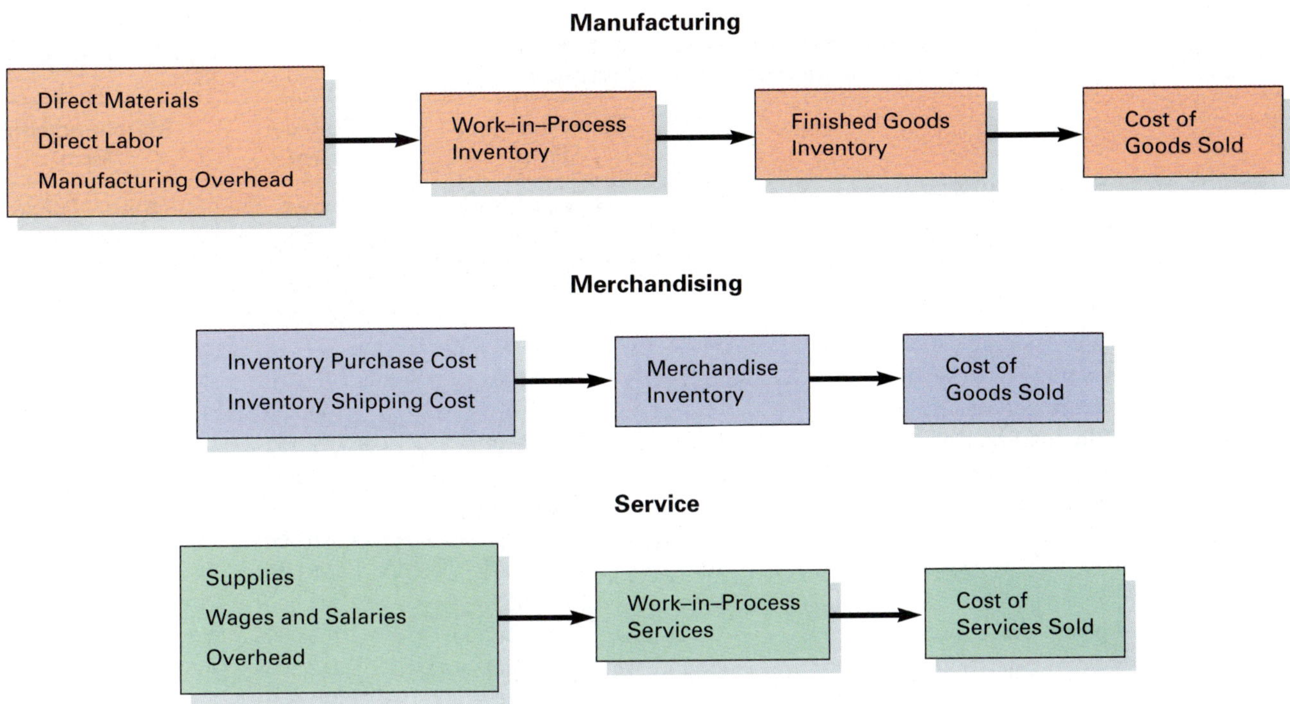

You should note two important items in Mason Tool's cost of goods sold calculation versus Brown Engineering's cost of services calculation. First of all, notice that Brown is using a rather insignificant amount of supplies ($11,900) to create its service product, especially when compared with Mason Tool, which is using a very significant amount of raw materials ($1,182,000) to create its tools. This difference underscores the fact that some supplies are often used in the process of creating and delivering a service product, but these costs are typically not a significant component of cost of services. Secondly, note that Brown Engineering does not hold finished service products for later sale to its customers. The very nature of a service business determines that a completed service is "delivered" to the customer almost instantly. In contrast, Brown Engineering does have a significant work-in-process inventory, representing service jobs that are not yet completed.

Smith Office Supply does not create the products it sells. As a result, Smith has no work-in-process inventory, and the cost of goods sold calculation only requires that Smith adjust the total amount of merchandise it purchased in 2003 by the change in its merchandise inventory account.

Balance sheet information for the three companies is presented at the bottom of Exhibit 6-2. As you can see, all three firms have accounts receivable, supplies inventory, and accounts payable accounts. Because Brown uses supplies directly in providing engineering services to its clients, this account is used in the cost of services calculation. On the other hand, cost of supplies for Mason Tool and Smith Office Supply is included in the overhead and administrative expenses accounts. In addition, you can see that Mason Tool has three inventory accounts; Smith Office Supply has one inventory account to record the costs of goods until the goods are sold to customers. Brown does not have a raw materials inventory, finished goods inventory, or merchandise inventory account. However, its work-in-process services account acts much like Mason Tool's work-in-process inventory account and is similarly used to adjust the Cost of Services account in Brown's income statement.

Exhibit 6-1 reviews the flow of costs through manufacturing, merchandising, and service organizations, and Exhibit 6-2 illustrates how these differing cost flows are reflected in the income

exhibit 6-2 Financial Statement Comparison: Manufacturing, Service, and Merchandising Firms

Income Statements for Different Types of Firms
For the Year Ended December 31, 2003

	Manufacturing Firm	Service Firm	Merchandising Firm
	Mason Tool Company	**Brown Engineering, Inc.**	**Smith Office Supply, Inc.**
Sales revenues	$4,000,000	$5,000,000	$2,500,000
Cost of goods sold/Cost of services:			
Cost of goods manufactured/Cost of services:			
Beginning raw materials/supplies inventory	$ 234,000	$ 2,300	
+ Purchases of raw materials/supplies	1,153,000	11,400	
Total raw materials/supplies available	$1,387,000	$ 13,700	
− Ending raw materials/supplies inventory	(205,000)	(1,800)	
Raw materials/supplies used	$1,182,000	$ 11,900	
+ Direct labor	445,000	1,890,000	
+ Manufacturing/service overhead	1,003,000	798,000	
Total manufacturing/service costs	$2,630,000	$2,699,900	
+ Beginning work in process	245,000	755,000	
− Ending work in process	(192,000)	(843,000)	
Cost of goods manufactured/Cost of services	$2,683,000	$2,611,900	
Underapplied overhead	307,000	22,100	
Adjusted cost of goods manufactured/Cost of services	$2,990,000	$2,634,000	
Merchandise purchases			$1,713,000
+ Beginning finished goods/merchandise inventory	354,000		378,000
− Ending finished goods/merchandise inventory	(407,000)		(356,000)
Total cost of goods sold/Cost of services	$2,937,000		$1,735,000
Gross margin	$1,063,000	$2,366,000	$ 765,000
Selling and administrative expenses:			
Selling expenses	$ 256,000	$ 367,000	$ 406,000
Administrative expenses	474,000	1,003,000	188,000
Total selling and administrative expenses	$ 730,000	$1,370,000	$ 594,000
Operating income	$ 333,000	$ 996,000	$ 171,000

Selected Balance Sheet Information
December 31, 2003

	Manufacturing Firm	Service Firm	Merchandising Firm
Accounts receivable	$744,000	$639,000	$ 39,000
Raw materials inventory	205,000		
Work-in-process inventory	192,000		
Work-in-process services		843,000	
Finished goods inventory	407,000		
Merchandise inventory			356,000
Supplies inventory	7,500	1,800	450
Accounts payable	298,000	106,000	489,000

statement and the balance sheet. In the remainder of this chapter, we will discuss how this cost information can be used to plan, control, and evaluate a company's operations. The extended production process of a manufacturing or service firm requires careful scrutiny of costs at each important stage of the process. For a merchandising company, cost management focuses on acquiring the right amount of inventory for the right price.

to summarize

Both manufacturing and service organizations maintain substantial production processes; an important managerial accounting function in these organizations is tracing the flow of costs through the various stages of production. Both manufacturing and merchandising organizations maintain significant inventory levels. These differences among manufacturing, merchandising, and service organizations are reflected in differences in their income statements and balance sheets.

2

Interpret a cost of goods manufactured schedule and analyze the levels of raw materials, work-in-process, and finished goods inventories in a manufacturing organization.

cost of goods manufactured schedule A schedule supporting the income statement; summarizes the total cost of goods manufactured during a period, including direct materials, direct labor, and manufacturing overhead.

COST OF GOODS MANUFACTURED SCHEDULE

The accounting for the flow of costs through a manufacturing organization was discussed in Chapter 3 of management accounting. In this section we will examine a single report, the cost of goods manufactured schedule, that summarizes the cost flows in a manufacturing organization during a given period. We will also see how this cost information can be used to evaluate both the management of costs incurred during the period and the levels of inventories that are maintained.

Exhibit 6-1 showed how manufacturing costs are accumulated in Work-in-Process Inventory, then flow to Finished Goods Inventory, and finally to Cost of Goods Sold. These costs are also usually summarized on a **cost of goods manufactured schedule**, which supports the cost of goods sold calculation on the income statement.

The cost of goods manufactured schedule shows the specific costs that have been incurred to manufacture goods during a period. Exhibit 6-3 shows the cost of goods manufactured schedule for Broyman Furniture Company, the hypothetical company that was used

exhibit 6-3 Cost of Goods Manufactured Schedule

Broyman Furniture Company
Cost of Goods Manufactured Schedule
For the Year Ended December 31, 2003

Raw materials:		
Beginning raw materials inventory	$ 50,000	
Add: Raw materials purchased	270,000	
Total raw materials available	$320,000	
Less: Ending raw materials inventory	30,000	
Raw materials used in production		$290,000
Direct labor		300,000
Manufacturing overhead:		
Indirect labor	$ 20,000	
Utilities	7,000	
Rent	72,000	
Depreciation	30,000	
Indirect materials	15,000	
Insurance	24,000	
Total actual manufacturing overhead	$168,000	
Add: Overapplied manufacturing overhead	6,000	
Applied manufacturing overhead		174,000
Total manufacturing costs		$764,000
Add: Beginning work-in-process inventory		90,000
Less: Ending work-in-process inventory		(80,000)
Cost of goods manufactured		$774,000

to illustrate manufacturing cost flows in Chapter 3 of management accounting. Most of the numbers in the schedule cannot be specifically traced back to the Chapter 3 illustration because it focused on the cost flows associated with the manufacture of one table. The important thing to focus on in Exhibit 6-3 is the format for summarizing and reporting manufacturing cost flows.

The cost of goods manufactured schedule provides the calculations that support the flow of costs for a manufacturing firm. In our example, the schedule shows that materials costing $290,000 were combined with direct labor costs of $300,000 and manufacturing overhead costs of $174,000 to transfer $764,000 of manufacturing costs to work-in-process inventory. This $764,000 amount of total manufacturing costs represents the new manufacturing costs incurred during the period and is a good representation of the level of production activity carried out during the period. The $764,000 was then adjusted for the beginning and ending work-in-process inventories to determine the $774,000 cost of goods manufactured for the period. The amount of cost of goods manufactured represents the total cost of items for which production was completed during the period; this cost includes some costs incurred in prior periods (from beginning work-in-process inventory) and some costs incurred during this period. Knowing the total cost of goods manufactured makes it easy to determine the total cost of goods sold. The cost of goods manufactured amount is added to beginning finished goods inventory (assume $60,000) and adjusted for any over- or underapplied manufacturing overhead (assume $6,000 overapplied) to arrive at cost of goods available for sale of $828,000. The ending finished goods inventory (assume $40,000) is then subtracted to determine the cost of goods sold ($788,000). This calculation of cost of goods sold is shown below.

caution

Remember that over- or underapplied overhead is usually charged to Cost of Goods Sold. Thus, in the cost of goods sold calculation, underapplied overhead is added to cost of goods manufactured, and overapplied overhead is subtracted from cost of goods manufactured.

Cost of Goods Sold

Beginning finished goods inventory	$ 60,000
Add: Cost of goods manufactured	774,000
Less: Overapplied manufacturing overhead	(6,000)
Total cost of goods available for sale	$828,000
Less: Ending finished goods inventory	(40,000)
Cost of goods sold	$788,000

Total cost of goods manufactured should include only those costs that have gone through the work-in-process inventory account during the period. Thus, as shown in Exhibit 6-3, applied (rather than actual) overhead costs are included in the cost of goods manufactured schedule. As illustrated, Cost of Goods Sold is then adjusted for the amount of over- or underapplied overhead.

Analyzing Production Costs and Inventory Levels

In the above example, cost of goods sold was determined to be $788,000. You should note that this is a summary number that is used in the financial statements and is the number to which auditors will attest. However, because it is a summary number, it is not useful for detailed internal decision making. To be useful, management would want to determine the cost of goods manufactured on a product-by-product basis, a period-by-period basis, and a department-by-department basis. By breaking costs down by product, period, and department, management can determine which units and products are performing well and which are performing poorly. For example, examine the table and bookcase production cost data for Broyman Furniture in Exhibit 6-4. The data are listed by month, and comparisons to the production cost in the same month in the preceding year are included. First, note that the production cost per unit for both the tables and the bookcases declines during the summer months; this seasonal decline probably occurs because the factory facility is used more heavily during these months, resulting in fixed production costs being spread over a larger number of manufactured units. Notice that, for the tables, the increase in production cost in 2003, relative to the same month in 2002, is

exhibit 6-4 Monthly Cost Information, by Product

Tables—Average Production Cost per Unit, by Month

	Jan.	Feb.	Mar.	Apr.	May	June	July	Aug.	Sep.	Oct.	Nov.	Dec.
2003	$310.12	$312.75	$308.49	$311.71	$306.23	$301.87	$298.44	$297.03	$305.60	$313.45	$315.79	$314.32
2002	300.37	302.24	298.24	302.04	297.81	293.49	292.12	288.43	294.05	306.32	310.89	309.75
Change in 2003	$9.75	$10.51	$10.25	$9.67	$8.42	$8.38	$6.32	$8.60	$11.55	$7.13	$4.90	$4.57
Percentage change	3.2%	3.5%	3.4%	3.2%	2.8%	2.9%	2.2%	3.0%	3.9%	2.3%	1.6%	1.5%

Bookcases—Average Production Cost per Unit, by Month

	Jan.	Feb.	Mar.	Apr.	May	June	July	Aug.	Sep.	Oct.	Nov.	Dec.
2003	$77.53	$78.18	$77.12	$77.92	$76.55	$75.46	$74.61	$74.25	$76.40	$78.36	$78.94	$78.58
2002	75.65	76.27	75.26	75.82	74.42	72.69	71.88	71.04	72.58	73.94	73.99	73.15
Change in 2003	$1.88	$1.91	$1.86	$2.10	$2.13	$2.77	$2.73	$3.21	$3.82	$4.42	$4.95	$5.43
Percentage change	2.5%	2.5%	2.5%	2.8%	2.9%	3.8%	3.8%	4.5%	5.3%	6.0%	6.7%	7.4%

much lower near the end of the year than at the beginning of the year. This evidence suggests that the production manager for the tables has improved the control of costs as the year has progressed. The bookcase numbers present exactly the opposite picture: cost per unit was up 7.4% in the month of December compared to the year before, whereas the cost increases in the early months of the year were just 2.5%.

Our brief analysis of the production cost data in Exhibit 6-4 is just the beginning of a thorough investigation into the performance of the table and the bookcase production units. As will be discussed in Chapter 9 of management accounting, cost variance analysis can be used to determine exactly which costs (material, labor, or manufacturing overhead) are causing the production cost per unit for bookcases to increase so dramatically.

inventory turnover (stock-turns) The number of times the inventory in the organization "turns over" during a period of time. It is often easier to think of inventory turnover as the number of times a dollar invested in inventory is sold during a period of time. Inventory turnover is computed as cost of goods sold divided by average inventory value.

days in inventory Average number of days of sales that can be made using only the supply of inventory on hand.

Management would also use the manufacturing cost and inventory numbers to evaluate the levels of raw materials, work-in-process, and finished goods inventories. Two measures used to evaluate a company's inventory management practices are **inventory turnover** and **days in inventory**. Selected information from Exhibit 6-3 is repeated in Exhibit 6-5 and used to illustrate the computations of inventory turnover and days in inventory.

The inventory turnover measures indicate how many times during the year Broyman has completely replenished or replaced the inventory, given the rate at which costs are flowing through the production process. For example, Exhibit 6-5 shows that the raw materials inventory "turned over" or was replaced 9.7 times during the year. Inventory turnover measures the intensity with which Broyman is managing its inventory—low inventory turnover indicates lots of idle inventory lying around whereas high inventory turnover indicates extremely active management with little excess inventory. The days in inventory measure provides an alternative measure of this same concept. For example, Exhibit 6-5 shows that Broyman's average manufacturing cost per day is $2,093.15. Given that the ending work-in-process inventory amount is $80,000, the amount of inventory still in process at the end of the year represents 38.2 days ($80,000 ÷ $2,093.15) days of manufacturing. A very streamlined production process would result in a low number of days of manufacturing in work-in-process inventory; a long, complex manufacturing process (such as the construction of a ship) could have more than a year's worth of manufacturing costs tied up in unfinished products.

fyi

Both inventory turnover and days in inventory measure the same thing. This can be seen by the fact that another way to compute days in inventory is as follows: Days in inventory = 365 ÷ Inventory turnover.

In evaluating products and departments, cost is only one criterion examined by management. In most cases, management is just as interested in indicators of product quality and production speed as in costs of production. Exhibit 6-6 shows cost, quality, and time data that would be examined by management for a hypothetical company with three divisions and six products. Obviously, management could have many different measures for

exhibit 6-5 Analysis of the Levels of Raw Materials, Work-in-Process, and Finished Goods Inventories

Raw Materials Inventory	
Ending raw materials inventory	$30,000
Total amount used during the year	$290,000
Average amount used per day (365 days)	$794.52
Inventory turnover (yearly cost ÷ inventory)	9.7
Days' supply of raw materials in ending inventory (inventory ÷ average daily cost)	37.8 days
Work-in-Process Inventory	
Ending work-in-process inventory	$80,000
Total manufacturing costs during the year	$764,000
Average manufacturing cost per day (365 days)	$2,093.15
Inventory turnover (yearly cost ÷ inventory)	9.6
Days of manufacturing represented by ending work-in-process inventory (inventory ÷ average daily cost)	38.2 days
Finished Goods Inventory	
Ending finished goods inventory	$40,000
Total cost of goods sold during the year	$788,000
Average cost of goods sold per day (365 days)	$2,158.90
Inventory turnover (yearly cost ÷ inventory)	19.7
Days of sales in ending inventory (inventory ÷ average daily cost)	18.5 days

the cost, quality, and time attributes it monitors. In this hypothetical example, the summary information suggests that both products in Division B have improved performance on each dimension (cost, quality, and time) over the last period, while both products in Division C show decreased performance over the prior period. Obviously, comparing performance with the last period is only one measure that could be used. Management may want to compare the performance of products versus each other or "benchmark" the performance of its products with those of other companies.

exhibit 6-6 Divisional Performance Report

	Division A		**Division B**		**Division C**	
	Product 1	**Product 2**	**Product 3**	**Product 4**	**Product 5**	**Product 6**
Cost to produce	Higher than last period	Same as last period	Lower than last period	Lower than last period	Higher than last period	Higher than last period
Quality of product	Happier customers, fewer defects	No change in customer attitudes	Happier customers, fewer defects	Happier customers, fewer defects	Increase in complaints	Increase in complaints
Average time to produce	Same as last period	One day less	Two days less	One day less	Two days more	Six days more

to summarize

Manufacturing costs are summarized on a cost of goods manufactured schedule. The cost of goods manufactured is added to the beginning finished goods inventory to determine cost of goods available for sale. Ending finished goods inventory is then subtracted from this number to compute cost of goods sold. Cost of goods sold is a summary number that is audited and used in the financial statements, but is not very useful for internal management decision making. For decision making, management would examine costs, as well as quality and time measures, on a product-by-product, period-by-period, and department-by-department basis. Inventory turnover measures can be used to evaluate the levels of raw materials, work-in process, and finished goods inventories.

3
Understand how merchants manage cost information in their organizations.

MANAGING COST INFORMATION

As discussed in the preceding section, cost data can be used in a manufacturing firm to evaluate the appropriateness of the levels of raw materials, work-in-process, and finished goods inventories. Merchants, or managers of merchandising organizations, are also very conscious of the total amount of inventory that is currently in the retail store or in the distribution center. Managing this inventory takes careful and detailed planning. The detail in these plans results from merchants having *many* different types of inventory items, each with its own particular supplier source and targeted customer. Merchants must also be very careful in planning their inventory levels because having either too little or too much inventory can involve critical issues. These issues are listed in Exhibit 6-7. If accountants are aware of these issues, they can help their organizations avoid a variety of unnecessary out-of-pocket costs or opportunity costs.

Carrying Too Much Inventory

holding costs The financial opportunity costs that result from investing money in an asset such as inventory. Whatever income the money could generate in an alternative investment is the holding cost of the current investment.

Having inventory is certainly necessary for most merchants if they expect to do business with their customers. However, accumulating as much inventory as possible is *not* the purpose of merchandising (or manufacturing) companies. Good business management entails having the right assets at the right place in the right time and in the right quantity (always a challenging endeavor!). The advent of the just-in-time (JIT) inventory management concept has clearly taught us that too much inventory creates a lot of management problems. First of all, clearly many out-of-pocket costs are involved in having inventory on site, including costs of storage, security, and record keeping. What may not be as clear is the financial opportunity cost (sometimes called the **holding cost**) of the inventory investment. Every dollar that is invested in inventory cannot be used in alternative business investments, such as expanding another part of the business

exhibit 6-7 Inventory Management Issues

Carrying Too Much Inventory	Carrying Too Little Inventory
• Increased overhead costs	• Increased risk of lost sales
• Increased financial holding costs	• Increased ordering costs
• Increased risk of loss of market value	• Increased risk of supplier price increases
• Decreased inventory flexibility	• Increased exposure to nondelivery
• Increased inventory shrinkage	• Decreased bulk order discounts

or simply investing in the stock market or in a bank savings account. Whatever money we *could* make by investing the money elsewhere is the holding cost of the current inventory investment. Accountants measure and report holding costs all the time. We will demonstrate the calculation of holding costs in the expanded material section of this chapter.

Increased overhead costs and holding costs are not the only issues involved in carrying too much inventory. The more inventory a merchant elects to carry, the more risk the merchant faces that the inventory will decrease in market value before it can be sold (of course, inventory may unexpectedly increase in market value as well). In addition, when a merchant invests in a lot of one type of inventory, it becomes difficult to shift to another inventory type that customers may suddenly want to buy. Finally, every merchant understands the tough reality that inventories "shrink" over time. **Inventory shrinkage** happens in a lot of ways. The type of shrinkage we hear about most often is theft (either by customers or employees). However, when inventory is being moved, stacked, stored, retrieved, and rotated, things get broken, parts get lost, and items become mislabeled. Liquid and gas stocks spill or evaporate. Cloth material becomes soiled. Grocery items spoil or become stale. As inventory is piled up around the store or distribution center, this disorder, spoilage, and theft are revealed every time the company takes an annual inventory count, resulting in additional out-of-pockets costs to replace the inventory.

inventory shrinkage The disorder, spoilage, and theft that result when a company chooses to maintain inventory on site, resulting in additional out-of-pocket costs to replace inventory.

fyi

In 1999, FRUIT OF THE LOOM reported that it experienced inventory shrinkage totaling $70.4 million. This represented a 25% increase in shrinkage compared to the prior year. Fruit of the Loom attributed the shrinkage increase to its expansion of its network of contractors (factories where its clothing items are produced).

Carrying Too Little Inventory

Clearly, having too much inventory is a poor use of resources. However, poor planning that results in not having enough inventory on hand can also be a source of trouble. It is obvious to most managers and owners that they lose potential sales when they have to turn away customers because of a lack of inventory. Accountants can support good inventory management when they are able to quantify these opportunity costs for decision makers. As can be seen in Exhibit 6-7, however, an organization that has inadequate inventory levels also incurs other costs. For example, initiating an order with a wholesaler or manufacturer for the delivery of goods often requires a number of business processes, including counting inventory, preparing purchase orders, receiving and inspecting shipments of goods, and initiating payments for purchases. Most merchants have to initiate and pay for each of these steps every time they purchase inventory. Merchants that maintain low inventory levels by buying in smaller quantities will generally have to make more purchases, and pay for additional employee time, to replenish their stock.

Prices for most types of inventory increase with time. Some items are particularly susceptible to sudden price increases. Have you ever awakened to hear the morning newscast report that automobile gasoline prices have suddenly surged? When you go out to your car and discover the gas tank nearly empty, don't you wish you had filled the tank yesterday? One reason some merchants purchase large amounts of inventory is to temporarily protect themselves from sudden increases in prices. Companies without similar foresight will experience greater out-of-pocket expenses if prices do increase. Companies that keep very low levels of inventory are most likely to have to pay for every price increase. In addition, these same companies are much more dependent on their suppliers to *always* meet their delivery commitments. If a supplier is late in making promised shipments or delivers inventory that is damaged or of the wrong type, the merchant may miss making sales to some customers. Finally, merchants that regularly purchase large levels of inventory often enjoy price discounts from their suppliers. Merchants making smaller purchases should be aware of the opportunity cost related to missing these potential bulk purchase discounts.

fyi

How important is the Christmas buying season for a toy merchant? The 1999 annual report for TOYS "R" US, INC., reports that approximately 42% of its sales occur in the months of November, December, and January.

Example of Inventory Management Costs

We'll use the fictitious example of two large retailers of children's toys, Kids N Toys, Inc., and Child's Delight, Inc., to illustrate the issues and costs involved in inventory management for merchandising organizations. As you might expect, the Christmas buying season is a big deal for a toy retailer. Management and buyers for these companies study trend reports and catalogs all year in order to properly plan their investments for December. Both companies have limited resources that can be invested in inventory for the holiday season. Given the necessary **lead time**, as well as the size of the investment, these decisions are absolutely critical to both companies.

lead time Generally, the time interval between initiating a request and finally fulfilling the request.

Once December has arrived, it becomes very difficult to make many adjustments to preplanned inventory types and levels.

A wholesaler of children's dolls has announced the availability of a new doll for Christmas this year, the Burzee Doll. Based on the manufacturer's reputation, as well as the fact that the manufacturer of the doll intends to do a lot of promotional advertising, the wholesaler is confident that the Burzee Doll will sell very well this year. To help make planning decisions, each retailer has its management accountants prepare some forecasts on potential revenues and costs related to the issues listed in Exhibit 6-7. Based on the projections of its management accountants, Kids N Toys, Inc., decides to invest very heavily in the Burzee Doll and orders 50,000 dolls for delivery on November 1. Because of the size of its order, the wholesaler offers Kids N Toys a discount of $2 per doll. On the other hand, the management accountants' projections of revenues and costs at Child's Delight, Inc., are not as optimistic. As a result, Child's Delight orders only 5,000 dolls and pays the full wholesale price of $12 per doll. Both retailers follow the manufacturer's recommendation to set the customer price at $30 per doll.

net work

TOYS "R" US is the largest toy retailer in the United States. With its toysrus.com Web site, a partnership with **AMAZON.COM**, it has also sought to expand its success to the Internet. As discussed in the chapter, effective management of a merchandising company requires information about both profitability and inventory management. Go to the corporate Web site for Toys "R" Us at **http://www.toysrus.com** and find the company's most recent earnings press release. In addition to discussing the company's profitability, does this press release also discuss inventory management?

Exhibit 6-8 outlines all the Burzee Doll events that take place during the holiday season, as well as the resulting revenues and costs for the two companies. As it turns out, the Burzee Dolls are a real hit during the holiday buying season. Child's Delight keeps running out of inventory and must reorder dolls three times during the season. As you can see in Exhibit 6-8, each time Child's Delight reorders dolls, it is not hard for the accountants to note the amount of inventory shrinkage. Occasionally, dolls are stolen, misplaced, or destroyed in the process of moving, sorting, and stacking. On the other hand, Kids N Toys has dolls all over the store, making it difficult to know much about shrinkage without taking a very expensive inventory count. The accountants at Kids N Toys elect to wait until all the inventory is sold before measuring inventory shrinkage.

By the end of December, Child's Delight has sold all of its dolls and elects not to place a fifth order. On the other hand, Kids N Toys still has a large number of dolls remaining. Since the buying craze for Burzee Dolls appears to be finished, Kids N Toys puts the dolls on sale at cost ($10 per doll) in mid-January. At the end of January, the store liquidates the remaining 4,400 dolls to another retailer at $3 per doll.

STOP & THINK These two companies now have very different levels of inventory in Burzee Dolls. With its very large inventory investment, what additional inventory costs are now a factor for Kids N Toys? What additional inventory costs is Child's Delight susceptible to with its relatively small inventory investment?

THE GROSS MARGIN REPORT When all Burzee Doll sales are totaled, Kids N Toys sold 48,400 dolls (indicating inventory shrinkage over the last three months of 1,600 dolls); Child's Delight sold 19,850 dolls (indicating inventory shrinkage of 150 dolls). Which of the two retailers did better with the Burzee Dolls? Exhibit 6-9 provides a gross margin report based on what each company spent on inventory purchases and received in inventory sales. When you look at the gross margin of $793,200 for Kids N Toys, it appears that this company did a much better job selling Burzee Dolls than its competitor, Child's Delight, based on its gross margin of only $325,500.

RETURN ON INVESTMENT (ROI) The gross margin numbers presented in Exhibit 6-9 suggest that Kids N Toys outperformed Child's Delight. However, if you had money to invest in these companies, you might actually like Child's Delight's retail work on Burzee Dolls better than the work done by Kids N Toys. Think about the average size of the inventory investment each company maintained. Kids N Toys initially spent $500,000 to acquire 50,000 dolls. By the end of January, this inventory had been fully liquidated back into cash. Hence, Kids N Toys had quite a bit of cash tied up in Burzee Doll inventory! On average, how much cash did it have invested in this inventory during its selling period? On November 1, Kids N Toys had $500,000 in Burzee Doll inventory. On January 30, it had no Burzee Doll inventory. On average, Kids N Toys had about a $250,000 investment in inventory during its three-month selling period ($500,000 ÷ 2).[2]

STOP & THINK Is there anything wrong with using the gross margin analysis presented in Exhibit 6-9 to evaluate management performance in these two companies? What costs may be missing?

2 Be careful with this calculation! The fact that Kids N Toys held its doll inventory for three months (or two months, or four months) does not change the fact that average inventory for the company is $250,000. The formal calculation here is (Beginning balance + Ending balance) ÷ 2. Instead of having no inventory, what if Kids N Toys still had $50,000 worth of Burzee Dolls on January 31? The average inventory investment would then be $275,000 [($500,000 + $50,000) ÷ 2].

exhibit 6-8 Management Events in the Burzee Doll Inventory

Date	Event	Kids N Toys, Inc.	Child's Delight, Inc.
Nov. 1	Retailers prepare the Burzee Doll inventory.	Company buys 50,000 dolls at $10 per doll. Customer price is set at $30.	Company buys 5,000 dolls at $12 per doll. Customer price is set at $30.
30	Sales on the doll start increasing.	Company has sold 7,500 dolls.	Company has sold 4,950 dolls and is out of stock. Reorders another 5,000 dolls at $12 per doll.
Dec. 10	Sales on the doll are really strong.	Company has sold another 12,000 dolls.	Company has sold another 4,970 dolls and is out of stock again. Reorders another 5,000 dolls at $15 per doll (supplier has increased price).
20	Sales on the doll continue to be very strong.	Company has sold another 15,000 dolls.	Company has sold another 4,990 dolls and is out of stock again. Reorders another 5,000 dolls at $15 per doll.
31	Sales have nearly halted in the last few days.	Company has sold another 7,000 dolls.	Company has sold another 4,940 dolls and is out of stock again. Chooses not to reorder.
Jan. 15	Sales are nearly nonexistent.	Company has sold another 500 dolls and now puts dolls on sale at cost ($10).	Out of Burzee Doll business.
30	Sales pick up a little.	Company has sold another 2,000 dolls and now sells the remaining 4,400 usable dolls to a small merchant for $3 per doll.	Out of Burzee Doll business.
31	Evaluate inventory shrinkage.	Sold a total of 48,400 units indicating that 1,600 units were lost due to shrinkage.	Sold a total of 19,850 units indicating that 150 units were lost due to shrinkage.

How does Kids N Toys' average inventory investment compare to its competitor's investment? Rather than one large inventory purchase at the beginning of November, Child's Delight made four smaller investments as needed during November and December. The average inventory purchase amount was $67,500 [($60,000 + $60,000 + $75,000 + $75,000) ÷ 4]. On December 31, it had no Burzee Doll inventory. On average, then, Child's Delight had only about a $33,750 investment in inventory during its two-month selling period ($67,500 ÷ 2).

exhibit 6-9 Gross Margin Report on the Burzee Doll Inventory

	Kids N Toys, Inc.		Child's Delight, Inc.	
	42,000 units × $30	$1,260,000		
	2,000 units × $10	20,000		
	4,400 units × $3	13,200		
Sales revenue		$1,293,200	19,850 units × $30	$595,500
			10,000 units × $12	
Cost of purchases	50,000 units × $10	(500,000)	10,000 units × $15	(270,000)
Gross margin		$ 793,200		$325,500

Obviously, the difference between the two companies' gross margins reported in Exhibit 6-9 is dramatic. However, the difference in Kids N Toys' average inventory investment of $250,000 versus the $33,750 average inventory investment at Child's Delight is also impressive. Remember from Chapter 1 of management accounting, that the DuPont approach to business recognizes that it is just as important to manage the money outflow for asset investment as it is to manage the money inflow from profits. This is the logic underlying Pierre du Pont and Donaldson Brown's ROI (return on investment) formula. Remember that the ROI formula has two parts (see Exhibit 1-2 if you need a review):

$$\underset{\text{(Profit} \div \text{Revenue)}}{\text{Profit margin}} \times \underset{\text{(Revenue} \div \text{Total assets)}}{\text{Asset turnover}} = \text{ROI}$$

Based on ROI, which of these two companies has created the most revenue for each dollar invested in its Burzee Doll inventory asset? Answering this question is really a function of the "asset turnover" section of the ROI formula. Notice, however, that rather than *total* revenue and *total* assets, we are focusing only on Burzee Doll revenue and the value of the Burzee Doll inventory asset. This fact really doesn't present a problem. Rather than measuring how much total revenue is generated per dollar of total assets, we will simply measure *how much specific revenue is generated per dollar of a specific inventory item.* Hence, how many times does Kids N Toys turn over its Burzee Doll inventory compared to Child's Delight?

Kids N Toys: Revenue ÷ Average inventory
$1,293,200 ÷ $250,000 = 5.17

Child's Delight: Revenue ÷ Average inventory
$595,500 ÷ $33,750 = 17.64

Note that organizations have a limited amount of resources to invest. Using the ROI formula, the **DUPONT COMPANY** was able to wisely manage the task of maximizing the value of its investments by knowing where in the massive organization to invest its resources. Looking at the asset turnover numbers above, you can see that Child's Delight made the better use of limited purchasing dollars to manage the Burzee Doll inventory to create sales revenue.[3]

Combining the gross margin and inventory turnover data yields the following ROI calculations for Kids N Toys and Child's Delight:

(Gross margin ÷ Revenue) × (Revenue ÷ Inventory) = Return on investment in inventory

Kids N Toys: ($793,200 ÷ $1,293,200) × ($1,293,200 ÷ $250,000) = 317%

Child's Delight: ($325,500 ÷ $595,500) × ($595,500 ÷ $33,750) = 964%

These ROI numbers suggest that although Child's Delight generated a lower gross margin, it actually performed better than Kids N Toys because of superior inventory management. By the way, if these ROI numbers (317% and 964%) seem high to you, then you should congratulate yourself for paying attention. These numbers *are* high because we have focused on the utilization of just one asset—inventory. In order to sell Burzee Dolls, each merchandiser must also invest in buildings, store shelving and displays, cash registers, and so forth. However, these ROI numbers give a strong indication that, regardless of what the overall ROI of each company is, it appears that Child's Delight has been more effective at managing its acquisition and sales of Burzee Dolls.

The day-to-day effort to manage the Burzee Doll inventory involves many other important issues (as listed in Exhibit 6-7). Even the ROI measures above do not provide Kids N Toys and

3 In this case, inventory turnover was measured by dividing a retail number (revenue) by a wholesale, or purchase cost, number (inventory). As illustrated in the preceding section, inventory turnover is frequently measured using cost of goods sold rather than sales or revenue. Conceptually, comparing a wholesale number (inventory) to a wholesale number (cost of goods sold) makes more sense than comparing a wholesale number to a retail (sales) number. However, as long as a consistent approach is used, the insights gained are the same.

Child's Delight management with the data necessary to address all issues as they *plan* for future inventory investments and *control* and *evaluate* the current inventory acquisition and selling process. This is where good management accounting can provide real value in management's effort to improve a merchandising operation. Exhibit 6-10 provides a management accounting view of the two companies' retail work with the Burzee Doll line of operations. Study both Exhibit 6-10 and Exhibit 6-7 for a moment. What information in Exhibit 6-10 could help a manager trying to work with some of the issues described in Exhibit 6-7?

THE MANAGEMENT ACCOUNTING REPORT ON KIDS N TOYS' NET OPERATING PROFIT As you can see in Exhibit 6-10, we are identifying some additional out-of-pocket costs on the Burzee Doll operation for each company. Note that the gross margin for each company is the same as that calculated in the gross margin report in Exhibit 6-9. However, we're approaching the calculation of gross margin differently, as well as identifying some other relevant costs to calculate **net operating profit** for each company. Net operating profit is useful in measuring the performance of these operations. Much more important, though, are the insights gained in the management accounting numbers used to calculate gross margin and net operating profit. These numbers, presented in Exhibit 6-10, are extremely useful for planning, controlling, and evaluating the Burzee Doll retail operations.

net operating profit The difference between normal business sales and normal business expenses.

Let's work with Kids N Toys first. This company originally purchased 50,000 units with the intent of selling all of them for $30. Why didn't it then have $1.5 million in revenue? This question cannot be answered using the gross margin report in Exhibit 6-9, but the answer is obvious in the management accounting report in Exhibit 6-10. Somehow, 1,600 dolls that Kids N Toys planned to sell were broken, misplaced, or stolen. Based on an intended $30 selling price, this cost the company $48,000 in lost revenue. In addition, the market demand changed while Kids N Toys still had dolls to sell. As a result, the store had to sell some dolls for prices lower than the planned $30. Specifically, Kids N Toys reduced expected revenue by $40,000 when it sold 2,000 dolls for $10, and reduced expected revenue by another $118,800 when it sold 4,400 dolls for $3. This loss of market value is a risk that Kids N Toys management should consider when planning for next year's purchases. Further, management

exhibit 6-10 Management Accounting Report on the Burzee Doll Inventory

In addition to cost of purchases, note the following additional inventory costs:

- Average inventory overhead costs are $1.10 per unit per month.
- Average costs to initiate and receive a purchase order are $1,250 per event.

	Kids N Toys, Inc.		Child's Delight, Inc.	
Expected revenue	50,000 units × $30 standard price	$1,500,000	20,000 units × $30 standard price	$600,000
Shrinkage loss	1,600 units × $30	(48,000)	150 units × $30	(4,500)
Market loss	2,000 units × ($30 − $10) + 4,400 units × ($30 − $3)	(158,800)		(0)
Actual revenue		$1,293,200		$595,500
Purchase costs	50,000 units × $10 standard cost	(500,000)	20,000 units × $10 standard cost	(200,000)
Lost discount		(0)	20,000 units × $2 lost discount	(40,000)
Price increase		(0)	10,000 units × $3 price increase	(30,000)
Gross margin		$ 793,200		$325,500
Overhead costs	50,000 units ÷ 2 = 25,000 average inventory level × $1.10 × 3 months	(82,500)	5,000 units ÷ 2 = 2,500 average inventory level × $1.10 × 2 months	(5,500)
Order costs	1 order × $1,250	(1,250)	4 orders × $1,250	(5,000)
Net operating profit		$ 709,450		$315,000

should also evaluate the information on inventory shrinkage to better control the inventory operation.

We briefly discussed the concept of activity-based costing (ABC) in Chapter 3 of management accounting. We'll spend a lot of time on this concept in Chapter 7 of management accounting. Briefly, ABC is an approach to tracking the relationship between activities and costs that is generally used to better allocate manufacturing overhead costs to products. This concept can also be used to analyze overhead costs in merchandising organizations. Managing the Burzee Doll inventory requires some overhead costs. In this example, let's assume an ABC analysis reveals that the cost for storage, security, and other supervisory activities works out to be about $1.10 per doll per month. In addition, the effort to count inventory and prepare the purchase order, as well as to receive and pay for the inventory, requires about $1,250 in administrative costs each time inventory is purchased. In a standard income statement, only the direct cost of inventory purchases would be used to measure gross margin. Those overhead and purchasing costs related to managing the Burzee Doll inventory are typically combined with all other administrative costs to form Selling and Administrative Expenses on the income statement. However, the management accounting report in Exhibit 6-10 has specifically identified and related these costs to the Burzee Doll inventory. This information allows management to see exactly how the Burzee Doll product line is contributing to Kids N Toys' overall net operating profit. Further, management can evaluate how having a lot of inventory leads to higher overhead costs. On the other hand, though, purchasing all these dolls at once saved Kids N Toys additional purchasing costs.

THE MANAGEMENT ACCOUNTING REPORT ON CHILD'S DELIGHT'S NET OPERATING PROFIT Now let's evaluate operations at Child's Delight using the management accounting report in Exhibit 6-10. During November and December, Child's Delight purchased a total of 20,000 units with the intent of selling all of them for $30. Similar to Kids N Toys, the difference between expected revenue and actual revenue is explained by the inventory shrinkage of 150 units. Compared to Kids N Toys, why does Child's Delight have a much lower percentage of dolls being broken, misplaced, or stolen? It seems reasonable to expect that Child's Delight found it much easier to maintain and keep track of its much smaller level of inventory. Can this shrinkage be further reduced? Child's Delight should carefully consider this question as it plans for the next buying season.

As noted in Exhibit 6-7, keeping the inventory levels low helps protect the organization against certain types of costs and risks. However, this can be a challenging balance because other costs occur as a result of low inventory levels; Child's Delight incurred three of these costs. First, because Child's Delight made small inventory purchases, bulk discounts were unavailable to the company. The effect of losing these discounts, $40,000, was to pay $2 more per doll (20,000 dolls × $2). Second, each time Child's Delight ran out of inventory and had to reorder, it had to pay the current market rate. Given the high popularity of Burzee Dolls during the holiday buying spree, it is not surprising that the manufacturer raised the price. This cost was passed through the distributor to Child's Delight, which had to pay an additional $3 per doll for its last two shipments. Overall, this resulted in an additional $30,000 in cost (10,000 dolls × $3). Finally, each purchase event at Child's Delight adds to the management activities that must take place. If we assume that both companies have similar inventory acquisition activities, then Child's Delight must have $5,000 in purchase order costs (4 purchases × $1,250 activity costs). Again, though, low inventory levels have their advantage. Because Child's Delight orders only 5,000 dolls at a time, its inventory will range from 0 to 5,000 dolls. On average, it will generally have 2,500 dolls on hand. Based on an average monthly overhead cost of $1.10 per doll, selling Burzee Dolls led to relatively low overhead costs of $5,500 (again, assuming similar ABC costs for storage, security, and other supervisory activities for Child's Delight and Kids N Toys). Clearly, Child's Delight management should pay attention to all these numbers as it evaluates this year's operations and make plans for next year.

Remember that the format and content of financial accounting reports are standardized in order to allow external users to compare reports from many different companies. In contrast, the format and content of internal management accounting reports differ across organizations because each organization customizes the reports to fit specific needs. Hence, the format of the management accounting report in Exhibit 6-10 is not regulated by anyone! The accountants for one particular retailer will customize the report to best support their own management processes of planning, controlling, and evaluating. The cost calculations displayed in Exhibit 6-10 are used by many, but not all, organizations in the merchandising industry. In this case, we saw that a simple comparison of gross margins does not necessarily indicate which company, Kids N Toys (gross margin of $793,200) or Child's Delight (gross margin of $325,500), made the better decisions. By including information on inventory management, we concluded that Child's Delight had more successfully combined the activities of profitable sales with efficient asset utilization. The more detailed profit analysis contained in Exhibit 6-10 enabled us to look more closely at the specific factors affecting the net operating profit of Kids N Toys and Child's Delight.

to summarize

Because wholesalers and retailers generally do not have to deal with raw materials or work in process, the process of accounting for inventory in a merchandising business is not nearly as complicated as it is in a manufacturing business. However, *managing* inventory costs is both complicated and critical for a merchant. Having too much inventory creates unnecessary overhead costs, financial holding costs, costs due to loss of market value, and costs due to inventory shrinkage. Not having enough inventory may result in unnecessary ordering costs and loss of bulk order discounts, as well as opportunity costs due to lost sales and increased supplier prices. While measuring some of these costs presents a challenge to accountants, the information is very important to the processes of planning, controlling, and evaluating gross margins and net operating profits for individual product lines.

4

Measure profitability and personnel utilization in a service organization.

COST MANAGEMENT IN SERVICE ORGANIZATIONS

As discussed in Chapter 3 of management accounting, service organizations have many characteristics in common with manufacturing organizations. Both types of organizations engage in a substantial production process before delivering the final product to the customer. In a manufacturing organization, this production process involves people assembling materials using equipment located in factories. In a service organization, materials are of much smaller importance, and the production process focuses on people delivering a service within an infrastructure of tangible assets (hotels, delivery trucks, barbershops, doctors' offices, etc.). In some service organizations, such as airline service, the focus is on the tangible asset infrastructure—while the pilots, flight attendants, and ticket agents are important, most of our interest centers around the reliability of the planes and the baggage handling equipment. In other service organizations, such as legal services, the focus is on person-to-person delivery of customized service—we don't really care how nice the attorney's office is, as long as the attorney gives us good legal counsel. In this section, the evaluation of cost management will be discussed in the context of a service organization.

Characteristics of a Service Organization

Service organizations can be broadly categorized into three basic types: professional services, service shops, and mass services.[4] A professional services organization is associated with people pro-

4 See Lin Fitzgerald, Robert Johnson, Stan Brignall, Rhian Silvestro, and Christopher Voss, *Performance Measurement in Service Businesses* (London: CIMA, 1991).

A family doctor clinic is categorized as a professional services organization because the doctor provides a highly customized service—treatment is tailored to individual patients.

viding a highly customized service process. For example, a good family doctor tailors the treatment to the specific patient, after developing a personal rapport with the patient and carefully extracting a thorough case history. At the other end of the continuum, a mass service organization provides a standardized product with little emphasis on the person delivering the product. For example, **MCDONALD'S** has developed its fast-food business around the delivery of standard-quality food in a predictable atmosphere; we are pleased when the person serving us is competent and cheerful, but we are primarily interested in the taste of the food and the cleanliness of the restrooms. A service shop is somewhere between a professional service and a mass service. For example, in a large-scale laser eye surgery clinic, there is more emphasis on standardization and on the equipment itself than one finds in a family doctor clinic. Also, in a high-end sit-down restaurant, the taste of the food is still important, but the quality of the personal service is at least as important.

The different characteristics of professional services, service shops, and mass services are summarized in Exhibit 6-11. Professional services are those services that emphasize person-to-

exhibit 6-11 Characteristics of Service Organizations

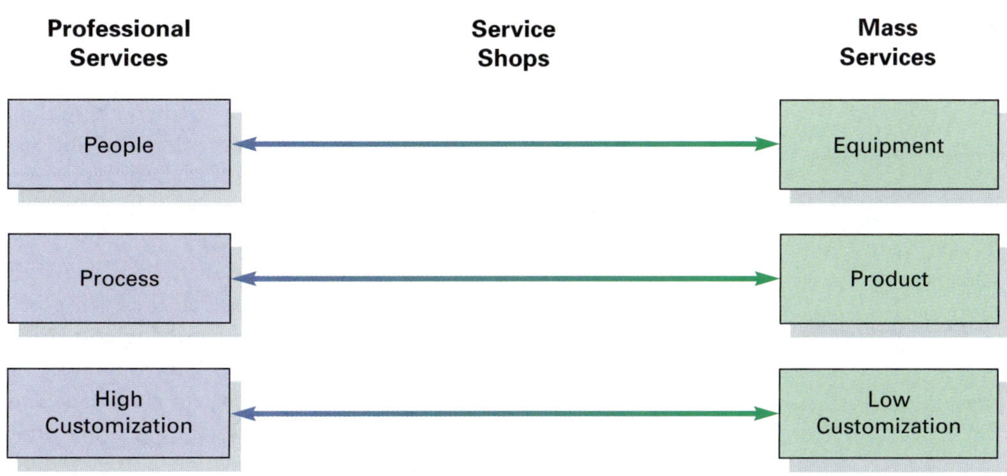

person delivery, that focus on the process of service delivery rather than the creation of some final, tangible product, and that are highly customized. Mass services are those services that rely on equipment more than people in delivering the service, that result in the customer taking away a tangible product, and that do little, if any, tailoring to individual customer needs. Service shops provide a mixture of the three dimensions of people/equipment, process/product, and high/low customization.

Cost Management in a Service Organization

As we saw earlier in the chapter in our discussion of cost management in manufacturing and merchandising organizations, it is important for an organization to evaluate the magnitude of its costs and the degree to which it is efficiently utilizing its resources. We looked at cost and profitability measures, as well as at indicators of inventory management (such as inventory turnover). The same two concepts—evaluation of profitability and efficiency—will be used in developing cost management tools for services organizations.

The magnitude of an organization's costs can be evaluated in at least three ways. First, the trend in the costs over time can be examined. For example, back in Exhibit 6-4, we evaluated the performance of Broyman Furniture by looking at the patterns in its monthly production cost numbers. Second, actual costs can be compared to budgeted costs. Preparation and use of cost budgets were discussed at length in Chapter 5 of management accounting. Finally, the magnitude of a cost can be evaluated by comparing it to the associated revenue. For example, as part of our evaluation of the sale of Burzee Dolls by Kids N Toys and Child's Delight, we looked at the gross margin (retail sales less wholesale cost of goods sold). In our illustration of cost management in a service organization in this section, we will use this latter approach of comparing costs to revenues in order to evaluate costs. Remember, however, that time-series cost trends and comparison of budgeted costs to actual costs can also be used.

For a manufacturing organization, key resources used in the production process are raw materials, machine hours, factory space, and labor. For a merchandising organization, the management of the level of inventory is crucial to the efficient use of the organization's resources. For a service organization, the management of materials inventories, building space, and equipment usage is also important. However, to emphasize the importance of people in service organizations, our illustration in this chapter will identify one way in which a service organization can measure the degree to which it is efficiently using its people.

Illustration: Cost Management in an Audit Firm

A large audit firm is a good example of a professional services organization. Actually, an "audit" firm is better characterized as being a professional services firm in the businesses of advising companies on how to improve their operating systems and processes; providing specialized accounting, tax, and information systems consulting; and conducting audits of financial statements. In fact, the broad-based nature of the services provided by audit firms has gotten them into a bit of trouble with the Securities and Exchange Commission (SEC)—in November 2000, the SEC adopted new regulations restricting the type of consulting services that an audit firm can provide to a company that it also audits.

The illustration in this section is for the hypothetical audit firm of LeviForrester. This illustration will center on the audit services offered in one large regional office of the firm. The office employs approximately 200 professionals and another 100 support staff. We will examine the costs associated with the professionals in the office. The costs of the support staff, as well as the training, recruiting, marketing, and technical analysis costs charged to the regional office by the national headquarters of LeviForrester, are also very important to the overall profitability of the regional office. However, assigning these support costs and national charges to specific jobs is quite difficult. The task of identifying cost drivers, common costs, and other concepts important to the proper treatment of these indirect support costs will be undertaken in Chapter 7 of management accounting, where we discuss activity-based costing. For the example in this chapter, we will restrict our attention to personnel costs that can be directly traced to specific client engagements.

The regional office of LeviForrester employs five types of professionals, as listed below.

	Average Years of Service with the Firm	Number of Professionals in the Office
Partner	More than 12 years	10
Senior manager	9 to 12 years	15
Manager	6 to 8 years	20
Senior	3 to 5 years	50
Staff	1 to 2 years	100

The partners exercise overall oversight of the audit practice. They review and approve the supporting documents (in electronic form) for each audit. They also seek to build the business by finding new clients. One of the 10 partners is designated the "managing partner" and is responsible for running the office and setting the strategic direction for the practice in that area. The senior managers and the managers are the professionals who are the primary interface between the audit firm and the clients. These managers keep the client informed about the progress of the audit and also supervise the other members of the audit team (the seniors and staff). The seniors spend much of their time at the clients' offices supervising and performing the actual work of the audit. The staff accountants do the bulk of the routine work of the audit.

Partners are expected to spend about half of their time working on specific client jobs during the year. This works out to be 1,000 hours out of the potential 2,000 working hours (50 weeks × 40 hours per week) during the year. At other times, partners are cultivating new client relationships and making proposals in order to get new client engagements. Senior managers and managers are expected to spend 75% of their time working on specific client engagements; seniors and staff are expected to spend all of their time working on specific client engagements. In fact, an important responsibility within the audit firm is the planning of the demands of various audit engagements to make sure that all of the seniors and the staff are always scheduled for specific engagements and are not sitting around the main office because of "unassigned" time.

These expectations about how much of a professional's time is to be spent in serving specific clients are used to develop billing rates and job cost charges. The computation of these billing rates and job cost charges is shown in Exhibit 6-12. The job cost charges are computed as a professional's total annual compensation divided by the number of client hours to be worked during a year. For example, a partner's annual compensation is $400,000, and each partner is expected to work on specific client engagements for 1,000 hours during a year. Thus, the partner compensation cost assigned to a job is $400 per hour ($400,000 ÷ 1,000 hours). These job cost charges are used by LeviForrester to compute the professional labor cost associated with each audit engagement.

exhibit 6-12 Billing Rates and Job Cost Charges for LeviForrester

	Annual Compensation	Expected Billable Hours	Compensation Cost per Billable Hour	Client Billing Rate per Billable Hour
Partner	$400,000	1,000	$400	$500
Senior manager	130,000	1,500	87	300
Manager	100,000	1,500	67	225
Senior	50,000	2,000	25	150
Staff	40,000	2,000	20	100

The billing rates are used in computing how much is to be charged to a client for an audit engagement. As explained in Chapter 3 of management accounting, the billing rate for professional services is large enough to cover both the payment to the professional and general administrative costs such as secretarial support, computers, supplies, travel, and so forth. LeviForrester's billing rates for each type of professional are shown in Exhibit 6-12. As you can imagine, the determination of these billing rates is an extremely important element in LeviForrester's success. Billing rates that are too high will drive away potential customers whereas billing rates that are too low will lead to low profitability and, perhaps, the inability to appropriately compensate the professionals.

On October 5, the managing partner for the regional office of LeviForrester received the profitability report contained in Exhibit 6-13. The report is generated in early October because LeviForrester's fiscal year ends on September 30—it is impossible for LeviForrester to analyze its own business operations at the end of the normal calendar year because January is the busiest month of the year for audit firms as they perform audit work for their clients with December 31 year-ends. The managing partner used the data in the profitability report to compute profit percentage from professionals (PPP), which is the fundamental measure of profitability used by LeviForrester. PPP is computed as follows:

$$\begin{aligned} \text{PPP} &= (\text{Revenue} - \text{Professional compensation cost}) \div \text{Revenue} \\ &= (\$60{,}975{,}000 - \$14{,}450{,}000) \div \$60{,}975{,}000 \\ &= 76.3\% \end{aligned}$$

The managing partner is quite pleased with this report because the firm-wide goal for PPP is just 73.0%. As the various regional offices within LeviForrester are evaluated, each region's PPP is used to allocate a firm-wide bonus pool—the professionals in regions with PPP in excess of 73.0% can expect to receive higher-than-average year-end bonuses.

The managing partner also received the personnel utilization report contained in Exhibit 6-14. The report contains personnel utilization rates (PUR) for each category of professional within the firm. The contents of this report are somewhat disturbing. The managing partner sees that the partners in the office spent only 82.0% of the time that they should have on specific client engagements. In addition, the hours billed by managers, seniors, and staff accountants were well in excess of 100% of the expected amount. This personnel utilization pattern suggests at least two potential future problems. First, existing clients may become concerned that the LeviForrester partners are not spending as much time with them as they had anticipated. The clients may feel that the LeviForrester partners are now spending too much time finding new clients and not enough time attending to the needs of the existing clients. Second, the high utilization rates for the managers, seniors, and staff are a warning sign that these key professionals may be being worked too hard. Hiring and training new professionals is an expensive process, and LeviForrester does not want to overwork its young professionals, resulting in abnormally high employee turnover.

exhibit 6-13 Profitability Report for LeviForrester

	Number of Professionals	Actual Billable Hours	Billing Rate	Total Revenue	Total Compensation Cost
Partners	10	8,200	$500	$ 4,100,000	$ 4,000,000
Senior managers . .	15	20,000	300	6,000,000	1,950,000
Managers.	20	35,000	225	7,875,000	2,000,000
Seniors.	50	120,000	150	18,000,000	2,500,000
Staff.	100	250,000	100	25,000,000	4,000,000
Total.				$60,975,000	$14,450,000

exhibit 6-14 Personnel Utilization Report for LeviForrester

	Actual Billable	Budgeted Billable	Utilization Rate
Partners	8,200	10,000	82.0%
Senior managers	20,000	22,500	88.9%
Managers	35,000	30,000	116.7%
Seniors	120,000	100,000	120.0%
Staff	250,000	200,000	125.0%

The two specific measures used in this example—PPP and PUR—are intended only as illustrations; measures with these specific names are not in use in any real professional services firm. However, measures similar to these are very commonly used in service organizations. These two measures are representative of a broad class of measures that indicate the performance of service organizations on two important dimensions—profitability and personnel utilization.

to summarize

Three broad types of service organizations are professional services, service shops, and mass services. The dimensions on which these types of organizations differ are people/equipment, process/product, and high/low customization. As with manufacturing and merchandising organizations, it is important to measure both profitability and resource utilization in a service organization. In a professional services firm, profitability is measured by comparing the service revenues with the compensation costs associated with the professionals. It is also important to monitor the degree to which the professionals are appropriately utilized within the firm.

expanded material

As mentioned earlier in the chapter, an important element of cost management is the evaluation of whether an organization is utilizing its resources efficiently. In the expanded material section of this chapter, you will learn further details about resource management. In particular, the expanded material discusses ways to determine the appropriate level of inventory that should be maintained by an organization.

5 Calculate and interpret holding costs in merchandising and service businesses.

OPPORTUNITY COSTS IN MANAGING INVENTORY AND WORK-IN-PROCESS SERVICES

Let's return to our Burzee Doll example to discuss opportunity costs involved in managing inventory. As discussed in Chapter 1 in management accounting, there are many types of costs involved in managing an organization. All the costs that we discussed in the management accounting report for Kids N Toys and Child's Delight involved out-of-pocket costs (see Exhibit 6-10). However, there are several cost issues listed in Exhibit 6-7 that we did not include in the earlier analysis for these two companies. For example, inventory flexibility involves potential opportunity costs related to investing in a lot of inventory. Kids N Toys tied up a lot of money in securing 50,000 Burzee Dolls for the Christmas season—a shopping season that is particularly critical for retailers in the United States. Kids N Toys may have been fortunate that the Burzee Doll line sold as well as it did. If fickle shopper tastes had turned instead to another toy, it would have been difficult for Kids N Toys to shift this part of its inventory investment out of Burzee Dolls and into an alternative item in time to take advantage of the Christmas shopping rush. Kids N Toys may not have had any real problems in this area, but it needs to pay attention to this issue in planning for next year.

Child's Delight was also exposed to some opportunity costs. For example, because it kept its inventory of Burzee Dolls much lower than its competitor, Child's Delight was much more at risk of losing sales due to problems with supplier delivery and other logistics beyond its control. We'll assume in this case that all its deliveries were on time and without problems. However, another opportunity cost that Child's Delight was clearly not so fortunate in avoiding was lost sales due to lack of inventory. During the same period of time that Child's Delight sold its 19,850 dolls, Kids N Toys sold 41,500 dolls. If these retailers were at all similar in terms of competitive factors such as location and advertising, then it appears certain that Child's Delight could have sold more dolls *if* it had had more dolls! How many more dolls could have been sold? Frankly, this is a very difficult number to measure—even for a good management accountant. You won't see it measured on any of the management accounting reports in this chapter. That does not at all imply that this number is less important than the others. There is a lot of discussion (and disagreement) on how to measure this number. The important thing is to somehow make decision makers aware of this cost. However, there is so much disagreement in practice as to how to specifically calculate this number that it is best in a textbook such as this to simply make you aware of this particular opportunity cost issue.

Holding Costs and Economic Profit in Merchandising Organizations

economic profit The difference between net operating profit and holding costs of inventory and other asset investments. Note that generally accepted accounting principles (GAAP) do not formally recognize opportunity costs such as holding costs.

cost of capital The weighted-average cost of a firm's debt and equity capital equals the rate of return that a company must earn in order to satisfy the demands of its owners and creditors.

Another opportunity cost that both companies in our example experienced is financial holding costs. Financial holding costs are very well defined in practice. We'll use this cost to calculate for these two merchants a third income number called **economic profit**. As we calculated before, during the three-month period of November, December, and January, Kids N Toys had an average of $250,000 invested in Burzee Doll inventory. (See pages 309–311 if you need help remembering how to calculate average inventory levels.) This money could alternatively have been earning money in a financial investment, or it could have been used to pay off loans or retire stock that Kids N Toys currently has outstanding. Every business has a **cost of capital** that relates to its cost of using money. In fact, you likely have your own individual cost of capital. Do you have any loans? What is the average interest rate on those loans? Let's assume it is 15%. Hopefully, you understand that as long as you have loans, every dollar you use for anything besides paying down your loan(s) costs you 15%. This 15% rate is your cost of capital. To be specific, for every dollar you spend buying a new stereo system, your loan(s) will increase by $0.15 at the end of the year. Hence, buying the stereo had better be worth this implicit financial holding cost. Even if you don't have any loans, you probably (hopefully!) have a savings account. Your cost of capital would then be the interest rate on your investment in the savings account. Let's assume you get a 4% return on your account. In this case, for every dollar you delay putting into the account (such as money spent on your new stereo), at the end of the year, your account will be $0.04 less than it could have been. Obviously, this cost information is important to all decisions involving the investment of limited resources. The formula to calculate a financial holding cost is the same approach traditionally used to calculate interest costs. We'll assume that the cost of capital for both Kids N Toys and Child's Delight is 20%. The financial holding cost of the average Burzee Doll inventory investment for Kids N Toys can be calculated in the following manner:

Financial holding cost = Average investment × Annual rate × Number of periods
$250,000 × 20% × 3/12 year = $12,500

The financial holding cost for Child's Delight can also be calculated. Remember, we calculated earlier that Child's Delight had a much lower average investment in inventory. In addition, this company's investment in Burzee Dolls lasted only for two months—November and December. As a result, its financial holding cost was much lower than Kids N Toys and is calculated as follows:

$33,750 × 20% × 2/12 year = $1,125

The financial holding cost is as much a cost of being in the business of selling Burzee Dolls as any other cost we calculated and listed earlier in Exhibit 6-10. Most accountants recognize that measuring financial holding costs is important to managing the economic well-being of the organization. Hence, in Exhibit 6-15 we have expanded the original management accounting report on the Burzee Doll inventory to include financial holding costs in order to calculate the organization's economic profit.

Before we leave this example and move on to discuss holding costs in service organizations, take one more opportunity to compare the gross margin report in Exhibit 6-9 and the management accounting report in Exhibit 6-15. These two merchandising reports would look basically the same regardless of whether Child's Delight and Kids N Toys were retailers or wholesalers of toys. You should now have a pretty clear understanding of how dramatically

exhibit 6-15 Expanded Management Accounting Report on the Burzee Doll Inventory

In addition to cost of purchases, note the following additional inventory costs:

- Average inventory overhead costs are $1.10 per unit per month.
- Average costs to initiate and receive a purchase order are $1,250 per event.
- Average costs of capital are 20%.

	Kids N Toys, Inc.		Child's Delight, Inc.	
Expected revenue	50,000 units × $30 standard price	$1,500,000	20,000 units × $30 standard price	$ 600,000
Shrinkage loss	1,600 units × $30	(48,000)	150 units × $30	(4,500)
Market loss	2,000 units × ($30 − $10) + 4,400 units × ($30 − $3)	(158,800)		(0)
Actual revenue		$1,293,200		$ 595,500
Purchase costs	50,000 units × $10 standard cost	(500,000)	20,000 units × $10 standard cost	(200,000)
Lost discount		(0)	20,000 units × $2 lost discount	(40,000)
Price increase		(0)	10,000 units × $3 price increase	(30,000)
Gross margin		$ 793,200		$ 325,500
Overhead costs	50,000 units ÷ 2 = 25,000 average inventory level × $1.10 × 3 months	(82,500)	5,000 units ÷ 2 = 2,500 average inventory level × $1.10 × 2 months	(5,500)
Order costs	1 order × $1,250	(1,250)	4 orders × $1,250	(5,000)
Net operating profit		$ 709,450		$ 315,000
Holding costs	$500,000 in purchases ÷ 2 = $250,000 average inventory investment × 20% × 3/12 year	(12,500)	($60,000 + $60,000 + $75,000 + $75,000) ÷ 4 = $67,500 average purchase ÷ 2 = $33,750 average inventory investment × 20% × 2/12 year	(1,125)
Economic profit		$ 696,950		$ 313,875

segment Any part of an organization requiring separate reports for evaluation by management.

Economic Value Added (EVA®) A commercialized performance measurement system that emphasizes the incremental profits an organization creates over and above the profit required to cover the costs of capital.

management accounting can differ from financial accounting in analyzing results of merchandising organizations. It is also important to point out that the reports in Exhibits 6-9 and 6-15 are both **segment** reports that are specific to inventory lines in these companies. A complete net operating profit analysis of all operations at either company should obviously include revenues and costs that are specific to all other inventory lines and overhead costs that are common across the organization (for example, the salaries for company executives). A complete economic profit analysis (sometimes called an **Economic Value Added** or **EVA**®) would include a "holding cost" on all assets belonging to the company (cash, investments, equipment, buildings, land, etc.).

Service Organizations and Holding Costs

Something you should realize about GAAP and the service industry is that there typically has *not* been nearly as much emphasis on measuring and reporting work-in-process costs as compared to the manufacturing industry. However, it is important that the management accountant support the management process by reporting on the costs invested in work-in-process services. Think about the economic facts of work-in-process services for a moment. What do these costs represent? They represent significant investments in services provided to a client that typically have yet to provide any kind of a ROI in terms of cash receipts. Work in process is obviously necessary in many service companies. However, service companies cannot allow work-in-process services to build up in their organizations without restraint. Otherwise, resources are tied up that could otherwise be used to provide additional salable services. These opportunity costs eventually reduce profits in the company. Doesn't this sound a lot like the same risk of holding costs we described for merchandising companies earlier in this section? Accountants can and should measure holding costs on large service projects. Such measures provide decision makers with the insight to assess the effects of not properly planning and controlling large service projects. For example, consider a large accounting firm that is planning an audit which is expected to take three months to complete. Suppose that by the end of the three months, this large accounting firm has invested $400,000 in supplies, labor, and overhead for the audit project. Because most service companies have outstanding debts that are accruing interest costs or investment opportunities that have a measurable rate of return, these companies will incur a cost of capital just like merchants and manufacturers. If the accounting firm's cost of capital is 20%, the holding costs on this project are:

fyi

A study on cost accounting in the service industry reported that 65% of service companies have significant levels of work in process at the end of their reporting periods.

Average investment during the three-month period—($0 + $400,000) ÷ 2 = $200,000

Holding cost—$200,000 × 20% × 3/12 months = $10,000

What if the accounting firm has not completed the audit at the end of three months? At this point, it appears that the audit will require another month and another $40,000 in costs to complete. What are the additional holding costs of this extra month?

Average investment during the fourth month—($400,000 + $440,000) ÷ 2 = $420,000

Additional holding cost—$420,000 × 20% × 1/12 months = $7,000[5]

Computing and understanding these cost data provide a lot of incentive for the audit manager to complete the job and collect fees as quickly as possible. In providing these data, the accountant is supporting good planning and control of work in process in the audit service process.

5 Note that ($440,000 ÷ 2) × 20% × (4/12) < $10,000 + $7,000. This is because the costs on this audit contract are building much faster in the first three months ($400,000 in three months) than in the last month ($40,000 in one month). Similarly, using $400,000 ÷ 2 assumes that the $400,000 in costs is growing evenly over the three-month period ($133,333 per month). A more accurate method of computing the total holding costs for the four-month period would involve calculating and summing the holding costs for each individual month.

to summarize

Both merchandising and service firms often experience several types of opportunity costs, such as lost sales due to not having enough inventory or delays in completing work in process for customers. These costs are extremely difficult to measure. One important category of opportunity costs that management accountants can measure is financial holding costs, which is a measure of the costs of having money tied up in inventory (for merchants) or in work-in-process services (for service companies). Measuring holding costs requires that the company's cost of capital first be identified. The holding cost formula is Average investment in inventory or Work-in-process services × Annual rate × Number of periods. Financial holding costs can be deducted from net operating profit to measure economic profit for a particular product line.

6

Use classic quantitative tools in inventory management (economic order quantity, reorder point, and safety stock).

QUANTITATIVE INVENTORY MANAGEMENT METHODS

We have spent a lot of time in this chapter discussing the many types of costs involved in managing inventory for merchants. These issues are listed in Exhibit 6-7. Generally, service companies do not carry significant levels of inventory and do not need to pay as much attention to inventory management costs. However, many manufacturing companies carry significant inventory levels of raw materials, work in process, and finished goods. These companies need to pay attention to issues involved in managing costs of carrying too much versus too little inventory. The primary question here is, "How much inventory should a company have?" This section will describe some quantitative methods that can be useful to accountants working to answer this question. We will use the example of a merchandising company to illustrate these methods; however, these inventory management calculations are equally applicable to manufacturing companies.

economic order quantity (EOQ) A specific calculation used to determine the most cost-effective size of a purchase order. The EOQ balances the costs of placing an order against the costs of carrying inventory in the organization.

Economic Order Quantity

It is a significant challenge to balance the costs (in Exhibit 6-7) of carrying too much inventory against the costs of carrying too little inventory. Determining how much inventory a company should have involves two important issues: (1) knowing *how much* inventory to order and (2) knowing *when* to place the inventory order. One well-known method used to handle the first issue is the **economic order quantity (EOQ)**. In calculating the optimal size of an inventory order, the EOQ attempts to balance the costs of carrying inventory (e.g., overhead costs, holding costs, risk of lost market values, shrinkage, etc.) against the costs involved in purchasing inventory.

caution

It is important that you understand that the purchase costs used to calculate the EOQ are *not* the inventory purchase prices, but the overhead costs involved in handling a purchase order (e.g., preparing purchase orders, receiving and inspecting shipments, initiating payment for purchases, etc.).

We'll use the Burzee Doll example to demonstrate how to balance carrying costs and purchasing costs to calculate EOQ. First, we need to determine a cost per doll that includes all the costs of carrying Burzee Dolls during the two-month holiday buying season (November and December). Look back at Exhibit 6-15. Carrying costs should include the cost due to shrinkage loss, cost due to market loss, overhead costs, and holding costs. You should realize that combining all these carrying costs into a single cost per unit requires a great deal of analysis and intuition on the part of the accountant. However, let's assume that carrying costs are approximately \$5 per doll. In addition, purchase order costs are \$1,250 per order. Finally, we'll assume that a merchant can sell as many as 40,000 dolls during the holiday buying season. Exhibit 6-16 demonstrates one method of calculating EOQ using a cost schedule approach. As you can see, as the order quantity gets higher, the average inventory level in the store increases, and total carrying costs increase; in addition, the total purchase orders for the buying season are reduced, resulting in lower total ordering costs. By calculating the total of both carrying and ordering costs, the accountant can get a general idea of the optimal (i.e., economic) order quantity. According to the numbers in Exhibit 6-16, it appears that the store should request approximately 4,500 dolls for each of its nine orders during the buying season.

STOP & THINK Think about EOQ and the relationship between the costs of carrying inventory versus the costs involved in purchasing inventory. As costs of carrying inventory increase, should the organization increase or decrease the size of its purchase orders? As costs of purchasing inventory increase, should the organization increase or decrease the size of its purchase orders?

There is an alternative, and more precise, approach to calculating the EOQ using a formula (derived by calculus). Without working through the calculus derivation, the EOQ formula is:

$$\text{EOQ} = \sqrt{\frac{2QP}{C}}$$

Q = The market demand in units for the period
P = The overhead cost of placing one order
C = The total carrying cost for one unit for the period

By inserting our Burzee Doll data into the EOQ formula, we can calculate the precise EOQ as follows:

$$\text{EOQ} = \sqrt{\frac{2(40{,}000)(\$1{,}250)}{\$5}} = \sqrt{\frac{\$100{,}000{,}000}{\$5}} = \sqrt{20{,}000{,}000} = 4{,}472 \text{ dolls}$$

Now that we have the EOQ, we can calculate the following exact costs:

Total carrying costs = 4,472 ÷ 2 = 2,236 average inventory × $5 = $11,180
Total ordering costs = 40,000 ÷ 4,472 = 9 orders × $1,250 = $11,250
Total inventory management costs = $11,180 + $11,250 = $22,430

Using the EOQ formula is much faster and more precise than working through an EOQ cost schedule. With the EOQ, we can resolve the first of two important issues involved in determining how much inventory a company should have—knowing *how much* inventory to order. Now we will turn our attention to the second issue—knowing *when* to place the inventory order.

exhibit 6-16 Calculating EOQ Using a Cost Schedule

Base data:

- Total market demand for dolls for the period: 40,000 dolls
- Average carrying cost per doll for the period: $5
- Average overhead costs per purchase order: $1,250

Order Quantity	**1,500**	**2,250**	**3,000**	**3,750**	**4,500**	**5,250**	**6,000**	**6,750**
	÷ 2	÷ 2	÷ 2	÷ 2	÷ 2	÷ 2	÷ 2	÷ 2
Average inventory level	750	1,125	1,500	1,875	2,250	2,625	3,000	3,375
× Carrying cost	$ 5	$ 5	$ 5	$ 5	$ 5	$ 5	$ 5	$ 5
Total Carrying Costs	**$ 3,750**	**$ 5,625**	**$ 7,500**	**$ 9,375**	**$11,250**	**$13,125**	**$15,000**	**$16,875**
Total demand	40,000	40,000	40,000	40,000	40,000	40,000	40,000	40,000
÷ by Order quantity	1,500	2,250	3,000	3,750	4,500	5,250	6,000	6,750
Number of orders (rounded up)	27	18	14	11	9	8	7	6
× Costs per order	$ 1,250	$ 1,250	$ 1,250	$ 1,250	$ 1,250	$ 1,250	$ 1,250	$ 1,250
Total Ordering Costs	**$33,750**	**$22,500**	**$17,500**	**$13,750**	**$11,250**	**$10,000**	**$ 8,750**	**$ 7,500**
Total Costs	**$37,500**	**$28,125**	**$25,000**	**$23,125**	**$22,500**	**$23,125**	**$23,750**	**$24,375**

Reorder Point and Safety Stock

Knowing *when* to place the inventory order involves the reorder point and the desired safety stock. Assume for a moment that you are the manager of the Kids N Toys store. Now that you have calculated the EOQ, you need to know exactly when to place your order. You don't want to reorder Burzee Dolls too soon, or you'll end up with more inventory on hand than you need. This will result in unnecessary overhead costs, holding costs, and possibly increased inventory shrinkage. On the other hand, if you wait until you're nearly out of dolls before you place the order, you'll probably run out of inventory before the next shipment arrives. This will result in lost sales—a serious opportunity cost. Walking through your store, you watch the levels of dolls on your shelves and in your storeroom decline as customers make purchases. In terms of level of Burzee Doll inventory, at what point do you place your next order? Essentially, you need to calculate a **reorder point**. The calculation is quite simple:

reorder point The point at which the inventory level in the organization drops low enough to trigger a new purchase order.

Reorder point = Average lead time in days × Average daily sales

Lead time, in this case, is the time between when store management initiates a purchase order and when the inventory is finally delivered and ready for sale. Lead time for Burzee Dolls would include the time it takes for Kids N Toys to process any necessary paperwork to initiate the purchase order, for the distributor to process the purchase order and deliver the goods, and for Kids N Toys to receive and prepare the dolls for aisle display. Let's assume that lead time for the Burzee Doll is three days. Further, Kids N Toys sells, on average, 800 dolls per day. The reorder point calculation is:

Reorder point = 3 days × 800 dolls = 2,400 dolls

When the inventory falls to 2,400 dolls, you need to initiate a new purchase order. By the time the order arrives, the store should be selling its last doll.

At this point, a couple of things about this reorder point number may be bothering you. One possible problem is that the reorder point calculation is assuming a perfect world. In other words, the reorder point calculation shown assumes that sales are *always* 800 dolls per day and that the lead time is *always* three days. A sudden surge in customer demand or any problems in order processing or shipping could result in empty shelves. As manager for Kids N Toys, you may think you should build a little cushion into your reorder point calculation to allow for any unexpected problems. This is the purpose of **safety stock**. The calculation of the amount of safety stock has two parts: (1) to handle possible problems in the reorder process and (2) to handle an unexpected spike in sales demand. Let's assume that problems in the reorder process could result in a maximum lead time of four days. Further, as many as 875 dolls could sell in one day. The safety stock calculation would be as follows:

safety stock The minimal level of inventory required to ensure against the organization running out of inventory in the case of unforeseen problems in receiving its next purchase order.

Maximum lead time	4 days	
Average lead time in days	3 days	
Surplus	1 day	
Average expected sales per day	× 800 dolls	
Safety stock for reorder problem		800 dolls
Maximum expected sales per day	875 dolls	
Average expected sales per day	800 dolls	
Surplus	75 dolls	
Maximum lead time	× 4 days	
Safety stock for demand changes		300 dolls
Total safety stock		1,100 dolls

Based on these numbers, Kids N Toys will always want to keep at least 1,100 dolls on hand to handle unexpected situations involving either its suppliers or its customers. Hence, this safety stock number should be added to the original reorder point calculation, resulting in a new reorder point calculation that includes a cushion for safety stock:

Reorder point with safety stock = (Average lead time in days × Average daily sales) + Safety stock
= (3 days × 800 dolls) + 1,100 dolls = 3,500 dolls

You've likely noticed that the reorder point calculation that includes safety stock can be directly calculated as:

Reorder point with safety stock = Maximum lead time in days × Maximum daily sales
= 4 days × 875 dolls = 3,500 dolls

Combining these two calculations into one simple calculation is acceptable, assuming that management is not interested in knowing the specific level for safety stock. Usually, though, store management wants to know when sales are eating into the safety stock. Such a situation signals that special attention is needed to ensure that the store does not run out of stock and miss some customer sales. Exhibit 6-17 graphically depicts these relationships.

caution

Perhaps you've heard of the saying "Garbage in, garbage out!" The quality of these three quantitative inventory management models (like all decision models and systems in business) is only as good as the quality of the information that is used in the calculations. Before using the EOQ, reorder point, or safety stock calculations, the accountant needs to be sure that all costs and risks of carrying and ordering inventory are understood. Current JIT thinking suggests that accountants in the past may have severely understated the costs of carrying inventory, resulting in unnecessarily large inventory orders and high levels of inventory in the organization.

to summarize

Balancing costs of carrying too much inventory against the costs of carrying too little inventory is a significant challenge for accountants in both merchandising and manufacturing organizations. The economic order quantity, reorder point, and safety stock calculations can help. Exhibit 6-17 graphically summarizes the relationship between EOQ, reorder points, and safety stock inventory levels. Consider Exhibit 6-17 in light of the inventory management issues in Exhibit 6-7. The EOQ model is a useful tool for managing carrying costs (e.g., overhead costs, holding costs, losses

exhibit 6-17 Graphical Display of EOQ, Reorder Points, and Safety Stock Inventory Levels

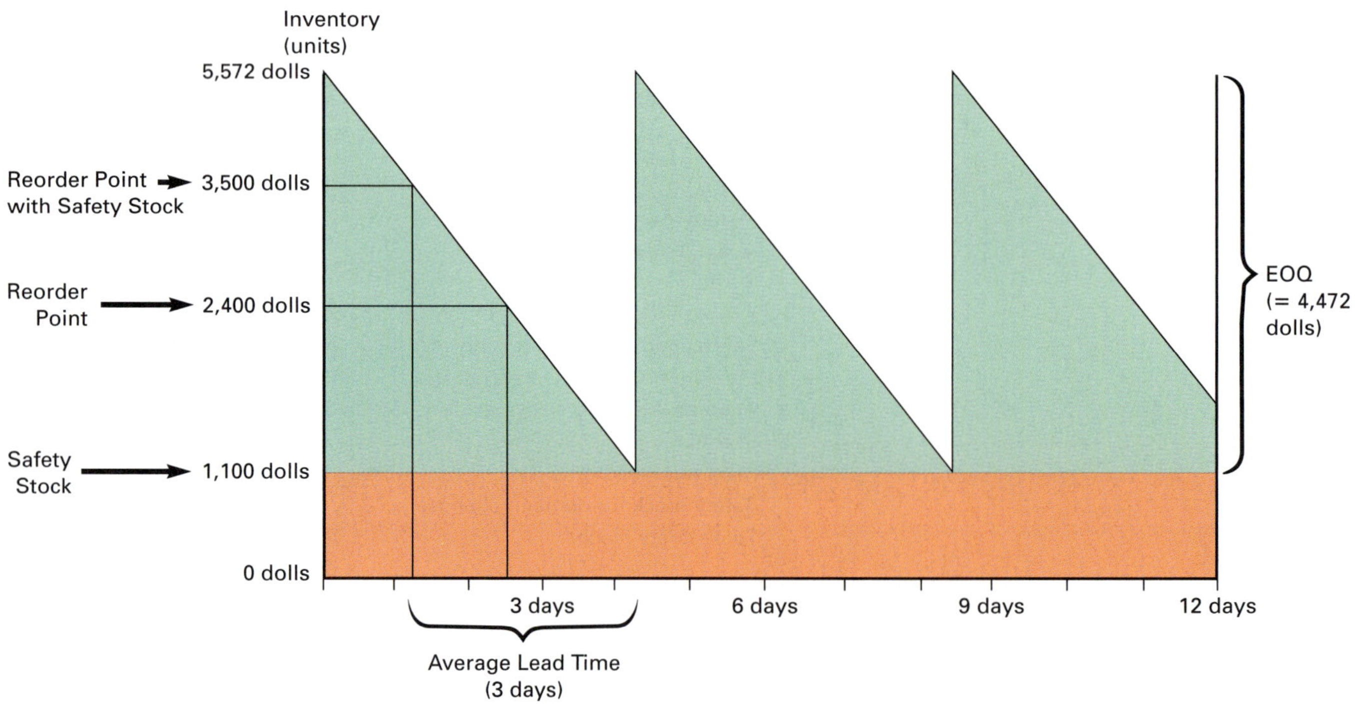

due to decreased market value, and the cost of inventory shrinkage). The EOQ model balances these carrying costs against ordering costs. In addition, the EOQ should be combined with intelligent calculations of reorder points and safety stock in order to guard against excessive risk of lost sales due to delivery problems and fluctuating market demand.

---

review of learning objectives

1 **Outline the different cost flow patterns in manufacturing, merchandising, and service organizations and understand how these costs are reflected in the income statement and balance sheet.** Both manufacturing and service organizations maintain substantial production processes. As a result, both types of organizations report work-in-process inventory in the balance sheet. In addition, the computation of cost of goods sold can be quite complex for these types of organizations because the computation involves combining information about materials, labor, and overhead costs. The computation of cost of goods sold in a merchandising organization is relatively simple because inventory is purchased in its final form and no substantial additional costs are incurred in getting it ready to sell. Both manufacturing and merchandising organizations maintain significant levels of ending inventory that are reported in the balance sheet.

2 **Interpret a cost of goods manufactured schedule and analyze the levels of raw materials, work-in-process, and finished goods inventories in a manufacturing organization.** Manufacturing costs are summarized on a cost of goods manufactured schedule. The total manufacturing cost for a period is the sum of the direct materials and direct labor costs incurred, as well as an addition for the amount of overhead applied to the goods in production during the period. The cost of goods manufactured is the cost of goods completed and transferred out of work-in-process inventory during the period. The cost of goods manufactured is added to the beginning finished goods inventory to determine cost of goods available for sale. Ending finished goods inventory is then subtracted from this number to compute cost of goods sold. Inventory turnover measures can be used to evaluate the levels of raw materials, work-in-process, and finished goods inventories. The level of raw materials inventory is compared to the amount of materials used during the period. Work-in-process inventory is compared to the total manufacturing costs incurred during the period. The level of finished goods inventory is compared to the cost of goods sold during the period.

3 **Understand how merchants manage cost information in their organizations.** Because merchants basically purchase inventory in a finished state, the process of accounting for inventory in a merchandising business is not nearly as complicated as it is in a manufacturing business. There are a number of important issues associated with managing the inventory in order to maximize sales and minimize a variety of inventory costs. For example, having too much inventory creates unnecessary overhead costs, financial holding costs, costs due to loss of market value, and costs due to inventory shrinkage. Not having enough inventory may result in unnecessary ordering costs and loss of bulk order discounts, as well as opportunity costs due to lost sales and increased supplier prices. Measuring these costs allows management accountants to prepare detailed cost reports that support effective management of gross margins and net operating profits for individual product lines.

4 **Measure profitability and personnel utilization in a service organization.** Like a manufacturing organization, a service organization involves a substantial process before delivering a final product to the customer. Three types of service organizations are professional services, service shops, and mass services. Professional service firms emphasize people-to-people service over automation, the delivery of a process rather than a final tangible product, and high customization. A mass service organization emphasizes the standardized, automated delivery of a tangible product. Service organizations, similar to manufacturing and merchandising organizations, must measure profitability and resource utilization. A professional services firm uses profitability measures based on a comparison of revenues to the compensation cost of the professionals. Personnel utilization can be measured by comparing the number of billable hours actually worked to the number that was expected.

expanded material

5 **Calculate and interpret holding costs in merchandising and service businesses.** Although opportunity costs can be extremely difficult to measure, one important type of opportunity cost that accountants can measure is financial holding costs. Financial holding costs measure the costs of having money tied up in inventory (for merchants) or in work-in-process services (for service companies). Measuring holding costs requires that the company's cost of capital first be identified. The holding cost formula is Average investment in inventory or work-in-process services × Annual rate × Number of periods. Financial holding costs can be deducted from net operating profit to measure economic profit for a particular product line. Measuring economic profit for an entire company is sometimes called Economic Value Added (EVA™).

6 Use classic quantitative tools in inventory management (economic order quantity, reorder point, and safety stock). Both merchandising and manufacturing organizations have significant investments in inventory costs. Accountants can balance the costs of carrying too much inventory against the costs of carrying too little inventory by calculating the economic order quantity (EOQ), reorder point, and safety stock. The EOQ model is a useful tool for managing carrying costs (e.g., overhead costs, holding costs, losses due to decreased market value, and the costs of inventory shrinkage). The EOQ model balances these carrying costs against ordering costs. The EOQ is combined with reorder point and safety stock calculations in order to guard against excessive risk of lost sales due to delivery problems and fluctuating market demand.

key terms and concepts

cost of goods manufactured schedule 303
days in inventory 305
holding costs 307
inventory shrinkage 308
inventory turnover (stockturns) 305
lead time 308
net operating profit 312

expanded material

cost of capital 320
economic order quantity (EOQ) 323
economic profit 320
Economic Value Added (EVA) 322
reorder point 325
safety stock 325
segment 322

review problem

Cost Management in a Service Business

[Note: This Review Problem combines the cost flow accounting tools learned in Chapter 3 of management accounting with the service organization cost management skills learned in this chapter.]

Columbus & Hercules, a public accounting firm, is computing the overhead rates to use when billing customers and bidding on jobs. Columbus & Hercules provides the following estimates relating to overhead costs for the year 2003:

Utilities	$ 12,000
Rent	30,000
Equipment depreciation	22,000
Office supplies	20,000
Support staff salaries	120,000
Total estimated overhead costs	$204,000

In addition, Columbus & Hercules offers the following annual estimates (based on a 50-week work year) regarding the salaries and estimated hours associated with the professionals employed by the firm:

Position	Total Estimated Salaries	Total Estimated Billable Hours
Partners (2 × $100,000)	$200,000	4,400
Managers (3 × $70,000)	210,000	6,600
Seniors (6 × $50,000)	300,000	13,200
Staff auditors (10 × $25,000)	250,000	22,000

Columbus & Hercules computes a chargeable hourly rate for each position that is the sum of the following: (1) each position's hourly rate (based on salary), (2) an overhead rate, and (3) a markup of 20% of (1) and (2). The overhead rate allocates estimated overhead costs to each position, then relates the allocated costs to the hours expected to be worked by each position. Travel and materials costs are directly traceable and billed to each job.

Columbus & Hercules have no client projects in process on January 1, 2003. During January of 2003, Columbus & Hercules worked on several auditing and accounting jobs and incurred the following costs:

Jan. 1 Paid rent for January, $2,500.
4 Purchased office supplies on account, $1,200.
9 Paid $4,500 for payables from last year.
15 Paid office support salaries, $5,000.
15 Paid biweekly salaries of professionals: partners, $8,000; managers, $8,400; seniors, $12,000; staff, $10,000.
15 Applied overhead costs based on billable hours: partners, 170 hours; managers, 270 hours; seniors, 500 hours; staff, 900 hours.
18 Used office supplies totaling $800 to prepare client materials.
21 Purchased office supplies on account, $1,100.
25 Received and paid invoice from office supply store for purchase on January 4.
27 Billed clients for the following jobs using the computed hourly rate for each position:

	Job #1	Job #2
Partner	90 hours	80 hours
Manager	150 hours	140 hours
Senior	320 hours	200 hours
Staff	560 hours	400 hours

28 Transferred costs from Work-in-Process Services to Cost of Services based on information from January 27.
31 Estimated utility costs for the month of January to be $1,000.
31 Paid office support salaries, $5,400.
31 Made an adjusting entry for the depreciation of office equipment, $1,900.
31 Paid biweekly salaries of professionals: partners, $8,000; managers, $8,400; seniors, $12,000; staff, $10,000.
31 Applied overhead costs based on billable hours: partners, 180 hours; managers, 280 hours; seniors, 525 hours; staff, 950 hours.

During the month, the 10 staff accountants were assigned to one of the three managers for the entire month. Managers 1 and 2 were assigned three staff accountants each; Manager 3 was assigned four staff accountants. At the end of the month, the following staff utilization report was generated:

Staff Working for:	Budgeted Billable Hours	Actual Billable Hours
Manager 1	528	690
Manager 2	528	530
Manager 3	704	630
Total	1,760	1,850

Required:

1. Compute the billing rate to be used for each position.
2. Provide the journal entries made by Columbus & Hercules for January.
3. Compute the ending balance in Work-in-Process Services.

4. Compute the ending balance in Overhead.
5. Using the January 27 billing and cost data for Jobs 1 and 2 (combined), compute a profitability percentage for the jobs. The profitability percentage is computed as [(Revenue − Cost) ÷ Revenue]. Comment, given that the target profitability percentage is 23%.
6. Use the staff utilization numbers to evaluate the staff usage practices by the three managers.

Solution

1. Billing rate

Overhead allocation rate: $204,000 ÷ $960,000 = $0.2125 per dollar of salary.

Position	Estimated Salaries	Preliminary Rate	Allocated Overhead	Hours	Overhead Rate per Hour
Partner	$200,000	$0.2125	$ 42,500	4,400	$9.66
Manager	210,000	0.2125	44,625	6,600	6.76
Senior	300,000	0.2125	63,750	13,200	4.83
Staff	250,000	0.2125	53,125	22,000	2.41
Total	$960,000		$204,000		

Billable Rate for Each Position

Position	Hourly Rate (1)	Overhead Rate (2)	Markup [(1) + (2)] × 0.20 = (3)	Billable Rate (1) + (2) + (3)
Partner	$45.45[1]	$9.66	$11.02	$66.13
Manager	31.82[2]	6.76	7.72	46.30
Senior	22.73[3]	4.83	5.51	33.07
Staff	11.36[4]	2.41	2.75	16.52

[1]$200,000 ÷ 4,400 hours = $45.45 per hour.
[2]$210,000 ÷ 6,600 hours = $31.82 per hour.
[3]$300,000 ÷ 13,200 hours = $22.73 per hour.
[4]$250,000 ÷ 22,000 hours = $11.36 per hour.

2. Journal entries

Date	Account	Debit	Credit
Jan. 1	Overhead	2,500	
	Cash		2,500
	Paid rent for the month of January.		
4	Office Supplies	1,200	
	Accounts Payable		1,200
	Purchased office supplies on account.		
9	Accounts Payable	4,500	
	Cash		4,500
	Paid accounts payable from prior period.		
15	Overhead	5,000	
	Cash		5,000
	Paid office support salaries.		
15	Work-in-Process Services	38,400	
	Cash		38,400
	Paid salaries of professionals.		

Partners	$ 8,000
Managers	8,400
Seniors	12,000
Staff	10,000
Total	$38,400

Date	Account		Debit	Credit
15	Work-in-Process Services		8,051	
	Overhead			8,051
	Allocated overhead based on billable hours.			
	Partners—170 hours × $9.66	$1,642		
	Managers—270 hours × $6.76	1,825		
	Seniors—500 hours × $4.83	2,415		
	Staff—900 hours × $2.41	2,169		
	Total	$8,051		
18	Work-in-Process Services		800	
	Office Supplies			800
	Used office supplies on behalf of clients.			
21	Office Supplies		1,100	
	Accounts Payable			1,100
	Purchased office supplies on account.			
25	Accounts Payable		1,200	
	Cash			1,200
	Paid for supplies purchased on Jan. 4.			
27	Accounts Receivable		57,724	
	Service Revenue			57,724
	Billed clients for Jobs #1 and #2.			
	Partners—170 hours × $66.13	$11,242		
	Managers—290 hours × $46.30	13,427		
	Seniors—520 hours × $33.07	17,196		
	Staff—960 hours × $16.52	15,859		
	Total	$57,724		
28	Cost of Services		48,107	
	Work-in-Process Services			48,107
	Transferred completed work in process to cost of services; comprised of each position's hourly rate and overhead rate.			
	Partners—170 hours × ($45.45 + $9.66)	$ 9,369		
	Managers—290 hours × ($31.82 + $6.76)	11,188		
	Seniors—520 hours × ($22.73 + $4.83)	14,331		
	Staff—960 hours × ($11.36 + $2.41)	13,219		
	Total	$48,107		
31	Overhead		1,000	
	Utilities Payable			1,000
	To record estimated utilities expense for the month.			
31	Overhead		5,400	
	Cash			5,400
	Paid office support salaries.			
31	Overhead		1,900	
	Accumulated Depreciation—Office Equipment			1,900
	To record depreciation expense for the month.			
31	Work-in-Process Services		38,400	
	Cash			38,400
	Paid salaries of professionals.			
	Partners	$ 8,000		
	Managers	8,400		
	Seniors	12,000		
	Staff	10,000		
	Total	$38,400		

31	Work-in-Process Services	8,458	
	Overhead		8,458

Allocated overhead based on billable hours.

Partners—180 hours × \$9.66	\$1,739
Managers—280 hours × \$6.76	1,893
Seniors—525 hours × \$4.83	2,536
Staff—950 hours × \$2.41	2,290
Total	\$8,458

3. Ending balance in Work-in-Process Services

Work-in-Process Services

1/15	38,400	1/28	48,107
1/15	8,051		
1/18	800		
1/31	38,400		
1/31	8,458		
End. bal.	46,002		

4. Ending balance in Overhead

Overhead

1/1	2,500	1/15	8,051
1/15	5,000	1/31	8,458
1/31	1,000		
1/31	5,400		
1/31	1,900		
		End. bal.	709

5. Profitability percentage

[(\$57,724 − \$48,107) ÷ \$57,724] = 16.7%

The profitability percentage for Jobs 1 and 2 is just 16.7%, compared to the target of 23.0%. Columbus & Hercules should look at two things. First, was there anything about the way the firm did business this month that would have caused its costs to be unusually high? Second, if the firm's business practices during the month were the same as usual, the client engagements for Jobs 1 and 2 should be reevaluated to determine whether Columbus & Hercules has underbid for the jobs.

6. Staff utilization ratios

Staff Working for:	Budgeted Billable Hours	Actual Billable Hours	Staff Utilization Ratio
Manager 1	528	690	130.7%
Manager 2	528	530	100.4%
Manager 3	704	630	89.5%

Manager 3 was given four staff accountants for the month; it is apparent that Manager 3 did not have enough work to keep all four of those individuals occupied for the entire month. In addition, Manager 1 may be putting an excessive workload on the staff assigned to him or her. Manager 1 should be reminded that good staff accountants are expensive to replace, and excessively long hours can cause them to look elsewhere for work.

discussion questions

1. What similarities are there in the inventories of a manufacturing and a merchandising organization? What are the differences?
2. What similarities are there in the inventories of a manufacturing and a service organization? What are the differences?
3. How does the work-in-process inventory in a manufacturing organization differ from that in a service organization?
4. What is represented by total manufacturing cost?
5. What is represented by total cost of goods manufactured?
6. Why is the total cost of goods sold number of limited usefulness for detailed internal decision making?
7. What amount is compared to the level of raw materials inventory in computing a useful measure of raw materials inventory turnover? Of work-in-process inventory turnover? Of finished goods inventory turnover?
8. Name three problems associated with carrying too much inventory.
9. Name three problems associated with carrying too little inventory.
10. What is inventory shrinkage? Name three things that can cause inventory shrinkage.
11. How can the ROI formula be used to evaluate the management of inventory?
12. What are the three basic types of service organizations?
13. The different types of service organizations vary in the emphasis they place on three dimensions. What are these three dimensions?
14. The same two concepts that underlie cost management in manufacturing and merchandising organizations are also used in developing cost management tools for service organizations. What are these two concepts?
15. What are three ways in which the magnitude of an organization's costs can be evaluated?

expanded material

16. What causes holding costs to exist? How is it that holding costs exist in the service industry, which typically does not have inventories?
17. What are the advantages of purchasing inventory in large quantities? What are the advantages of purchasing it in small quantities?
18. What are carrying costs in the denominator of the economic order quantity (EOQ) formula? How do large carrying costs affect the economic order quantity?
19. Explain the reasoning behind the reorder point formula, Reorder point = Lead time × Average daily sales.

discussion cases

CASE 6-1

BUYING INVENTORY FOR THE HOLIDAY SELLING SEASON

Ryan Baird owns a small retail shop. Historically, her annual sales have been about $250,000, with 60% of that coming in the holiday selling season of November and December. This year on a buying trip to southern China, Ryan discovered an item that she is certain will be in huge demand. The item is a mechanical cricket powered by a photovoltaic cell—the cricket automatically silences at night when it gets dark and then starts chirping in the morning when the sun's rays hit it. Ryan can buy the crickets from her Guangdong supplier for $1.00 each; she plans to sell them for $9.95 each.

Ryan is trying to decide how many of the crickets she should order. If she orders 30,000 or more, she can get a volume discount and pay just $0.80 each. However, she does not have room to store that many crickets, and she will have to rent storage space for $3,000 per month (three-month minimum). Also, the Guangdong supplier will only accept cash, and, because Ryan does not have very good credit, she will have to pay 17% annual interest on any money she borrows. She expects any loan to be outstanding for about two months.

Ryan has come to you for advice about whether she should buy a large quantity of crickets or play it safe and order just 10,000. What advice would you give her?

expanded material

CASE 6-2

FINANCIAL HOLDING COSTS

You work in the accounting department of Cox Company. You are having a debate with one of your co-workers about holding costs. Your co-worker insists that holding costs should not be considered in making decisions because they do not involve any cash flows. He believes that cash flows are all that the business really cares about. How do you respond to him?

exercises

EXERCISE 6-1

TOTAL MANUFACTURING COSTS AND COST OF GOODS MANUFACTURED

The following information is for Kiev Derrald Company:

Manufacturing overhead (actual)	$100,000
Ending raw materials inventory	12,000
Manufacturing overhead (applied)	95,000
Beginning work-in-process inventory	55,000
Manufacturing overhead (applied)	40,000
Ending work-in-process inventory	47,000
Beginning raw materials inventory	10,000
Direct labor costs	60,000

1. Compute total manufacturing costs.
2. Compute cost of goods manufactured.

EXERCISE 6-2

Spread-Sheet Software

TOTAL MANUFACTURING COSTS, COST OF GOODS MANUFACTURED, AND COST OF GOODS SOLD

The following information is for MTC Harry Company:

Beginning raw materials inventory	$ 25,000
Raw materials *used* in production as direct materials	110,000
Ending raw materials inventory	40,000
Manufacturing overhead (actual)	300,000
Beginning work-in-process inventory	150,000
Ending work-in-process inventory	180,000
Direct labor costs	95,000
Beginning finished goods inventory	71,000
Ending finished goods inventory	86,000
Underapplied manufacturing overhead	19,000

1. Compute total manufacturing costs.
2. Compute cost of goods manufactured.
3. Compute cost of goods sold.

EXERCISE 6-3

INVENTORY TURNOVER IN A MANUFACTURING COMPANY

The following information is for Pecos Yo Company:

Raw materials used during the year	$200,000
Ending raw materials inventory	25,000
Applied manufacturing overhead	350,000
Direct labor costs	100,000
Ending work-in-process inventory	60,000
Cost of goods sold	600,000
Ending finished goods inventory	40,000

Compute the following:

1. Inventory turnover for ending raw materials inventory.
2. Days' supply of raw materials in ending inventory.
3. Inventory turnover for ending work-in-process inventory.
4. Days of manufacturing represented by ending work-in-process inventory.
5. Inventory turnover for ending finished goods inventory.
6. Number of days' sales in ending finished goods inventory.

EXERCISE 6-4

INVENTORY TURNOVER IN A MERCHANDISING COMPANY

Beanie Company is a merchandising company. Beanie had the following financial data for the years 2002 and 2003:

	2003	2002
Revenues	$200,000	$180,000
Cost of goods sold	110,000	109,000
Gross margin	$ 90,000	$ 71,000
Inventory	$ 40,000	$ 50,000

Calculate Beanie Company's turnover for inventory for 2003 and explain what it means.

EXERCISE 6-5

INVENTORY TURNOVER IN A MERCHANDISING COMPANY

Both Dave and Kelly own auto parts stores. The following information is available for 2002 and 2003:

	Dave	Kelly
Revenue		
2002	$150,000	$300,000
2003	130,000	350,000
Ending inventory		
2002	75,000	225,000
2003	55,000	255,000

1. Calculate each company's turnover for inventory for 2003.
2. Which owner manages inventory better? Explain your answer.

EXERCISE 6-6

PROFITABILITY IN A SERVICE ORGANIZATION

Lorien Company is an engineering firm composed of five engineers. The annual compensation for each engineer is $200,000. It is expected that each engineer will work 2,000 hours during a year on client jobs. To cover overhead costs, the billing rate per engineering hour has been set at $175 per hour. At the end of the most recent year, the managing partner of the engineering firm found that total billable hours during the year for the five engineers had been 9,200. Use this information to compute the firm's profitability percentage, computed as follows:

$$[(\text{Revenue} - \text{Compensation cost}) \div \text{Revenue}]$$

EXERCISE 6-7

PERSONNEL UTILIZATION IN A SERVICE ORGANIZATION

Magily Company is a mathematical model consulting firm. Magily's services are sought by oil exploration companies for interpreting seismic data, by NASA for deciphering signals from deep space probes, and by Wall Street derivatives speculators who want to predict the weather in order to know whether to buy or sell soybean futures. Magily has the following numbers of mathematicians on its professional staff:

	Number of Individuals	Client Billable Hours Expected to Be Worked per Year
Full mathematicians	5	700
Associate mathematicians	10	2,100
Assistant mathematicians	40	2,600

During the most recent year, full mathematicians worked a total of 3,000 hours; associate mathematicians worked a total of 25,000 hours; and assistant mathematicians worked a total of 140,000 hours. Compute personnel utilization ratios for each class of mathematician.

expanded material

EXERCISE 6-8

FINANCIAL HOLDING COSTS

On January 1, 2003, Owen Corporation has $350,000 in inventory. On May 1, 2003, Owen's inventory is at $400,000. Owen's cost of capital is 13%. What were Owen's financial holding costs for January through April?

EXERCISE 6-9

FINANCIAL HOLDING COSTS

Brady Company sells imported goods made in India. One product it sells is a wooden music box. The music boxes cost Brady $65, and Brady charges its customers a price of $250. Brady's cost of capital is 12%. On average, an entire year elapses between the time Brady pays for a music box and the time Brady collects the cash from the sale of the music box. What are Brady's annual financial holding costs per unit for the wooden music boxes?

EXERCISE 6-10

ECONOMIC ORDER QUANTITY

Pace Retailers' best-selling item is its reinforced bicycle tires. Pace sells 4,745 of these tires each year. Pace pays $200 to place an order, and it costs Pace $2.50 per year to hold one tire. The retail price of the tires is $12.50. What is the economic order quantity of tires Pace should order at one time?

EXERCISE 6-11

REORDER POINT

Refer to Exercise 6-10. Suppose the lead time for reinforced bicycle tires is 13 days. To ensure adequate inventories at all times, Pace maintains a safety stock of 80 tires. Assuming Pace sells the 4,745 bicycle tires uniformly over the 365 days of the year, what is Pace's reorder point?

EXERCISE 6-12

ECONOMIC ORDER QUANTITY

For the past three years, Hawkeye Army Surplus Store has had excessive inventory holding costs. Management believes the excessive costs are due to the large orders the company places. The company hires a consultant, Brad Miles, to analyze the problem and suggest a solution. Information about two products, combat boots and backpacks, is as follows:

	Combat Boots	Backpacks
Annual market demand	20,000 pairs	5,000
Cost per unit	$20	$55
Annual carrying cost per unit	$7	$16
Ordering cost	$500	$500

How many pairs of combat boots should Brad suggest Hawkeye purchase at a time? How many backpacks?

EXERCISE 6-13

REORDER POINT

Avery Grocery Store is the only grocery store in Rayville, a small town populated mostly by college students. Students have been complaining lately because Avery always runs out of macaroni and cheese, the students' favorite food. Avery management decides it needs to calculate a more suitable reorder point. Information about the macaroni and cheese is as follows:

Average daily sales	500 boxes
Average lead time	5 days
Avery's cost per unit	$0.30
Price charged to customers	$0.75

1. What should be the reorder point if Avery does not want to maintain any safety stock?
2. What should be the reorder point if Avery wants to maintain a safety stock of 1,000 boxes of macaroni and cheese?

problems

PROBLEM 6-1

COST OF GOODS MANUFACTURED

The following data apply to the Newton and Alexander Companies:

	Newton	Alexander
Raw materials inventory, January 1, 2003	(1) $_____	$ 4,000
Raw materials purchased	21,000	(4) _____
Raw materials inventory, December 31, 2003	6,000	3,000
Manufacturing overhead (actual)	8,000	(5) _____
Manufacturing overhead (applied)	(2) _____	16,000
Selling and administrative expenses	14,000	25,000
Work-in-process inventory, January 1, 2003	(3) _____	20,000
Work-in-process inventory, December 31, 2003	16,000	22,000
Direct (raw) materials used in production	15,000	(6) _____
Direct labor costs	25,000	30,000
Cost of goods manufactured	49,000	55,000
Overapplied (or underapplied) manufacturing overhead	(2,000)	4,000

Fill in the unknowns for the two cases. (*Hint:* Indirect materials are not used in either company.)

PROBLEM 6-2

COST OF GOODS MANUFACTURED SCHEDULE

[Note: The journal entries required as Part (1) of this problem are also a requirement in Problem 3-7 in management accounting.]

Itsu Manufacturing Company applies manufacturing overhead on the basis of direct materials costs. The estimates for 2003 were:

Direct materials costs	$500,000
Manufacturing overhead	150,000

Following are the transactions of Itsu Manufacturing Company for 2003:

a. Raw materials purchased on account, $550,000.
b. Raw materials issued to production, 90% for direct use and 10% for indirect use, for a total of $350,000.

c. Direct labor costs, $500,000.
d. Indirect labor costs, $50,000.
e. Administrative and sales salaries, $140,000 and $90,000, respectively.
f. Utilities, $21,000; plant depreciation, $40,000; maintenance, $15,000; miscellaneous manufacturing overhead, $4,000. (These costs are allocated on the basis of plant floor space—administrative facilities, 500 square feet; manufacturing, 2,500 square feet; sales facilities, 1,000 square feet.)
g. Manufacturing equipment depreciation, $12,000.
h. Additional raw materials issued to production for direct use, $250,000.
i. Manufacturing overhead is applied.
j. Recorded factory foreman's salary, $54,000.
k. Ninety percent of existing Work-in-Process Inventory is transferred to Finished Goods Inventory. (Work-in-Process beginning inventory was $30,000.)
l. All finished goods are sold. (Assume no beginning or ending inventories. Sales are marked up 50% of cost.)
m. Over- or underapplied manufacturing overhead is closed to Cost of Goods Sold.

Required:

1. Prepare a journal entry for each of the transactions. (Assume that all manufacturing overhead is a product cost.)
2. Given the following beginning inventory amounts, prepare a cost of goods manufactured schedule for 2003 for Itsu Manufacturing Company. Assume all beginning and ending raw materials amounts include only direct materials.

Raw materials inventory	$80,000
Work-in-process inventory	30,000
Finished goods inventory	-0-

PROBLEM 6-3

COST OF GOODS MANUFACTURED SCHEDULE

Delta Manufacturing Company applies manufacturing overhead to jobs on the basis of machine hours. The 2003 estimates of manufacturing overhead and machine hours were:

Manufacturing overhead	$1,825,000
Machine hours	365,000

Delta had the following transactions for October 2003:

a. Raw materials of $420,000 were purchased on account.
b. Raw materials of $400,000 were issued to production; 90% were direct materials, and the balance was indirect materials.
c. Direct labor costs incurred, $300,000.
d. Indirect labor costs incurred, $55,000.
e. Selling, general, and administrative expenses incurred, $150,000.
f. Manufacturing overhead costs incurred:

Plant depreciation (factory)	$25,000
Equipment depreciation (factory)	14,000
Utilities (factory)	7,000
Factory maintenance	9,000
Factory taxes and insurance	5,000
Miscellaneous manufacturing overhead	6,000

g. Machine hours for the month, 30,400.
h. Eighty-five percent of Work-in-Process Inventory was transferred to Finished Goods Inventory. Assume that beginning Work-in-Process Inventory amounted to $95,000.
i. *All* finished goods are sold. (There is no beginning or ending finished goods inventory.)
j. Over- or underapplied manufacturing overhead is charged to Cost of Goods Sold, and the overhead account is closed.

Required:

1. Prepare journal entries to reflect the flow of costs incurred during October.
2. Assuming that beginning raw materials inventory was $16,000 and beginning work-in-process inventory was $95,000, prepare a cost of goods manufactured schedule for October 2003.

PROBLEM 6-4

ANALYSIS OF MANUFACTURING COST FLOWS

The following T-accounts represent manufacturing cost flows for Kanton Manufacturing Company for the year 2003.

Direct Materials Inventory

	Debit	Credit
1/1	70,000	250,000
	210,000	
12/31	30,000	

Work-in-Process Inventory

	Debit	Credit
1/1	80,000	700,000
	250,000	
	310,000	
	140,000	
12/31	80,000	

Finished Goods Inventory

	Debit	Credit
1/1	90,000	740,000
	700,000	
12/31	50,000	

Manufacturing Overhead

Debit	Credit
30,000	140,000
22,000	
16,000	
38,000	
40,000	

Required:

1. Compute the following amounts for 2003:
   a. Direct labor cost.
   b. Cost of goods manufactured.
   c. Cost of goods sold.
   d. Actual manufacturing overhead costs.
2. Prepare a cost of goods manufactured schedule for 2003.
3. Prepare a cost of goods sold schedule for 2003.
4. **Interpretive Question:** Explain how the over- or underapplied manufacturing overhead is usually accounted for.

PROBLEM 6-5

INVENTORY TURNOVER IN A MANUFACTURING COMPANY

The following information is for Bun MaScare Company:

Beginning raw materials inventory	$ 25,000
Raw materials purchased	110,000
Ending raw materials inventory	15,000
Manufacturing overhead (actual)	300,000
Beginning work-in-process inventory	50,000
Ending work-in-process inventory	40,000
Direct labor costs	90,000
Beginning finished goods inventory	200,000
Ending finished goods inventory	270,000
Overapplied manufacturing overhead	15,000

Required: Compute the following:

1. Inventory turnover for ending raw materials inventory.
2. Days' supply of raw materials in ending inventory.
3. Inventory turnover for ending work-in-process inventory.
4. Days of manufacturing represented by ending work-in-process inventory.
5. Inventory turnover for ending finished goods inventory.
6. Number of days' sales in ending finished goods inventory.
7. **Interpretive Question:** What conclusions can you draw from your inventory turnover calculations?

PROBLEM 6-6

Spread-Sheet Software

PROFITABILITY AND PERSONNEL UTILIZATION IN A SERVICE COMPANY

Diggy Company specializes in caring for the pets of the rich and famous. Diggy gives personal care to each and every pet, and its professional animal "consultants" are on call 24 hours per day. Some details about Diggy's business are given below.

	Number of Individuals	Client Billable Hours Expected to Be Worked per Year	Annual Compensation	Billing Rate
Partners	5	500	$500,000	$400
Consultants	40	2,500	35,000	250

During the most recent year, the five partners billed a total of 3,000 hours, and the 40 consultants billed a total of 56,000 hours.

Required:

1. Compute personnel utilization ratios for each of the two classes of professionals within the firm.
2. Compute the firm's profitability percentage as follows: [(Revenue − Compensation cost) ÷ Revenue].
3. **Interpretive Question:** Speculate on why the 40 consultants worked the number of billable hours that they did.

expanded material

PROBLEM 6-7

Spread-Sheet Software

INVENTORY MANAGEMENT

Watersports, Inc., sells high-performance water skis. Because its sales are seasonal, Watersports calculates and uses different reorder points for summer and winter months. The following information is available:

	April–October	November–March
Lead time (days)	3	7
Total customer demand for the period	1,600	400

The water skis cost $150 each, and Watersports sells them to its customers for $300. Watersports' supplier charges $500 for each order placed. Watersports incurs an *annual* holding cost of $17 per set of skis.

Required: Calculate the appropriate economic order quantities and reorder points for the two seasons.

competency enhancement opportunities

- Analyzing Real Company Information
- International Case
- Ethics Case
- Writing Assignment
- The Debate
- Internet Search

The following additional assignments provide opportunities for students to develop critical thinking, ethical perspectives, oral and written communication skills, experience with electronic research, and teamwork through group and business activities.

ANALYZING REAL COMPANY INFORMATION

• *Analyzing 6-1 (Microsoft)*

1. For the year ended June 30, 1999, MICROSOFT's total cost of revenue was $2.814 billion. Can you compute Microsoft's total manufacturing costs for the year? Cost of goods manufactured for the year? Explain.
2. As of June 30, 1999, Microsoft reported the following about the number of its employees:

Employees engaged in research and development	12,090
Employees in sales and marketing	15,186
Employees in administration	2,850
Other employees	1,270
Total	31,396

Refer to Microsoft's income statement in Appendix A and compute the following:

a. Total revenue per employee.
b. Total R&D cost per R&D employee.
c. Total sales and marketing cost per sales and marketing employee.
d. Total administrative cost per administrative employee.

• *Analyzing 6-2 (Wal-Mart)*

1. Through its Retail Link™ system, WAL-MART gives its suppliers access to detailed sales information "store by store, item by item, day by day." What advantages are there to Wal-Mart in sharing this kind of detailed data with suppliers? What disadvantages?
2. Wal-Mart reports (in its 2000 10-K report filed with the Securities and Exchange Commission) that 83% of the goods sold in Wal-Mart stores and Supercenters is first shipped to one of Wal-Mart's 45 regional distribution centers and then shipped to the individual stores. On the other hand, SAM'S CLUBS receive the majority of their goods directly from the supplier. Why is there a difference in the distribution procedure for these two groups of stores?
3. In recent years, SAM'S Clubs sales, as a percentage of total Wal-Mart sales, have decreased, from 19% of sales in fiscal 1997 to 15% of sales in fiscal 2000. What impact do you think this change in sales mix has had on Wal-Mart's overall gross margin percentage? Explain.

INTERNATIONAL CASE

• *Arthur Andersen*

ARTHUR ANDERSEN is one of the largest professional services firms in the world. In 2000, the company reported revenues of $8.4 billion generated from its various business units—assurance and business advisory, tax and legal advisory, business consulting, and global corporate finance. Arthur Andersen has 385 offices in 83 countries, and over half of its revenues are generated outside North and South America.

1. What does Arthur Andersen sell?
2. Arthur Andersen has an office in Quito, Ecuador. What type of company operating in Ecuador would hire Arthur Andersen instead of a local Ecuadorian professional services firm?
3. Review the chapter discussion of cost information for service companies. What costs would be important to Arthur Andersen in deciding how much to bid on a consulting contract for a potential new client?

ETHICS CASE

• Performance Evaluation: The Illusion of Objectivity?

You are a store manager for a large, regional department store chain. You have been asked by company headquarters to submit an evaluation of the performance of two of your assistant managers. The company is considering promoting one of them to be the manager of another store in the chain.

One of the assistant managers heads the Electronics department in your store. She is a long-time friend of yours and you would like her to get the promotion. The other candidate heads the Home and Garden department; she is a good assistant manager but you just don't know her well. You decide to recommend your friend, the head of the Electronics department, for the promotion.

In order to support your recommendation with objective evidence, you include the following departmental profit numbers for the most recent year:

	Electronics	Home and Garden
Sales	$500,000	$300,000
Net profit	$100,000	$ 40,000
Profit percentage	20%	13%

On this basis, arguing that the Electronics department has generated higher sales, higher net profit, and a higher profit margin percentage, you recommend that the promotion be given to your friend. However, you are a little troubled by the following two additional pieces of information:

1. The average value of inventory held in the Electronics department at any given time is $1.2 million. The comparable number for the Home and Garden department is $250,000.
2. The profit percentage in the Electronics department has been fairly stable over the last five years. On the other hand, the profit percentage in the Home and Garden department is at a 10-year high; the increase coincides with the hiring of the current head of the Home and Garden department.

Is it ethical for you to recommend the promotion for your friend, the head of the Electronics department? How should you use the numerical evidence in support of your recommendation?

WRITING ASSIGNMENT

• Consultant's Report for a Small-Town Supermarket

You have been hired as a financial consultant by a small-town supermarket. The supermarket is considering building a new, larger store and requests your expertise in evaluating the feasibility of the project. You know that the construction of the store will cost $3 million. You also know that the average gross margin percentage in supermarkets is 27%.

Draft a one-page memo to the owner of the supermarket requesting additional cost information to be used in your analysis. The store owner is a clever businessperson but has no experience in using quantitative data in making decisions. Therefore, your memo must be very specific in identifying the information that you will need to perform a useful analysis.

THE DEBATE

• *Overutilization of Young Professionals*

As seen in this chapter, an important dimension of performance for a manufacturing, merchandising, or service organization is the efficient utilization of resources. The more intensively resources are used, the greater a company's return on investment. However, when talking about a service organization, this "resource" is often the time of young professionals who are just starting their careers. Competitive pressures on companies can translate into 70- and 80-hour work weeks for college graduates in the first few years of their careers. These work pressures make it difficult for young professionals to develop their lives outside work.

Divide your group into two teams and prepare a two-minute oral presentation supporting the following views.

- One team supports "Work/Life Balance." This group believes that young professionals should not be viewed as "resources" to be utilized but as human beings to be respected.
- The other team supports "Survival of the Fittest." This group believes that it is a dog-eat-dog world out there, and that those young professionals who can't stand the long hours should get out of the way of those who can.

INTERNET SEARCH

International

• *The Peninsula Hotel in Hong Kong*

The **PENINSULA HOTEL** is Hong Kong's oldest and finest hotel. The hotel epitomizes service. For example, the Peninsula maintains a fleet of chauffeur-driven Rolls-Royce limousines to transport guests to and from the Hong Kong airport. Access the Web site for the Peninsula Hotel at **http://www.peninsula.com/hotels/hk/hk.html**. Sometimes Web addresses change, so if this address doesn't work, access the Web site for this textbook (**http://albrecht.swcollege.com**) for an updated link. Once you've gained access to the site, answer the following questions:

1. Hong Kong is divided into three main parts: Hong Kong Island, Kowloon, and the New Territories. In which of these is the Peninsula Hotel located?
2. In its description of its "Accommodations," the Peninsula Hotel describes some of the special features offered to guests in the Peninsula, Garden, and Marco Polo suites. What are these special features?
3. What is the daily rate for the cheapest room at the Peninsula Hotel? For the most expensive room?
4. The Peninsula Hotel in Hong Kong is owned by the Peninsula Group. What other hotels does this group own?

Management Accounting Information in the New Business Environment

chapter **m7**

learning objectives

After studying this chapter, you should be able to:

1. Explain the fundamentals of activity-based costing (ABC) and activity-based management (ABM).
2. Describe total quality management (TQM) and costs of quality (COQ).
3. Describe how just-in-time (JIT) management systems integrate with and extend ABC and TQM using time-based performance measures.

expanded material

4. Compute the opportunity cost of lost sales.

setting the stage

You most likely wouldn't want to be in Phil Condit's shoes anytime in the next few years; then again, maybe you would.[1] Condit is CEO of **BOEING COMPANY**, the largest manufacturer of commercial airplanes in the world. If you have ever flown on a commercial jet, odds are you were in one of Condit's (or one of his predecessor's) products. In fact, a Boeing airplane is taking off somewhere in the world every 3.5 seconds. By the end of each day, Boeing jets fly over 17 million miles; that's the equivalent of 35 round trips to the moon! With its $16.3 billion merger with **MCDONNELL DOUGLAS**, Boeing commands approximately two-thirds of the $65 billion global market for commercial planes with 100 seats or more. Further, just prior to the McDonnell Douglas merger, Boeing completed a $3.1 billion acquisition of the defense and space operations of **ROCKWELL INTERNATIONAL**, making Boeing the largest builder of military aircraft in the world, as well as the number one supplier of goods and services to both the Pentagon and NASA. Boeing is basically sitting in the catbird seat. So, why might you hesitate to take Condit's job right now if it were offered to you?

If you had taken a walking tour of Boeing's 747, 767, and 777 plant in Everett, Washington, within the last couple of years, two things would likely have impressed you. First, this cavernous plant is monstrous, able to house 74 football fields! Second, for the largest company in the world dealing in commercial and military aircraft technology, as well as a significant player in space rockets and satellites, there isn't much in the Everett plant that suggests a "future world" of production technology. You won't find robotics, flashing lights, or laser-guided tools. In fact, the place looks a lot like a very large version of a repair bay at your local automobile service station. Planes are everywhere in various stages of completion, and *a lot* of mechanics are running around with nothing more complicated than a set of hand tools. Is this the way a production operation works that builds something as sophisticated as a 747-400 jet, capable of flying 420 people in a three-class configuration across the Atlantic Ocean? In 1998, Boeing likely had one of the most inefficient large-scale production operations in the world. Phil Condit, and everyone else at Boeing, was painfully aware of this fact. In fact, one vice president said at that time, "You know the Baldrige prize for the manufacturing processes? Well, if there was a prize for the opposite, this system would win it hands down."

Boeing's Everett plant turns out four massive jets per month, each priced at about $170 million. Each jet is tailor-made to the desires of each customer. The company has always prided itself on giving customers *exactly* what they want. This customization doesn't end with engine specifications and landing systems. It includes choice of paint colors (e.g., if you want white, Boeing offers nearly 110 shades to choose from) and location in the cockpit where the pilot's clipboard will be placed. However, don't get the impression that these are simple adjustments. Every alteration, even a seemingly minor one such as moving the location of an emergency flashlight holder, consumes thousands of hours of engineering time, requires hundreds of pages of detailed drawings, and costs hundreds of thousands, if not millions, of dollars to execute. Much of this cost of product complexity is compounded by the fact that Boeing *manually* tracks many of the parts that go into each plane.

Today's air transportation market is changing. The profits of commercial airlines are no longer protected by government regulations. The once free-spending Department of Defense has had its wings clipped by Congress. Boeing's customers have become extremely cost-conscious, leading to major pricing battles with Boeing's last remaining major competitor, **AIRBUS INDUSTRIE** (a European consortium). The three-fold *strategic imperatives* of cost, quality, and time are more important to Boeing than ever before. Boeing has responded to new market demands by implementing a complete reengineering of all processes, information systems, and management procedures involved in the manufacturing of its products. It is working to better manage costs by reducing and streamlining activities in the production process. No longer can Boeing customers select every option in their plane without paying extra. The company is reducing parts and work-in-process inventories in order to significantly increase stockturns. It is working to correct problems

1 Information from "Boeing's BIG Problem," *Fortune*, January 12, 1998, pp. 96–103; Boeing Company's home page at http://www.boeing.com; "The Incentives Airbus Is Using to Sell Its A380 Now May Backfire Later," *Business Week*, March 5, 2001, pp. 52–53.

with receiving shipments of parts on time from suppliers and getting completed planes out the door on time to customers. And all these changes must be accomplished without diminishing the absolute quality that is expected of aircraft technology that carries satellites into space, carries military weapons into battle, and (most importantly) carries two million people daily—a number that exceeds the world's population over an eight-year period! If Phil Condit and his reformation team succeed, Boeing, a manufacturer of world-class airplanes, may become a world-class company—perhaps even a Baldrige Award winner.

The biggest challenge for Boeing, however, is increased competition from Airbus. Airbus is aggressively promoting its new superjumbo jet, the A380, touted to seat nearly 550 passengers (Boeing's 747 seats 416 passengers) and fly more efficiently than any Boeing aircraft. When questioned on the surprisingly low cost of the A380 (currently offered at a discount of $140 million), Airbus executives claim their factories and turnaround times are more efficient than Boeing's. The A380 poses a significant threat to Boeing, which has no plans for an airplane that would directly compete with the size of the A380. Some analysts view this battle between Boeing and Airbus as the "dogfight of the century." So the future certainly does look very exciting for Phil Condit. What do you think? Still want to trade places with him?

caution

Just because the science of product costing was first developed over 100 years ago, don't assume that there are no new issues today. Business is now more complicated and more competitive than ever before. Management accounting systems are expected today to provide cost and performance measures that are more accurate, more relevant, and more strategically focused than ever before!

If there is one thing that is constant in the history of business (and, for that matter, history at large), it is change. A hundred years ago, the executives and management accountants of successful companies such as ***CARNEGIE STEEL*** *and* ***DUPONT*** *created cost accounting and performance measurement systems that were so new and unique at the time that the decision makers in these companies were able to plan, control, and evaluate critical business processes better than most of their competition. However, these management accounting practices are now well understood and serve as a minimum expectation of most organizations desiring to remain competitive and viable in today's business environment. New management accounting theories and techniques are being developed constantly and tested in the laboratory of the current international market economy. Some of these new ideas are gaining a lot of attention, and you need to be aware of them. This chapter will introduce three important topics that have had a significant impact in the last 10 to 20 years on the types of information that many management accounting systems are now providing to the management process in an effort to keep organizations competitive. These topics are activity-based costing (ABC), costs of quality (COQ), and just-in-time (JIT). In Chapter 10 of management accounting, we will introduce a new model of strategic performance measurement that has come into the spotlight in just the last five or six years. This new innovation, called the Balanced Scorecard, is getting a lot of attention and may be the next significant step in the innovation of management accounting.*

1

Explain the fundamentals of activity-based costing (ABC) and activity-based management (ABM).

ACTIVITY-BASED COSTING

In the late 1800s, Andrew Carnegie competed very strongly in the steel market with an almost fanatical emphasis on product cost information. Since then, product costing has been a primary purpose of management accounting. Manufacturing processes of today don't look at all like the manufacturing processes of the late 1800s, however. Advances in technology, combined with increasingly intense global competition, have resulted in manufacturing systems that are very complex compared to their predecessors. Because the companies that best understand their costs generally compete well in the economy, product costing has also undergone some important changes that we will consider in this chapter. It is important, though, to remember that the economy has shifted dramatically since the days of Andrew Carnegie. Service companies, such as transportation, consulting, and financial institutions, are the dominant force in today's economy. As you know from your study of Chapter 3 of management accounting, the service provided by these companies to their clients is a "product" that requires a product costing system very similar to that of manufacturing companies. In fact, service companies are some of the heaviest users of the management accounting techniques discussed in this chapter.

activity-based costing (ABC) A method of attributing costs to products based on first assigning costs of resources to activities and then costs of activities to products.

One major development in product costing is **activity-based costing (ABC)**. Basically, ABC identifies and uses a number of critical activities within the organization to measure product costs. For many types of manufacturing and service companies, ABC is a more accurate product costing system than the traditional product costing systems introduced in Chapter 3 of management accounting. However, ABC requires more time and expense to administer than traditional costing systems.

Product Costing Review

Consider, for example, a small ice cream shop that is owned and managed by one person. Lucas, the owner, hires college students to run the daily operations of preparing and selling his various ice cream desserts. Lucas must decide how to properly price his ice cream desserts. One of his employees, Sally, who just completed her first economics class, tells him to simply "charge whatever the market will bear." Yet this advice provides Lucas only with a price ceiling. Obviously, he cannot charge more than his customers will pay. However, in response to important matters of profitability such as competition and market share, Lucas wonders about his price floor—how low can he go? The obvious answer is that he cannot price below cost (except on occasion). But this begs the elemental question: What does it *cost* Lucas to make each of his ice cream desserts? Frankly, despite being in the ice cream business for several years, Lucas is not sure.

In relatively "simple" operations like Lucas's ice cream shop, as well as in complex operations such as a car manufacturer or a large law firm, product costing is a critical management issue. Today, cost accountants are paid rather well to answer the question, "What does it cost to make a product ready to sell?" In working with Lucas and his ice cream shop, the classic approach to this question is to apply the traditional product cost models that we studied in Chapter 3 of management accounting. Essentially, for a manufacturing organization, this model states that:

Cost of product = Direct materials + Direct labor + Manufacturing overhead

conversion costs The costs of converting raw materials to finished products; include direct labor and manufacturing overhead costs.

prime costs The direct costs that are "primarily seen" in the product (i.e., direct materials and direct labor).

To calculate the direct materials cost of a banana split, for example, Lucas needs simply to determine the cost of materials directly involved in making a banana split; in other words, the cost of ingredients. The process of converting these "raw" materials into a banana split (the conversion process) requires direct labor and overhead costs, known together as **conversion costs**. Direct labor is simply the hourly wage Lucas pays his employees to physically assemble the ingredients of each dessert sold. Clearly, because each type of dessert requires different ingredients and different amounts of time to create, each will have a different set of direct materials and direct labor costs. Direct materials and direct labor, the **prime costs**, are obvious components in the ice cream dessert production process. Prime costs are easily understood and, typically, can be directly traced to each type of product produced.

The second cost of the conversion process, overhead, is a little more difficult to understand and directly trace to the dessert production operation. Typically, in a "manufacturing" company like Lucas's shop, manufacturing overhead costs are thought of as "manufacturing support costs." In order to produce banana splits and other desserts, Lucas must have several other components in place besides ice cream and an ice cream scooper. Lights, heat, and other utilities must be present in the kitchen area. Equipment, such as blenders and freezers, must be purchased and maintained. Indirect materials, such as cleaning supplies and light bulbs, must be provided. Likely, Lucas will have other personnel on the payroll besides the counter help. A shop manager and a nightly cleanup crew add additional production costs in the form of indirect labor. All these costs are necessary for Lucas to produce his wares; hence, all are included in manufacturing overhead. As you understand after studying previous chapters, manufacturing overhead is, in essence, a catchall category. In other words, the total cost of a product or service is the cost of everything necessary to produce the product or service. In the case of a manufacturing company, after identifying direct materials and direct labor costs, any remaining product costs are manufacturing overhead costs.

Direct materials, direct labor, and manufacturing overhead do not comprise the total set of costs in Lucas's ice cream shop. Traditionally, product costs are defined as only those costs necessary to actually produce the product. There are other nonproduction costs in Lucas's ice cream shop. These include selling costs, such as costs of advertising the shop and maintaining an area for customers to enjoy their ice cream. General administrative expenses, such as office expenses and Lucas's own salary, are also costs that must be planned and controlled. Because these selling and general administrative costs are not directly connected to any aspect of the production process, they are typically not included in the product cost category. Nonetheless, these are still essential costs. If Lucas does not invest in selling and general administrative activities, soon there will be no production. Costs related to selling and general administration come under the heading of "period costs." In contrast to product costs, which are incurred as products are produced, period costs seem to be strictly related to the passage of "periods" of time.

Hence, we can summarize all these costs (originally defined in Chapter 1 of management accounting) as follows:

- *Direct materials:* The cost of the materials that actually become part of the product.
- *Direct labor:* Wages paid to those who physically work to assemble direct materials into the finished product.
- *Manufacturing overhead:* All costs required to produce a product *other than* direct materials and direct labor.
- *Product costs:* Direct materials + Direct labor + Manufacturing overhead.
- *Period costs:* All costs in the company *other than* the product costs.

Hopefully, this quick discussion of Lucas's ice cream shop is simply a review of what you already understand about product costing. At this point, you may feel that it should be a simple task to track the total costs Lucas spends on direct materials, direct labor, and manufacturing overhead in order to answer his question, "What does it cost to make a dessert?" Frankly, tracking Lucas's *total* product costs in his shop is a fairly simple task. However, the key issue for Lucas (and all other product and service managers) is to break those total product costs down for *each type* of product being created. For an ice cream shop that makes and sells many types of desserts, the product cost question becomes much more difficult to answer. It is precisely this question that accountants and managers have been struggling to answer for the last several decades.

SeatJoy, Inc., Is in Trouble!

Consumers are better informed and more demanding than ever before. In addition, competition is increasing as industries are deregulated, technology improves, and national barriers to worldwide competition are removed. The bottom line in this business environment is that margins on goods and services are becoming increasingly tighter. In terms of the ROI model, because most companies cannot sell their goods and services for more money, they need to sell more of their products faster (i.e., increase turnover) in order to remain profitable. What does this mean to an organization that sells a large variety of goods or services? Basically, it means that the organization could be losing money on some of its products and not even realize what is happening. In addition, it may choose to stop providing a particular product based on the false assumption that the product is a money loser. We can better demonstrate this point with an example that we will use for the remainder of this section.

Exhibit 7-1 displays the 2002 operating results for SeatJoy, Inc. (a fictitious company in the business of making high-quality leather desk chairs). As you can see, SeatJoy has three lines of reclining desk chairs. The Cushman model is its "bread and butter" product. This is the original chair that SeatJoy introduced in 1989 when the company started business. Shortly thereafter, SeatJoy introduced a similar chair that included a swing-out leg rest when the chair reclined. SeatJoy called this chair the Cushman II. More recently (2000), SeatJoy came out with a premium chair made from exotic leathers called the Luxor. Compared to the Cushman lines, the Luxor production process requires closer supervision, as well as more specialized production equipment.

SeatJoy follows a traditional approach of applying manufacturing overhead to products using an overhead application rate based on direct labor hours. The computation of the 2002 over-

exhibit 7-1 SeatJoy, Inc.: 2002 Operating Results

Manufacturing Overhead Cost Analysis

Annual manufacturing overhead	$18,240,000
Total annual direct labor hours	÷ 456,000
Manufacturing overhead rate per direct labor hour	$40

Labor Cost Analysis

	Cushman	Cushman II	Luxor	Total
Direct labor hours per product	10.0 hours	15.0 hours	12.5 hours	
Annual sales volume	× 18,000 chairs	× 14,400 chairs	× 4,800 chairs	
Total annual direct labor hours	180,000 hours	216,000 hours	60,000 hours	456,000 hours
Wage rate per hour	× $20	× $20	× $20	× $20
Total annual direct labor costs	$3,600,000	$4,320,000	$1,200,000	$9,120,000

Individual Unit Analysis

	Cushman	Cushman II	Luxor
Sales price	$1,000	$ 1,500	$ 3,000
Direct materials per product	$ (335)	$ (650)	$(1,395)
Direct labor per product	(200)	(300)	(250)
Manufacturing overhead per product	(400)	(600)	(500)
Total cost per product	$ (935)	$(1,550)	$(2,145)
Margin per product	$ 65	$ (50)	$ 855
Margin percent	6.5%	(3.3)%	28.5%

Total Annual Results

	Cushman	Cushman II	Luxor	Total
Sales revenue	$ 18,000,000	$ 21,600,000	$ 14,400,000	$ 54,000,000
Total direct materials	$ (6,030,000)	$ (9,360,000)	$ (6,696,000)	$(22,086,000)
Total direct labor	(3,600,000)	(4,320,000)	(1,200,000)	(9,120,000)
Total manufacturing overhead	(7,200,000)	(8,640,000)	(2,400,000)	(18,240,000)
Total product costs	$(16,830,000)	$(22,320,000)	$(10,296,000)	$(49,446,000)
Total margin	$ 1,170,000	$ (720,000)	$ 4,104,000	$ 4,554,000
Selling and administrative expenses				(4,000,000)
Operating profit				$ 554,000

head rate is shown first in Exhibit 7-1. Now take a moment to look through all the numbers in SeatJoy's 2002 operating results. Based on an analysis of 2002 results, it appears that the Cushman II line is dragging down company profits. After evaluating these numbers, the management team decides to drop the Cushman II product line. As a result, some suppliers are notified that SeatJoy will be reducing or canceling orders for certain raw materials. Further, one supervisor and the entire Cushman II labor crew are laid off. These are difficult decisions, but management feels strongly that SeatJoy should not absorb in 2003 another $720,000 reduction in operating profit (the total loss on the Cushman II line in 2002). SeatJoy is now in a position to realize a significant jump in operating profit in 2003. Or is it?

As the accountant prepares and provides the first few monthly profit reports in 2003, it is obvious that there are problems in the operations of the remaining two product lines, particularly

STOP & THINK What do you think is the source of the problem with operations at SeatJoy, Inc.? Should SeatJoy now drop the Cushman product line? Why or why not?

in the Cushman line. By the end of the year, when the annual operating results are put together (Exhibit 7-2), the debacle is confirmed. SeatJoy is in serious trouble! What happened? Sales of both the Cushman and the Luxor product did not change from 2002 results. Further, labor and materials costs per product stayed consistent with 2002 costs, and total manufacturing overhead decreased in 2003. Why didn't company profits improve as management expected after making the decision to drop the Cushman II product line? It looks as if SeatJoy should now consider dropping the Cushman product line in order to save the company.

Comparing the operations reports for 2002 and 2003 should reveal the problem. Take a second look at the manufacturing overhead numbers at the top of each exhibit, particularly the overhead rate per direct labor hour. Yes, manufacturing overhead costs did decrease in 2003, as

exhibit 7-2 SeatJoy, Inc.: 2003 Operating Results

Manufacturing Overhead Cost Analysis

Annual manufacturing overhead	$11,920,000
Total annual direct labor hours	÷ 240,000
Manufacturing overhead rate per direct labor hour	$49.67 (rounded) (Note: All computations below are based on rounding the overhead rate to the nearest penny.)

Labor Cost Analysis

	Cushman	Luxor	Total
Direct labor hours per product	10.0 hours	12.5 hours	
Annual sales volume	× 18,000 chairs	× 4,800 chairs	
Total annual direct labor hours	180,000 hours	60,000 hours	240,000 hours
Wage rate per hour	× $20	× $20	× $20
Total annual direct labor costs	$3,600,000	$1,200,000	$4,800,000

Individual Unit Analysis

	Cushman	Luxor
Sales price	$ 1,000.00	$ 3,000.00
Direct materials per product	$ (335.00)	$(1,395.00)
Direct labor per product	(200.00)	(250.00)
Manufacturing overhead per product	(496.70)	(620.88)
Total cost per product	$(1,031.70)	$(2,265.88)
Margin per product	$ (31.70)	$ 734.12
Margin percent	(3.2)%	24.5%

Total Annual Results

	Cushman	Luxor	Total
Sales revenue	$ 18,000,000	$ 14,400,000	$ 32,400,000
Total direct materials	$ (6,030,000)	$ (6,696,000)	$(12,726,000)
Total direct labor	(3,600,000)	(1,200,000)	(4,800,000)
Total manufacturing overhead	(8,940,600)	(2,980,224)	(11,920,824)
Total product costs	$(18,570,600)	$(10,876,224)	$(29,446,824)
Total margin	$ (570,600)	$ 3,523,776	$ 2,953,176
Selling and administrative expenses			(4,000,000)
Operating loss			$ (1,046,824)

expected since some costs were saved by dropping the Cushman II product. However, these costs did not drop nearly as much as the direct labor hours, resulting in a sharp increase in the overhead application rate per direct labor hour ($40 in 2002 versus nearly $50 in 2003). When the management team decided to drop the Cushman II line, why didn't manufacturing overhead costs decrease as much as expected? Obviously, the current manufacturing overhead application system based on direct labor hours does not provide very accurate insight on cost behavior, particularly in decision-making situations that have strategic implications like adding or dropping a major product line. When management made the decision to drop the Cushman II line, it failed to consider two very important issues:

- First, if the allocation system based on direct labor hours is improper, then it is possible that the Cushman II product line was actually subsidizing some manufacturing overhead costs that should have been assigned to one or both of the other products (a problem called product cost **cross-subsidization**). When a poor cost accounting system allows cross-subsidization of product costs, then the management process of planning, controlling, and evaluating is severely compromised.
- Second, some manufacturing overhead costs (known as **common costs**) simply do not relate directly to any particular product line. Examples of these common costs include executive salaries, rent or property taxes on administrative buildings, and general liability insurance. Common costs cannot be allocated meaningfully to products without potentially creating confusion as the organization works to manage its costs effectively.

cross-subsidization A distortion of costs that occurs when costs of one product are erroneously assigned to another product.

common costs Manufacturing overhead costs, such as executive salaries or property taxes, that cannot be attributed to products. Costs of facility support activities are common costs.

Hierarchical Product Cost Model A method of categorizing costs based on types of activities. Activity types include unit-level activities, batch-level activities, product line activities, and facility support activities.

ABC-based accounting systems are designed to avoid problems related to cross-subsidization effects and common costs allocations by categorizing and assigning manufacturing overhead costs based on the **Hierarchical Product Cost Model**. Essentially, the Hierarchical Product Cost Model provides management accountants with a method for categorizing costs according to the types of activities those costs support. One important benefit of ABC and the Hierarchical Product Cost Model is the way these tools affect our view of variable and fixed costs (more on this below).

The ABC Hierarchical Product Cost Model

We provided some very simple definitions of fixed and variable costs in Chapter 1 of management accounting. Chapter 2 of management accounting spent considerable time describing how much variety there actually is in fixed and variable costs. The important thing to understand in this chapter is that, in practice, very few costs can be definitely categorized as fixed or variable with respect to a single type of activity in the organization, such as direct labor hours, machine hours, or units produced. In fact, every organization has many different kinds of activities, each of which directly affects certain costs. Stated differently, *given enough time and with respect to a particular activity, nearly every cost in the organization can be considered variable.* This is really quite an important concept in the theory of ABC. Before you can predict a cost behavior (which is necessary before you can begin managing the cost), you need to identify the activity that actually drives the cost in question.

Let's return to the situation at SeatJoy, Inc. As you now know, the traditional approach SeatJoy is using to assign manufacturing overhead costs to its products appears to be causing problems. This approach is demonstrated in Exhibit 7-3. As you can see, SeatJoy simply sums together all manufacturing overhead costs within the organization and assigns those costs to products based on a single activity, direct labor hours. However, consider the variety of costs that are being combined into a single pool of costs. The purpose of a manufacturing overhead allocation rate (in this case, based on direct labor hours) is to *meaningfully* allocate costs to products in a manner that relates to the behavior of the costs. Think about property taxes on the production facility for a moment. Do these costs adjust at all based on changes in total direct labor hours within the organization? Of course not! Neither do the costs of insuring these facilities against damage and liability claims. Perhaps engineering costs and supervision costs, as well as costs to set up a production run and perform quality checks on the output, are related to direct labor hours, but the relationship is not very strong. There likely are other activities in

exhibit 7-3 Traditional Overhead Costing at SeatJoy, Inc.

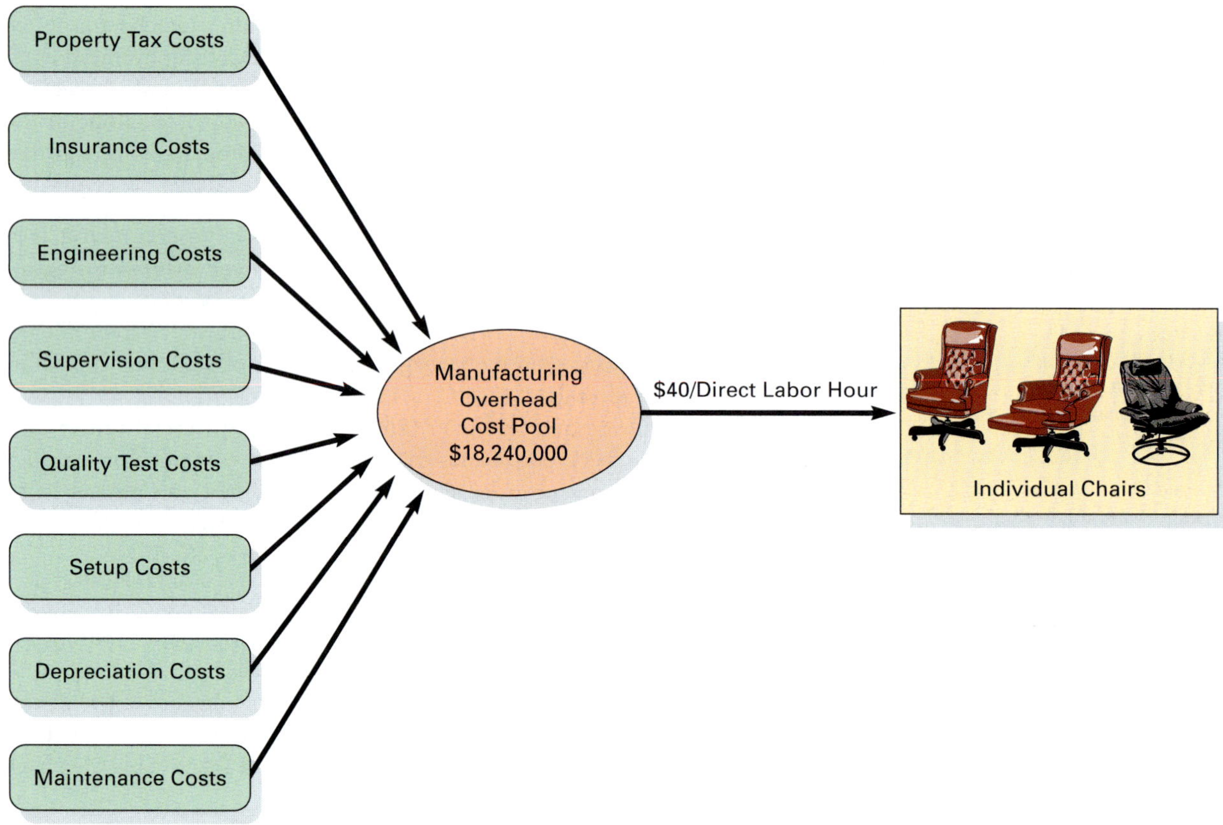

the SeatJoy organization that relate more closely to increases and decreases in these costs than direct labor hours. Identifying these activities is the intent of the Hierarchical Product Cost Model.

Look back at Exhibit 7-1 for a moment. How does SeatJoy determine how many direct labor hours are used in the plant? As you can see in the second table, annual labor hours for each product line are really just a function of how many chairs SeatJoy intends to produce and sell. Allocating manufacturing overhead on the basis of the number of direct labor hours per chair is essentially the same thing as allocating manufacturing overhead on the basis of the number of chairs produced. How much of manufacturing overhead costs will be assigned to the Luxor product line? Well, that really depends on how many units SeatJoy will produce in this product line (which then determines how many direct labor hours will be used). Because the allocated manufacturing overhead is really a function of the number of units produced, we call this method of allocating manufacturing overhead costs **unit-based costing (UBC)**. Think back to Chapter 3 of management accounting. Isn't this the basic approach we used in that chapter to allocate overhead in both manufacturing and service companies? UBC is a very traditional cost accounting method used in many types of organizations, and it is the cost allocation approach currently used by the SeatJoy organization in this example. UBC is a good method of cost allocation *in the right context.* However, a UBC approach usually creates problems in an organization with multiple products and services. Cost distortions can develop that make both strategic and short-term planning decisions difficult. The distortions are the result of using an oversimplified information system to represent the complex realities of modern business processes.

unit-based costing (UBC) The traditional method of allocating manufacturing overhead using an approach that is essentially based on the number of units produced.

STOP & THINK We have stated that the overhead allocation rate per direct labor hour for SeatJoy is really just a rate per chair (i.e., unit). Hence, we call this a UBC allocation system. Look at Exhibit 7-1. What is the manufacturing overhead allocation rate per chair (i.e., per unit)?

You have probably noticed by now that allocating manufacturing overhead costs to products is a two-stage process. First, we gather all the manufacturing overhead costs into a common pool of costs. Second, we allocate these costs to products based on a (hopefully) appropriate allocation rate. This rather simple UBC two-stage allocation process is characterized by the following relationship:

caution

Don't get the idea from the SeatJoy example that UBC is always a "bad" cost allocation method. On the contrary, UBC is a very good cost allocation method for manufacturing and service organizations with overhead that essentially does change based on the number of units of goods and services produced. Further, compared to ABC, UBC is typically easier and less costly. However, if UBC is causing reported product costs to be distorted, the management process in the organization can be seriously affected.

Costs → **Production Department(s)** → Products

You can see this relationship demonstrated in Exhibit 7-3. All the support costs related to the production department at SeatJoy are gathered into a single cost pool. The costs are then allocated to individual chairs using a UBC rate based on direct labor hours.

The two-stage UBC relationship seems to say that products consume costs in production departments. However, that is not true. Costs are consumed by activities. And activities are necessary to create and deliver products and services. Based on this fact, the activity-based costing (ABC) method of allocating manufacturing overhead costs (which is also accomplished in two stages) makes a rather subtle change to the UBC relationship. The ABC two-stage allocation process is characterized by the following relationship:

Costs → **Activities** → Products

In the ABC relationship, costs are first attributed to activities. Then, each activity is studied to determine its relationship to the product, and product costs are determined based on these activities. Using this relationship allows the management accountant to refine the categorization of costs as either variable or fixed. The UBC approach, with its focus on production units, strictly defines variable costs as those that proportionally shift when an additional unit is produced. This approach probably works well with direct labor, direct materials, and *some* overhead costs. All other remaining costs are then considered fixed and allocated to units using a unit-based driver such as direct labor hours.

cost driver A factor that determines an activity cost. An activity can have more than one cost driver.

However, in today's complex manufacturing and service environments, production costs are determined by many types of activities, not by the production of single units. An activity that affects a particular cost is called a **cost driver** for that cost. Given the right cost drivers and enough time, most costs are variable. For instance, many costs in a manufacturing organization are variable based on the number of and type of *batches* produced or the number of and the characteristics of *product lines* within the company's product mix. Conversely, these costs are fixed based on the number of units produced. Nearly every cost has at least one cost driver (an activity). Effectively managing costs of providing a product means that *activities, not products,*

An activity that affects a particular production cost is called a cost driver. Given the right cost drivers, most costs are variable. Many costs in a manufacturing organization, such as a candy factory, are variable based on the number of and type of batches produced.

must be managed. The bottom line is that the traditional management accounting approach to product costs, which states that

Individual cost of product = Direct materials + Direct labor + Manufacturing overhead,

may not be the best perspective of production costs when making planning decisions such as the one facing SeatJoy. Notice, though, that this is the approach used by SeatJoy's management accountants to analyze individual unit costs and total annual operating results in Exhibit 7-1. ABC recommends a different view of production costs based on production activities. Using the Hierarchical Product Cost Model, we can see that production costs are a function of many types of activities. As shown in Exhibit 7-4, there are four categories of activities that result in production costs. Rather than focusing on the cost for an individual product, the Hierarchical Product Cost Model recognizes that an organization's total production costs are a function of these four categories of activities. As a result, these categories need to be well understood in order to manage the costs related to production. We need to spend some time discussing these four types of activities in order to better assess the situation at SeatJoy, Inc. We'll start at the top with unit-level activities and work our way down.

unit-level activities Activities that take place each time a unit of product is produced.

UNIT-LEVEL ACTIVITIES In the Hierarchical Product Cost Model, activities that are performed each time a unit of a product or service is produced are classified together and called **unit-level activities**. Think about the SeatJoy production setting. Obviously, direct materials are released and direct labor is used each time a chair is produced. Perhaps many of the production processes are automated, minimizing the amount of direct labor involved in the production of a single chair. Nevertheless, each chair produced increases the amount of operating time on the machinery. Operating SeatJoy's assembly, sewing, and packing equipment generates machine maintenance activities. If SeatJoy uses the unit-based depreciation method on its machinery, then depreciation charges occur as chairs are produced. Energy costs required to run the production machinery are also directly tied to the number of hours the machines are operated. Costs related to all these activities are categorized as unit-based costs. Note that in the traditional UBC approach, all costs are treated as if they took place at the unit level. Direct materials and direct labor are attributed to each unit produced. Additionally, all manufacturing overhead is allocated to each unit produced. In the ABC approach, direct materials, direct labor, and *some types* of manufacturing overhead are handled at the unit level. Traditionally, these

exhibit 7-4 Hierarchical Product Cost Model

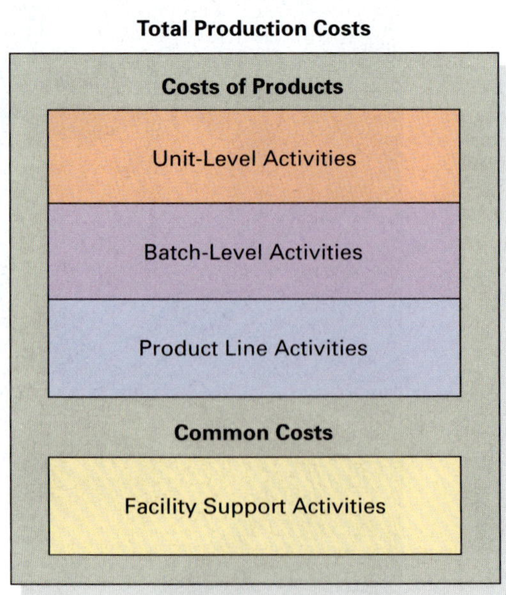

costs are considered to be the variable costs of production. The remaining manufacturing overhead costs are traditionally considered fixed. In ABC, however, these fixed manufacturing costs are related to batch-level, product line, or facility support activities. It is really this categorization, illustrated in Exhibit 7-5, that makes ABC quite different from UBC.

Let's assume that the accountants at SeatJoy determine that \$3,420,000 of the \$18,240,000 in annual manufacturing overhead costs is related to unit-level activities. SeatJoy can continue to use direct labor hours to allocate these costs to chairs. Based on 456,000 annual direct labor hours, this works out to \$7.50 per direct labor hour (\$3,420,000 ÷ 456,000 hours). As a result, a Cushman II chair is allocated \$112.50 in manufacturing overhead for unit-level activities (based on 15 direct labor hours per Cushman II chair).

As you can see in Exhibit 7-5, ABC takes a hard look at manufacturing overhead costs historically considered fixed. Remember that ABC is based on the premise that, once the proper cost driver is identified, most costs can be managed as variable costs. In terms of both the traditional UBC approach and the more modern ABC approach, unit-level costs are variable. As a product unit is produced or a service is performed, unit-level costs increase. Traditional management accounting using UBC then maintains that all other costs are fixed. Frankly, if we're talking about using individual units of the product as a cost driver, then these costs are fixed. However, the ABC Hierarchical Product Cost Model looks for other activities, required by the production process, that make many (though not all) fixed costs act variable. The result is the categorization of batch-level and product line activities and their related costs.

BATCH-LEVEL ACTIVITIES Let's consider batch costs. Many production runs flow in batches. An automotive production line builds a particular line of cars until market orders are met. Then the current production line is changed over to produce a different car. A steel mill or a flour mill mixes different components into customized batches, then packages the output to meet customer specifications. These attempts to individually satisfy customer demands result in the need for batch setups on the production line. During setup, production must pause while employees recalibrate or install different machines. The new batch often requires a different mix of raw materials. Ordering, paying for, and moving raw materials into production position entail time and expense. Often some inspection takes place, such as testing the first item of the batch run, to ensure that the configuration and quality of the product are acceptable. These

exhibit 7-5 Relationship between Unit-Based Costs and Activity-Based Costs in a Manufacturing Organization

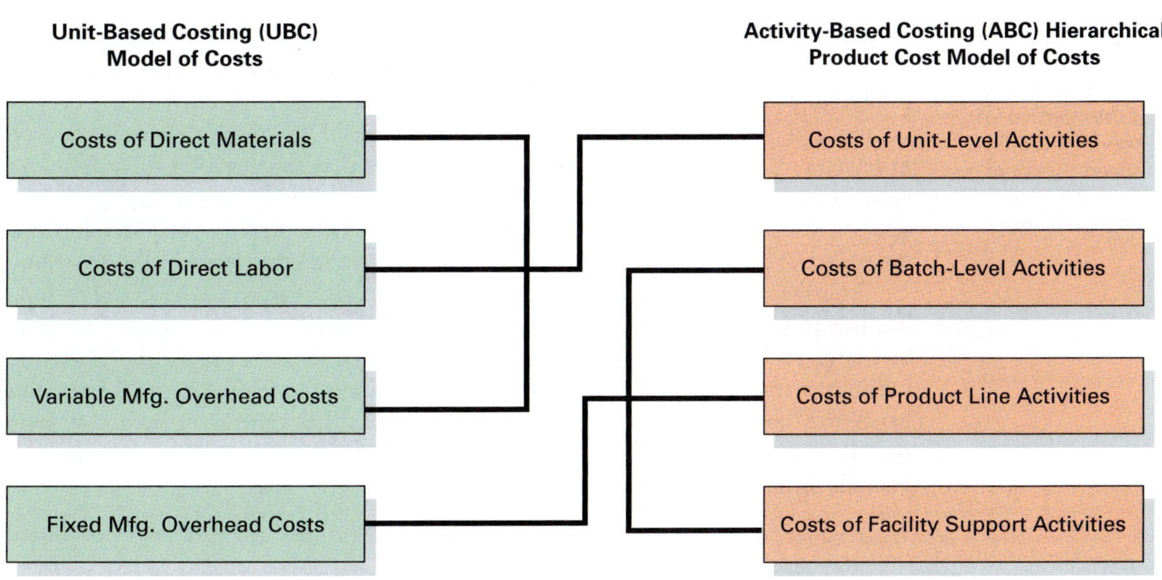

batch-level activities Activities that take place in order to support a batch or production run, regardless of the size.

activities that are necessary each time products or services are processed as a batch are known as **batch-level activities**.

Batch-level activities are more common in service firms where there is a lot of customization of the product for customers. A public accounting firm undertakes a lot of setup activities before work can begin on an audit, tax, or consulting job. A trucking company must perform many activities related to setting up a contract and organizing pickup and delivery details before transportation work can begin for a customer. A radio station that sells advertising often does a lot of design work before it can begin running a customer's advertising spot.

Regardless of the size of the batch (1 or 10,000 units, miles, or broadcasts), batch activities must take place, and batch-related costs must be spent. Each organization must evaluate its production operation to determine if and what activities take place to support a batch run. Then, the individual costs of each of these activities are determined. In line with the two-stage cost attribution process of ABC, once costs are assigned to activity cost pools, then batches that require a particular activity are assigned the attending costs. Examples of batch activities at a manufacturing company like SeatJoy include:

- number of setups,
- setup hours,
- movements of materials,
- orders for nonstocked items,
- purchase orders,
- number of inspections, and
- inspection hours.

By tracking batch costs in this manner, much product cost cross-subsidization is avoided. Batch costs can then be averaged out across the number of units in the batch (if desired). Units in small batches will then be required to carry a larger burden of these costs. Units in larger batches will experience favorable economies of scale. The cost information system begins reflecting what most managers and supervisors already know: poor scheduling leading to unnecessary production setups results in wasted resources. With this information available, managers can make better-informed decisions concerning the trade-off of large, cost-efficient batches versus production flexibility and low inventory levels. Later we will work through some calculations that demonstrate the negative impact that product cost cross-subsidization can have on decisions.

PRODUCT LINE ACTIVITIES Henry Ford infamously said that his customers were welcome to have their Model T car in any color, so long as it was black! That position has obviously changed at **FORD MOTOR COMPANY**, as well as at many other companies. Products, including the huge airplanes produced at **BOEING**, are often customized to satisfy rather small pockets of customers. This leads to the third level of activities in the Hierarchical Product Cost Model—product line activities. **Product line activities** are required to supply a particular product type to the market. These activities are constant regardless of the number of units or batches produced. The number of product line activities is tied to the diversity of the company's product mix and the individual complexity of each product. Organizations with many types of goods or services will require many more of these activities than organizations that produce only a few types of goods or services. As part of the effort to diversify the risk of market fluctuations and satisfy a myriad of demanding and informed customers, companies must develop and provide a diverse set of products. This results in increased overhead costs related to product line activities.

product line activities Activities that take place in order to support a product line, regardless of the number of batches or individual units actually produced. Costs of product line activities are also known as capability costs.

Management must be constantly aware of the costs of activities necessary to support an expanding product mix. As with batch activities, management must intelligently trade off the value of a large product mix against the cost of providing a variety of products. There are great opportunities for product cost savings through evaluating the inefficient use of resources by both batch-level and product line activities. Product lines that experience such cost savings should then be able to compete in the market at reduced prices. Sources of product line activities in a manufacturing firm like SeatJoy might include:

- engineering departments where product design changes in a product or production process take place,
- warehouses where materials necessary to each product line are stored and managed,

- supervisors who are dedicated to managing a particular product line,
- purchasing departments that initiate purchase orders, and
- receiving and shipping docks that receive raw materials and ship finished products.

In service organizations like a public accounting firm, a transportation company, or a bank, product line activities might include:

- in-house training resources dedicated to specific audit, tax, or consulting services,
- safety specialists dedicated to managing transportation of hazardous material, and
- loan officers dedicated to home mortgages versus commercial lending.

Only when the organization decides to permanently eliminate the product from its product mix can product line activities and their related costs be removed. Costs of product line activities are also referred to as **capability costs**—costs necessary to the capability of providing a particular product or service to the market.

capability costs Costs necessary to have the capability to produce a particular product or to provide a particular service. Capability costs are also known as the costs of product line activities.

facility support activities Activities necessary to have a facility in place in order to participate in the development and production of products or services. However, these activities are not related to any particular line of products or services. Costs of facility support activities are often called common costs.

FACILITY SUPPORT ACTIVITIES Up to this point we have discussed the top three layers of activities in the Hierarchical Product Cost Model: unit-level, batch-level, and product line (see Exhibit 7-4). The final level of activities in the Hierarchical Product Cost Model is facility support activities. Essentially, **facility support activities** are those activities that must be in place before development and production of any product or service can begin. Most of these activities are administrative in nature. Facility support activities are the source of the true common costs in the production facility. No single product or product line is responsible for the creation of these costs. Facility support activities are necessary for a business to create any products or services. Examples of facility support costs for a company like SeatJoy include:

- property taxes,
- plant security,
- landscaping,
- accounting, and
- salaries of the general administration (e.g., the vice president of manufacturing) and support staff.

The extent of facility support activities is unrelated to production volume or diversity. Therefore, it is impossible to sensibly relate these costs to the production of any particular product or product line. In the ABC model, there is no intervening activity that can connect costs of facility-sustaining activities to the products. Any assignment of these costs to products is doomed to be arbitrary. Therefore, the ABC approach is to *not* allocate these costs to products.[2] Allocating these costs simply distorts management's view of the relevant costs to be considered when strategically managing a product or product line.

Costs of facility support activities should be pooled together and kept separate from the other product costs. Only the costs of activities at the unit, batch, and product line levels are relevant to the production and management of a particular product line. For this reason, costs of facility support activities are part of the total production costs, but they should not be included in the costs of any specific line of products. Separating the costs of facility support activities from specific product costs is illustrated in the Hierarchical Product Cost Model in Exhibit 7-4.

Exhibit 7-6 illustrates how the two-stage ABC model is blended with the Hierarchical Product Cost Model. As you can see, the total manufacturing overhead costs shown in Exhibit 7-3 have been split into four separate cost pools based on how the costs relate to types of activities. The manufacturing overhead allocation rates per direct labor hour, per batch run, and per product line are discussed in the next section.

Resolving Cost Distortions

Poor management accounting can create tremendous problems within an organization, particularly when the competition starts driving down market prices. As profit margins are reduced

2 Actually, the idea that allocating common costs cannot be done sensibly does not belong solely to ABC theory. The traditional theory of responsibility accounting also supports not allocating the costs of facility support activities to products.

exhibit 7-6 Activity-Based Costing at SeatJoy, Inc.*

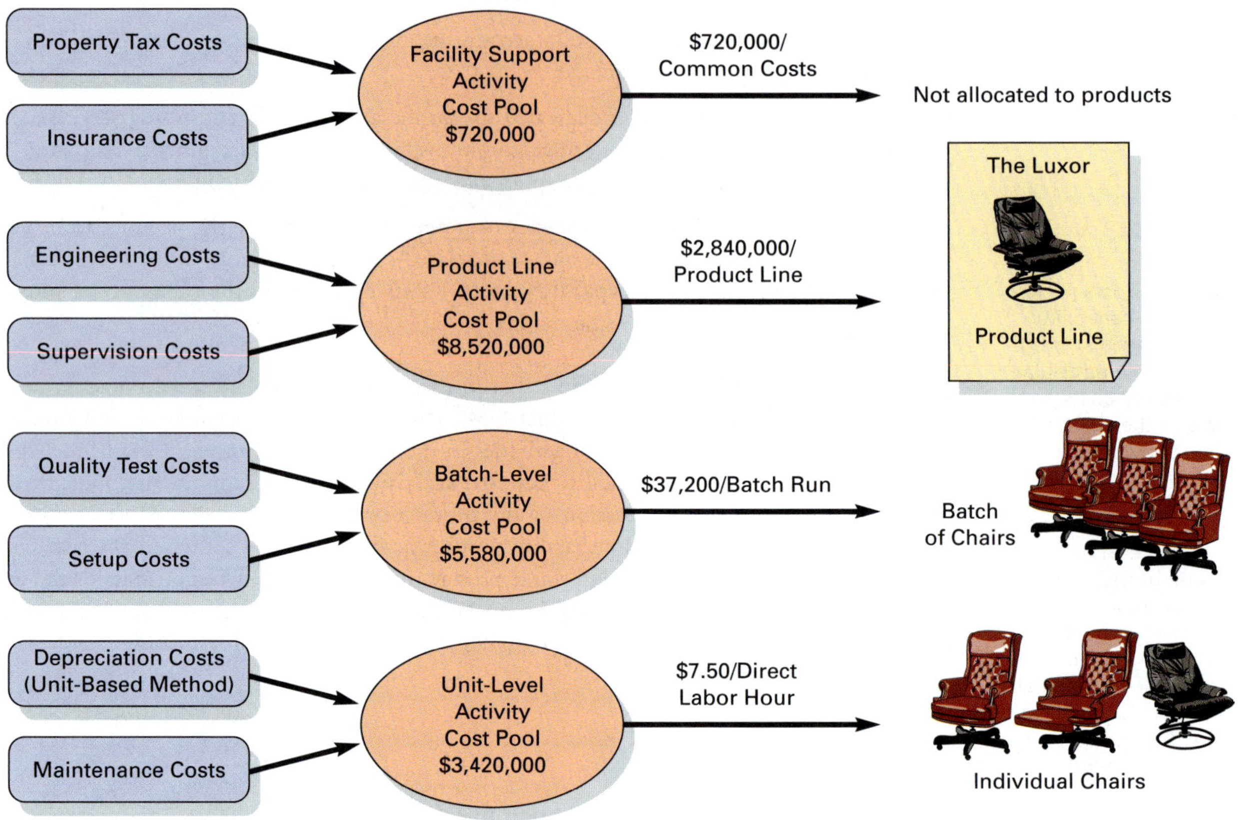

*Calculation of ABC allocation rates is demonstrated in Exhibit 7-7.

in a competitive market, it becomes increasingly more important for a manufacturing, merchandising, or service firm to accurately identify its product costs. The Boeing Company situation described at the beginning of this chapter is a classic example of an organization that produces multiple types of products in an environment with many batch-level and product line activities. Competition is pressuring Boeing to reduce its prices, requiring that Phil Condit and the other executives and managers at Boeing fully understand all production costs *and* how these costs relate to the aircraft they are manufacturing. There is little room for error. To the extent that management accountants provide poor data because of inappropriate cost allocation methods, Boeing will be susceptible to cost distortions such as cross-subsidization and inappropriate allocation of common costs. Each of these cost distortions can lead to decisions that reduce, rather than enhance, the organization's competitive strength.

PRODUCT COST CROSS-SUBSIDIZATION Let's return to SeatJoy, Inc. The production supervisors at SeatJoy have organized the production process by producing one batch run of each product each week. Typically, production workers spend Monday mornings setting up equipment to produce Cushman chairs. Once everything is set, some chairs are produced and evaluated for quality assurance. With the inspectors' OK, the production process begins, and company employees work until enough chairs are produced to fill all orders placed that week. Sometime Tuesday afternoon or Wednesday morning, they switch to producing Cushman II chairs, and all the setup and quality assurance activities again take place. Hopefully, by Friday morning SeatJoy can begin setting up the production equipment to make Luxor chairs. As you can see in Exhibit 7-3, SeatJoy has specific costs related to performing setup and quality test activities. Currently, SeatJoy combines these costs with all other manufacturing costs in order to create its manufacturing overhead allocation rate. However, because the weekly batch run of

Luxor chairs is much smaller than the weekly batch run of either Cushman or Cushman II chairs, some of the batch costs related to producing Luxor chairs are being subsidized by the other two products.

With a little additional data, we can compute the size of the product cost cross-subsidization taking place at SeatJoy. Of the $18,240,000 in 2002 manufacturing overhead costs, SeatJoy's management accountant determines that $5,580,000 is related to batch-level activities. SeatJoy works 50 weeks a year and produces one batch of each product weekly, which works out to 150 total batches each year (50 weeks × 1 batch per week × 3 product lines). As a result, SeatJoy should establish a manufacturing overhead allocation rate of $37,200 *per batch* ($5,580,000 ÷ 150 batches). The average cost *per chair* for batch-level activities at SeatJoy is computed as follows.[3]

MANUFACTURING OVERHEAD ALLOCATION USING BATCH-LEVEL ACTIVITIES

$5,580,000 ÷ 150 batches = $37,200 Manufacturing Overhead Costs per Batch

	Cushman	Cushman II	Luxor
Annual sales volume in chairs	18,000	14,400	4,800
Annual number of batches	÷ 50	÷ 50	÷ 50
Average batch size in chairs	360	288	96
Overhead costs per batch	$37,200	$37,200	$37,200
Average batch size in chairs	÷ 360	÷ 288	÷ 96
Average batch costs per chair	$103.33	$129.17	$387.50

How do these costs per chair compare when we allocate the $5,580,000 based on direct labor hours? Total direct labor hours for 2002, as well as the average number of direct labor hours per chair, are provided in Exhibit 7-1. The UBC allocation is computed below.

MANUFACTURING OVERHEAD ALLOCATION USING UNIT-LEVEL ACTIVITIES

$5,580,000 ÷ 456,000 hours = $12.24 Manufacturing Overhead Costs per Direct Labor Hour (rounded)

	Cushman	Cushman II	Luxor
Manufacturing overhead costs per direct labor hour	$ 12.24	$ 12.24	$ 12.24
Direct labor hours per product	× 10.0	× 15.0	× 12.5
Average batch costs per chair	$122.40	$183.60	$153.00

Look carefully at the difference in the calculations when using batches versus direct labor hours as the cost driver. If these manufacturing overhead costs are truly determined by batch-level activities, then the first set of calculations is more accurate than the second set. However, in Exhibits 7-1 and 7-2, SeatJoy is allocating manufacturing overhead costs using direct labor hours. As a result, Luxor chairs are receiving only *some* of the $387.50 average batch-level overhead costs per chair that this product is actually creating. The rest of these costs are being inappropriately allocated to the Cushman and Cushman II products. In other words, Luxor product costs are being *cross-subsidized* by the Cushman and Cushman II product lines. The result of this product cost cross-subsidization is that Cushman and Cushman II products will look less profitable than they really are, and conversely, Luxor chairs will look more profitable than they should.

Just like the product cost cross-subsidization that resulted from using direct labor hours to allocate costs of batch-level activities, SeatJoy is also likely cross-subsidizing costs of product line activities. Of the $18,240,000 in 2002 manufacturing overhead costs at SeatJoy, it is determined

3 It is critical to remember that we are computing *average* costs per chair here. Hence, because these are batch-level activities, SeatJoy *cannot* change these costs by changing the number of chairs produced. The cost driver for these costs is batches, not units (i.e., individual chairs).

that $8,520,000 is related to product line activities. That means that each product line should receive $2,840,000 of these costs ($8,520,000 ÷ 3 product lines). The average cost per chair for these manufacturing overhead costs is computed as follows:

PRODUCT LINE MANUFACTURING OVERHEAD ALLOCATION USING PRODUCT LINE ACTIVITIES

$8,520,000 ÷ 3 lines = $2,840,000 Manufacturing Overhead Costs per Product Line

	Cushman	Cushman II	Luxor
Manufacturing overhead costs per product line	$2,840,000	$2,840,000	$2,840,000
Annual sales volume in chairs	÷ 18,000	÷ 14,400	÷ 4,800
Average product line costs per chair	$ 157.78	$ 197.22	$ 591.67

How do these costs per chair compare when we allocate the $8,520,000 based on direct labor hours? Again, total direct labor hours for 2002, as well as the average number of direct labor hours per chair, are provided in Exhibit 7-1. The UBC allocation is computed below.

PRODUCT LINE MANUFACTURING OVERHEAD ALLOCATION USING UNIT-LEVEL ACTIVITIES

$8,520,000 ÷ 456,000 hours = $18.68 Manufacturing Overhead Costs per Direct Labor Hour (rounded)

	Cushman	Cushman II	Luxor
Manufacturing overhead costs per direct labor hour	$ 18.68	$ 18.68	$ 18.68
Direct labor hours per product	× 10.0	× 15.0	× 12.5
Average product line costs per chair	$186.80	$280.20	$233.50

business environment essay

City of Indianapolis Uses ABC Mayor Steve Goldsmith of Indianapolis understands the power of correctly allocating costs to their drivers. In his tenure as mayor of the twelfth largest city in the United States, Goldsmith has saved the local taxpayers roughly $400 million, has decreased the city's debt 3%, and has created nearly 30,000 jobs. How? Through ABC.

Before Goldsmith, ABC in the public sector was unexplored. Previously, the city of Indianapolis had broken down its costs only by function. In other words, the old accounting system identified money spent on salaries, equipment, capital investments, and professional service contracts, but never identified what specific activities were actually using these costs. But with his pioneering spirit and determination to save the taxpayers' money, Goldsmith undertook the challenge of painstakingly relating each cost to its appropriate activity by identifying the relevant cost driver. The result was significant insight into how money was being spent in his city.

With the help of KPMG (one of the "Big 5" CPA firms), Goldsmith and his finance team completed the analysis and then trained city employees on the importance of accounting correctly for money spent. The taxpayers of Indianapolis may not fully understand the power of ABC, but they are glad that Mayor Steve Goldsmith does!

Source: Adapted from H. Mayer, "Indianapolis Speeds Away," *Journal of Business Strategy,* May–June 1998, p. 41.

As you can see, there is a significant difference in the average costs per chair based on allocating these manufacturing overhead costs using product lines rather than direct labor hours. If these manufacturing overhead costs are truly determined by product line activities, then the first set of calculations is more accurate than the second set. However, since SeatJoy is allocating manufacturing overhead costs using direct labor hours, Luxor chairs are receiving only *some* of the \$591.67 product line manufacturing overhead costs. Just like the previous situation involving batch-level activities, some of the product line manufacturing overhead costs belonging to Luxor products are being inappropriately allocated to the Cushman and Cushman II products. Luxor product costs are being *cross-subsidized* by the Cushman and Cushman II product lines in the case of manufacturing overhead costs related to both batch-level and product line activities.

By understanding that batch and product line activities act as cost drivers, costs previously considered to be fixed are actually variable with respect to these types of activities. Products that require these activities should be assigned the burden of these costs. As you can see, product cost cross-subsidization occurs when unit-level cost drivers such as direct labor costs are used to allocate costs of batch-level and product line activities.

ALLOCATING COMMON COSTS AND THE DEATH SPIRAL Suppose, for example, that it is a company's practice to allocate a share of the cost of property taxes to each product. Neither the product manager nor the production line supervisor has any control over this cost (other than to argue vehemently in management meetings for smaller allotments of this cost). When the company is trying to manage product lines to new levels of cost effectiveness and customer satisfaction, this cost allocation serves only to cloud the issues. The product line is not responsible for creating activities that lead to property taxes, so these costs should not be combined with costs of unit-level, batch-level, and product line activities in determining product costs.

Some individuals argue that allocating facility support costs is useful because these activities result in very real costs and must be "covered" by product revenues if the company is to be profitable. It is true that these costs are real. Management must be constantly aware of these costs and should be constantly working to ensure that all facility support activities are cost effective. However, consider a simple example. Suppose that a company's annual property taxes are \$100,000 and are allocated evenly across four products (Products A, B, C, and D). The product cost information system indicates that the Product D line is generating a \$10,000 loss. After several unsuccessful attempts to make the product more profitable, it is discontinued. However, property taxes remain unchanged and are now allocated evenly over the remaining three product lines. Thus, where the three remaining product lines were each previously receiving \$25,000 in allocated common costs (\$100,000 ÷ 4 product lines), now each receives \$33,333 (\$100,000 ÷ 3 product lines). Suppose that, with the new allocation, Product C turns unprofitable. Should management now consider discontinuing Product C?

It is doubtful that anyone would be fooled into making the mistake of discontinuing Product C in the simple example above. Hopefully, few would have originally discontinued Product D either. Such imprudent decisions result in a classic case of "death spiral." Essentially, a **death spiral** begins when a company does not fully understand its costs and then attempts to reduce costs by cutting products or other business segments that in fact do not create the costs in question. This results in the remaining costs being reallocated over fewer product lines. So, although the Product D line may be displaying a \$10,000 loss, once the unavoidable \$25,000 allocation is removed, it is clear that the Product D line is actually contributing \$15,000 to help "cover" the \$100,000 tax cost and provide overall profit for the company. Removing this product from the company only results in other products having to carry an even larger burden of facility support costs. Continuing to drop products in such a manner will leave the company with \$100,000 in property taxes and no revenue-generating products.

death spiral A series of management decisions based on bad information that results in reducing or removing activities or segments from the organization that are actually profitable.

Given this simple example, you might expect few to fall into a death spiral trap. However, the product mix of most large-scale organizations is much more complex than this example. For example, the situation at Boeing Company involves many activities and much cost complexity. It would be quite easy to become confused about cost relationships in such a setting. There are several cases of companies falling into this trap and seriously damaging their competitive position before realizing what was happening.

The situation at SeatJoy certainly looks like the beginning of a death spiral. As demonstrated earlier, the accountants are allocating costs of batch-level and product line activities to the Cushman and Cushman II product lines that should belong to the Luxor product line. When SeatJoy management elects to drop the Cushman II product line, the Luxor manufacturing overhead costs being subsidized by the Cushman II line are reallocated to the remaining products. The result is that the Cushman product now looks as if it is unprofitable. Remember, though, that the Cushman line is subsidizing some Luxor costs. In addition, some common costs (i.e., costs of facility support activities) are being allocated to all three products. As demonstrated in Exhibit 7-6, property tax and insurance costs are facility support costs that really shouldn't be allocated to any of the products. Similar to the product cost cross-subsidization situation, dropping the Cushman II product line results only in a reallocation of these common costs. This reallocation also contributes to the Cushman product becoming unprofitable in 2003 as shown in Exhibit 7-2. Of the $18,240,000 in manufacturing overhead at SeatJoy, $720,000 is facility support costs. The average facility support cost per chair as allocated by the traditional manufacturing overhead allocation system is computed below.

FACILITY SUPPORT MANUFACTURING OVERHEAD ALLOCATION USING UNIT-LEVEL ACTIVITIES

$720,000 ÷ 456,000 hours = $1.58 Manufacturing Overhead Costs per Direct Labor Hour (rounded)

	Cushman	Cushman II	Luxor
Manufacturing overhead costs per direct labor hour	$ 1.58	$ 1.58	$ 1.58
Direct labor hours per product	× 10.0	× 15.0	× 12.5
Average facility support costs per chair	$15.80	$23.70	$19.75

As you can see, the UBC allocation approach assigns $23.70 per chair in common costs to the Cushman II product line. These costs, if removed from the 2002 operating results in Exhibit 7-1, would go a long way toward reversing what appears to be a loss in this product line. In fact, as you might suspect, once we have corrected accounting problems related to product cost cross-subsidization, removing these common costs should demonstrate that Cushman II is not an unprofitable product line. Exhibit 7-7 combines all the ABC allocations we've discussed into a new view of the 2002 operating results. With this information, SeatJoy management should clearly see that dropping the Cushman II product line is not a good decision and will drive overall SeatJoy operations into a loss situation in the year 2003. With the information shown in Exhibit 7-7, managers at SeatJoy should understand that to improve profits, they must focus on better controlling existing costs rather than making plans to drop any specific line of products.

Activity-Based Management (ABM)

Once SeatJoy has identified and classified activities according to the Hierarchical Product Cost Model, it is in a position to use the ABC data it has gathered to begin the process of improving activities. Remember that ABC is basically a two-stage process. The first stage of ABC involves tracing the flow of resources (and their costs) to activities. The result of the first stage of ABC is activity cost pools. Exhibit 7-6 illustrates activity cost pools for SeatJoy, Inc. It looks like a simple process to establish activity cost pools for an organization, right? Actually, this work can be both difficult and time-consuming. Allocating costs using UBC can often be done simply by using available records (such as payroll sheets or production reports) to identify the number of direct labor hours or number of chairs produced. All manufacturing overhead costs are then averaged across the total number of hours or units. On the other hand, to find out how costs *really* flow (i.e., to trace costs to activities), the accountant must leave the office and go out on the production floor or into the service area. Interacting with those

exhibit 7-7 SeatJoy, Inc.: ABC Analysis of 2002 Operating Results

	Unit-Level	Batch-Level	Product Line	Facility-Support
Activity cost pools	$3,420,000	$5,580,000	$8,520,000	$720,000
Cushman activity units	180,000 hours	50 batches	1 product line	
Cushman II activity units	216,000 hours	50 batches	1 product line	
Luxor activity units	60,000 hours	50 batches	1 product line	
Total activity units	456,000 hours	150 batches	3 product lines	1 facility
Cost per activity	$7.50 per direct labor hour	$37,200 per batch	$2,840,000 per product line	$720,000 in common costs

Labor Cost Analysis

	Cushman	Cushman II	Luxor	Total
Labor hours per product	10.0 hours	15.0 hours	12.5 hours	
Annual sales volume	× 18,000 chairs	× 14,400 chairs	× 4,800 chairs	
Total annual direct labor hours	180,000 hours	216,000 hours	60,000 hours	456,000 hours
Wage rate per hour	× $20	× $20	× $20	× $20
Total annual direct labor costs	$3,600,000	$4,320,000	$1,200,000	$9,120,000

Total Annual Results

	Cushman	Cushman II	Luxor	Total
Sales revenue	$ 18,000,000	$ 21,600,000	$ 14,400,000	$ 54,000,000
Total direct materials	$ (6,030,000)	$ (9,360,000)	$ (6,696,000)	$(22,086,000)
Total direct labor	(3,600,000)	(4,320,000)	(1,200,000)	(9,120,000)
Unit-level overhead	(1,350,000)	(1,620,000)	(450,000)	(3,420,000)
Batch-level overhead	(1,860,000)	(1,860,000)	(1,860,000)	(5,580,000)
Product line overhead	(2,840,000)	(2,840,000)	(2,840,000)	(8,520,000)
Total product-related costs	$(15,680,000)	$(20,000,000)	$(13,046,000)	$(48,726,000)
Total product margin	$ 2,320,000	$ 1,600,000	$ 1,354,000	$ 5,274,000
Facility support overhead				(720,000)
Selling and administrative expenses				(4,000,000)
Operating profit				$ 554,000

Individual Unit Analysis

	Cushman	Cushman II	Luxor
Sales price	$1,000.00	$ 1,500.00	$ 3,000.00
Direct materials per product	$ (335.00)	$ (650.00)	$(1,395.00)
Direct labor per product	(200.00)	(300.00)	(250.00)
Average unit-level OH per product	(75.00)	(112.50)	(93.75)
Average batch-level OH per product	(103.33)	(129.17)	(387.50)
Average product line OH per product	(157.78)	(197.22)	(591.67)
Total cost per product	$ (871.11)	$(1,388.89)	$(2,717.92)
Margin per product	$ 128.89	$ 111.11	$ 282.08
Margin percent	12.9%	7.4%	9.4%

involved (department managers, line supervisors, etc.) is the only way to gather accurate insight about activities.

The second stage of ABC is assigning costs now pooled by activities to products. In the work of tracing resources to activity cost pools, much of the insight necessary to establish the second ABC stage is also developed. Typically, a budgeted cost is established for each activity. The expected use of the activity is also determined (e.g., number of direct labor hours for unit-level activities, number of batches for batch-level activities, number of product lines for product line activities). Similar to the traditional manufacturing overhead allocation rate, an activity cost allocation rate is established and used to transfer costs as an activity is actually employed.

For example, think of the activity "purchasing" for a merchandising company. The accountants and managers using ABC must assimilate what costs are required to purchase inventory for the company. The total cost of purchasing activities, as well as the number of expected purchase orders, is budgeted for the year. Using this information, costs per purchase order are set. Then, each time a purchase order is initiated, the costs are assigned to the object requiring a purchase order. Most merchants purchase inventory in large lots, or batches. If this is the case, then costs of purchase orders are related to batch-level activities. Hence, using ABC, the accountants and managers may be able to demonstrate and understand clearly that it is batches of products that must carry (and cover) the costs of purchasing. If the company wants to know the average purchasing costs of a particular inventory item, this is simply a function of the number of product units in each batch of products purchased.

ABC does not provide all the information a company needs to *manage* the costs of purchasing, however. Other things besides number of purchase orders requested may be driving the costs of purchasing activities. Further, the merchant also needs to manage the performance (i.e., the quality and timeliness) of its purchasing activities. With ABC, our focus is on activities. However, effectively tracing costs to products is a separate issue from managing the activity process. In order for the accountant to provide useful information for managing activities within the organization, we need to expand our ABC model as shown below.

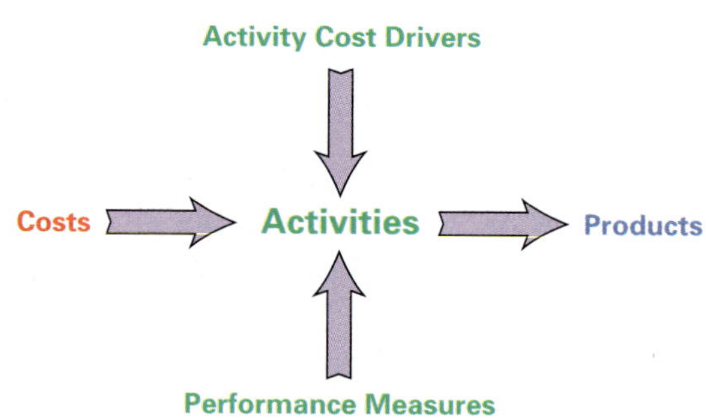

Assume that for our purchasing activity example, the ABC team finds that the number of line items in the purchase order and the amount of lead time provided for the purchase order drive the level of costs supporting this activity. In managing costs, it is important that this set of cost drivers be related to the purchasing activity. To better control costs, management needs to concentrate on controlling needlessly high levels of the cost drivers.[4]

In addition, activity performance measures should be established. The drive to improve the overall company so that it can better compete within its market means that every critical activity in the organization, not just those directly affecting customers, must be continuously improved. Every activity has a customer—either inside or outside the company. Performance measures used to evaluate the quality of purchasing might include the amount of time required to complete an order (i.e., lead time) and the level of errors in filling an order. Endeavoring to become a world-class merchandiser (or manufacturer or service provider) requires a company to

4 Often the allocation rate used to assign activity costs to cost objects is also included in the total set of activity cost drivers used to evaluate and control activity costs. However, an activity pool's set of cost drivers and the allocation rate used to assign its cost to products do not have to be the same.

clearly identify its strategy and then intelligently build performance measures that support the attainment of strategic goals.

activity-based management (ABM) The identification and use of cost drivers and performance measures to manage the costs, quality, and timeliness of activities.

Identifying and using multiple cost drivers and performance measures to manage an activity is called **activity-based management (ABM)**. As you can see in the previous diagram, ABM expands the basic ABC model by separating the task of product costing using activity-based relationships (Costs → Activities → Products) from the task of directly managing activities in order to achieve cost efficiencies and to enhance quality in business processes (Activity Cost Drivers → Activities ← Performance Measures). Using ABM, opportunities for cost efficiencies are created by separately tracking multiple cost drivers for each critical activity. Continuous improvement of the organization is then achieved using performance measures for strategically important activities in the organization. As you can see, managing activity cost drivers and performance measures for a particular activity is a management task that is actually exclusive of the processes of tracking a single cost driver that allocates the activity's costs to products. Exhibit 7-8 illustrates the application of ABM for two activities at SeatJoy.

exhibit 7-8 Activity-Based Management at SeatJoy, Inc.

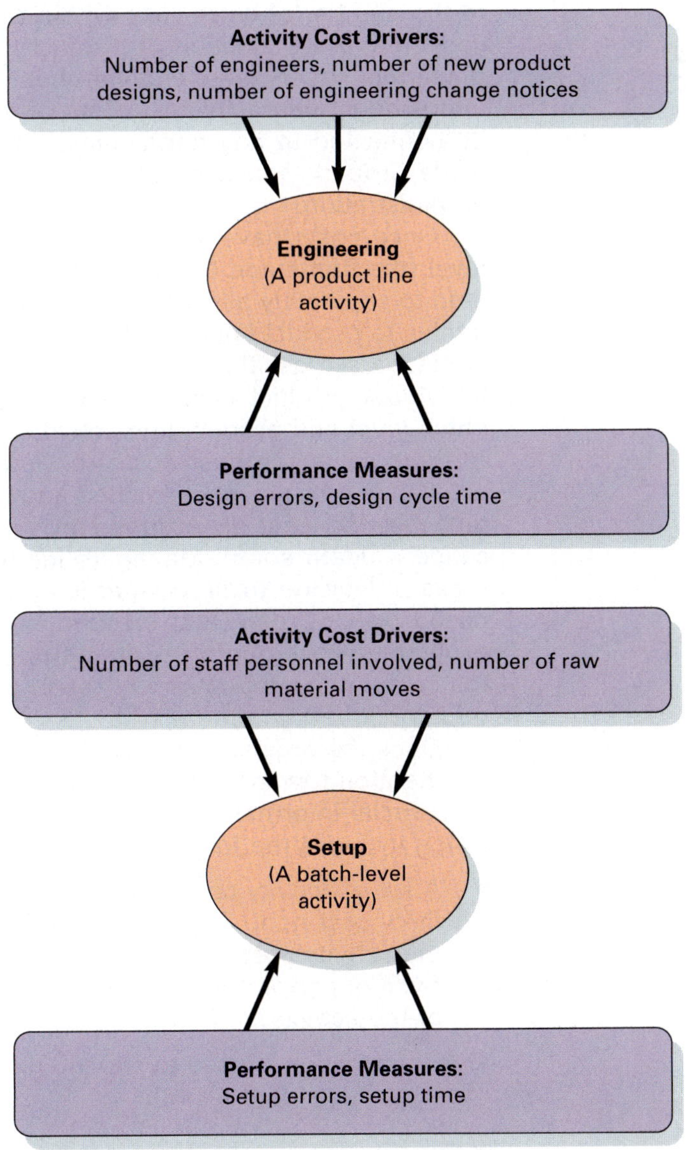

to summarize

Traditional product cost models generally focus on allocating overhead costs based on some measure that is a function of the number of products being produced or the amount of service being provided in the organization. This approach, called unit-based costing (UBC), works well in fairly simple settings with little diversity in the types of products or services offered to customers. In contrast, activity-based costing (ABC) recognizes that activities are the causes of costs. By understanding how activities relate to products, a manufacturing company with a diverse set of products and processes, such as Boeing Company, can more intelligently allocate manufacturing overhead costs to products.

Activities can be categorized across four levels: unit-level activities, batch-level activities, product line activities, and facility support activities. Generally, variable manufacturing overhead, such as machine maintenance or energy costs to run production equipment, is a function of the number of units produced. Setup costs, materials purchase orders, and route planning are examples of costs traditionally considered fixed that actually are variable in relation to the number of batch runs within the organization. Manufacturing overhead costs that are a function of product line activities are generally related to engineering, supervision, and warehousing. In contrast to unit-level, batch-level, and product line activities, costs of facility support activities cannot sensibly be connected to any particular product line. Examples of these activities include property taxes, plant security, landscaping, accounting, and executive administration.

Once costs have been pooled together according to the proper activity level (the first stage of ABC), new overhead allocation rates can then be created to separately allocate costs of unit-level, batch-level, and product line activities to product lines (the second stage of ABC). Costs of facility support activities are classified as common costs and should *not* be allocated to individual product lines; otherwise, product costs are distorted. If costs of batch-level and product line activities are allocated using UBC, then cost distortions called product cost cross-subsidization can also take place as one product is erroneously allocated another product's cost in the accounting system. Product cost distortions can lead to a series of management decisions called a death spiral. Managers inadvertently involved in a death spiral will make a decision to drop what is actually a profitable product or service line based on UBC data that erroneously suggest this product or service is unprofitable. Once one product line is dropped, the reallocation of overhead to the remaining products may result in another product looking unprofitable, thereby continuing the spiral.

Once the organization has developed an accurate ABC system, it can turn its attention toward improving activities that support its competitive strategy. The crucial information to be developed for important activities in the organization includes the following:

- A set of activity cost drivers that provides the greatest influence on the activity cost pool. The cost drivers become the focus of effort in controlling the activity cost pool.
- A set of performance measures used to evaluate the quality and timeliness of the activity.

This information is used to expand the ABC model in order to perform activity-based management (ABM).

2

Describe total quality management (TQM) and costs of quality (COQ).

TOTAL QUALITY MANAGEMENT

total quality management (TQM) A management philosophy focused on increasing profitability by improving the quality of products and processes and increasing customer satisfaction, while promoting the well-being and growth of employees.

We ended the last section on ABC by introducing the important concept that tracking and effectively allocating activity costs is not sufficient for managing activities. In today's highly competitive global markets, managing both the cost *and the performance* of activities is critical to the success of most organizations. This fact supports the importance of ABM to the management process of planning, controlling, and evaluating activities within the organization. In the last 20 years, an important management model known as **total quality management (TQM)** has had significant impacts on modern management accounting. TQM is a management philosophy that seeks to increase profitability by improving the quality of products and processes and increasing customer satisfaction while promoting the well-being and growth of the employees of the organization. Most managers, if asked, would say that their company seeks to improve quality, increase customer satisfaction, and take care of its employees. Implementing TQM, however, requires more than just endorsing the importance of quality in the company. An organization that has truly implemented TQM exhibits two defining characteristics. First, quality and continuous improvement are emphasized above all else within the organization. The premise here is one of priority. A company focused on TQM manages itself with the assumption that if product quality is high, customers will be satisfied and employees will be happy, and *then* profits can be expected. This contrasts with the assumption that the company cannot focus on quality until it is performing well financially. Second, TQM in the organization is the result of continuously planning, controlling, and evaluating improvement using specific measures. It is in this second assumption that accounting systems built to perform ABM can interface well with TQM. By tracking costs and performance related to TQM activities, the management accountant provides important support of this critical trend in business management.

TQM Comes to the United States

W. Edward Deming is widely credited with leading the quality revolution in Japan that started in the 1950s. Ironically, Deming received little attention as a consultant to U.S. companies prior to 1950. In contrast, the Japanese began to heed his advice on controlling processes, improving systems, and empowering workers in 1950. Soon, Deming moved to Japan where he remained for approximately 30 years. In honor of his work, Japan established the national Deming Prize to annually honor companies making significant improvements in the TQM process.

During the 1980s, concerns about American competitiveness spurred many U.S. companies to take a new interest in quality. Several companies invited Deming, then in his eighties, back to the United States to challenge the "old way" of thinking about costs and quality. A hundred years ago Andrew Carnegie essentially built an empire in the steel industry with the following motto: "Watch the costs and the profits will take care of themselves." Deming essentially revised this phrase to "Watch the *quality* and the profits will take care of themselves." The effect he and his colleagues have had on the way organizations work and compete is profound. Deming passed away in December 1993 at the age of 93.

TQM and Management Accounting

statistical process control (SPC) A statistical technique for identifying and measuring the quality status of a process by evaluating its output to determine if serious problems exist in the process.

Perhaps you've heard the term *statistical process control.* **Statistical process control (SPC)** is a technical tool that provides users with the ability to study, control, and improve processes of all types. Using statistical probability analysis, SPC provides management with the ability to know whether the errors in a production or service process are a signal that a serious problem exists in the process. Deming refined this early engineering tool and placed it squarely in the center of his TQM theory of management. Basically, Deming recognized that variation is a regular fact of life. No matter how carefully the fry cook at your local MCDONALD'S prepares a set of hamburgers, each one will be slightly different from the others. This is a natural fact of variation. Frankly, it's probably not very important to you as a consumer that every McDonald's hamburger you purchase is *exactly* like every other hamburger made that day in that store. However, if you're in the business of manufacturing or purchasing baseballs to be used in major league games throughout the summer, you're probably quite interested in consistent product

business environment essay

AT&T Is a Double Prize Winner! In 1951, the Union of Japanese Scientists and Engineers (JUSE) created the Deming Prize to commemorate the philosophy of W. Edward Deming. This distinguished award is given to companies that best exemplify Deming's methods by achieving outstanding quality management.

For years, Americans did not really grasp Deming's quality methods. It was not until the success of Japanese industries started to seriously affect America's world market share in the late 1970s that the American attitude regarding quality management changed. Now, American companies such as AT&T are impressing the Japanese. In 1994, AT&T received the two most prestigious quality awards—the U.S. Baldrige Award and the Japanese Deming Prize. AT&T is the first American manufacturer to receive the Deming Prize. Commenting on this accomplishment, AT&T's chairman, Robert E. Allen, said, "Receiving these awards is like winning both the World

net work

The NATIONAL INSTITUTE OF STANDARDS AND TECHNOLOGY (NIST) sponsors a site for the Malcolm Baldrige National Quality Award program at http://www.quality.nist.gov. This site will keep you up-to-date on the latest quality award winners, quality programs for students, presidential speeches on "Baldrige" quality, and descriptive portfolios of the award winners. Check out this site to answer the following fundamental question: Who was Malcolm Baldrige, and why is the award named after him?

quality. If you're in the business of manufacturing or purchasing surgical scalpels, computer chips, or rocket boosters for the U.S. Space Shuttle Program, then consistent product quality may be even more important.

SPC is having a large effect on management accounting in many organizations today. An accountant usually doesn't need to perform statistical analysis and probability procedures in order to participate in the TQM effort. SPC work is typically the responsibility of engineers and statisticians. Nevertheless, using SPC to support TQM in a company involves a lot of cost management issues. It costs money to create low-variation, high-quality products and services. It costs money to inspect and measure processes in order to know when problems exist. Finally, Deming and others have taught us that it costs a great deal of money to allow high-variation, low-quality products and services to exist in our organizations. Tracking and managing these costs is an important part of the TQM effort and is often the responsibility of accountants.

Costs of Quality (COQ)

Let's use baseball manufacturing to help understand exactly how management accounting works with SPC to measure and report quality costs. You may be interested to learn that, although China produces 80% of the world's baseballs, every single baseball pitched in the major leagues is made in a Costa Rican factory owned by RAWLINGS SPORTING GOODS COMPANY. A Rawlings baseball begins life as a "pill," a small sphere of cork and rubber enclosed in a rubber shell. The pill is tightly wound with three different layers of wool yarn, then finished with a winding of cotton/polyester yarn. This "core" is then coated with a latex adhesive. Over this gooey, hard lump, an extremely tight-fitting jacket of leather must be sewn. Sewing on the cover is a major effort. No one has been able to successfully create a machine that can automatically stitch the cover on a professional baseball. Hence, Rawlings employs about 1,000 baseball sewing experts. In its factory, top sewing pros can sew four to six baseballs an hour, achieving perfect string tension by feel. A wooden press rolls the seams flat, and finished balls are stored in a dehumidifying room that shrinks the covers tight and protects the balls from tropical humidity that might make them bloat illegally. Baseballs are carefully inspected at the Rawlings plant before being packed for shipping. A baseball that turns out too skinny, too hefty, or otherwise off-spec is "blemmed." It's stamped "blem" for blemish and sold as a practice ball.[5]

To be used in the major leagues, a Rawlings baseball should weigh 5.10 ounces and be 9.15 inches in diameter. As we pointed out, however, regardless of how hard the Rawlings Sporting

5 Hannah Holmes, "The Skinny on Sewing Up Baseballs," at http://www.discovery.com.

Series and the World Cup on the same day." AT&T's commitment to total quality management (TQM) that began in 1990 definitely paid off!

The Malcolm Baldrige National Quality Award was established in 1988 to recognize U.S. manufacturing, service, and small business companies that excel in quality management. The award's threefold purpose is to promote awareness of quality as an important competitive element, recognize quality achievements of U.S. companies, and publicize successful quality strategies. The award can be presented to a maximum of six companies each year that exemplify these characteristics. Due to the award's strict criteria, however, the Baldrige Award has *never* been given to six companies in one year.

Sources: "AT&T Wins Baldrige Award and Deming Prize in Quality Coup" and "Power Systems Is First U.S. Manufacturer to Win Deming Prize," AT&T Press Releases, October 18, 1994, http://www.att.com/press/; The Baldrige National Quality Program, http://www.quality.nist.gov.

fyi

A Rawlings baseball doesn't last long in a major league game (average life is about six minutes), but it has to be as perfect as possible. When a professional pitcher hurls a ball toward homeplate at nearly 100 miles per hour, the slightest blemish in stitching, size, or weight can be the difference between a strike and a home run, the difference between winning a Pennant and having a disappointing season.

Goods Company works to make sure its sewers are consistently producing baseballs of the perfect weight and size, variation occurs.[6] For the Rawlings plant, the important thing is to distinguish simple random variations in baseball weight and size that occasionally occur in a well-controlled production environment from systematic variations that occur more often when a poorly trained sewer is working or when low-quality leather is being used. Consider the following hypothetical example. Using probability rules, Rawlings has determined upper and lower control limits for a baseball. Specifically, baseballs must weigh between 5 and 5.25 ounces and have a circumference between 9 and 9.25 inches. Exhibit 7-9 shows an SPC chart of measurements of daily baseball weights at Rawlings. As you can see, some of these measurements are outside the control limits, indicating that there are potentially serious quality problems in the factory. Although getting the production process back in control will require some management effort, the problem cannot go on unchecked. Blemmed baseballs cost Rawlings money because the balls cannot be sold at game prices. Worse, though, is the cost to Rawlings' reputation. If Major League Baseball switches to another supplier because of inconsistent quality at Rawlings, the long-term opportunity costs to Rawlings could be devastating.

Before Rawlings' production managers can begin working on a potential quality problem on the production floor, the management accountants need to answer a couple of important questions: "What is it costing Rawlings when it produces blemmed baseballs? What will it cost to get the production process back within control limits?" These questions are the initial step in identifying an important set of costs called "costs of quality." **Costs of quality (COQ)** are costs spent to achieve TQM, as well as costs spent when products and processes fail to have high quality. Once activities that relate to quality in the organization have been identified, the accountant must be able to track the costs of those activities in order to measure COQ. Joseph M. Juran, another American quality guru who, like Deming, was enormously influential in the Japanese quality movement, originally identified COQ as an important accounting concept. Eventually, Juran also returned from Japan to the United States with his COQ theories to guide notable companies such as TEXAS INSTRUMENTS, DUPONT, and XEROX. He understood that organizations need to balance costs of achieving quality against the costs of poor quality. Most importantly, he specifically defined four types of quality costs that form the COQ model: prevention costs, appraisal costs, internal failure costs, and external failure costs.

costs of quality (COQ) Costs spent to achieve high quality of products and services, as well as costs spent when products fail to have high quality. The four types of costs of quality are prevention costs, appraisal costs, internal failure costs, and external failure costs.

6 *Note:* This example uses fictitious production standards and results in the setting of an actual company. Data used to illustrate quality concepts in this text should not be construed as actual production standards and results for the Rawlings Sporting Goods Company.

exhibit 7-9 Rawlings Baseball Production: Deming's SPC Analysis of Daily Operating Results

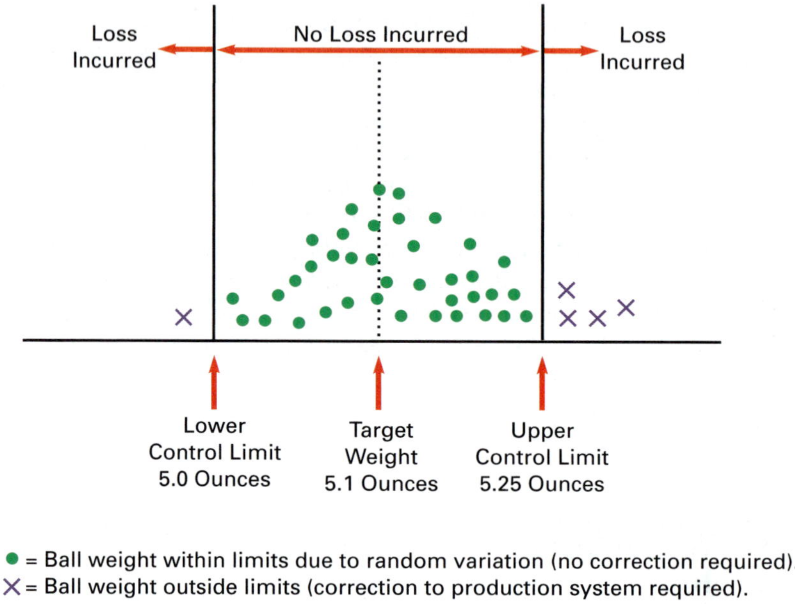

prevention costs Costs of quality that specifically relate to the effort to ensure that processes are performed correctly the first time and that products and services meet customers' expectations.

PREVENTION COSTS **Prevention costs** are costs incurred to ensure that tasks are performed correctly the first time and that the product or service meets customer requirements. Examples of prevention costs include costs of process or product design, employee training, education of suppliers, preventive maintenance, and other quality improvement meetings and projects. In the case of Rawlings Sporting Goods, the quality of its baseballs is highly dependent on the quality of its raw materials and on the expertise of those who stitch on the leather covers. This company will likely spend a lot of money working with its suppliers and training its employees to build a quality product.

appraisal costs Costs of quality that specifically relate to the effort of inspecting, testing, and sampling activities performed in order to identify and remove low-quality products and services from the system.

APPRAISAL COSTS **Appraisal costs** are the amounts spent on inspection, testing, and sampling of raw materials, work in process, and finished goods and services. They include overhead expenses for quality inspectors, costs to adjust measuring and test equipment, and costs of associated supplies and materials. Rawlings performs extensive inspections to gather data similar to that shown in Exhibit 7-9. These inspections require individuals to invest time using special equipment to evaluate each ball for size, weight, color, stitching, etc. Both appraisal and prevention costs can be viewed as investments in the process of providing quality baseballs to Major League Baseball.

internal failure costs Costs of quality that specifically relate to the expenses that occur when low-quality products and services fail before production and delivery to customers.

INTERNAL FAILURE COSTS Juran categorizes all the scrap and rework costs that are incurred to dispose of or fix defective products *before* they are shipped to the customer as **internal failure costs**. Costs of downtime or reduced yield due to production of defective parts or services are also included in this cost category. For example, if a Rawlings employee spends 10 minutes sewing a baseball, only to have the cover suddenly rip because of poor-quality leather, the company has lost money due to both the scrapped leather and the wages paid for 10 minutes of sewing a useless ball. In addition, all the materials and labor time spent previously winding, coating, and fitting the ball before the stitching work started are lost and become part of the internal failure costs. Clearly, Rawlings wants to be able to reduce scrap and sell more baseballs. Investments in prevention and appraisal work should reduce internal failure in the organization.

external failure costs Costs of quality that specifically relate to the costs that occur when low-quality products and services fail after production and delivery to customers.

EXTERNAL FAILURE COSTS Internal failure costs are very expensive. Nevertheless, Rawlings would *much* rather experience an internal failure than an external failure (defined as failure after the product has been delivered to the customers). **External failure costs** are generally the highest costs of a poor-quality process. Some examples are the costs of processing complaints, customer returns, warranty claims, product recalls, field service, and product liability. The most serious type of external failure cost likely results from unhappy customers; because bad news travels fast, defects found by a customer can cause the firm to lose both market share and future profits. In fact, a FORD MOTOR COMPANY survey indicates that a dissatisfied customer tells, on average, six other people. Sometimes the bad news can travel even faster. If a cover of a Rawlings baseball is pulled loose by a pitcher in the act of throwing a knuckleball during a game, the ball is immediately removed from the game. Obviously, more than six people instantly know about the product failure. Worse, though, is when product failure leads to news announcements and discussion in the media. In the last few years, you may recall some famous examples of publicized product failure involving software with bugs, unsafe tires on vehicles, and medicine or medical procedures with unexpected side effects.

fyi

Most experts agree that losses on gross sales due to poor quality range from 20% to 30%. Most executives underestimate these losses because they consider only the most obvious costs such as scrap and rework to be the costs of low quality.

Source: K. G. Rust, "Measuring the Costs of Quality," *Management Accounting*, August 1995, pp. 33–37.

Juran originally related all four of these COQ categories back to Deming's SPC model. He taught that if companies really understood the extent of failure costs, they would be willing to invest more in appraisal and prevention costs to keep more of their products performing within established control limits. Accountants should track these costs so that they can better manage the important relationship between costs of low-quality products and costs required to create high-quality products. This is an important relationship to manage. Obviously, high quality saves the company a lot of money as both internal and external product failures are reduced. On the other hand, high quality may require high investments in appraisal and prevention costs. Even though TQM requires that managers focus first on quality and then on profits, managers still need to understand how their commitment to TQM affects the company's bottom line (i.e., its profits). The dollar amounts involved in COQ are often quite large. Accountants add important competitive value to the organization when they are able to provide this important cost information. Hence, the ABC/ABM accounting system should identify appraisal and prevention activities, track the cost drivers of these activities, and establish performance measures that relate to reductions in failure costs and activities as a result of appraisal and prevention activities.

COQ Example

Let's return to our hypothetical example involving the production of baseballs at Rawlings Sporting Goods Company. Rawlings has invested expensive time and equipment to inspect all baseballs represented on the graph in Exhibit 7-9. As you can see, there are a few baseballs whose individual weights are outside the control limits. Balls failing the test are marked "blems" and sold very cheaply as practice balls. Other balls are not even usable as practice balls and must be scrapped. (Remember that weight is not the only quality criterion at Rawlings. The company is inspecting and scrapping balls for size, stitching, and color problems as well.) In addition to the balls failing the SPC tests, as displayed in Exhibit 7-9, Rawlings may also occasionally deal with complaints from merchants, athletes, and other organizations involving balls that fail in "the field" (pardon the pun). Because of the company's high commitment to customer satisfaction, it incurs significant costs in handling these calls, providing replacement balls, and investigating the cause of the product failure back at the factory. To counter these problems, Rawlings is considering making a large investment in its inspection equipment and in better training for its factory workers. Additionally, it is considering a new supplier for some of its raw materials, but significant costs are involved in establishing a new supplier relationship. Rawlings has a difficult planning decision to make that will likely require an intelligent evaluation of the trade-offs across all its quality costs. Rawlings will invest in an increasing level of appraisal and prevention costs in order to increase the percentage of baseballs that conform to all control limits. However, as the quality of baseballs increases, failure costs decrease dramatically. Balancing the decreasing costs of product failure with the increasing costs of high quality requires combining *all* costs in order to compute total COQ. The idea is to find the quality level where COQ is minimized. As an example, look at the fictitious cost numbers in the following table. As the percentage of baseballs that comply with all control limits (color, weight, diameter) increases, total appraisal and prevention costs increase. On the other hand, as the percentage of baseballs that comply with all control limits decreases, total failure costs increase. Rawlings needs to balance these costs by focusing on the appropriate level of quality in its production process. As you can see by inspecting the numbers presented, all quality costs are minimized in this example at 94% conformance where total COQ equals $2,237,155.

% of balls within all control limits	84%	86%	88%	90%	92%	**94%**	96%	98%	100%
Total appraisal & prevention costs	$ 100,037	$ 122,554	$ 156,347	$ 211,347	$ 311,850	**$ 530,663**	$1,164,270	$4,214,198	$44,172,984
Total failure costs	52,100,456	7,927,472	3,713,274	2,549,005	2,018,342	**1,706,492**	1,495,145	1,338,798	1,216,244
Total costs of quality (COQ)	$52,200,493	$8,050,026	$3,869,621	$2,760,352	$2,330,192	**$2,237,155**	$2,659,415	$5,552,996	$45,389,228

Locating COQ in the Accounting Records

It is important to see that tracking COQ within traditional accounting records can be challenging. Essentially, if the accountant desires to provide COQ data, most of these data are generally buried in the accounting records. As we discussed in previous chapters, many organizations traditionally categorize product costs as direct materials, direct labor, and overhead; and they categorize period costs as selling or general administrative. Quality costs used in the COQ model are typically spread throughout these traditional categories as shown below.

Prevention Costs		Appraisal Costs		Internal Failure Costs		External Failure Costs	
Cost Type	**Where Found**	**Cost Type**	**Where Found**	**Cost Type**	**Where Found**	**Cost Type**	**Where Found**
Process or product design	General administrative	Quality inspectors	Overhead	Scrap	Direct materials	Processing complaints & returns	Selling
Employee training	Overhead	Purchasing test equipment	Overhead (depreciation)	Rework	Direct labor	Product recalls	Selling or general administrative
Educating suppliers	General administrative	Adjusting test equipment	Overhead	Downtime	Direct labor and overhead or general administrative	Product liability	General administrative
Preventive maintenance	Overhead	Special supplies and materials	Overhead	Reduced yield	Direct materials and direct labor	Lost sales	Not found in the accounting system

Companies using a traditional cost accounting system may have some difficulty separating quality costs from other costs. However, companies using an ABC system should have already identified activities related to each of these quality processes. Often, it is much easier to implement a COQ accounting system in an organization that uses ABC. Note that lost sales (one type of failure costs) are *not* found in the accounting system. Remember that lost sales are an opportunity cost, and opportunity costs are typically not tracked within most accounting systems. Nevertheless, these are extremely important costs for the accountant to measure and provide to decision makers trying to plan, control, and evaluate the quality process in the organization. Lately, there has been some progress in the effort to track these important opportunity costs. Measuring the costs of lost sales is discussed in the expanded material section of this chapter.

to summarize

W. Edward Deming was extremely influential in helping companies understand that quality is an important competitive necessity in business. One of the main TQM (total quality management) tools he prescribed was SPC (statistical process control). Companies use SPC to identify an acceptable range of variation in their products and services. When the variation in the product or service exceeds the control limits established by the firm, then managers begin working to increase the quality of the production process.

A contemporary of Deming, Joseph M. Juran, developed a new categorization of costs called COQ (costs of quality) that can be used to manage decision making based on SPC. Keeping products or services in conformance with control limits requires investing in two types of quality costs: prevention costs (such as good product design and employee training) and appraisal costs (such as inspection and testing). When the production process starts creating variation outside the control limits, two types of quality costs result: internal failure costs (such as scrap and employee downtime) and external failure costs (such as handling complaints and product recalls). Perhaps the most important external failure costs are the opportunity costs of lost sales.

The COQ information that accountants provide managers should illustrate how decreasing failure costs may be offset by increasing prevention and appraisal costs. The level of quality conformance in a production process should be at the point where total quality costs are minimized. Identifying quality costs can be a challenge because these costs are generally intermingled across all the product and period costs within many organizations' accounting systems. Of all the quality costs identified in the COQ model (i.e., appraisal, prevention, internal failure, and external failure costs), the external failure costs are most difficult to measure because these costs include the opportunity costs of lost sales due to customer dissatisfaction.

3

Describe how just-in-time (JIT) management systems integrate with and extend ABC and TQM using time-based performance measures.

JUST-IN-TIME

Now that you are familiar with some of the newest concepts for managing costs and quality, it is "time" to talk about some modern methods of managing time. When discussing TQM in the previous section, we mentioned that managing quality was fundamentally a Japanese concept that was adopted by the United States in the 1980s. Remember that management accounting has evolved as a result of competition. When one company or industry (or, in the new global economy, country) develops a better management accounting technique or measure, it then competes more strongly in the marketplace. Eventually, the success of the innovator puts pressure on other organizations to adopt the same or a similar approach to their own management accounting systems. This was exactly the situation when U.S. companies began adjusting their management teams and management accounting systems to focus on quality and timeliness. In the 1980s, American manufacturers faced an assault from Japanese companies such as TOYOTA and NEC. These Japanese companies had mastered quality and inventory control, as well as speedier ways to get products to market. Western CEOs studied the competition, deconstructed what made it so good, adopted the better features of their rivals, and changed their management systems. Since then, this new management focus on quality and timeliness has had an impact on management accounting and has spread into U.S. merchandising and service industries, as well as into industries in other countries around the world.

business environment essay

The Japanese Focus on Inventory Henry Ford, the famous automotive production industrialist, lifted the FORD MOTOR COMPANY to great success during the early and mid-1900s by achieving tremendous cost efficiencies in producing cars. He believed in long production runs where low-skilled workers could build the same car part over and over again. As a result, high manufacturing costs per automobile plummeted, and he was able to offer cars to the public at extremely competitive prices. However, this production approach required high levels of raw materials, work-in-process, and finished goods inventories.

Meanwhile, across the ocean in Japan, Taiichi Ohno, an industrial scientist, and Eliji Toyoda, an executive vice president at TOYOTA MOTOR CORPORATION (and the son of the founder of Toyota), were experimenting with a different approach to large-scale production. While other Toyota executives thought that Toyoda's ideas were impractical, in 1949, in a machine shop in Koromo, Eliji Toyoda began experimenting with a new production control approach

JIT Inventory Systems

just-in-time (JIT) A management philosophy that emphasizes removing all waste of effort, time, and inventory costs from the organization. One obvious result of JIT is the reduction or removal of needless inventory in a production system.

The effort of management to compete on measures of time and to make improvements involving time is captured in the concept of **just-in-time (JIT)** management processes. To understand JIT, you need to first understand how JIT is used to manage inventory, including raw materials inventory, work-in-process inventory, and finished goods inventory. Let's talk for a moment about inventory. What is the purpose of inventory in a manufacturing plant? This may seem obvious. In the past, manufacturers stockpiled inventories in order to avoid shutdowns or slowdowns and to meet customer needs if suppliers were late or if production or delivery was slow. Occasionally (sometimes more than occasionally!), suppliers deliver raw materials that contain some defects, or the production process ruins some work-in-process, or a customer returns an unacceptable product. How do we deal with these unexpected surprises? Again the answer has been to "have a little extra on hand" so that bad parts or products can be replaced without having to interrupt the manufacturing process. Not surprisingly, production managers can get a little nervous when inventory levels get too low.

Because of concerns about risks due to scheduling and quality problems, companies establish policies to keep inventory levels at or above some minimal level. This minimum level of inventory is usually called a "safety stock" (as was discussed in the expanded material section of Chapter 6 of management accounting). However, several years ago some cagey accountants and business owners in Japan created a new competitive view of inventory management. They (like everyone else) realized that maintaining these inventories can be very expensive because of warehousing costs, interest costs incurred to finance inventory, and the opportunity cost of money tied up in stockpiled inventory. The real insight these Japanese business professionals had was that inventories are really only "buffers" that mask inefficient operations or product quality problems. Eliminate these timing and quality problems, and you no longer need the inventory buffers. By concentrating on improving product quality and timely deliveries, many Japanese companies became much more efficient and profitable at the same time that inventories were kept to a minimum or even eliminated. The emerging inventory systems that allow for the elimination of inventory stockpiles, inefficiency, and waste are referred to as just-in-time inventory systems. The competitive value of these new management systems eventually caught on and came to America.

JIT began as a management tool for manufacturing. So, when first learning about JIT, it's probably best to think of it in this context. In a manufacturing setting, JIT is a process by which only enough materials to satisfy immediate production are shipped to the job site. When JIT is functioning perfectly, companies take delivery from suppliers only as raw materials are needed for production and complete all inventory started during the day. In addition, inventory is completed only as it is ordered by customers and can be shipped immediately. As the name implies,

using the concepts of a just-in-time (JIT) inventory system. By 1953, the Koromo machine shop had a fully implemented *Kanban* system, which was based on the concept that supplies should be "pulled" through the production process as they are needed. (*Kanban* is essentially a signaling system that pulls parts forward through the production system.) Interestingly, Toyoda copied this idea from the sales methods of U.S. supermarkets. He was able to demonstrate that *Kanban* eliminated waste due to the overproduction of parts, reduced or eliminated the need for buffer inventories in the plant, and dramatically reduced production defects. In 1963, top management decided on the full application of *Kanban* as a means of transforming the production control system. Cost accountants were charged with developing and maintaining performance measures that tracked defects, excess inventory, and throughput time. Eliji Toyoda became chairman of Toyota in 1983. The rest, as they say, is history.

Source: M. Udagawa, "The Development of Production Management at the Toyota Motor Corporation," *Business History*, 1995, pp. 107–120.

materials are delivered "just in time" for production, and goods are manufactured "just in time" to meet customers' needs. As described earlier, JIT inventory systems started in Japan and have now been adopted successfully by a number of U.S. organizations. The results of JIT implementation are often dramatic. For example, one AT&T shop realized 54% improvement in quality yield, a 12-fold decrease in manufacturing time, an 88% reduction in scrap and rework, and a 95% increase in on-time deliveries.[7]

JIT and Value-Added Activities

Benefits such as those experienced by AT&T occur because companies that have adopted JIT have been able to avoid buildups of parts and materials and still ensure a smooth and orderly flow of goods to customers. JIT-based environments manage the flow of goods using a "pull" process. Essentially, this means that the final assembly stage for a product sends a signal (a *Kanban*; see the Business Environment Essay above) to the preceding workstation indicating what parts and materials will be needed during the next few hours. The preceding workstation then sends similar signals all the way back through the manufacturing cycle, ensuring an orderly flow of products. Thus, the demand at the final assembly stage "pulls" the inventory through the production process only as it is needed. Using this system, nothing is produced unless customers demand it. At all stages, inventories are eliminated or reduced to the lowest possible level. Obviously, then, progress toward successful implementation of JIT is inventory-related. Inventory reduction is not the primary purpose of JIT, but it generally is a consequence of JIT efforts to eliminate waste. The goal is to add value to the product or service and reduce or eliminate activities that do not. To be specific, **value-added activities** are essentially defined as those activities for which the customer is willing to pay. On the other hand, **non-value-added activities** are those for which the customer is not willing to pay. For example, clients in a law office are *not* interested in paying for the time spent running the payroll, organizing the file room, or computing billable hours. These are non-value-added activities. However, these clients should be willing to pay for court time and consultation time. These are clearly value-added activities that the law firm should emphasize. Under JIT, waste is considered to be anything other than the minimum amount of equipment, materials, parts, space, and workers' time that is essential to add desired value to a product. This results in careful management of time spent on value-added activities such as machining and assembly operations (for a manufacturer) and customer service and contact activities (for a service firm). More importantly, the JIT focus on eliminating waste emphasizes removing as much as possible the time spent on non-value-added activities such as setup work, materials handling, and inspection.

value-added activities Necessary activities in a production or service process that customers identify as valuable and for which they are willing to pay.

non-value-added activities Unnecessary activities in a production or service process that customers typically do not see or care about and for which they are unwilling to pay.

7 F. B. Green, F. Amenkhienan, and G. Johnson, "Performance Measures and JIT," *Management Accounting*, February 1991, pp. 50–54.

business environment essay

JIT and Speed, Speed, Speed The JIT philosophy originally focused on inventory. The objective of JIT was to reduce the amount of inventory on hand. Businesses learned that time is money, and if they could reduce the amount of time that inventory sat in storage, they could make more money. The JIT strategy was eventually incorporated into other areas of business as well. For **BANK OF BOSTON CORPORATION** (now part of **FLEETBOSTON FINANCIAL**), the objective was to reduce the time for processing mortgage applications. For **GILLETTE COMPANY**, it was accelerating the speed at which it introduces products.

Businesses are now differentiating themselves on speed. The faster they can provide a product or service, the more likely they are to obtain and retain business. As Kim Sheridan, chairman of **AVALON SOFTWARE INC.**, said, "It's not the big companies that eat the small; it's the fast that eat the slow." **BELL HELICOPTER** obtained a $113 million Army con-

JIT and Time

Like ABC and COQ, the JIT management model focuses a lot of attention on cost and quality. It is important to understand that JIT also encourages accountants to emphasize providing time-based performance measures to management. Critical success factors for many JIT manufacturing, service, and merchandising firms include improving timeliness of customer delivery and increasing the product or service provider's flexibility in handling customers' needs. Exhibit 7-10 provides a sample of appropriate performance measures that support these factors of success, which are particularly important in today's dynamic, customer-oriented environment.

How JIT Works with ABC and COQ in the New Business Environment

Initially, JIT inventory systems dramatically changed the cost structures of many manufacturing companies. JIT has also had significant impacts on management processes at many merchandising and service companies. Inventory balances have been reduced significantly (including work-in-process in service organizations), and product costs have decreased, primarily because of increased efficiency and reduced costs of handling inventory. JIT systems support both ABC and COQ. All three systems work to improve quality and productivity and to reduce costs. All are focused on increasing the accuracy and relevance of product costing and thus provide better information for management decision making. COQ helps identify activities that either add value or do not add value to providing a product or service. JIT also improves quality, as well as reducing the number of costs that must be allocated, by eliminating non-value-added activities. ABC more accurately assigns the remaining value-added costs that must be allocated. Together, these new management methods and their resulting changes in the way we do management accounting today have dramatically improved overall planning, controlling, and evaluating processes. JIT, ABC, and COQ are being combined in an increasing number of companies today to create a win-win situation for everyone. With these methods, product costs are more accurate, quality is increased, and timeliness of product and service delivery improves as companies experience better control over their business processes.

---

to summarize

Fundamentally, just-in-time (JIT) is a method of removing all waste from a production or service process. Originally a Japanese management system, JIT has

tract to build helicopters by emphasizing the speed at which it could build its products. It reduced its production time from 24 months to 12 months between 1991 and 1994.

By pushing speed, CHRYSLER (now part of DAIMLERCHRYSLER) was able to introduce its small car, the Neon, in just 33 months. Typical development time for a new car is four to six years. It was also able to reduce by almost half the number of people required to develop a new car model—from 1,400 people to 741. Did this push for speed reduce quality at Chrysler? Quality ratings provided by J. D. POWER & ASSOCIATES indicated that quality improved by as much as 15% for cars such as the Dodge Intrepid, the Chrysler Concorde, and the Eagle Vision.

No longer is the focus of JIT on inventory alone. Companies are just-in-timing just about everything—including time itself.

Source: *The Wall Street Journal*, December 23, 1994, p. A1.

exhibit 7-10 Time-Based Performance Measures in a JIT Firm

Customer Delivery Success Factor (On-time delivery to customers can be affected by suppliers, product design time, and the production process and distribution time.)

Measure	Computation Method
Customer on-time delivery	Number of on-time deliveries divided by total deliveries. Goal: higher
Supplier on-time delivery	Number of on-time deliveries divided by total deliveries. Goal: higher
Design cycle time	Amount of time from initial idea to readied plans. Goal: lower
Number of contract changes	Number of times a contract is changed. Goal: lower
Schedule attainment	Number of unchanged schedules divided by total schedules. Goal: lower
Lead time	Amount of time from customer's initial request to final product or service delivery. Goal: lower
Setup time*	Amount of time required to set up a production run. Goal: lower
Throughput time*	Amount of time from beginning of production or service process until process conclusion. Goal: lower

Provider Flexibility Success Factor (Manufacturing, service, and merchandising flexibility includes the ability to respond quickly to changes in customer demand and product design changes.)

Measure	Computation Method
Lead time for new product introduction	Amount of time from idea to readiness for sale. Goal: lower
Parts and product availability	Number of times a part or product is unavailable when requested. Goal: lower
Number of common parts	Number of parts in a product design common to other products. Goal: higher
Inventory level	Average level of inventory. Goal: lower
Capacity utilization	Percentage of process capacity used in current operations. Goal: higher
Downtime	Amount of time a manufacturing or service process was unavailable. Goal: lower
Setup time*	Amount of time required to set up a production run. Goal: lower
Throughput time*	Amount of time from beginning of production or service process until process conclusion. Goal: lower

*Note that some performance measures are important to both customer delivery and flexibility success factors.

Source: Adapted from J. A. Hendricks, "Performance Measures for a JIT Manufacturer," *Management Accounting*, January 1994, pp. 26–30.

made a significant impact on the way manufacturing, service, and merchandising companies in the United States and other nations are managed. Like ABC and COQ, JIT has a strong emphasis on costs and quality. However, JIT adds an important third dimension to the management process—management of timeliness and flexibility. In a manufacturing setting, demand at the final assembly stage "pulls" the inventory through the production process only as it is needed. Using this system, nothing is produced until customers demand it.

The main goal of JIT is to add value to the product or service and to reduce or eliminate activities that do not. By focusing on removing non-value-added activities and managing time spent on value-added activities, inventories and costs are reduced, while quality and timeliness are improved. Timeliness issues include emphasis on reducing customer delivery times and increasing flexibility within the production, service, or merchandising process.

JIT, ABC, and COQ all interact well in manufacturing, merchandising, and service operations to support managers in the new business environment. COQ helps identify value- and non-value-added activities. JIT improves quality and timeliness by eliminating non-value-added activities. ABC more accurately assigns costs to the remaining value-added activities.

---

expanded material

The focus of this chapter is to introduce you to some of the "cutting-edge" issues in management accounting today. The topics in this chapter are organized around the threefold strategic imperatives of costs (e.g., activity-based costing or ABC), quality (e.g., total quality management or TQM), and time (e.g., just-in-time or JIT). Remember that management accounting is not dictated by some regulatory agency. Management accounting practice is determined by competition and the strategic needs of each organization. Accounting tools such as ABC and COQ essentially focus on new ways of measuring and reporting costs. These costs are often recorded somehow in the traditional accounting system. In this expanded section, we will explore a *very* new way of thinking about and reporting the opportunity costs of lost sales. The interesting thing about measuring the costs of lost sales is that this is a measure of costs that is rarely recorded anywhere within the traditional accounting system.

4
Compute the opportunity cost of lost sales.

MEASURING COSTS OF LOST SALES

Want to set a manager's teeth on edge? If you're in manufacturing, show the manager a pile of scrapped work-in-process inventory due to low-quality materials or mistakes made in the production process. If you're in merchandising, show the manager a pile of merchandise that can't be sold due to low-quality materials, poor design, or damage during shipping. These piles represent wasted costs and opportunities and translate into lost profits. The accountant using COQ in a manufacturing or merchandising organization will report these costs as internal failure costs. However, identifying internal failure costs within service companies is more challenging. Where are the piles of scrapped inventory in a service company? Actually, there is often no distinction between internal failures and external failures for a service company such as an airline, a law firm, or a bank. Baggage is misplaced, a client's phone calls are not returned, or deposits are recorded in the wrong account. Internal processes have failed at these service companies, and external customers are *immediately* affected. Instead of scrapped inventory that can't be sold, service companies identify their own kind of scrap heap: customers who will not come back. Frankly, all three types of companies (service firms, merchants, and manufacturers) experience lost opportunities due to disgruntled customers. Perhaps the most significant impact of the TQM revolution across businesses is an increasing determination to make sure the customers' experience with the company is exemplary. (Hopefully, you've had some personal experience as a customer with this corporate resolution.)

As we discussed earlier, disappointed customers can lead to a number of external failure costs, including costs of processing complaints, customer returns, warranty claims, product recalls, field service, and product liability. Many of these costs don't apply to service companies. As a result, these companies naturally focus on the effect of losing the goodwill of their customers, which in turn leads to loss of future sales. However, the risk to manufacturers and merchants is that they will focus too much on external failure costs that are easy to measure and will fail to fully appreciate the opportunity cost of lost sales.

Robust Quality

If the accountant is somehow able to identify and measure the cost of lost sales, then managers can use this information in better planning, controlling, and evaluating the process of delivering the products that customers want. What kinds of products do customers want? Let's return to our earlier discussion about baseball manufacturing. Think about a baseball player pitching for the Chicago Cubs. Does he care if a RAWLINGS baseball appropriately weighs between 5 and 5.25 ounces and has a circumference between 9 and 9.25 inches? Actually, no. What he cares about is that the baseball, when pitched, will perform as he intends—that it will have the desired curve, fade, slide, drop, or heat. Referring back to the SPC chart in Exhibit 7-9, a ball that weighs between 5 and 5.25 ounces and has a circumference between 9 and 9.25 inches has no defects. However, one-tenth of an ounce is pretty important to a professional baseball pitcher trying to throw a split-fingered fastball. Pitching performance will improve and be more consistent as Rawlings works to reduce variation in the weight and size of baseballs—even if the variation is within the limits imposed by Major League Baseball.

robust quality The capability of a product to perform according to customer expectations regardless of surroundings and circumstances.

The effort to reduce all variation is related to the concept of robust quality. **Robust quality** essentially means that the product will perform for the customer under all kinds of circumstances. In other words, you and I really don't care if the stereo, shirt, or sports car we buy was manufactured within some set of control limits or specifications. For us, the proof of a product's quality is in its performance when it is rapped, overloaded, stretched, or soaked. We all prefer stereos that continue to power up (even after a lightning storm has sent electrical surges throughout our neighborhood); we all prefer clothes that don't tear (even when a small child yanks on the sleeve to get our attention); we all prefer cars designed to steer safely and predictably (even on roads that are wet or full of potholes). We say these products are robust. They gain steadfast customer loyalty.

In the mid-1980s, FORD MOTOR COMPANY had a valuable experience with the importance of robust quality.[8] At that time, Ford owned 25% of MAZDA and asked the Japanese company to help build some of the transmissions for a car Ford was selling in the United States. Both Ford and Mazda built their transmissions using the same specifications. Yet, after the cars with Ford-built transmissions had been on the road for a while, they began developing much

8 G. Taguchi and D. Clausing, "Robust Quality," *Harvard Business Review*, January–February 1990, pp. 65–75.

higher warranty costs and more customer complaints about noise than the cars with Mazda-built transmissions. As a result, Ford engineers disassembled and inspected transmissions made by both companies. They were astounded at the comparison. The Ford transmissions were all built within the range of engineering specifications, but the Mazda transmissions displayed absolutely no variability from the target measures. The Ford transmissions that were breaking down were those shipped with components built quite close to the manufacturing control limits. Because the Mazda plant was working hard to reduce all variance—even variance within the acceptable control limits—its transmissions had lower production, scrap, rework, and warranty costs.

Taguchi's Quality Loss Function

Taguchi quality loss function A method developed by Genichi Taguchi for estimating the actual size of all external failure costs, particularly the opportunity costs of lost customer sales that result from dissatisfied customers.

Genichi Taguchi is a very famous Japanese quality expert who made an important adaptation to SPC charts that allows management accountants to actually measure the external failure costs of lost customers. U.S. companies have used Taguchi's famous quality loss function since the early 1980s. Essentially, the **Taguchi quality loss function** is a method of relating the amount of variation in a product to external failure costs due to dissatisfied customers. Managers and accountants who use the Taguchi quality loss function recognize that shipping a product that barely satisfies the corporate standard gains you virtually nothing over shipping a product that fails. Translation: There is a lot more difference between baseballs that weigh 5.10 ounces versus 5.24 ounces (both balls are within Major League Baseball tolerance specifications) than there is between baseballs weighing 5.24 ounces versus 5.26 ounces (only one ball is within tolerance specifications). Nevertheless, using the upper and lower limit controls displayed in Exhibit 7-9 would have Rawlings feeling just as confident shipping a baseball to the National League weighing 5.24 ounces as shipping a baseball weighing 5.10 ounces. Can you see why this might create a performance problem for Rawlings' customers? The Taguchi motto is: "Don't just try to stay within specifications, get on target!" Every time Rawlings ships a baseball that is more or less than the perfect size and weight, robust quality is reduced, and the likelihood increases that the ball will not perform in the field as expected. The result of being off target is dissatisfied customers, and dissatisfied customers talk to other customers, which can significantly reduce future sales.

The quality loss, as defined by Taguchi, is all the costs of external failure (including costs of lost customer sales). A simple formulation of Taguchi's loss function looks a bit like Einstein's

business environment essay

Real Customer Satisfaction Arrives at Ford Motor Company In 1981, FORD MOTOR COMPANY decided it was time to investigate what was behind the success of Japanese manufacturers. Japanese companies were quickly becoming the leaders in the car industry as well as other manufacturing industries. Edward Deming and Genichi Taguchi were responsible for making the Japanese companies strong competitors in the world economy. Using total quality management (TQM) and the Taguchi quality loss function enabled a company to achieve high levels of quality without the high costs. For example, Taguchi methods enabled some Japanese manufacturers to realize a large increase in quality gains—up to 80%!

Ford Motor Company was struggling to compete against the Japanese, so the company decided it was better "to join the cause than to fight the cause." In 1981, Taguchi first presented his ideas to Ford on how quality should be based on customer needs. After listening to Taguchi's presentation, Ford was motivated to become much more aggressive in implementing quality strategies and information.

Some time later, Ford began its Ford 2000 initiative to drastically reduce the number of defects per manufactured car made between 1995 and 2000. To make this goal possible, managers were provided with up-to-date, accurate information via the company's Intranet. The company's efforts did not go unnoticed. Customer satisfaction, the best measurement of reduction in external failure costs, increased. In

fyi

A recent study of the performance of Rawlings baseballs notes that even balls within Major League Baseball specifications (i.e., weigh between 5.00 and 5.25 ounces) can have approximately a 10% performance difference. In other words, the study showed that balls at the lightest and liveliest end of the tolerance specifications would typically travel 49.1 feet farther on a 400-foot hit than the heavier balls. That's within Major League Baseball's own specifications and could mean the difference between a lazy fly ball and a home run.

Source: J. Kaat, "Baseball's New Baseball," *Popular Mechanics*, October 13, 2000.

theory of relativity formula (remember $E = MC^2$?). Using Taguchi's formula, the cost of external failures is computed as follows:

$$L = CD^2$$

L = total quality loss due to external failures.
C = costs required to fix the problem and get the product back on target.
D = distance from the target measured in standard units.

If your geometry skills are reasonably fresh, you might note that this formula is a quadratic function (because of the D^2 term). If it has been a while since your last geometry class, you just need to note that quality loss increases very quickly as the distance between the product and the target increases. The implication here is that if management decides not to incur the voluntary expenses of reducing variation, it involuntarily incurs several times that amount in the form of warranty costs, lost sales due to customer ill will, and so forth. One important idea behind Taguchi's quality loss function is that it disagrees with the traditional notion of quality control limits. Look back at the SPC chart in Exhibit 7-9. This chart says that there is no loss as long as baseballs weigh between 5.0 and 5.25 ounces. Since the SPC chart is reporting that very few balls being shipped to the major leagues are outside the weight specifications, the data suggest that probably little loss is being incurred. But how much is Rawlings really losing in external failure costs, and how much would be saved if Rawlings reduced weight variation in baseballs? This is difficult to know precisely. Remember that Rawlings is trying to manufacture baseballs that weigh exactly 5.10 ounces. Let's assume that it would cost Rawlings $10,000 in prevention and appraisal costs to reduce average variation by each 0.01 ounce. Therefore, if baseballs varied on average only 0.01 ounce from the target of 5.10 ounces (i.e., from 5.09 to 5.11), then it would require only $10,000 to correct the problem. According to the Taguchi quality loss function, Rawlings would then save approximately $10,000 in external failure costs by making this reduction. It looks like an even trade-off between costs and cost savings, doesn't it? Remember, though, that Rawlings would also save some internal failure costs as well (waste, scrap, downtime, etc.). Now look at the chart of numbers on the following page. As you can

1997, the J. D. Power Initial Quality Study recognized the drastic leap in consumer quality ratings of Ford cars. In addition to the improved rankings, Ford's Atlanta plant received the Power's Platinum Award, which is given to the car manufacturing plant with the fewest facility problems.

The rankings and award seemed to confirm the company's efforts toward quality improvements and have acted as a catalyst to further inspire Ford to become a worldwide quality leader. However, the emphasis on quality improvements has not come without serious trade-offs. As part of the Ford 2000 initiative, a majority of management efforts concentrated on the North American market. The initial success of the program has aroused enthusiasm for the effort, pushing it forward. However, the emphasis on the North American market has come at an enormous cost in the foreign markets where Ford is engaged. Ford's net income in its foreign divisions dropped from a profit of $300 million in 1997 to a loss of $300 million in 1999. It seems that Ford's efforts to address the critical factor of quality have enabled it to compete with other car makers in North America, but have been less successful elsewhere. However, no one ever said that managing large companies such as Ford is easy. Ford will continue to work to implement quality performance measures while balancing its efforts across a global market.

Sources: M. Larson, "Ford Puts Quality Data in Human Hands," *Quality Magazine*, December 1997, http://www.qualitymag.com; D. Winter, "Ford's Nasser Still Upbeat Despite Firestone Fallout," *Ward's Auto World*, December 2000.

see, it will cost Rawlings more to get the baseball weight on target as the distance between the target weight and the actual weights increases. However, the opportunity loss (i.e., external failure costs) is much larger as the variation (i.e., the distance from target) increases. Hence, the Taguchi quality loss function really emphasizes the importance of reducing variation in order to increase robust quality within products and services.

Cost per 0.01 ounce unit to correct	$10,000	$10,000	$10,000	$10,000	$10,000	$10,000
Average distance from target	× 1 unit	× 2 units	× 3 units	× 4 units	× 5 units	× 6 units
Total cost to correct	$10,000	$20,000	$30,000	$40,000	$50,000	$60,000
Cost per 0.01 ounce unit to correct (C)	$10,000	$10,000	$10,000	$10,000	$10,000	$10,000
Distance squared (D^2)	× 1 unit	× 4 units	× 9 units	× 16 units	× 25 units	× 36 units
Total quality loss (L)	$10,000	$40,000	$90,000	$160,000	$250,000	$360,000

fyi

In 1989, Genichi Taguchi received the Ministry of International Trade and Industry (MITI) Purple Ribbon Award from the emperor of Japan for his contribution to Japanese industrial standards.

Obviously, Taguchi's quality loss measures are not very precise and objective. He is making general *approximations* about how quality problems affect all companies. Some companies may experience more or less loss due to quality problems than Taguchi suggests. Nevertheless, using the quality loss function, the management accounting system can provide a valuable signal to companies about the importance of continuously improving the quality of their goods and services. Measuring deviations from specifications has always been the job of engineers. However, by taking those deviations and translating them into costs, the accountant is able to draw a lot of attention to the problem.

Is Quality Free?

Before we leave this section on quality, you need to know that there is some disagreement in the profession on how to measure quality costs. In fact, you may have even noticed a discrepancy in the section you just read. Remember that earlier we discussed the importance of identifying the proper level of quality in the organization by offsetting prevention and appraisal costs against internal and external failure costs in order to minimize total costs of quality (COQ). It appears, therefore, that COQ trade-offs will typically justify a level of quality that is less than 100% conformance to all control limits. On the other hand, our discussion of measuring the costs of lost sales using the Taguchi quality loss function seems to indicate that "quality is free!" In other words, when one understands the *full extent* of external failure costs, the minimal quality cost trade-off point is very close to or exceeds 100% conformance. Hence, using the Taguchi quality loss function, companies should spend whatever it takes to have absolute quality and customer satisfaction. Remember that this is the essence of TQM—that quality is emphasized above all else, including costs. Not everyone feels this strongly about TQM. Some managers and accountants disagree with a "field of dreams" approach to managing quality costs (i.e., "if you build *perfect* quality, profits will come"). You should pay attention to this current debate, as there is good logic on both sides. The real test of this concept is in the competitive marketplace. In any event, management accounting systems need to measure COQ, including the cost of lost sales, in order to add competitive value to the organization's TQM efforts.

to summarize

The Taguchi quality loss function attempts to measure external failure costs using a formula where L (quality loss) = C (cost to correct) × D^2 (distance from target). The quality loss function is not a precise measure of external failure costs, but it provides an approximate signal of the significant opportunity costs organizations experience when less-than-perfect goods and services are provided to customers. Using the quality loss function, accountants can provide important insight to help their companies better compete in the marketplace. Some TQM advocates suggest that organizations should strive for 100% quality conformance. These individuals defend this position by suggesting that most organizations underestimate failure costs as a product or service process moves away from 100% quality conformance. Nevertheless, there is currently an active debate on the issue of whether perfect quality is too costly to achieve.

---

review of learning objectives

1 Explain the fundamentals of activity-based costing (ABC) and activity-based management (ABM). Unit-based costing (UBC) systems generally allocate all manufacturing overhead costs based on some measure related to the number of products being produced or the amount of service being provided in the organization (e.g., direct labor hours). In settings with little diversity in the types of products or services offered to customers, UBC may be an appropriate tool. On the other hand, activity-based costing (ABC) recognizes that activities are the causes of costs. Activities can be categorized across four levels: unit-level activities, batch-level activities, product line activities, and facility support activities. Generally, variable overhead such as machine maintenance or energy costs to run production equipment is a function of the number of units produced. Setup costs, materials purchase orders, and route planning are examples of costs traditionally considered fixed that actually are variable in relation to the number of batch runs within the organization. Overhead costs that are a function of product line activities are generally related to engineering, supervision, and warehousing. Once activity cost pools have been created, costs of unit-level, batch-level, and product line activities can be assigned to products. If costs of batch-level and product line activities are allocated using UBC, then some products may be inappropriately assigned costs that actually belong to another product. This particular cost distortion is referred to as product cost cross-subsidization.

Costs of facility support activities (e.g., property taxes, plant security, landscaping, accounting, and executive administration) cannot be sensibly connected to any particular product line. These costs (otherwise known as common costs) should *not* be allocated to individual product lines. Otherwise, product costs are distorted, which can lead to a series of management decisions called a death spiral. Managers inadvertently involved in a death spiral will make a decision to drop a product or service line based on UBC data that erroneously suggest that these products or services are unprofitable.

The point of ABC is to appropriately *assign* costs to products. However, ABC does not really provide useful information for managing activities. To *manage* costs of activities, a set of activity cost drivers that provides the greatest influence on the activity cost pool is identified. To manage activity performance, a set of quality- and time-based measures is also created and related to each critical activity in the organization. The process of managing activities using cost drivers and performance measures is called activity-based management (ABM). ABC and ABM combine to form the following model of activities:

Activity Cost Drivers
↓
Costs → Activities → Products
↑
Performance Measures

2 Describe total quality management (TQM) and costs of quality (COQ). Total quality management (TQM) is a philosophy in which (1) product and process quality is emphasized over profits and (2) quality must be measured in order to be realized. Using SPC (statistical process control), W. Edward Deming became one of the pioneers of TQM in both Japan and America. SPC establishes control limits. When the variation in the product or service exceeds the control limits established by the firm, then managers begin work to increase the quality of the production process. Joseph M. Juran expanded the process of SPC in order to manage four specific types of costs of quality (COQ). Prevention and appraisal costs are viewed as investments in the process of keeping products and services within established control limits. When the production process starts creating variation outside the control limits, internal failure costs (such as scrap and employee downtime) and external failure costs (such as handling complaints and product recalls) occur. If increasing prevention and appraisal costs offset decreasing failure costs, then management accountants should help companies understand how to minimize total quality costs. Identifying quality costs can be a challenge, however, because these costs are generally intermingled across both product and period costs within most organizations' accounting systems. Costs of lost sales due to customer dissatisfaction are important opportunity costs, yet they are particularly difficult to measure.

3 Describe how just-in-time (JIT) management systems integrate with and extend ABC and TQM using time-based performance measures. Just-in-time (JIT) has become an important tool for managing manufacturing, service, and merchandising companies across the world. In a manufacturing setting, demand at the final assembly stage "pulls" the inventory through the production process only as it is needed. Using this system, nothing is produced until customers demand it. Like ABC and COQ, JIT puts a strong emphasis on costs and quality. However, JIT also focuses on management of timeliness and flexibility. The main goal of JIT is to add value to the product or service and reduce or eliminate activities that do not. By focusing on removing non-value-added activities and reducing time spent on value-added activities, inventories and other costs are reduced, while quality and timeliness are improved. It is important to point out that JIT, ABC, and COQ all interact well to support managers in the new business environment. COQ helps identify value and non-value-added activities. JIT improves quality and timeliness by eliminating non-value-added activities. ABC more accurately assigns costs to the remaining value-added activities.

expanded material

4 **Compute the opportunity cost of lost sales.** The Taguchi quality loss function provides a means of approximately measuring the impact of *all* external failure costs on the company's costs—including the opportunity costs of lost sales due to customer dissatisfaction. The Taguchi quality loss function measures these costs using a formula where L (quality loss) = C (cost to correct) × D^2 (distance from target). Using this formula, accountants can provide an important signal of the significant opportunity costs organizations experience when less-than-perfect goods and services are provided to customers. Currently, in light of the likely size of cost of external failure, there is some debate on whether prevention and appraisal costs can ever increase enough to justify having less-than-perfect conformance to control limits (i.e., perfect quality).

key terms and concepts

activity-based costing (ABC) 347
activity-based management (ABM) 365
appraisal costs 370
batch-level activities 356
capability costs 357
common costs 351
conversion costs 347
cost driver 353
costs of quality (COQ) 369
cross-subsidization 351
death spiral 361
external failure costs 371
facility support activities 357
Hierarchical Product Cost Model 351
internal failure costs 370
just-in-time (JIT) 374
non-value-added activities 375
prevention costs 370
prime costs 347
product line activities 356
statistical process control (SPC) 367
total quality management (TQM) 367
unit-based costing (UBC) 352
unit-level activities 354
value-added activities 375

expanded material

robust quality 379
Taguchi quality loss function 380

review problem

ABC versus Conventional Product Costing

Willett Company makes two types of products: Product A and Product B. The company's management accountants accumulated the following production cost information for 2003:

	Product A	Product B	Total
Production volume (units)	1,000	500	
Number of engineering changes per product line	4	8	
Total cost of engineering changes			$12,000
Direct labor hours per unit	3	2	
Direct materials cost per unit	$5	$7	
Direct labor cost per hour	$6	$12	

Required: Assume Product A sells for $42 each and Product B sells for $50 each. Assume also that engineering changes are the only manufacturing overhead cost Willett Company incurs. If all products are sold, what is the gross margin of each product assuming the following:

1. Engineering change costs are allocated on the basis of direct labor hours.
2. Engineering change costs are allocated on the basis of the number of engineering changes made.

Solution **1. Allocation on the Basis of Direct Labor Hours**

	Product A (1,000 units)	Product B (500 units)
Sales	$42,000 (1,000 × $42)	$25,000 (500 × $50)
Cost of goods sold:		
Direct materials	$ 5,000 (1,000 × $5)	$ 3,500 (500 × $7)
Direct labor	18,000 (1,000 × 3 hr × $6)	12,000 (500 × 2 hr × $12)
Manufacturing overhead	9,000 (1,000 × 3 hr × $3*)	3,000 (500 × 2 hr × $3*)
Total cost of goods sold	$32,000	$18,500
Gross margin	$10,000	$ 6,500

*Overhead allocation per direct labor hour:

$$\frac{\$12{,}000 \text{ total costs}}{4{,}000 \text{ total direct labor hours}} = \$3 \text{ per direct labor hour}$$

Product A (1,000 × 3 hr) = 3,000
Product B (500 × 2 hr) = 1,000
Total 4,000 direct labor hours

2. Allocation on the Basis of Engineering Changes

Sales	$42,000	$25,000
Cost of goods sold:		
Direct materials	$ 5,000	$ 3,500
Direct labor	18,000	12,000
Manufacturing overhead	4,000*	8,000*
Total cost of goods sold	$27,000	$23,500
Gross margin	$15,000	$ 1,500

*Overhead allocation per engineering change:

$$\text{Cost per change: } \frac{\$12{,}000}{12} = \$1{,}000 \text{ per change}$$

Overhead allocations per product:
Product A: 4 changes × $1,000 per change = $ 4,000
Product B: 8 changes × $1,000 per change = 8,000
Total $12,000

discussion questions

1. What is the lowest price that a company should charge its customers?
2. What is the difference between a product cost and a period cost?
3. Traditionally, what basis has been used to allocate manufacturing overhead costs to products?
4. What type of incorrect decision can be made if a cost accounting system allows cross-subsidization of product costs?
5. "Given enough time, every cost is fixed." Do you agree or disagree? Explain.

6. In what context does a unit-based costing (UBC) system cause problems?
7. Under a Hierarchical Product Cost Model, what are the four classifications of production costs?
8. Give three examples of batch-level activities.
9. In general, which type of fast-food outlet would have higher overhead costs: an outlet selling hamburgers, pizza, and chicken or an outlet selling only hamburgers? Explain.
10. Give three examples of facility support costs.
11. How can the allocation of common costs potentially cause a death spiral?
12. ABC (activity-based costing) uses activity allocation rates in product costing. How are activity cost drivers used in ABM (activity-based management)?
13. In what way do Edward Deming's ideas of total quality management (TQM) change Andrew Carnegie's slogan, "Watch the costs and the profits will take care of themselves"?
14. Briefly describe the four types of costs in costs of quality (COQ).
15. Why are external failure costs generally the highest of the costs of quality (COQ)?
16. How did the concept of just-in-time (JIT) change the view of most companies that maintaining a minimum level of inventory was desirable? Use the measures of cost, quality, and time as you prepare your answer.
17. "The purpose of just-in-time (JIT) is to reduce inventory." Do you agree or disagree? Explain.

expanded material

18. Describe the concept of robust quality.
19. According to the Taguchi quality loss function, what happens to the total loss due to external failure as a product's quality gets further from target specifications?

discussion cases

CASE 7-1

PARAMOUNT SKIS

Paramount Skis produces three models of skis: Novice, Straightaway, and Mogulist. Sales and costing information for the three models are as follows:

	Novice	Straightaway	Mogulist
Selling price per unit	$130	$250	$300
Units produced	13,000	8,000	6,000
Direct materials cost	$780,000	$400,000	$240,000
Direct labor cost	$130,000	$52,000	$42,000

In the past, manufacturing overhead has been allocated based on number of units produced. Manufacturing overhead for the period is $1,620,000, and the predetermined overhead rate is $60 per unit produced.

Based on this information, management has determined that the Novice is barely breaking even. Because the market for skis is quite competitive, the price for each model is set by the market—not by management. Thus, increasing the price charged for products is not an option. As a result, management is considering discontinuing the Novice. Before making a final decision, management has come to you for advice. You collect the following information regarding manufacturing overhead:

Manufacturing Overhead	Manufacturing Overhead Costs	Allocation Bases
Engineering	$ 250,000	Engineering changes
Quality control	750,000	Number of units produced
Manufacturing support	620,000	Number of setups
Total overhead	$1,620,000	

Allocation Bases	Novice	Straightaway	Mogulist
Engineering changes	3	7	5
Number of units produced	13,000	8,000	6,000
Number of setups	29	78	63

Determine the gross profit for each model under the current manufacturing overhead allocation scheme. Determine the manufacturing overhead cost for each model using the information relating to activities. Determine the gross profit for each model using the ABC allocated manufacturing overhead. What recommendation would you make to management regarding its decision to discontinue the Novice?

CASE 7-2

COSTS OF QUALITY (SLEEPY INN MOTELS)

You are the leader of a group of investors that is planning to open a nationwide chain of low-cost motels that you will call "Sleepy Inn Motels." You are preparing for a strategy meeting that will be held tomorrow. The investor group is considering two strategies for how the motel chain will be operated. One strategy, which you have titled "Quality," proposes to market the motel chain as the quality leader among low-cost motels. The motels will be located in good neighborhoods, will offer swimming pools and other amenities, and will have well-appointed rooms. The motels will also have good maid service, a trained manager on site 24 hours per day to handle guest complaints, and a national troubleshooting team that will promptly fly to any location to investigate consistent patterns in customer complaints received via a toll-free complaint hotline.

You have titled the other strategy "Quick and Dirty." The motels will be located wherever cheap real estate can be found, will be staffed with the lowest-cost labor possible, and will offer no amenities, no reservations, and low-budget room furnishings. There will be no mechanism for receiving customer complaints, and the night manager will not be authorized to do anything more than distribute room keys and collect cash.

A significant portion of the investor group advocates the "Quick and Dirty" strategy, arguing that it offers the lowest operating costs and, therefore, the highest profit. You are worried that these investors may not have thought carefully about all the costs associated with this strategy. Using the costs of quality (COQ) categories, outline some of the major costs that will differ between these two motel strategies.

exercises

EXERCISE 7-1

PRODUCT COSTING REVIEW

Mad Dog Enterprises manufactures computer game control devices such as joysticks and steering wheels. Following is a list of the costs incurred by Mad Dog in 2003:

Wages paid to assembly workers	$100,000
Cost of plastic used in making devices	25,000
Insurance on factory building	12,000
Salary of factory supervisor	57,000
Interest on money borrowed to finance operations	34,000
Wages paid to factory maintenance workers	61,000
Cost of computer/controller boards installed in devices	38,000
Advertising costs	127,000
Cost of electricity used in factory	46,000

Compute the total cost for each of the following categories:

1. Direct materials
2. Direct labor
3. Manufacturing overhead
4. Period costs

EXERCISE 7-2

IMPORTANCE OF MANUFACTURING OVERHEAD ALLOCATION

The percentages of product costs comprised by direct materials, direct labor, and manufacturing overhead for three companies are as follows:

	Company A	Company B	Company C
Direct materials	45%	31%	13%
Direct labor	22	62	8
Manufacturing overhead	33	7	79
	100%	100%	100%

Based on this information, which of these three companies would probably improve its product-costing accuracy most by converting to activity-based costing (ABC)? Explain your answer.

EXERCISE 7-3

PRODUCT COST HIERARCHY

For the following list of costs, indicate by the appropriate letter which category of activities each cost applies to: unit level (U), batch level (B), product line (P), or facility support (F):

a. Machine fine-tuning adjustment cost (required after the production of each unit)
b. Salary of vice president of finance
c. Machine inspection cost (required after the completion of each day's production)
d. Cost of the external audit firm
e. Direct labor
f. Product testing cost (performed at the start of each day's production)
g. Direct materials
h. Factory security cost
i. Machine straight-line depreciation cost (Generally, machines are dedicated to producing a particular type of product.)
j. Warehousing cost (Each type of product has its own warehouse.)
k. Employee training cost (Training is generally specific to different types of products.)

EXERCISE 7-4

IDENTIFYING CROSS-SUBSIDIZATION

Cottrell Company manufactures three products. Gross margin computations for these three products for 2003 are given below.

	Product A	Product B	Product C
Sales	$ 300,000	$500,000	$600,000
Direct materials	(50,000)	(250,000)	(200,000)
Direct labor	(150,000)	(50,000)	(100,000)
Manufacturing overhead*	(225,000)	(75,000)	(150,000)
Gross margin	$(125,000)	$125,000	$150,000

*Manufacturing overhead is allocated to production based on the amount of direct labor cost.

Cottrell has reexamined the factors that cause its manufacturing overhead costs and has discovered that the annual amount of manufacturing overhead is more closely related to the number of product batches produced during the year than it is to direct labor costs. The number of batches of the three products for 2003 was as follows: Product A, 10 batches; Product B, 60 batches; Product C, 30 batches.

1. Prepare gross margin calculations for Cottrell's three products assuming that manufacturing overhead is allocated based on the number of batches.
2. Under the direct labor cost method of manufacturing overhead allocation, one of Cottrell's products received a cross-subsidization from the others. Which product received the subsidization, and what was the amount of the subsidization?

EXERCISE 7-5

Spread-Sheet Software

ALLOCATING BATCH-LEVEL AND PRODUCT LINE MANUFACTURING OVERHEAD COSTS

Grantsville Company has two divisions. Gross margin computations for these two divisions for 2003 are given below.

	Industrial Products	Consumer Products
Sales	$600,000	$900,000
Direct materials	(100,000)	(150,000)
Direct labor	(300,000)	(300,000)
Manufacturing overhead*	(250,000)	(250,000)
Gross margin	$ (50,000)	$200,000

*Manufacturing overhead is allocated to production based on the amount of direct labor cost.

Grantsville has determined that its total manufacturing overhead cost of $500,000 is a mixture of batch-level costs and product line costs. Grantsville has assembled the following information concerning the manufacturing overhead costs, the annual number of production batches in each division, and the number of product lines in each division:

	Total Mfg. Overhead Costs	Industrial Products	Consumer Products
Batch-level manufacturing overhead	$300,000	10 batches	40 batches
Product line manufacturing overhead	200,000	5 lines	15 lines
	$500,000		

1. Prepare gross margin calculations for Grantsville's two divisions assuming that manufacturing overhead is allocated based on the number of batches and number of product lines.
2. Under the direct labor cost method of manufacturing overhead allocation, which division received a cross-subsidization, and what was the amount of the cross-subsidization?

EXERCISE 7-6

COMMON COSTS AND THE DEATH SPIRAL

Blaine Avenue Company manufactures three products. Gross margin computations for these three products for 2003 are given below.

	Product X	Product Y	Product Z
Sales	$800,000	$700,000	$ 600,000
Direct materials	(50,000)	(150,000)	(200,000)
Direct labor	(50,000)	(200,000)	(250,000)
Manufacturing overhead*	(80,000)	(320,000)	(400,000)
Gross margin	$620,000	$ 30,000	$(250,000)

*Manufacturing overhead is allocated to production based on the amount of direct labor cost.

Blaine Avenue has reexamined the activities that relate to its manufacturing overhead costs and has discovered that $500,000 of the annual amount of manufacturing overhead is directly related to the number of product batches produced during the year. The number of batches of the three products for 2003 was as follows: Product X, 100 batches; Product Y, 100 batches; Product Z, 50 batches. The remaining $300,000 in overhead is for facility support (property taxes, security costs, general administration, etc.) and does not vary at all with the level of activity.

1. Prepare gross margin calculations for Blaine Avenue's three products assuming that manufacturing overhead is allocated based on the number of batches. Also, show a "total" column. Facility support costs are not to be allocated to any of the products, but are to be subtracted in the "total" column in the computation of total company operating profit.
2. Using the gross margin numbers prepared under the direct labor cost method of manufacturing overhead allocation, Blaine Avenue's board of directors has tentatively decided to discontinue the Z product line. Assume that this was done at the beginning of 2003. What would have happened to total company operating profit for the year? Explain.

EXERCISE 7-7

COSTS OF QUALITY

Some of the costs in the list below are costs of quality. For each cost, indicate by the appropriate letter what type of cost it is: prevention cost (P), appraisal cost (A), internal failure cost (I), external failure cost (E), or not a cost of quality (N/A).

a. Cost of raw materials used in discarded, defective products
b. Salary of the president of the company
c. Cost to purchase product testing equipment
d. Lawsuit costs stemming from the sale of defective products
e. Cost to repair defective products before shipment
f. Employee quality training costs
g. Employee downtime caused by production halts to repair defective products
h. Cost of sampling raw materials to ensure quality
i. Customer warranty costs
j. Property taxes
k. Cost of lost reputation (i.e., lost sales)
l. Cost to help suppliers improve their product shipping procedures
m. Interest cost on short-term loans
n. Production process design costs

EXERCISE 7-8

OPTIMAL LEVEL OF COSTS OF QUALITY

Leslie Angel is planning to open her own textbook publishing company. Leslie is trying to decide whether to provide low-quality textbooks, average-quality textbooks, or high-quality textbooks. Leslie has analyzed the costs of quality related to publishing textbooks and has developed the following analysis of the costs of quality:

- *Prevention costs:* The best way to ensure the quality of a textbook is to hire good authors and to increase the amount of time the authors spend on researching and writing the text material. Of course, high-quality authors cost more.
- *Appraisal costs:* To improve the quality of the text material, Leslie can hire independent verifiers to determine whether the text is readable and correct and whether the homework problems are solvable.
- *Internal failure costs:* Sometimes an error in the text is found just before the book is to be printed. In such a case, Leslie must require the authors to spend extra time fixing the text.
- *External failure costs:* If a textbook containing lots of errors is sold, the bad reputation created will hurt potential future sales. To counteract this effect, Leslie must spend more on advertising.

Leslie has gathered the following numerical information about the costs of quality in relation to publishing textbooks:

	Low Quality	Average Quality	High Quality
Prevention costs:			
Author hours spent on text	100 hours	500 hours	1,000 hours
Author salary rate	$50/hour	$60/hour	$70/hour
Appraisal costs:			
Verifier hours spent on text	50 hours	200 hours	800 hours
Verifier salary rate	$20/hour	$20/hour	$20/hour
Internal failure costs:			
Author hours spent fixing text	400 hours	200 hours	20 hours
Author salary rate	$50/hour	$60/hour	$70/hour
External failure costs:			
Cost of advertising	$60,000	$20,000	$5,000

Which type of textbooks—low-, average-, or high-quality—should Leslie publish in order to minimize her total costs of quality? Show your calculations.

EXERCISE 7-9

JIT INVENTORY

The president of Penman Corporation, John Burton, has asked you, the company's controller, to advise him on whether Penman should develop a just-in-time (JIT) inventory system. Your research concludes that there is a high cost associated with inventory storage facilities; that inventories use a large portion of the company's cash flow; and that because of the nature of the inventory, there is a significant amount of shrinkage. Research also shows that neither of Penman's two competitors uses a JIT inventory system. Most of Penman's employees are trained to do only one job and belong to a local union. The union is strong and, in the past, has opposed major production changes. The union believes major changes will result in the loss of union employees' jobs. Your research indicates that Penman's major production item (a fairly new product in the market) should continue to have strong sales growth.

1. Using the information provided, advise John Burton to either continue the present system or work to develop a JIT inventory system.
2. Assume John decides to develop an inventory management system. He plans to evaluate the system after one year. List at least four possible performance measures John could use to evaluate the effectiveness of the system. Describe what information these measures would provide John.

EXERCISE 7-10

VALUE-ADDED AND NON-VALUE-ADDED ACTIVITIES

Below is a list of activities performed by the Ibapah Bijou, a movie theater. Indicate whether each activity is a value-added activity (VA) or a non-value-added activity (NVA).

a. Redesigning the staff uniforms.
b. Cooking popcorn.
c. Counting the ticket stubs at night to make sure no one got in free.
d. Servicing the quadraphonic speaker system.
e. Paying for the rights to show the next movie starring Julia Roberts.
f. Paying a management fee for the employee pension fund.
g. Renting a storage facility to store the excess inventory of candy, uncooked popcorn, and soft drinks.
h. Paying the accounts payable.
i. Cleaning the white movie screens.
j. Scrubbing the theater floor to remove the sticky residue of spilled soft drinks.

expanded material

EXERCISE 7-11

TAGUCHI QUALITY LOSS FUNCTION

Cooley Lane Company manufactures computer disk drives. Occasionally, a defective disk drive (one that spins at the wrong revolutions per minute) is shipped to a customer. Cooley Lane's policy is to fix the drive for free when it is returned by a complaining customer. Cooley Lane has a standardized statistical defect measure whereby each defective drive is given a score of 0 through 5 to indicate how bad it is, with 5 being the worst. A perfect drive receives a score of 0. The direct material and direct labor cost to fix a defective drive is only $25.

The manager in charge of product quality has recently been reading about the Taguchi quality loss function, and she thinks that Cooley Lane is underestimating the external failure costs associated with a defective disk drive. She thinks that Cooley Lane should consider increasing the amount it spends on prevention and appraisal in order to reduce the number of defective drives returned by customers. In the past month, 15 drives have been returned by customers. The drives had the following standardized defect scores:

Standardized Defect Score	Number of Defective Drives
1	2
2	1
3	1
4	4
5	7

Using the Taguchi quality loss function, estimate the dollar value of the quality loss associated with the external failure of these defective drives.

problems

PROBLEM 7-1

IDENTIFYING CROSS-SUBSIDIZATION

Dugway Company has three operating divisions. Gross margin computations for these three divisions for 2003 are given below.

	Division R	Division S	Division T
Sales	$300,000	$200,000	$150,000
Direct materials	(50,000)	(100,000)	(40,000)
Direct labor	(150,000)	(30,000)	(70,000)
Manufacturing overhead*	(105,000)	(21,000)	(49,000)
Gross margin	$ (5,000)	$ 49,000	$ (9,000)

*Manufacturing overhead is allocated to production based on the amount of direct labor cost.

Dugway has determined that its total manufacturing overhead cost of $175,000 is a mixture of batch-level costs and product line costs. Dugway has assembled the following information concerning the overhead costs, the annual number of production batches in each division, and the number of product lines in each division:

	Total Mfg. Overhead Costs	Division R	Division S	Division T
Batch-level overhead	$100,000	10 batches	40 batches	50 batches
Product line overhead	75,000	5 lines	15 lines	20 lines
	$175,000			

Required:

1. Prepare gross margin calculations for Dugway's three divisions assuming that manufacturing overhead is allocated based on the number of batches and the number of product lines.
2. Under the direct labor cost method of manufacturing overhead allocation, one or more of Dugway's divisions received a cross-subsidization from one or more of the others. Which division(s) received subsidizations, and what was the amount of the subsidizations?
3. After preparing the gross margin calculations in part (1), what advice do you have for Dugway concerning whether it should shut down any of its three divisions? Is this the same advice that would come from looking at the original gross margin calculations using manufacturing overhead allocated according to direct labor cost? Why is there a difference?

PROBLEM 7-2

ALLOCATING UNIT-LEVEL, BATCH-LEVEL, AND PRODUCT LINE MANUFACTURING OVERHEAD COSTS

Solar Salt Company has two divisions. Gross margin computations for these two divisions for 2003 are given below.

	Agricultural Products	Retail Products
Sales	$1,600,000	$900,000
Direct materials	(100,000)	(50,000)
Direct labor	(900,000)	(500,000)
Manufacturing overhead*	(450,000)	(250,000)
Gross margin	$ 150,000	$100,000

*Manufacturing overhead is allocated to production based on the amount of direct labor cost.

Solar Salt has determined that its total manufacturing overhead cost of $700,000 is a mixture of unit-level costs, batch-level costs, and product line costs. Solar Salt has assembled the following information concerning the manufacturing overhead costs, the annual number of units produced, production batches, and number of product lines in each division:

	Total Mfg. Overhead Costs	Agricultural Products	Retail Products
Unit-level overhead	$210,000	13,500 units	7,500 units
Batch-level overhead	280,000	90 batches	50 batches
Product line overhead	210,000	18 lines	10 lines
	$700,000		

Required:

1. Prepare gross margin calculations for Solar Salt's two divisions assuming that manufacturing overhead is allocated based on the number of units, number of batches, and number of product lines.

2. Comment on the comparison between the original overhead allocation done using direct labor cost and the manufacturing overhead allocation done in part (1).
3. Repeat part (1), assuming the following information concerning the number of units, batches, and product lines in each division.

	Total Mfg. Overhead Costs	Agricultural Products	Retail Products
Unit-level overhead	$210,000	13,500 units	7,500 units
Batch-level overhead	280,000	50 batches	90 batches
Product line overhead	210,000	10 lines	18 lines
	$700,000		

PROBLEM 7-3

IDENTIFYING AND USING VOLUME-BASED AND ACTIVITY-BASED COST ALLOCATION RATES

Rane Company produces electronic fish finders. It makes two different fish finders: the standard model, which is produced in bulk and sells for $150, and the deluxe model, which comes in various configurations and sells for $300. Rane's engineering and design overhead cost for 2003 is $60,000. The following information relates to production in 2003:

Number of different machine setups needed for a standard model production run	4
Number of different machine setups needed for a deluxe model production run	11
Number of standard fish finders produced	22,000
Number of deluxe fish finders produced	8,000
Average batch size per production run for standard model	400
Average batch size per production run for deluxe model	200

Required:

1. Determine the engineering and design costs to be assigned to standard and deluxe fish finders using the following allocation methods:
   a. Number of units produced
   b. Number of setups required
2. Which allocation method do you believe is more equitable?

PROBLEM 7-4

COMMON COSTS AND THE DEATH SPIRAL

Clark Street Company manufactures three products. Gross margin computations for these three products for 2003 are as follows:

	Product J	Product K	Product L
Sales	$800,000	$700,000	$ 600,000
Direct materials	(150,000)	(50,000)	(200,000)
Direct labor	(50,000)	(200,000)	(250,000)
Manufacturing overhead*	(80,000)	(320,000)	(400,000)
Gross margin	$520,000	$130,000	$(250,000)

*Manufacturing overhead is allocated to production based on the amount of direct labor cost.

Clark Street has reexamined the factors that cause its manufacturing overhead costs and has discovered that $300,000 of the annual amount of manufacturing overhead is directly related to the number of product batches produced during the year. The number of batches of the three products for 2003 was as follows: Product J, 150 batches; Product K, 100 batches; Product L, 50 batches. The remaining $500,000 in manufacturing overhead is for facility support (property taxes, security costs, general administration, etc.) and does not vary at all with levels of manufacturing activity in the company.

Required:

1. Assume that Product L was eliminated at the start of the year. Estimate what the gross margin for the remaining two products would have been. Use the direct labor cost method of overhead allocation.
2. Now, assume that both Product K and Product L were eliminated at the start of the year. Estimate what the gross margin for the remaining product, Product J, would have been. No manufacturing overhead allocation is needed because there is only one product.
3. In light of your answers in parts (1) and (2), what problems can arise when facility support manufacturing overhead costs are allocated?
4. Prepare gross margin calculations for Clark Street's three products assuming that manufacturing overhead is allocated based on the number of batches. Also, show a "total" column. Facility support costs are not to be allocated to any of the products, but are to be subtracted in the "total" column in the computation of total company operating profit.

PROBLEM 7-5

MANUFACTURING OVERHEAD ALLOCATION USING ACTIVITY-BASED COSTING

The following information is given for the Greenbaum Manufacturing Company:

	Product A	Product B	Product C	Product D
Units produced	3,000	3,450	2,875	2,400
Direct materials cost	$135,000	$169,050	$149,500	$103,200
Direct labor cost	$75,000	$124,200	$117,875	$93,600

Manufacturing Overhead	Mfg. Overhead Costs	Relevant Activities
Engineering	$209,950	Engineering changes
Quality control	129,500	Number of setups
Maintenance	41,065	Maintenance hours worked in each area of production
Manufacturing support	93,800	Production volume (units produced)

Activities	Product A	Product B	Product C	Product D
Engineering changes	300	150	275	125
Number of setups	12	5	9	11
Maintenance hours worked in each area of production	45	49	56	41
Production volume	3,000	3,450	2,875	2,400

Required:

1. Determine the ABC allocation rate for each activity (i.e., each manufacturing overhead cost pool).
2. Determine the manufacturing overhead cost for each product.
3. If products A, B, C, and D sell for $130, $125, $156, and $166, respectively, determine the gross margin for Greenbaum's four products. Assume all units are sold.

PROBLEM 7-6

MANUFACTURING OVERHEAD ALLOCATION USING ACTIVITY-BASED COSTING

Twigco Transmission Company manufactures three different automobile transmissions. The first model is an automatic transmission, the second model is a 4-gear manual transmission, and the third model is a 5-gear manual transmission. Relevant information for each transmission is provided as follows:

	Automatic		4-Gear		5-Gear	
	Total	Per Unit	Total	Per Unit	Total	Per Unit
Units produced	10,000		8,000		6,000	
Direct materials cost	$2,000,000	$200	$1,200,000	$150	$1,050,000	$175
Direct labor cost	$2,700,000	$270	$1,600,000	$200	$1,350,000	$225
Sales price		$505		$425		$455
Purchases per year	22		26		27	
Number of machine setups per unit	30		34		40	
Engineering change orders	36		42		50	

Total manufacturing overhead cost pools:

Engineering	$304,000
Quality control	260,000
Purchasing costs	150,000
Machine maintenance costs	240,000
Total costs	$954,000

Required:

1. Determine the gross margin for each product allocating manufacturing overhead costs on the basis of production volume (units produced).
2. Identify appropriate allocation bases for each of the four pools of manufacturing overhead costs.
3. Determine the ABC allocation rates for each of the four cost pools suggested in part (2).
4. Using the allocation bases suggested in part (2), determine manufacturing overhead costs per product.
5. a. Determine the gross margin per product using the manufacturing overhead costs determined in part (4).
   b. **Interpretive Question:** Which of the methods (unit-based costing or activity-based costing) is the better method to allocate the manufacturing overhead costs?

PROBLEM 7-7

MANUFACTURING OVERHEAD ALLOCATION WITH MULTIPLE PRODUCTS

Schmidt Electronics produces two products: CD105 and HD210. Relevant costing information for each product is as follows:

Per Unit	CD105	HD210
Direct materials	$10.50	$17.25
Direct labor	$10.00	$15.00
Direct labor hours per unit	1	2
Total number of machine setups	400	200
Units produced	6,000	7,000

Manufacturing overhead costs and associated ABC allocation bases are as follows:

	Mfg. Overhead Costs	Allocation Bases
Product inspection	$30,000	Units produced
Materials management	48,000	Number of machine setups
Manufacturing support	16,000	Product lines

Required:

1. If manufacturing overhead is allocated on the basis of direct labor hours, compute the cost per unit for CD105 and HD210.
2. Determine the allocation rate per activity for each ABC allocation basis.
3. Determine the manufacturing overhead cost for each product using your answer to part (2).
4. Using your answer to part (3), compute the cost per unit for CD105 and HD210.
5. Compare your answers to part (1) and part (4). Why the difference in costs?

PROBLEM 7-8

ACTIVITY-BASED COSTING AND GROSS MARGIN CALCULATIONS

Stafford Manufacturing, Inc., produces two different products. Product 1 sells for $950 each, and Product 2 sells for $700 each. Estimated annual production and sales for Product 1 and Product 2 are 2,100 units and 2,900 units, respectively. Direct materials are $350 for Product 1 and $200 for Product 2. Direct labor costs are $300 for Product 1 and $310 for Product 2. Stafford purchases materials for Product 1 every month and for Product 2 every two months. On average, Stafford performs 10 setups each month for Product 1 production and 8 setups each month for Product 2 production. The following are manufacturing overhead costs incurred by Stafford Manufacturing:

Quality control	$150,000
Purchasing costs	74,880
Miscellaneous manufacturing overhead	62,640

Required:

1. Assuming that the allocation bases for the three manufacturing overhead costs are production volume for quality control, number of purchases for purchasing costs, and number of setups for miscellaneous manufacturing overhead, calculate the cost per unit of each allocation basis.
2. Determine total manufacturing overhead costs for each product.
3. Determine the gross margin percent for Stafford Manufacturing for each product it produces.

PROBLEM 7-9

ALLOCATION OF MANUFACTURING OVERHEAD WITH MULTIPLE PRODUCTS

Central, Inc., is a manufacturing firm that manufactures two types of airplane motors. The Type 1 motor is a jet engine that is designed for medium-size military aircraft. Because of a long-term contract with the military, Type 1 motors need no modifications. Type 2 motors are designed for larger commercial aircraft. Because the Type 2 motor is designed for several different models of airplanes and the mounting hardware is different for each, retooling is regularly required. Costs for the two types of engines are presented here:

	Type 1 Engine (400 Units Produced)		Type 2 Engine (180 Units Produced)	
	Total	**Per Unit**	**Total**	**Per Unit**
Direct materials cost	$108,000,000	$270,000	$70,200,000	$390,000
Direct labor cost	72,000,000	180,000	46,800,000	260,000
Manufacturing overhead costs:				
Engineering costs				$576,000,000
Quality control				155,520,000
Utilities and maintenance				5,220,000

Required:

1. Determine the amount of manufacturing overhead to be assigned to each unit of activity assuming the following ABC information:

Manufacturing Overhead Cost	*Allocation Bases*
• Engineering costs	• Engineering change orders per unit
• Quality control	• Machine setups per unit
• Utilities and maintenance	• Production volume

Type 1 Engines
- 0 engineering change orders per unit
- 18 machine setups per unit
- 400 units produced

Type 2 Engines
- 16 engineering change orders per unit
- 32 machine setups per unit
- 180 units produced

2. Determine the amount of manufacturing overhead to be assigned to each type of engine.
3. Compute the gross margin on Type 1 and Type 2 engines assuming selling prices of $1 million and $4 million, respectively.

PROBLEM 7-10

ALLOCATION OF MANUFACTURING OVERHEAD WITH MULTIPLE PRODUCTS

Macey Sprinkling Company produces two types of pipe: (1) lawn sprinkler pipe and (2) building sprinkler pipe. Relevant information for the production of the two types of pipe for 2003 is as follows:

	Lawn Sprinkler Pipe	Building Sprinkler Pipe
Feet produced	325,000	150,000
Prime costs	$243,750	$123,000
Manufacturing overhead costs:		
Utilities	$ 75,000	$ 40,000
Support staff	63,000	35,750
Quality control	8,000	4,060
Purchasing	19,200	10,250

Macey allocates utilities and support staff costs on the basis of production volume, quality control costs on the basis of number of machine setups required, and purchasing department costs on the basis of number of purchase orders. During 2003, volume of these various activities per *product line* was:

	Lawn Sprinkler Pipe	Building Sprinkler Pipe
Production volume	325,000 ft.	150,000 ft.
Machine setups	12	24
Purchase orders	1	30

Required:

1. Determine the cost per unit for each cost driver.
2. Determine the amount of manufacturing overhead to be assigned to the two types of sprinkler pipe.
3. Determine the total cost for each type of pipe produced for the year.

PROBLEM 7-11

COSTS OF QUALITY

DeeAnn Martinez is preparing to open her own CPA firm. DeeAnn is a smart businessperson and wants to maximize her profits. She has not yet decided whether to run a low-quality CPA firm (basically offering to sign the financial statements of anyone who will pay her fee), an average CPA firm, or a premium-quality CPA firm (competing head-to-head with the large international accounting firms such as PRICEWATERHOUSE COOPERS).

DeeAnn has analyzed the costs of quality related to operating a CPA firm and has developed the following analysis:

- *Prevention costs:* The best way to ensure the quality of the audit is to increase the quality of the staff hired and to increase the time that the staff spends on each audit. DeeAnn realizes that hiring higher-quality staff will cost more.
- *Appraisal costs:* DeeAnn plans to inspect the work of the staff auditors by having audit managers review the work. The average salary rate for an audit manager (including all fringe benefits) is $50 per hour.

- *Internal failure costs:* Sometimes the audit team will do such a poor job that one of DeeAnn's audit partners will have to personally supervise the completion of the audit work. The average salary rate for an audit partner is $100 per hour.
- *External failure costs:* If investors or creditors rely on financial statements that later prove to be false, the audit firm that approved those financial statements will probably be sued. Of course, the frequency of being sued, and the cost of each lawsuit, will be higher if DeeAnn decides to provide low-quality audits.

DeeAnn has gathered the following numerical information about the costs of quality in relation to operating a CPA firm:

	Low Quality	Average Quality	Premium Quality
Prevention costs:			
Staff hours spent on audit	10 hours	30 hours	100 hours
Staff salary rate	$20/hour	$25/hour	$35/hour
Appraisal costs:			
Manager review of audit work	1 hour	5 hours	20 hours
Internal failure costs:			
Frequency of bad audits	1 in 3	1 in 10	1 in 50
Partner time to fix bad audit	10 hours	5 hours	3 hours
External failure costs:			
Frequency of lawsuits	1 in 5	1 in 40	1 in 100
Expected loss on each lawsuit	$200,000	$100,000	$100,000

Required:

1. Assume that the revenue from each audit is the same no matter what the quality of the audit. Therefore, in order to maximize her profits, DeeAnn must minimize the expected cost of each audit. Which type of audit firm—low quality, average quality, or premium quality—should DeeAnn operate in order to maximize her expected profit per audit? Show your calculations.
2. Comment on whether the assumption about revenue made in part (1) seems appropriate.

expanded material

PROBLEM 7-12

TAGUCHI QUALITY LOSS FUNCTION

TAC Computers is a nationwide distributor of personal computers for home and business use. Its main sales channels are the Internet and telephone sales. Customers either call in to TAC's customer sales center or log on to TAC's Web site to place orders for custom-made computers. One of TAC's distinguishing marketing strategies is its three-year 24 × 7 customer support call center. All TAC customers have the ability to call the customer support center 24 hours a day, seven days a week to receive technical assistance with their machine. TAC prides itself on the high quality of service in this call center. Every customer call is immediately followed with either an e-mail or a postcard survey that asks the customer to provide feedback on the experience and answer the following questions:

1. Was your concern or question thoroughly resolved by the TAC technician?
2. Did the TAC technician handle your call with courtesy and professionalism?

Technicians' performance on the first question is referred to as the "error rate." Performance on the second question is referred to as the "care rate." The customer support call center management team uses performance on the error rate and care rate to manage operations and determine additional training needed by individual call center technicians. Performance on these two measures has been quite good for TAC. The TAC standard for each technician is to have no more than 1% complaints per month on the first question and no more than 0.5% complaints per month on the second question (a full-time technician handles 600 calls per month on average). Management feels that 99% quality on error and 99.5% quality on care is an excellent performance level for this industry.

Currently, few technicians need additional training each month. However, if a technician's error rate exceeds 1% of any month's call volume, that technician goes through a skills verification test to identify areas of weakness in handling specific technical issues, then undergoes some customized training. The cost of running a technician through this analysis and training process is estimated to be about $600. In the event that a technician's care rate exceeds 0.5% of a month's call volume, a manager is assigned to observe the technician in order to identify specific problems in working with customers. Then the technician works through a specialized training program based on the manager's assessment. The average cost of running a technician through this process is about $900.

As the controller for TAC Computers, you've been reading lately about the opportunity costs of low quality, and you're concerned that management of the customer support call center may not recognize the significant cost of lost sales that result when the company's reputation is hurt by technician error or lack of care for the customer.

Required:

1. Assuming that the Taguchi quality loss function is approximately accurate in measuring TAC's quality loss due to the external failure of handling customer calls, calculate the opportunity cost of lost sales when a technician's error rate hits 1%. Calculate the opportunity cost of lost sales when a technician's care rate hits 0.5%.
2. Explain to the management team of the customer support call center how they should interpret and use these Taguchi calculations to improve the operations in their center.

competency enhancement opportunities

- Analyzing Real Company Information
- International Case
- Ethics Case
- Writing Assignment
- The Debate
- Internet Search

The following additional assignments provide opportunities for students to develop critical thinking, ethical perspectives, oral and written communication skills, experience with electronic research, and teamwork through group and business activities.

ANALYZING REAL COMPANY INFORMATION

• *Analyzing 7-1 (Microsoft)*

MICROSOFT, like most other companies, is continually striving to appropriately allocate costs and to increase the quality of its products. We have studied Microsoft's financial statements in past chapters. Now it is time to think beyond the numbers and examine other factors that might affect a firm's performance. Use your knowledge of Microsoft and the computer software industry to answer the following questions:

1. What types of overhead costs might Microsoft incur associated with its software products? Identify several cost drivers that Microsoft might consider in allocating overhead using the ABC method of overhead allocation.
2. What sort of product quality issues might Microsoft face associated with its software? Identify the various costs of quality associated with a faulty software product.

• ***Analyzing 7-2 (Techtronics Technologies)***

Techtronics Technologies (a hypothetical company) produces mass storage devices for computers. The company produces three models: Model HD110, Model HD220, and Model HD330. Sales and costing information for these three products is as follows:

	HD110	HD220	HD330
Selling price per unit	$169	$185	$199
Units produced	2,500	3,800	4,100
Direct materials cost	$235,000	$444,600	$574,000
Direct labor cost	$37,500	$64,600	$77,900

In the past, manufacturing overhead has been allocated based on direct labor costs. Manufacturing overhead for this period is $416,000, and the predetermined overhead rate is $40 per unit produced.

Based on this information, management has determined that Model HD330 is barely breaking even. Because the market for mass storage devices is quite competitive, the price for each model is set by the market—not by management. Thus, increasing the price charged for products is not an option. As a result, management is considering discontinuing Model HD330. Before making a final decision, management has come to you for advice. You collect the following information regarding manufacturing overhead:

Mfg. Overhead	Mfg. Overhead Costs	Allocation Bases
Engineering	$198,000	Engineering changes
Quality control	34,000	Number of units produced
Manufacturing support	184,000	Number of setups
Total manufacturing overhead	$416,000	

Activity	HD110	HD220	HD330
Total number of engineering changes	210	114	126
Total number of units produced	2,500	3,800	4,100
Total number of setups	30	27	23

1. Determine the gross margin for each model under the current manufacturing overhead allocation scheme.
2. Determine the manufacturing overhead cost for each model using the information related to cost drivers.
3. Determine the gross margin for each model using cost drivers to allocate manufacturing overhead.
4. What recommendation would you make to management regarding their decision to discontinue Model HD330?

INTERNATIONAL CASE

• *Deming in Japan*

As noted in this chapter, the ideas of W. Edward Deming received little attention in the United States in the late 1940s and early 1950s. Deming then moved to Japan where his ideas were accepted and implemented almost immediately. The result was that industries in Japan, such as automobile production, quickly developed a reputation for producing quality products. In the 1980s, the United States found itself trying to catch up to the Japanese in the race for quality products. Can you speculate as to why Deming's ideas were not readily accepted in the United States, yet were quickly adopted in Japan? To answer this question, you may need to recall your world history during the 1940s.

ETHICS CASE

• *Minuteman Enterprises*

You are the controller for Minuteman Enterprises, a manufacturer of rocket booster engines and various aerospace products. Though there are many commercial customers for most of the company's products, the federal government is the only buyer of your rocket booster engines. Because you are the only provider for the engines, the government has agreed to buy these engines at a price equal to your cost plus a 10% markup.

As the controller, you have recently been studying the accuracy of your product costs. Traditionally, manufacturing overhead has been allocated on the basis of direct labor hours. Using this method, rocket boosters have borne a high percentage of manufacturing overhead because they take many more direct labor hours than do the other products.

You have just been presented an analysis by one of your staff members that shows that direct labor hours is not a very relevant base for allocating manufacturing overhead costs. Rather, she has made a very convincing case that manufacturing overhead should be allocated using activity-based costing with multiple cost drivers. Using her suggested approach, however, you discover that the rocket boosters bear a much smaller portion of manufacturing overhead costs, and therefore, the total cost of the boosters is considerably less than the amount you had been using to determine the price charged to the government.

You know that her calculations using ABC are likely more accurate than the current cost allocation method and that the commercial products should bear a larger amount of manufacturing overhead costs. Yet, you also know that by using ABC and the more accurate cost drivers, your profits from both the boosters and the commercial products will be reduced.

1. What should you do?
2. Is it ethical to continue to allocate manufacturing overhead costs on the basis of direct labor hours?
3. Would it be ethical to use direct labor hours if that were the basis used by other government contractors?
4. If you decide to switch to ABC, should you inform the government that you have overcharged it and return the excess profits?

WRITING ASSIGNMENT

• *Advantages and Disadvantages of ABC*

Your boss recently attended a conference where activity-based costing was discussed. She is intrigued by the ABC concept and wonders if the company is appropriately costing its products. Your company produces and sells four different styles of briefcases. The production process differs for each briefcase, as different features require different equipment. She returns from the conference and asks you to summarize the advantages and disadvantages of ABC. Your assignment is to write a two-page memo addressing these issues.

THE DEBATE

• *ABC or Bust!*

As the text indicates, activity-based costing has received much attention from businesses around the world. Yet some firms still resist adopting an ABC system, and others have adopted ABC and then reverted to their more traditional costing systems. Divide your group into two teams and prepare five-minute presentations defending the following positions:

- Team One is "In Support of ABC." Your team's task is to identify the benefits of using an activity-based product costing system. Briefly explain the advantages that a company will realize if it adopts ABC.
- Team Two is "In Support of Tradition." Your team's task is to identify the benefits of using a more traditional product costing system based on, for example, direct labor hours. Explain the advantages of a traditional system that cause many firms to still choose it over ABC.

INTERNET SEARCH

International

• *Toyota Motor Corporation*

W. Edward Deming helped **TOYOTA** become the company it is today. Go to Toyota's Web site at **http://www.toyota.com**. Sometimes Web addresses change, so if this Toyota address doesn't work, access the Web site for this textbook (**http://albrecht.swcollege.com**) for an updated link to Toyota. Once you have gained access to Toyota's Web site, answer the following questions:

1. Access Toyota's operations section and locate the company's history timeline. When did Toyota begin selling in North America? When did this company sell its millionth car in North America?
2. Next, look for the criteria and mission of Toyota's community-funding program. What is the mission of this program? Identify a couple of points in the funding guidelines that would limit a community's or a program's chance for funding.

part 4

Evaluation

Evaluating Products and Processes

chapter

m8

learning objectives

After studying this chapter, you should be able to:

1 Explain how evaluation leads to planning and why products and processes must be continuously evaluated.

2 Understand why benchmarking is so important and how it is conducted.

3 Understand the concept of differential costs and revenues, and be able to identify those costs and revenues that are relevant to making product and process decisions.

4 Identify several examples of product and process evaluation decisions, and be able to analyze and select the best alternative for each example.

expanded material

5 Understand the theory of constraints and how focusing on scarce resources can direct activities in manufacturing companies.

setting the stage

Every day in *The Wall Street Journal* and other publications, we read about companies that are either expanding into new business lines, dropping existing products, entering new markets, exiting existing markets, or making other major business decisions. These kinds of decisions have historically been referred to as nonroutine decisions. Take the October 6, 2000 issue of *The Wall Street Journal,* for example. On just the front page, there were stories about:

- **TIME WARNER** and **EMI** scrapping plans for a $20 billion music joint venture because of tough antitrust scrutiny from the European Commission.
- **PRICELINE.COM**'s decision to close its **WEBHOUSE** service that allowed customers to bid for groceries and gasoline online.
- **OWENS CORNING** filing for Chapter 11 bankruptcy court protection, blaming escalating asbestos liability claims.
- **SMITHKLINE**'s bid to acquire **BLOCK DRUG** for about $1.2 billion. (Block is the maker of Sensodyne and other dental products.)
- **GENERAL MOTORS' SATURN** division's plans to unveil and produce a new sports utility vehicle as part of its $1.5 billion investment to expand Saturn into a full-line automobile brand.
- **POLO RALPH LAUREN**'s closing of its Polo Jeans stores and some Club Monaco outlets to focus on wealthier customers.
- **TWA**'s plans to revamp its route network, including dropping flights from New York's Kennedy Airport to Milan, Italy, and Lisbon, Portugal.

Each of these actions represents a major product or process decision by the company. Consider the Priceline.com decision, for example. One year earlier, Priceline.com founder Jay Walker said that his "name-your-own-price system" would encompass every category of goods. His prediction that "there is no category we won't be in" turned out to be less than accurate. By shutting down its name-your-own-price grocery and gasoline sales operations, Priceline and its subsidiary, WebHouse Club, Inc., wrote off an investment of over $363 million.

In Chapter 1 of management accounting, you learned that management decision making involves the three functions of planning, controlling, and evaluating. Thus far, we have discussed the planning and controlling functions. You have learned that planning involves long-run planning, including strategic planning and capital budgeting, and short-run planning, including production prioritizing and operational budgeting. You have learned that controlling involves tracking actual performance in terms of costs, quality, and timeliness measures. These tracked measures (costs, quality, and timeliness) are then used in the evaluating process to compare against budgets previously prepared. Evaluating involves analyzing results, providing feedback to managers and other employees, rewarding performance, and identifying problems. One specific type of evaluation focuses on products and processes. As you learned in Chapter 1, managers need to assess the performance of their products or services, as well as the processes that are in place to create those products or services. A second type of evaluation focuses on the personnel and their divisions within the organization. Upper-level management must evaluate how well lower-level managers perform the activities assigned to them in the planning stages. In this chapter, we focus on the evaluation of products, services, and processes. In Chapter 9 of management accounting, we focus on evaluating personnel and their divisions.

EVALUATING PRODUCTS AND PROCESSES

1 Explain how evaluation leads to planning and why products and processes must be continuously evaluated.

Evaluation brings us back to the point where we started—planning. Information gained through the evaluation process is used for planning during the following period. When managers are evaluating last period's performance, they are also probably making planning decisions that will affect, and hopefully improve, performance in the next period. This planning, controlling, and evaluating cycle is diagrammed on the following page.

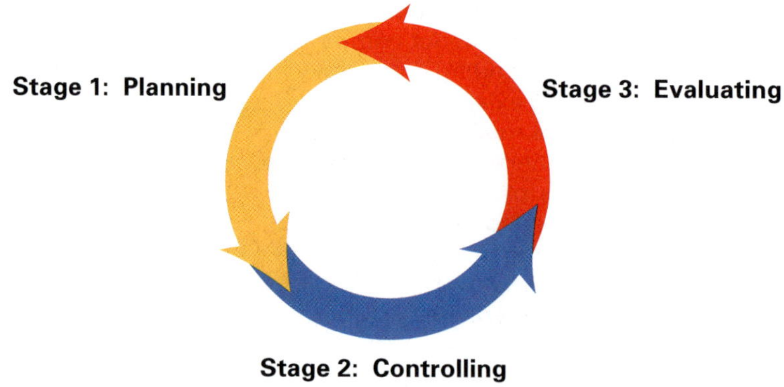

The evaluation of products, services, and processes leads to decisions that will affect future operations, including whether to enter or exit a market for a particular service or product, whether to make or buy a component, whether to sell a product before or after additional processing, and what prices to charge for services and products. In the opening scenario, most of the examples cited involved entering or exiting markets.

The evaluation decisions we will discuss in this chapter can have a significant impact on the profitability, quality, and timeliness of the products of an organization for several periods and so must be considered very carefully. In a manufacturing company, for example, evaluation can help a company decide whether to accept a special order, whether to make or buy manufacturing components, whether to build or sell plants, and how to best use limited raw materials in the manufacturing process. In a merchandising company, evaluation can lead to decisions about how to use limited store shelves and whether to open a new store. In a service company, evaluation can help the company decide whether to hire a particular specialist or contract that service to another firm, how to use scarce labor resources, and whether to merge with another company. In a governmental unit, evaluation can affect decisions about whether to collect garbage

business environment essay

A Better Bumper Factory Shahid Khan is the founder and owner of **BUMPER WORKS** in Danville, Illinois. Bumper Works designs and manufactures bumpers for lightweight pickup trucks for Japanese automakers, including **TOYOTA MOTOR CORPORATION**, whose standards are very exacting. "There was nothing Toyota could teach us," says Khan, "about engineering low-cost bumpers." But on how to run a bumper factory, Khan is more humble. "We had benchmarked ourselves against American industry," he says. "I don't think we knew how bad we were."

Toyota, a world leader in factory efficiency, did know. But rather than take its business elsewhere, Toyota dispatched a team of manufacturing experts to the bumper plant to conduct a crash course in the Toyota system. Productivity at Bumper Works rose 60% from the previous year, and the number of defects was reduced by 80%.

Khan made sales calls to Toyota for five years before landing his first contract with the company in 1985. Then, in 1987, Khan and two other bumper makers were told by Toyota to design new bumpers considerably more durable than the Big Three (**GM**, **CHRYSLER**, and **FORD**) specifications required. Such demands from Japanese companies are common. "We were the only company that could demonstrate we could do that," Khan says. As a result, in 1988, his firm became the sole supplier of bumpers to U.S. facilities where Toyota attaches rear bumpers and other accessories to trucks made in Japan.

In 1989, Toyota made additional demands. Toyota wanted annual price reductions despite rising costs for materials and labor. It also wanted better bumpers

at the curb or at the house site, whether to hire an in-house lawyer or contract out all legal services, and whether to develop a water system or buy water from a nearby community. In a dot.com company, evaluation could lead to decisions about how to price banner ads, whether to charge an access or user fee, or whether to add or drop existing lines (such as Priceline.com's decision to drop groceries and gasoline).

To illustrate how evaluation (and help from customers and vendors) can help companies improve their competitive position, see the Business Environment Essay below. Especially note the types of actions taken by **BUMPER WORKS** to improve product quality, cut production time, acquire new equipment, reduce inventory, and increase worker participation. All these actions involved changes in the fundamental operating process that Bumper Works had been using. The decisions made by Bumper Works enabled the company to continue to be successful in a very competitive market.

Why Evaluation Is So Important

Today, we live in an age when information is transmitted worldwide almost instantaneously and change is occurring faster than ever before. With accurate and timely information so readily available, it is absolutely critical that companies produce the highest-quality products at the lowest possible price and faster than anyone else. If a U.S. automobile manufacturer produces a car that is more expensive or of lower quality than cars made in Japan or Germany, for example, consumers will buy foreign automobiles because information about the Japanese and German cars is readily available to U.S. car buyers. Likewise, if a U.S. automobile company can buy higher-quality tires at a lower price from a Korean tire manufacturer than it can from a U.S. tire manufacturer, it will buy Korean tires because information about the foreign tires is easily accessible. Similarly, if investors have a limited amount of money to invest, they can just as easily buy stocks of European or Asian companies as stocks of U.S. companies because the information is available and the markets are easily accessible.

This increased availability of up-to-date information and the ease with which products, services, and investments can be acquired internationally have made it critically important that

and more punctual deliveries. Toyota wanted to help Khan meet these demands, but little could be done until Bumper Works cut the time it took to change dies in the metal-stamping presses from 90 minutes or more to less than 22 minutes. Only then would Bumper Works be flexible enough to make 20 different bumper models each day. Bumper Works could not afford new presses with quick-change features, so, with Toyota's help, Khan's workers improvised. They welded homemade metal tabs to their nine-ton dies to facilitate lining up the dies on pins attached to the presses. Workers also videotaped die-change procedures and produced an instruction manual—a Bumper Works first. "We had no organization," recalls the die coordinator. "There were a lot of simple things we didn't think about until the Toyota team came in."

By July 1990, Bumper Works achieved the die-change objective. Toyota then dispatched two more consultants from Japan to lead what Khan calls "boot camp." In about two weeks of 16-hour days, the plant was turned upside down. Virtually every piece of equipment, except the massive metal presses, was moved. Employees had to relearn their jobs. Toyota's goal was for a piece of raw steel to come in one end of the building and go out the other end on the same day as a finished bumper. The employees now schedule their own work rather than wait for a supervisor's direction. When a batch of Toyota bumpers is shipped, a card is returned to the press operators, and they press out more. Bumper quality improved significantly, and costs came down.

Source: Adapted from "Japanese Auto Makers Help U.S. Suppliers to Become More Efficient," *The Wall Street Journal*, September 9, 1991.

fyi

Much of the continuous improvement literature had its origin in Japan with Japanese companies. As a result, even in U.S. management accounting literature, you will frequently encounter the Japanese term *kaizen,* which means "continuous improvement." Continuous improvement can take the form of continuous reductions in product defects, delivery time, material waste, inventory size, setup time, and so on. Under continuous improvement programs, one of the major responsibilities of managers and workers is to reduce total costs by continuous improvement in both monetary and nonmonetary standards.

companies operate as efficiently and effectively as possible. Because it is so important to be a high-performing or "world-class" company, organizations are placing more and more emphasis on evaluating their performance and continuously improving. Managers recognize that, in this information age, it is "survival of the fittest" and that only the best-performing companies will be able to compete in the long run.

Companies can be poor performers for several reasons. Some companies do not perform well because they fail to develop appropriate corporate strategies or goals or because they lack vision (planning). Some companies do not perform well because their evaluation methods are poor or do not fit their organizational structures and, therefore, fail to accurately assess how well they are doing. Perhaps most commonly, some companies do not perform well because they fail to execute their strategies and planned actions.

In this chapter, we will discuss several ways companies organize and set goals and then evaluate their performance against those goals. As was the case with product cost determination discussed in Chapter 2 of management accounting, performance evaluation has been the subject of considerable research in the past few years and has undergone significant changes. Much emphasis has been placed on developing evaluation systems that align performance evaluation with an organization's strategic plan and objectives and that focus on customer and employee needs. Historically, many performance measures have been backward looking and have tended to report results too late to allow corrective action to be taken. New evaluation systems link daily activities with measures that help organizations guide decisions and actions.

Obviously, to effectively evaluate performance, organizations must have goals, objectives, or benchmarks against which to assess their performance. Most organizations establish these goals and benchmarks through a process called strategic planning, which we have already discussed.

Quality and Time Standards

In evaluating performance, it is important to focus on both monetary and nonmonetary measures. For example, one well-known fast-food chain's managers are evaluated not only on the profitability of their unit, but also on such quality standards as cleanliness and the kind of service provided to customers. In another company, some managers receive more points for developing new technologies and making innovations than for keeping costs in line. At another company, production employees are rewarded on how much they can reduce the delivery time of products to customers. Other nonmonetary measures of performance include creating good employee morale and maintaining equipment in good running order.

Fast-food managers can be evaluated on the kind of service provided to customers. Thus, it is important that employees offer fast service with a smile.

For an evaluation system to be successful, the criteria by which products and processes are evaluated should be well defined, objective, and measurable. Usually, qualitative criteria are much harder to evaluate than objective cost measures and resulting variances, but that does not diminish their importance. In fact, quality and time standards are often as important to a firm's success as financial results. Those companies that can deliver the highest-quality products quickest and at the most competitive price will usually be the most successful. Some companies have even developed "best supplier" awards to recognize those suppliers that deliver products at the lowest price, with the highest quality and with the fewest late orders. Criteria used in making these awards usually include such elements as cost reductions, delivery improvement (frequency as well as timeliness), and percentage of defects.

In evaluating quality and time considerations, quality is usually defined as the total features and characteristics of a product or service that bear on its ability to satisfy stated or implied needs. Generally, as a final measure, quality must be viewed from a customer perspective as determined by acceptance in the marketplace. One writer has suggested that quality includes the following eight dimensions:[1]

1. *Performance*—a product's primary operating characteristic. Examples are automobile acceleration and a television set's picture clarity.
2. *Features*—supplements to a product's basic functioning characteristics, such as power windows on a car.
3. *Reliability*—a probability of not malfunctioning during a specified period.
4. *Conformance*—the degree to which a product's design and operating characteristics meet established standards.
5. *Durability*—a measure of product life.
6. *Serviceability*—the speed and ease of repair.
7. *Aesthetics*—how a product looks, feels, tastes, and smells.
8. *Perceived quality*—as seen by a customer.

As an example of how management might apply these quality components to a specific product, consider an automobile tire. Its quality may be measured by tread-wear rate, handling, traction, impact on gas mileage, noise levels, resistance to punctures, and appearance. As another example, the tax service of a CPA may be measured by timely completion of tax returns, tax savings, number of audits or letters from the IRS, suggestions made for future investment opportunities, fees charged, and personal attention given.

This discussion of quality suggests that performance evaluation must be viewed more broadly and from a different perspective than it has been in the past. Controlling costs is still essential, but the emphasis should also be on quality and improvement in processes, products, and services. Some people argue that the competitive advantage of some Japanese companies is the direct result of acceptance of this quality philosophy, attributed to W. Edwards Deming. The Deming chain reaction is depicted in Exhibit 8-1.

With a broader perspective, managers can seek ways to measure all aspects of company performance. The emphasis should be on the critical activities of the company. The goal is to identify and concentrate on those activities that add the most value to products or services.

In addition to quality, performance evaluation now often considers the time it takes to get a product to the marketplace. By using technology and re-engineering processes, most companies today can deliver goods to customers faster than ever before.

The challenge is to integrate cost, quality, and speed considerations into evaluation systems effectively. The objectives of zero defects, continuous improvement, decreasing manufacturing and delivery time, and meeting customer expectations of quality are admirable. Developing and effectively implementing performance measures that help achieve these objectives is not an easy task, but it is certainly worthy of management's effort. In the end, those organizations that develop the most appropriate performance measures and provide the necessary encouragement and motivation for employees to achieve the organization's objectives will be the most successful.

STOP & THINK What do you think researchers mean when they say that current evaluation methods do not give enough consideration to intangible capabilities and focus too much on financial returns?

1 David A. Garvin, "Competing on the Eight Dimensions of Quality," *Harvard Business Review* 65 (November–December 1987): pp. 101–109.

exhibit 8-1 Deming Chain Reaction

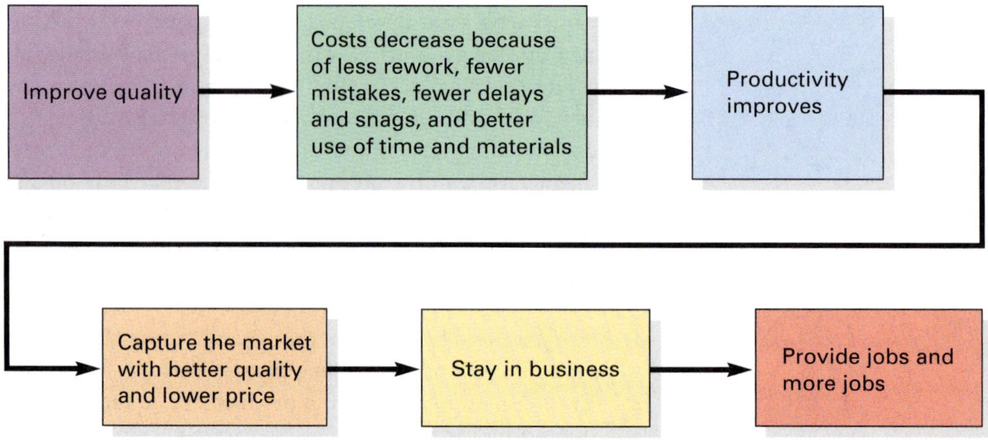

to summarize

In an age when information is inexpensive and readily available, it is important that companies offer the highest-quality products at the lowest possible price and faster than their competitors. Because quality, speed, and price are so important, it is critical that organizations establish good evaluation methods and continuously improve. A company cannot improve its performance until it knows how it is doing. Evaluation helps an organization plan better and control its operations more effectively. In addition to cost considerations, nonmonetary measures should be used in evaluating performance. To be effective, these criteria must be well defined, objective, and measurable. New approaches to performance evaluation include quality and time considerations. The new approaches are required because all aspects of a company's performance need to be monitored. In the final analysis, those organizations that can deliver the highest-quality products to their customers at the lowest

business environment essay

Nonmonetary Standards at Xerox Customer surveys at **XEROX**'s Omaha district indicated that 18% of customers were dissatisfied with billing accuracy. This figure prompted an evaluation that revealed that district's billing error rate was 3.54%. Further, estimates were made of the costs required to correct billing errors and the amount of revenues lost due to the cancellation of contracts by those dissatisfied because of billing problems. The total cost to the company was estimated to be almost $200,000 during a six-month test period.

A team with representatives from the different departments that participated in the billing process was formed to improve billing performance. The team followed a multistep problem-solving process. First, the problem was identified and analyzed. During this stage, team members identified all those who might have an impact on billing errors and the likely causes of those errors. Next, possible solutions were con-

prices and in the shortest amount of time will be the most successful. Significant challenges exist in implementing new performance evaluation approaches.

2

Understand why benchmarking is so important and how it is conducted.

benchmarking A performance evaluation process used by companies to target areas for improvement by comparing the company's financial and operating performance against the performance of other companies or by comparing the performance of internal departments against each other.

BENCHMARKING

In recent years, there has been an evaluation revolution. Several new evaluation methods have been developed. In this chapter, we will describe only one—benchmarking. Two others (the balanced scorecard and the concept of continuous improvement) will be discussed in future chapters.

Benchmarking involves comparing a company's financial and operating performance against a competitor's performance or comparing the performance of various internal departments against each other. The benchmarking process usually consists of four steps. Step 1 is to analyze the company's practices, procedures, and performance in a given process and to set forth goals and objectives for improving them. Analysis of the company's practices and procedures is crucial because the practices of other firms will not prove very revealing unless a company has determined its own strengths and weaknesses.

Step 2 involves the selection of a benchmark (or benchmarks). These benchmarks can be departments within a company or competing companies that perform the process under analysis optimally. This step is critical as selection of the wrong benchmarks can result in identifying inappropriate procedures and unrealistic goals for a firm.

In step 3, detailed information on the benchmarks' practices and procedures for that process is collected and shared. Although collecting such data on competing companies may prove difficult, various sources offer benchmark data, and companies are often willing to share information with each other.

In step 4, a company must carefully analyze the data collected in step 3 to determine which of the policies and procedures used by benchmarked companies can best be employed.

Internal versus External Comparisons

The standards of comparison used for benchmarking can be based on the performance of departments or divisions within the same company or appropriate departments from other companies. When using internal units as benchmarks, a company can begin by identifying its

sidered. Here the focus was on ways to educate personnel about correct billing input and procedures. In the solution-planning stage, the team chose to create a cartoon character, Captain Xero, to attract attention to the improvement program and to convey the program's message. Cartoons would be published weekly to educate personnel about billing. Finally, the team implemented the program and evaluated its results.

The focus on improving billing accuracy paid off handsomely. During a one-year period, billing errors were reduced 52% as the billing error rate fell from 3.54% to 1.71%. Surveys revealed that customer satisfaction with billing accuracy also improved significantly. The estimated reduction in costs associated with billing errors exceeded $100,000 during the second six-month period after the program was implemented.

Source: Adapted from David M. Beuhlmann and Donald Stover, "How Xerox Solves Quality Problems," *Management Accounting*, September 1993, pp. 33–36.

best-performing units and then analyze their strategies and practices for performance. Once the approaches have been determined and quantified, less effective departments are encouraged to adopt the practices of the more successful units.

A drawback to internal comparisons alone, however, is that they may foster complacency and may not afford a realistic picture of a unit's potential within the industry. Internal comparisons are often of limited value because a company may be unable to recognize its own shortcomings and faults. Also, although one department within a company may outperform other departments substantially, that fact is not indicative of its performance relative to the industry as a whole. In essence, the department may be outperforming other units within the company, but still be falling short of the performance yields found in other similar companies. For example, it is easy to assume that a growth rate of 4 percent a year is satisfactory; yet, if outside competitors are realizing growth rates of 8 percent, there is clearly great room for improvement.

A second approach to benchmarking is to compare a company against top competitors. Most experts believe that this approach is the most relevant point of comparison for both services and products. As mentioned above, a major stumbling block is that obtaining the necessary data for an effective comparison may be difficult. Nevertheless, this type of analysis, peer group benchmarking, is beneficial because it not only allows a company to compare itself to another company with a similar set of attributes, but it may also afford a more invigorating view of what is possible within the industry. Thus, to the extent that key result measurement ratios of individual companies can be compared with averages of a select group of companies with generally similar attributes, peer group examinations can be quite revealing.

A third form of benchmarking is to compare a company with the "best-in-class." This approach entails comparing a company with top-performing firms sharing comparable functions or philosophies, although they may not be in the same industry. The advantage of this type of cross-industry comparison is that practices and procedures followed in other industries may prove very beneficial, even though they have not been used previously in the same industry. Best-in-class comparisons can bring new ideas, new thoughts, and even new concepts. On the downside, however, the introduction of new concepts is somewhat speculative. There is risk whenever a company adapts a new concept or procedure. Because a process performs well in one industry does not necessarily mean it can be carried over effectively to a different industry. This limitation has to be considered before implementing any new ideas.

Benchmarking can yield great benefits in the education of executives and the realized performance improvements of operations. In addition, benchmarking can be used to determine strategic areas of opportunity. In general, it is the application of what is learned in benchmarking that delivers the impressive results so often noted.

The benefits of benchmarking are realized when companies employ recommendations and embark on a change process leading to marked improvements in productivity, costs, and revenues. The following are examples of how companies improved their results through benchmarking:

- GLAXO WELLCOME had over 80 toll-free telephone numbers, over half of which failed to ring anywhere. By eliminating all but one telephone number, Glaxo greatly reduced customer frustration and confusion.
- NORWEST (now WELLS FARGO), the nation's largest mortgage company, embarked on a benchmarking campaign and was able to quantify the following benefits:
    - Sales brochure consolidation: $430,000 in savings.
    - Customer and direct mail consolidation: $1 million in savings.
    - Opportunity lending: $20 million in added growth.
    - Teller referrals: up 15%, 33% of which result in additional sales.
    - Use of sales road maps: sales increase up to 102%.
    - Use of partner letters: 150% increase in commercial sales.
    - Performance coaching: 5.08 products per new customer.
- MARRIOTT improved its guest check-in service process 500% by benchmarking the patient admittance process used by hospital emergency rooms.
- SOUTHWEST AIRLINES saved millions of dollars a year and was able to put more aircraft in the air while reducing the number on the ground by benchmarking Indy 500 pit crews.

- XEROX dramatically improved its warehouse order-picking process by benchmarking L.L. BEAN, a catalog order company.
- KPMG PEAT MARWICK borrowed the concept of a supermarket's express checkout to start an express line in its word-processing pools. The change enabled teams with minor document changes to go through an expedited process, which was of great value to the word-processing department and solved a long-standing problem of work assignments.[2]

to summarize

Several new performance measures have been developed in recent years. In this chapter we discuss one—benchmarking. Benchmarking is the process of comparing a unit's performance with other units either within or outside the company. Benchmarking can result in marked improvements in productivity, costs, and revenue.

3

Understand the concept of differential costs and revenues, and be able to identify those costs and revenues that are relevant to making product and process decisions.

DIFFERENTIAL COSTS AND REVENUES

differential costs Future costs that change as a result of a decision.

Evaluation of products and processes usually leads to consideration of alternative courses of actions. For example, the evaluation of a particular product may lead a company to believe that it must expand capacity, outsource production, or even drop a product in favor of an alternative product. It may also result in the company deciding to buy a competitor. In the rest of this chapter, we provide examples of how products and processes are evaluated to make better decisions. These concepts are probably best understood by examining examples of decisions to change, add, or drop products or processes. Before you can understand how evaluation can lead to better product and process decisions, however, a framework is necessary. In building a framework, we will focus mostly on costs and revenues. Do not forget, however, that the evaluation of timeliness and quality must be considered as well. In making decisions about products and processes, the costs and revenues that are different for, and hence relevant to, various alternative courses of action must be identified. When evaluating costs and revenues, analysis of **differential costs** and revenues is the key to properly evaluating both products and processes. As discussed in Chapter 1 of management accounting, the differential costs of a decision are the future costs that change as a result of that decision. For example, recently GM estimated that it would cost nearly $4 billion to close some plants and lay off some employees. By doing so, however, it expected to save hundreds of millions of dollars in future years by being more efficient. The term *differential* is also commonly applied to future revenues that will be affected by these decisions.

To illustrate, assume that you own the Speedy Print Shop. A customer wants you to print 500 copies of a one-page flyer immediately. To price the job, you need to know what it will cost. Exhibit 8-2 includes both an incorrect and a correct analysis of the available cost data. The left column (the incorrect analysis) includes all costs; the right column (the correct analysis) includes only the differential costs. We will explain each cost and how we determined whether it was relevant to the pricing decision.

1. *Paper.* The cost of the paper for the printing job is differential because it is a future expenditure that must be made as a result of the decision to accept the order. In a sense, therefore, it is a cost that changes as a result of the decision. If we do not accept the order, we do not need to purchase the paper. Note also that paper is a variable cost—its total cost increases proportionately to the size of the order.

2 These examples were taken from "Benefits and Values of Benchmarking," Best Practices, LLC, 6320 Quadrangle Drive, Suite 200, Chapel Hill, NC 27514.

exhibit 8-2 Speedy Print Shop Rush Order Analysis

	Incorrect Analysis (all costs)	Correct Analysis (differential costs)
Variable costs:		
Paper (500 at 10¢)	$ 50	$ 50
Printing labor (5 hours at $16; 5 hours at $24)	80	120
Fixed costs:		
Printing plates	100	100
Printing press depreciation (5 hours at $10)	50	
Manager's salary (5 hours at $20)	100	
Totals	$380	$270

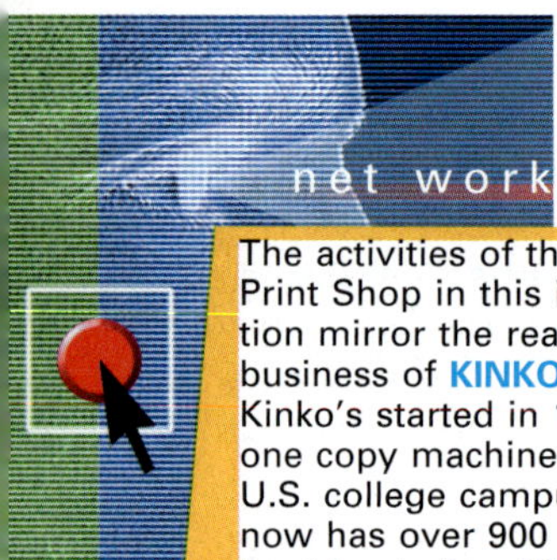

The activities of the Speedy Print Shop in this illustration mirror the real-life business of KINKO's. Kinko's started in 1970 with one copy machine near a U.S. college campus and now has over 900 branches in at least nine different countries. Access Kinko's Web site at http://www.kinkos.com and identify which college campus Kinko's opened next to and in which countries it now operates.

2. *Printing labor.* Accepting the order will require a future expenditure for additional labor to operate the press. This again obviously represents a change from the existing situation—without the order, we would not incur the cost of labor. Also, this example illustrates another important point about measuring future costs. Since this rush order will have to be printed during overtime hours, the appropriate labor rate is time and a half. (Given a normal hourly rate of $16, the labor rate for this job would be $24.) It is easy to overlook this and assume that the normal labor cost per hour ($16) applies. The differential cost of $24 per hour that will be incurred as a result of the decision, however, is the appropriate cost to use. Like paper, printing labor is a variable cost that increases in total proportionately to the size of the order.
3. *Printing plates.* New printing plates must be prepared for this order, so it is a future expenditure that changes as a result of the decision to accept the order. The important point here is that printing plates are a fixed cost (you can print as many copies as you want from the same set of plates), but the cost is still differential because it is an additional expenditure for this order. A common but incorrect assumption is that only variable costs are relevant (that fixed costs do not have to be taken into account). This is not the case. All future costs that change as a result of accepting the order, whether fixed or variable, are differential.
4. *Printing press depreciation.* This cannot be a differential cost because it is not a future cost (depreciation is an allocation of a past cost), and it does not change as a result of the decision to accept the order. (Assuming a time-based depreciation method, the press depreciates over time, whether or not it is used.) Costs such as depreciation, which are past costs and do not change, are referred to as **sunk costs**. No decision can change past, or sunk, costs; they are never relevant to a decision.
5. *Manager's salary.* Although the manager's salary is a future cost (we will be paying for future services), it will be paid whether or not the order is accepted. Consequently, the manager's salary is not a differential cost; it does not change as a result of the decision to accept this order.

sunk costs Costs, such as depreciation, that are past costs and do not change as the result of a future decision.

The differential costs for this rush order total $270. This means that in pricing the job, Speedy Print Shop will be losing money unless it charges at least this much. Similarly, if Speedy Print Shop declines the job at an offered price of $300 because that price is less than the incorrectly calculated differential cost of $380, the company will experience an opportunity cost (loss) of $30.

To further illustrate the role of differential and sunk costs in making a product or process decision, we assume that Dixon Wholesale Company is thinking of purchasing a delivery truck with an estimated useful life of five years. Following are the costs of acquiring and operating a truck:

Original cost		$10,000
Variable costs per mile:		
Gasoline and oil	$ 0.25	
Repairs and maintenance	0.03	
Tires	0.02	
Total variable costs per mile		$ 0.30
Fixed costs per year:		
Insurance	$ 500	
Licenses	110	
Depreciation expense ($10,000 ÷ 5 years)	2,000	
Total fixed costs per year		$ 2,610

These variable and fixed operating costs are incurred each year the truck is used. However, they are not all differential costs; they are not all relevant to every decision made about the truck. For the following decisions, we identify the differential costs, the sunk costs, and the reason for the classifications.

DECISION 1 Should the truck be purchased? Whether to purchase the truck is really a capital budgeting decision, a topic we discussed in Chapter 4 of management accounting. But the decision is based on differential (future) costs to be incurred if the truck is purchased.

- **Differential costs:** All variable costs (30 cents per mile driven); all fixed costs except depreciation (which is already included in the purchase cost); and the purchase cost ($10,000).
- **Sunk costs:** None.
- **Comment:** All costs except depreciation are differential costs because the truck has not yet been purchased; all costs can be avoided by an alternative decision.

DECISION 2 Let's now jump forward in time two years. The truck has now been owned and used for two years, but it has not been licensed or insured for the current (third) year. Should it be licensed and insured, or should some other means of transportation be used? (Assume for now that the truck will not be sold, even if not used.)

- **Differential costs:** All variable costs (30 cents per mile driven) and some fixed costs (insurance, $500; licenses, $110).
- **Sunk costs:** Remaining book value of the truck ($6,000 at the beginning of the year).
- **Comment:** As soon as the truck is purchased, its cost becomes a sunk cost. During its estimated life, its remaining book value is a sunk cost if we assume, for simplicity, that the truck has no resale value. The company must absorb the cost of the truck either by using the truck (and depreciating its cost each year) or by writing off the entire cost. All costs except depreciation and the remaining book value are, therefore, differential costs.

DECISION 3 The truck has been owned and used for two years and has been licensed and insured for the current (third) year. Should the truck be used for transporting inventory this year? Should other means be arranged?

- **Differential costs:** All variable costs (30 cents per mile driven) and no fixed costs.
- **Sunk costs:** Insurance ($500); licenses ($110); remaining book value ($6,000 at the beginning of the year).
- **Comment:** If insurance and license fees are not refundable, these are sunk costs, as is the remaining book value.

Analysis of the costs that are relevant in making these three decisions should help you understand how differential costs are determined. As you can see, variable costs are *usually* differential; fixed costs are *sometimes* differential; and past costs are *never* differential.

Total Costs versus Differential Costs

total cost The total variable and fixed costs incurred in making a product or providing a service.

In trying to improve performance, managers usually prefer to use the differential-cost approach; that is, they disregard sunk costs and other costs that are the same for each alternative being considered. This approach highlights costs that make a difference, takes less time, and reduces the chance of error in the calculation (fewer numbers reduce the chances for mistakes). In some cases, however, a manager may want to review the **total cost** to ensure that some relevant costs are not overlooked.

To illustrate this total-cost approach, we will assume that Dixon Wholesale Company has another decision to make about its truck.

DECISION 4 The truck has been owned for four years, but it has not yet been licensed or insured for the current (fifth) year. Should the truck be used for the last year of its economic life, or should it be traded for a new truck that will be driven five years?

Pertinent information is presented in the following table:

	Old Truck	New Truck
Original cost	$10,000	$12,500
Current book value	2,000	
Current resale value	1,700	
Resale value at end of year	0	10,000
Variable operating costs	$0.30 per mile	$0.27 per mile
Annual fixed costs:		
Insurance	$ 500	$ 550
Licenses	110	110
Depreciation expense	2,000	2,500
Estimated mileage per year	50,000 miles	50,000 miles

On the basis of this information, the total cost of operating the old truck and the total cost of operating a new truck are shown in Exhibit 8-3.

Note that the total cost of operating the old truck includes the yearly $2,000 depreciation expense. If the new truck is bought, the $2,000 book value of the old truck must still be writ-

exhibit 8-3 Total-Cost Analysis for the Current Year: Keeping the Old Truck versus Selling It and Buying a New Truck*

Total Costs	Old Truck	Difference	New Truck
Variable costs:			
$0.30 × 50,000 miles	$15,000		
$0.27 × 50,000 miles			$13,500
Fixed costs:			
Insurance	500		550
Licenses	110		110
Depreciation expense	2,000		2,500
Book value of old truck to be written off			2,000
Resale value of old truck	0		(1,700)
Total cost	$17,610		$16,960
Difference		$650	

*Be aware that in order to emphasize the total-cost and differential-cost approaches, this analysis ignores the time value of money and related income tax effects, which we discussed in Chapter 4 of management accounting.

ten off. Thus, the $2,000 is a sunk cost and is the same under both alternatives, so it is not relevant to the decision at hand. The current resale value of the old truck, however, is a reduction in cost that will occur only if the new truck is purchased.

Two observations should be made about the total-cost approach to analyzing alternatives. First, it highlights the more attractive alternative in terms of cost only. In our example, the data appear to favor buying a new truck. However, this requires an investment of additional funds, which forces consideration of other factors. Because these factors were covered in Chapter 4 of management accounting, we have tried to keep our example simple by assuming a fair market value of $10,000 for the new truck at the end of one year. This means that the new truck's annual depreciation expense of $2,500 is equal to the difference between its original cost and its resale value after one year. Had the drop in value been greater than the depreciation expense, the excess would have been an additional cost of using the new truck during its first year.

Second, the total-cost approach is time-consuming because it involves differential costs as well as costs that are the same for all alternatives under consideration. With the differential-cost approach, only costs that are different need to be accumulated and analyzed. Thus, the costs of licensing both trucks and the $2,000 book value of the old truck to be depreciated or written off would not be considered. Exhibit 8-4 provides a list of the differential costs taken from Exhibit 8-3.

Although the differential-cost approach accumulates comparative costs and revenues that are different from those of the total-cost approach, it does not alter the relative attractiveness of the alternatives. Both the total and the differential analyses show a savings of $650 if the new truck is purchased. Thus, the acquisition of the new truck should bring future benefits to the company.

It should be noted that in both the total analysis and the differential analysis, the resale value of the old truck was treated as a negative cost. Instead, it could have been treated as a differential revenue from which the differential costs had been subtracted. It should also be noted that since both methods of analysis provide the same answer, it is likely that a firm will use the differential analysis method to save time in the collection and analysis of data. The total-cost revenue method will likely be used only when there is considerable uncertainty about whether all differential costs and revenues have been accounted for in the differential-cost approach.

Qualitative Considerations

As has been the case with all management accounting decisions discussed in this book, the effect of product or process decisions on the time and quality with which products or services can be delivered must be considered. In deciding whether to accept the rush print job, for example, Speedy Print Shop must consider the possibility that while accepting the job might lead to additional business, it could affect the quality of printing services to other customers. Likewise, if accepting the rush print job will slow down service to other customers, accepting the job may not be a good decision, no matter how financially attractive it seems to be.

In making a final decision, the cost and qualitative factors may lead you to the same conclusion. If they do not, you must decide what to do to enhance your company's overall profitability

exhibit 8-4 Differential-Cost and Revenue Analysis for the Current Year: Operating the Old Truck versus Selling It and Buying a New Truck

Differential Costs and Revenues	Old Truck	New Truck	Difference
Variable costs	$15,000	$13,500	$ 1,500
Insurance	500	550	(50)
Depreciation expense		2,500	(2,500)
Resale value of old truck	0	(1,700)	1,700
Total differential costs and revenues	$15,500	$14,850	$ 650

in the future. You might decide, for example, to accept the rush print job for an amount near or even below your differential cost to ensure that you get the order.

---

to summarize

Differential costs are the future costs that change as a result of a decision. Differential costs and revenues are those costs and revenues that are relevant to decisions. Sunk costs are never relevant because they are past costs that cannot be changed. Care must be exercised when estimating future costs because past cost relationships may not continue into the future. Some future costs may not be differential because they do not change as a result of a decision. Both variable and fixed costs may be differential.

There are two approaches to analyzing alternatives: total cost and differential cost. With the total-cost approach, all costs (including sunk costs) are accumulated. The differential-cost approach excludes sunk costs and all common costs, dealing only with costs that are different for the alternatives being considered. Once the quantitative analysis has been completed, qualitative factors must be considered.

4
Identify several examples of product and process evaluation decisions, and be able to analyze and select the best alternative for each example.

special order An order that may be priced below the normal selling price in order to utilize excess capacity and thereby contribute to company profits.

EXAMPLES OF PRODUCT AND PROCESS EVALUATION DECISIONS

The concept of differential costs applies to all evaluation decisions covered in this and the next chapter. In the remainder of this chapter, we will apply differential costing to several examples of short-term product and process evaluation decisions. First, we will consider the issue of evaluating special orders. A **special order** is an order that may be priced below the normal price in order to utilize excess capacity, thus contributing to company profits. We will look at special orders from the perspective of both the buyer and the seller. Second, we will look at the decisions, based on evaluation of products, competition, and the like, of exiting or entering a market (dropping or adding plants, segments, product lines, geographic territories, etc.). Third, we will look at how an organization might evaluate the use of scarce resources, such as limited raw materials in a manufacturing firm, limited shelf space in a merchandising company, and limited expertise or labor in a service firm. Fourth, we will consider how firms evaluate the pricing of regular products and services. In the expanded material section of the chapter, we will discuss the theory of constraints and how focusing on critical, constrained resources can result in more efficient manufacturing processes. On the text Web site at **http://albrecht.swcollege.com**, you will find a discussion of another major decision for some companies: deciding how manufacturers of joint products decide at what stage to sell the products.

STOP & THINK In addition to the specific examples covered in this chapter, identify two other types of decisions that organizations make that would involve evaluating products and/or processes.

Special Orders

In the opening scenario, we mentioned that SATURN is introducing a new sports utility vehicle (SUV) as part of its effort to become a full-line automobile brand. In making SUVs, Saturn will have to decide which parts and services to outsource to suppliers and which to make itself. TOYOTA, for example, makes only 30% of its automobile parts while GM makes 65% of its parts. The decision to outsource the making of parts or services is the first decision we cover in this chapter. It would be made after calculating all the costs and other factors involved in outsourcing versus making the parts internally. These types of special order decisions can involve long-term purchase and sales arrangements (as would be the case with Saturn) or only one-time orders (as in the Speedy Print Shop example). In either case, both the buyer (Saturn in the opening scenario) and the seller (the parts manufacturer) have decisions to make. These decisions can be outlined as in the following diagram:

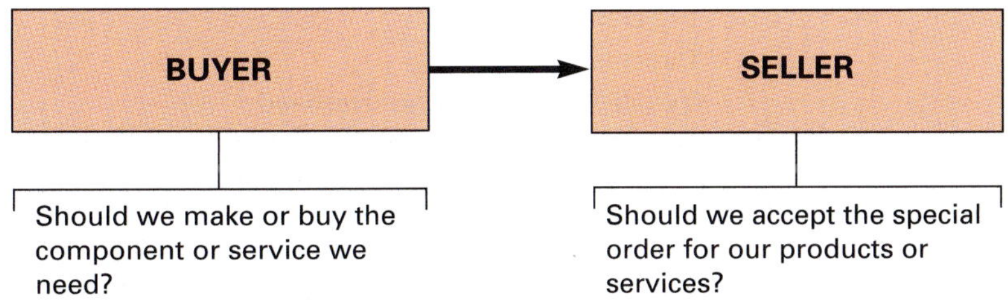

As the diagram shows, special orders can involve products or services. For example, in manufacturing companies, the special order might involve buying parts on a one-time basis from other companies because of a sudden surge in demand; or it could involve a company outsourcing or purchasing its internal audit services from a CPA firm. When parts are involved, both companies are manufacturing firms. When a service (such as internal auditing) is involved, the buyer may be a manufacturing, merchandising, or service company, but the provider is always a service company.

We will first look at special order decisions from the perspective of the buyer. Then, we will look at special order decisions from the perspective of the seller. In both cases, we will examine buying and selling products and services.

SPECIAL ORDERS—THE BUYER'S DECISION Many companies outsource virtually everything. Many Internet businesses, for example, are "virtual outsourcers." They take orders from customers and relay those orders to manufacturers, which, in turn, ship the products directly to the customers. Other organizations make or provide most of their products and services internally. In the following section, we describe the factors companies must consider when deciding whether to make or to buy products and services.

Making or Buying Manufactured Parts Companies, such as Toyota and Saturn, must decide which products and services they will produce and offer internally and which ones they will outsource or buy from outsiders. With respect to manufactured products, if a product consists of a number of parts, management must decide for each component whether to produce it or purchase it from an outside supplier. Over time, and based on a consideration of the relevant quantitative and qualitative factors, management develops a long-term policy regarding the use of its facilities to produce components for its products.

The fact that a long-term policy has been established does not mean that the issue is permanently closed. In fact, management is always reconsidering its decisions and looking for new ways to save money, improve quality, or speed up manufacturing and delivery processes. If a firm has idle facilities, for example, management may wish to find a use for those facilities. One possibility is to manufacture components that are normally purchased. Whether this decision is wise depends not only on cost considerations but also on a number of qualitative factors, such as the likely effect on the regular source of supply, the company's ability to produce a high-quality component, speed of delivery, and management's interest in keeping workers on the payroll. Thus, even though a firm has a long-term policy of purchasing some components and producing others, certain situations may require decisions that alter that policy.

Assuming that the qualitative factors favor the use of idle facilities to produce the part, what costs are relevant to a make-or-buy decision? In general, the purchase cost and all other costs that can be avoided if the part is manufactured are differential costs. Any cost that will be incurred regardless of whether the part is purchased or manufactured is not a differential cost and is irrelevant.

To illustrate how the differential costs in such a decision are identified, we assume that Ritter Manufacturing Company has excess capacity that could be used in producing wheel bearings. The accounting department has compiled the following projected total-cost figures for producing the bearings:

	Cost per Unit	Costs for 1,000 Units
Direct materials	$ 3.00	$ 3,000
Direct labor	8.00	8,000
Variable manufacturing overhead	4.00	4,000
Fixed manufacturing overhead, direct	2.50	2,500
Fixed manufacturing overhead, indirect	5.00	5,000*
Total costs	$22.50	$22,500

*Total indirect fixed costs are the same under both alternatives.

The company has been buying this bearing from a regular supplier in 1,000-unit quantities at a price of $19 per unit. Should Ritter continue to buy or start making the bearings? To answer this question, management must identify the differential costs of each alternative, taking into account any additional resources that may be needed, as well as alternative uses for the currently idle facilities. Two possible situations are presented here.

SITUATION 1 The currently idle facilities have no alternative uses. If the idle facilities do not have any practical alternative use, the opportunity cost is zero. With no opportunity cost, the differential costs would be the costs strictly associated with manufacturing (direct labor, direct materials, and so on).

The costs of the two alternatives can be presented on a total-cost or a differential-cost basis, as shown in Exhibit 8-5. Although each analysis produces different total costs, both demonstrate that the firm would save $1,500 per 1,000 units ($1.50 per unit) by making the component rather than buying it. The company's final decision would depend, of course, on whether there were negative qualitative factors that would, in the opinion of management, more than offset the $1.50 unit-cost advantage of making the part.

SITUATION 2 The idle facilities can be rented for $4,000 if they are not used to manufacture bearings. Management estimates that, if the facilities are used for manufacturing, 1,000 wheel bearings could be manufactured during this time.

In this case, the opportunity cost of producing the bearings is $4,000, or an average cost of $4 per unit ($4,000 ÷ 1,000 units). This opportunity cost is an important consideration in the firm's decision whether to buy or make the part, as shown in Exhibit 8-6. When the opportunity cost is considered, the cost of producing the part is $2,500 more than the cost of buying it.

exhibit 8-5 Analyses of the Costs of Using Idle Facilities (Situation 1)

	Total-Cost Analysis (per 1,000 Units)		Differential-Cost Analysis (per 1,000 Units)	
	Buy	Make	Buy	Make
Purchase cost	$19,000		$19,000	
Direct materials		$ 3,000		$ 3,000
Direct labor		8,000		8,000
Variable manufacturing overhead		4,000		4,000
Fixed manufacturing overhead:				
Direct		2,500		2,500
Indirect	5,000	5,000		
Total cost	$24,000	$22,500	$19,000	$17,500
Difference	$1,500		$1,500	

exhibit 8-6 The Effect of an Opportunity Cost on Analyses (Situation 2)

	Total-Cost Analysis (per 1,000 Units)		Differential-Cost Analysis (per 1,000 Units)	
	Buy	Make	Buy	Make
Purchase cost	$19,000		$19,000	
Direct materials		$ 3,000		$ 3,000
Direct labor		8,000		8,000
Variable manufacturing overhead		4,000		4,000
Fixed manufacturing overhead:				
Direct		2,500		2,500
Indirect	5,000	5,000		
Opportunity cost, rental		4,000		4,000
Total cost	$24,000	$26,500	$19,000	$21,500
Difference	$2,500		$2,500	

Unless there are quality, time, or other qualitative factors that override this cost, Ritter should buy the bearing and rent the idle facilities. Remember, the essence of the make-or-buy problem is management's desire to achieve the best utilization of existing facilities in the short term.

Because opportunity costs do not represent actual transactions, they are not recorded in the accounts. Yet they are always significant in the decision-making process because each situation has at least two alternatives. Thus, opportunity costs provide a good illustration of why a manager cannot rely solely on the data collected for external financial reports.

Purchasing Services or Providing Them Internally In recent years, companies have not only outsourced product parts, but more and more they are also outsourcing services such as cafeteria service, internal auditing, garbage removal, payroll accounting, legal services, and even basic accounting. In deciding whether to acquire services or provide them internally, companies go through the same kind of analysis as if they were buying products. That is, they consider the differential costs of each alternative, as well as qualitative factors, such as the quality of the service, whether space exists to house the service, whether services can be delivered on a timely basis, and management's interest in keeping workers on the payroll. Assuming management believes it can acquire high-quality services both within and outside the company, what costs are relevant to the purchase-or-provide decisions? Costs that will be incurred regardless of whether the service is purchased or provided internally are not differential costs and are irrelevant to the decision.

To illustrate how the differential costs are identified, we assume that Ritter Manufacturing Company is considering outsourcing its internal audit function. The following annual cost information relating to internal auditing is available.

Costs of Internal Auditing Department	
Salaries of internal audit employees	$1,200,000
Travel costs	1,400,000
Training costs	100,000
Depreciation on internal audit offices	50,000
Utilities for internal audit offices	40,000
Computers, software, and supplies	150,000
Other variable costs	75,000
Total costs of internal audit	$3,015,000

business environment essay

The Outsourcing Rage in America In recent years, organizations have outsourced more and more of their manufacturing and administrative functions. **GENERAL MOTORS**, for example, has outsourced its accounting functions. The **U.S. POST OFFICE** has outsourced much of its sales function and has asked supplier firms to teach customers how they can use the Post Office to ship their products. Everyone seems to be outsourcing everything, keeping only core activities in-house.

One exception to this trend is **WALT DISNEY**. Recognizing that it has a strong brand name, Disney decided that it could effectively sell clothes and other merchandise to customers. It had to decide whether to own its own retail outlets or enter into licensing agreements with other retailers. If it chose licensing, it would face some risk that contractual protections would be insufficient to prevent the licensee from degrading the value of the brand or from attempting to extract money from Disney by threatening to do so. On the other hand, entering into a new line of business, retail stores, where the company had no expertise was problematic as well. Disney chose to develop its own stores, but to enter into a long-term promotional relationship with **MCDONALD'S**.

Source: Information obtained from **http://as3.lib.byu.edu:8686/universe/document?_ansset=GeHauKO-EVYRMsSEVYRUUBRI** (accessed on September 29, 2000).

fyi

In recent years, major CPA firms have become professional service firms and are offering all kinds of new services. In fact, in other countries where accountants can practice law, three of the world's largest law firms are "Big 5" CPA firms. One of the fasting-growing services being offered by CPA firms is internal audit services for major corporations, such as the example in this chapter.

A CPA firm has offered to perform the internal audit services for $3,100,000 per year. You have determined that if internal audit services were contracted out to the CPA firm, the space currently used by the internal auditors could be used by the purchasing department, which is currently occupying rented space in a nearby city. The rent paid for offices used by the purchasing department is $10,000 per month.

Should Ritter continue to have its own internal audit department, or should it outsource its internal audit function to the CPA firm? From a strictly financial point of view, Ritter should not outsource, as shown below.

Cost of outsourcing:		
CPA firm cost		$3,100,000
Rent saved by relocating purchasing department ($10,000 per month × 12 months)		(120,000)
Net cost of outsourcing		$2,980,000
Cost of maintaining internal audit department:		
Total cost of internal audit department		$3,015,000
Less: nondifferential costs (incurred under either alternative)		
Depreciation expense	$50,000	
Utilities	40,000	
Total nondifferential costs		(90,000)
Differential cost of maintaining internal audit department		$2,925,000
Excess cost incurred by outsourcing internal auditing		$ 55,000

Of course, the one-year cost analysis is really an incomplete analysis. In making the decision, management must determine what the future costs of each alternative will be. If, for example, management can lock into a five-year commitment of $3,100,000 annually and it believes costs of keeping the internal audit department will rise $100,000 per year, from a cost perspective, the company may want to outsource even though the cost is higher in the current year.

In addition to costs, management must consider many other factors. For example, will the outside CPA firm provide audit services of the same or higher quality as those provided by the internal auditors? Having good internal audit services is important because the auditors can help ensure the efficiency and effectiveness of operations, assure that controls are implemented and

> **caution**
>
> Be careful to consider all differential costs and revenues in making evaluation decisions and to exclude the nondifferential costs. For example, in this internal audit example, if depreciation and utilities (which will be incurred whether or not internal audit services are outsourced) are not considered, an incorrect decision will be made.

followed, and even prevent and detect fraud and other problems. Quality of services is very important in an area like internal auditing, where it is difficult for management to judge whether the company is getting value for its money. Management would also want to consider other factors: (1) Will the CPA firm be able to provide the services in the long run? (2) Can the company use the displaced internal audit employees in other positions, or is the company willing to lay off employees? (3) Will outsourcing the internal audit services affect the cost of other services received by the company (for example, will outsourcing internal audit services reduce the cost of the external audit or the cost of cafeteria or other services)? (4) If internal auditing was used as a management trainee development area (as it is in many companies), are there other efficient and effective ways to train future managers?

SPECIAL ORDERS—THE SELLER'S DECISION If a seller can sell its services profitably at market prices, the decision is an easy one—provide the service. After all, that is the purpose of being in business. Where the difficulty comes is in deciding whether to reduce the normal price of a product or service in order to obtain a special order. Typical situations involving a possible price reduction when idle capacity exists are:

1. A manufacturer sells products under its own brand name, as well as to retail chain stores for sale under the chain's brand name.
2. A firm, such as a building contractor or an equipment manufacturer, sells its products or services in a competitive bidding situation.
3. A firm sells a product under distress conditions, for instance, when there has been a sharp decline in demand for its products because of a new product offered by a competitor.
4. A product has significant sales potential with a foreign distributor, whose market demands lower prices than those in the United States.
5. A provider of a service has extra capacity and has the opportunity to sign a large contract, at a lower-than-normal price, that would consume the excess capacity.

In each of these situations, we assume that a firm has available capacity that can be utilized to fill the special order. The relevant costs for this decision are the additional, or incremental, costs necessary to produce and deliver the special order. Management must therefore know the incremental costs. This information will indicate the lowest price at which the special order will begin to contribute to the firm's profits.

To illustrate, we will assume that Kent Electronics, which usually sells hand calculators for $19, receives an order from a large department store chain for 10,000 calculators at a price of $13 each. The requested calculators are to be sold under the store's brand name. Kent currently has excess capacity that could be used in producing enough calculators to fill the order. Should the company accept the order?

The answer to this question does not, of course, depend on cost and price factors alone. An obvious consideration, for example, would be whether the order would result in a significant loss of sales of the company's own brand of calculators. Let's assume that this is not a problem.

If the accounting department presents the data on a total-cost basis, the manager might erroneously reject the order. It appears from the following that the firm would have a loss if it accepted the special order:

Special Order for Calculators—Total-Cost Approach

Sales price		$ 13
Manufacturing costs:		
Direct materials	$3	
Direct labor	4	
Manufacturing overhead	9	
Total manufacturing costs		16
Loss per unit		$ (3)
Number of units in order		× 10,000
Expected loss exclusive of selling and administrative expenses		$(30,000)

It is not unusual for managers to base decisions on total-cost information because the data are readily available, having been collected in order to prepare financial statements and income tax returns. Unfortunately, such information may lead management to the wrong conclusion—in this case, to reject the order.

The only differential costs, however, are those future costs that change if the order is accepted. These include the variable product costs as well as the direct fixed costs. Fixed costs that are incurred regardless of whether the order is accepted should not be considered. The following analysis, prepared on a differential-cost basis, shows that Kent Electronics should accept the order.

Special Order for Calculators—Differential-Cost Approach

Sales price		$ 13
Variable and differential fixed costs:		
Direct materials	$3	
Direct labor	4	
Variable manufacturing overhead costs	2	
Differential fixed overhead costs	1	
Variable selling and administrative expenses	1	
Total variable and differential fixed costs		11
Remaining margin to cover fixed costs and provide a profit		$ 2
Number of units in order		×10,000
Expected contribution to fixed costs and profit		$ 20,000

These data assume that additional fixed costs of $1 per unit will be incurred if the order is accepted. If no additional fixed costs would be incurred, the margin would increase to $3. The analysis clearly suggests that, from a financial point of view, management should accept the order. This approach identifies not only the differential costs but also a price floor (the total variable and differential fixed costs of $11) below which management should probably not accept an order. As long as the price exceeds total variable and differential fixed costs, the firm will increase its profits by accepting the order. This analysis assumes that the company has no better alternative uses for its excess capacity and that special sales by the chain will have no adverse effect on Kent's normal sales. But what if regular customers hear about this special order and insist on lower prices, thus disrupting the normal pricing structure? Or, what if filling the special order will have an adverse effect on the quality of current products or the speed with which products can be offered to regular customers? These and other qualitative factors must also be considered.

A manager must also consider whether acceptance of such an order would be a violation of the Robinson-Patman Act. This legislation, enacted in 1936, prohibits firms from quoting different prices to competing customers for the same goods unless differences in price can be attributed to differences in cost. In the case of Kent Electronics, the sale is probably legal because the calculators are to be sold under the store's brand name, and the department store will assume all advertising costs.

The differential-cost approach to pricing can also be used in explaining why theater tickets are less expensive for matinees than for evening performances, why airline economy fares are less expensive than business-class fares, and why it is cheaper to make telephone calls at night and on weekends than on weekdays. If there is excess capacity that can be used to provide a service or make a product that will generate more revenue than the variable cost of providing the service or making the product, the firm will increase its profits by the amount of the margin remaining after deducting differential costs.

A few words of caution are in order when making these types of decisions. First, in some situations, there may also be some additional fixed costs that are relevant to the pricing decision. Second, a company must not accept too many orders that barely cover variable costs, or it will not be able to cover all its fixed costs. Third, using all extra capacity to fill a special order at a lower-than-normal price may prevent a company from being able to accept additional work at higher prices in the future. Fourth, accepting a special order may force a company to cut corners with normal customers, resulting in lower-quality products or services to those customers or decreasing the speed at which other customers are served.

to summarize

In choosing whether to make or buy a component or service, management must compare the differential costs of making the part or providing the service (including the opportunity costs of alternative uses of the facilities) with the cost of purchasing (outsourcing) the part or service. Qualitative factors must also be considered because they may be significant enough to reverse a decision based only on quantitative considerations. In deciding whether to accept special orders, the differential-cost approach is appropriate. Using this approach, only variable costs and differential fixed costs are considered.

Exiting or Entering a Market

The decision of whether to exit or enter a market is usually based on careful evaluation, although companies seem to be buying and selling businesses quite often these days. We will first consider the decision of whether to exit a market and then the decision of whether to enter a market.

EXITING A MARKET When a segment (product or line of products) is losing money, management must decide whether to drop it, as PRICELINE.COM did with its grocery and gasoline business. Such decisions are particularly difficult because the differential costs are not easy to identify, and this can lead to analyses based on invalid assumptions, as the following example demonstrates.

To illustrate, we will assume that Augusta Retail Company is thinking of closing one of its stores. The question of the store's value arose because of the July financial results for the company's three stores (amounts are in thousands):

	Store 1	Store 2	Store 3	Total
Sales revenue	$250,000	$90,000	$60,000	$400,000
Cost of goods sold	170,000	40,000	30,000	240,000
Gross margin	$ 80,000	$50,000	$30,000	$160,000
Operating expenses	55,000	30,000	35,000	120,000
Net income (or loss)	$ 25,000	$20,000	$ (5,000)	$ 40,000

If Store 3 is closed, it would seem reasonable to assume that Augusta Retail Company's profits will increase by $5 million, as shown here.

	Store 1	Store 2	Total
Sales revenue	$250,000	$90,000	$340,000
Cost of goods sold	170,000	40,000	210,000
Gross margin	$ 80,000	$50,000	$130,000
Operating expenses	55,000	30,000	85,000
Net income	$ 25,000	$20,000	$ 45,000

business environment essay

Dropping a Product Line In October 2000, **CIRCUIT CITY** suddenly decided that it would no longer sell major home appliances, such as washers, dryers, and dishwashers. Why would it make such a dramatic decision when sales of major appliances totaled $1.7 billion in 1999? According to Circuit City strategists, appliances were dropped for two reasons: (1) other companies such as **SEARS**, with 35% of the market; **HOME DEPOT**, quickly becoming a billion-dollar player; and **LOWE'S**, the number two seller, were too aggressive in their pricing and competitive strategies; and (2) softening volume, lower margins, and dim prospects for appliances were discouraging, especially compared to the higher margins on consumer electronic products. In dropping appliances, Circuit City embarked on a three-year plan to remodel virtually all of its 616 stores to concentrate exclusively on consumer electronics and home office equipment. The plan would cost about $1.2 billion and entail laying off about 1,000 employees. The price of Circuit City's stock dropped by 7% soon after the plan was announced.

Source: Information obtained from **http://library.northernlight.com/NC20000816060003696.html?inid=d1xbRwcTFkB5D34VBm** (accessed on October 2, 2000).

This analysis is based on three assumptions:

1. That all costs shown are differential and therefore relevant to the decision. In other words, there are no joint costs (costs that are common to two or more stores).
2. That the sales of the other stores will not be affected by dropping Store 3.
3. That no qualitative factors have a bearing on the decision.

Before closing Store 3, the company's general manager should check the validity of these assumptions. For simplicity, suppose that the second and third assumptions are valid, and that only the first assumption needs verification. First, the accounting department must separate the total costs of each store into variable costs, direct fixed costs, and indirect (or unavoidable) fixed costs. With this new information, the accounting department might prepare the following modified report for July (amounts are in thousands).

business environment essay

Avon Cosmetic Products in Department Stores? One of the most important decisions a company faces is what distribution channels to use to sell its products. Take Avon cosmetics, for example. **AVON PRODUCTS** is the world's largest direct seller of cosmetics. The company has sold its products through door-to-door sales representatives for the past 115 years. "Ding-dong, Avon calling," which debuted in 1954, is one of the best-known commercials and sales pitches. Now, for the first time, Avon will begin selling products in department stores. The Avon line will be called "Becoming," as in "Avon lets me become the woman that I am." Some 400 new products are being developed for the new line that will be sold in about 150 to 200 **J.C. PENNEY** and **SEARS, ROEBUCK** stores beginning in summer 2001.

Avon's retail strategy is part of its plan to reach new customers. Although Avon is the world's leading

	Store 1	Store 2	Store 3	Total
Sales revenue	$250,000	$90,000	$60,000	$400,000
Variable costs	190,000	50,000	40,000	280,000
Contribution margin	$ 60,000	$40,000	$20,000	$120,000
Direct fixed costs	20,000	15,000	18,000	53,000
Segment margin	$ 40,000	$25,000	$ 2,000	$ 67,000
Indirect fixed costs (not allocated)				27,000
Net income				$ 40,000

The manager can use this modified report to determine whether Store 3 made a positive contribution toward covering the indirect (unavoidable) fixed costs. In looking at this modified report, the manager would immediately see that the segment margin for Store 3 is a positive $2 million. This means that Store 3 is contributing $2 million to the company's overall profit. Thus, if Store 3 is dropped, profits will decrease by $2 million unless another store with greater profit potential is added or Store 3 can be sold to another company. To illustrate the potential decline in profits if Store 3 is dropped, the manager might ask the accounting department to prepare a report to indicate what the company's July financial results would show without Store 3. This pro-forma report would show the following information (amounts are in thousands):

	Store 1	Store 2	Total
Sales revenue	$250,000	$90,000	$340,000
Variable costs	190,000	50,000	240,000
Contribution margin	$ 60,000	$40,000	$100,000
Direct fixed costs	20,000	15,000	35,000
Segment margin	$ 40,000	$25,000	$ 65,000
Indirect fixed costs (not allocated)			27,000
Net income			$ 38,000

Although the original report suggested that profits would increase by $5 million if Store 3 were dropped, total profits would actually decrease by $2 million ($40 million − $38 million). The reason is that Store 3 is generating revenues that are $2 million greater than differential costs (variable costs and avoidable fixed costs). This analysis suggests that Store 3 should not be

direct seller of beauty and related products with sales of $5.3 billion in 1999, the company believes that it is missing sales to women who prefer to buy cosmetics in stores. The new line will be priced significantly higher than Avon's core direct selling brand, but well below prestige brands. For example, the new line may charge $7.50 for a tube of lipstick—higher than the $3 charged by Avon's core brand but lower than the $14 charged for most department store brands. Although the new distribution strategy may reach new customers, some people believe it will alienate committed, long-time, door-to-door sales representatives who have been the bread-and-butter sales force of the company. Only time will tell if the new distribution process is a good one.

Source: Information obtained from http://www.businessweek.com/reprints/00-38/b3699003.htm.

dropped, unless it can be replaced by another store or business that will contribute more than $2 million to cover unavoidable indirect fixed costs. (Obviously, we have not considered any sales price Augusta could receive from selling Store 3. Any money received from selling Store 3 would need to be deducted from the $2 million annual contribution Store 3 is making toward covering indirect costs.)

ENTERING A MARKET The considerations involved in deciding whether to enter a market are quite similar to those when deciding whether or not to exit a market. From a financial perspective, if adding a product line (segment) will contribute to the income of a firm, it is generally a good decision. The contribution can come in several forms. First, entering a new market can reduce the current cost of doing business. For example, assume that Augusta is considering purchasing a wholesale distribution company that will allow the company to buy directly from manufacturers, rather than from other wholesalers, when acquiring merchandise for its stores. Even if the new wholesale company is not profitable on its own, if it could reduce Augusta's costs enough so that overall profits are higher, the decision to buy might be a good one. Buying a new company or entering a new market could increase overall company profits by having the new segment cover some of the indirect fixed costs now being borne entirely by existing businesses. From a financial perspective, the important point to consider is whether total profits will be higher or lower after the purchase.

In addition to the financial considerations, organizations consider the effects on quality and time to deliver products to customers when deciding whether to enter a market. For example, suppose a small company has superior-quality products, manufacturing knowledge, or other attributes that could enhance the quality of the organization's products. Would it be wise to buy this smaller company even if the purchase doesn't increase overall short-term profits? Probably so. Or, what if a company occupies a strategic location for serving an organization's customers and buying the company would allow the organization to deliver its products more quickly to customers? Would buying the strategically located company be a good decision even if short-term overall profits aren't increased? Again, probably so. Both purchases would allow the organization to serve its customers better by increasing quality and decreasing delivery time. Hopefully, the result of both purchases would be a larger market share and higher profits in the long run. Unfortunately, it is hard to quantify by how much quality and/or delivery time must improve before a purchase is a good one. Because quality and time decisions are subjective, we will focus on the short-term financial considerations in deciding whether to enter a market. You should realize, however, that quality and time considerations are very important, and in considering some purchases, they may be the overriding factors that outweigh short-term financial considerations.

To illustrate entering a new market, assume that Augusta Retail Company now has only two stores. Further, assume that it is considering purchasing the wholesale company just discussed. The following data are available for Augusta Retail Company prior to making the purchase (amounts are in thousands):

	Store 1	Store 2	Total
Sales revenue	$250,000	$90,000	$340,000
Cost of goods sold	170,000	40,000	210,000
Other variable costs	20,000	10,000	30,000
Contribution margin	$ 60,000	$40,000	$100,000
Direct fixed costs	20,000	15,000	35,000
Segment margin	$ 40,000	$25,000	$ 65,000
Indirect fixed costs (not allocated)			27,000
Net income			$ 38,000

As these data show, Augusta currently makes a net income of $38 million. Now, assume that Augusta can purchase a wholesale company that will allow Augusta to buy directly from manufacturers, thus decreasing its cost of goods sold by 30%. However, the wholesale company is currently losing $10 million per year. Should Augusta buy the wholesale company? The following analysis shows that, from a financial perspective, buying the wholesale company would be a good decision (again, amounts are in thousands).

Effect on Current Stores

	Store 1		Store 2		Total (before and after purchase)		Wholesale Company	Total (including wholesale company)
	Before	After	Before	After	Before	After		
Sales revenue	$250,000	$250,000	$90,000	$90,000	$340,000	$340,000	$110,000	$450,000
Cost of goods sold	170,000	119,000[1]	40,000	28,000[2]	210,000	147,000	70,000	217,000
Other variable costs	20,000	20,000	10,000	10,000	30,000	30,000	15,000	45,000
Contribution margin	$ 60,000	$111,000	$40,000	$52,000	$100,000	$163,000	$ 25,000	$188,000
Direct fixed costs	20,000	20,000	15,000	15,000	35,000	35,000	35,000	70,000
Segment margin	$ 40,000	$ 91,000	$25,000	$37,000	$ 65,000	$128,000	$ (10,000)	$118,000
Indirect fixed costs (not allocated)					27,000	27,000	—	27,000
Net income					$ 38,000	$101,000	$ (10,000)	$ 91,000

[1]$170,000 − (0.3 × $170,000) = $119,000.
[2]$40,000 − (0.3 × $40,000) = $28,000.

fyi

Pick up practically any business newspaper or periodical and you'll read about companies exiting or entering markets. For example, the front page of the November 6, 2000 *Wall Street Journal* carried stories about VIACOM agreeing to buy BET, the nation's biggest African American–controlled media company; PEPSICO's offer to purchase QUAKER OATS; and the plans of BANK OF AMERICA, IBM, and PRUDENTIAL to purchase stakes in a Web firm that helps link tenants directly with landlords.

This analysis shows that even though the wholesale company is losing $10 million per year, purchasing the wholesale company will increase overall company profits by $53 million ($91 million − $38 million). Of course, this elaborate analysis really wasn't necessary since many costs (other variable costs, direct fixed costs, and indirect fixed costs) stayed the same. In fact, the only differential costs were the decrease in cost of goods sold (facilitated by being able to buy directly from manufacturers instead of wholesalers) and the $10 million loss the wholesale company incurs. Focusing only on the differential costs, you can see that the net income of the company would be increased by $53 million upon buying the wholesale company (numbers are in thousands).

Differential Costs of Deciding to Enter a Market

Decrease in cost of goods sold of Store 1	$51,000
Decrease in cost of goods sold of Store 2	12,000
Loss incurred by wholesaler	(10,000)
Increase in income from buying wholesaler	$53,000

This analysis suggests that, from a financial perspective, the wholesale company should be purchased. The decreases in cost of goods sold that will result in Store 1 and Store 2 more than compensate for the losses currently being incurred by the wholesaler.

to summarize

In deciding whether to exit or enter a market, the effect on profits, quality, and speed of delivery should be considered. When focusing on the financial aspects of exiting or entering a market, only the differential costs and revenues need be considered. A product or line of products should not be dropped unless it does not make a contribution toward covering indirect fixed costs. An alternative product or line of products can be added that will contribute more toward covering unavoidable indirect fixed costs. A segment should be added if it increases overall company profits. The increase in overall company profits can come from reduced costs in existing segments or from the profitable margin of the acquired segment.

Selecting the Best Use of a Scarce Resource

Organizations are often faced with the decision of how to best use scarce resources. In a manufacturing company, the scarce resource might be limited raw materials or limited production capacity. For a retail merchandising firm, such as WAL-MART, the scarce resource might be limited shelf space. For a service firm, the scarce resource might be limited expertise. We will illustrate the concept of scarce resources using limited shelf space for a retail merchandising firm.

When a retail merchandising firm sells more than one product and store shelves are inadequate to display all products equally, management has to decide to which products the store should allocate shelf space and how much space should be allocated to each product. With limited shelf space, stocking one product means that another product cannot be stocked or will have to be stocked on a more limited basis. In deciding which products to stock, management needs to know which products and how much of each product to stock in order to maximize net income. A retail store will normally maximize net income by stocking those products that contribute the most toward covering fixed costs and providing profit in relation to the "critical resource factor," in this case, shelf space. The **critical resource factor** is the resource that limits operating capacity by its availability. For example, in a manufacturing company, if machine hours are the most critical resource, a company should concentrate on the product for which revenues exceed variable costs by the highest margin per machine hour. Other critical resources in manufacturing companies might include labor hours, floor space, or special raw materials. Because shelf space is the critical resource factor for our retail store example, from a financial point of view, management should stock those products for which revenues exceed variable costs by the highest margin per square foot of shelf space.

critical resource factor The resource that limits operating capacity by its availability.

To illustrate, we assume that Bolten Retail Company stocks potato chips and cookies. Let's further assume that its capacity, at least in the short term, is limited by the availability of only 20 square feet of shelf space for these two products. The revenue and cost data for one package each of potato chips and cookies are:

	Potato Chips	Cookies
Selling price	$3.10	$3.50
Variable costs	2.48	3.15
Contribution margin per unit	$0.62	$0.35
Percentage contribution margin (contribution margin ÷ selling price)	20%	10%

On the basis of this limited information, it would appear that potato chips are more profitable than cookies. The sale of one bag of potato chips will contribute $0.62 toward fixed costs, whereas the sale of one package of cookies will contribute only $0.35.

Before Bolten can decide whether or not to emphasize potato chips, however, management must consider the extent to which each product uses the critical resource, limited shelf space. If a bag of potato chips takes up twice as much space as a package of cookies (two bags of potato chips occupy one square foot of shelf space, while four packages of cookies can occupy the same one square foot of shelf space), the sale of cookies will make a greater total contribution to profits than the sale of potato chips, as shown by the following calculations:[3]

3 We are assuming that the company can sell all the potato chips and cookies it stocks. If it can't, or if one product sells faster than the other, rate of turnover must be considered.

	Potato Chips	Cookies
Contribution margin per unit	$0.62	$0.35
Packages per square foot	× 2	× 4
Contribution margin per square foot of shelf space	$1.24	$1.40

STOP & THINK Why do you think that most grocery stores allocate more space to breakfast cereals than to most other products?

Even though potato chips have a higher contribution margin per unit of product ($0.62 versus $0.35), cookies have a higher contribution margin per square foot of shelf space ($1.40 versus $1.24), which is the critical resource. The management of Bolten Retail Company should stock cookies rather than potato chips, assuming that the company's only critical resource is shelf space.

However, if the demand for cookies is limited and Bolten never has potato chips for sale, will customers start shopping at other stores? In that case, Bolten should stock as many cookies as it can sell and use the balance of the critical resource for stocking potato chips. To illustrate, we assume that the market demand for cookies is 1,800 packages per month or an average of 60 per day. Because it takes only 15 square feet of shelf space (60 packages ÷ 4 packages per square foot) to store one day's worth of cookies, 5 square feet of shelf space are available to stock potato chips. This means that 10 bags of potato chips can be stocked. Assuming all 10 bags are sold during each day, the combined sales of cookies and potato chips will contribute $27.20 to cover fixed costs and provide a profit, as shown below.

caution

It is essential to carefully and accurately identify the scarce resource and the quantity of the scarce resource consumed by each product. For example, in the store shelf space decision, if you don't carefully calculate the amount of space needed for cookies and potato chips and instead look only at the contribution margin per unit, an incorrect decision will be made. It is only when you consider the contribution margin per square foot of shelf space that the correct decision is made.

	Daily Contribution Margin
Packages sold:	
Potato chips (10 bags × $0.62 per bag)	$ 6.20
Cookies (60 packages × $0.35 per package)	21.00
Total	$27.20

This analysis shows that from a financial perspective, the best use of the 20 square feet of shelf space is to use 15 square feet for cookies and 5 square feet for potato chips. Because demand for cookies is limited, only a $21 daily contribution margin can be earned by selling cookies. The other 5 feet of shelf space should be used to stock potato chips. Obviously, nonfinancial factors, such as customer satisfaction, would also have to be considered in making the final decision of how much of each product to stock.

The foregoing analysis dealt with only two constraints: store shelf space and product demand. If a firm is further limited by other factors (such as the ability to buy certain amounts of particular products), management generally has to use the quantitative techniques of linear programming or simulation to help decide how many of each product to produce and/or sell. You can learn about this technique in advanced accounting or business management courses. Regardless of the number of constraints, though, the essence of the decision is to achieve the best short-term utilization of available resources.

In the expanded material section of this chapter, you will find a discussion of the theory of constraints, a philosophical approach to focusing on "constraints" as a way to allocate limited resources and improve management processes.

to summarize

In deciding how to make the best use of critical resource factors, management should choose the item that provides the greatest contribution margin per unit of the most critical resource.

Setting Selling Prices

Some people argue that a discussion of setting prices in a book such as this is a waste of time because the market sets the price and there is nothing management can do to affect prices. Others argue that, especially in some markets, management does set prices or at least influence prices. In this section, we assume that management can influence prices and discuss those factors management should consider.

Pricing a product is partly a matter of guesswork because managers rarely know with any precision how price affects demand (e.g., how many more units could be sold if the price were to be lowered by a certain amount). In addition, other factors, such as advertising and packaging, affect the sale of a product.

The pricing process is further complicated by the fact that there are several broad categories of pricing decisions and the same cost information is not appropriate for all of them. Earlier, we considered the pricing of special orders. In this section, we cover the pricing of normal products. Other pricing categories, including the pricing of new products, are covered in advanced accounting and marketing texts.

NORMAL PRICING OF PRODUCTS In deciding whether to accept special orders, we stated that the price must be high enough to cover variable and incremental fixed costs. The price normally charged for a product or service, however, must be high enough to cover all costs (including production, selling, and administrative costs) and still provide a reasonable return on the owners' investments. Therefore, all costs (variable, as well as a fair share of fixed costs) are relevant to the pricing decision. In some cases, however, the final price may be set somewhat above or below the price suggested by total cost plus a reasonable return. This occurs when pricing decisions are based primarily on supply and demand, competition, and other market factors. For example, textbook prices are strictly competitive. Whether it costs $250,000 or $500,000 to produce a textbook, its price has to be close to that of the nearest competitors.

In supplying cost data to aid management in normal pricing decisions, accountants may use a functional approach, summarizing costs by function (manufacturing, selling, or administrative), or a contribution approach, classifying costs by behavior (fixed or variable). To illustrate the two approaches, we assume that Kent Electronics (from the calculator example earlier in the chapter) is pricing a desk calculator. The relevant costs for each approach are as follows:

Functional Cost Approach	
Direct materials	$ 6
Direct labor	8
Manufacturing overhead (200% × direct labor cost)	16
Total manufacturing cost	$30
Markup to cover selling and administrative expenses and provide a reasonable return on investment (0.40 × selling price)	20
Estimated normal selling price	$50

Contribution Approach	
Direct materials	$ 6
Direct labor	8
Variable manufacturing overhead	7
Variable selling and administrative overhead expenses	4
Total variable costs	$25
Markup to cover fixed costs and provide a reasonable return on investment (0.50 × selling price)	25
Estimated normal selling price	$50

The markups calculated here are based on the selling price because marketing people generally use this approach. How do we calculate the markup as a percentage of the selling price before that price is known? If the markup is to be 40% of the selling price, as in our first example, the total manufacturing cost must be 60% of the selling price. So we simply divide the manufacturing cost by 60% to get the selling price ($30 ÷ 0.60 = $50). Then, the selling price minus the manufacturing cost is the markup ($50 − $30 = $20).

If a functional cost approach is used, the markup must be large enough to cover all selling and administrative costs and provide a reasonable return on investment. If a contribution approach is used, the markup must be large enough to cover all fixed costs and generate a reasonable return on investment.

to summarize

For normal pricing of products, management should consider all costs, not just differential costs (as was the case with pricing special orders). The markups applied must be high enough to cover all costs and expenses and provide a reasonable return on investment.

expanded material

Thus far in this chapter, we have discussed how and why organizations evaluate products and processes, including the concepts of benchmarking and differential costs and revenues. We have also provided several examples of evaluation decisions, such as whether to accept special orders, whether to outsource or provide services and products internally, whether to continue or discontinue existing product lines or expand into new product lines or geographic regions, how best to use critical resources, and how to set selling prices. Another evaluation decision, whether to sell or continue processing products developed from joint manufacturing processes, is discussed on the Internet if you are interested. In the chapter, we have explained how to make product and process evaluation decisions by focusing on differential costs and revenues. In this expanded section, we discuss another approach to making product and process evaluation decisions—the theory of constraints. This approach or philosophy, which has gained in popularity in recent years, was developed during the 1980s and involves making production decisions by focusing on bottleneck resources. The theory of constraints advocates that only constraint resources should operate at full capacity.

5

Understand the theory of constraints and how focusing on scarce resources can direct activities in manufacturing companies.

theory of constraints (TOC)
A management philosophy that focuses on constraint resources and holds that they should operate at full capacity.

THEORY OF CONSTRAINTS

To compete against global rivals in the early 1980s, managers from a variety of industries worked hard to revitalize their manufacturing practices. During this period, a manufacturing philosophy called the **theory of constraints (TOC)** or optimized production technology (OPT) received considerable attention. TOC was popularized by Eliyahu Goldratt, an Israeli physicist, in his book *The Goal.* Goldratt claimed that by scheduling production by focusing on bottleneck resources, a firm could develop and maintain a manufacturing-based competitive advantage over other firms. The premise of TOC is that only constraint resources should operate at full capacity. That is, a facility can produce a finished product no faster than the constraint resource can process the materials that go into the product. The constraint resource acts as the "drum," setting the production pace for the entire operation. Once material has been processed on the constraint resource, it should not sit idle but should be kept moving until shipped to the customer. By following a few basic rules, each of which focuses management's attention on the firm's constraint resource, managers can use TOC to maximize the throughout (amount of product produced in available facilities) of their production facility. The result is that the firm is better able to meet its customers' needs.

Constraint management can improve a company's competitive position by helping it better schedule and utilize its productive resources. When the constraint resource becomes the focal point, nonconstraint operations will operate below capacity, facilitating several positive outcomes. For example, nonconstraint resources no longer produce excess work-in-process (WIP) inventory; shop floor clutter and confusion are thereby reduced, production quality is improved, preventive maintenance activities are enhanced, and more time is available for employee training. By identifying the constraint resource and using it as the reference point for decision making, management can alter the very nature of key assumptions regarding product costing, performance measurement, product and process design, and make-versus-buy decisions. In general, the theory holds that more accurate assumptions lead to better decisions and enhanced competitiveness.

Employing TOC requires five basic steps:

1. *Understand the system's constraints.* The constraint may be a manufacturing process, a delivery process, or any other aspect of the process from taking delivery of raw materials to making sure finished products are sold and delivered.
2. *Decide how to exploit the system's constraints.* Production and pricing decisions should be based on the throughput yield per unit of constraint resource.
3. *Subordinate everything else to keeping the constraint resource operating at optimal capacity.* All nonconstraint activities should be coordinated with the constraint resource. This often requires a dramatic shift in managerial mindset, including allowing workers and machinery to sit idle or perform other, unrelated activities when not needed.
4. *Elevate the constraint.* By focusing on the constraint, it may be possible to offload some work to nonbottlenecks by acquiring more equipment or outsourcing some bottleneck work.
5. *If a constraint has been broken, go back to step 1.* Do not allow nonaction or inertia to cause a system constraint. Bottlenecks can, and will, shift around within an organization. Not properly identifying the relevant and current constraint can lead to a return of process inefficiencies and confused management policies.

Examples of companies that have adopted TOC are plentiful in the literature. For example, before employing TOC, a privately held metal tool manufacturing company used the ratio of indirect to direct labor hours as its key performance measure. Focusing on this measure caused the company to develop a "keep the workers busy at all costs" attitude, resulting in piles of excess WIP inventory, production inefficiencies, and a poorly focused pricing strategy. Under TOC, nonconstrained resources are allowed to sit idle, and the company uses this idle time to cross-train employees. As another example, a packing company struggled for a period of time with employees at nonbottlenecks who tried to stay busy by releasing WIP too early to the bottleneck operation. By implementing new, TOC-consistent performance measures, the company was able to eliminate buildups of WIP inventory and become more efficient.

As a simple example of the TOC, assume that Wilton Company requires five processes to make treadmills. The first process involves purchasing materials such as metal, rubber, and electronic components. There is no constraint on the amount of any of these materials that can be purchased. The second process involves manufacturing the various components of the treadmills. The equipment and personnel available to manufacture the components can produce parts for 20 treadmills per hour. The third process involves painting the various components. Painting equipment and personnel can process 18 treadmills per hour. The fourth process involves assembling the finished parts into completed treadmills. Assembly requires specially manufactured equipment that can process only 15 treadmills per hour. Finally, the fifth process, testing, has unlimited capacity because it involves labor only and additional workers can be hired. The following diagram shows the manufacturing processes and their capacities.

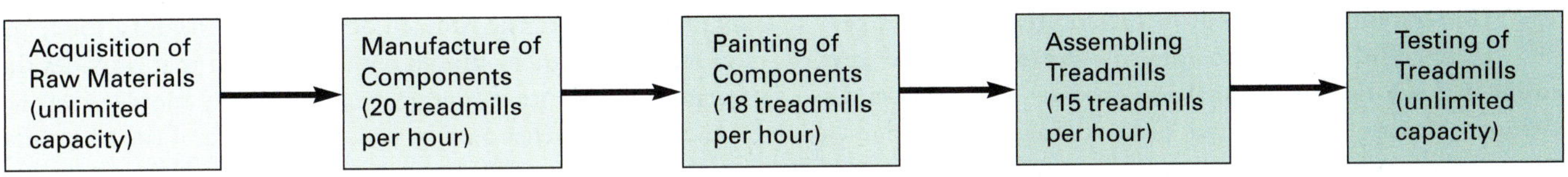

As you can see, if each process operated at full capacity, every hour the components for two treadmills would be produced that painting couldn't process, and three treadmills would be painted that couldn't be assembled. WIP inventory would accumulate in both the third and fourth processes, making production less efficient.

By focusing on the constraint resource—assembling in this case—the company might choose to purchase another specialized assembly machine, outsource some assembly, use the extra time in manufacturing components and painting to complete other jobs or cross-train, or even have some of the idle employees help out in testing treadmills. By focusing on constraint resources, management will know exactly where its bottlenecks are and can take action to fix the problem. Of course, if the constraint resource—assembly—is allowing the company to meet customer demands for treadmills, management may choose to undertake promotional campaigns or add additional products that can be made using excess capacity in component manufacturing and painting.

to summarize

TOC is a management philosophy that focuses management's attention on the bottlenecks or constraint resources. Other measures can result in excess WIP inventory or other inefficiencies. TOC helps management understand the kinds of decisions that will make the firm more productive.

review of learning objectives

1 Explain how evaluation leads to planning and why products and processes must be continuously evaluated. Evaluation is designed to improve the efficiency and cost-effectiveness of existing operations related to products and operating processes. Such decisions usually are in the form of corrective actions regarding machinery efficiency, reduction of waste, efficient task performance, and overcoming bottlenecks. Evaluation takes place regularly, often daily, weekly, or monthly. Sometimes evaluation leads to strategic decisions that deal with changes in the product or the processes. These decisions might be related to the type or quality of the company's products, fundamental changes in the production process, changing suppliers or types of raw materials, or changing the product distribution system.

2 **Understand why benchmarking is so important and how it is conducted.** Benchmarking involves comparing a company's financial and operating performance against a competitor's performance or comparing the performance of various internal departments against each other. It consists of four steps: (1) analyzing the company's practices, procedures, and performance in a given process; (2) selecting a benchmark or benchmarks; (3) gathering information on the benchmark's practices and procedures; and (4) analyzing the data collected in step 3 to determine which policies and procedures used by the benchmarked companies can best be employed.

3 **Understand the concept of differential costs and revenues, and be able to identify those costs and revenues that are relevant to making product and process decisions.** Making product and process decisions involves a consideration of differential costs and revenues. These are future costs and revenues that will change as a result of the decision and therefore are the relevant costs in determining whether the decision to change should be made. Differential costs may be variable, fixed, or both. Past costs that do not change as a result of a decision are not relevant to the decision and are called sunk costs.

4 **Identify several examples of product and process evaluation decisions, and be able to analyze and select the best alternative for each example.** Examples of product and process decisions are (1) special orders (including whether to make or buy a component or service and whether to accept special orders), (2) whether to exit or enter a market, (3) how to best utilize a critical resource, and (4) setting normal selling prices. In choosing whether to make or buy a component or service, management must compare the differential costs of making the part or providing the service (including the opportunity cost of alternative uses of the facilities or labor) with the cost of purchasing the part or service. In deciding whether or not to accept a special order in situations where there is excess capacity, the price should be high enough to provide a positive contribution toward covering normal fixed costs and increasing profit. A product or product line should not be dropped or a market exited unless that unit does not make a positive contribution toward covering indirect fixed costs. An alternative product or line of products can be added that will contribute more toward covering unavoidable indirect costs. A market should be entered only if it contributes to the overall profitability of the firm. In deciding how to use a scarce resource, management should choose the item that provides the greatest contribution margin per unit of the most critical resource. A product should be processed further if the additional revenues from further processing will exceed the additional costs of further processing. For normal pricing, management should consider all costs, not just differential costs.

expanded material

5 **Understand the theory of constraints and how focusing on scarce resources can direct activities in manufacturing companies.** The theory of constraints (TOC) suggests that management should focus on the few "constraints" that are found in any management setting. The premise of TOC is that only constraint resources should operate at full capacity and that a facility can produce a finished product no faster than the constraint resource can process the materials that go into the product.

key terms and concepts

benchmarking 413
critical resource factor 432
differential costs 415
special order 420
sunk costs 416
total cost 418

expanded material

theory of constraints (TOC) 436

review problem

Whether to Make or Buy a Part

Schill Manufacturing Company makes lawn mowers. It has been buying a component from a regular supplier for $11.50 per unit. Because Schill recently has been operating at less than full capacity, the president is considering whether to make the part rather than purchase it. The estimated total cost of making the part under the company's costing system is $14.40, computed as follows:

Direct materials	$ 3.20
Direct labor	5.60
Manufacturing overhead (100% of direct labor cost)	5.60
Estimated total cost to make	$14.40

Variable manufacturing overhead costs are estimated to be 40% of direct labor cost. Fixed manufacturing costs that are not differential are 60% of direct labor cost.

Required: Decide whether Schill should make or buy the component.

Solution

Differential-Cost Analysis

	Cost to Make	Cost to Buy
Purchase price		$11.50
Direct materials	$ 3.20	
Direct labor	5.60	
Variable manufacturing overhead (40% of direct labor cost)	2.24	
Differential cost to make the part	$11.04	
Differential cost to buy the part		$11.50
Cost savings by making the part	$ 0.46	

Total-Cost Analysis

	Cost to Make	Cost to Buy
Purchase price		$11.50
Direct materials	$ 3.20	
Direct labor	5.60	
Variable manufacturing overhead (40% of direct labor cost)	2.24	
Fixed manufacturing overhead	3.36	3.36
Total cost to make	$14.40	
Total cost to buy		$14.86
Cost savings by making the part	$ 0.46	

Calculations:

$5.60 × 0.40 = $2.24 variable manufacturing overhead

$5.60 × 0.60 = $3.36 fixed manufacturing overhead

Unless qualitative factors override the cost estimate, Schill should make the part rather than purchase it. The decision will be the same whether the calculation is based on differential costs only or on total costs. Note that the fixed manufacturing overhead cost applies to both making and buying the part under the total-cost analysis because these costs will be incurred whichever alternative is selected.

discussion questions

1. Why is it so important to continuously evaluate products and processes?
2. Many accounting systems are designed to collect financial information for the purpose of preparing financial statements. What problem does this create for an accountant who is asked to compile relevant data for use by managers to make product and process decisions? Explain.
3. What is a differential cost? Give an example of how differential costs are used by managers making product and process decisions.
4. Distinguish between variable costs and differential costs. Why is the distinction important?
5. Can a fixed cost be relevant to a decision? Explain.
6. What is a sunk cost? Why are sunk costs irrelevant in product and process decision making?
7. In deciding whether to replace an old asset with a new one, which of the following are differential revenues and costs?
   a. Cost of the new equipment
   b. Resale value of the old equipment
   c. Resale value of the new equipment
   d. Book value of the old equipment
   e. Operating costs of the new equipment
8. Distinguish between the total-cost approach and the differential-cost approach to analyzing data for product and process decisions.
9. What is the major limitation in using the total-cost approach to analyze data for product and process decisions?
10. Why must business decisions be based on qualitative as well as quantitative information? Explain.
11. Explain what costs are generally relevant to make-or-buy decisions.
12. Explain why opportunity costs are not included in the accounting records.
13. What is the significance of idle capacity in determining the price of a special order?
14. If total manufacturing costs, including fixed manufacturing overhead, are larger than the price offered by a purchaser for a special order, the order should not be accepted because the profits of the company will be adversely affected. Do you agree? Explain. (Ignore qualitative factors.)
15. In deciding whether to exit or enter a market, what factors should be considered?
16. When should a segment (product, product line, division, etc.) be dropped? When should a segment be added?
17. Why is the contribution margin per unit of a critical resource more important than the contribution margin per unit of product in deciding which products to produce and sell?

expanded material

18. Why does employing the TOC in manufacturing processes lead to less WIP inventory?
19. Proponents argue that the TOC helps management make better use of production resources and better decisions about whether or not to outsource and how to use employees effectively. Explain why this is so.

discussion cases

CASE 8-1

BUYING FROM INSIDE OR OUTSIDE THE COMPANY

E & B Company has two divisions, processing and finishing. The Finishing Division has been purchasing certain products from the Processing Division at a price of $80 per unit. (A unit consists of 100 yards of material.) The Processing Division has announced that, starting next month, it will raise its price to $100 per unit. As the manager of the Finishing Division, you object to this price and have indicated that you are planning to purchase these units of material from outside suppliers at a price of $85 per unit. You have asked the accounting department to furnish cost data to help you understand why the Processing Division's price has to be raised to $100 per unit. Following is the information supplied about the Processing Division's operations:

Units produced for Finishing Division	2,000
Variable production costs per unit	$60
Indirect fixed costs allocated to the Processing Division	$50,000
Normal profit per unit in Processing Division	$15

If the Finishing Division buys from outside suppliers, the facilities used by the Processing Division to manufacture these units for the Finishing Division will remain idle.

Answer the following questions:

1. If the Processing Division is successful in imposing the $100 price and the Finishing Division elects to buy from outside suppliers, what impact does this action have on the overall profit of E & B Company?
2. Explain why the variable production costs, the fixed costs, and the normal profit are, or are not, each relevant to this decision. (You are not being asked to discuss whether the $100 price is an appropriate price or whether the division managers should be allowed to maintain an autonomous posture in this decision.)
3. What additional factors should E & B Company's top management consider in resolving this matter?

CASE 8-2

SUNK COSTS

Sam Love owns and manages a small but growing service business. In fact, this year has been so good that Sam is moving his office to a larger, more centrally located site. In an effort to save on moving costs, Sam employs his brother Dan (who owns a large truck) to haul his office furniture and equipment. Unfortunately, Dan doesn't properly secure the rear door of the truck, and one of Sam's two copy machines winds up in a million pieces in the middle of the highway. As the two brothers survey the damage, Sam's office manager approaches and says, "Well, look on the bright side, the machine was half depreciated."

Should Sam take comfort from this statement? Explain your answer.

CASE 8-3

WHY MOST COMPANIES WANT TO BENCHMARK

Everyone wants to benchmark these days. Assume you are the dean of a business school with a highly successful MBA program. You have enjoyed increasing numbers of highly qualified applicants, recruiters love your students, and both *Business Week* and *U.S. News and World Report* have ranked you in the top 10 business schools in the United States. You have just been contacted by the deans of two other business schools, whose MBA programs rank well below yours. They would like to spend a couple of days at your school benchmarking against your admissions, advising, placement, and other services, as well as studying your curriculum, faculty development processes, and other ingredients of your success. You would like to help them but are not sure you want to reveal why you have been so successful. If you don't expose your secrets of success, however, their visits would largely be a waste of time. What should you do? Should you welcome your competitors with open arms, or should you refuse to allow them to benchmark against you? Or, should you allow them to come but hide your best secrets from them?

exercises

EXERCISE 8-1

CLASSIFYING DECISIONS

Indicate whether each of the following activities appears to be mostly related to planning, controlling, or evaluating:

1. Operational budgeting
2. Production prioritizing
3. Providing feedback to managers
4. Tracking performance
5. Strategic planning
6. Rewarding performance
7. Capital budgeting

8. Comparing costs, quality, and timeliness against previously prepared budgets
9. Analyzing results
10. Identification of problems

EXERCISE 8-2

RELEVANT COSTS

Quick Serve Company provides janitorial services for office buildings. Last year the firm acquired a cleaning machine for $100,000. The firm expected to use the machine for five years. However, this year a new, more efficient machine has been introduced on the market. The accountant for Quick Serve has determined that the annual total operating costs for the old machine are $240,000. The annual operating costs for the new machine would be $200,000, and the purchase price is $130,000. The president of Quick Serve feels the company should not buy the new machine. He points out that the operating costs of $200,000 and the purchase price of $130,000 for the new machine, plus the original cost of the old machine of $100,000, are greater than the operating costs of the old machine.

1. Do you agree with the president?
2. What type of cost is the $100,000 purchase price of the old machine?

EXERCISE 8-3

QUALITATIVE FACTORS

Sturdy Chair Company manufactures wooden chairs. In producing the chairs, a great deal of scrap wood is created. The company currently uses the wood as fuel in a factory furnace. However, it has the opportunity to send the scrap wood to a subcontractor, who would turn it into pressed board to be used to produce small end tables as a new product of Sturdy Chair.

Identify any qualitative factors that Sturdy Chair Company might want to consider in deciding how to use the scrap wood.

EXERCISE 8-4

SPECIAL-ORDER PRICING

You are the controller for Comfort Shoe Company. The company has excess shoes, which it has not been able to market through its own distribution outlets. To utilize the excess capacity, the president is negotiating with a large department store chain to sell Comfort shoes. He has asked you to estimate the minimum selling price below which Comfort should not accept an order from the retail chain. Cost information per pair of shoes is:

Direct materials	$8
Direct labor	5
Manufacturing overhead:	
Variable	3
Fixed	2
Selling and administrative expenses:	
Variable	1
Fixed	3

The fixed costs are the same whether or not the order is accepted.

1. What is the minimum selling price the company should accept based solely on cost information (not considering qualitative factors)?
2. Assume that the president agrees to sell 20,000 pairs at a price of $19 per pair. What would be the expected increase in profit?

EXERCISE 8-5

MAKE-OR-BUY DECISIONS

Tiny Toy Company needs 40,000 miniature engines to complete its toy fire trucks. If Tiny Toy Company buys rather than makes the part, some of the facilities still cannot be used in another manufacturing activity. Twenty-five percent of the fixed manufacturing overhead costs are indirect and will still be incurred regardless of which decision is made. The costs of making and buying the part are:

Cost to make the part:	
Direct materials	$ 5.00
Direct labor	10.00
Variable manufacturing overhead	7.00
Fixed manufacturing overhead	8.00
	$30.00
Cost to buy the part from another company	$28.80

Identify the differential costs of making the part as a basis for deciding whether to make or buy it.

EXERCISE 8-6

MAKE-OR-BUY DECISIONS

Miller Manufacturing builds and markets personal computers for home and small business use. The company has been approached by an outside supplier offering to provide monitors to the company for $65 each. The company's marketing director negotiated the deal personally and is thrilled about how much cheaper it will be to purchase the monitors from outside. Producing the cost data outlined below, the manager proudly proclaims, "Look, a $9 per-unit savings!"

	Per Unit	15,000 Units per Year
Direct materials	$28	$ 420,000
Direct labor	10	150,000
Variable manufacturing overhead	3	45,000
Fixed manufacturing overhead, direct	6	90,000
Fixed manufacturing overhead, indirect	27	405,000
Total cost	$74	$1,110,000

1. Assuming zero opportunity costs, should the company accept the outside offer?
2. If the monitors are purchased from outside, Miller can produce an alternative product that will contribute $250,000 per year toward covering indirect fixed overhead. Will this affect your decision in item (1) above?

EXERCISE 8-7

MAKE-OR-BUY DECISIONS

Alta Company has been manufacturing 8,000 units of part X for its products. The unit cost for the part is as follows:

Direct materials	$ 3
Direct labor	8
Variable manufacturing overhead	4
Fixed manufacturing overhead	6
Total	$21

A supplier has offered to sell 8,000 units of part X to Alta for $18 each. If the part is purchased, Alta can use its facilities to manufacture another product, which would generate a contribution margin of $4,000. Seventy-five percent of the fixed manufacturing overhead costs are indirect and will still be incurred even if the part is purchased.

Compute the net differential cost in deciding whether to make or buy the part.

EXERCISE 8-8

PURCHASING SERVICES FROM OUTSIDE

Dr. Anderson, a local dentist, is considering reducing his office staff and outsourcing the management of his accounts receivable. Currently, he has an office manager and two part-time workers on his staff. One part-time employee spends almost 100% of her time sending out billing notices and following up on collections. Even then, Dr. Anderson is able to collect on only about 80% of the receivables. A collection agency wants Dr. Anderson's business. It will handle all billing and collection details for a monthly fee of $1,500. The agency believes it can deliver a 90% collection of receivables. Another firm, We Collect, Inc., has approached Anderson with a proposal that would shift all accounts receivable risk to We Collect, Inc. Anderson would receive 85% of all receivables automatically. Additional information follows:

Anderson's average yearly accounts receivable	$400,000
Anderson's average annual bad debt expense	80,000
Part-time accounts receivable employee salary	12,000

Which of the following alternatives should Anderson pursue concerning his accounts receivable?

1. Maintain status quo (part-time employee handling accounts receivable).
2. Outsource to collection agency.
3. Outsource to We Collect, Inc.

EXERCISE 8-9

Spread-Sheet Software

DISCONTINUING A PRODUCT LINE

Swanton Company currently sells three products: desk calendars, pen sets, and paper-clip holders. The company is thinking of discontinuing the production and sales of paper-clip holders. However, because many customers buy the products as a set, Swanton estimates that the sales of the other two products will decrease by 20% if the paper-clip holders are discontinued.

Current data on each of the three products are provided below.

	Desk Calendars	Pen Sets	Paper-Clip Holders	Total
Units	40,000	20,000	12,000	
Sales revenue	$280,000	$240,000	$24,000	$544,000
Variable costs	160,000	160,000	26,000	346,000
Direct fixed costs	40,000	20,000	5,000	65,000
Indirect fixed costs	30,000	40,000	6,000	76,000

1. What is the segment margin of the paper-clip holders?
2. **Interpretive Question:** Would you recommend dropping the paper-clip holder product line? Why or why not?

EXERCISE 8-10

ADDING A NEW PRODUCT

Lipston Corporation is thinking about adding a new product line. Marketing surveys indicate that sales of the new product would be 200,000 units. Each unit sells for $4. Direct variable costs would be $2.80 per unit, direct fixed costs would be $120,000, and $90,000 represents the company's indirect fixed costs. The company does not expect the new product to affect the sales of its other products.

Should Lipston add the new product? Why or why not?

EXERCISE 8-11

CONTRIBUTION MARGIN PER UNIT OF A CRITICAL RESOURCE

Santana Sports Company produces two products, soccer balls and volleyballs. Both products are extremely popular, and the company can sell as many of either ball as it can produce. Santana Sports can produce only a limited number of balls, however, because only 12,000 direct labor hours are available due to the isolated location of the community. It takes two hours of direct labor to produce a soccer ball and one-and-one-half hours to produce a volleyball. The selling price of a soccer ball is $34, and the variable costs are $20. The selling price of a volleyball is $26, with variable costs of $14.

Which product should Santana Sports Company produce if its direct labor hours are limited?

EXERCISE 8-12

CRITICAL RESOURCE CONSTRAINTS

Whiz Kids manufactures two computer games. Far Out is a quiz game about astronomy, and Dynamite is a mystery game. The company has a limited supply of skilled labor and has been able to obtain only a limited number of "chips," a necessary part in the production process.

Information on each product is as follows:

	Far Out	Dynamite
Contribution margin per unit	$4	$3
Units produced per hour	2	3
Units produced per 100 chips	80	60

Anticipated sales exceed capacity for both products.
Total labor hours available: 9,000 hours
Total chips available: 30,000 chips

1. Identify the critical resource constraint under which Whiz Kids must operate.
2. Which product should be produced?

EXERCISE 8-13

PRICING REGULAR PRODUCTS

Medical Care, Inc., is considering what price to charge for Sparkle, a toothpaste that is sold in its leased store at a hospital. The accountant has been asked to prepare an estimated normal selling price based on the costs that Medical Care incurs in making the product in a factory it operates. Costs of producing one tube of Sparkle are 20 cents for direct materials, 10 cents for direct labor, 20 cents for variable manufacturing overhead, and 10 cents for variable selling and administrative costs. Total direct fixed costs are $10,000. The company estimates that a markup of 40% of the selling price is necessary to cover the fixed costs and provide a reasonable return on investment.

1. Calculate the estimated normal selling price.
2. Would you recommend that the company obtain any other information before establishing a sales price?

expanded material

EXERCISE 8-14

THEORY OF CONSTRAINTS

Rudyard Company makes replacement engines for jet aircraft. Making the engines involves four processes: (1) purchasing materials, (2) assembling the engines, (3) testing the engines, and (4) delivering the completed engines to customers. Although each of these processes is critical, delivery to customers is very difficult because of the weight of the engine, the sensitivity of the calibration, and the stabilization required for shipment. Rudyard has no problem purchasing component parts for the engines. Upon order, suppliers can deliver needed parts in any quantity within one day. Assembling engines, however, requires highly skilled employees. Currently, the company has three employees who can each assemble one engine every three days. Testing also requires highly skilled engineers who use simulators made to the company's specifications. Right now, Rudyard has two simulators, each of which can test one engine every four days. Currently, there is only one trucking company that can deliver the engines to customers and ensure that they will be treated with the necessary care. The trucking company can haul three engines per truck, but given the location of customers, it can deliver only 15 engines per month.

1. What is the constraint resource in this company?
2. How many engines should Rudyard be making per month?
3. How much excess time is available in the other processes?
4. How would you suggest the company use its excess resources?

problems

PROBLEM 8-1

SPECIAL-ORDER PRICING

Midwest Company manufactures portable radios. Shop Smart, a large retail merchandiser, wants to buy 200,000 radios from Midwest Company for $12 each. The radio would carry Shop Smart's name and would be sold in its stores.

Midwest Company normally sells 420,000 radios a year at $16 each; its production capacity is 540,000 units a year. Cost information for the radios is as follows:

Production costs:	
Variable production costs	$7
Fixed manufacturing overhead ($2,100,000 ÷ 420,000 units)	5
Selling and administrative expenses:	
Variable	1
Fixed ($420,000 ÷ 420,000 units)	1

The $1 variable selling and administrative expenses would not be applicable to the radios ordered by Shop Smart because that is a single large order. Shop Smart has indicated that the company is not interested in signing a contract for less than 200,000 radios. Total fixed costs will not change regardless of whether the Shop Smart order is accepted.

Required:

1. Identify any opportunity costs that Midwest Company should consider when making the decision.
2. Determine whether Midwest Company should accept Shop Smart's offer.
3. **Interpretive Question:** What qualitative factors might be relevant to this decision?

PROBLEM 8-2

MAKE-OR-BUY DECISIONS

Logan Company manufactures several toy products. One is a large plastic truck, which requires a plastic truck body, two metal axles, and four rubber wheels. Logan currently manufactures and assembles all the parts.

Another toy company has offered to sell the parts to Logan at $1.70 per truck if 20,000 or more parts are purchased each year, and at $2 per truck if less than 20,000 parts are purchased. Logan is considering this offer. The space used in producing the parts could be used for a new toy, which is scheduled to begin production next year. If Logan continues to produce the parts for the plastic truck, the company will have to lease space from another company in an adjacent building to produce the new toy. The rent would be $8,000 per year.

Other information related to the truck is:

	Produce Parts	Assemble Truck	Total
Direct materials	$1.10	$0.20	$1.30
Direct labor	0.30	0.20	0.50
Variable manufacturing overhead	0.20	0.15	0.35
Fixed manufacturing overhead	0.20	0.40	0.60
Total manufacturing costs	$1.80	$0.95	$2.75

The marketing department has estimated that sales for the plastic truck will be approximately 16,000 units per year for the next three years. The fixed manufacturing overhead is indirect and will still be incurred regardless of which decision is made.

Required:

1. Describe Logan Company's two alternatives for this decision.
2. What costs are relevant to the decision?
3. Which alternative should Logan Company select?
4. What would be the best decision had Logan not planned to produce the new toy?
5. **Interpretive Question:** What are some of the qualitative factors that Logan Company might consider in making the decision?

PROBLEM 8-3

CHOOSING BETWEEN TWO MACHINES

Tasty Burger is thinking of making the hamburger rolls for its chain of fast-food restaurants. Two machines, A and B, are being considered for purchase. The company now purchases the rolls from an outside supplier for 12 cents each. The cost information for producing the rolls would be:

	Machine A	Machine B
Variable costs per roll	$0.08	$0.07
Annual fixed costs	$1,750	$2,500
Initial cost of machine	$5,000	$12,000
Salvage value at end of five years	$0	$4,000
Estimated life of machine	5 years	5 years

Required:

1. At a sales volume of 300,000 rolls per year, which of these alternatives is best—buying the rolls, using machine A, or using machine B? (Ignore the time value of money, and assume straight-line depreciation.)
2. At what level of production would you be indifferent between machine A and machine B? Which machine is preferable if production exceeds this volume?

PROBLEM 8-4

PURCHASING SERVICES FROM OUTSIDE

Northeast Reinsurance Company is growing rapidly. As it has grown, it has added legal staff to provide for its legal services. One of the principals of the company is an attorney who has provided oversight over the growing legal department. However, she is now too busy to continue this "legal counsel" role. She suggests that the senior company attorney become an officer of the company and be given the title "legal counsel and secretary." Another of the principals is good friends with an attorney at a prestigious regional law firm. That law firm has offered to provide Northeast with legal services for an annual retainer of $500,000 plus an average billing rate of $100 per hour for all work done over 5,000 hours per year. It is expected that legal work, whether done inside or outside the company, will require about 6,000 hours this coming year and will probably increase by 10% a year thereafter. The current company legal staff may be able to handle the work load for two years before it will have to hire another attorney (at an expected salary and benefit package of $100,000). Other variable costs are expected to increase by 5% a year.

Additional information follows:

	Current Costs of Internal Legal Department
Salaries and benefits of legal staff	$350,000
Travel costs	80,000
Required continuing education costs	10,000
Legal support costs (library, computers, software, supplies, etc.)	100,000
Other variable costs	25,000
Allocated office overhead (depreciation, utilities, etc.)	40,000
Total costs of legal department	$605,000

Required:

1. What are the relevant costs for Northeast to consider in making this decision?
2. From a financial standpoint, should Northeast continue to use its own legal department for legal services or outsource this function to the regional law firm?
3. What other factors might Northeast consider in making this decision?

PROBLEM 8-5

Spread-Sheet Software

UNIFYING CONCEPTS: MAKE-OR-BUY DECISIONS (DIFFERENTIAL COSTS AND OPPORTUNITY COSTS)

Snow Corporation manufactures freezers for residential use. The company is planning to produce a new freezer suitable for apartments. These smaller freezers require a component that Snow Corporation can either make or buy from a subcontractor. The subcontractor will sell the part for \$46. The costs for making 12,000 units of the part are as follows:

Direct materials	\$20 per unit
Direct labor	\$15 per unit
Variable manufacturing overhead	\$10 per unit
Fixed manufacturing overhead	\$40,000*

*The \$40,000 fixed manufacturing overhead includes \$24,000 of indirect fixed costs allocated to the part and \$16,000 for a production manager.

If the part is produced, Snow Corporation will use an idle machine it already owns. If the part is bought, the company plans to rent the machine and the factory space to another company for \$8,000 and \$14,000 a year, respectively.

Snow expects that, if the part is produced, the company will be able to schedule production so that no warehouse space will be needed. However, if the part is bought, Snow will need to use warehouse space, for which it will have to pay \$2,000 a year in rent.

Required:

1. Identify any opportunity costs relevant to the decision to make or buy the component.
2. Determine the differential costs of making the product.
3. Determine the differential costs of buying the product.
4. **Interpretive Question:** Would you recommend that Snow make or buy the component? Why?

PROBLEM 8-6

DROPPING A PRODUCT LINE

Mountain Land, Inc., manufactures skis, ski boots, and ski poles for downhill skiing. The company is thinking of dropping ski poles as a product line. The following report was prepared by the accounting department:

	Skis	Ski Boots	Ski Poles	Total
Sales revenues	\$480,000	\$210,000	\$50,000	\$740,000
Variable costs	(370,000)	(140,000)	(24,000)	(534,000)
Contribution margin	\$110,000	\$ 70,000	\$26,000	\$206,000
Direct fixed costs	(40,000)	(20,000)	(27,000)	(87,000)
Segment margin	\$ 70,000	\$ 50,000	\$ (1,000)	\$119,000
Indirect fixed costs	(35,000)	(20,000)	(5,000)	(60,000)
Net income	\$ 35,000	\$ 30,000	\$ (6,000)	\$ 59,000

Required:

1. Should the ski pole line be dropped? Why or why not?
2. **Interpretive Question:** What qualitative factors should be considered in deciding whether to drop the ski pole line?

PROBLEM 8-7

ADDING AND DROPPING PRODUCT LINES

Hansig Manufacturing Company has been producing three products: A, B, and C. Now that the plant has been shifted to an assembly-line operation, a fourth product, D, has been added.

Each product has its own assembly-line operation, producing 10,000 units. Total indirect fixed costs of $23,000 are divided proportionately, based on the space allocated to each assembly line. Other pertinent information is given below.

	A	B	C	D
Selling price per unit	$3.00	$2.50	$2.70	$1.50
Variable cost per unit	$2.00	$1.80	$1.80	$1.30
Number of square feet	800	600	500	400

Required:

1. Prepare a schedule that shows net income for each product line.
2. Would total company income increase if product D were dropped? Why or why not?
3. **Interpretive Question:** If you could double the production of A, B, or C in place of having D, which would you choose? Why?

PROBLEM 8-8

SHUTTING DOWN OR CONTINUING OPERATIONS

End Trail Campground is open year-round. However, 80% of its revenues are generated from May through October. Because only 20% of the revenues are generated from November to April, the campground is considering closing during those months. The yearly revenues and cost information expected by End Trail for next year if the campground does not close are:

Camping fees	$1,800,000
Variable costs	990,000
Fixed costs ($40,000 per month)	480,000

The cost to close the campground at the end of October would be $20,000, and the cost to reopen in May would be $50,000. If the campground is closed, the total fixed costs are only $25,000 per month, rather than the $40,000 per month when the campground is open.

Required: Determine whether End Trail Campground should close from November to April or remain open for the entire year.

PROBLEM 8-9

DETERMINING PRODUCTION WITH A CRITICAL RESOURCE LIMITATION

Clarity Corporation produces three sizes of television sets: 10-inch screen, 19-inch screen, and 24-inch screen. The revenues and costs per unit for each size are as follows:

	Screen Size		
	10-inch	19-inch	24-inch
Selling price	$195	$325	$450
Variable costs:			
Direct materials	$ 55	$100	$126
Direct labor	80	120	180
Variable manufacturing overhead	40	60	90
Total variable costs	$175	$280	$396
Contribution margin	$ 20	$ 45	$ 54
Units ordered for next week	200	150	75

The company has a constraint on the amount of skilled labor available to produce television sets. Direct labor employees are paid $8 per hour. The total amount of labor time available for next week's production is 2,700 hours.

Required: Given the units ordered for next week, which size or sizes of television sets should be produced and sold to maximize the company's profit?

PROBLEM 8-10

DETERMINING PRODUCTION WITH A CRITICAL RESOURCE LIMITATION

A company is examining two of its products, X-121 and Y-707. The following information is being reviewed:

	X-121	Y-707
Unit selling price	$28.50	$21.00
Materials required per unit	$3.00	$1.50
Direct labor required per unit	$2.50	$1.25
Variable manufacturing overhead per unit	$0.50	$1.00
Production time per unit (in hours)	1.5	1

Required:

1. Which item should the company manufacture if there is no constraint on hours of production?
2. If full production capacity is 1,500 hours, and if the company can sell all the units it makes, which item should it manufacture? Why?

PROBLEM 8-11

CONTRIBUTION MARGIN PER UNIT OF A CRITICAL RESOURCE

Dresser, Inc., manufactures three super-sports-hero dolls: Super Dunk, Pete Tulip, and Zonk. Production, however, is limited by the skilled labor necessary to produce these unique dolls. Data on each of the dolls are as follows:

	Super Dunk	Pete Tulip	Zonk
Contribution margin per doll	$6	$4	$5
Dolls produced per hour	20	28	25
Expected total market volume (units)	20,000	9,000	100,000
Total skilled labor hours available: 4,500 hours.			

Required:

Assuming that there are no relevant qualitative factors, how many dolls of each type should Dresser produce?

PROBLEM 8-12

UNIFYING CONCEPTS: PRODUCTION AND ADVERTISING

Cole Company manufactures only two products—a battery charger and a testing machine for automobile engines. An average of 30,000 chargers and 50,000 testers are sold each year. This year, the company can afford only $60,000 for advertising the products, which is just enough to advertise one product effectively. The marketing manager expects that the sales of chargers will increase by 20% if they are advertised and that the sales of testers will increase by 10% if they are advertised.

The following information about the two products has been provided by the accountant:

	Charger	Tester
Selling price per unit	$70	$90
Variable cost per unit	$30	$40
Fixed cost per unit	$30	$40
Production time per unit (in hours)	2	4

Required:

1. If Cole had an unlimited number of labor hours, would you recommend that it advertise either of its products? If yes, which one and why?

2. Assume that Cole has a capacity of 260,000 labor hours. Should Cole still advertise? If so, which product should it advertise?

PROBLEM 8-13 NORMAL SELLING PRICE

TeleCom Products manufactures desktop and wall-mounted telephone units. The company is seeking to come up with a reasonable price for its desktop slimline model. Production costs for each unit follow:

Direct materials	$3.50 per unit
Direct labor	0.5 hour per unit
Direct labor rate	$6 per hour
Variable manufacturing overhead	$4 per labor hour
Variable selling and administrative costs	$1 per unit
Fixed overhead (direct)	$1.50 per unit
Markup of selling price to cover indirect overhead and expected profit	40%

Required: Calculate the estimated normal selling price.

expanded material

PROBLEM 8-14 THEORY OF CONSTRAINTS

Dalton Enterprises makes several products, including microwave ovens, dishwashers, and vacuum cleaners. Each manufacturing process requires several production processes. Right now, the company has large amounts of money tied up in work-in-process inventory at various locations throughout the company. Although Dalton has tried to eliminate this inventory, each month the inventory seems to increase. In addition, the company has a salary incentive system that pays production employees bonuses if they meet budgeted production quotas. The bonuses pay increasingly higher amounts for each unit that is produced in excess of the quota. In recent years, employees have been receiving large production bonuses under the incentive plan, so management knows that the employees are working hard and being productive. These higher bonuses, combined with the money tied up in work-in-process inventory, are creating a cash flow problem for the company.

You have been hired to help the company fix its cash flow problems. You have just attended a conference on the theory of constraints.

Required: Explain how you could apply what you have learned to help the company with its problems.

competency enhancement opportunities

- Analyzing Real Company Information
- International Case
- Ethics Case
- Writing Assignment
- The Debate
- Internet Search

The following additional assignments provide opportunities for students to develop critical thinking, ethical perspectives, oral and written communication skills, experience with electronic research, and teamwork through group and business activities.

ANALYZING REAL COMPANY INFORMATION

• *Analyzing 8-1 (Microsoft)*
Go to the annual report for **MICROSOFT** provided in Appendix A at the back of this textbook. Read through the report to determine how many segments of business exist within Microsoft. What approach does Microsoft appear to use in identifying operating segments within the company at large?

• *Analyzing 8-2 (Main Line Pictures, Inc. versus Kim Basinger)*
Hollywood produces a lot of entertainment, including accounting entertainment! In early 1993, the Superior Court of the State of California (Los Angeles County) heard a litigation suit filed by **MAIN LINE PICTURES, INC.**, against the actress Kim Basinger for breach of contract. At issue was Basinger's decision to withdraw from a film project after making a verbal commitment to appear in it. The film, released in September 1993, was *Boxing Helena.* Didn't see it? That was the point of Main Line's lawsuit: the studio claimed a lot of people didn't see *Boxing Helena* because the actress who replaced Basinger (Sherilyn Fenn) did not have nearly the same box office appeal.

Main Line claimed damages due to an incremental difference in revenues and costs, which led to actual profits being less than expected, all due to not having Basinger in the film. An expert economist and an expert in film finance were called to testify regarding the appropriate size of the incremental revenue and cost differences. Hence, the case essentially became an accounting argument.

Main Line's lawyers argued that their client lost between $5.1 million and $9.7 million as a result of Basinger's withdrawal. The $5.1 million loss calculation is shown below (all amounts are in millions).

Minimum Damages, Plaintiff

	With Basinger	Without Basinger	Difference
Foreign presales	$ 7.60	$ 2.70	$4.90
Domestic presales	3.00		3.00
Total revenue	$10.60	$ 2.70	$7.90
Production costs	(7.60)	(4.80)	(2.80)
Profit (loss)	$ 3.00	$(2.10)	$5.10

To understand the numbers above, you need to know a couple of things about revenues and costs in the movie business and this film in particular.

- It is extremely difficult to predict what a film will actually earn when released. There are *plenty* of examples of big budget films that did poorly at the box office, as well as inexpensive, independent films that have done very well. Hence, presale revenue (guaranteed minimum payments by a film distributor to the film producer) is the only sure revenue the producer can bank on when budgeting costs of making the film. If the film does well, then the distributor and producer share in the profits.
- After Basinger dropped out of the film, one of Main Line's partners loaned $1.7 million to the project, to be repaid out of domestic revenues.
- Often the producer will contract to share profits from presales, as well as incremental profits, with key actors. Basinger was to be paid a guaranteed $1 million to star in the film. In addition, she, her proposed co-star Ed Har-

ris, and writer/director Jennifer Lynch were to be paid a total of 20.5% of the producer's net profits. On the other hand, Sherilyn Fenn and her co-star, Julian Sands, each received only a $100,000 guaranteed salary.

- After Basinger dropped from the film project, the producer made some changes to scale back production costs by $1.9 million.
- Often a movie project has many investing partners. Main Line had a partnership with Philippe Caland, who was, essentially, to receive 50% of net profits (after participation payments to the actors and writer), up to a maximum of $2 million.
- After withdrawing from *Boxing Helena,* Basinger received $3 million from a separate producer to star in *Final Analysis.*

Do you agree with the numbers presented above by the plaintiff? Consider all the information provided above and adjust the incremental profit analysis if needed. Be sure to defend your decision to use or not use each piece of information provided.

Source: Adapted from T. L. Barton, W. G. Shenkir, and B. C. Marinas, "Main Line vs. Basinger: A Case in Relevant Costs and Incremental Analysis," *Issues in Accounting Education,* Spring 1996, pp. 163–174.

International

INTERNATIONAL CASE

• *Ameripill Company*

Located in Bartow, Alabama, the Pharmaceutical Division of **AMERIPILL COMPANY** ranks among the top 15 drug companies in the world. The European Unit of the Pharmaceutical Division is divided into three markets: United Kingdom (U.K.), Germany, and France. Actual and budgeted operating reports for two recent years are presented below for these three markets.

	United Kingdom		Germany		France	
	Year 2 Budget	**Year 1 Actual**	**Year 2 Budget**	**Year 1 Actual**	**Year 2 Budget**	**Year 1 Actual**
Sales	$49,960	$48,080	$156,840	$137,440	$108,720	$102,560
Cost of sales	(21,982)	(21,155)	(65,872)	(57,995)	(53,414)	(50,254)
Direct expenses	(14,658)	(14,512)	(50,286)	(46,603)	(31,529)	(29,742)
Other income/expenses	(1,499)	(1,155)	(300)	(210)	(946)	(1,026)
Responsibility earnings	$11,821	$11,258	$ 40,382	$ 32,632	$ 22,831	$ 21,538
Interest income/expense*	(358)	(241)	(1,312)	(939)	(1,033)	(1,047)
Exchange gain/loss**	(142)	(338)	(150)	(210)	(272)	(286)
Division charges***	(1,629)	(1,640)	(4,700)	(4,123)	(3,262)	(3,077)
Earnings before taxes	$ 9,692	$ 9,039	$ 34,220	$ 27,360	$ 18,264	$ 17,128
Segment assets	$84,500	$88,860	$ 73,760	$ 72,900	$ 74,220	$ 73,460
Earnings before taxes	19.4%	18.8%	21.8%	19.9%	16.8%	16.7%
Return on assets	11.5%	10.2%	46.4%	37.5%	24.6%	23.3%

* Based on locally incurred debt.

** Based on the average Year 1 exchange rate with the United States.

*** Fixed charge negotiated annually between the Bartow Division and the market subsidiary.

1. Analyze these reports carefully. Assuming that Ameripill requires a minimum ROA of 12%, should the company consider dropping the U.K. market?
2. Ameripill currently has a problem with one of the drugs sold in France. In the French market, Saincoeur is a highly successful treatment for heart-attack victims. (It is also sold under other names in all of Ameripill's markets.) Because of regulatory pressure in France, Saincoeur is being sold at a much lower price in France than in Germany or the U.K. Despite the price ceiling, Saincoeur is a profitable product (barely) in France. However, word of the lower price is creating a lot of pressure in the neighboring markets to reduce the prices to a level similar to that of the French market. Saincoeur is a very profitable product in both Germany and the U.K. How do these facts affect your previous decision regarding the U.K. market in (1)?

Source: Adapted from S. F. Haka, B. A. Lamberton, and H. M. Sollenberger, "International Subsidiary Performance Evaluation: The Case of the Ameripill Company," *Issues in Accounting Education*, Spring 1994, pp. 168–190.

ETHICS CASE

• *Play World, Inc.*

Roger Smith, the controller of Play World, Inc., a toy company, has just completed an analysis of a make-or-buy decision with respect to a particular part for one of the new toys the company is planning to manufacture. The result of the analysis clearly shows that the company should buy the part from one of the three available suppliers (based on written price quotations received from those suppliers within the past few weeks). Based on this analysis, Smith and the division manager, Kate Pfirman, agreed to proceed with placing an order. They issued instructions to the purchasing department indicating that the order should be placed for a price not higher than $3.40 per part. A few days later, Smith received a phone call from the purchasing department indicating that all three suppliers had raised their price to $4.00 per unit. It was a normal business practice to raise prices after written quotations had been issued.

It was immediately clear to Smith that it would be disadvantageous to his company to buy the part at the higher price. He discussed the new information with Pfirman, and they agreed to proceed with manufacturing plans to make the part internally. Smith thought it was rather strange that all three suppliers had raised their price to the same amount, but felt there was nothing he could do about it.

A few days later, Smith's secretary, Lynn Berry, asked if she could have a private conversation with him. Berry was obviously upset, so Smith asked her to come into his office and shut the door. Berry told him she was good friends with the secretary for the president of one of the suppliers from which Play World had planned to buy the part for the new toy. Berry's friend had casually mentioned that her boss had been on the phone with the other suppliers and they had agreed to raise the price for certain parts they were manufacturing to specified dollar amounts. Berry said she was reluctant to tell Smith because she didn't want her friend to get in trouble for revealing confidential information outside her company. For Smith, this information was the missing piece that explained why the price for the part had been raised to $4.00 by all three companies. Smith thanked Berry for the information and told her not to worry; he would keep the information to himself but would give some thought to what he would eventually do with what she had told him.

1. Who are the parties that are affected by this bid-rigging scheme?
2. What should Smith do with the information he received from Berry (keep in mind his responsibilities to the accounting profession, to his company, and to Berry)?

WRITING ASSIGNMENT

• *Airline Ticket Prices*

If you have ever shopped for airline tickets, you are aware of the tremendous diversity in ticket prices for the same flight, even for those who sit in the same section (first-class, coach, etc.) Much of the difference is based on two factors: (1) when you bought your ticket and (2) whether you plan to stay over a Saturday night.

Write a one- to two-page paper describing why airline companies have so many different ticket prices. Also, why do you think it is important to the airline that clients fly back from their business trips on Sunday instead of Saturday?

THE DEBATE

• *Total Costs versus Differential Costs*

As discussed in this chapter, a management accountant can choose whether to present information using total costs or differential (e.g., incremental) costs. Divide your group into two teams. Each group will defend cost analysis for relevant decision making using either total costs or differential costs.

- One team represents "Total Costs." Present the advantages of using total costs for decision making. What are the disadvantages of using differential costs?
- The other team represents "Differential Costs." Present the advantages of using differential costs for decision making. What are the disadvantages of using total costs?

INTERNET SEARCH

• *Benchmarking in Europe*

Early in the chapter we discussed the concept of benchmarking, a new evaluation method that has been used extensively in recent years. We discussed benchmarking in the context of one company comparing its financial and operating performance against a competitor's performance or comparing the performance of various internal departments against each other. However, benchmarking is a concept that can be used in any type of organization or even for yourself. Take the **EUROPEAN COMMISSION**, for example. Since the mid-1990s, the commission has undertaken a number of benchmarking initiatives so that member countries can compare best practices at three levels: country and business environment, company or enterprise, and industry or sector. The European Commission discusses its benchmark initiatives at the following Web site: **http://www.benchmarking-in-europe.com**. (Sometimes Web addresses change, so if this address does not work, access the Web site for this textbook, **http://albrecht.swcollege.com**, for an updated link.) Go to this site and answer the following questions:

1. List the four basic steps in benchmarking it identifies.
2. Identify the objective of enterprise policy benchmarking.
3. What method has been used to benchmark in the area of enterprise policy?

Evaluating Personnel and Divisions

chapter **m9**

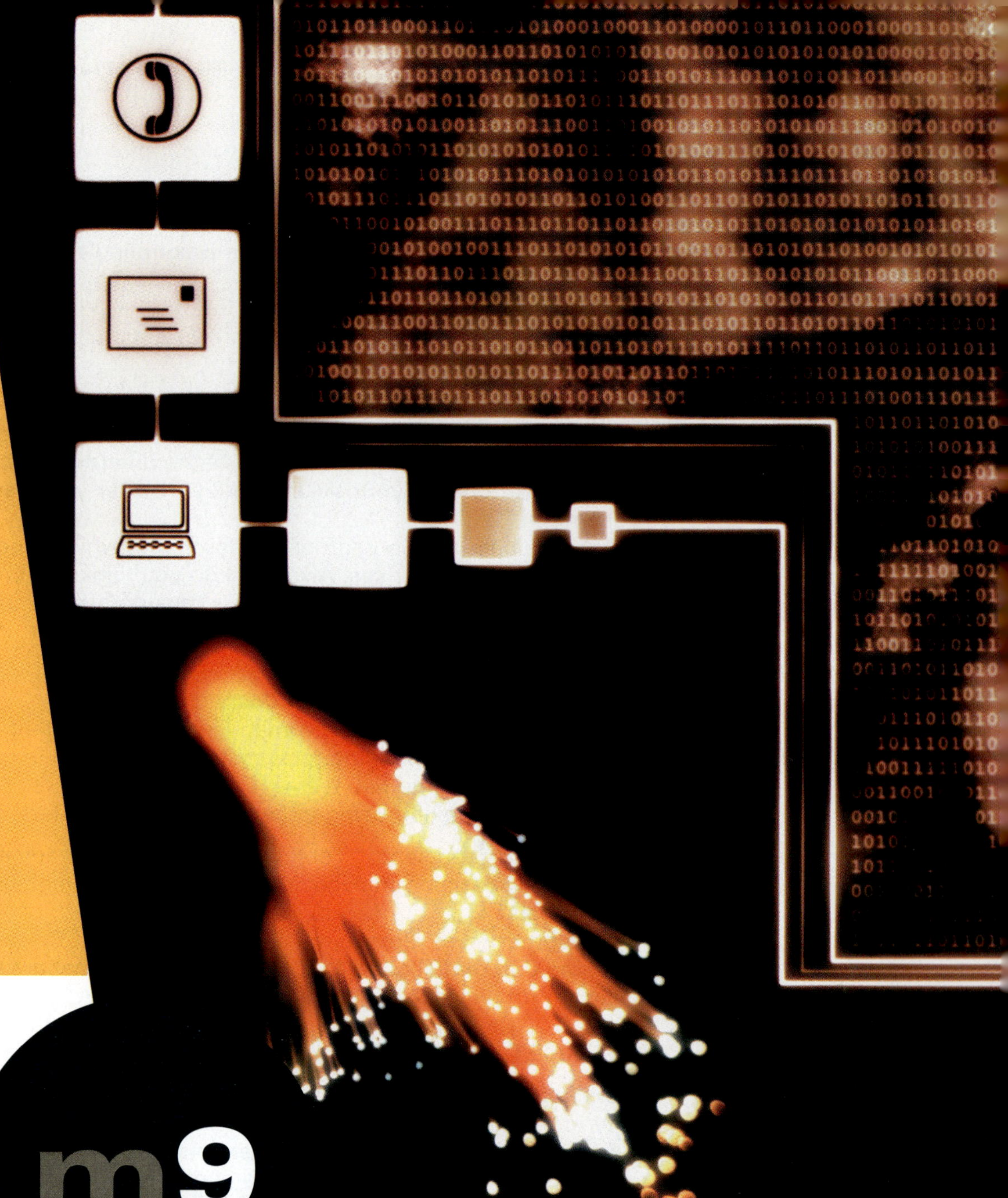

learning objectives After studying this chapter, you should be able to:

1 Explain why evaluating personnel and divisions is such an important activity in organizations.

2 Identify different kinds of organizational units in which evaluation occurs.

3 Explain how performance is evaluated in cost centers.

4 Explain how performance is evaluated in profit centers.

5 Explain how performance is evaluated in investment centers.

expanded material

6 Compute and interpret variable overhead variances in cost centers.

setting the stage

In deciding where to invest their money, potential investors, whether they are individuals or professionally managed investment funds, try to evaluate the company and its management. This evaluation has never been harder than with Internet or high-tech companies. Take the case of **ICG COMMUNICATIONS INC.**, for example.[1] ICG Communications is a provider of Internet services based in Englewood, Colorado. After being a high flier on Wall Street, its stock was selling for $.44 a share in January 2001, down from a high of $39.25 in March 2000. What went wrong, and why didn't investors do a better job of evaluating potential returns?

ICG is a story of big ambition and big money gone awry. The company borrowed heavily to grow as fast as possible, while paying too little attention to the details needed to manage its growth, such as customers, investment bankers, industry analysts, and current and former employees. While ICG's expansion made it one of the biggest players providing access to the Internet—by early 2000, 10% of Internet traffic crossed the ICG network—it overpromised and then underdelivered on its service. As a result, key customers, such as **MICROSOFT**, **NETZERO, INC.**, and **EARTHLINK, INC.**, responded to customer complaints about blocked connections, busy signals, and cutoff connections by shifting their business to ICG competitors.

ICG's strategy was to provide the systems—networks of switches, modem banks, and fiber-optic cable—that linked people at home via their local telephone company with the high-speed fiber-optic lines that carry Internet traffic. If the Internet is a superhighway, ICG would build the ramps that carried traffic from the local roads—i.e., the Baby Bells—onto the superhighway. Because more and more people wanted to get onto the Internet, the demand for the ramps was practically unlimited, ICG said, and it intended to dominate the ramp business.

ICG planned to get the bulk of its revenue in two ways: by getting paid for its systems and service by Internet providers such as NetZero, and by collecting a small toll from the local phone company for each minute a customer spent connected to the Internet through ICG's system. But building ramps was not going to be cheap. So, ICG went where the money is—Wall Street. With the help of **MORGAN STANLEY DEAN WITTER & COMPANY**, the company raised $2 billion starting in 1995. While some of the money was used to build ramps, some of it was used to build ICG's striking new headquarters, a tower that the architect described as "the curve of a ship's prow looking toward the mountains."

Meanwhile, in addition to leading the company, the CEO, J. Shelby Bryan, was hobnobbing on the social and political circuits in New York and Washington. Although the company was headquartered in Colorado, Bryan lived in Manhattan where he held fund-raising parties for President Clinton and Al Gore. In July 1999, Clinton named Bryan to the President's Foreign Intelligence Advisory Board where he was awarded top-secret security clearance. He also served as national finance chair of the Democratic Senatorial Campaign Committee in 1997 and 1998. Unfortunately, Bryan's growing public profile began to rankle investors, making it harder to raise new capital. One major investor nixed an earlier investment in 1999, in part due to its concerns that Bryan had too many distractions to keep a close eye on the company.

Today, although the company still hopes to solve its network problems and arrange a large credit line to make sure it is able to keep operating and pay new supplier debts and employees, ICG's frustrated investors have taken to ridiculing the company on Internet message boards. One ditty making the rounds, meant to be sung to the tune of the "Addams Family," goes:

Their tower's a museum
With art that's ad nauseam
The stockholders could scream
The Gang at ICG.

On November 14, 2000, ICG filed for Chapter 11 bankruptcy protection from creditors. Chapter 11 is a plan that allows the company some time to try to work out its financial matters.

With ICG, some investors have not only not earned a positive return, they have experienced a 98% loss on their investment. This case illustrates well the importance of the two topics that will be discussed in this chapter—the need to evaluate both divisions (or companies in

1 Paul M. Sherer and Gary McWilliams, "How a Brash Provider of Internet Services Became Unplugged," *The Wall Street Journal*, November 13, 2000, p. A1. Also, see Paul M. Sherer, "ICG Files for Protection from Creditors," *The Wall Street Journal*, November 15, 2000, p. A1.

this case) and people. In this case, the company seems to have overpromised and underperformed. Similarly, Bryan, the CEO, appears to have been distracted by political and social ambitions and interests. If the allegations of investors and potential investors are correct, this fixation on interests outside the company made it impossible for Bryan to perform to his best ability.

In this chapter, we will be examining ways that investors, managers, and others evaluate how well organizational units and their managers are performing. In Chapter 8 of management accounting, we focused on the performance of products and processes and introduced various evaluation methods, including benchmarking. Benchmarking and other overall evaluation methods are appropriate for divisions and units as well, but will not be repeated in this chapter. Rather, we will concentrate on evaluation measures that focus exclusively on the performance of divisions and people.

In evaluating divisions and people, it is often difficult to separate the performance of a unit from the performance of its managers. As a result, managers are most often evaluated on how well their units perform. If managers are responsible for costs only, they are usually evaluated on how well they control costs. If they are responsible for revenues and costs, they are usually evaluated on how profitable their units are. And, if they are responsible for costs, revenues, and investments, they are most frequently evaluated on the return those investments generate. In the case of ICG and CEO Bryan, he was responsible for costs, revenues, and investments. Since the company lost large sums of money, neither Bryan nor ICG would be evaluated very positively.

1

Explain why evaluating personnel and divisions is such an important activity in organizations.

EVALUATING PERSONNEL AND DIVISIONS

Today, we live in a new and different economy. At least three major developments have dramatically changed the environment in which businesses operate. First, new technology has made information inexpensive. While low-cost, high-speed digital and cable video and data transmission hardware produces information quickly and easily, new software has made preparation, data, and communication tools available to individuals who previously did not have access to needed information. With these technology developments, time, space, and other temporal constraints on information have been reduced and, in many cases, eliminated.

A second major development that has significantly affected business has been globalization. Faster methods of transportation, together with instantaneous information, have allowed the world to become one giant marketplace. Consumers can now buy products from foreign firms as easily as from a local store. Organizations such as GENERAL MOTORS have to worry not only about what CHRYSLER and FORD are doing, but also about what TOYOTA, VOLKSWAGEN, and BMW are doing as well. In fact, Chrysler is not just "Chrysler" anymore. It is now a conglomeration of European, North American, and Asian manufacturers known as DAIMLERCHRYSLER. Instead of having only two major American competitors, General Motors and all other business organizations now have to compete with similar companies throughout the world. In addition, with the increased availability of inexpensive information, more is known about these competitors and about General Motors than ever before. If a GM product has deficiencies, for example, the world knows about and can act on those problems instantly. If GM or one of its units is not performing well, investors will be reluctant to invest money and even GM's management will direct its resources to other operating units.

A third major change is the concentration of power in certain market investors, primarily large mutual and pension funds. Mutual funds such as FIDELITY and VANGUARD and pension funds such as CALPERS, for example, now hold major stock positions in many companies. The influence of these major market players is so significant that, if they are displeased, corporate executives will find that their positions within the company are in jeopardy. Armed with easily available and inexpensive information about investees and their competitors, large institutional investors raise the competitive bar very high and shorten the periods over which success is measured.

While these change drivers have significantly affected everything we do, including the way we live, they have had two dramatic effects on business and on how we evaluate business units and their managements. First, they have eliminated the old model that assumed information is expensive. Today, anyone, armed with the right access to data sources, can know almost as much about companies as corporate insiders. In addition, with better and more timely information, investors can make evaluations that tell them where they should put their money and which organizations are performing best. Second, these developments have dramatically increased the level of competition among organizations. Institutional investors and business executives want the best performance, and they want it now. They demand that organizations be market leaders and be highly profitable. Because global competitors often have different cost structures that can be exploited to render historically successful business models obsolete, and because information about all organizations is widely available, only organizations that are truly the best survive and remain successful.

A number of business developments have occurred because of these changes. Some of the most obvious are:

- An increased pace of change in the business world
- Shorter product life cycles and shorter competitive advantages
- A requirement for better, quicker, and more decisive actions by management
- The emergence of new companies and new industries
- The emergence of new professional services
- Outsourcing of non-value-added, but necessary, services
- Increased uncertainty and the explicit recognition of risk
- Increasingly complex business transactions
- Increased focus on customer satisfaction

To be able to react to fast-paced business changes, managers and investors must make timely evaluations of units and their managements. They must know as early as possible whether a unit's profit or market share is decreasing. They must be able to assess trends and changes in performance quickly. They must know when new competitors are getting stronger and encroaching on the business's success. They must know when management is performing in ways that are resulting in the organization losing ground to competitors. Only if they have accurate information about how well management and various organizational units are performing, can they make effective personnel, resource, and other decisions. In addition, as we have stated previously, good evaluation leads to good planning, which leads to good control. If managements do not accurately evaluate how they are doing, what needs to be improved, and where resources must be placed and withdrawn, their organizations will most likely be unsuccessful in the future. The result of faster-paced changes is that evaluations must be performed quicker and more frequently than ever before.

---

to summarize

The business world is changing faster than ever before. These fast-paced changes require that decision makers (managers and investors) have better information and perform more timely evaluations of organizational units and the individuals responsible for the organizations. Good evaluation leads to better planning and control decisions and the better allocation of resources.

---

business environment essay

Reducing Trauma Unit Costs As an example of how good evaluation can lead to better decisions and better performance, consider the case of the **UNIVERSITY OF MICHIGAN MEDICAL CENTER**'s trauma unit. Evaluation of the trauma (emergency) unit resulted in subdividing costs into six categories: (1) nursing, (2) surgery, (3) pharmacy, (4) laboratory, (5) radiology, and (6) emergency. Because medical practice continues to be pressured by increasing patient demands and decreasing reimbursement, and because trauma services are especially vulnerable to cost pressures as the ability of their patients to pay is often marginal and the care provided is extremely resource intensive, the medical center decided to work hard to reduce trauma unit costs.

Take nursing services, for example. To reduce costs, the hospital developed a coherent discharge plan for each patient early during hospitalization. The physician leader was responsible for coordination and oversight of the nursing staff, residents, case man-

2

Identify different kinds of organizational units in which evaluation occurs.

EVALUATION OF DIVISIONS AND PERSONNEL IN DIFFERENT TYPES OF OPERATING UNITS

segments Parts of an organization requiring separate reports for evaluation by management.

Most companies are made up of a number of relatively independent **segments** or subunits, sometimes called groups, divisions, or subsidiaries.

As an example, Exhibit 9-1 shows an organizational chart for a hypothetical company that we will call International Manufacturing Corporation (IMC). IMC has three operating (subsidiary) companies: Acme Computer, Edison Automobile, and Jennifer Cosmetics. Although each of these companies has several divisions and other subsegments, only a few of those for Edison Automobile are shown. Edison has three geographic bases: the United States, the Far East, and Europe. The making and selling of automobiles in the Far East division is further broken down into the Japanese and Korean units. The Japanese unit is separated into sales, manufacturing, and service. Edison Automobile's other geographic divisions have similar subsegments.

You will notice that IMC uses different criteria to define its segments at each level. At the highest level, product group (computers, autos, cosmetics) is used, probably because there is a significant difference in the business knowledge needed to produce and sell these products. At the middle level, segments are defined geographically because of the unique needs of each market and the distances involved. At the lowest level, each country unit is subdivided by function—sales, manufacturing, and service.

Given the organizational chart in Exhibit 9-1, how much autonomy should the executives of each division be granted by corporate management? If each company (Acme, Edison, and Jennifer) has its own president, vice presidents, and other officers, should these executives be allowed to operate independently of one another? If Acme, for example, is the most profitable company, should it be given more operating capital than Edison and Jennifer, or less? Should a decision for Acme to expand into hand-held computers be made by Acme's executives or by IMC's corporate officers? Within Edison Automobile, how much autonomy should each of the geographic offices have? Should a decision to double the advertising budget or offer consumer rebates in the Far East operations be made by the manager of that division, by the top management of Edison Automobile, or by the president of IMC?

decentralized company An organization in which managers at all levels have the authority to make decisions concerning the operations for which they are responsible.

Questions such as these are difficult to answer. In fact, it would probably be difficult to find two companies that would answer them the same way. Assuming that IMC is basically a **decentralized company**, managers at all levels will have the authority to make decisions concerning the operations for which they are directly responsible. Regarding the question of rebates

agers, and discharge planners in the discharge process. The net effect of the shorter stays was reduced nursing costs. As another example, radiology costs were reduced by utilizing outside hospital examinations and substituting less costly examinations for more expensive tests (abdominal ultrasound instead of abdominal CT, for example). The medical center also developed protocols for X-ray utilization so as to minimize "routine films." As a result, the center stopped performing lateral C spines in the trauma bays and discontinued routine daily chest X-rays in the ICU. Through close evaluation and follow-up in other areas, the overall variable cost of care per patient was reduced by 25%. The mean length of patient stay decreased from 8.72 days to 7.06 days, and significant cost reduction was achieved in all six cost areas. Nursing costs decreased 24%; surgical costs, 5%; laboratory costs, 27%; radiology costs, 7%; pharmacy costs, 57%; and emergency services, 36%.

Source: Information was obtained from http://www.chcecon.org/traumacostpaper.asp.

exhibit 9-1 An Organizational Chart

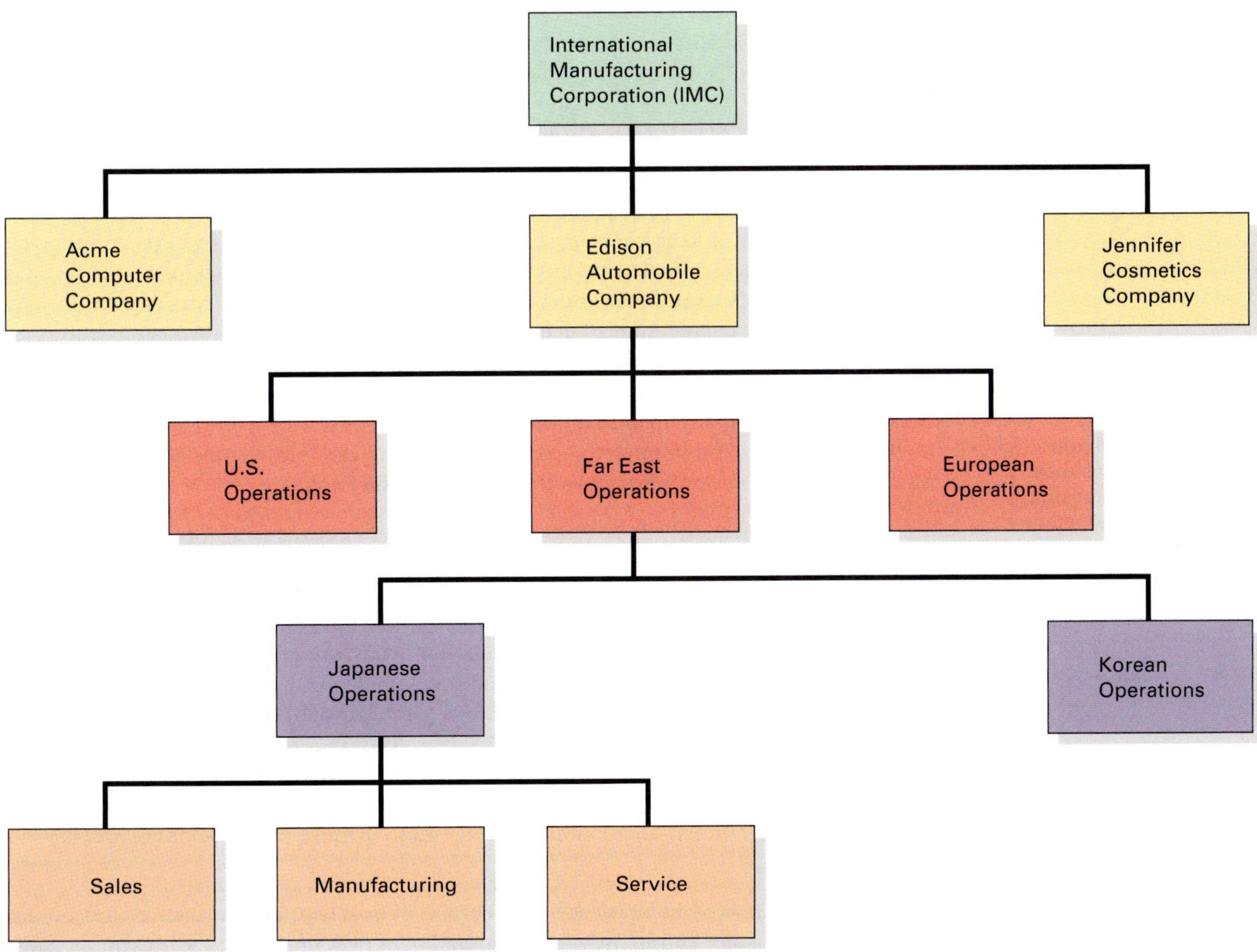

business environment essay

Berkshire Hathaway As an example of how businesses are divided into segments, consider BERKSHIRE HATHAWAY, INC., which is primarily owned by Warren E. Buffett, one of the richest individuals in the United States. In a 2000 SEC filing, Berkshire stated that its most important business is the property and casualty insurance business, which includes GEICO CORPORATION, the sixth largest auto insurer in the United States, and GENERAL RE CORPORATION, one of the four largest reinsurers in the world. In addition, it identified several other types of businesses, including the publication of a daily and Sunday newspaper in western New York (BUFFALO NEWS); the manufacture and sale of boxed chocolates and other confectionery products (SEE'S CANDIES); diversified manufacturing and distribution; the retail sale of home furnishings (NEBRASKA FURNITURE MART, R.C. WILLEY HOME FURNISHINGS, STAR FURNITURE COMPANY, and JORDAN'S, INC.); the manufacture, import, and distribution of footwear (H.H. BROWN SHOE COMPANY, LOWELL SHOE, INC., DEXTER SHOE COMPANY, and JUSTIN BRANDS); the retail sale of fine jewelry; the providing of training to operators of aircraft and ships throughout the world; the providing

in the Far East, for example, the operating manager of that geographic division should probably decide whether to offer them. Likewise, the manager of the Japanese Manufacturing division should decide where to buy engine parts, and the manager of the Service division should have primary responsibility for setting the price to charge for repairing a muffler in Japan. These managers would also be held accountable for the consequences of their decisions.

Benefits and Problems of Decentralization

To what degree should a company decentralize? BERKSHIRE HATHAWAY, for example, is very decentralized, allowing managers of its various business units to operate nearly autonomously. Clearly, a large company employing thousands of people in different geographic areas could not remain completely centralized, with top management making all the decisions. The president of IMC would not know enough about the costs and varieties of paint in Japan, for example, or have enough time to make all the operating decisions for the manufacturing subsegment of the Japanese operations of Edison Automobile. Though such decisions would never be made by the president of a large international company, they would be made at a higher level in a **centralized company** than in a decentralized one.

centralized company An organization in which top management makes most of the major decisions for the entire company rather than delegating decisions to managers at lower levels.

Currently, the trend in most companies is to decentralize. The reasons often cited for making decisions at the lowest possible level in an organization are:

1. Segment managers usually have more information about matters within their area of responsibility than do managers at higher levels.
2. Segment managers are in a better position to see current problems and to react quickly to local situations.
3. Higher-level management can spend more time on broader policy and strategic issues because the burden of daily decision making is distributed.
4. Segment managers have a greater incentive to perform well because they receive the credit (or blame) for performance resulting from their decisions.
5. Employees have greater incentives and motivation to perform well because there are more opportunities for advancement into leadership positions when a company is decentralized.
6. Managers and officers can be evaluated more easily because their responsibilities are more clearly defined.

Decentralization has its drawbacks as well. Decisions made by managers of decentralized units are sometimes not consistent with the overall objectives of the firm. For example, Edison

of fractional ownership programs for general aviation aircraft; the licensing and servicing of almost 6,000 DAIRY QUEEN stores; the rental of furniture and accessories; and the manufacturing and production of face brick and concrete masonry products.

In addition to its own business segments, Berkshire Hathaway also owns large segments of AMERICAN EXPRESS COMPANY, THE COCA-COLA COMPANY, FEDERAL HOME LOAN MORTGAGE CORPORATION, THE GILLETTE COMPANY, THE WASHINGTON POST COMPANY, and WELLS FARGO COMPANY. Warren Buffett is generally believed to be one of the most astute investors in the United States. As he states in his annual report, "We are interested in making investments that meet the following conditions:

1. It is a large purchase (at least $25 million of before-tax earnings).
2. The company has demonstrated consistent earning power.
3. The business earns a good return on equity with little or no debt.
4. The management of the company is good and in place.
5. The company is involved in a 'simple business.'
6. There is an offering price which is realistic."

Automobile might find it less expensive to buy computer parts for its automobiles from an outside source than from Acme Computer, or the Service division of Japanese operations may find it cheaper to buy repair parts from outsiders rather than from the Manufacturing division. Such decisions would allow the buying divisions to report lower costs, but the decisions might decrease the company's overall profitability.

There are two ways to prevent such problems. First, certain decisions should be centralized. For example, all decisions related to insurance coverage, which benefits the entire company, should probably be made at the corporate level. Second, a system of responsibility accounting should be established so that a manager's decisions will benefit not only the segment but also the firm as a whole. This **goal congruence**, whereby the goals of the company and all its segments are in harmony, can be achieved only if the responsibility accounting system is well designed.

goal congruence The selection of goals for responsibility centers that are consistent, or congruent, with those of the company as a whole.

responsibility accounting A system of evaluating performance; managers are held accountable for the costs, revenues, assets, or other elements over which they have control.

Responsibility Accounting

Responsibility accounting is a system in which managers are assigned and held accountable for certain costs, assets, and/or revenues. There are two important behavioral considerations in assigning responsibilities to managers. First, the responsible manager should be involved in developing the plan for the unit over which the manager has control. Current research indicates that people are more motivated to achieve a goal (budget or standard) if they participate in setting it. Such participation assures that the goals will be reasonable and, more importantly, that they will be perceived to be reasonable by the managers.

Second, a manager should be held accountable only for those costs, assets, or revenues over which the manager has substantial control. Some costs may be generated within a segment, but control over them lies outside that unit. The manager of the Japanese Manufacturing division, for example, may be responsible for labor costs, but employee wages may be determined by a union scale controlled elsewhere. Admittedly, determining "substantial control" requires a judgment based on the circumstances, but if all relevant factors are considered, careful and fair judgments can be made.

RESPONSIBILITY ACCOUNTING REPORTS Regardless of the degree of autonomy given to managers at various operating levels, responsibility accounting (performance) reports are needed at all levels of the organization. At the lowest levels, these reports tell managers where corrective action must be taken to control their segments' operations. At top levels, these reports

exception reports Reports that highlight variances from, or exceptions to, the budget.

keep management informed of the activities of all segments. The reports are then used to reward past performance and set incentives for future performance.

Exhibit 9-2 illustrates the kind of responsibility accounting reports a company might use. Note that reporting begins at the bottom and works upward, with each manager receiving information on the operations for which that manager is responsible, as well as summary information on the performance of lower-level managers. Note also that these reports are **exception reports**, meaning that variances from, or exceptions to, the budget are highlighted. In the report, unfavorable or negative variances are labeled "U" while favorable variances are labeled "F." Such reports direct management immediately to the areas requiring corrective action. To keep

exhibit 9-2 Responsibility Accounting Reports for Edison Automobile Company of IMC

President, Edison Automobile	Responsibility Centers	Budgeted Costs	Actual Costs	Variance*
The president receives from each geographic area of operations a report summarizing its performance. The president can see where corrective action needs to be made by tracing the differences between budget and actual downward to their sources.	General Administration	x	x	x
	United States	x	x	x
	Far East	$58,000	$65,000	$7,000 U
	Europe	x	x	x

Far East Operations	Responsibility Centers	Budgeted Costs	Actual Costs	Variance
The manager of Far East operations receives a report from each country segment's head. These reports are then summarized and passed on to the president of Edison Automobile.	Japanese Operations	$21,000	$23,000	$2,000 U
	Korean Operations	x	x	x
	Total costs	$58,000	$65,000	$7,000 U

Japanese Operations	Responsibility Centers	Budgeted Costs	Actual Costs	Variance
The manager of Japanese operations receives from each unit a report summarizing its performance. These reports are combined and sent up to the next level, the manager of Far East operations.	Sales	x	x	x
	Manufacturing	$ 9,000	$10,200	$1,200 U
	Service	x	x	x
	Total costs	$21,000	$23,000	$2,000 U

Japanese Manufacturing Division	Variable Costs of Manufacturing	Budgeted Costs	Actual Costs	Variance
The Manufacturing division supervisor receives a performance report on the supervisor's center of responsibility. The totals from these reports are then communicated to the manager of Japanese operations, the next level of responsibility.	Direct materials	$ 2,000	$ 2,500	$ 500 U
	Direct labor	6,000	6,400	400 U
	Manufacturing overhead	1,000	1,300	300 U
	Total costs	$ 9,000	$10,200	$1,200 U

*U means unfavorable.

the example simple, Exhibit 9-2 focuses only on costs. In a real company, some units would report their profitability and even a return on investment.

Responsibility accounting reports prepared for lower-level managers contain greater detail than those for upper-level managers. This is because lower-level managers are responsible for the detailed operations of the firm and need to take immediate action when some aspect of operations gets out of control; upper-level managers perform more of an overall review function. Furthermore, the responsibility accounting reports of lower-level managers in a decentralized operation would contain more items than they would in a centralized operation; with decentralization, managers are given broader areas of responsibility.

RESPONSIBILITY CENTERS In our example, the president of IMC is responsible for the entire organization and should be held accountable for the company's overall successes and failures. At lower levels, the president of Edison Automobile Company, the manager of Edison's operations in the Far East, the manager in charge of Japanese operations in Edison's Far East operations, and the manager of the Japanese Manufacturing division, for example, would be held responsible for operations within their respective units.

responsibility center An organizational unit in which a manager has control over and is held accountable for performance.

cost center An organizational unit in which a manager has control over and is held accountable for costs.

profit center An organizational unit in which a manager has control over and is held accountable for both costs and revenues.

investment center An organizational unit in which a manager has control over and is held accountable for costs, revenues, and assets.

Each unit is referred to as a **responsibility center**, and, depending on the operation, it may be a cost, profit, or investment center. As the name implies, a **cost center** is any organizational unit in which the manager of that unit has control over the costs incurred. The manager of a cost center has no responsibility for revenues or assets, either because revenues are not generated or because they are under the control of someone else. The manufacturing unit of Japanese operations of IMC, for example, could be designated a cost center. A **profit center** manager, however, has responsibility for both costs and revenues. Profit centers are usually found at higher levels in an organization than are cost centers. The geographic regions (United States, Far East, and Europe, as well as various country operations within the Far East region) of Edison Automobile would probably be profit centers.

In an **investment center**, the manager is responsible for costs, revenues, and assets. This means that the manager is responsible not only for operating costs, but also for determining the amount of funds to be invested in the center's plant and equipment and for the rate of return earned on those investments. Investment centers are usually found at relatively high levels in organizations. The different companies in IMC (Acme Computer, Edison Automobile, and Jennifer Cosmetics) would probably be investment centers.

---

to summarize

Most companies are divided into segments with specific responsibilities assigned to each segment manager. In a centralized organization, top management makes most of the operating decisions; in a decentralized organization, decision-making authority is delegated down the corporate ladder to the managers most immediately responsible. It is very important in a decentralized company that the goals of the company and all its segments are in harmony. This concept is referred to as goal congruence.

Regardless of the degree of decentralization, almost all companies use performance reports that show variances from budgeted amounts for each division, department, and unit. These reports pass upward through an organization so that supervisors and managers at all levels can assess the performance of the units serving under them. Decentralized companies are divided into fairly independent responsibility centers. There are three types of responsibility centers: cost, profit, and investment. Managers of responsibility centers usually have control over, and are held accountable for, the performance of the center.

3
Explain how performance is evaluated in cost centers.

EVALUATING PERFORMANCE IN COST CENTERS

As stated in the last section, managers of cost centers are responsible for costs incurred. Most cost centers usually have one type of cost that is more significant than any other. In service organizations, salaries are generally the major cost. In wholesale and retail businesses, the cost of merchandise purchased for resale is often the most significant cost. In manufacturing firms, costs incurred to make products (direct materials, direct labor, and manufacturing overhead) are usually most significant.

If managers are to be held responsible for the costs incurred in their centers, they must have control over those costs, have relevant information about those costs, and have a system that focuses on or engineers in effective cost controls. Historically, companies have used a *standard costing* system that isolates differences between actual and standard costs to determine whether costs are too high or too low, whether they are improving (decreasing) or getting worse (increasing), and whether they will allow the company to be competitive. With this method, standard costs are compared to actual costs, and variances are computed. Standard cost systems have been used effectively in service, merchandising, and manufacturing firms.

target costing A costing approach that designs a product to meet specific cost objectives based on target market prices less the target margin.

In recent years, however, some leading management accountants have argued that companies using standard costing have been missing out on a valuable competitive tool in controlling costs. They argue that instead of assessing, after the fact, whether costs were appropriate, it is more effective to design or engineer appropriate cost levels into products and services. They advocate a **target costing** approach that evaluates costs before production begins. Basically, target costing involves designing products based on prespecified costs by gathering marketing input on customer needs and getting everyone in the company to work toward hitting the target costs.

In this section, we will first cover standard costing systems and will then introduce the revolutionary target costing approach being advocated and tried by some accountants and companies.

Standard Cost System

standard cost system A cost-accumulation system in which standard costs are used as product costs instead of actual costs.

Companies that use standard costing design their accounting systems to incorporate standard costs and variances. This type of system, called a **standard cost system**, is a cost-accumulation process based on costs that should have been incurred rather than costs that were actually incurred. The steps in establishing and operating a standard cost system are:

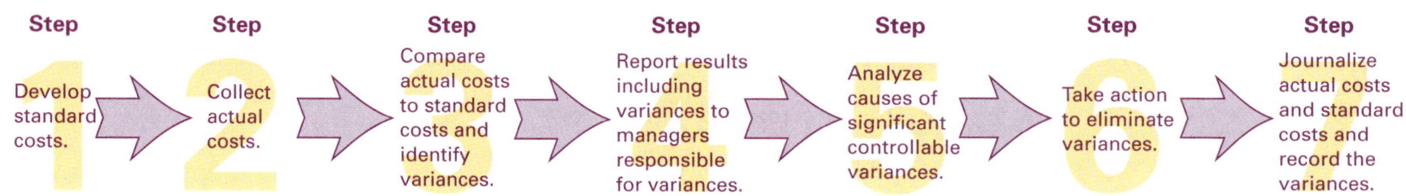

These steps describe a typical standard cost system. You can find some or all of these elements in most organizations, but you will not likely find all seven elements in all firms. You are most likely to find an extensive standard cost system in manufacturing firms, which usually have standard costs for direct materials and direct labor and, to a lesser extent, for manufacturing overhead. These standard costs usually are reported on **standard cost cards**, often stored in a computer. A standard cost card for Smell-Good Perfume made by Jennifer Cosmetics, a subsidiary of IMC, is shown in Exhibit 9-3. The data in Exhibit 9-3 will be used to illustrate how variances are calculated and analyzed.

standard cost cards An itemization of the components of the standard cost of a product.

DETERMINING STANDARD COSTS AND IDENTIFYING VARIANCES In a manufacturing firm, standard costs are determined on the basis of careful analysis and the experience of many people, including accountants, industrial engineers, purchasing agents, and the managers of the departments to be judged. Accountants play an important role in developing standard costs because they have the data needed to determine how costs have changed in the past in re-

exhibit 9-3 Standard Cost Card

Jennifer Cosmetics
Standard Cost Card—Smell-Good Perfume

	(1) Standard Quantity	(2) Standard Price or Rate	(3) Standard Cost (1) × (2)
Inputs:			
Direct materials	2 ounces	$ 2.000	$ 4.00
Direct labor	2 hours	16.000	32.00
Manufacturing overhead:			
Variable	2 hours	1.500	3.00
Fixed	2 hours	2.375	4.75
Total standard cost per unit.			$43.75

lation to levels of activity. This is not an easy task. Changes in methods of production, technology, worker efficiency, and plant layout, for example, can affect the behavior of costs. Before they can serve as standard costs, past costs often have to be adjusted to take changes in operating conditions into account. These changes sometimes occur gradually and may not be easily noticeable, making it difficult for management accountants to identify cost characteristics that will be useful in setting standards for the future.

Engineers are often involved in setting standard costs because of their knowledge of the most efficient way of performing each task in relation to the existing technology of the operation. Managers who will be judged by the standard costs should be involved in the standard-setting process; they are more likely to be motivated to meet standards if they have participated in setting the standards and have accepted them. Of course, the participation of such managers also makes effective use of their experience and judgment.

Once management has established a standard quantity and a standard price for each resource (direct materials, direct labor, and manufacturing overhead), the standard quantity is multiplied by the standard price to arrive at a standard dollar cost for the manufactured product. Actual costs are then compared with these standards to calculate the **variance**, the amount by which the actual cost differs from the standard. This variance, if significant, is a signal to management that costs may be "out of control" and that corrective action should be taken to eliminate the variance. This process of using variances from a standard to isolate problem areas is called **management by exception**. It is the basis of the control function.

variance Any deviation from standard.

management by exception The strategy of focusing attention on significant deviations from a standard.

Because standard costs have a price (or rate) component and a quantity (or usage) component, a comparison of actual and standard costs can result in two variances: a price (rate) variance and a quantity (usage) variance. These variances are usually computed for direct materials, direct labor, and variable manufacturing overhead.

STOP & THINK Is it possible for a company to have positive variances (actual costs are less than standard costs) and still have problems?

Exhibit 9-4 is a general model for calculating variances. This model has two important characteristics. First, it is applicable to each of the manufacturing cost elements—direct materials, direct labor, and variable manufacturing overhead. Second, the analysis is essentially an input-output analysis. The price (rate) variance compares actual inputs used at the actual and standard prices. The actual quantities are used to isolate the effect of the price change on the cost of the resources actually acquired or used. The price variance, then, is the difference between the actual price and the standard price, times the actual quantity. The quantity (usage) variance compares the inputs actually used at the standard price with the inputs that should have been used at the standard price to produce the actual output. The standard price is used so that the quantity variances will not be influenced by price changes. The quantity variance is the difference between the actual quantity and the standard quantity, times the standard price.

exhibit 9-4 General Model for Variance Analysis

(1)	(2)	(3)
AQ × AP	**AQ × SP**	**SQ × SP**
(Actual quantity of inputs × Actual price)	(Actual quantity of inputs × Standard price)	(Standard quantity of inputs allowed for actual output × Standard price)

Price (rate) variance
(Materials price variance)
(Labor rate variance)
(Manufacturing overhead spending variance)

Quantity (usage) variance
(Materials quantity variance)
(Labor efficiency variance)
(Manufacturing overhead efficiency variance)

Total Variance

to summarize

Standard cost systems are used to accumulate costs based on standards rather than actual costs. Standard costs are predetermined costs that serve as benchmarks for judging what actual costs should be. Standard costs are usually expressed as the per-unit cost of materials, labor, and manufacturing overhead and are used by managers for planning, implementing, and controlling decisions. The total variance between actual and standard costs is made up of price or rate and quantity or efficiency variances. Standard costs are based on careful analysis by many people, including accountants, engineers, and managers. Standard costs are compared with actual costs incurred to determine variances, the amounts by which actual costs differ from standards. Significant variances alert management to specific problem areas that may require corrective action. The strategy of focusing on significant variances, called management by exception, is essential to the controlling function.

DIRECT MATERIALS VARIANCES Variance analysis is an essential part of an effective standard cost system. We will first explain how direct materials variances are computed and analyzed. Then, we will explain the computation and analysis of direct labor variances. The more complex variances for manufacturing overhead will be discussed and illustrated in the expanded material section of this chapter.

To illustrate the computation of the price and quantity variances for direct materials, we will assume the following actual results of Smell-Good Perfume made by Jennifer Cosmetics:

Direct materials purchased	10,000 ounces at $1.85 per ounce
Direct materials used	8,300 ounces
Bottles of perfume produced	4,000

Keep in mind throughout the following discussion that the standard cost card (Exhibit 9-3) specifies that materials should cost $2 for each ounce and that each bottle produced should require 2 ounces of material. (Obviously, many ingredients would be mixed together to make perfume. To keep the example simple, we are assuming only one ingredient is used.)

materials price variance
The extent to which the actual price varies from the standard price for the quantity of materials purchased or used; computed by multiplying the difference between the actual and standard prices by the quantity purchased or used.

Materials Price Variance The **materials price variance** reflects the extent to which the actual price varies from the standard price for the actual quantity of materials purchased or used. Although the price variance can be calculated either when materials are purchased or when they are used, it is generally best to isolate the variance at purchase and report the variance to the purchasing manager who has responsibility for controlling the purchase price. If management waits until the materials are used before calculating variances, the information needed by the purchasing managers to take corrective action is delayed.

In calculating the materials price variance, the standard price per unit of materials should reflect the final, delivered cost of materials, net of any discounts taken. For example, Jennifer Cosmetics may have determined its standard materials price per ounce as follows:

Purchase price	$ 1.84
Freight	0.17
Handling costs	0.04
Less purchase discounts	(0.05)
Standard materials cost per unit	$ 2.00

The standard cost above assumes that the materials were purchased in certain lot sizes (for example, 50-gallon quantities) and delivered a certain way (by rail, for example). Handling costs and purchase discounts have also been included.

Assuming that variances are determined when materials are purchased and that 10,000 ounces of materials are purchased, the price variance is computed as follows:

Materials Price Variance
(based on quantity purchased)

AQ × AP (Actual quantity of inputs × Actual price)	**AQ × SP** (Actual quantity of inputs × Standard price)	**SQ × SP** (Standard quantity of inputs allowed for actual output × Standard price)
10,000 oz. × $1.85 = $18,500	10,000 oz. × $2.00 = $20,000	

Price variance
10,000 × ($2.00 − $1.85) = $1,500 F

This variance indicates that the company spent $1,500 less than the standard cost for the direct materials purchased. Because less money was spent than the standard cost, the variance is labeled "F" meaning "favorable." If the amount expended had exceeded the standard cost, the variance would have been "unfavorable," designated with a "U."

Isolating materials price variances at the time of purchase has the advantage of providing immediate information on purchasing decisions. This also allows companies to carry inventory in the accounting records at the standard cost. Some companies, however, prefer to compute materials price variances at the time the materials are transferred to Work-in-Process Inventory. If 8,300 ounces were used in production, the variance would be based on that amount rather than on the 10,000 ounces purchased. In this case, a favorable price variance of $1,245 would result, as shown below.

Materials Price Variance
(based on quantity transferred to production)

AQ × AP (Actual quantity of inputs × Actual price)	**AQ × SP** (Actual quantity of inputs × Standard price)	**SQ × SP** (Standard quantity of inputs allowed for actual output × Standard price)
8,300 oz. × $1.85 = $15,355	8,300 oz. × $2.00 = $16,600	

Price variance
8,300 × ($2.00 − $1.85) = $1,245 F

materials quantity variance
The extent to which the actual quantity of materials varies from the standard quantity; computed by multiplying the difference between the actual quantity and the standard quantity of materials used by the standard price.

Materials Quantity Variance The standard quantity of materials should reflect the amount needed for each completed unit of product but should allow for normal waste, spoilage, and other unavoidable inefficiencies. The standard cost card indicates that 2 ounces of direct materials are allowed for each bottle of perfume produced. Because Jennifer Cosmetics produced 4,000 bottles of Smell-Good perfume last period, the standard quantity allowed is 8,000 ounces (2 ounces × 4,000 bottles). Actual use of materials amounted to 8,300 ounces. The computation of the **materials quantity variance** is:

Materials Quantity Variance
(based on quantity transferred to production)

AQ × AP (Actual quantity of inputs × Actual price)	**AQ × SP** (Actual quantity of inputs × Standard price)	**SQ × SP** (Standard quantity of inputs allowed for actual output × Standard price)
	8,300 oz. × \$2.00 = \$16,600	8,000 oz. × \$2.00 = \$16,000

Quantity variance
\$2.00 × (8,300 − 8,000) = \$600 U

The company used 300 more ounces of material than expected, resulting in an unfavorable quantity variance of \$600 (300 ounces × \$2 per ounce).

Controlling Materials Variances Materials price variances are usually under the control of the purchasing department. The purchasing function involves getting a variety of price quotations, buying in economic lot sizes to take advantage of quantity discounts, buying and paying on a timely basis to obtain cash discounts, and paying attention to alternative forms of delivery to minimize shipping costs. Some of these factors will be less important when there are few suppliers or when purchase contracts with suppliers are for long periods. In any case, the existence of unfavorable price variances may suggest a problem that needs correcting.

The buyer responsible for these purchases should be able to explain the variance even though the buyer may not be able to control its occurrence. This may be the case, for example, when market prices change after the standard is set, which could be the explanation for the favorable price variance. Or materials may be damaged, requiring the reorder of a small quantity on a rush basis; this usually raises the price of the materials as well as the cost of shipping, causing an unfavorable price variance. The point is that the cause of any significant variance must be explained and steps taken to avoid such variances in the future. The purpose of variance analysis is not to browbeat employees for failing to meet impossible expectations, but rather to provide information that will help management identify ways of improving the production process.

Materials quantity variances may be caused by quality defects, poor workmanship, poor choice of materials, inexperienced workers, machines that need repair, or an inaccurate materials quantity standard. Just as the purchasing manager must explain significant price variances, generally the production manager must analyze significant quantity variances to determine their cause. If the material is of inferior quality, the purchasing manager, rather than the production manager, may be responsible for the variance. Again, the point is that the cause of the variance must be determined; only then can it be decided what action, if any, to take to prevent its recurrence. Production managers can be made aware of materials quantity variances on a timely basis if the company uses materials requisition forms. These forms should indicate when materials withdrawals from the storeroom exceed the standard quantity of materials specified for that production run. If the standard amount of materials for the production run is known at the start of the run, additional requisitions of materials can be "red-flagged" as being excessive. By using an excess materials requisition procedure as a nonmonetary standard, production managers will be alerted to a materials quantity variance before the monetary measure of the materials quantity variance is available. Thus, production managers can take quicker action to correct a problem than would be the case if they had to wait until the end of the reporting period to learn of materials quantity variances. Corrective action may involve returning excess materials to the storeroom rather than being careless about control in the production area, which could lead to waste or theft.

Accounting for Materials Variances The journal entries for recording the purchase and use of materials, as well as the materials price variance (isolated at purchase) and the quantity variance (isolated when materials are used), are:

Materials Price Variance:		
Direct Materials Inventory ($2.00 × 10,000 ounces).	20,000	
Materials Price Variance [($2.00 − $1.85) × 10,000 ounces].		1,500
Cash (or Accounts Payable) ($1.85 × 10,000 ounces).		18,500
Purchased 10,000 ounces of direct materials at $1.85 per ounce and entered the materials in inventory at the standard price of $2.00 per ounce.		
Materials Quantity Variance:		
Work-in-Process Inventory (8,000 ounces × $2.00)	16,000	
Materials Quantity Variance [(8,300 ounces − 8,000 ounces) × $2.00]. .	600	
Direct Materials Inventory (8,300 ounces × $2.00)		16,600
Transferred 8,300 ounces of materials out of inventory and recorded standard usage of 8,000 ounces of materials to produce 4,000 bottles of perfume.		

As shown, Materials Price Variance and Materials Quantity Variance are debited when the variances are unfavorable; they are credited when the variances are favorable. An unfavorable variance can be thought of as an expense; a favorable variance can be considered an expense reduction or savings. Note that the $16,000 debit to Work-in-Process Inventory is the standard cost for the 4,000 bottles (standard 8,000 ounces of materials × $2 standard price per ounce). The actual cost deviations from the standard costs are now in variance accounts. The variance accounts are usually transferred to Cost of Goods Sold at the end of the period. Thus, the income statement reports actual costs, where Work-in-Process Inventory and Finished Goods Inventory include only the standard costs of materials. Alternatively, as explained in Chapter 2 of management accounting, when variances are significant in amount, variance account balances at the end of a period should be allocated among Cost of Goods Sold, Work-in-Process Inventory, and Finished Goods Inventory instead of just transferred to Cost of Goods Sold.

to summarize

The difference between actual and standard costs of materials for a given production level can be separated into a materials price variance and a materials quantity variance. The materials price variance can be computed when the materials are purchased or when they are used in production. The managers responsible for the variances must determine their causes and, if the variances are outside an acceptable range, take action to eliminate them. The materials variances (price and quantity) are recorded in individual accounts when materials are acquired and used. The accounts for materials variances are generally closed into Cost of Goods Sold; work-in-process inventory and finished goods inventory accounts include only standard materials costs.

DIRECT LABOR VARIANCES A direct labor rate variance and a direct labor efficiency variance are usually determined for manufacturing labor when a standard cost system is being used. These variances are computed in a manner similar to the materials price and quantity variances.

labor rate variance The extent to which the actual labor rate varies from the standard rate for the quantity of labor used; computed by multiplying the difference between the actual rate and the standard rate by the quantity of labor used.

Labor Rate Variance A **labor rate variance** is a price variance; it shows the difference between actual and standard wage rates. Unfavorable labor rate variances may occur when skilled workers with high hourly pay rates are placed in jobs intended for less skilled or lower-wage-rate employees. Unfavorable labor rate variances may also occur when employees work overtime at premium pay (time and a half or double time). Conversely, favorable labor rate variances occur when less skilled or lower-wage-rate employees perform duties intended for higher-paid workers.

For Jennifer Cosmetics, the standard cost card (Exhibit 9-3) indicates that the standard direct labor rate per bottle of perfume was 2 hours at $16 per hour. Actual labor used during the month to make 4,000 bottles was 8,352 hours at $16.20 per hour. The labor rate variance was thus $1,670 unfavorable, computed as follows:

Labor Rate Variance

AH × AR (Actual hours of input × Actual rate)	**AH × SR** (Actual hours of input × Standard rate)	**SH × SR** (Standard hours allowed for output × Standard rate)
8,352 hours × $16.20 = $135,302	8,352 hours × $16.00 = $133,632	

Labor rate variance
8,352 hours × ($16.20 − $16.00) = $1,670 U

As this variance indicates, $1,670 more than the standard amount for the actual number of hours used was spent for direct labor because actual labor rates were higher than standard rates by $0.20 per hour. The company's guidelines would determine whether the variance should be investigated. Depending on the firm's hiring policies, and the degree of authority given to operating managers in setting wage rates and assigning workers to particular jobs, the operating managers may or may not be responsible for this labor rate variance. In general, labor rates are the responsibility of the manager who makes staffing decisions.

labor efficiency variance The extent to which the actual labor used varies from the standard quantity; computed by multiplying the difference between the actual quantity and the standard quantity of labor by the standard rate.

Labor Efficiency Variance The **labor efficiency variance** is a quantity variance. It measures the cost (or benefit) of using labor for more (or fewer) hours than prescribed by the standard. Computed in the same manner as the materials quantity variance, the labor efficiency variance computation is illustrated in the following schedule for Jennifer Cosmetics. Note that total standard hours are computed by multiplying the standard hours per unit by the actual number of bottles produced (2 hours × 4,000 bottles = 8,000 standard hours allowed).

Labor Efficiency Variance

AH × AR (Actual hours of input × Actual rate)	**AH × SR** (Actual hours of input × Standard rate)	**SH × SR** (Standard hours allowed for output × Standard rate)
	8,352 hours × $16 = $133,632	8,000 hours × $16 = $128,000

Labor efficiency variance
$16 × (8,352 − 8,000) = $5,632 U

The manufacturing division used 352 more direct labor hours than the standard, which caused an unfavorable efficiency variance of $5,632 (352 hours × $16).

The labor efficiency variance shows how efficiently the workers performed and, hence, how productive a department was. The variances might be unfavorable for a variety of reasons, including poorly trained employees, poor-quality materials that require extra processing time, old or faulty equipment, and improper supervision of employees. Note that the labor efficiency variance is probably the most important and closely watched manufacturing variance. It has become even more important in recent years as U.S. industries have tried to increase their productivity to match that of Japan, Korea, and other countries.

fyi

Organizations often try to encourage employees to work harder and faster by offering them rewards for productivity increases. However, employees are skeptical about whether rewards will actually be received. In 1997, for example, a survey reported the following results:

- 81% of workers surveyed said they would not receive any reward for productivity increases.
- 60% of managers surveyed felt their compensation would not increase if their performance improved.
- Only 3% of base salary separated average from outstanding employees at the companies surveyed.

Source: Craig Eric Schneider, "Capitalizing on Performance Management, Recognition, and Rewards Systems," *Compensation and Benefits Review,* March–April 1997, p. 23.

Controlling Labor Variances Whereas a materials price variance is usually the responsibility of the purchasing department, labor "price" or rate variances are normally the responsibility of either the production manager who is responsible for employees' work assignments or the personnel responsible for hiring employees. As indicated, rate variances are likely to be due to (1) certain tasks being performed by workers with different pay rates or (2) working overtime at rates higher than the normal wage rate. These variances may be manageable if care is taken in assigning workers to jobs that are consistent with their skills and pay scales. Deviations may be necessary in certain situations because of vacations, sickness, or absences of other employees. If the variances are caused by factors beyond the manager's control, he or she should not be held responsible for the unfavorable variance.

In a labor-intensive company, the labor efficiency variance is much more important than in a company that has low labor costs. The labor efficiency variance can be expressed in standard hours for a given activity or in monetary terms (standard hours × standard labor rate). If time standards are set for each activity and workers are required to report their actual hours of work on time tickets, managers have a basis for checking labor efficiency by comparing standard hours with the actual hours shown on time tickets. The variances can be separated into categories by causes so that judgments can be made about what corrective action should be taken. Some typical causes of labor inefficiency variances are absenteeism, machinery breakdowns, poor-quality materials, poor work environment, inadequate machinery, lack of employee skills on a given job, poor employee attitudes, lazy employees, and inaccurate standards. If these causes can be identified by analyzing time tickets, corrective action can be taken promptly. If the labor efficiency variance is expressed in monetary terms, the variances may not be available until end-of-period accounting reports are issued.

caution

When computing variances, be careful not to confuse actual and standard hours and actual and standard rates. The rate variance is always the difference between the standard and actual rate times the actual hours. (To multiply it times standard hours would not tell you how much the rate increase actually cost or saved the company in total.) On the other hand, the efficiency variance is a time-based variance; therefore, it is the difference between the standard and actual hours times the standard rate.

Accounting for Labor Variances Because the labor rate and labor efficiency variances are both computed for a given period of time or for a given amount of production, the labor costs and variances for Jennifer Cosmetics can be accounted for in a single journal entry.

Work-in-Process Inventory (8,000 hours × $16.00).	128,000	
Labor Rate Variance [($16.20 − $16.00) × 8,352 hours]	1,670	
Labor Efficiency Variance [(8,352 hours − 8,000 hours) × $16.00] . .	5,632	
Wages Payable (8,352 hours × $16.20)		135,302
To charge Work-in-Process Inventory for standard labor hours at the standard wage rate to produce 4,000 bottles of perfume; to set up unfavorable labor rate and efficiency variances to reflect the use of 352 hours above standard at an average wage rate of $0.20 above standard.		

As with all production variances, labor variances are closed to Cost of Goods Sold at the end of the period or allocated among Cost of Goods Sold, Work-in-Process Inventory, and Finished Goods Inventory. By closing variances from standard into Cost of Goods Sold, actual cost of goods sold will be reported on the income statement. Work-in-Process Inventory and Finished Goods Inventory include only the standard costs of labor.

business environment essay

Satisfied Employees Are More Productive For many companies, labor costs are the highest cost. This is certainly true for service firms and may even be true for manufacturing firms. Labor rate and labor efficiency variances provide information about whether labor rates are higher than expected or standard and whether workers are performing as efficiently as expected or standard. Many labor costs that are not usually explicitly considered can significantly affect both of these ratios, however, and result in higher costs than expected. Take employee turnover, for example. Common estimates are that employee turnover costs range from $10,000 to $40,000 per person, depending on the position, while employee retention actually increases revenues. In addition, it has been estimated that a 5% increase in employee retention can result in a 10% decrease in labor costs and lead to productivity increases ranging from 25 to 65%.

Because of the high costs of employee turnover, most companies work hard to increase employee retention. The most common approach is to "buy" employee satisfaction with increased pay and benefits.

A nonmanufacturing organization sometimes expresses standards in quantitative terms. For example, a hospital might have standard times for activities such as taking blood samples.

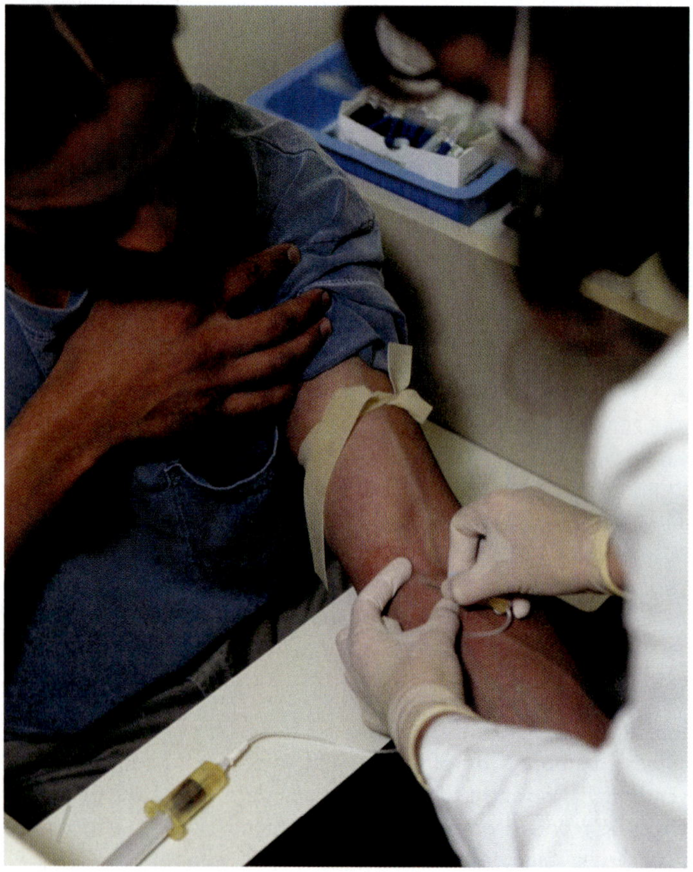

to summarize

The labor rate variance is the difference between the actual and the standard labor rates multiplied by the actual hours worked. The labor efficiency variance is the difference between actual and standard hours multiplied by the standard wage rate. Labor variances are usually controllable by manufacturing division managers. The labor variances (rate and efficiency) are recorded in individual accounts when labor costs are incurred. Like materials variances, labor variances are closed to Cost of Goods Sold so that the work-in-process inventory and finished goods inventory accounts include only standard labor costs.

STANDARD COSTS IN NONMANUFACTURING FIRMS In nonmanufacturing environments, standards are sometimes expressed only in quantitative terms; in other situations, the quantitative standards are converted to monetary standards as a basis for identifying monetary variances. For example, automobile service centers have standard times and standard labor costs for automobile repairs, tune-ups, oil changes, muffler replacements, and so forth. Organizations might have standard times for such activities as cleaning hotel rooms, taking blood samples, completing income tax returns, and meeting delivery schedules. These types of standards can be applied in not-for-profit and service organizations as well as in restaurants and merchandising firms. In the fast-food area, for example, franchises, such as MCDONALD'S and BASKIN-ROBBINS, have standard quantities for meat in hamburgers and ice cream in cones.

However, a 1998 survey of 206 medium-to-large companies conducted by WILLIAM M. MERCER, INC., found that in organizations with high turnover, compensation was the most common reason for dissatisfaction. In companies with very low turnover, 40% of the respondents said that emotional factors (work satisfaction, good relationships with managers and other employees) were the sole reasons for their retention; only 21% attributed their retention to financial factors (satisfaction with compensation and benefits).

This evidence suggests that creating a workplace where employees feel better about themselves is extremely important. If a work environment constantly raises employees' self-esteem to a higher level than they experience elsewhere, they will want to spend more time at work and will enjoy very high job satisfaction. It certainly makes sense: people do more of what they enjoy and less of what they don't enjoy. The consequence is that people who enjoy working are more productive.

Source: "Increasing Employee Satisfaction," http://www.performance-unlimited.com/satisfy.htm.

EVALUATION OF STANDARD COSTING Standard cost systems, such as those discussed here, have many advantages and disadvantages. The advantages include the following:

1. The setting of standard costs requires a careful analysis of operations. Such an analysis can lead to efficiencies and economies even before the standard cost system is fully operative.
2. Standard costs are useful for planning overall materials and labor.
3. A standard cost system is simpler to operate than a system using actual costs because the cost flows are recorded at standard.
4. A standard cost system helps identify and control problem areas; this leads to increased production efficiency.
5. Standard costs provide a basis for measuring performance by assigning variances to the responsible manager.
6. A standard cost system is compatible with the principle of management by exception, which contributes to the effective utilization of management's time and effort.

The disadvantages of standard costing include the following.

1. A standard cost system is expensive and time-consuming to develop.
2. It is easy to misinterpret the causes of a variance because so many factors are involved.
3. Standard costs must be changed as conditions change (e.g., as the product, the materials, or the production methods change). Sometimes these changes occur so quickly that standards become out-of-date before management realizes it.
4. Workers tend to view measures of efficiency with mistrust. Responsibility for significant variances may be erroneously assigned, leading to morale problems.
5. The setting of standards is not an exact science. Standards are reported as specific figures but are treated by managers as ranges of acceptable performance. Random fluctuations are to be expected but often are hard to distinguish from situations requiring action.
6. Standards do not support continuous improvement.
7. Standard costs are based on the simplistic cost model in which every cost has to be treated as either fixed or variable. In the real world, however, many costs do not behave according to these idealized models, which means that managers can always legitimately point to shortcomings in the variance analysis and standard costing.

Although the disadvantages noted here are real and should not be minimized, standard cost systems have generally been cost-beneficial and are widely used, even for nonmanufacturing activities. You should recognize that standards are also used for planning and controlling in nonmanufacturing activities and organizations. Manufacturing firms use standards and budgets for their nonmanufacturing activities, as do merchandising and service businesses. In essence, the concepts of standards and cost systems apply to all types of organizations in varying degrees.

to summarize

Standard costs can be used in nonmanufacturing firms, as well as manufacturing firms. Standard cost systems have both advantages and disadvantages. Most advantages center on achieving greater accuracy and efficiency. Most disadvantages center on the costs involved in setting standards and the inability to establish exact standards in a changing environment.

Target Costing

target market price The price that consumers will pay for a product or service.

Target costing is an alternative to standard costing. With this approach, the company designs a product based on prespecified costs by gathering input on customer needs and then gets everyone in the company to work toward hitting those target costs. Target costing begins by determining the **target market price**, the price required to win the customer's business, then subtracts the target profit to arrive at the target cost. Target costing has all the ingredients of strategic cost management: quality, cost, and time. It manages costs before they are incurred by setting a target cost for the product or service based on the market, the customer, and the amount of profit desired. It is externally focused on the competition. It organizes workers from different departments into cross-functional teams that strive for the same cost goal and form an integrated planning and execution system.

Target costing involves the following six steps:

1. *Establish the target market price.* The price consumers will pay for a product or service is based largely on the value they perceive in the item and the qualities that contribute to their perception. Target costing uses a product's or service's features to pin down a market price and involves assessing how similar products already on the market are priced. The goal is to determine customers' preferences, collect information about similar products marketed by competitors, and apply that information during the design phase.
2. *Determine the target profit margin.* Target profit margins should reflect the company's strategic business objectives and should be sufficient to offset the life-cycle costs of the product.
3. *Examine the reliability of current cost-management techniques.* A key step in the product-planning phase is analyzing the quality and accuracy of cost information and subsequently generating reliable estimates. For companies with existing products that are similar to the proposed product, cost information from the old product can be used to estimate the new costs.
4. *Establish the target cost.* The difference between the target price and the target profit margin is the allowable cost that the company can commit to the product or service. This cost goal should be attainable, but should still require considerable effort to achieve.
5. *Achieve the target cost.* Making the target cost a reality requires designing excess costs out of the product. Cost reduction efforts do not end with design considerations. Rather, they include eliminating waste, such as scrap and rework, and striving to make operational processes more cost-efficient.
6. *Identify further cost reductions once production begins.* Target costing is a continuous process. As product design unfolds, it is important to compare the target costing objects to actual costs. Companies need to ask: Are competitors still behaving as expected? Are customers' needs still being met? Maintaining an accurate assessment of current costs is also a key to staying on track.

Target costing assumes that companies have little power over customer behavior. Certainly, customers have more options than ever before. Continuing improvements in technology and reduced costs of logistics have not only expanded customer choices but have also created unrelenting downward pricing pressure. If companies are to remain profitable, they must operate with the assumption that the market sets the prices of products and services and that the customer is the ultimate judge in the marketplace.

The roots of target costing trace back to World War II when, due to a shortage of materials, U.S. manufacturers made an organized effort to build the most function into a product for the lowest cost. This approach was called value engineering. The Japanese adopted and expanded the concept in the 1960s, and target costing was born as a long-term profit-planning system that is customer driven and price led.

Today, target costing is used by 80 to 85% of Japanese manufacturing companies, including such well-known names as **SONY**, **TOYOTA**, **NISSAN**, **CANON**, **NEC**, and **OLYMPUS**. Historically, American companies have been slow to adopt target costing. Today, however, major companies such as **DAIMLERCHRYSLER** and **BOEING** are making concerted efforts to adopt target costing. Boeing has implemented target costing in producing the new 757-300, an innovative airplane design that stretches 24 feet longer than the standard passenger plane and is 10% more economical for airlines on a per-seat basis. Using target costing, DaimlerChrysler has established a program to reduce the total cost of the extended enterprise by eliminating stifling bureaucratic procedures, redundant checking and testing, and other practices that have historically hampered customer-supplier relationships. Companies that are adopting target costing believe that technology and globalization have given customers more power than ever before and that to be competitive, a company must adopt target costing.

As a specific example of the value of target costing, consider the case of a major manufacturing company that found itself on the losing end of a bidding competition. To respond, the company broke down the costs and compared them to the target cost allowed by the market. Although the company performed well in most areas, it determined that its cost for the product's power supply was grossly higher than the competition's. Further investigation revealed that the company produced unique power supplies for many of its different products. In contrast, the competitor had standardized its power supplies, which resulted in far less complexity and far higher production volumes. These two benefits allowed the competitor to drive down the overall cost of power supplies as well as the overall market price for the finished product. The manufacturing company's choices were clear—standardize power supplies to reduce costs or consider outsourcing the manufacturing of power supplies to a company that could produce them at the allowable component cost.

With target costing, companies can avoid the problem of producing a product, only to discover that the price they must charge to make a profit is too expensive for their customers. Standard costs that are too high, whether they are achieved or not, result in lost customers if other suppliers can meet customers' targeted costs. Because target costing is customer driven, it can improve customer satisfaction. Target costing also allows more people in the company to understand the company's objectives and how they are going to be achieved because it encourages people with different functions to work on the same team to meet the collective target costing goals. Ideally, target costing arrives at a price that works for the company as well as the customer. That makes it a more effective way to do business, and companies that have used target costing have found that they reach their profit goals more effectively.

IMPLEMENTING TARGET COSTING Although nearly everyone can see the advantages of a system that promises greater customer satisfaction and profitability, putting target costing into practice and getting all employees to accept a new way of doing their jobs can be difficult. Among the problems experienced by companies that have adopted or tried to adopt target costing are the following:

- The company may fail to clearly explain the reasons for implementing target costing. Specifically, the connection to business strategy may not be made clear.
- Top management may not support target costing.
- The company may underestimate the effort required to implement target costing and dedicate insufficient resources to its implementation.

- People may not be ready for change—old ideas change slowly.
- Managers may not respond quickly to the changes target costing brings.
- The company may not be able to accurately determine acceptable market prices.

Unlike standard costing, where the methods of setting standards and computing variances can be covered in this text, there is no easy template for teaching how target costing is performed. Whereas standard costing looks at actual costs and compares them to predetermined standards, implementing target costing involves determining what prices customers will support, specifying appropriate profit levels, and then engineering production processes and costs so that acceptable customer prices can be met. The way organizations complete that process varies from company to company, depending on the specific manufacturing processes the company uses and the individuals involved in the process. Further, some companies implement target costing only on an incremental basis whereas others use a more revolutionary approach, making it one of their highest priorities.

ADVANTAGES OF TARGET COSTING Companies that have successfully implemented and maintained an effective target costing system have experienced the following advantages:

- More effective determination of the expected cost of manufacturing a product or providing a service.
- Greater cost efficiencies.
- Spending money where it had the greatest impact.
- Appropriate identification of customers' real needs.
- Matching of the firm's activities to customers' requirements.
- Increased customer satisfaction.
- Better understanding of cost objectives among co-workers.
- Participation of co-workers in setting quality, cost, and time targets.
- Transformation of the image of management accountants into that of valued partners working on everyone's behalf.
- Greater ability to compete globally.

to summarize

Target costing is an approach that attempts to determine the price customers will pay for products and services, subtracts an appropriate level of profits, and then engineers and designs production and other processes so that predetermined costs can be met. Target costing involves cross-functional teams working together to meet target costs. While most people agree that target costing has great appeal, implementing it can often be very difficult. As a result, although target costing has been widely used by Japanese companies, American companies have been slow to adopt it.

4

Explain how performance is evaluated in profit centers.

EVALUATING PERFORMANCE IN PROFIT CENTERS

As defined earlier, a profit center is an organizational unit (segment) in which a manager has responsibility for both costs and revenues. Profit centers both produce and market goods or services. For example, the U.S., Far East, and European operations of the Edison Automobile Company of IMC, illustrated in Exhibit 9-1, might be profit centers.

The Segment-Margin Income Statement

To evaluate the performance of profit centers and to decide how limited resources will be divided among profit centers, management needs a report that compares the revenues and costs

segment-margin income statement An income statement that identifies costs directly chargeable to a segment and further divides them into variable and fixed cost behavior patterns.

direct costs Costs that are specifically traceable to a unit of business or segment being analyzed.

indirect costs Costs normally incurred for the benefit of several segments or activities.

caution

Many students confuse the terms *variable* and *fixed costs*, *controllable* and *noncontrollable costs*, and *direct* and *indirect costs*. Costs are variable if they fluctuate with activity. If they don't fluctuate with activity, costs are fixed. Costs are controllable if they can be adjusted by the activity manager. If they can't be adjusted by the activity manager, costs are noncontrollable. Costs are direct if removing the activity results in the costs being eliminated. Costs that remain after an activity is eliminated are indirect.

of the profit centers being evaluated. One such report that is often used is the **segment-margin income statement**, such as the one presented in Exhibit 9-5 for IMC on pages 480-481.

To keep Exhibit 9-5 simple, we are assuming that IMC has only two divisions: Acme Computer and Edison Automobile. Further, we have included only the regions of Edison Automobile. You will note that it includes three geographic regions; the Far East Region has operations in two countries—Japan and Korea. As you read across, note that the segment focus becomes narrower: from divisions to geographic regions to countries within geographic regions.

Before reviewing specific aspects of this segment-margin income statement, we want to remind you of a very important management accounting principle—segment managers should receive information about, and be evaluated on, only the items they can control or influence.

As was the case with cost centers, in evaluating profit centers it is important that managers be held responsible only for the controllable costs; the costs and revenues over which they have control are usually called **direct costs**. In Exhibit 9-5, we apply responsibility accounting to IMC by including in each segment report only the revenues and costs controlled by that segment manager. This implies that some costs, **indirect costs**, will not be assigned to a particular segment because the manager cannot control them. Company-wide, indirect costs total $1.5 million, which might include the president's salary and interest on company debt, for example.

Similarly, when Edison Automobile is broken down into smaller segments for analysis, we see an additional $200,000 of indirect costs that are not assigned to Edison Automobile's three regions. Costs such as the division manager's salary and advertising for all regions are not controlled by the division manager and so are not allocated to the regions. You will note that as we move down the organizational hierarchy, from divisions to geographic regions to countries, indirect costs increase in total; managers at the lower levels have the narrowest range of responsibility and the fewest costs to control. The manager of manufacturing in Japan, for example, will be responsible for the items ordered for that unit but not for setting the salary of the manager of Far East operations; this is the responsibility of the manager of Edison Automobile. The salary of the manager of Far East operations is thus a direct and controllable cost of Edison Automobile and is an indirect and noncontrollable cost to Japanese operations.

Managing Costs and Revenues in Profit Centers

Profit center managers manage their costs the same way cost center managers evaluate and manage costs. That is, they use either the standard or target costing concepts that we have already discussed. Unlike cost center managers, however, profit center managers are also responsible for managing revenues because the segment profit they are evaluated on is a function of both costs and revenues. In the next section, we examine one way management analyzes its revenues.

MANAGING REVENUES AND REVENUE VARIANCES A segment's actual and expected revenues may differ for several reasons including the following:

- Sales prices were higher or lower than expected.
- Sales volume was higher or lower than expected.
- The company's market share was higher or lower than expected.
- The industry, as a whole, sold fewer products than expected.
- The mix of products sold was different than expected.

Because management is interested in knowing which of these factors contributed to differences between actual and expected or standard[2] revenues, variances that help isolate these fac-

2 In this discussion, the terms *standard* and *expected* are used interchangeably. Some people refer to these prices and volumes as standard; others refer to them as expected because they aren't under the complete control of the company.

sales price variance The difference between the actual price and the expected or standard price multiplied by the actual quantity; measures the part of the difference between expected and actual sales revenue that is due to differences between expected and actual prices of goods.

sales volume variance The difference between the actual quantity and the expected quantity multiplied by the expected or standard price; measures the part of the difference between expected and actual sales revenue that is due to the difference between expected and actual volume of goods sold.

market share variance The part of the sales volume variance that accounts for the difference between the actual market share of each product sold and the expected market share of each product sold.

tors are calculated. To illustrate how revenue variances are calculated, assume the following data for one of Acme Computer's divisions. Assume that the division sells two types of computing devices: hand-held and laptop. Market share, industry volume, and sales data for the two computing devices are as follows:

Actual Data (in thousands)

	Units	Sales Prices	Total Market	Percent of Market
Hand-held	800	$240	9,500 units	8.42%
Laptops	2,300	290	10,100 units	22.77%
Total	3,100	277*	19,600 units	15.82%

*Weighted average price rounded to the nearest dollar. Calculated as [(800 × $240) + (2,300 × $290)]/3,100.

Expected Data (in thousands)

	Units	Sales Prices	Total Market	Percent of Market
Hand-held	900	$200	10,000 units	9.00%
Laptop	2,100	300	10,000 units	21.00%
Total	3,000	270*	20,000 units	15.00%

*Weighted average price rounded to the nearest dollar. Calculated as [(900 × $200) + (2,100 × $300)]/3,000.

exhibit 9-5 A Segment-Margin Income Statement

International Manufacturing Corporation (IMC)
Segment-Margin Income Statement
September 2003
(in thousands of dollars)

	Corporation as a Whole	Corporation Breakdown into Two Companies: Acme Computer	Corporation Breakdown into Two Companies: Edison Automobile
Net sales revenue	$25,000	$15,000	$10,000
Variable costs:			
Cost of goods sold	$15,000	$ 9,000	$ 6,000
Selling and administrative costs	3,000	1,700	1,300
Total variable costs	$18,000	$10,700	$ 7,300
Contribution margin	$ 7,000	$ 4,300	$ 2,700
Less fixed costs controllable by segment managers	2,000	1,300	700
Segment margin	$ 5,000	$ 3,000	$ 2,000
Less company indirect costs	1,500		
Net income	$ 3,500		
Segment-margin ratio		20%	20%

industry volume variance The part of the sales volume variance that accounts for the difference between the expected market share of the total market and the expected or standard quantity of goods sold.

Using these data, we can compute the **sales price variance** and the **sales volume variance.** Note that when actual sales exceed expected or standard sales, the variance is favorable. This is the opposite of the cost variances, where an actual cost that exceeds a standard cost was deemed to be an unfavorable variance. Once we have calculated the sales price variance and sales volume variance, we can then split the sales volume variance into a **market share variance** and an **industry volume variance.** These calculations are shown below and on the next page.

Sales Price Variance and Sales Volume Variance
For Hand-Helds

Actual quantity × Actual price	Actual quantity × Standard price	Standard quantity × Standard price
800 × $240 = $192,000	800 × $200 = $160,000	900 × $200 = $180,000

Sales price variance $32,000 F | **Sales volume variance** $20,000 U

Market Share Variance and Industry Volume Variance

Actual quantity × Standard price	Total actual market × Expected market share × Standard price	Standard quantity × Standard price
800 × $200 = $160,000	9,500 × .09 × $200 = $171,000	900 × $200 = $180,000

Market share variance $11,000 U | **Industry volume variance** $9,000 U

International Manufacturing Corporation (IMC)
Segment-Margin Income Statement (continued)
September 2003
(in thousands of dollars)

Possible Breakdown of Edison Automobile (Only)				Possible Breakdown of Edison Automobile (Far East Operations)		
Not Allocated	**U.S. Operations**	**Far East Operations**	**European Operations**	**Not Allocated**	**Japanese Operations**	**Korean Operations**
—	$5,000	$2,000	$3,000	—	$1,200	$800
—	$2,900	$1,100	$2,000	—	$ 700	$400
—	700	300	300	—	170	130
—	$3,600	$1,400	$2,300	—	$ 870	$530
—	$1,400	$ 600	$ 700	—	$ 330	$270
$ 200	250	100	150	$ 30	60	10
$(200)	$1,150	$ 500	$ 550	$(30)	$ 270	$260
	23%	25%	18%		23%	33%

Sales Price Variance and Sales Volume Variance For Laptops

Actual quantity × Actual price	Actual quantity × Standard price	Standard quantity × Standard price
2,300 × \$290 = \$667,000	2,300 × \$300 = \$690,000	2,100 × \$300 = \$630,000
Sales price variance \$23,000 U	Sales volume variance \$60,000 F	

Market Share Variance and Industry Volume Variance

Actual quantity × Standard price	Total actual market × Expected market share × Standard price	Standard quantity × Standard price
2,300 × \$300 = \$690,000	10,100 × .21 × \$300 = \$636,300	2,100 × \$300 = \$630,000
Market share variance \$53,700 F	Industry volume variance \$6,300 F	

Summarizing these variances, we see that the revenue variances for Acme's two products are as follows:

Variances	Hand-Held	Laptops	Total
Sales price	\$32,000 F	\$23,000 U	\$ 9,000 F
Sales volume	20,000 U	60,000 F	40,000 F

Breakdown of Sales Volume Variance

	Hand-Held	Laptops	Total
Market share	\$11,000 U	\$53,700 F	\$42,700 F
Industry volume	9,000 U	6,300 F	2,700 U

The sales price variance informs users whether actual sales prices were higher or lower than expected. The sales volume variance informs users whether the number of units sold was more or less than expected. The market share variance informs users whether the company's share of the total market was higher or lower than expected. Finally, the industry volume variance informs users whether the actual total market was higher or lower than expected.

Thus far, the revenue variance analysis has been on a product-by-product basis. By looking at products individually, we have answered four of the five questions raised earlier. We know from the sales price variances that the sales price for hand-held computers was higher than expected and the sales price for laptops was lower than expected. We know that sales volume for hand-held computers was less than expected and that the sales volume for laptops was greater than expected. In further analyzing the reason for the \$20,000 negative sales volume variance for hand-held computers, we see that \$11,000 was due to Acme's share of the market being less than expected and that \$9,000 was due to the total market being less than expected. With respect to the \$60,000 favorable sales volume variance, we know that \$53,700 was due to Acme's share of the market being greater than expected and that \$6,300 was due to the total market being higher than expected.

The one question we haven't answered relates to the sales mix of the two products. To answer the mix question, it is necessary to combine the analysis of the two products. We do this as follows:

Sales Price Variance and Sales Volume Variance
Hand-Helds and Laptops Combined

	Actual quantity × Actual price	Actual quantity × Standard price	Standard quantity × Standard price
Hand-held	800 × $240 = $192,000	800 × $200 = $160,000	900 × $200 = $180,000
Laptops	2,300 × $290 = $667,000	2,300 × $300 = $690,000	2,100 × $300 = $630,000
Total	3,100 × $277.09677* = $859,000	3,100 × $274.19354* = $850,000	$3,000 × $270* = $810,000

Sales price variance $9,000 F | **Sales volume variance** $40,000 F

*Weighted average price

sales mix variance The part of the sales volume variance that accounts for the difference between the actual quantity of each product sold and the percentage of the actual total products sold that was expected to be represented by each product based on expected market share of the products.

Note that the sales price variance and the sales volume variance for the two products combined is equal to the sum of the two products individually.

Now, we can split the sales volume variance into a **sales mix variance** and a **sales yield variance** (sometimes called the final sales volume). The sales mix variance is caused by selling a different mix (proportion) of hand-helds and laptops than expected. Note that the standard weighted average price for the two products at the expected sales volume is $270 per unit.

Actual quantity × Standard price	Actual total quantity × Standard weighted average price	Standard quantity × Standard price
800 × $200 = $160,000		900 × $200 = $180,000
2,300 × $300 = $690,000		2,100 × $300 = $630,000
3,100 × $274.19354* = $850,000	3,100 × $270 = $837,000	3,000 × $270* = $810,000

Sales mix variance $13,000 F | **Sales yield variance** $27,000 F

*Weighted average price

By examining the sales volume variance on a combined product basis, we see that the mix of products sold was positive—more of the higher-price laptops were sold than expected while fewer of the lower-price hand-held computers were sold.

A final analysis is to split the sales yield variance into the market share variance and industry volume variance, as follows:

Actual total quantity × Standard weighted average price	Total actual market × Expected market share × Standard price	Standard quantity × Standard price
		900 × $200 = $180,000
		2,100 × $300 = $630,000
3,100 × $270 = $837,000	19,600 × .15 × $270 = $793,800	3,000 × $270* = $810,000

Market share variance $43,200 F | **Industry volume variance** $16,200 U

*Weighted average price

On a weighted product basis, you can see that the sales yield variance is positive because of the positive market share variance, meaning that Acme sold a higher share of the weighted market than was expected. The sales yield variance is made lower because the total market in the industry was less than expected.

sales yield variance On a combined product basis, that part of the sales volume variance that is not explained by the mix of products sold. The sales yield variance is the amount of sales volume variance explained by differences between actual and expected market share and total industry sales. The sales yield variance is further broken down into the industry volume variance and market share variance and is also referred to as the "final volume variance."

Using this analysis, if we were evaluating the manager of this segment, we would probably:

- Congratulate him or her for:
  - Selling more laptops than expected.
  - Selling hand-helds at a higher price than expected.
  - Having a positive sales mix.
  - Getting a larger share of the combined market than was expected.
  - Gaining market share for laptops.
- Criticize him or her for:
  - Selling fewer hand-helds than expected.
  - Selling laptops at a lower price than expected.
  - Losing market share in the hand-held market.

When combined with cost variances, revenue variances can inform managers why the income or profit margin of a division or company wasn't as high as it should have been. It will tell them whether the lower net income is caused by expenses that are too high or revenues that are too low. Revenue variance information can help managers take corrective actions to improve their performance. If revenues, for example, are the problem, maybe an aggressive advertising campaign is warranted. If costs are the problem, maybe some cost-cutting or efficiency measures need to be implemented. With these variances, profit center managers now have the information they need to make intelligent planning, controlling, and evaluating decisions.

Interpreting Profit Center Performance Results

segment margins The difference between segment revenue and direct segment costs; a measure of the segment's contribution to cover indirect fixed costs and provide profits.

segment-margin ratios The segment margin divided by the segment's net sales revenue; a measure of the efficiency of the segment's operating performance and, therefore, of its profitability.

contribution-margin ratio The percentage of net sales revenue left after variable costs are deducted; the contribution margin divided by net sales revenue.

Given that the segment-margin income statement in Exhibit 9-5 was prepared in light of the principles of controllable and direct costs, how does management use the information it contains? First, the net income figure provides management with concrete information for evaluating the performance of the company as a whole. Second, the **segment margins** enable management to analyze company results by evaluating the performance of each segment.

We are now ready to examine the operations of IMC segments in detail. In absolute terms, Edison Automobile has a smaller segment margin than Acme Computer ($3 million versus $2 million). U.S. operations has earned more than the Far East and European operations; the Japanese operations has a larger segment margin than the Korean operations. Absolute profits, however, often favor those segments with a larger asset base—with larger manufacturing facilities, for example. A larger facility with more manufacturing capacity should naturally have higher production and higher sales and, hence, a higher segment margin and higher income. A more equitable way to assess performance is to compare **segment-margin ratios** (segment margin divided by net sales), because ratios focus on relationships rather than absolute dollar amounts. For example, though the segment margin of European operations is larger than that of Far East operations, the latter has a higher segment-margin ratio (25% versus 18%). Far East operations also has a higher **contribution-margin ratio** [30% versus 23% ($600 ÷ $2,000 = 30% for Far East; $700 ÷ $3,000 = 23% for Europe)].

In using segment-margin income statements to evaluate profit centers, it is important to review performance over several periods or months. A single period or month may not be typical of overall performance. In our example, September might have been an unusually bad profitability month for the Korean unit of Far East operations because of a slump in the Korean economy or a labor strike. In fact, the performance can be evaluated only by looking at cost and profit trends over several periods, and by comparing the results of these units with those of other similar units. (This comparison is consistent with the process of benchmarking introduced in Chapter 8 of management accounting.)

to summarize

Profit center managers are usually evaluated on both costs and revenues. The most common profit center measurement tool is the segment-margin income statement. This statement identifies both direct and indirect costs and charges only the direct costs to segments. Segment-margin income statements subdivide direct costs into their variable and fixed cost components. Nonmonetary as well as monetary measures should be used to evaluate profit centers. Costs in profit centers are analyzed and managed the same way they are in cost centers—using standard or target costing. Because profit center managers are also held responsible for revenues, a revenue variance analysis procedure that breaks down differences between actual and expected revenues into sales price variances, sales volume variances, sales mix variances, market share variances, and industry volume variances is used.

STOP & THINK Is it possible that a manager could be doing a poor job of managing revenues and revenue growth even though revenues were increasing from period to period?

5

Explain how performance is evaluated in investment centers.

EVALUATING PERFORMANCE IN INVESTMENT CENTERS

An investment center was defined earlier as an organizational unit in which a manager has responsibility for costs, revenues, and assets. Overall, companies would be considered investment centers, as would the independent segments of decentralized companies. For example, the Acme Computer, Edison Automobile, and Jennifer Cosmetics subsidiaries of IMC (see Exhibit 9-1) would probably all be investment centers. Officers of such segments are responsible for acquiring and managing the assets required to manufacture and market their products, as well as for managing the revenues and costs related to those products. The assets include inventory, accounts receivable, and long-term operating assets such as equipment and delivery trucks.

In business, the distinction between profit and investment centers often becomes blurred or even nonexistent. Many companies refer to segments as profit centers when they are really investment centers. Nevertheless, because the distinction between profit and investment centers is useful for defining responsibilities and determining how performance will be evaluated, we discuss them separately.

There are several methods of evaluating the performance of an investment center. When a segment operates almost as a separate company, the rate of return on invested assets and the residual income are usually measured.

Return on Investment (ROI)

return on investment (ROI) A measure of operating performance and efficiency in utilizing assets; computed in its simplest form by dividing net income by total assets.

As you will recall, we discussed **return on investment (ROI)** (sometimes called return on total assets[3]) to evaluate a company's overall performance. ROI is a measure of how much has been earned on the assets of a company; it is equal to net income divided by total assets. For example, if a company earned $1,000 on $10,000 of assets for one year, its ROI would be $1,000 ÷ $10,000, or 10%.

Because an investment center operates as if it were an independent company, its performance can also be evaluated using ROI. In calculating the ROI for an investment center, however, management must be sure to consider only the assets, revenues, and costs controlled by that center. In other words, assets used and costs incurred for the benefit of several investment centers should not be included in the calculation. To stress this concept, we will restate the basic ROI formula as:

$$\text{Investment center ROI} = \frac{\text{Investment center income}}{\text{Investment center assets}}$$

3 In this chapter, we will use the term *ROI* instead of *return on total assets* because it is more commonly used in management decision making. We also use total assets instead of average total assets to keep the calculations simple.

Generally, when an investment center's ROI is analyzed, this formula is divided into its components—the operations performance (sometimes called profit margin) and asset turnover ratios—as follows:

$$\text{Profit margin} \times \text{Asset turnover} = \text{ROI}$$

$$\frac{\text{Net income}}{\text{Revenue}} \times \frac{\text{Revenue}}{\text{Total assets}} = \frac{\text{Net income}}{\text{Total assets}}$$

Note from this formula that the new element is total assets or investments. Net income, which is a function of costs or expenses and revenues, and revenues were considered in profit centers. In evaluating investment centers, where management has responsibility for assets as well as profits, the ROI formula can be used where it couldn't be used before. It is this ROI calculation that investors commonly use to evaluate companies in which they are considering investing.

Clearly, in the above calculations, we could have eliminated the two revenue figures because they cancel each other out, making ROI equal to net income divided by total assets. However, including revenue draws attention to the important concept that ROI is a function of both operating performance and asset turnover.

profit margin (operating performance) ratio An overall measure of the profitability of operations during a period; computed by dividing net income by revenue.

asset turnover ratio An overall measure of how effectively assets are used during a period; computed by dividing revenue by total assets.

The expanded formula shown above helps us identify the three ways an investment center can improve its ROI: (1) it can decrease costs to increase its **profit margin (operating performance) ratio** (net income divided by revenue), (2) it can decrease assets to increase its **asset turnover ratio** (revenue divided by total assets), or (3) it can increase revenue with a corresponding increase in net income. An investment center requiring a major investment in assets (such as a steel mill) will necessarily have a low asset turnover and will therefore have to rely primarily on a higher operating performance to increase its return. An investment center with few operating assets (such as a grocery store) has a more rapid asset turnover and can sustain a lower profit margin ratio while still earning an attractive ROI. For example, a grocery store might make only 2 cents profit per dollar of product sold, but its asset turnover of 12 times a year makes its ROI 24%. A steel mill with an asset turnover of 2 times a year would have to earn 12 cents per dollar of sales to produce an ROI of 24%.

To illustrate the three ways of increasing ROI, we will assume that Acme Computer has revenue of $10,000,000, net income of $1,000,000, and total assets of $5,000,000. The ROI is:

$$\text{Profit margin} \times \text{Asset turnover} = \text{ROI}$$

$$\frac{\$1{,}000{,}000}{\$10{,}000{,}000} \times \frac{\$10{,}000{,}000}{\$5{,}000{,}000} = \text{ROI}$$

$$10\% \times 2 = 20\%$$

The following examples show how each of the three alternatives increases ROI:

1. Increase ROI by reducing expenses by $400,000, providing a net income of $1,400,000:

$$\frac{\$1{,}400{,}000}{\$10{,}000{,}000} \times \frac{\$10{,}000{,}000}{\$5{,}000{,}000} = \text{ROI}$$

$$14\% \times 2 = 28\%$$

2. Increase ROI by reducing total assets to $4,000,000:

$$\frac{\$1{,}000{,}000}{\$10{,}000{,}000} \times \frac{\$10{,}000{,}000}{\$4{,}000{,}000} = \text{ROI}$$

$$10\% \times 2.5 = 25\%$$

3. Increase ROI by increasing revenue to $12,000,000 (assume that profits increase proportionately):[4]

$$\frac{\$1{,}200{,}000}{\$12{,}000{,}000} \times \frac{\$12{,}000{,}000}{\$5{,}000{,}000} = \text{ROI}$$

$$10\% \times 2.4 = 24\%$$

Although ROI is an effective way of evaluating managers of investment centers, it has certain drawbacks. For example, assume that an investment center currently has an ROI of 22%, but the company has an overall ROI of only 16%. If a new project or investment that promises a return of 19% becomes available to the investment center manager, it might be rejected because the center's ROI would be reduced, even though the company's overall ROI would be increased.

Residual Income

residual income The amount of net income earned above a specified minimum rate of return on assets; used to evaluate investment centers.

Although ROI is widely used to evaluate investment centers, because of its drawbacks, some companies use a closely related measure called **residual income**, which is the amount of net income an investment center is able to earn above a certain minimum rate of return on assets. Exhibit 9-6 compares the residual income and ROI approaches. Assuming that the specified minimum rate of return on assets is 15% and that an investment center earns a $25,000 net income on total assets of $100,000, we see that residual income is $10,000 ($25,000 net income − $15,000 minimum return on assets).

To further illustrate why many companies prefer to use residual income over ROI for evaluating investment center performance, assume that the division for which data were given in Exhibit 9-6 has an opportunity to invest $40,000 in a new project that will generate a return of 20% ($8,000 per year). A manager being evaluated on ROI would probably reject this investment opportunity because, as the following analysis shows, it would reduce the division's overall ROI from 25 to 23.6%.

	Without the New Investment	The New Investment	With the New Investment
Total assets	$100,000	$40,000	$140,000
Net income	$ 25,000	$ 8,000	$ 33,000
ROI	25%	20%	23.6%

exhibit 9-6 A Comparison of ROI and Residual Income

	ROI	Residual Income
Total assets	$100,000	$100,000
Net income	$ 25,000	$ 25,000
ROI ($25,000 ÷ $100,000)	25%	
Minimum rate of return on assets (15% × $100,000)		15,000
Residual income		$ 10,000

4 As discussed in Chapter 2 of management accounting, because of the concept of operating leverage, profits are likely to increase more than proportionately when revenue rises. When revenue increases 10%, fixed costs may remain the same. The result is that both the operating performance and asset turnover ratios are likely to increase when revenue goes up. We are ignoring these CVP considerations in order to keep the example simple.

On the other hand, a manager being evaluated on residual income (with a minimum rate of return of 15%) would probably be quite enthusiastic about the project because it increases residual income from $10,000 to $12,000.

	Without the New Investment	The New Investment	With the New Investment
Total assets	$100,000	$40,000	$140,000
Net income	$ 25,000	$ 8,000	$ 33,000
Minimum rate of return	15,000*	6,000**	21,000
Residual income	$ 10,000	$ 2,000	$ 12,000

*$100,000 × 15% = $15,000
**$40,000 × 15% = $6,000

Whether or not the investment should actually be made also depends on several other factors, including what other alternatives are or will be available. The advantage of residual income is that it encourages managers to make as much profit as possible rather than merely achieving a certain ROI; this means making investments that benefit not only their centers but also the company as a whole.

to summarize

Managers of investment centers are usually held responsible for costs, revenues, and assets. The most common performance measures used in investment centers are ROI and residual income. ROI is a function of both operating performance and asset turnover. Residual income is the amount of net income left over after a certain minimum rate of return has been earned on assets. Both ROI and residual income must be used with care because they can encourage managers to maximize short-run profits at the expense of long-term profitability.

expanded material

Earlier in the chapter, you were introduced to standard costing as a way to evaluate performance in cost centers and were shown how standard costing can be used to compute variances for materials and labor. Information relating to these material and labor variances can be used by decision makers to evaluate the acquisition and use of these important resources. In this expanded material section, we introduce you to the variances associated with variable manufacturing overhead costs. (Fixed overhead variances, which are more complicated and less useful, will be left for future courses.) While the computations associated with variable overhead variances are similar to those used for materials and labor, they are generally more complicated. As a result, interpreting the results and assigning responsibility must be done with caution.

6

Compute and interpret variable overhead variances in cost centers.

VARIABLE MANUFACTURING OVERHEAD VARIANCES IN COST CENTERS

Manufacturing overhead is the third type of product cost that must be controlled and accounted for. Manufacturing overhead includes such costs as indirect materials, indirect labor, utilities, and repairs and maintenance. Like direct materials and direct labor, variable manufacturing overhead is measured and controlled by establishing standard costs, measuring actual costs, analyzing variances from standard, and reporting the variances to managers so they can take necessary corrective action.

Measuring and Controlling Variable Manufacturing Overhead Costs

As you study this expanded material, keep in mind that we are covering only variable overhead in this book. Fixed overhead and its associated variances will be covered in later courses. In studying variable overhead, remember that the formal costing system generates only monetary variances, called spending and efficiency variances. In addition to these variances, control is often achieved by physical observation of activities and by using quality and time measures of results, such as scrap rates for materials, downtime for machines, overtime hours, defective parts, kilowatt-hour usage, and the number of hours needed for repairs. These nonmonetary measures are cost drivers that should be monitored on a regular basis to ensure efficient operations.

IDENTIFYING VARIABLE OVERHEAD ELEMENTS, COST DRIVERS, AND PER-UNIT COSTS The first step in controlling variable manufacturing overhead is to study the behavior of each overhead cost to determine whether it is fixed, variable, or mixed. (You will recall that the analysis of costs was discussed in Chapter 7 of management accounting.) The second step is to develop a cost driver (for each variable manufacturing overhead element) that relates the variable manufacturing overhead cost to specific activities or volume changes. As we explained in Chapter 7 of management accounting, traditional cost drivers have usually been output measures (number of items produced) or input measures (number of direct labor hours worked, machine hours used, or direct labor dollars spent). In Chapter 7 of management accounting, we introduced you to new product costing methods, including activity-based costing, where multiple cost drivers are used. For simplicity in illustrating variable overhead variances, we will assume that variable manufacturing overhead costs vary with direct labor hours. However, you should be aware that, where possible, costs are assigned to activities based on cost drivers that reflect the actual usage of costs for each activity. Thus, instead of using one cost driver, such as direct labor hours, a company might identify different cost drivers for each type of variable overhead cost.

To illustrate the calculation of variable manufacturing cost variances using direct labor hours as the cost driver, we will again use the Jennifer Cosmetics example discussed earlier in the chapter. Assume that, for Jennifer Cosmetics, direct labor hours worked fluctuate between 7,000 and 9,000 hours each month. A study of cost behavior patterns over this relevant range has revealed the following variable rates for each of the variable manufacturing overhead items:

Variable Manufacturing Overhead Items	Standard Variable Rates (per direct labor hour)
Indirect materials	$0.44
Indirect labor	0.38
Utilities	0.19
Repairs and maintenance	0.49
Total	$1.50

Summing these amounts, a total standard variable manufacturing overhead rate of $1.50 per direct labor hour is developed. The amount of standard variable overhead applied to each unit is $1.50 times the number of standard direct labor hours allowed for each bottle of perfume manufactured. Because Jennifer Cosmetics allows 2 standard direct labor hours for each bottle of perfume, the applied variable manufacturing overhead cost is $3.00 per unit ($1.50 × 2 hours).

VARIABLE MANUFACTURING OVERHEAD VARIANCES To illustrate how variances are calculated for variable manufacturing overhead costs, assume again that Jennifer Cosmetics actually used 8,352 direct labor hours to produce 4,000 bottles of perfume during the month. Also assume that the actual results, including the total variable manufacturing overhead costs incurred, are summarized as follows:

Bottles of perfume produced	4,000
Direct labor hours used	8,352
Standard direct labor hours for bottles produced (2 hours × 4,000 bottles)	8,000
Actual variable manufacturing overhead costs incurred:	
Indirect materials	$ 3,370
Indirect labor	2,900
Utilities	1,500
Repairs and maintenance	4,200
Total variable manufacturing overhead costs	$11,970

total variable manufacturing overhead variance The extent to which actual variable manufacturing overhead varies from the amount included in Work-in-Process Inventory; the difference between actual and applied variable manufacturing overhead.

On the basis of 8,000 standard direct labor hours to produce an actual output of 4,000 bottles, the standard cost for variable manufacturing overhead is $12,000 (8,000 hours × $1.50 per hour). The difference between the $11,970 actually incurred and the $12,000 standard cost is the **total variable manufacturing overhead variance**. This variance is the amount of under- or overapplied variable overhead. In this example, variable manufacturing overhead has been overapplied by $30 ($12,000 − $11,970). As with direct materials and direct labor, the total variable manufacturing overhead variance is separated into two major variances: spending and efficiency. The spending and efficiency variances are computed as follows:

Variable Manufacturing Overhead Variances

AH × AR (Actual hours of input × Actual rate)	AH × SR (Actual hours of input × Standard rate)	SH × SR (Standard hours allowed for output × Standard rate)
$11,970	8,352 hours × $1.50 = $12,528	8,000 hours × $1.50 = $12,000

Spending variance
$12,528 − $11,970 = $558 F

Efficiency variance
$12,528 − $12,000 = $528 U
[or $1.50 × (8,352 − 8,000)]

Total variable manufacturing overhead variance $30 F

variable manufacturing overhead spending variance The difference between actual manufacturing overhead incurred and the standard manufacturing overhead for the actual activity level.

Variable Manufacturing Overhead Spending Variance The **variable manufacturing overhead spending variance** ($558 F) is the difference between the actual variable manufacturing overhead costs incurred ($11,970) and the amount that should have been incurred at the actual activity level [$12,528 (8,352 direct labor hours × $1.50 standard rate)].

Because manufacturing overhead contains several different cost items, it is possible to compute a spending variance for each overhead item. This analysis helps managers determine which costs are creating the variances. For Jennifer Cosmetics, the analysis would be as follows:

	Actual Costs	Actual Hours of Input × Standard Rate	Variance
Indirect materials	$ 3,370	$0.44 × 8,352 hours = $ 3,675	$305 F
Indirect labor	2,900	0.38 × 8,352 hours = 3,174	274 F
Utilities	1,500	0.19 × 8,352 hours = 1,587	87 F
Repairs and maintenance	4,200	0.49 × 8,352 hours = 4,092	(108)U
	$11,970	$12,528	$558 F

Looking at the variance column, we see a $305 favorable variance for indirect materials, a $274 favorable variance for indirect labor, an $87 favorable variance for utilities, and a $108 unfavorable variance for repairs and maintenance. The favorable variances mean that less was spent than was expected for the actual hours worked, indicating either that spending is in control or that the standards are too high. The unfavorable variance for repairs and maintenance indicates that spending exceeded the standard and that there may be a problem. In both cases, managers and others responsible for any significant variances (favorable or unfavorable) should be asked to explain the reasons for their existence. Of course, this example assumes that variable overhead is a function of direct labor hours. If direct labor hours is not a good cost driver of (does not influence) variable overhead costs, the variances are highly suspect.

variable manufacturing overhead efficiency variance The difference between manufacturing overhead costs at actual hours and manufacturing overhead costs expected at standard hours.

Variable Manufacturing Overhead Efficiency Variance The $528 unfavorable **variable manufacturing overhead efficiency variance** is the standard variable overhead rate times the difference between the standard and actual activity levels [$1.50 × (8,352 actual direct labor hours − 8,000 standard)]. When direct labor hours are used as the basis for assigning manufacturing overhead, the efficiency variance indicates the number of dollars saved (or spent) as a result of using fewer (or more) actual direct labor hours than the standard number of hours for the actual output. As you will recall, the same relationship was used in computing the direct labor efficiency variance. The reason for computing the two efficiency variances is to show that inefficient use of labor causes variances not only in labor costs but also in variable manufacturing overhead. If you use more direct labor hours than planned, more variable manufacturing overhead cost is assigned to products. Since Jennifer Cosmetics' direct labor efficiency variance is unfavorable ($5,632), the variable manufacturing overhead efficiency variance also is unfavorable. Conversely, of course, a favorable direct labor efficiency variance would have produced a favorable variable manufacturing overhead efficiency variance. Again, it is important to note that we are assuming that direct labor hours is an appropriate cost driver for variable overhead costs.

The manager responsible for the control of direct labor hours should be held responsible for an unfavorable manufacturing overhead efficiency variance because the variance is a measure of the efficiency with which direct labor is used. Thus, the manufacturing overhead efficiency variance is really an additional aspect of the direct labor efficiency variance when using direct labor hours as the cost driver to assign variable overhead.

to summarize

Historically, standard costs for variable manufacturing overhead items have been developed using an input measure, such as direct labor hours or machine hours, as a cost driver. Recently, however, cost drivers that relate to individual overhead items have been used to reflect how overhead costs relate to activities. Regardless of the cost drivers used, standard overhead costs are computed for each variable overhead item to determine a standard variable rate that is used in applying variable manufacturing overhead to each unit of product.

The total variable manufacturing overhead variance can be segregated into two variances: spending and efficiency. The variable manufacturing overhead spending variance measures the difference between the costs actually incurred and the amount that should have been incurred at the actual activity level. The variable manufacturing overhead efficiency variance is the difference between variable manufacturing overhead costs at the actual and standard activity levels. Because the spending variance highlights the differences between actual costs incurred and standard amounts for individual manufacturing overhead items, it is generally the more useful overhead variance to analyze for control purposes.

---

review of learning objectives

1 Explain why evaluating personnel and divisions is such an important activity in organizations. Today, information about how efficiently and effectively an organization is operating is easily accessible worldwide. For a company to survive in this information age, it must deliver the highest-quality products to its customers at the least possible price in the shortest amount of time. The only way an organization can continue to improve on these dimensions is to assess its performance and identify areas for improvement. This need for continuous improvement makes performance evaluation more important than ever before.

2 Identify different types of organizational units in which evaluation occurs. Most companies are divided into segments with responsibilities assigned to segment managers. These segments may be defined in terms of product line, geographic area, or function, for example. In a centralized organization, top management makes most of the important operating decisions; in a decentralized organization, decision-making authority is delegated to lower-level managers as well. The current trend is toward decentralization because it usually results in better, more informed decisions.

With responsibility accounting, managers are held accountable for the costs, assets, or revenues over which they have control. The three types of responsibility centers are cost, profit, and investment. Cost centers are usually found at relatively low levels in the organization, and the managers are held accountable for the costs they incur. Profit and investment centers are found at higher levels, and the managers are held accountable for the profits or the return on investments in assets they generate.

3 Explain how performance is evaluated in cost centers. Traditionally, performance has been evaluated in cost centers using standard costs. In recent years, some organizations, including most Japanese companies, have adopted an alternative called target costing. A standard cost system involves setting standard (predetermined) costs that serve as a benchmark for judging what actual costs should be. Standard costs are usually expressed as the per-unit cost of materials, labor, and manufacturing overhead and are used by managers for planning, implementing, and controlling decisions. Standard costs are developed on the basis of careful analysis using the experience of many types of staff, including engineers, supervisors, accountants, purchasing agents, and others. Standard costs have a quantity component and a price component. A comparison of actual and standard costs usually results in two variances: a price (rate) variance and a quantity (usage) variance. Significant variances alert management to specific problem areas that require corrective action. The strategy of focusing on significant variances, called management by exception, is essential to the control function. A standard cost system is designed to accumulate actual costs, to compare actual and standard costs to identify variances, and to report operating results (including variances) to management for review and for corrective action when significant variances occur. Manufacturing firms make extensive use of standard costing systems. A complete standard cost system includes standards for materials, labor, and manufacturing overhead. Materials variances are usually called price variances and quantity variances. The materials price variance reflects the extent to which the actual price varies from the standard price for the actual quantity of materials purchased or used. The materials quantity variance measures the extent to which the quantity of materials used varies from the standard quantity allowed for the achieved level of production. Labor variances are called rate variances and efficiency variances. The labor rate variance is the difference between the actual and the standard labor rates multiplied by the actual hours worked. The labor efficiency variance is the difference between actual and standard hours multiplied by the standard wage rate. Target costing is a customer-focused approach that attempts to determine the price customers will pay for products and services. It involves six steps: (1) establishing target market prices, (2) determining target profit margins, (3) examining the reliability of current cost-management techniques, (4) establishing target costs, (5) achieving targeted costs, and (6) identifying further cost reductions once production begins. With target costing, cross-functional teams work together to meet the target costs. Although most people agree that target costing has great appeal, implementing it can often be very difficult. As a result, while target costing has been widely used by Japanese companies, American companies have been slow to adopt it.

4 Explain how performance is evaluated in profit centers. Profit center managers are responsible for revenues as well as costs. The best measure of performance in a profit center is a segment-margin income statement, which distinguishes between indirect and direct costs and reports a segment margin that is controllable by segment managers. Segment-margin income statements also divide direct segment costs into their variable and fixed components in order to compute the segment's contribution margin. Nonmonetary factors often must also be considered in assessing the performance of a profit center. In profit centers, costs are analyzed in the same way they are in cost centers. Revenues are analyzed by calculating sales price and sales volume variances. The sales volume variance is further broken down into market share and industry volume variances. And, in cases where profit centers sell more than one product, a sales mix variance can also be calculated.

5 Explain how performance is evaluated in investment centers. Investment centers are usually found at higher levels in an organization than profit centers. The managers of investment centers are responsible for costs, revenues, and assets. Commonly used measures of investment center performance are return on investment (ROI) and residual income. ROI is calculated by dividing net income by total assets. An investment center can improve its ROI by (1) decreasing its costs to increase its operating performance ratio, (2) decreasing its assets to increase its asset turnover ratio, or (3) increasing revenue with a corresponding increase in net income. Residual income is the amount of net income an investment center is able to earn above a certain minimum rate of return on assets. The problem with both ROI and residual income is that they tend to encourage managers to make decisions that increase short-run profits but may diminish profits in the long run.

expanded material

6 Compute and interpret variable overhead variances in cost centers. Using an appropriate cost driver, standard costs are computed for each variable overhead item to determine a standard variable overhead rate that is used in applying variable manufacturing overhead to each unit of product. The variable overhead variances may be divided into spending and efficiency variances. The spending variance measures the difference between the costs actually incurred and the amount that should have been incurred at the attained level of activity. The efficiency variance is the difference between variable manufacturing overhead costs at the actual and standard activity levels.

key terms and concepts

review problems

Material and Labor Variances

The standard cost sheet for Kendra Box Company shows the following unit costs for direct materials and direct labor for each box made:

Direct materials (4 board feet of lumber @ $2)	$ 8
Direct labor (2 standard hours @ $6)	12
Total standard cost per unit (excluding overhead)	$20

During the month of October, 83,000 board feet of lumber were used to produce 20,000 boxes, and the following actual costs were incurred:

Lumber purchased (100,000 board feet @ $2.20)	$220,000
Direct labor (39,600 hours @ $6.05)	$239,580

Required: Compute the materials and labor variances.

Solution

Materials Variances

The price variance is computed when the lumber is purchased, and the quantity variance is computed when the lumber is used.

Materials price variance:

Purchase price per board foot for 100,000 feet	$ 2.20	
Standard price per board foot	(2.00)	
Difference	$ 0.20	U
Feet of lumber purchased	× 100,000	
Total price variance	$ 20,000	U

Materials quantity variance:

Actual lumber used	83,000	feet
Standard lumber required (20,000 boxes × 4 feet)	(80,000)	feet
Difference	3,000	feet U
Standard cost per board foot	× $2.00	
Total quantity variance	$ 6,000	U

Labor Variances

The labor rate and labor efficiency variances are both based on direct labor hours used; thus, they are computed at the same point in time.

Total direct labor variance:

Actual direct labor cost (39,600 hours at $6.05)	$239,580
Standard direct labor cost	
(20,000 boxes × 2 hours = 40,000 hours × $6.00)	240,000
Total direct labor variance	$ 420 F

Labor rate variance:	
Actual rate	$ 6.05
Standard rate	(6.00)
Difference	$ 0.05 U
Actual hours	× 39,600
Total labor rate variance	$ 1,980 U
Labor efficiency variance:	
Actual direct labor hours	39,600
Standard direct labor hours	40,000
Difference	400 F
Standard direct labor rate	× $6.00
Total labor efficiency variance	$ 2,400 F

expanded material

Variable Manufacturing Overhead Variances

Use the information given above, plus the following information, to address issues associated with Kendra Box Company's manufacturing overhead variances.

The company's budget shows the following monthly variable manufacturing overhead costs at several production levels:

	Percent of Standard Capacity		
	80%	90%	100%
Expected number of boxes	20,000	22,500	25,000
Expected direct labor hours	40,000	45,000	50,000
Variable manufacturing overhead costs	$80,000	$90,000	$100,000

The company normally produces at 100% of capacity. In addition to the information given above relating to production and the use of materials and overhead, the following actual information is also available:

Variable manufacturing overhead	$83,000

Required:

1. Compute variable manufacturing overhead cost rate (a) per box and (b) per direct labor hour.
2. Compute the variable manufacturing overhead spending and efficiency variances for October.

Solution

1. **Variable Manufacturing Overhead Cost Rates**

		Cost per Unit	Cost per Hour
Flexible budget at normal capacity:			
Boxes produced per month	25,000		
Labor hours per month	50,000		
Variable manufacturing overhead costs	$100,000	$4	$2

2. **Variable Manufacturing Overhead Variances**

The following diagram shows the computation of the variable overhead spending and efficiency variances:

AH × AR (Actual hours of input × Actual rate)	AH × SR (Actual hours of input × Standard rate)	SH × SR (Standard hours allowed for output × Standard rate)
$83,000	39,600 hours × $2 = $79,200	40,000 hours × $2 = $80,000

Spending variance $3,800 U

Efficiency variance $800 F

Total variable overhead variance $3,000 U

The variable overhead efficiency variance can also be computed by multiplying the difference between standard labor hours and actual labor hours by the standard variable overhead rate per hour (39,600 − 40,000 = 400 favorable hours × $2 variable overhead rate = $800 F).

discussion questions

1. Why is evaluating personnel and divisions so important to a business, especially in today's economy?
2. Why is it practically impossible for a firm to be completely centralized, that is, to have top management making all operating decisions?
3. Why is a system of responsibility accounting necessary in most businesses?
4. What are some important behavioral factors that must be considered when responsibilities are assigned to managers?
5. Why are most performance reports called exception reports?
6. What is the difference between a cost center and a profit center? Between a profit center and an investment center?
7. What is a standard cost?
8. What is the purpose of a standard cost system?
9. Who is responsible for the development of the standards to be used in a standard cost system?
10. What is a variance from standard?
11. What is the relationship of a standard cost system to the principle of management by exception?
12. What are the steps in establishing and operating a standard cost system?
13. What purpose is served by dividing the total direct materials variance into a price and a quantity variance, and dividing the total direct labor variance into a rate and an efficiency variance?
14. Who is usually responsible for each of the following variances?
    a. Direct materials price variance
    b. Direct materials quantity variance
    c. Direct labor rate variance
    d. Direct labor efficiency variance
15. What are the major advantages and disadvantages of a standard cost system?
16. What are the major advantages and disadvantages of using target costing?
17. If a profit center has a net loss, does that mean it is not making a contribution to the company as a whole?
18. What are the variances used to analyze revenues in profit and investment centers?
19. What is the major disadvantage of using ROI to evaluate the performance of investment centers?
20. What is the major advantage of using residual income to evaluate the performance of investment centers?

expanded material

21. What are the two steps in developing standards and measures for use in controlling variable manufacturing overhead?
22. What is a variable manufacturing overhead spending variance, and what does it indicate about variable manufacturing overhead costs?
23. What is a variable manufacturing overhead efficiency variance, and how does it relate to the labor efficiency variance?

discussion cases

CASE 9-1

CONTINUOUS IMPROVEMENT NEEDED

One evening after a strenuous day at the office, Janis Walker, president of Western Mills, Inc., a leading textile manufacturing firm, was out jogging to help relieve the tensions of that day's work. While jogging, she focused her thinking on the firm's commercial carpeting division. The major customers of the division are companies that are building new office buildings, hotels, and motels and need quality carpet in their buildings. The carpet division is doing quite well, but Walker has a nagging feeling that the division could be doing better. She decided to discuss the performance of the division with the division manager. When she arrived home after jogging, Walker called the division manager and arranged a meeting for the next day.

At the meeting, Walker asked the division manager how long it took to deliver an order to the building site after production started. The manager's answer was 17 days. Walker then asked what the industry average was for delivery. The answer was 15 days. Walker wanted to know why Western Mills took longer than competitors to meet order requirements. The manager answered that its product was of a higher quality, so customers were willing to wait longer for the order to be filled. With this information in hand and without hesitation, Walker said, "I will give you six months to reduce the delivery time to 10 days! You study the problem and tell me what resources you need to meet this 10-day delivery goal. I want a report from you as soon as possible."

1. Assuming that the division already has a standard cost system, what limitations of that system resulted in two more days of delivery time than its competitors?
2. Assuming this company has a standard cost system, what changes is the division manager likely to make in order to meet the president's 10-day delivery mandate?
3. How could the use of target costing have helped this company?

CASE 9-2

USING SEGMENT DATA TO MAKE KEY DECISIONS

Sure-Check Company, a calculator manufacturer, is considering dropping one of its calculator product lines because of consistent losses from this model over the past three years. The recent poor performance of this product (known as model A) is shown here (in thousands).

	2001	2002	2003
Revenue (average price $100 per unit)	$14,600	$14,400	$14,200
Variable costs:			
Direct materials cost ($40 per unit)	$ 5,840	$ 5,760	$ 5,680
Direct labor cost ($20 per unit)	2,920	2,880	2,840
Variable manufacturing overhead costs ($15 per unit)	2,190	2,160	2,130
Selling expenses (10% of sales)	1,460	1,440	1,420
Total variable costs	$12,410	$12,240	$12,070
Contribution margin	$ 2,190	$ 2,160	$ 2,130
Less fixed costs controllable by segment managers	2,022	1,997	1,972
Segment margin	$ 168	$ 163	$ 158
Less company indirect fixed costs	438	432	426
Operating loss	$ (270)	$ (269)	$ (268)

Revenue and fixed costs (controllable by segment managers) are expected to decrease again in 2004 by $200,000 and $25,000, respectively, whereas direct materials and direct labor are expected to increase by 5% unless the production department purchases a new attachment with a two-year life for $150,000. This new attachment would replace an attachment purchased only two years ago for $200,000 with, at that time, an expected four-year life. If the new attachment is purchased, direct materials and direct labor will not increase in 2004.

1. Assuming that the new attachment is not purchased, should Sure-Check Company continue to manufacture and sell the model A calculator? Explain.
2. Should the new attachment be purchased? Explain.
3. How, if at all, would the production capacity made available by discontinuing model A affect your decision regarding the purchase of the attachment?
4. What qualitative factors could affect your responses to (1) and (2)?

CASE 9-3

WHY IS MY GROSS MARGIN DECREASING?

Jenson Company sells three products: (1) a health food called *Gro-Gain,* (2) diet supplements called *Muscular,* and (3) a liquid medication called *Yupi Juice* that supposedly cures arthritis. Gro-Gain sells for $5 per bottle, Muscular sells for $10 for a package of 50 pills, and Yupi Juice sells for $15 per bottle. Gro-Gain has 2% of the health food market, Muscular has 10% of its niche market, and Yupi Juice has 50% of the liquid arthritis medication market. The gross margins are 20% for Gro-Gain, 25% for Muscular, and 30% for Yupi Juice. Even though total sales increased this period over last period while total industry sales and the expected and actual sales prices of the three products remained constant, Jenson's gross margin decreased slightly. You suspected that the cause of the decreased gross margin was an increase in costs of the three products. However, an investigation revealed that costs for the three products remained the same as they were last period. Considering the data given, what do you believe is causing the decreased gross margin?

CASE 9-4

WHAT ARE MY COSTS ANYWAY?

You have recently been promoted to be the manager of the camera division of a large corporation. Your most profitable product is an instant camera that takes pictures and then develops them immediately. Historically, the pictures taken by the camera were of a poor quality, but due to large investments in research and new breakthroughs in technology, the instantly developed pictures are of increasingly higher quality. You have just received your segment financial statements for the period, which report the following:

Revenue	$81,000,000
Cost of products sold	40,000,000
Gross margin	$41,000,000

On the basis of this performance you are due to receive a $3 million bonus. The top executives of the company are ecstatic about your performance because you have increased quality, reduced defects, and dramatically increased the productivity of your segment. Having studied management accounting, however, you know that the manufacturing costs are not the only ones that add value to your products. In fact, in your heart, you believe that were it not for research and development costs, aggressive marketing, and good customer service subsequent to sales, your segment would not be nearly so profitable. Yet, these costs are tracked in other departments and are not your responsibility.

As a manager who is benefiting from traditional performance evaluation methods, you wonder whether you should inform management that they are actually giving you a bonus that is too high. Apparently, you are the only one in your company that is aware that these other value-adding costs should be included in your performance evaluation. What should you do? Do you let well enough alone or should you go to management and let them know that you are probably being overpaid?

exercises

EXERCISE 9-1

RESPONSIBILITY ACCOUNTING REPORTS

Lorlily Company is an agricultural supply firm. The management of the company is decentralized, with division managers heading the two operating divisions: Machinery and Seed/Fertilizer. Within each division, the sales are split between the two states of Indiana and Illinois.

The following data are applicable to revenue in 2003:

	Budget	Actual
Machinery—Indiana	$800,000	$750,000
Seed/Fertilizer—Illinois	500,000	580,000
Seed/Fertilizer—Indiana	400,000	530,000
Machinery—Illinois	350,000	250,000

1. Prepare a responsibility accounting report for the head of the Machinery division. For each of the two geographic areas (Indiana and Illinois), show whether the variance between budgeted and actual machinery revenue is favorable or unfavorable.
2. Prepare a responsibility accounting report for the head of the entire company. The company head wants to see only the overall results for each of the two operating divisions (Machinery and Seed/Fertilizer); a detailed breakdown by geographic area is not requested.

EXERCISE 9-2

MATERIALS PRICE VARIANCE

Hogan Manufacturing Company has just adopted a standard cost system. You have been asked to analyze the materials purchases and usage for the month of August to determine the materials price variance to be recorded at the end of the month. During August, 5,000 gallons of a chemical were purchased at $3.20 per gallon. Only 4,200 gallons were put into production. The standard price per gallon is $3.15. Compute the following variances:

1. The materials price variance if the chemical is carried in inventory at standard price.
2. The materials price variance if the chemical is carried in inventory at actual price and is charged to Work-in-Process Inventory at the standard price.

EXERCISE 9-3

MATERIALS PRICE AND QUANTITY VARIANCES—JOURNAL ENTRIES

Genesis Enterprises produces one product—MX4. The following information relating to raw materials is available for the month of March:

Beginning direct materials inventory	1,500 pounds @ $3.10 per unit
Purchases made during the month	11,000 pounds @ $3.10 per unit
Direct materials placed in production	11,750 pounds

The standard materials usage for one unit of MX4 is 2 pounds with a standard price per pound of $3. Genesis produced 6,000 units of Product MX4 during the month.

1. Compute the materials price and quantity variances for Genesis assuming the materials price variance is computed at the time of purchase.
2. Provide the journal entries required to record:
   a. The purchase of direct materials and the materials price variance.
   b. Placing the direct materials in production and the materials quantity variance.

EXERCISE 9-4

DIRECT MATERIALS PURCHASED AND USED

Mary Clarke is concerned about her performance as a recently employed purchasing agent. The accounting department has provided her with the following data for the month of August:

Units produced	2,000
Materials used	1,078 tons
Materials purchased	1,400 tons at $43 per ton

The standard materials usage set by management for one unit of product is half a ton of materials per unit, at $45 per ton. Her performance report shows the following variances:

Used (1,078 tons − 1,000 tons standard) × $45 per ton	$3,510 U
Purchased ($45 per ton standard − $43 per ton actual) × 1,400 tons	2,800 F
	$ 710 U

If you were Mary Clarke, how would you explain this report, which indicates a $710 unfavorable variance?

EXERCISE 9-5

ANALYZING MATERIALS COST

Mr. Rogers, the production manager, has received a report showing a $16,500 unfavorable total materials variance. He knows that production used 10,000 pounds less than the budgeted amount for direct materials. Mr. Rogers also knows that the standard price for direct materials was determined to be 80 cents per pound.

What was the actual cost of direct materials used during the period if the budgeted amount was estimated to be 500,000 pounds?

EXERCISE 9-6

MATERIALS PRICE AND QUANTITY VARIANCES

John Clarke, production manager, has just received a report stating that the total materials variance for last month was $3,000 unfavorable. However, he is not certain whether the production foremen are overdrawing from inventory or the purchasing department has been unable to acquire materials at reasonable prices. The information he needs is contained in the following report:

Standard production	150,000 units
Actual production	146,000 units
Standard materials per unit	2 pounds
Materials used in March	300,000 pounds
Standard price for materials	$1.50 per pound
Actual price for materials	$1.47 per pound

1. Compute the materials price and quantity variances for the month.
2. **Interpretive Question:** What was the cause of the unfavorable variance, and what recommendation would you make to Mr. Clarke?

EXERCISE 9-7

MATERIALS PRICE AND QUANTITY VARIANCES—JOURNAL ENTRIES

Starship Enterprises produces and sells calibrators. The company began the period with the following inventory of raw material:

200 units at $5.50 per unit (the materials price variance is taken at the time of purchase)

A standard of four units of material for each calibrator produced has been established. During the period, Starship purchased an additional 1,500 units of material at a total cost of $8,220. The dollar amount of materials transferred to Work-in-Process Inventory during the period was $8,800. At the end of the period, Starship had an ending materials inventory of 50 units.

1. Provide the journal entry required to record the materials price variance.
2. Provide the journal entry required to record the materials quantity variance.

EXERCISE 9-8

LABOR RATE AND EFFICIENCY VARIANCES

To produce one unit of Product OU812 requires four hours of labor at a standard cost per hour of $8.50. During the month of September, 15,000 units were produced. Actual hours and costs for the month are as follows:

Actual direct labor hours	58,800
Actual direct labor costs	$498,000

1. Compute the actual cost per hour of direct labor for the month of September.
2. Compute the labor rate variance.
3. Compute the labor efficiency variance.

EXERCISE 9-9

RESPONSIBILITY FOR LABOR COSTS

Raymond Stone, a recent business school graduate, has taken a job with Farben Corporation as production manager. His job is to see that production is efficient. After his first month, he is given this memo.

Performance Report	
Ray Stone:	$8,000 Unfavorable

Given the following data, what justification would you give if you were in his position, keeping in mind that Stone is not responsible for hiring, firing, and wage rates?

Units produced	750 units
Direct labor used	7,600 hours at $20
Standard direct labor hours per unit	10 hours at $16

EXERCISE 9-10

RESPONSIBILITY FOR LABOR RATES

In Exercise 9-9, what is theoretically wrong with the conclusion that Raymond Stone is not responsible for labor rates?

EXERCISE 9-11

LABOR VARIANCES

During the year, Thompson Plastics was in negotiation with the local union over wages. A settlement was finally reached, and the average wage per hour was increased to $32.80. Production fell to 145,000 units, and 220,000 hours were incurred. Standard production has been set at 150,000 units; 1.5 hours of labor were expected to produce one unit at a standard labor cost of $48.75 per unit. Actual labor cost for the period was $7,216,000.

1. Calculate the labor variances at Thompson Plastics.
2. Prepare the journal entry to enter labor costs in Work-in-Process Inventory and set up the rate and efficiency variances for labor.
3. **Interpretive Question:** Are these variances significant in light of the new wage agreement?

EXERCISE 9-12

EMPLOYEE MORALE AND PRODUCTION EFFICIENCY

Crest Fabrics is a nonunion textile firm. Employee morale and production efficiency have dropped in the last few weeks, causing management some concern. Further, quality control problems have resulted in a 10% increase in rejects in the last two weeks. The following information may help management identify the causes of current problems:

Employee Production Efficiency Report (in percentages)

Employee	Wk 14	Wk 15	Wk 16	Wk 17	Wk 18	Wk 19	Wk 20
Baker	96	100	86	93	91	89	85
Johnson	101	97	89	90	93	91	87
Becker	105	109	93	96	95	92	90
Howard	99	98	88	93	97	94	88
Kettle	92	93	81	85	90	91	90

Additional information:

a. Standards for measuring worker efficiency were raised at the start of week 16.
b. Crest Fabrics changed its source of supply of materials in week 15.

1. From the production efficiency report can you identify trends in the efficiency of individual workers? Which ones might have low morale?
2. **Interpretive Question:** What clues to the causes of the diminishing efficiency and quality can you draw from the information given?

EXERCISE 9-13

LABOR VARIANCES

Compute the missing amounts.

Total labor variance	$ 47,500 U
Labor efficiency variance	42,000 U
Actual labor hours incurred	110,000
Standard labor hours allowed	(a)
Units produced	50,000
Standard hours allowed per unit	2
Total actual labor costs	$467,500
Actual labor cost per hour	(b)
Actual labor cost per unit	(c)
Labor rate variance	(d)
Standard labor cost per hour	(e)
Standard labor cost per unit	(f)

EXERCISE 9-14

TARGET COSTING AT NASA

By the time the National Aeronautics and Space Administration (NASA) launched the Viking missions to Mars, its costs had skyrocketed into the billions. So, as preparations were being made for the next Mars exploration mission, Pathfinder, NASA was told to tighten its belt considerably. NASA had a target cost goal (for Pathfinder) that was one-fifteenth of the cost of the Viking mission, which forced the agency along a different design path. One of the changes NASA's engineers made that saved huge amounts of money was to use inflated balloons to land the spacecraft rather than retro rockets, which the Viking mission had employed.

1. Why was NASA able to reduce costs so significantly when preparing for the Pathfinder mission?
2. Do you think applying target costing is easier for NASA than for for-profit organizations such as General Motors or General Mills? If so, why?

EXERCISE 9-15

SEGMENT-MARGIN INCOME STATEMENTS

Professional Management, Inc., is a company that sponsors seminars for executives. It has two profit centers, or divisions: a time-management group and a money-management group. Financial information for the two divisions for the year just ended follows:

	Time Management	Money Management
Revenue	$842,000	$965,000
Mailing costs	48,000	102,000
Printing costs	146,000	98,000
Hotel rental costs	425,000	501,000
Travel expenses	72,000	60,000
Advertising costs	108,000	106,000

Of these costs, printing and advertising are direct fixed costs, whereas mailing, hotel rental, and travel are variable costs. Using this information, prepare segment-margin income statements for the two divisions.

EXERCISE 9-16

Spread-Sheet Software

EVALUATING PERFORMANCE WITH SEGMENT AND CONTRIBUTION MARGINS

Damond Corporation's three profit centers had the following operating data during 2003:

	North	East	West
Revenue (at $10 per unit)	$100,000	$150,000	$200,000
Fixed costs:			
Costs unique to the division	30,000	61,000	70,000
Costs allocated by corporate headquarters	20,000	30,000	40,000
Variable costs per unit	6	6	4

Damond's management is concerned because the company is losing money. They ask you to:

1. Calculate each profit center's contribution and segment margins, and overall company profits.
2. Determine, on the basis of these calculations, which center(s), if any, should be discontinued. (Assume that the 2003 performance is indicative of all future years. Ignore all nonfinancial factors.)

EXERCISE 9-17

MEASURING PERFORMANCE USING SEGMENT AND CONTRIBUTION MARGINS

El Pico Company has two divisions: Maya and Aztec. During 2003, they had the following operating data:

	Maya Division	Aztec Division
Revenue	$100,000	$120,000
Fixed costs:		
Costs unique to the division	50,000	45,000
Costs allocated by corporate headquarters	11,000	10,000
Variable costs per unit	4	4
Unit sales price of division's product	10	8

1. Compute each division's contribution and segment margins, and the contribution each makes to overall company profits.
2. **Interpretive Question:** Based on only the financial information given, should either division be discontinued? Why?

EXERCISE 9-18

REVENUE VARIANCES

Sweets, Inc., makes two products: caramel wafers and chocolate wafers. Actual and standard or expected revenue data for the two products are as follows:

Actual Data (in 000s)			
	Units	Sales Price	Total Actual Market
Caramel wafers	5,000 boxes	$20.00	50,000 boxes
Chocolate wafers	4,000 boxes	25.00	60,000 boxes
Total	9,000 boxes	22.22	110,000 boxes

Standard Data (in 000s)			
	Units	Sales Price	Expected Market Share
Caramel wafers	4,500 boxes	$22.00	12%
Chocolate wafers	4,400 boxes	26.00	7%
Total	8,900 boxes	23.98	10% (given)

Using the above data, calculate the sales price and sales volume variances for caramel and chocolate wafers for Sweets, Inc.

EXERCISE 9-19

REVENUE VARIANCES

Using the data in Exercise 9-18 and assuming that the sales volume variance for caramel wafers is $11,000 favorable and for chocolate wafers is $10,400 unfavorable, compute the market share and industry volume variances for both caramel and chocolate wafers.

EXERCISE 9-20

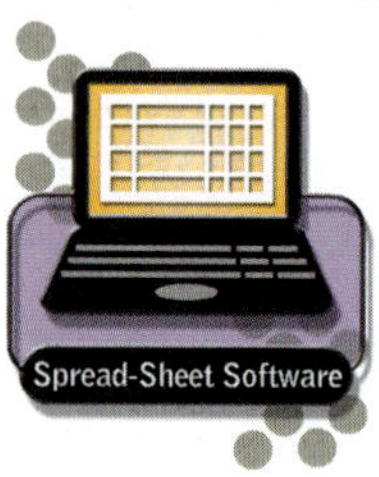

REVENUE VARIANCES

Using the data in Exercise 9-18, calculate the sales mix variance for Sweets, Inc.

EXERCISE 9-21

RETURN ON INVESTMENT

Compute the missing data, items (a) through (i), in the following table:

	Division X	Division Y	Division Z
Revenue	$600,000	$500,000	$ (g)
Net income	30,000	25,000	(h)
Total assets	(a)	100,000	200,000
Operating performance ratio	(b)	(d)	10%
Asset turnover ratio	(c)	(e)	4 times
ROI	12%	(f)	(i)

EXERCISE 9-22

RETURN ON INVESTMENT

During 2003, the North and South divisions of Mayberry Company reported the following:

	North Division	South Division
ROI	18%	20%
Operating performance ratio	6%	5%
Revenue	$60,000	$80,000
Total assets	$20,000	$20,000

1. What was each division's asset turnover ratio in 2003?
2. What operating performance ratio would each division need in order to generate an ROI of 25%?

EXERCISE 9-23

MEASURING PERFORMANCE: RESIDUAL INCOME AND ROI

McCormick Corporation measures the performance of its divisions by using the residual income approach, with a minimum accepted rate of return of 16%. In 2003, the printing division, which has total assets of $250,000, generated a net income of $55,000, or 8% of sales. The operating results are expected to be the same in 2004. In early 2004, the printing division receives a proposal for a $50,000 investment that would generate an additional $10,000 of income per year.

1. Should the manager of the printing division make the investment?
2. Would your answer to (1) be different if McCormick Corporation used the ROI approach to evaluate the performance of its various divisions? Why or why not?

EXERCISE 9-24

MEASURING PERFORMANCE: RESIDUAL INCOME AND ROI

An investment center of Southwick Corporation made three investment proposals. Details of the proposals follow.

	Proposals		
	1	2	3
Required investment	$80,000	$50,000	$65,000
Annual return	13,000	9,000	9,500

Southwick Corporation uses the residual income method to evaluate all investment proposals. Its minimum rate of return is 15%.

1. As president of Southwick Corporation, which of the investments, if any, would you make? Why?
2. Assuming that Southwick Corporation uses the ROI approach to evaluate investment proposals, which investments, if any, would you make? (Southwick Corporation's current return on assets is 20%.)

expanded material

EXERCISE 9-25

VARIABLE MANUFACTURING OVERHEAD SPENDING AND EFFICIENCY VARIANCES

Lauder Company manufactures one product. The standard capacity is 20,000 units per month. Manufacturing overhead costs are budgeted on the basis of direct labor hours. At standard capacity, the monthly variable overhead budget would be $50,000 at two direct labor hours per unit. During February, 18,000 units of product were manufactured, and $46,000 of variable manufacturing overhead was incurred. Actual direct labor hours were 35,000.

Compute the variable manufacturing overhead spending and efficiency variances.

EXERCISE 9-26

VARIABLE MANUFACTURING OVERHEAD VARIANCES

Rollins Manufacturing Company estimates variable manufacturing overhead for the month of November to be $80,000 with an estimated activity level (in direct labor hours) of 10,000 hours. At standard capacity, each unit of finished product requires two direct labor hours to complete. During November, 4,900 units of finished product were produced at an actual overhead cost of $77,500. Actual direct labor hours during the month were 9,850.

1. Compute the amount of variable overhead applied during November.
2. Compute the amount of under- or overapplied overhead for the month.
3. Compute the variable manufacturing overhead spending and efficiency variances.

problems

PROBLEM 9-1

RESPONSIBILITY ACCOUNTING REPORTS

Ryhan Company is a multinational computer services firm. The management of the company is decentralized, with division managers heading the following three divisions: Europe, Asia, and the Americas. Within each division, the three sources of revenue are software sales, service contracts, and consulting fees.

The following data are applicable to revenue in 2003:

	Budget	Actual
Europe—software sales	$200,000	$230,000
Asia—software sales	200,000	130,000
Americas—software sales	350,000	420,000
Europe—service contracts	120,000	90,000
Asia—service contracts	70,000	80,000
Americas—service contracts	250,000	190,000
Europe—consulting fees	40,000	90,000
Asia—consulting fees	50,000	35,000
Americas—consulting fees	100,000	60,000

Required:

1. Prepare a responsibility accounting report for the head of the Europe division. For each of the three revenue sources (software sales, service contracts, and consulting fees), show whether the variance between budget and actual is favorable or unfavorable.
2. Prepare a responsibility accounting report for the head of the entire company. The company head wants to see only the overall results for each of the three geographic divisions (budget versus actual); a detailed breakdown by revenue source is not requested.

PROBLEM 9-2

MATERIALS AND LABOR VARIANCES

The standard cost data for Madison Machinery Company show the following costs for producing one of its machines:

Direct materials	400 pounds at $8 = $3,200
Direct labor	150 hours at $15 = $2,250

During April, four machines were built, with actual total costs as follows:

Materials purchased	2,000 pounds at $8.20 = $16,400
Materials used	1,700 pounds
Direct labor incurred	625 hours at $14.80 = $9,250

Required:

1. Compute the following variances:
   a. Materials price variance (inventory is carried at standard cost)
   b. Materials quantity variance
   c. Labor rate variance
   d. Labor efficiency variance
2. Record the standard materials and labor costs in Work-in-Process Inventory, and enter the variances in appropriate journal entries.

PROBLEM 9-3

MATERIALS AND LABOR VARIANCES

Gemini, Inc., provides the following standard cost data for one of its products:

Direct materials	5 pounds at $4.25 per pound
Direct labor	2 hours at $6.00 per hour

During the month of August, the following actual cost data were accumulated:

Materials purchased	16,000 pounds at $4.15 per pound
Materials used	14,500 pounds
Direct labor incurred	6,450 hours at a total cost of $38,571
Units produced	3,150 units

Required: Compute the following variances:

1. Materials price variance (this variance is computed at the time of purchase)
2. Materials quantity variance
3. Labor rate variance
4. Labor efficiency variance

PROBLEM 9-4

MATERIALS AND LABOR VARIANCES

Actual materials	2,000 tons
Actual hours used	1,500 hours
Standard materials for output (tons)	(a)
Standard hours for output	(b)
Actual cost per ton of material	(c)
Standard cost per ton of material	$ 4
Actual cost per direct labor hour	$ 4
Standard cost per direct labor hour	(d)
Total direct labor variance	$1,625 U
Total direct materials variance	$ 400 F
Direct materials price variance	(e)
Direct materials quantity variance	$ 0
Direct labor rate variance	$ 750 U
Direct labor efficiency variance	(f)

Required: Compute the missing amounts.

PROBLEM 9-5

MATERIALS AND LABOR VARIANCES

Sports Manufacturing, Inc., produces and sells footballs. The standard cost for materials and labor for one regulation-size football is as follows:

Direct materials	2 feet of leather at $5.50 per foot
Direct labor	½ hour at $9.00 per hour

During the period, Sports Manufacturing recorded a materials price variance of $100 U and a materials quantity variance of $380 F. In addition, the company recorded a labor rate variance and a labor efficiency variance of $1,200 U and $450 U, respectively. Seven thousand footballs were produced during the period, and the materials inventory did not change during the period.

Required:

1. Compute the actual costs for materials and labor during the period.
2. Provide the journal entries to record the materials price and quantity variances. (Hint: the amount of materials purchased and used is the same.)
3. Provide the journal entries to record the labor rate and efficiency variances.

PROBLEM 9-6

MATERIALS AND LABOR VARIANCES

The following information was taken from the records of Liberty Manufacturing Company for the month of July:

Materials (actual):	
Purchases of material A:	1,300 pounds × $5.25
Purchases of material B:	750 pounds × $2.50
Used 900 pounds of material A	
Used 525 pounds of material B	
Direct labor (actual):	
Manufacturing:	1,050 hours × $8.90
Assembly:	450 hours × $4.50

Standard cost per unit:

Material A: 2 pounds × $5.20 per pound	$10.40
Material B: 1 pound × $2.60 per pound	2.60
Direct labor—manufacturing: 2 hours × $8.50	17.00
Direct labor—assembly: 1 hour × $4.60	4.60
Standard cost per unit	$34.60

Units produced: 500

Required:

1. Calculate the materials price and quantity variances, assuming that the materials price variance is recognized at the time of purchase.
2. Calculate the labor rate and labor efficiency variances.
3. **Interpretive Question:** What is the advantage, if any, of calculating the materials price variance at the time of purchase rather than at the time of use?

PROBLEM 9-7

MATERIALS AND LABOR VARIANCE ANALYSIS

Cooke Manufacturing Company produces high-quality men's pajamas for several large retail stores. The standard cost card for each dozen pairs of pajamas is as follows:

Direct materials, 30 yards at $0.80	$24
Direct labor, 4 hours at $5.00	20
Manufacturing overhead:	
Variable cost: 4 direct labor hours at $2.00	8
Fixed cost: 30% of direct labor cost	6
Total product cost per dozen pairs	$58

During the month of September, the company filled three orders of pajamas at the following costs:

Order	Number of Dozens	Yards Used	Labor Hours
8	400	12,200	1,500
9	900	26,750	3,750
10	500	15,450	2,140
	1,800	54,400	7,390

The following additional information involving materials and labor was supplied by the accounting department:

a. Purchases of materials during the month amounted to 60,000 yards at $0.82 per yard.
b. Total direct labor cost for the month was $37,689.

Required:

1. Compute the materials price variance for September. (Materials are carried in Direct Materials Inventory at standard.)
2. Compute the materials quantity variance for September.
3. Compute the labor rate and labor efficiency variances for September.

PROBLEM 9-8

DETERMINING HOW VARIANCES ARE COMPUTED

HIC Company uses a standard cost system in its accounting for the manufacturing costs of its only product. The standard cost information for materials and labor is as follows:

Direct materials: 3 pounds at $4	$12
Direct labor: 1 hour at $6	6

During April of its first year of operation, the company completed 4,400 units and had the following materials and labor variances:

Materials price variance	$ 700 F
Materials quantity variance	3,200 U
Labor rate variance	900 U
Labor efficiency variance	600 U

There was no Work-in-Process Inventory at the beginning or end of April.

Required: Compute the following amounts:

1. The amount of materials and labor debited to Work-in-Process Inventory during April.
2. The pounds of materials used in production.
3. The actual hours of labor used in production.
4. The actual labor rate per hour.

PROBLEM 9-9

TARGET COSTING

Hotstone, Inc., makes tires for automobiles and other vehicles. The company is currently under tremendous pressure by customers to hold down costs, increase quality, and provide tires on a more timely basis. Automakers have informed Hotstone that if improvements are not made soon, they will start using other providers. While one large customer is very concerned about the prices Hotstone charges for the tires, it is particularly concerned about the quality and safety of the tires. There have been several incidents where one particular type of tire has experienced rubber separation, resulting in costly and deadly rollovers of a particular type of sports utility vehicle.

In a meeting of Hotstone's top executives to determine how to meet these almost unrealistic customer demands, two proposals have emerged. The first, made by a marketing vice president, is that costs can be reduced and quality improved only by tightening the standards imposed on factory employees for costs, productivity, and quality. The marketing vice president believes that there is a lot of slack in the manufacturing process, that employees are enterprising, and that the employees will find ways to meet the standards if sufficient rewards are attached to meeting them. Others point out that the standards now in effect were established after significant time and motion studies and suggest that they cannot be arbitrarily tightened without significant employee unrest and compromises in quality.

As an alternative, a manufacturing vice president, who recently returned from studying several Japanese companies, argues that the only way to lower costs and simultaneously increase quality and timeliness is to engineer cost savings and quality into products using a process called target costing. She argues that it is essential to involve employees in a target costing effort so that they will understand the customers' demands for prices and quality and will work creatively on ways to reengineer the entire manufacturing process. She believes that significant cost reductions, quality improvements, and shortened manufacturing and delivery times can be developed if enough smart people work together to solve the problem. She argues that a target costing approach is the only way to make meaningful, long-term changes and to meet customer demands.

Required: As the CFO of Hotstone, Inc., you have been assigned to lead the effort to reduce costs, increase quality, and decrease manufacturing and delivery times. Considering the costs and benefits of the two proposed approaches, what should you do? Write a memo to the CEO informing him of your plan to adopt the target costing approach.

PROBLEM 9-10

EVALUATION OF PROFIT CENTERS—SEGMENT MARGIN

Della Brown is the manager of one of the stores in the nationwide EatRite supermarket chain. The following information has been gathered about the performance of Della's store in the most recent quarter:

Operating Departments	Revenue	Contribution-Margin Ratio
Groceries	$600,000	20%
Fresh produce	200,000	40%
Dry goods	500,000	35%
Fixed costs controllable by:		
Manager of grocery department	$ 50,000	
Manager of fresh produce department	70,000	
Manager of dry goods department	80,000	
Store manager	100,000	
Corporate headquarters	100,000	
Total	$400,000	

Required: Prepare a segment-margin income statement for corporate headquarters' use in evaluating the store manager, Della Brown, and which Della can use to evaluate the managers of the three departments within the store.

PROBLEM 9-11

EVALUATION OF PROFIT CENTERS—SEGMENT MARGIN

Derrald Pearl Company has two divisions, Computer Consulting and Construction. During the most recent year, the two divisions had the following operating data:

	Computer Consulting	Construction
Revenue	$600,000	$250,000
Contribution-margin percentage	45%	15%
Fixed costs controllable by division managers	$200,000	$30,000
Fixed costs allocated by corporate headquarters	$100,000	$100,000

Required:

1. Prepare a segment-margin income statement for Derrald Pearl Company. Include three columns—one for the company total and one for each of the two divisions.
2. Based on the segment-margin income statement prepared in (1), what would happen to overall company profits if the Construction Division were to be discontinued?
3. Should either of the divisions be discontinued? Explain.

PROBLEM 9-12

REVENUE VARIANCES

Menendez Company is a merchandiser that sells three products: Product X, Product Y, and Product Z. The following are the actual and expected (standard) data for the three products:

	Actual Data		
	Units	Sales Price	Total Actual Market
Product X	530	$5.00	2,250 units
Product Y	760	4.00	10,000 units
Product Z	660	7.00	2,500 units
Total	1,950	5.29	14,750 units

Standard Data			
	Units	Sales Price	Total Market Share
Product X	500	$6.00	25%
Product Y	900	3.00	10%
Product Z	600	5.00	20%
Total	2,000	4.35	Total market = 20% (assumed)

Required:

1. Compute the sales price variance, the sales volume variance, the market share variance, and the industry volume variance for Product X.
2. Compute the sales price variance, the sales volume variance, the market share variance, and the industry volume variance for Product Y.
3. Compute the sales price variance, the sales volume variance, the market share variance, and the industry volume variance for Product Z.
4. Compute the sales price, sales volume, sales mix, market share, and industry volume variance for the three products combined.

PROBLEM 9-13

ROI AND CONTRIBUTION-MARGIN ANALYSIS

Macro Data Corporation's three divisions had the following operating data during 2003:

	Fax Machine	Calculator	Computer
Revenue	$100,000	$150,000	$200,000
Variable costs	50,000	90,000	135,000
Fixed costs	45,000	56,000	53,000
Total assets	50,000	38,000	120,000

Required:

1. Compute the contribution margin for each division.
2. Compute the segment margin for each division.
3. Compute the ROI for each division.
4. Which division had the highest operating performance ratio?
5. **Interpretive Question:** Which division had the best performance in 2003? Why?

PROBLEM 9-14

ROI

Marcos Trade Corporation has two divisions: the Pacific division and the Atlantic division. Following are their operating data for 2003:

	Pacific Division	Atlantic Division
Revenue	$100,000	$100,000
Net income	8,000	7,000
Total assets	50,000	40,000
Stockholders' equity	24,000	16,000
Long-term debt	23,000	20,000

1. Calculate the ROI for each division.
2. **Interpretive Question:** On the basis of this return, which division appears to have the better performance? Why?

PROBLEM 9-15

ROI

The following information for 2003 applies to the two sales divisions of Ward Enterprises:

	Division A	Division B
Total inventory	$33,333	$37,500
Operating performance ratio	12%	16%
Net income	$12,000	$10,000

Required:

1. Calculate each division's revenue.
2. Calculate each division's asset turnover ratio assuming that controllable assets include inventory only.
3. **Interpretive Question:** Which division had the better performance for the period? Why?

PROBLEM 9-16

ROI AND RESIDUAL INCOME

Pacific Corporation has a number of autonomous divisions. Its real estate division has recently reviewed a number of investment proposals.

a. A new office building would cost $450,000 and would generate yearly net income of $80,000.
b. A computer system would cost $350,000 and would reduce bookkeeping and clerical costs by $50,000 annually.
c. A new apartment house would cost $900,000 and would generate yearly net income of $150,000.

The real estate division currently has total assets of $1.8 million and net income of $350,000.

Required:

1. Assuming that the performance of the manager of the real estate division is evaluated on the basis of the division's ROI, evaluate each of the independent proposals, and determine whether it should be accepted or rejected.
2. Assuming that the manager's performance is evaluated on a residual income basis, determine whether each of the proposals should be accepted or rejected. (The division's minimum accepted rate of return is 15%.)

PROBLEM 9-17

ROI AND RESIDUAL INCOME

Albertson Furniture Company is a retailer of home furnishings. It currently has stores in three cities—San Francisco, Los Angeles, and Phoenix. Operating data for the three stores in 2003 were as follows:

	San Francisco	Los Angeles	Phoenix
Revenue	$1,500,000	$1,900,000	$1,800,000
Variable costs	900,000	1,200,000	1,200,000
Fixed costs	300,000	350,000	250,000
Total assets	1,800,000	2,500,000	1,300,000

Required:

1. Compute the segment margin for each store.
2. Compute the operating performance ratio for each store.
3. Compute the asset turnover for each store.
4. Compute the ROI for each store.
5. Compute the residual income for each store. (The minimum rates of return for the stores are San Francisco, 15%; Los Angeles, 13%; and Phoenix, 18%.)

PROBLEM 9-18

ROI AND RESIDUAL INCOME

	Division W	Division X	Division Y	Division Z
Revenue	$100,000	$300,000	$ (i)	$850,000
Net income	$ (a)	$ 90,000	$ (j)	$ (m)
Total assets	$ 85,000	$ (e)	$550,000	$ (n)
Operating performance ratio	15%	(f)	6%	(o)
Asset turnover ratio	(b)	0.75 times	(k)	4.0 times
ROI	(c)	(g)	(l)	21%
Minimum accepted rate of return	13%	(h)	15%	12%
Residual income	$ (d)	$ 12,000	$ 17,500	$ (p)

Required: Compute the missing data, labeled (a) through (p).

PROBLEM 9-19

MEASURING PERFORMANCE: RESIDUAL INCOME AND ROI

The gaming division of Nevada Corporation had income of $550,000 and total assets of $3 million in 2003. The figures are expected to be similar in 2004. The manager of the gaming division has an opportunity to purchase some new gambling machines for $250,000. He concludes that the new machines would increase annual net income by $44,000.

Required:

1. Calculate the current ROI and the expected return on the proposed investment.
2. Calculate the gaming division's current residual income and the expected residual income on the proposed investment. (Assume that the division's minimum accepted rate of return is 17%.)
3. Should the new machines be purchased:
   a. If the division uses the ROI method?
   b. If the division uses the residual income method?

PROBLEM 9-20

ROI AND RESIDUAL INCOME

The manager of the manufacturing division of Minolta Company is evaluated on a residual income basis. He is in the process of evaluating three investment proposals.

a. Pay $500,000 for a new machine that will increase production substantially. This will result in an increased income of $80,000 annually.
b. Pay $350,000 for a new machine that will reduce labor costs by $70,000 annually.
c. Pay $800,000 for a new machine that will increase annual net income by $115,000.

The manufacturing division currently has total assets of $1.2 million and net income of $200,000. Its minimum accepted rate of return is 15%.

Required:

1. Evaluate the three investment proposals independently, and determine which should be accepted.
2. Assuming that the division manager is evaluated on the basis of the division's ROI, determine whether each of the proposals should be accepted or rejected.

expanded material

PROBLEM 9-21

VARIABLE MANUFACTURING OVERHEAD VARIANCES

Engraph Manufacturing Company uses standard direct labor hours as a basis for charging variable manufacturing overhead to Work-in-Process Inventory. The following data were taken from the records:

Data for August:	
Budgeted units	9,000
Budgeted hours	36,000
Actual variable manufacturing overhead	$217,000
Actual units produced	8,000
Actual direct labor hours	33,000
Variable manufacturing overhead data (annual):	
Estimated variable manufacturing overhead cost	$2,560,000
Estimated direct labor hours	400,000
Estimated units of production	100,000

Required:

1. Compute the annual variable manufacturing overhead rate to be used to apply variable overhead to Work-in-Process Inventory per direct labor hour.
2. Determine the variable overhead spending variance for August.
3. Determine the variable overhead efficiency variance for August.
4. Prepare the journal entry to transfer standard variable overhead costs to Work-in-Process Inventory.

PROBLEM 9-22

VARIABLE MANUFACTURING OVERHEAD VARIANCES

Piedmont Tile Company attempts to control manufacturing overhead costs through the use of a flexible budget. Standards are set by studying historical overhead cost data, which are shown here. Actual total overhead costs for each month of the third quarter are also shown.

Standards:
Variable overhead: $1.70 per direct labor hour

Months	Direct Labor Hours	Total Variable Overhead Costs (actual)	Standard Hours Allowed
July	50,000	$150,000	47,500
August	60,000	185,000	60,500
September	40,000	90,000	39,000

Required:

1. Compute the variable overhead spending variance for each month.
2. **Interpretive Question:** Give several reasons why the variable overhead spending variances for all three months might be unfavorable.

PROBLEM 9-23

VARIABLE MANUFACTURING OVERHEAD SPENDING AND EFFICIENCY VARIANCES

The following production information is available for the Porter Corporation:

Standard production	150,000 units
Actual production	145,000 units
Actual variable manufacturing overhead	$175,000
Variable manufacturing overhead applied	$0.80 per machine hour
Actual machine hours	220,000 hours
Standard machine hours per unit produced	1.5 machine hours

Required:

1. Calculate the variable manufacturing overhead spending and efficiency variances for the Porter Corporation.
2. **Interpretive Question:** Explain how the spending variance and the efficiency variance are used to control overhead costs.
3. Identify cost drivers other than machine hours that might be better measures of spending and efficient use of variable overhead costs.

competency enhancement opportunities

- Analyzing Real Company Information
- International Case
- Ethics Case
- Writing Assignment
- The Debate
- Internet Search

The following additional assignments provide opportunities for students to develop critical thinking, ethical perspectives, oral and written communication skills, experience with electronic research, and teamwork through group and business activities.

ANALYZING REAL COMPANY INFORMATION

• ***Analyzing 9-1 (Microsoft)***

In the 2000 annual report for MICROSOFT (accessible at http://www.Microsoft.com), you will find Segment Information in footnote #16 in the Notes to the Financial Statements. That footnote is shown below:

Notes to Financial Statements continued (in millions)
Segment Information
Year Ended June 30

	Windows Platforms	Productivity Applications and Developer	Consumer and Other	Reconciling Amounts	Consolidated
1998					
Revenue	$6,236	$ 7,458	$ 1,765	$ (197)	$15,262
Operating income . .	3,661	4,824	(1,050)	(1,021)	6,414
1999					
Revenue	$8,570	$ 8,636	$ 1,854	$ 687	$19,747
Operating income . .	5,476	4,950	(1,241)	743	9,928
2000					
Revenue	$9,265	$10,089	$ 2,718	$ 884	$22,956
Operating income . .	5,813	4,935	(1,455)	1,644	10,937

The Company's organizational structure and fundamental approach to business reflect the needs of its customers. As such, Microsoft has three major segments: Windows Platforms; Productivity Applications and Developer; and Consumer and Other. Windows Platforms includes the Windows Division, which is primarily responsible for developing and marketing Windows NT Workstation, Windows 2000 Professional, Windows 98, Windows 95, Windows NT Server, and Windows 2000 Server. Productivity Applications and Developer includes the Business Productivity Division, which is responsible for developing and marketing desktop applications, server applications, and developer tools. Consumer and Other products and services include primarily learning, entertainment, and PC input device products; WebTV and PC online access; and portal and vertical properties. Assets of the segment groups are not relevant for management of the businesses nor for disclosure. Segment information is presented in accordance with SFAS 131, Disclosures about Segments of an Enterprise and Related Information. This standard is based on a management approach, which requires segmentation based upon the Company's internal organization and disclosure of revenue and operating income based upon internal accounting methods. The Company's financial reporting systems present various data for management to run the business, including internal profit and loss statements (P&Ls) prepared on a basis not consistent with generally accepted accounting principles. Reconciling items include certain elements of unearned revenue, the treatment of certain channel inventory amounts and estimates, and the classification of revenue from product support and consulting. Additionally, the internal P&Ls use accelerated methods of depreciation and amortization. In fiscal 2000, the Company's internal P&Ls included the Black-Scholes value of employee stock option grants, amortized over the remaining months of the fiscal year of the grant, as well as minor changes to the segments' composition due to various internal reorganizations during the year. Fiscal 1999 disclosures have been restated for consistent presentation. It is not practicable to restate fiscal 1998 for these changes.

Revenue attributable to U.S. operations includes shipments to customers in the United States, licensing to OEMs and certain multinational organizations, and exports of finished goods, primarily to Asia, Latin America, and Canada. Revenue from U.S operations totaled $10.1 billion, $13.7 billion, and $15.7 billion in 1998, 1999, and 2000, respectively. Revenue from outside the United States, excluding licensing to OEMs and certain multinational organizations and U.S. exports, totaled $5.2 billion, $6.0 billion, and $7.3 billion in 1998, 1999, and 2000, respectively.

Long-lived assets totaled $1.5 billion and $1.8 billion in the United States in 1999 and 2000 and $154 million and $126 million in other countries in 1999 and 2000.

1. As you can see, Microsoft has three different segments: Windows Platforms, Productivity Applications and Developer, and Consumer, Commerce, and Other. How do you think Microsoft primarily evaluates these segments—as cost centers, as profit centers, or as investment centers?
2. Compute the margin (operating income/revenue) for the three divisions for 1998, 1999, and 2000. Which segment is the most profitable? Which is growing the fastest?

• *Analyzing 9-2 (Petersen Pottery)*

Just outside Elkins, West Virginia, Clive Petersen has been making ceramic bathroom fixtures (sinks, toilets, and bathtubs) since 1960. Petersen fixtures had become known over the years for their distinctive customer features, their high quality, and their long life. **PETERSEN POTTERY** started out as a two-man operation. By 1980 it had grown to 20 master potters. By this time, Clive Petersen felt that he had expanded to a point that he needed to institute a formal accounting control system. The insistence of his banker that he get a "real" management accounting system in place was also compelling. As a result, Petersen hired a formally trained management accountant who began working with his most experienced master potters to design cost standards. After some research, Petersen's accountant arrived at the following cost standards for a toilet (note that variable manufacturing overhead is allocated based on direct labor hours):

Direct materials:		
Raw clay	25 lb. × $0.95 per lb. =	$23.75
Glazing mix	5 lb. × $0.75 per lb. =	3.75
Direct labor:		
Molding	1.0 hr. × $15.00 per hour =	15.00
Glazing	0.5 hr. × $15.00 per hour =	7.50
Variable manufacturing overhead	1.5 hr. × $3.00 per hour =	4.50
Total per fixture		$54.50

After six months of operations, Petersen was disturbed over the lack of attention paid to the standards by his potters. He felt that the potters were just too set in their ways to adhere to the new system. Many of the potters told Petersen that the new system was "confusing" and didn't help them in their work. In reviewing the June production results, the following actual costs were noted in connection with manufacturing 1,145 toilets:

Materials used:	
Raw clay	28,900 lb. @ $0.92 per lb.
Glazing mix	5,900 lb. @ $0.78 per lb.
Direct labor:	
Molding	1,200 hr. @ $15.25 per hour (average)
Glazing	600 hr. @ $15.00 per hour (average)
Actual variable manufacturing overhead	$5,120

1. Compute all cost variances for the month of June.
2. What suggestions do you have for Mr. Petersen regarding his new standard cost system?

Source: Adapted from J. K. Shank, "Petersen Pottery" case, *Cases in Cost Management: A Strategic Emphasis* (Cincinnati: South-Western, 1996).

INTERNATIONAL CASE

• *Target Costing in Japan*

Japan is always a good place for useful insight on innovative management accounting practice and technique. From early on, the Japanese recognized that the most efficient way to keep costs down was to *design* them out of their products, not to reduce them after the products entered production. This realization reflects a fundamental reality of cost management in Japan; the majority of a product's costs (as much as 90 to 95% according to some experts) are "designed in." Consequently, effective cost control programs in a Japanese business typically focus heavily on the design process for a particular product. This is done primarily through target costing and value engineering (VE). Target costing is used to determine what the market is willing to pay for a product, then VE is used to design the product in order to achieve a prespecified targeted level of costs.

What do you think is the effect of target costing and VE on the use of variances? Specifically, will materials usage variances and labor efficiency variances be more or less important to a firm that strictly uses target costing and VE versus a traditional firm that is more focused on controlling daily production processes?

ETHICS CASE

• *Cool Air, Inc.*

Jack Lear, an internal auditor for Cool Air, Inc., met with Paul Marsh, the manager of the cost accounting department, to discuss a concern about a possible "glitch" in the standard cost system. Jack explained that he had been reviewing the employee time cards in the company division where air-conditioning units and refrigerators were assembled. The time cards reflected how much employee time was devoted to the assembly of air-conditioning units and how much time applied to refrigerators. Jack's concern was that the hours actually charged for each of these operations always seemed to be right on target with the standard labor times for each air-conditioning unit and each refrigerator unit assembled; yet Jack had been told a number of times by employees in the assembly department that the standard hours for assembling air-conditioning units were too low. The employees felt that they could not meet these standards without "fudging" their time cards or sacrificing some quality work in the assembly process. Since company policy emphasized product quality, Jack suspected that time sheets were being modified by shifting hours worked on air-conditioning units to the time sheets for assembling refrigerators.

Paul Marsh, the cost manager, thought for a minute about what Jack was telling him and then made an interesting observation. He said that he had been concerned about the fact that the company's prices for its air-conditioning units were generally lower than its competitors' prices for the same size and quality of units, whereas its prices for refrigerators were generally higher than those of its competitors. He wondered if the company's pricing structure, which was tied to its standard costs, was out of line with competition. This position was reinforced when Paul and Jack looked at the company's sales of each of these products. Over the past year or so, the company had gained market share in air-conditioner sales and had lost market share in refrigerators! Based on this information, Paul asked Jack to do some "detective" work on the time cards in the assembly division and report back his findings.

A few days later, Jack reported that he had found convincing evidence that the foremen in the assembly division had been in collusion to "doctor" employee time sheets in order to more closely meet the time standards for both air-conditioner and refrigerator assembly.

1. Who are the stakeholders affected by the "doctoring" of time sheets?
2. What are the ethical issues in this situation?
3. What should Paul do?

WRITING ASSIGNMENT

• *Qualitative Variance Analysis*

With the push for continuous improvement, stable standards may become a thing of the past. As companies strive for and achieve zero defects and no waste, variances quantifiable in terms of dollars become more and more difficult to obtain. To determine variances from a standard, firms are now turning their attention to qualitative measures such as the number of customer complaints or the number of machine setups. In a one- to two-page paper, identify three standards that might be used in a manufacturing environment and three standards that might be used in a service environment that cannot be readily quantifiable in dollars. Discuss how each of those standards would be measured, as well as how variances from those standards would be measured.

THE DEBATE

• *When Might a Favorable Variance Turn "Bad"?*

Consider the labor efficiency variance. As you now understand after working through this chapter, a labor efficiency variance occurs when the hours actually used are more or less than the standard hours allowed based on actual production output. Assume that a team of internal auditors was able to complete a particular auditing project in one of the company's divisions in fewer hours than originally expected. Does this team have a favorable labor efficiency variance? More importantly, assuming there is a favorable labor efficiency variance, is this a good or a bad thing?

Divide your group into two teams and prepare a two-minute defense of your team's assigned position.

- One team represents "Favorable labor efficiency variance—GOOD!" Answer the following questions in your discussion. (1) Is measuring the difference between auditing hours *originally* budgeted and the actual hours used the proper way to measure a labor efficiency variance? (2) Your team should take the position that favorable labor efficiencies are a *good* result in this operation. What positive aspects concerning the audit team's work are indicated by a favorable labor efficiency variance?
- The other team represents "Favorable labor efficiency variance—BAD!" Answer the following in your discussion. (1) Respond to Team 1's report on whether measuring the difference between auditing hours *originally* budgeted and the actual hours used is the proper way to measure a labor efficiency variance. If you disagree, provide a correct response. (2) Your team should take the position that favorable labor efficiencies may *not* be a good result in this operation. What negative aspects concerning the audit team's work could be indicated by a favorable labor efficiency variance?

INTERNET SEARCH

• Motivating Employees to Be More Productive

In addition to evaluating employees, as was discussed in this chapter, it is also important to motivate employees and managers by providing appropriate incentives. Many companies provide consulting services to organizations to help them create winning incentives for their employees. For an example of the kinds of services that are offered and some examples of incentives that seemed to work, go to **http://www.goalmanager.com**. Sometimes Web addresses change, so if this address does not work, access the Web site for this textbook (**http://albrecht.swcollege.com**) for an updated link. Once you've gained access to the site, look over some of the success stories and answer the following questions:

1. Describe one employee motivation success story described at this Web site.
2. What was the key to motivating employees in that organization?

comprehensive problem 8-9

C-V-P Analysis, Variance Analysis, and Budgeting

Gonzales Company makes compact discs, which it sells to music companies. The following data are available for the company:

Expected sales in units:	
January	1,200 discs
February	1,400 discs
March	1,800 discs
Selling price	$10.00 per disc
Beginning accounts receivable balance, January 1	$4,000.00
Desired finished goods inventory, March 31	380 discs
Beginning finished goods inventory, January 1	300 discs*
Beginning direct materials inventory, January 1	400 ounces*
Desired direct materials inventory, March 31	600 ounces
Standard direct materials needed per disc	4 ounces
Standard direct labor time per finished product	10 minutes
Standard direct materials cost per ounce	$0.50
Standard direct labor cost per hour	$18.00

*The beginning inventory numbers for January were based on the best estimate of January sales in December. The expectations changed in January, and the new expected sales numbers should be used to estimate beginning inventory on hand for February and March.

Additional information:

- Of a month's sales, 60% is collected by month-end; the remaining 40% is collected the following month.
- The desired finished goods inventory each month is 20% of the next month's sales.
- The desired direct materials inventory every month is 10% of next month's production needs.

Required:

1. Using the standard costs for making the discs, prepare the following:
   a. Sales forecasts for January, February, and March (in dollars).
   b. Cash collections budgets for January, February, and March (in dollars). Assume that all sales are on credit.
   c. Production budgets for January, February, and March (in units).
   d. Direct materials usage budgets for January, February, and March (in ounces).
   e. Direct materials purchases budgets for January, February, and March (in ounces).
   f. Direct labor budgets for January, February, and March (in dollars).
2. Assume that actual usage of direct materials to make the discs was $4\frac{1}{2}$ ounces at a cost of $0.60 per ounce. Compute the materials price and quantity variances for each month.
3. Assume that actual labor costs to make the discs were 12 minutes of labor at a cost of $19 per hour. Compute labor rate and efficiency variances for each month.
4. Assuming again that Gonzales is able to make the discs at the standard costs, how much will profits increase if it raises its price to $12 per disc in January, February, and March? Assume total fixed costs of $5,000 per month.
5. Assuming again that Gonzales is able to make the discs at its standard costs, if sales decrease by 300 discs during the three months at the increased price of $12 per disc, should Gonzales raise its price?

Continuous Improvement in Management Accounting

chapter

m10

learning objectives

After studying this chapter, you should be able to:

1 Explain the fundamentals of building a Balanced Scorecard.

2 Anticipate that both management accounting and financial accounting are poised for important changes.

setting the stage

It has been said, "knowledge is power!" The ability to compete effectively in the economy has always been a function of the knowledge and abilities that a company can pull together and emphasize in the process of creating new products, making good decisions, and implementing effective processes. Throughout this text, we have generally classified organizations as manufacturers, merchandisers, or service providers. However, in this new age, more and more successful companies really can't be classified in one of these three categories. We've often used **MICROSOFT** as an example company in this textbook. What kind of company is Microsoft? Does this company manufacture products? Does it distribute merchandise? Does it sell services? Actually, Microsoft does all three things, but that still doesn't adequately describe this company. Microsoft is one of the key citizens in what might be called a "New Economy" that runs more on intangible assets, such as intellectual property, than tangibles such as plants, equipment, and distribution channels. A lot of these New Economy companies have comparatively little in tangible assets, and yet they are obviously considered to be very valuable by the stock market. What this tells you is that traditional accounting models aren't capturing the value. Accounting, in other words, no longer delivers accountability.

Knowledge assets are very expensive both to acquire and to develop. And they're extremely difficult to manage. When a drug passes its clinical tests, huge value is created—but there's no transaction. Nothing changes hands. Nobody buys anything, and nobody sells anything. As a result, accounting, by tradition, does not measure or report this kind of information to managers (or investors). When software passes a beta-test, it suddenly becomes valuable—but there's no transaction, so there's no reporting. Or think about how value is destroyed: when a big, old company is late in figuring out how to enter the world of e-commerce, huge value is destroyed—but there's no transaction, and the company continues to be reported by accountants to its managers as doing well. Traditional measures of performance may ignore intangible corporate capabilities that can often lead to higher long-term returns than plant and equipment assets. In short, technology has created far more data than ever before. But what we all need—and what accounting now needs to work on—is the transformation of data into valuable information and knowledge.

For example, Bill Gates and Microsoft are continually hiring many of the world's smartest scientists and creating a giant research laboratory. Their goal is to control the future of computing. In the process, the value of Microsoft as a company rises and falls based on progress and problems in its (research and development) process. For example, a conflict is currently raging at Microsoft regarding its flagship Windows™ product and a rising new software called ".Net"—a technology that can link thousands of Web sites together in an Internet-style bucket brigade. This new software promises that one mouse click will have the wallop of dozens of steps on the Web today. Putting an accurate value on the Windows technology at Microsoft is difficult, but no one can question that much of the market value of Microsoft, one of the most important companies in the world today, is based on Windows—a proprietary technology that Microsoft guards with the ferocity of a rottweiler. However, .Net technology may be the biggest threat to the future of Windows that Microsoft has ever seen. And ironically, .Net is Microsoft's own technology. So far, about 4,000 of Microsoft's 40,000 employees are working exclusively on .Net. By the end of 2001, Bill Gates expects that virtually all of the company will be focused on creating new .Net products or updating old products with the new technology. In fact, Gates is committing half of Microsoft's current $4 billion budget to .Net breakthroughs. Not everyone at Microsoft, though, is committed to the vision of .Net. In fact, many key executives and scientists, including Bill Gates himself, have worried that .Net could totally undercut the value of Windows in the marketplace long before Microsoft is actually able to sell .Net products and technology to the world. The result of such a scenario could be significant reductions in Microsoft's revenues. On this argument, some key employees have even left Microsoft to join or start other companies that would directly compete with their former employer.

In the midst of all this effort and diverging opinions, the economic value of Microsoft is changing, though traditional accounting has no effective way of measuring or helping to manage these very real changes in the company's critical intangible assets. Only the future will reveal how Microsoft's bottom line will be affected by the efforts of its research teams and the strategic decisions of its executives. One thing is certain, however, traditional performance evaluation systems don't consider these kinds of changes.

Sources: A. Webber, "New Math for a New Economy," *Fast Company* (January–February 2000); J. Greene, "Microsoft's Big Bet," *Business Week* (October 30, 2000).

Competitive pressures in the marketplace require that companies continually look for ways to improve their information systems in order to obtain better insights into how to operate their businesses more effectively and more efficiently. Management accounting, being at the core of business information systems, is always evolving. Managers want management accounting information that supports the strategy of the company. They do not want the information limited to financial measures of performance only. Quality and time measures of performance in customer service (e.g., timely deliveries), internal business processes (e.g., production defects), and growth in the organization (e.g., employee education levels) are becoming more important all the time. As a result, we are at the intersection of new directions in accounting. It's time we take a brief look at the future of management accounting.

You are now in the last chapter of this textbook. You've spent a lot of time studying many details concerning the process of creating and using accounting to add value to an organization. We've established that the management process involves planning, controlling, and evaluating business activities in order to compete well on issues involving cost, quality, and time. We've also discussed managing these concerns across three different types of firms: manufacturing, merchandising, and service. It should be clear to you now that the accountant must customize a great variety of information sources to fit the specific strategic and operating needs of decision makers. Perhaps you're feeling a bit overwhelmed. Of all the information that is possible (and we've presented in this text only a subset of a growing list of possibilities), what information is best for a particular company? Does a model exist that helps accountants and managers identify specific performance measures critical to surviving and thriving in the fast-paced, highly competitive, worldwide economy of the twenty-first century? More importantly, how does management accounting continue to improve performance measures in pace with innovations in products and processes and changes in markets and competition? Actually, there's been a lot of discussion recently among managers and management accountants on this very question. One approach to answering this question is gaining attention in many companies. The approach is called the "Balanced Scorecard," and no education on management accounting is really complete without some awareness of this approach. We'll spend most of this chapter illustrating this new performance measurement model and how it could affect the nature of both management accounting and financial accounting.[1]

LET'S TAKE A FLIGHT!

Imagine that a friend of yours is getting her airplane pilot's license and has invited you to sit in the passenger seat of the airplane during her next pilot's lesson. Your friend has not been taking flying lessons very long. However, as you listen to her enthusiastic description of past lessons as the two of you drive out to the airfield the next afternoon, you begin to really look forward to the experience. After parking the car and walking to the Cessna plane that waits on the tar-

1 The Balanced Scorecard Model was first presented in a series of articles in the *Harvard Business Review* by Robert S. Kaplan and David P. Norton: "The Balanced Scorecard—Measures That Drive Performance" (January–February 1992); "Putting the Balanced Scorecard to Work" (September–October 1993); "Using the Balanced Scorecard as a Strategic Management System" (January–February 1996). The most complete discussion on this theory is found in Kaplan and Norton's *The Balanced Scorecard: Translating Strategy into Action* (Boston, MA: Harvard Business School Press, 1996) and *The Strategy-Focused Organization: How Balanced Scorecard Companies Thrive in the New Business Environment* (Boston, MA: Harvard Business School Press, 2001).

mac, your friend introduces you to the flight instructor, and the three of you climb into the plane. Soon after you take your seat and buckle the seatbelt, your friend revs the engine and the small plane surges forward. The instructor is sitting next to your friend, providing advice and guidance as the plane taxis down the runway gathering speed for takeoff. Suddenly, as you peer over the shoulders of the instructor and your friend in front of you, you notice with some concern that the small plane's instrument panel is noticeably bare of the assortment of instruments, dials, gauges, and controls that are typically part of an airplane's cockpit. In fact, there appears to be only one gauge on the whole panel. Trying to make your question sound casual, you ask about the barren panel and the sole gauge. The instructor looks back over his shoulder to tell you that the gauge measures airspeed. The plane is nearing the end of the runway and is just about to lift off. After swallowing once or twice, you brave more questions about direction, altitude, fuel, temperature, and thrust. Aren't these items also important in flying a plane? Don't most planes have gauges to provide feedback to the pilot on details other than simply airspeed? The instructor agrees but indicates that your friend is currently concentrating on airspeed in her flying lessons. Once she excels at managing airspeed, perhaps the airspeed gauge will be switched for an altimeter, and she can then concentrate on managing altitude. The instructor tells you that he feels it's important to not make the pilot concentrate on too many things at the same time. You notice that your friend is concentrating very hard on the airspeed gauge as the plane noses up and lifts off from the ground. You swallow hard and tighten your seatbelt until it is very snug around your waist. For some reason, you're suddenly imagining about a hundred others places you'd rather be than sitting in this plane.

Flying an airplane is a complicated process. To do it successfully requires that the pilot process a lot of information about various performance aspects of both the equipment and the environment. Managing a company is certainly no less complicated. A lot has to happen at once in order for a company to perform well in its competitive environment as the demands of products, customers, and regulatory agencies change constantly. One of a management accountant's most important functions is to identify and implement **performance measures** that are focused on key strategic and operating plans established by management. These performance measures then become the primary means of controlling and evaluating business processes in the organization. What is the best performance measure for an accountant to provide for an organization? Frankly, there is no one best performance measure.

performance measures A general term used to describe all measures designed to capture information about performance related to a particular activity or process.

THE BALANCED SCORECARD

1

Explain the fundamentals of building a Balanced Scorecard.

Previous chapters and sections in this textbook have typically focused on subsets of management accounting issues such as merchandising, cost measurement, or the evaluating process. However, in this chapter we are not going to focus the discussion on any particular type of firm, strategic imperative, or management process. Instead, we present a *framework* that a management accountant can use to work with any of these issues. That framework is the Balanced Scorecard.

Balanced Scorecard A new management model designed to link together performance measures for financial, customer, internal process, and learning/growth perspectives that are unique to an organization's particular strategy.

The **Balanced Scorecard** is an approach to integrating performance measures in order to support directly the strategy an organization is trying to establish and follow. At first glance, this may not seem like a very new idea. Shouldn't all performance measures support the organization's strategy? Hasn't management accounting always been focused on supporting managers' and executives' efforts to create a profitable company? Actually, although the purpose of management accounting is to establish performance measures that add value to the organization, too often these measures have been limited to periodic reports composed solely of financial measures. Advances in computer systems technology today allow more information, more variety in information, and more timely information to be created and reported than ever before. The existence of better information capabilities provides an opportunity for accountants, working in conjunction with system technologists and organization executives, to significantly expand the definition of management accounting. As you study this chapter, you need to understand that the Balanced Scorecard is really a guiding theory of management, rather than an exact formula or blueprint that can be automatically implemented in any organization to improve its management processes. Once created, each organization's own Balanced Scorecard is a direct view of its strategy, its plans, and its management processes. The idea that a Balanced Scorecard is extremely personal for each organization is captured in the following comment made by an executive as his division completed work on its first Balanced Scorecard:

> In the past, if you had lost my strategic planning document on an airplane and a competitor found it, I would have been angry, but I would have gotten over it. In reality, it wouldn't have been that big a loss. Or if I had left my monthly operating review somewhere and a competitor obtained a copy, I would have been upset, but, again, it wouldn't have been that big a deal. This Balanced Scorecard, however, communicates my strategy so well that a competitor seeing this would be able to block the strategy and cause it to become ineffective.[2]

Hence, there is no such thing as a *standard* Balanced Scorecard that any organization can use to operate successfully in its environment. Therefore, as we use example performance measures throughout the chapter to describe the Balanced Scorecard theory, you should remember that each organization must design its own performance measures that support its own particular strategy.

Adding Value with Performance Measures

Think back on the last nine chapters involving management accounting and all the various performance measures we've studied involving cost, quality, and time. You should recognize that there are a number of problems associated with the performance evaluation methods currently used in many organizations. Some individuals argue that current performance measurement systems even encourage waste, inefficiency, and poor quality. For example, a measure that emphasizes purchase price may encourage the purchasing department to increase the purchase quantity to get a lower price but might ignore quality and speed of delivery. The results may be excess inventory, increased storage and other carrying costs, and failure to use suppliers with the best quality and service.

Another example may be allocating overhead costs based on direct labor hours. Direct labor may be a fixed cost that is small in relation to manufacturing overhead items, which are becoming more significant for many companies. The result of any overemphasis on direct labor as a mechanism for managing overhead costs may be missed opportunities for cost control since major overhead activities are not directly exposed to the management process of planning, controlling, and evaluating.

If machine utilization is the performance measure being emphasized, a supervisor may run a machine in excess of daily production requirements to maximize the performance measure. This may result in excess inventory or production that is not needed. Similarly, if only the number of units produced is the performance measure, poor-quality goods or inventory that is not desired by customers may be produced. A specific example from the former Soviet Union illustrates this point. Oil drillers, in competition with one another, received recognition and compensation based on the number of meters drilled. The award-winning team recognized by Pravda drilled meter upon meter but never struck oil. It seems that the first 100 meters of drilling do not require as much effort and expense as the second, third, fourth, and so on. The winning team drilled dry hole after dry hole. The depth of these wells never exceeded 100 meters.

Some prominent researchers believe that performance evaluation systems used in the United States are quite ineffective and have contributed to a decline in America's competitiveness. One major problem that these researchers identify with traditional performance evaluation methods is the limited focus of these methods. To be specific, they argue that current evaluation methods, which mostly focus on financial returns, are not designed to cope with such intangible corporate capabilities as an excellent work force, research and development, and information assets. They argue that we have moved from a manufacturing society to an information society and that performance evaluation systems have not kept pace. This argument certainly seems to have merit when considering the competitive position of **MICROSOFT** described at the beginning of this chapter. Are Mi-

2 R. S. Kaplan and D. P. Norton, *The Balanced Scorecard: Translating Strategy into Action* (Boston, MA: Harvard Business School Press, 1996), p. 148.

crosoft's real assets appropriately displayed on a balance sheet that focuses on inventory, equipment, and buildings? Does it make sense to evaluate performance at Microsoft based on controlling costs of materials, labor, and manufacturing overhead? Microsoft, like many other companies, needs a performance measurement system that is customized to fit its particular strategy.

Every company ultimately must perform well financially in order to survive. Even not-for-profit organizations must be able to consistently pay their bills, including payrolls and loans, in order to survive over time. Other companies must consistently show profits, build equity, and provide a return to stockholders. The DUPONT COMPANY made a lot of money by carefully tracking financial measures that contributed to consistent ROI and ROE performance. Remember, however, that successful management accounting methods are eventually copied by other organizations. Hence, strictly using ROI to manage an organization does not provide a competitive edge in today's economy. Organizations must continuously improve their management information processes in order to continue to compete. Traditional financial measures are now being vigorously supplemented in three new areas: customer service, internal process improvement, and learning and growth throughout the organization.

Customers

The first key to strong financial performance is customer satisfaction. When companies understand what their customers value and what services and products they are willing to pay for, then these companies can design customer-focused performance measures that lead to growth in market share, increased revenues, and long-term profits. There are two types of customer performance measures: leading measures and outcome measures. **Leading measures** focus on fulfilling customer expectations regarding cost, quality, and time factors. **Outcome measures** determine if the improvements in leading measures result in more satisfied, loyal customers. Therefore, it is important that there be a clear link between the company's efforts to provide low-cost, high-quality, timely products and services and customer response to these efforts as demonstrated by increased market share and customer profitability (i.e., the company is able to earn sufficient profits by serving its customers). Exhibit 10-1 provides measures of customer-focused performance.

leading measures Measures that, if successfully implemented, will support desired performance in other business activities. Note that some leading measures can also serve as outcome measures.

outcome measures Measures of desired outcome performance in activities critical to an organization's strategic goals. Note that some outcome measures are also leading measures to support desired performance in other business activities.

exhibit 10-1 Performance Measures of Customer Satisfaction

Leading Performance Measures

Cost

- Purchase cost to customer
- Delivery cost to customer
- Setup cost to customer
- Maintenance and repair cost to customer

Quality

- Returns by customers
- Quality rankings by other agencies
- Customer survey response

Time

Reliable Delivery

- Percentage of on-time deliveries
- Number of production interruptions

Fastest Delivery

- Average response time for service call
- Time to complete contract
- Production cycle time

Outcome Performance Measures

Customer Retention Rates

- Retention rates
- Number of defecting customers
- Costs to retain customers

Customer Acquisition Rates

- Acquisition rates
- Number of new customers
- Costs to recruit customers

Market Share

- Percent of total number of customers
- Percent of total dollars spent by customers
- Percent of total units sold to customers

business environment essay

Volant, Inc. Hank Kashiwa (a 1975 Olympic skier) and his brother Bucky (who holds a Ph.D. in fluid mechanics) decided to combine their expertise and create VOLANT, INC., a ski manufacturing company. The Kashiwas wanted to manufacture a revolutionary product—skis made from steel. Steel would resist lateral twisting in the pressure of a ski turn and give the skis a tighter grip on the snow, as well as decrease production costs. This design quickly became popular among skiers; however, the company's production problems were clouding its success.

That is when Volant, Inc., turned to Mark Soderberg, a former BOEING employee who was very familiar with the manufacturing process. As Soderberg walked into Volant's factory for the first time, the immense inventory piles and the excessive product scrapping shocked him. Soderberg decided the best way to begin the company makeover was to stop the daily production problems by shutting down the factory for a few weeks.

Soderberg involved the entire company as he created problem-solving and process-analysis teams to generate ideas and strategies. During some of the brainstorming sessions, he encouraged everyone to throw out any and every idea; as an incentive, he

LEADING MEASURES OF CUSTOMER SATISFACTION We have discussed cost, quality, and time measures throughout the last nine chapters of this textbook. Naturally, most customers desire low-cost products and services. However, customer satisfaction is the result of the right combination of cost, quality, and time. As customers, we are willing to balance our demands for these three objectives. For example, when you mail a package across the nation, you are probably very comfortable making a trade-off decision. The U.S. POSTAL SERVICE, like other package delivery companies, provides various delivery schedules (overnight, two days, three to five days), as well as some options regarding quality of service (contents insurance and registered delivery); each mailing option carries an appropriate price.

Most companies have spent a great deal of effort understanding how their customers perceive value in terms of timeliness, quality, and price. For many companies, customers are more concerned with reliability than with the fastest delivery. This is particularly true in a JIT environment. TOYOTA demands deliveries from its suppliers to assembly plants within a one-hour time window. Early arrivals of parts are as unacceptable as late deliveries. Hence, observers have sometimes witnessed delivery trucks driving around and around a Toyota assembly plant until it is time to deliver their goods. If you think about it, this is not really strange behavior. Have you ever scheduled a telephone repairperson to come to your home during the day? Your definition of "on time" is probably not sometime between 9:00 A.M. and 3:00 P.M., is it? Further, given a 1:00 P.M. appointment, you probably would not be particularly pleased at the repairperson's effort to "delight the customer" by arriving two hours early. Performance measures regarding reliability versus fastest delivery of goods or services depend on both the strategy of the company and the demands of its customers. A few examples of these types of measures are provided in Exhibit 10-1. You can look back at Exhibit 7-10 on page 376 in Chapter 7 of management accounting for more examples of time-based performance measures.

As you remember from Chapter 7, total quality management (TQM) has been firmly rooted in the United States since the 1980s. Commitment to quality is now generally assumed for most products and services—it is a competitive necessity. Companies not committed to the total quality effort will typically struggle to survive. Hence, organizations must pay careful attention to what quality factors are important to their customers and then build measures that accurately track performance of these quality factors.

As mentioned earlier, customers compare timeliness and quality factors with price to evaluate the real value of a product or service. Many companies realize, however, that the purchase

would hand out $100 bills to the participating employees.

Through Soderberg's strategic framework and involvement of company employees, Volant, Inc., began witnessing major quality improvements along with decreasing costs. In addition, the manufacturing process was eased through a simple design change in the skis. Volant's output quickened and the company started making on-time deliveries. The inventory piles, the poor-quality cycles, and delivery problems that plagued the business were eliminated. For the first time in Volant's history, the company finished its preseason shipments ahead of schedule.

The Kashiwa brothers had a great business idea, but the company lacked a good planning, controlling, and evaluating system. Soderberg says that, "it was just the basics of manufacturing" that helped turn this ski company around. It is the combination of these company basics, strategies, and visions that creates a customized performance measurement system that enhances operations management and creates a competitive advantage.

Source: Thomas Petzinger Jr., "The Front Lines," *The Wall Street Journal* (October 3, 1997), p. B1.

life cycle costing The process of measuring all costs involved in creating, producing, and using a product or service. Life cycle costing is not limited to costs incurred by the organization measuring these costs but also includes all costs incurred by the suppliers and the customers of the product or service.

price of their product often does not represent the total cost to their customer. If you own a car, you may be painfully aware of this fact. The purchase price of your car is only part of its total cost. Maintenance, repairs, gas mileage, and insurance also combine with the original purchase price to determine the total cost of owning your car. Perhaps you wish you had spent a little more (or less) when purchasing your car in order to better balance the subsequent costs of owning your car. In an effort to account for costs that are an essential part of the total value of a product, some firms are turning to a concept known as life cycle costing. Essentially, **life cycle costing** is a method of costing that focuses on all costs that will be incurred throughout the entire life of a product. The life cycle approach to costing helps to ensure that no costs are omitted when evaluating performance and value. Hence, when evaluating customer satisfaction, an

When you buy a car the purchase price represents only part of the total cost of car ownership. You must also consider such costs as maintenance, repairs, and gas. In an effort to account for all costs incurred throughout the entire life of a product, some companies use life cycle costing.

organization also needs to measure performance of its product or service in terms of *all* its costs for its customers. These cost measures are listed in Exhibit 10-1.

OUTCOME MEASURES OF CUSTOMER SATISFACTION An organization's focus on customers must be twofold. First, the company works to measure up to customer expectations regarding cost, quality, and time. Then the company must determine if its efforts are being rewarded with increased market share and customer profitability. **Market share** is the proportion of industry sales of a particular product or service that is controlled by a specific firm. Companies increase their market share in two ways: retaining current customers and acquiring new customers. Clearly, companies that cannot service their current customers better than competitors will be hard-pressed to maintain market share. Absolute customer satisfaction is key in this regard. Interestingly, when management accountants ignore expected future cash flows over a customer's life, they miss reporting the real cost (the opportunity cost) of losing customers. Exhibit 10-2 shows how much profit a customer generates over time in four different industries. As you can see, customer profitability over time really takes off *if* the company can retain its customers' loyalty. This increased profitability over time is the result of increased purchases or higher account balances, reduced operating costs, and profits from referrals. Hence, customer retention rates are very important outcome measures that result from good performance of leading measures related to customers' overall costs, quality of product, and timeliness of delivery.

market share The percentage share one company receives of the total sales revenue in the economy for a particular product or service.

caution

Research indicates that adequate scores on customer satisfaction surveys are not sufficient to create the kind of loyalty that results in high customer retention rates. Companies that cannot consistently *delight* their customers on the most valued performance factors will lose business.

Source: T. O. Jones and W. E. Sasser, "Why Satisfied Customers Defect," *Harvard Business Review* (November–December 1995), pp. 88–99.

fyi

On average, credit card companies spend $51 recruiting each new customer. Given the data in Exhibit 10-2, a company must then retain a new customer for about a year and a half in order just to pay back its initial investment in acquiring the customer.

Once the company has established leading measures that result in high customer retention, it can turn its attention to acquiring new customers in order to grow its market share. Obviously, there is a strong relationship between loyal customers who speak enthusiastically about the company's product and the company's ability to win new customers. As a result, many companies identify customer loyalty as the best way to acquire new customers. In addition, companies also spend a great deal of effort and resources recruiting new customers. Hence, tracking performance in customer acquisition is a strategy of growth in market share. It is important to understand that there are many ways to successfully maintain and increase market share through customer retention and acquisition. However, retaining and recruiting customers *profitably* is important to strong financial performance. Hence, companies must track the costs spent recruiting new customers, as well as the costs spent retaining current customers. Using activity-based costing (ABC) to track the costs of activities necessary to recruit and retain customers can provide a company with the necessary information to identify desirable customers and to make important decisions to drop certain unprofitable customers. Management accountants who provide outcome measures of their companies' efforts to profitably grow market share can add competitive value to the management process. These customer outcome measures are listed in Exhibit 10-1.

Internal Processes

Management accountants can help their organizations better understand how satisfying customers (using leading performance measures) relates to growth in customer profitabil-

exhibit 10-2 How Much Profit an Average Customer Generates over Time

Industry	Year 1	Year 2	Year 3	Year 4	Year 5
Credit cards	$ 30	$ 42	$ 44	$ 49	$ 55
Industrial laundry	144	166	192	222	256
Industrial distribution	45	99	121	144	168
Auto servicing	25	35	70	88	88

Source: Adapted from F. F. Reichheld and W. E. Sasser, "Zero Defections: Quality Comes to Services," *Harvard Business Review* (September–October 1990), pp. 105–112.

net work

J.D. POWER AND ASSOCIATES, headquartered in Los Angeles, has achieved international recognition for its marketing information and consulting in the areas of consumer opinion and customer satisfaction. You may be familiar with the annual customer satisfaction awards this company provides in the automobile industry. In the last few years, J.D. Power and Associates has branched out into the financial, telecommunications, and travel service industries. Go to its home page at **http://www.jdpower.com** and research the awards for the most recent year. What automotive brand had the highest owner loyalty? What credit card had the highest customer satisfaction? What long-distance telephone company had the highest customer satisfaction? What rental car agency had the highest customer satisfaction?

ity (using outcome measures). The next issue to be resolved is what processes within the organization must take place in order to satisfy the customer completely? Most of your work in the last nine chapters has focused on building performance measures to support the manager's efforts to plan, control, and evaluate processes within the company. However, building performance measures that effectively support the goal of customer satisfaction requires that the management accountant first understand that there are three types of processes that must be in place in order to take care of the customer: innovation processes, operations processes, and service-after-sale processes. Examples of performance measures for management of internal processes are provided in Exhibit 10-3.

INNOVATION PROCESS MEASURES We've talked very little in this textbook about planning, controlling, and evaluating the *innovation process*, which involves identifying new products and services, and then creating and bringing those products to market. The reason for this is that most of the management accounting effort has historically been focused on the operations process, which involves building goods or providing services that already exist. For example, accountants spend a great deal of effort developing budgets of operations, then measuring variances from standard costs of direct materials, direct labor, and manufacturing overhead. However, the innovation process of identifying and creating new products is where much of a company's competitive edge is created. This is why Microsoft spends so much money hiring some of the best minds in the software industry—to ensure that it will continue to create new products that retain and recruit customers. As we move further into the new century, many businesses are spending more in their research, design, and development processes than they do to support their production and operating processes. Microsoft is a great example of this trend. If you look at its income statements for 1998 through 2000, you will see that this company is now spending more money on research and development of new products than it is spending to provide goods and services to its current customers. These data are provided below.

	1998	1999	2000
Cost of sales	$2,460 million	$2,814 million	$3,002 million
Research & development	$2,601 million	$2,970 million	$3,772 million

Admittedly, many companies do not spend the kind of money on the innovation process that Microsoft does. Nevertheless, the resources invested in the innovation process for most companies are significant. It's important to the ultimate financial success of the organization that the critical effort to identify and develop new products and services is effectively managed. At some point, the money invested in the research and development (R&D) effort must provide

exhibit 10-3 Performance Measures of Internal Processes

	Innovation Processes	Operations Processes	Service-after-Sale Processes
Cost measures	• R&D costs per new product • Payback on R&D costs	• Unit-level costs • Batch-level costs • Product line costs	• Costs per service incidence • Costs of replacement parts
Quality measures	• Number of modifications required per design • Percentage of sales from new products	• Defects-per-million opportunities (six sigma) • Errors in customer service	• Customer requests handled on first call • Satisfaction survey responses
Time measures	• Lead time (idea to working model) • Design cycle time	• Lead time (order to delivery) • Production cycle time	• Lead time (request to fulfillment) • Repair cycle time

business environment essay

The Balanced Scorecard—Code Red! The job of managing a hospital is extremely difficult! On the one end, you must deal with doctors who oppose any monetary label on patient care, and on the other end you must make financial decisions that will keep the hospital operational. Some of these decisions can be agonizing, leaving you to wonder where you draw the line. For example, do you make the questionably unethical decision of turning away needy patients because of money? These were the very problems facing Dr. Jon Meliones, chief medical director of **DUKE CHILDREN'S HOSPITAL** in Durham, North Carolina, in the mid-1990s.

The hospital was $11 million in the red. Critical programs were being canceled, the number of patient beds was being reduced, and the quality of patient care was in a miserable state. Dr. Meliones, faced with the disastrous state of the hospital, came across the Balanced Scorecard strategy and instantly decided that applying the principles from the Balanced Scorecard was the solution. Upon learning that the Balanced Scorecard dealt with finance, customer service, learning and growth, and internal processes, Dr. Meliones saw this model as a perfect fit for his hospital. Not only did it deal with the financial administration of running a hospital, but it also took into consideration the very real needs of the patients and doctors who receive and provide the care.

"We wanted everyone—from accountants to physicians to therapists—focusing on a common goal, not individual goals," explained Meliones. "We needed to become a strategy-focused organization if our Balanced Scorecard was to succeed and, in turn, if the hospital was to succeed." The Balanced Scorecard effort at Duke Children's Hospital involved distributing daily "report

financial returns. However, an R&D project can require a very long payback period. Many organizations begin significant R&D projects expecting that financial returns will not be realized for many years. Sometimes basic research is done in organizations with no clear idea of what profitable product or service may eventually result. Occasionally, some of our society's most useful innovations have resulted from these kinds of R&D investments. On the other hand, with this strategy it is possible that a lot of resources and energy will be needlessly spent in the innovation process, which means that the strategic imperatives of cost, quality, and time still apply here. Given the size of the investments made, it is important that organizations develop measures to evaluate the costs of their innovation processes. In addition, organizations should assess the effectiveness (e.g., the quality) of innovation work.

Finally, without proper controls, R&D work is at risk of simply taking too long. You're likely familiar with the old adage that "time is money." Clearly, any project that requires time extensions will cost more to complete. You'll remember from Chapter 6 of management accounting that additional costs due to time overruns will also include increased holding costs. However, in the case of R&D, "time is opportunity!" The market is always moving. Organizations that take longer than their competitors to complete the research and development of new products or services may quickly find themselves seriously disadvantaged in the marketplace. Hence, organizations that manage well their innovation processes will compete well in the marketplace. Performance measures that support the management of the innovation process will typically be custom-built for each organization based on its strategic intent and on the particular nature of its R&D work. Exhibit 10-3 provides examples of cost, quality, and time-based measures for the innovation process.

OPERATIONS PROCESS MEASURES *Operations processes* involve all the activities a customer generally experiences, including receipt of customer order, creation of product, and delivery of product or service. Ever since Francis Cabot Lowell established his cotton mill in Waltham, Massachusetts, in 1814 and created the "Waltham system" of accounting to track manufacturing costs, accountants have focused on adding value to the operations processes by measuring cost, quality, and time performance. In the effort to support operations processes, many valuable accounting methods have been developed. As a result, several of the previous

cards" to all hospital employees to ensure they understood where they stood within the strategic goals of the hospital. These report cards empowered the hospital staff to find creative ways to reduce costs, increase the quality of patient care, and help hospital administrators see more than just the bottom line. For example, physicians received information pertaining to their own patient loads, such as average length of stay and average cost per patient. They could then evaluate the results themselves and determine where to cut costs rather than having to follow a mandate issued by someone in management who doesn't understand the medical issues involved in these kinds of decisions.

Not only did these report cards allow doctors and other medical staff to evaluate where they could cut costs, but it also empowered them to look for other ways to improve quality of care. For example, a chief complaint of patients' parents was not being able to identify their child's primary caregiver. So a secretary decided that as patients were admitted, labels with the names of each one's primary doctor and nurse would be placed on their doors. "Prior to this simple solution, only 42 percent of parents could identify their child's doctor," said Meliones. "But as soon as we began labeling, that number rose to 99 percent. The Balanced Scorecard began turning everyone into a chief strategy officer of some sort."

As a result of the cooperative effort between management and medical staff to implement a Balanced Scorecard, Duke Children's Hospital has gone from $11 million in the red to $4 million in the black, an incredible turnaround!

Source: SAS Institute, Inc., News and Events, "Life in the Balance: Duke Children's Hospital," http://www.sas.com/news/success/dukehosp.html (accessed March 5, 2001).

chapters have focused on helping you understand these methods. Though management accounting for operations processes has been in place for a long time, new methods continue to evolve in an effort to create information that has competitive value.

The concepts of activity-based costing (ABC) and the Hierarchical Production Model (discussed in Chapter 7 of management accounting) represent some of the important cost measures created recently to fulfill competitive needs for organizations. An example of a fairly new quality measure for manufacturing processes that is having an impact in the marketplace is "six sigma quality." One of the famous measures of quality, six sigma quality is now gaining attention as an operations management tool for merchandising and service firms. Sigma[3] is a statistical measure of variation in a product or process and is used in statistical process control (SPC) charts to evaluate upper and lower control limits (see Chapter 7 for a review of SPC charts). Sigma measures also provide insight about probabilities. Specifically, when the incidence of a single error in the product or service process occurs at a distance of six sigma from the target value, then the probability that the process itself has quality problems is very low. To be precise (without getting into all the statistics involved), an operation process is said to have **six sigma quality** when defects in the process are occurring at the low rate of 3.4 defects per million opportunities—now that's a high-quality process! Other measures of cost, quality, and time that have competitive value continue to be developed and refined. Exhibit 10-3 provides some measures that exemplify the continuous improvements we now see in cost, quality, and time measures to support operations processes.

six sigma quality A measure of quality based on statistical analysis. Products or services with six sigma quality have no more than 3.4 defects per million opportunities (e.g., parts or events).

SERVICE-AFTER-SALE PROCESS MEASURES *Service-after-sale processes* are of two types. One type of service-after-sale process involves the billing and collection of payments from customers. The other type involves the organization's commitment to warranty its product, including efforts to repair or replace products and provide post-sale support and guidance in the use of the product. If you've purchased a personal computer lately, you have likely had some experience with technical support to help you resolve a computer problem or simply to figure out how to better use your new computer. Depending on your experience with your computer merchant's technical support (or, for that matter, the post-sale support of any other product or service you've purchased), you

3 Sigma is the Latin symbol for a statistical measure more commonly known as "standard deviation."

fyi

LANDS' END is a garment mail-order merchant that exemplifies the growing trend of excellent service-after-sale to customers. Despite being a very large company (on an average day, close to 300 phone lines handle between 40,000 and 50,000 calls, and during peak seasons, close to 1,100 phone lines handle over 100,000 calls per day), it has established a strong reputation for customer service. Lands' End offers one of the simplest guarantees in the industry—"GUARANTEED. PERIOD.®" This means letting the customer return the product at any time, for any reason. As an example of the extent of its guarantee, customers who need additional buttons, have lost a belt, or need a piece of luggage repaired can receive all these services at any time after purchase, free of charge. Even if a child loses a mitten from Lands' End the same season it was purchased, the "Lost Mitten Club" will replace it at half the price of a pair, and Lands' End will pick up the costs of shipping.

probably have strong positive or negative feelings about the quality and timeliness of the support you received, and about the company itself! Do organizations create a competitive edge when they provide quality, timely post-sale support while controlling the costs of that support? You bet! Is it important to effectively control the process of billing and collecting payments from customers? If you remember our extensive discussion of holding costs in Chapter 6 of management accounting, you know that companies can spend a lot of time and resources creating customer invoices and then following up to ensure prompt collection. Poor management of service-after-sale processes can result in many opportunity costs. Hence, management accountants also pay attention to management of these processes using effective performance measures, some examples of which are provided in Exhibit 10-3.

Learning and Growth

Perhaps the most interesting example of continuous improvement in management accounting is found in the very recent trend for accountants to help management teams better understand the process of building learning and growth within the organization. In order to survive and thrive in this competitive economy, an organization must continue to learn and grow. Or, to be more specific, the organization's employees, system, and structure must learn, grow, and change in order to continuously build and improve internal processes and satisfy customers. Certainly, the demand of customers today is well described by the question, "What have you done for me lately?" Without learning and growth, internal processes stop improving, customers grow restless and defect, and financial performance stagnates. However, many might react rather strongly to the trend to create performance measures on learning and growth by challenging whether this kind of work is really management accounting at all! How does one measure learning and growth? Frankly, it's not a well-developed accounting discipline. However, because development in this area is rather slight, there is much opportunity for management accountants to create significant competitive value for their organizations by working to build good measures. Don't forget the lesson of Donaldson Brown and the DuPont ROI formula. Accountants who are able to provide information useful to plan, control, and evaluate critical business processes, regardless of the initial difficulty of the effort, will add the most value to their organization. By dividing this effort into leading measures and outcome measures (somewhat similar to the effort of managing an organization's work with its customers), the Balanced Scorecard Model suggests some interesting possibilities for measuring performance in the learning and growth effort. Exhibit 10-4 illustrates some example measures that can be used for managing learning and growth performance.

LEADING MEASURES OF LEARNING AND GROWTH The ultimate result of building learning and growth in the organization is based on developing employee productivity. Employee productivity then leads to internal process improvements. Related to employee productivity is employee retention and employee satisfaction. These three issues form the desired outcome measures of learning and growth. Therefore, the organization should track performance in the productivity, retention rates, and satisfaction of its employees. However, managing improvements in these important outcome measures requires that management accountants identify the factors that result in high employee productivity, retention, and satisfaction. These factors form *leading* measures in learning and growth: employee capabilities, information system capabilities, and organizational structure capabilities.

net work

Balanced Scorecards are often implemented with the help of an outside consultant. **METRUS GROUP** is an organization whose employees are experts in Balanced Scorecards and performance measurement strategies. Access the Web site at http://www.metrus.com and find "the balanced scorecard process" link, which will allow you to choose another link titled "Assessment." In what ways does the Balanced Scorecard approach open up opportunities for a firm's leaders?

Improvements in employee capabilities should lead to improvements in employee productivity. However, improving employee productivity does not necessarily mean that employees are satisfied with their work situation and are committed to staying with the company. To the extent investments in employee capabilities also lead to higher satisfaction and retention rates among employees, then companies may expect to see positive improvements in internal processes, customer care, and financial performance. Measures here can focus on the level of qualifications and certifications among employees, as well as investments made by the company in employee training and education.

In this information age, the strength of a company's information system structure is critical to employee productivity. To build an excellent organization, employees need relevant, accurate, and timely information on the effects of their efforts to improve processes, satisfy customers, and strengthen financial performance within the organization. In addition to information systems, modern technology continues to provide significant opportunities for directly improving various business processes in all kinds of organizations. Performance measures on information systems and other types of technologies can focus on the quality of systems, accessibility to systems, and investments in systems.

Poorly run organizations can quickly damage employee satisfaction, as well as create confusion that limits employee productivity. Factors that define a well-run organization include effective communication; alignment of goals (i.e., everyone understands and is working toward the same goals); integration of team efforts across departments; and clearly defined planning, controlling, and evaluating processes. Measuring performance and capability in organizational structures is likely the most undefined and challenging "next step" for management accountants today. Nevertheless, this is important work. Organizations usually work very hard to create effective communication channels, to obtain buy-in from employees on company goals, to form an environment where people will work together, and to establish good management processes. Surveys of employees' perspectives are one good way to measure performance on the drive to create good organizational structure.

STOP & THINK *Market value* for a company is computed as the number of shares of stock outstanding multiplied by the average price per share. Essentially, market value measures how much money stockholders believe the company is worth. MICROSOFT's stock price at the end of 1999 was $95.63 per share. Based on 5,028,000,000 common shares outstanding at the end of 1999, this works out to a market value of over $480 billion! However, if you look at Microsoft's 1999 balance sheet, you'll see that its net assets (total assets minus total liabilities) are valued at only $28.44 billion. Why the huge difference?

OUTCOME MEASURES OF LEARNING AND GROWTH Examples of leading and outcome measures of learning and growth are provided in Exhibit 10-4. As accountants track these measures, it is critical that good performance

exhibit 10-4 Performance Measures of Learning and Growth

Leading Performance Measures

	Employee Capabilities	Information Systems Capabilities	Organizational Structure Capabilities
Cost measures	• On-site training expense per employee • Off-site education expense per employee	• Total costs invested in computer systems within the organization • Systems R&D expense per total systems expense	• Costs invested in assessing and building new communication structures • Costs invested in activities to align goals within the company
Quality measures	• Number of new certifications or degrees • Percentage of employees participating in education activities	• System capability compared to competitor systems • Percentage of employees with access to personal computer	• Assessment of effective communication • Assessment of effective teamwork • Assessment of goal alignment
Time measures	• Average yearly training or education hours per employee • Time required to complete a training module	• Average life cycle time of personal computers (e.g., how often are machines upgraded?) • Time required to complete a system upgrade	• Amount of time spent in teamwork versus individual work • Average time to disseminate information or to receive employee feedback

Outcome Performance Measures

Employee Retention	Employee Satisfaction	Employee Productivity
• Employee turnover rate • Average employee years with company • Number of female managers • Average age of employees	• Survey of employee satisfaction • Percentage of employees having leadership opportunities • Management positions filled by inside versus outside recruits	• Output per employee • Billable hours per consultant • New ideas or patents per employee • Recognition of employees by customers

business environment essay

A Nose by Any Other Name . . . In 1996, GIVAUDAN ROURE (at that time a division of ROCHE HOLDINGS LTD., a $14 billion Swiss conglomerate) created a product that would go on to win two prestigious 1997 FiFi Awards. Haven't heard of the FiFi Awards? Are you also unfamiliar with Givaudan Roure or Roche Holdings? Don't worry. These are not exactly household names, but they are part of an industry with a very familiar "smell." FiFi Awards are given by the Fragrance Foundation, an international coalition of companies involved in the business of creating and selling perfume. Givaudan Roure is an inconspicuous research firm in Teaneck, New Jersey, whose business is perfumery—the art of blending natural and synthetic scents to make perfume. Givaudan Roure created Michael Jordan Cologne for BIJAN FRAGRANCES, INC. It was this cologne that won the two FiFi Awards—the industry's version of the Oscars: Men's Fragrance Star of the Year and Men's National Advertising Campaign of the Year. Givaudan Roure has had a major impact on the fragrance industry, having created CALVIN KLEIN's Obsession, CHRISTIAN DIOR's Poison, YVES SAINT LAURENT's Opium, CARTIER's So Pretty, ARMANI's Aqua di Gio, and HUGO BOSS's Hugo.

Remember the last time you smelled a perfume or cologne that you thought was really wonderful? Trying to describe the scent to another person is usually quite difficult—it must be experienced to be understood. Constantly inventing new scents to delight the noses of people across the world is a large, but financially rewarding, challenge. In 1999, the fragrance industry reported sales of approximately $8.3 billion in America alone. Givaudan Roure's CEO, Geoffrey Webster, understands that the success of his company is based on a strategy of learning and growth, and he is making significant investments in employee, systems, and organizational capabilities.

Givaudan Roure's main employees are perfumers who work in a perfumery laboratory. However, per-

in employee capabilities, information system capabilities, and organizational structure capabilities results in improvements in employee satisfaction, retention, and productivity. Obviously, then, management accountants can (and should) test the relationship between leading measures and outcome measures by evaluating satisfaction of employees using surveys; reporting on resignation trends within the company; and measuring employees' productivity in terms of volume, quality, and timeliness of output. When investments in employee education programs or improvements in information systems fail to improve employee outcome measures, then management accountants should provide useful information to better manage these critical processes. Otherwise, there is likely to be little improvement in internal processes, customer satisfaction, and (finally) financial performance. Are you getting the sense that linking together all performance measures within the organization may be a critical aspect of developing a Balanced Scorecard? If so, then you are on track with the final concept that we discuss in the next section.

Linking It All Together

So far in this chapter, and, for that matter, throughout this entire textbook, we have been discussing *a lot* of different performance measures! Do management accountants really need to track *all* these data in order to effectively support the management processes within their companies? Clearly, the answer is no. Too much information is often as harmful as too little. Managers and organizations can become overloaded with information. The key is to clearly identify the vision and strategy a company chooses to pursue, and then establish a set of performance measures that supports progress toward specific company goals. Thus far in this chapter, we have learned that a Balanced Scorecard approach recognizes that management of a company requires information on financial, customer, internal process, and learning and growth activities. Further, performance measures of these activities are not limited to financial measures, but should include nonfinancial measures as well (e.g., quality and time-based measures). Perhaps the most important aspect of a Balanced Scorecard approach is that all measures must *link together* to eventually support

fumers are not really scientists; they are artists who look everywhere for the necessary inspiration to design scent compounds called notes. Perfumers must complete a rigorous education that culminates in the ability to identify by smell nearly 3,000 synthetic natural scents. To make the most of these talents, Webster has designed an entire building to foster creativity among all perfumers. An immaculately kept Zen garden occupies the central courtyard in the New Jersey building. The building has a circular layout that is intended to inspire the circular process of fragrance invention. Givaudan Roure employees regularly participate in tasting sessions designed to inspire new combinations of fragrance notes. Edible floral sorbets, such as rose, lavender, and geranium, are some of the featured dishes prepared by the corporate chef. Some perfumers surround themselves with music to stimulate their creative abilities by listening for musical notes that can be replayed as fragrance notes.

In addition, Givaudan Roure is making significant investments in the capabilities of laboratory technologies. One important technological system is called ScentTrek. ScentTrek is used to identify previously undetected scents in nature. Using a clear plastic globe to surround a flower and take constant measures over a 24-hour period, ScentTrek is able to then reproduce natural scents too subtle to be consciously detected by the human nose. ScentTrek has been sent to golf courses, mountain glens, and seaside beaches to capture scents that can evoke for each of us pleasant memories and emotions. ScentTrek has even been used to analyze the wonderful smell of an old leather baseball glove. Using well-trained and inspired perfumers in combination with investments in advanced technologies like ScentTrek, Givaudan Roure is able to savor the sweet smell of success in a very competitive industry.

Source: Lisa Chadderdon, "The Sweet Smell of Success," *Fast Company* (April–May 1998), pp. 144–153.

the ultimate financial goals of a company.[4] Good performances on activities that do not directly or indirectly contribute to the ultimate goals the organization has established are obviously a waste of resources. Nevertheless, pointless investments in non-value-added activities probably occur in many organizations. Distinguishing non-value-added activities from value-added activities and identifying which performance measures successfully contribute to helping the company accomplish its strategic goals are the ideas behind linkages within a Balanced Scorecard.

To illustrate the importance of clearly linking performance measures in a Balanced Scorecard, look at Exhibit 10-5. It should be clear that the ability to achieve a positive ROI (return on investment) or ROE (return on equity) is closely linked to customer outcome measures (customer retention, customer acquisition, and market share). However, a company can increase its market share and still experience declining ROI because the type of customers it is serving, or the way it is serving its customers, does not lead to positive profits for the company. This is the concept of leading versus lagging indicators. **Leading indicators** are measures of performance that, if accomplished, should lead to a desired result. Measures of performance on the desired results are the **lagging indicators**. A company may desire positive ROI. However, the company does not really "manage" ROI directly; instead, it manages performance that *leads* to positive ROI. Hence, it is important that the company has clearly determined that there is a strong relationship between its leading and lagging indicators. In other words, a company may determine that high rates of customer acquisition should lead to improvements in its overall ROI. Nevertheless, if the company actually does acquire a lot of new customers but does not experience improved ROI performance, it likely needs to spend some time better identifying exactly what the real leading indicators are for improved profits in its industry.

leading indicators Measures that indicate the potential success of future business activities. Leading indicators are related to the concept "leading measures."

lagging indicators Measures that indicate the success of past business activities. Lagging indicators are related to the concept "outcome measures."

As you can see in Exhibit 10-5, cause-and-effect relationships between leading and lagging indicators should exist throughout a company's Balanced Scorecard. Customer outcome measures

4 The ultimate goals of an organization do not need to be financial profits in order to apply the Balanced Scorecard Model. For example, not-for-profit organizations (such as governments or charities) will likely emphasize service to constituents or clients as their ultimate strategic goals.

exhibit 10-5 Performance Measurement Linkages in a Balanced Scorecard

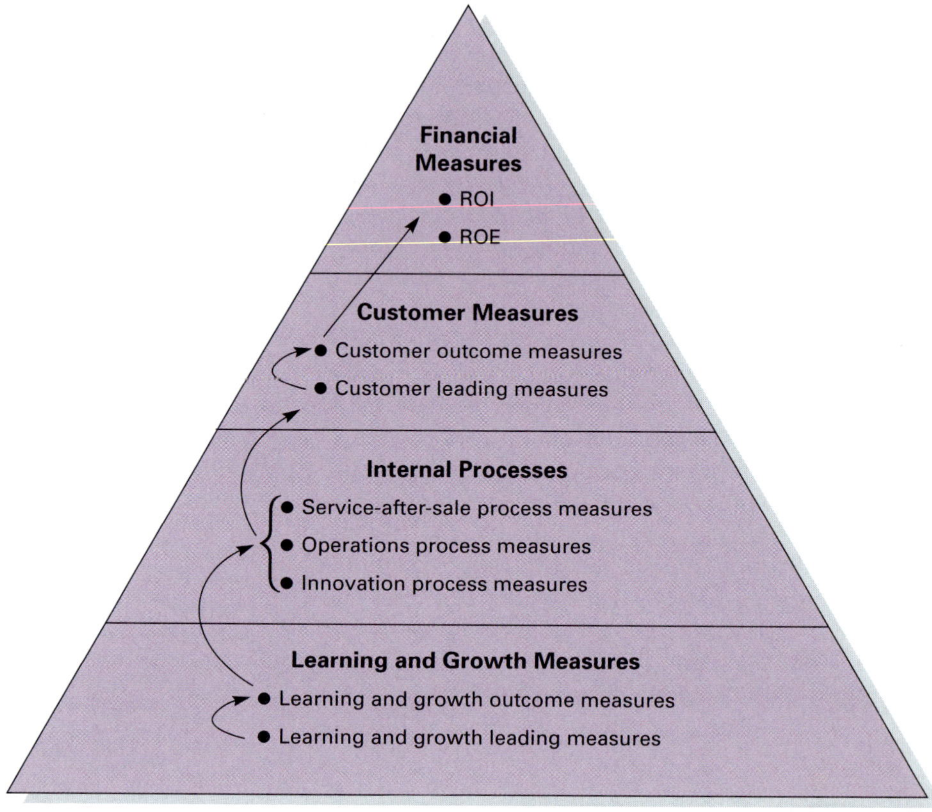

> **fyi**
>
> In Chapter 7 of management accounting, we described the Malcolm Baldrige National Quality Award for companies that have demonstrated excellence in quality management. Since 1988, 43 companies have received the Baldrige Award. However, high quality has not always translated into strong financial performance. Many Baldrige Award winners have struggled financially after winning the award. For example, **FEDEX** lost $1.5 billion on its European operation, the **WALLACE COMPANY** declared bankruptcy, and many **RITZ-CARLTON** hotels have lost money or become insolvent since winning the award. Furthermore, **GM**, **IBM**, **KODAK**, and **WESTINGHOUSE** each had Baldrige Award-winning divisions, yet each sustained substantial overall corporate losses that led to the replacement of their chairmen. Failure to invest in quality initiatives that translate (i.e., *link*) to desired financial performance may be one reason some Baldrige Award companies have struggled financially.
>
> *Source:* D. Benson and M. Swain. "A Study of the Impact of TQM on the Financial Performance of Firms," *Academy of Accounting and Financial Studies Journal* (Vol. 3, no. 1, 1999, pp. 145–159).

are leading indicators for financial measures. If the company identifies the cost, quality, and time factors that customers care about, then improved performance in these activities will lead to good outcomes in customer retention, acquisition, and market share. Similarly, effective innovation, operations, and service-after-sale processes should lead to improved performance in customer leading measures. Continuous improvements in these internal processes are then linked to learning and growth outcome measures (i.e., employee retention, satisfaction, and productivity), which are linked to investments in leading measures of employee, information systems, and organizational structure capabilities. Exhibit 10-5 illustrates that most performance measures serve as both leading and lagging indicators. When an accountant builds a performance measurement system based on this perspective, it should be clear that financial performance is no more important than performance related to internal processes or learning and growth effort. This is the concept of "balance" in a Balanced Scorecard.

To illustrate this idea of linkages, suppose that a company has identified that repeat and expanded sales to current customers (e.g., the result of customer retention) is the most important factor leading to improved ROI. Next, customer loyalty is assured by continuous improvement in product design, coupled with short lead times on customer orders. Finally, improving the process of product design and delivery requires committed and well-educated employees working with state-of-the-art computer systems in an organization with clear communication channels. These cause-and-effect relationships form the company's strategy. By building a Balanced Scorecard that focuses on this particular set of performance measures, a management accountant is able to clearly support the company strategy. Accountants do not *traditionally* perform this kind of work. However, according to a survey, 80 percent of large American companies want to change their performance measurement systems to better support competitive company strategies.[5]

5 B. Birchard, "Making It Count," *CFO* (October 1995), pp. 42–48.

Traditional financial measures such as net income or ROI are really "after the fact." The fact that a company is reporting either positive or negative profits is the result of *past* performance with customers, internal processes, and learning and growth efforts. Can an ROI measure be used to predict future performance? As illustrated in Exhibit 10-5, financial measures are the ultimate lagging indicators of a successful strategy. Managing an organization's strategy requires insight on leading performance measures. What we see from this reality is that the Balanced Scorecard is really a management system. Management accountants who want to add value to the organization must build and support effective management systems.

An Example Scorecard

Exhibit 10-6 shows the Balanced Scorecard for a small company (between 100 and 1,000 employees) in the biotechnology industry. This scorecard is in an ever-constant state of evaluation

exhibit 10-6 Sample Balanced Scorecard

Scorecard for a Biotechnology Firm

Strategic Goals	**Performance Measures**
Financial Perspective	
• Growth	• Percent increase in revenue of top line products
• Profitability	• Return on equity; earnings per share
• Industry leadership	• Market share
Customer Perspective	
Outcome:	
• New products	• Percent of sales from new products
• Early purchase of seasonal products	• Percent of sales recorded by early purchase date
Leading:	
• Early payment	• Percent of customers who pay early
• Product quality	• Product performance vs. industry quality standards
• Customer satisfaction	• Customer satisfaction surveys
Internal Processes Perspective	
Service-after-sale:	
• Accurate invoices	• Percent of error-free invoices
Operations:	
• Low-cost producer	• Unit cost vs. competitors
• Reduce inventory	• Inventory as percent of sales
Innovation:	
• New products	• Number of actual introductions vs. target
• New active ingredients	• Number of new ingredients identified by research program
• Proprietary positions	• Number of patents that create exclusive marketing rights
Learning and Growth Perspective	
Outcome:	
• Employee retention	• Average employee years with company
• Employee satisfaction	• Employee satisfaction surveys
Leading:	
• Employee capabilities	• Training costs invested per employee; percent of employees participating annually in training
• Organizational structure capabilities	• Average weekly hours in teamwork settings; survey of effective teamwork

Source: Adapted from C. W. Chow, K. M. Haddad, and J. E. Williamson, "Applying the Balanced Scorecard to Small Companies," *Management Accounting* (August 1997), Institute of Management Accountants, Montvale, NJ, pp. 21–27.

business environment essay

Citibank's Balanced Scorecard **CITIBANK PRIVATE BANK**, one of the largest private banks in the world, realizes that a Balanced Scorecard of performance measurements is a necessity for success. Recently, Citibank has achieved revenue growth of 20 percent each year partly due to its focus on its Balanced Scorecard.

The company's Balanced Scorecard includes five components, one of which is Strategic Cost Management (SCM). The overall goal of SCM is to improve efficiency and cut costs while maintaining a high-quality service. This strategy was implemented after noticing that downsizing and one-time cost cuts do not help companies maintain permanent low costs. Therefore, Citibank's SCM is designed to be a continuous cost-management process that encourages reinvesting the saved money into the company to sustain growth.

and redesign as the company works to better understand the right strategy and the right performance measures to use in implementing its strategy to succeed in its particular market. Take a moment to examine this scorecard. Can you recognize the factors this company has identified as important to its strategy? Can you identify linkages between its measures?

The financial goals and measures are rather generic for this firm. The majority of companies in most industries are working to build return on equity, earnings per share, and market share. However, this biotechnology company has determined that it needs to be particularly aggressive in revenue growth in its top line (i.e., best selling) products.

The customer goals are divided into leading and outcome measures. The company has linked early customer payment, product performance, and customer satisfaction as important to its percent of sales from new products and percent of sales taking place early in the buying season. Further, growth in new products should provide future top line products. Getting customers to buy early in the season also seems to be important to building market share and profitability.

Innovation is likely the most important factor in internal processes for a research-intensive firm (such as in the biotechnology industry). Accordingly, you can see that there are a number of measures encouraging successful efforts in innovation processes, which should support customer and financial goals for this company. Additionally, this firm also emphasizes keeping product costs and inventory levels low in order to further support the effort to improve return on equity and earnings per share. Finally, providing accurate invoices should encourage customers to pay early.

At the foundation of this company's business are its investments in learning and growth. It is making substantial investments in training and desires to continually train as many employees as possible. In addition, it is also focusing on teamwork efforts. The expectation is that these leading measures of learning and growth will link to improved employee retention and satisfaction, as well as support internal processes and customer service.

As you consider this scorecard, you may feel that some measures and linkages among measures may be missing. You may be right! Nevertheless, in contrast to being solely focused on short-term financial performance, the management accountants in this company are on their way to creating a performance measurement system that truly incorporates the entire strategy of their company. Studying this scorecard should make it clear to you that good performance measures can capture a unique strategy for a specific firm.

There Is No "Quick Approach"

The Balanced Scorecard approach to performance measurement recognizes that every organization is unique. Hopefully, this textbook has made it clear for you that a manufacturing com-

Citibank collects its cost structure improvement ideas from all branches of the company, both formally and informally. These improvement ideas have been as simple as reducing copying costs by using both sides of paper to complex strategies such as creating a predictive model for filtering loan-application data.

Citibank's management and internal consultants actively support and manage SCM. In 1999, for example, this strategy reduced Citibank's annualized expenses by $2 billion and has enabled the bank to grow globally. Citibank now has offices in more than 90 countries. Its future growth looks great—as long as Citibank maintains its Balanced Scorecard objectives.

Sources: William A. Brindley and Michael J. Bear, "The Citibank Private Bank's Portfolio Balancing Act," *The Journal of Business Strategy* (July–August 1997), pp. 12–17; Citigroup press release, January 18, 2000, http://www.citigroup.com.

pany will not manage itself the same as a merchandising or service company. Further, even companies competing within the same industry will each have different sets of goals, objectives, and strategies to attain a specific mission. The process of building a Balanced Scorecard takes time and effort. The management accountant must have a clear knowledge of both financial and management accounting concepts. Then the organization's specific strategy must be clearly and specifically defined in terms of cause-and-effect relationships (i.e., linkages) for its particular industry. What cost, quality, and time issues are important to compete successfully within a particular market? An organization cannot expect to be financially rewarded for world-class performance in response time to customer repair requests unless that type of response time is truly valued by its customers. Finally, measures must be developed, tested, and implemented into clear reporting systems that support effective planning, controlling, and evaluating procedures.

Management accountants can easily build elegant looking but irrelevant performance measurement systems. There are examples of this in far too many organizations. The best example of this bad situation is when accounting is determined to be a non-value-added activity in an organization, and managers simply ignore accounting data as they work on their own to build the company. One of the authors of this textbook is reminded of an experience of having dinner with a plant manager who had established his plant as the most successful division within the company. When asked how the plant controller's work figured into the division's successful implementation of cutting-edge management principles such as JIT and TQM, the plant manager smiled grimly and indicated that the controller really had only two jobs in the organization. First, the controller was responsible for handling all requests from the external auditors. Second, the controller was simply to "stay out of his way!" He felt that the controller (the chief accountant in the organization) provided no information useful to him in his efforts to implement and execute strategy. Clearly, both the controller and the plant manager were missing important opportunities. The division was making significant investments in its accounting system without receiving any competitive benefits. The controller's reports were irrelevant to the core activities of the organization. How long before one of the competitors in this division's market can effectively use management accounting to better implement its own strategy and seize the market?

Good management accounting requires that both managers and accountants work together to create information systems and performance measures that add value—that support the organization's unique strategy. This kind of work is not easy, nor is it done quickly. Management accountants must clearly understand the nature of critical business processes in the organization, as well as how managers and executives intend to strategically plan, control, and evaluate those processes. Linkages between activities must be tested. If performance in one activity does not lead to desired outcomes in customer service or financial performance, then relationships need to be reexamined. This is exciting work! The history of business in America has clearly demonstrated that successful organizations are willing to spend the necessary creative energy to really understand how the work they do adds value to the marketplace. The spirit of continuous improvement that is now prevalent throughout our economy requires that management accounting continue to identify and support opportunities to improve the cost, quality, and timeliness of the information it provides.

to summarize

The Balanced Scorecard is a new theory that explicitly supports strategy by integrating performance measures of financial, customer, internal process, and learning and growth activities within an organization. Both financial and nonfinancial measures are used throughout this new management model. A Balanced Scorecard, once created, is unique to each organization. The process of building a Balanced Scorecard requires that management accountants work closely with managers, executives, and information technologists in order to clearly understand how measures link together to eventually support successful financial results for the company. This idea of linkages across performance measures is critical to a successful Balanced Scorecard. Financial performance is linked to customer outcome measures of customer retention, customer acquisition, and market share. These customer outcome measures in turn are linked to leading measures on customer service involving cost, quality, and time. Supporting customer service are the internal processes that take place within an organization. These internal processes include innovation processes (identifying and creating new products), operations processes (obtaining customer orders and producing and delivering products), and service-after-sale

business environment essay

What's in a Name? The accounting profession is facing profound changes. The marketplace, clients, and professional expectations are suddenly different. Accountants must develop new competencies, including improved communication skills, business knowledge, and the capacity to make inferences from the relationship between business circumstances and economic and industrial trends. Further, accountants must redefine themselves as being concerned with the definition, acquisition, analysis, reporting, and use of all kinds of information (both financial and nonfinancial, internal and external). Expanding the relationship between accountants and the information that they use in their work will allow these professionals to more effectively operate, manage, and assess organizations and their various activities in a global economy that is being constantly reshaped by technology advances.

In the midst of the increasing pressure to change and adapt within this new economy, some people are proposing that the terms "accounting" and "accountancy" may no longer adequately describe a profession moving to higher levels of information management. For instance, it may be appropriate for the accounting profession to rename itself the "information consultancy" profession. The body of knowledge that would qualify a person as an "information consultant" should include management techniques, computers, computerized information systems, and the various functions needed by an organization to carry out its mission (including accounting). Most importantly, to understand and manage essentially *all* of the critical information needed to effectively run an organization, one must clearly understand *all* of the key underlying business activities and processes.

The American Institute of Certified Public Accountants (AICPA) is currently working with several other

processes (handling warranties and providing support to customers). In order to continually improve its internal processes, an organization must emphasize its employees by measuring outcome performance on employee retention, satisfaction, and productivity. Finally, these employee outcome measures are linked to important investments in the capabilities of employees, information systems, and organizational structure.

2 Anticipate that both management accounting and financial accounting are poised for important changes.

ACCOUNTING FOR TOMORROW

"There is a bulldozer of change moving across America and if you are not part of the bulldozer, you will be part of the road." The Balanced Scorecard is one important example of continuous improvement that is characteristic of a competitive world economy that is always growing and changing. Managers and accountants in many organizations are creating new performance measurement systems that support dramatic improvements in products, processes, and people. These professionals understand that measures should focus on monitoring *all* critical activities in an organization in order to anticipate and prepare for future decisions, rather than simply report the financial effects of past decisions. Hence, in harmony with the idea of an instrument panel on an airplane, some companies prefer to refer to their measurement systems as dashboards rather than scoreboards.

In this atmosphere of healthy competition and change, you can expect that new models and methods of management accounting will continue to be developed. Even financial accounting is beginning to move in this direction. Investors, creditors, and regulators are beginning to put a lot of pressure on companies to make public more relevant and more timely information than is now contained in annual reports prepared using the financial accounting model first developed by Italian merchants in the 1300–1400s. The American Institute of Certified Public Accountants

leading accountancy institutions around the world to create a new professional designation that is global in scope and focused on knowledge integration that creates economic value. This new designation is not intended to replace the CPA designation, or any other designation, but rather is intended to complement existing credentials. At the time of the printing of this textbook, those working on this project have not yet decided what to call this new designation. For now, it is simply referred to as the "XYZ" designation; and it will be defined by four critical characteristics. It will be:

1. global in reach (it will be recognized throughout the world, not just in the United States);
2. based on a wide range of disciplines (including accountancy, management consulting, information technology, business law, finance, financial planning, marketing, economics, risk management, human resources, actuarial services, and engineering);
3. bound by global ethical standards; and
4. based on global standards of competency, with a commitment to continuing learning and periodic evaluation to ensure currency of knowledge and skills.

Overall, the intent is that this "XYZ" designation will be a recognized emblem of experience and ability to integrate knowledge and business experience to provide strategic business insight that creates economic value. So watch for future developments here, including its actual name. This may be a professional designation that you will hold one day.

Sources: P. Lowell and R. Fremgen, "What's in a Name Change?" *Journal of Accountancy* (August 1999); "Key Features of XYZ: The Proposed Designation," *The CPA Letter* (February–March 2001).

exhibit 10-7 The Future of Financial Accounting in Public Reports

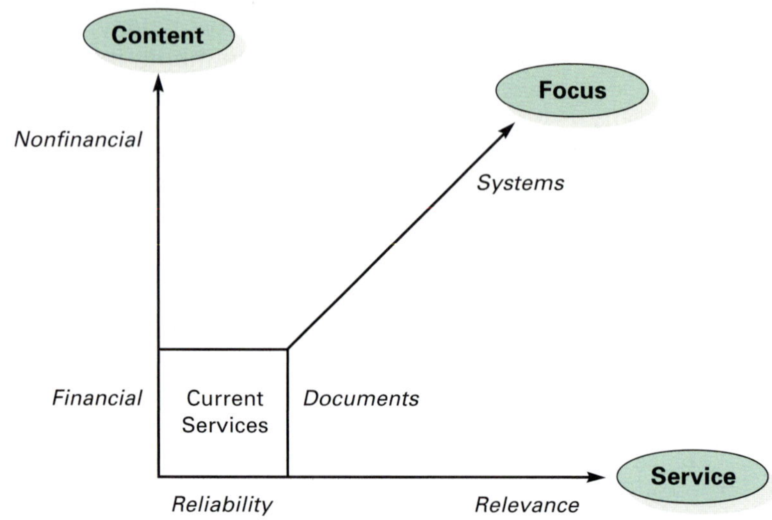

Source: From a 1996 presentation by Robert K. Elliott, Chairperson of the AICPA Special Committee on Assurance Services.

(AICPA) has commissioned special committees to study these demands for additional public data about companies and to propose new models of financial accounting. Robert Elliott, chairman of the AICPA in 2000/2001, represents many others in calling for accounting to continue to grow and mature as the global economy and technology grow. He describes the professional practice of a "new finance" that "encompasses hard-core management accounting topics such as cost management, discount rates, and capacity management; manufacturing issues including just-in-time production, distribution channel management, and competitive intelligence; and softer topics like benchmarking, performance measurement, and managing change." He says the new finance is "less about accounting and more about becoming strategic advisors and decision makers in our companies."[6]

Exhibit 10-7 illustrates one way to view the current direction of change that is necessary for accounting in today's marketplace. As you can see, the pressure on accounting to change is threefold. First, financial accounting is being pressured to provide *nonfinancial* data in public reports. Second, preparation of financial accounting reports has always focused on making reports objective, consistent, and reliable. However, users of financial accounting reports want these reports to emphasize more the *relevance* of information to important investing, lending, and regulatory decisions for individual companies. Finally, in an age when the Internet allows users to access and analyze huge amounts of data almost instantaneously, there is increased demand by decision makers trying to evaluate a company based on financial accounting to be able to access information *systems* throughout the year, rather than having to wait one to three months after the year-end for the company to release an annual report document; or, in the case of internal management accounting reports, having to wait days or weeks for cost, quality, and time analysis reports to be completed and delivered to management. It's difficult to predict how these demands will eventually affect the financial accounting reports provided by thousands of companies like **MICROSOFT**. However, it's not difficult to predict that changes are coming. This is a very exciting time to be preparing to enter the world of business. Regardless of whether you intend to actually work as an accountant, it is clear that accounting will dramatically impact the way you work. By understanding the concepts of financial and management accounting, as well as the great potential for continuous improvement in these areas, you will be better prepared to use accounting to personally add value to your organization.

6 P. Fleming, "Steering a Course for the Future," *Journal of Accountancy* (November 1999), pp. 35–38.

review of learning objectives

1 Explain the fundamentals of building a Balanced Scorecard. Competition requires that companies continually improve their performance measures in order to add value to the products and services they provide within their industries. Nonfinancial measures are growing in importance in today's marketplace as companies work to build better management systems. The Balanced Scorecard is being heralded as an important new management model that explicitly supports a successful strategy by integrating performance measures of financial, customer, internal process, and learning and growth activities within an organization. Management accountants must work closely with managers, executives, and information technologists in order to build a Balanced Scorecard that is unique to their own organization. One of the most important aspects of a successful scorecard is *linking* all performance measures either directly or indirectly to desired financial performance. The Balanced Scorecard approach to these linkages is to connect financial performance directly to customer outcome measures of customer retention, customer acquisition, and market share. These customer outcome measures in turn are linked to leading measures on customer service involving cost, quality, and time. Internal processes taking place within an organization that support value-added services expected by customers are then identified. These internal processes include innovation processes (identifying and creating new products), operations processes (obtaining customer orders and producing and delivering products), and service-after-sale processes (handling warranties and providing support to customers). Positive employee outcome performance in terms of employee retention, satisfaction, and productivity is necessary in order to support continual improvement of internal processes. Employee outcome measures on retention, satisfaction, and productivity are linked to important investments in the capabilities of employees, information systems, and organizational structure.

2 Anticipate that both management accounting and financial accounting are poised for important changes. This textbook has covered a lot of territory in an effort to introduce you to the world of accounting. You should understand that management accounting has always been a function of competitive need. In other words, the desire to compete well in the marketplace drives companies to develop better methods of management accounting. Hence, as you would expect, today's competitive markets continue to put pressure on both management and financial accounting to make some fundamental changes. The AICPA (American Institute of Certified Public Accountants) has commissioned special committees to investigate these trends. The pressure on accounting to grow and change involves three essential areas: (1) the need to include nonfinancial measures in public accounting reports; (2) the need to better emphasize relevant, rather than just reliable, data; and (3) the need to allow continual access to data systems rather than periodic report documents. Accountants, as well as other business professionals, who can anticipate these needs will be best positioned to add value to their organizations throughout the future.

key terms and concepts

discussion questions

1. Why is it unwise for a company to focus on only one performance measure while ignoring other performance measures?
2. Why do you think performance measures vary from company to company?
3. Why do you think there has been such a revolution in the way companies think about and measure their performance in recent years?
4. What is one way that traditional performance measurement systems, which have historically been tied to financial reporting, may be dysfunctional?

5. Why do you think some researchers argue that traditional performance measures are partly responsible for a decline in America's competitiveness?
6. Describe the two types of customer performance measures.
7. What are the key ingredients of customer satisfaction?
8. Why doesn't the purchase price of a product equal the product's total cost to customers?
9. What are two ways companies can increase the market share of their products?
10. What are the three types of processes that should be in place to effectively support customer satisfaction?
11. How can companies plan, control, and evaluate their innovation processes?
12. Is it possible for a company to spend more money on the innovation process than on providing goods and services to current customers?
13. What are the three leading measures of "learning and growth" in an organization?
14. What are some of the factors of effective organizational structures discussed in this chapter?
15. Why do you think the market value of many companies (as measured by per-share stock price times the number of shares outstanding) is greater than the book value of the net assets (as measured by total assets minus total liabilities) listed on the balance sheets of those companies?
16. How do companies go about managing their return on investment (ROI)?
17. Pressure to provide better information to support the competitive needs of today's marketplace is resulting in fundamental changes in the accounting information that is being provided to managers, investors, and creditors. Identify the three primary areas of change.

discussion cases

CASE 10-1

STRATEGY FOR DEVELOPING A BALANCED SCORECARD

A company is interested in developing a Balanced Scorecard approach to evaluating and enhancing its performance. It is looking at two ways of accomplishing the task. The first is for top management to develop the scorecard approach and impose it on managers throughout the organization. The second is to involve managers, customers, and other stakeholders in a grass-roots approach to determine what cost, quality, and time factors should be measured. Which of the two approaches would you recommend to the company?

CASE 10-2

HOW SOON CAN YOU MAKE US A BALANCED SCORECARD?

You are currently the controller for a large manufacturing company. The president of the company calls you to his office and states the following: "I just went to a round-table discussion with presidents of other companies, and they told me that the most important development they had made in their companies was to implement Balanced Scorecards. I want you to drop whatever you are doing this week and develop a Balanced Scorecard for our company." You are vaguely aware of the concept of Balanced Scorecards from your reading, but you aren't too sure what they are all about. As you begin to think about your upcoming task, you discover that your company does not have a strategic plan or mission statement. Is the task given you by the president one that can be accomplished in a week or accomplished at all? What is the effect of not having a strategic plan or mission statement on the development of a Balanced Scorecard for the company?

CASE 10-3

GET THOSE BUSINESS SCHOOL RATINGS UP!

You are the dean of the business school at North Central University. You have recently gone through a strategic planning process involving representatives from all your stakeholder groups (students, staff, faculty, recruiters, alumni, administration, etc.). The result is a newly refined strategic plan, including a mission statement, underlying values, specific objectives and strategies, and assessment outcomes (performance measurements). One of your objectives is to increase the ranking of your business school by *Business News*, a magazine that annually ranks business programs in your region. Given your understanding of the Balanced Scorecard approach and the material covered in this textbook, answer the following questions.

1. Even though it takes longer, is it wise to involve various stakeholders in developing your strategic plan? Why or why not?
2. What are some likely strategies that might be implemented to increase your business school ranking? Explain.

exercises

EXERCISE 10-1 CUSTOMER SATISFACTION PERFORMANCE MEASURES

The following are possible performance measures of customer satisfaction:

1. Purchase cost to customer
2. Customer defection rate
3. Returns by customers
4. Number of new customers
5. Time to complete contract
6. Percent of total units sold
7. Customer survey response
8. Costs to recruit customers

Identify which of these measures are most likely to be considered leading measures and which are outcome performance measures. Also, if they are leading performance measures, identify whether they relate to cost, quality, or time. If they are outcome performance measures, identify whether they relate to customer retention, customer acquisition, or market share.

EXERCISE 10-2 INTERNAL PROCESSES PERFORMANCE MEASURES

The following are possible performance measures of internal processes:

1. Cost of replacement parts
2. Lead time (order to delivery)
3. Lead time (idea to working model)
4. Payback on R&D costs
5. Percentage of sales from new products
6. Unit-level costs
7. Defects per million
8. Repair cycle time

Identify the type of performance measure (cost, quality, or time) and the related process (innovation, operations, or service-after-sale) for each of these measures.

EXERCISE 10-3 PERFORMANCE MEASURES OF LEARNING AND GROWTH

The following are performance measures of learning and growth:

1. Number of new certifications or degrees
2. Average life cycle time of personal computers
3. Assessment of effective communication
4. Employee turnover rate
5. Output per employee
6. Average yearly training or education hours per employee
7. Survey of employee satisfaction
8. Amount of time spent in teamwork versus individual work

Identify which of these learning and growth measures are leading performance measures and which are outcome performance measures. Also, if they are leading performance measures, identify whether they would be classified as cost, quality, or time measures and whether they relate to employee, information system, or organizational structure capabilities. If they are outcome performance measures, identify whether they relate to employee retention, employee satisfaction, or employee productivity.

EXERCISE 10-4 BALANCED SCORECARD LINKAGES

The following are examples of performance measures in a Balanced Scorecard:

1. ROI
2. Percentage of employees having leadership opportunities

3. Repair cycle time
4. Quality rankings by other agencies
5. ROE
6. Design cycle time
7. Six sigma
8. Systems R&D expense per total systems expense

Classify each of the above performance measures using the categories in Exhibit 10-5. For each measure, identify the type of lagging measure to which it links.

EXERCISE 10-5 CLASSIFYING BALANCED SCORECARD ELEMENTS

Listed below are a number of scorecard measures for a manufacturing company:

a. Number of new customers
b. Percentage of customers who place multiple orders
c. Percentage of on-time deliveries
d. Number of worker accidents
e. Number of customer complaints about products
f. Number of employees who attend training seminars
g. Percentage of product defects
h. Percentage of back-ordered products
i. Customer satisfaction, as measured through periodic surveys
j. Unit product cost
k. Percentage of revenues from new products
l. Earnings per share
m. Gross margin on products
n. Employee turnover
o. Costs to retain customers
p. Amount of time spent in teamwork

Classify each performance measure according to the following:

1. *Perspective:* financial, customer, internal processes, or learning and growth
2. *Focus:* cost, quality, time, or overall financial (*Note:* Some measures may have more than one focus.)
3. *Relationship:* leading or outcome (*Note:* As the measure relates to other measures within its own perspective)

EXERCISE 10-6 BALANCED SCORECARD AND INCENTIVES

Recall from the chapter the discussion of the oil drillers from the former Soviet Union who won a production competition based on the number of meters drilled. Those drillers determined that the first 100 meters of drilling were the easiest, so they simply drilled dry wells that never exceeded 100 meters in depth. Naturally, management would be upset when the drillers' tactics were exposed. After all, management's objective was to drill wells and find oil.

1. Can you suggest to management an incentive system that would have prevented such behavior and would instead encourage the desired behavior?
2. Do you consider what the drillers did to be wrong or smart?

EXERCISE 10-7 THINKING ABOUT THE BALANCED SCORECARD

Albert Einstein once commented that "sometimes what can be counted doesn't count, and what can't be counted is what really counts." A business executive stated, "The first indication we don't know what we are doing is a preoccupation with numbers." How do you think these two statements relate to the Balanced Scorecard approach to performance measurement?

problems

PROBLEM 10-1

APPLYING THE BALANCED SCORECARD TO MANUFACTURING

Martin, Inc., manufactures pleasure and fishing boats. Management's goals and objectives for the company are:

1. *Goal:* To maintain strong financial health
   Objectives:
   - Maintain sufficient cash balances to assure liquidity and solvency
   - Achieve continued growth in sales and profits
   - Provide a good return to investors
   - Increase market share
2. *Goal:* Provide excellent customer service
   Objectives:
   - Provide boats that meet customer needs
   - Meet customer needs on a timely basis
   - Exceed customer quality standards
3. *Goal:* Be the industry leader in product innovations
   Objectives:
   - Bring new boats and features to the market before competitors
   - Increase efficiency and productivity faster than competitors

Required: For each of these objectives, provide one measure of performance the company could use.

PROBLEM 10-2

APPLYING THE BALANCED SCORECARD TO A SMALL BUSINESS

You are an optometrist with your own practice. For the past 20 years, you have focused almost exclusively on profitability of your practice as your sole performance measure. In fact, you have been quite profitable. However, during the past two years, a number of new, low-cost, commercial optometric offices including LENSCRAFTERS, WAL-MART, SHOPKO, and even KMART have opened in your practice area. As a result, your profitability has decreased to the point where you are barely breaking even. Because of your concern for your practice, you have asked a business consultant what you should do.

She has told you that your single-minded focus on profitability is no different than that of your new commercial competitors and has convinced you that these competitors will be more successful than you in making profits because they have lower cost structures than you do. She has suggested that you read her recently published book on the Balanced Scorecard measurement system and respond to the following questions:

Required:

1. Are your current success measures mostly financial, internal processes, learning and growth, or customer focused?
2. Has your focus been on financial, quality, or time measures, or on an appropriate balance of the three?
3. Thinking about your performance perspective (financial, customer, internal processes, and learning and growth), how could you distinguish yourself from the commercial optometrists and create value for your customers?
4. Are there ways you should change your focus regarding cost, quality, and time measures?

PROBLEM 10-3

APPLYING THE BALANCED SCORECARD TO AN INTERNET COMPANY

OnRamp, Inc., is a technology company that provides connections for Internet service providers (ISPs) to the information highway. If U.S. WEST and other long-distance companies that own fiber optic cable are the information highway, OnRamp, Inc., views itself as the on- and off-ramps that provide access to the highway for ISPs, such as EARTHLINK, INC., and their customers. Two years ago, OnRamp, Inc., had an initial public offering (IPO) where it raised $500 million in operating capital. With that money, it built a new office building and developed much of the infrastructure needed to serve as the on- and off-ramp market leader. The company gets its revenue from charging ISPs a small user fee for each customer connected to the information highway. In its prospectus for the IPO, OnRamp, Inc., stated that its only critical performance measure of success was the number of users that it served. It stated that if, in two years, it serviced 2 million individual users, then it would consider itself to be successful. Now, two years later, there are 5 million individual customer accounts within OnRamp's system. Unfortunately, however, OnRamp, Inc., is still losing considerable amounts of money and is experiencing serious complaints about delayed Internet access and server problems.

Required:

1. What do you think about OnRamp, Inc.'s "number of ISP customers" performance measure?
2. If, in fact, OnRamp Inc., measures its success solely on the basis of number of individual ISP customers, what important performance measures is it ignoring?

PROBLEM 10-4 APPLYING THE BALANCED SCORECARD TO A UNIVERSITY

The dean of your business school has determined that there are four major drivers of success for her business school. Those success drivers are having outstanding (1) faculty, (2) students, (3) curricula, and (4) alumni and recruiter support.

Required: Based on these drivers of success, develop a Balanced Scorecard performance system that the dean could use to evaluate the operations of her school. Be specific and indicate the purpose of each measure. Make sure that you clearly include both leading and outcome measures in your Balanced Scorecard.

PROBLEM 10-5 APPLYING THE BALANCED SCORECARD TO A CHURCH

As an accountant and active member of a local church, you have been asked by your pastor to help him develop a Balanced Scorecard measurement system for the church. He is seriously interested in continuous improvement and believes that by identifying and monitoring the right performance measurements, the church will be more successful. In discussions with the pastor, you have determined that the scorecard should focus on the following four areas:

- Increase in learning and commitment of members
- Size of congregation and membership
- Respect in the community
- Amount of financial contributions

Required: Develop a performance measurement system for these four areas that includes both leading and outcome measures that could be used by the pastor and his church to grow and measure the success of his ecumenical efforts.

competency enhancement opportunities

- International Case
- Ethics Case
- Writing Assignment
- The Debate
- Internet Search

The following additional assignments provide opportunities for students to develop critical thinking, ethical perspectives, oral and written communication skills, experience with electronic research, and teamwork through group and business activities.

Note: Due to the nature of this chapter, there are no Analyzing Real Company Information problems.

INTERNATIONAL CASE

• *A Balanced Scorecard in Russia*

This chapter has discussed the need for companies to focus on more than just the numbers. Additional factors must be considered in addition to financial results. Thus, the concept of the Balanced Scorecard. Consider the case of a country where the economy is not as sophisticated as in the United States—Russia. Inflation runs rampant, shortages prevail, organized crime rules. How could a Balanced Scorecard approach help a company that finds itself in this situation? Or could it? Can you suggest areas from a Balanced Scorecard perspective that a company in Russia might emphasize?

ETHICS CASE

• *"Family" Business*

Martin Beemer is the purchasing manager for the police department in a large metropolitan city. The city has 13,000 police officers. The city currently purchases police uniforms from three different manufacturers, one of which is SunKing, International (a Korean company). Martin recently agreed (in private) with SunKing's vice president to give SunKing increased business if SunKing would hire his daughter as a "ghost" salesperson in the United States at a salary of $350,000 per year.

1. Do you believe the actions of Martin and SunKing are unethical? Fraudulent?
2. What internal process performance measures could the city have had in place in the purchasing department that could have revealed the kickback arrangement?

WRITING ASSIGNMENT

• *More Than Just the Numbers*

You have found in your study of accounting that accountants generally focus on the numbers. Their job is to summarize financial results and provide information for decision makers. In this chapter, you have read about additional measures that are critical to a company's success: items like customer loyalty and satisfaction and employee productivity. Your assignment is to prepare a one- to two-page memo summarizing the following points:

1. Select an internal process measure, like research and development, and map out how the careful monitoring of that process will eventually show up in a financial measure like ROI.
2. Are accountants the best people to collect information on items such as customer satisfaction and customer loyalty? If not, who in a business would be best suited to collect this type of information?

THE DEBATE

• *Quantitative vs. Qualitative*

The concept of the Balanced Scorecard suggests that instead of focusing on the financial aspects of business decisions, a company should manage such items as customer satisfaction, employee growth, and total quality, and the profits will follow. Divide your group into two teams. Each team should prepare a five-minute presentation addressing the following issues:

- One team supports "quantitative" measures. Defend the position that a company should manage by the numbers. The DuPonts and the Carnegies achieved the success they did because they focused on costs and profits. Provide reasons in support of your assigned position.
- The other team supports "qualitative" measures. Defend the position that a company's management should examine more than just the financial statement numbers. Other important information must be managed if a company is to be successful. In your presentation, identify some of that "other important information."

INTERNET SEARCH

• *Building a Balanced Scorecard*

How does one go about building a Balanced Scorecard? Let's go to the Internet to find some help. Go to **http://www.rens.com/viewpoint/papers.html** and access the site entitled "An Overview of The Balanced Scorecard." Sometimes Web addresses change, so if this address does not work, access the Web site for this textbook (**http://albrecht.swcollege.com**) for an updated link. Once you have gained access to this site, answer the following questions:

1. How do you recognize a "good" Balanced Scorecard?
2. How many steps are involved in developing a Balanced Scorecard? What are the steps?

appendix a

MICROSOFT CORPORATION
1999 ANNUAL REPORT

FINANCIAL HIGHLIGHTS

msft In millions, except earnings per share

Year Ended June 30	1995	1996	1997	1998	1999
Revenue	$6,075	$9,050	$11,936	$15,262	**$19,747**
Net income	1,453	2,195	3,454	4,490	**7,785**
Diluted earnings per share[1]	0.29	0.43	0.66	0.84	**1.42**
Cash and short-term investments	4,750	6,940	8,966	13,927	**17,236**
Total assets	7,210	10,093	14,387	22,357	**37,156**
Stockholders' equity	5,333	6,908	10,777	16,627	**28,438**

1 Diluted earnings per share have been restated to reflect a two-for-one stock split in March 1999.

FELLOW SHAREHOLDERS

> Microsoft continued to perform strongly in 1999. Our customers count on us to provide great software that helps them communicate more effectively, work more productively, learn more creatively, and make the most of their leisure time. We worked hard to meet those needs and to set the standard for features, functionality, simplicity, and seamless integration with the Internet in all of our products. The result was remarkable growth and record revenue.

In the years ahead, we will see accelerating change in the software industry, as the computing needs of our customers start to move beyond the PC into a "PC-Plus" world. The PC will undoubtedly remain at the heart of computing at home, work, and school, but it will be joined by numerous new intelligent devices and appliances, from handheld computers and auto PCs to Internet-enabled cellular phones. More software will be delivered over the Internet, and the boundary between online services and software products will blur. The Internet will continue to change everything by offering a level of connectivity that was unimaginable only a few years ago — and every home, business, and school will want to be hooked up to that incredible global database.

Microsoft's vision is to empower people through great software — any time, any place, and on any device. That means helping companies build friction-free knowledge-management systems, so information flows effortlessly through their businesses, and to implement flawless e-commerce operations. It means helping developers create great Web-enabled products for a wide range of devices. It means making PCs simpler and more reliable. It means helping consumers transform the Internet into their own "personal Internet" — a resource that learns from them over time and empowers them with all of the information they need, while protecting their privacy. Everything we do focuses on allowing people and organizations to create and manage their information.

BUILT AROUND YOU

> In a world of increasing technological complexity, one of our primary goals must be to make our products easier and more effective for customers to use. In part, this entails developing simpler interfaces, natural-language processing, and voice control to help hide the underlying complexity from users. We're working hard to achieve those breakthroughs. But it also means getting closer to our customers and working harder to understand their needs. We must help customers integrate technology by learning about how they work, how information flows through their organization, what they'll need in the future — and about where we're succeeding or failing. Customer-centric thinking must permeate everything we do.

Our growth is always forcing us to look at the best way to stay close to our customers and respond to their needs. This year we organized the company so that its structure is customer-based rather than product-based. The leaders of each of Microsoft's newly defined divisions now have end-to-end management accountability in their respective customer segments. Guided by the company's overall vision, they have total responsibility for setting a clear mission and priorities for their division, including all product planning and marketing strategies. The divisional leaders also have freedom to form business relationships both inside and outside Microsoft — freedom to work with the parties they need to do the best job for their customers.

Microsoft's mission has always been to connect customers with the information they need. But today there is more information to connect with than ever before, stored in more places than ever before, and accessible in more ways than ever before. By refocusing totally on offering customers what they want rather than what technology can provide, we will help them succeed in the PC-Plus world. We will also build a solid foundation for Microsoft well into the 21st century.

MANAGING KNOWLEDGE

> An organization's most valuable asset is its knowledge base. It is also the hardest to manage. For the majority of knowledge workers, getting the information they need is still more difficult than it should be. Mostly, it involves creating and distributing paper documents or telephoning and meeting with fellow employees. New digital approaches enabled by our software will make knowledge workers far more efficient.

With its Web-based collaboration tools, Microsoft® Office 2000 is already a powerful component of a knowledge management solution. In the coming year, we will augment it with several other key initiatives. Windows® 2000 Active Directory™ service will simplify administration and make it easier for knowledge workers to find resources throughout their organization. Future versions of Microsoft Exchange will offer both a platform for unified messaging and our Web Store technology, creating a powerful, centralized communications and knowledge management solution. In the future, we plan to introduce document library and search server technology that will help companies leverage their knowledge bases. Because 50% of work is now done in teams — compared with only 20% a decade ago — we have added team productivity features to the BackOffice® family and other products. And to help organizations realize the dream of a paperless office, our ClearType technology offers on-screen resolution and readability that equals or exceeds that of paper.

To help knowledge workers access information more efficiently, we're also developing what we call a digital dashboard. The digital dashboard is a customized Office 2000 solution that pulls together all of the information that is important to you — regardless of whether it's on your PC, corporate network, or the Internet — and makes it available in one place. A digital dashboard helps you manage and prioritize messages, tasks, information, meetings — in fact, whatever you want. It also gives you access to all of the analytical tools you need to process your data. And it makes all of this available wherever you are, whether on your handheld computer, PC, or smart telephone. The digital dashboard will bring the concept of empowerment any time, any place, and on any device even closer to reality.

CONNECTING EVERYWHERE

> Microsoft's fundamental vision for Windows is one of total scalability — from embedded operating systems in smart devices such as thermostats and light switches, through Windows CE on handheld PCs, and Web-enabled telephones, to the largest mission-critical server farms. Windows 2000, SQL Server™ 7.0, and the next version of Exchange will take our high-end scalability and around-the-clock availability

far beyond what was thought possible just five years ago, and we expect to make even greater progress in the years ahead. A key to this is using Windows 2000 breakthrough load-balancing to provide scaling and reliability beyond that of the most expensive systems of the past. Web sites can use Windows to easily add capacity and avoid having a single point of failure. The Windows 2000 load-balancing technology automatically redirects tasks to the server that is operating under the least load.

A core requirement of knowledge workers is access to their information wherever they are. Our IntelliMirror™ technology in Windows 2000 will help make that possible, by transparently and automatically backing up and synchronizing your data so that it is available on PCs or intelligent devices.

Your handheld computer, Web-enabled telephone, and PC will synchronize with each other wirelessly and automatically, whether you are in your office or on the road. At Microsoft, some of our employees already use Windows 2000 with a wireless network. When they walk into a meeting room, their laptop is automatically recognized and a "virtual workgroup" of everyone in the room is created. Wireless networks will transform the workplace.

Ubiquitous connectivity will also revolutionize the home, enabling consumers to leverage the power and richness of the PC on any intelligent device, thanks to fast, low-cost wireless networks that will make high-quality audio and video available in every room. For example, our Windows Media™ audio player downloads music twice as fast as previous formats, has double the storage capacity, and offers powerful anti-piracy protection. We're also evolving the WebTV Network™ service, which today has more than 800,000 subscribers, with on-demand programming, personalized viewing, more Web-enhanced content, great games, and powerful communications for the whole family. We aim to help millions of Americans enjoy the digital lifestyle at home as well as at work with exciting offerings such as the CarPoint™ online automotive service, HomeAdvisor™ online real estate service, MoneyCentral™ personal finance service, plus the MSN™ Hotmail Web-based e-mail service, which now has more than 40 million members.

EXPANDING BANDWIDTH

> Microsoft's vision of empowering people through great software — any time, any place, and on any device — depends on helping consumers and businesses advance from today's narrow-band world into a broadband future. Even now, the majority of consumers — along with many small and medium-sized businesses — still access the Internet via their regular telephone lines. The result is that the rich world of real-time interactivity remains a dream for most consumers, while many businesses are reluctant to put videoconferencing or multimedia on their networks, because they fear it will crowd out transaction traffic and other high-priority communications.

Our core strategy here is to make investments that will accelerate the deployment of high-speed broadband networks and to collaborate on the technology that will make interactive services for consumers and businesses run seamlessly across these networks. To that end, we are working with companies that will play a leading role in making broadband Internet and multimedia access widely available. We are enthusiastic about the many technologies that will deliver this, which is why we continue to invest in various infrastructures such as wired and wireless telecommunications, cable, and interactive television. Some of our exciting relationships include AT&T, Nextel Communications, NTL, Rogers Communications, WirelessKnowledge, Concentric Networks, Wink Communications, and more.

THE PC-PLUS ERA

> The enduring popularity of the PC — more than 100 million should be sold worldwide this year — is amazing, but not surprising. In a single, economical package, the PC offers individual students, knowledge workers, and consumers the kind of computing power that was found only in corporate computing departments just a decade ago. Whether you want to communicate, learn, work, or play, the PC can enrich and improve the experience.

In the new millennium, the remarkable power and flexibility of the PC will be available wherever it is needed. The PC-Plus era will be about connectivity, scalability, and simplicity. It will be an era when people are at the center, where technology is a natural extension of the way consumers and businesses think about themselves and their interactions with others. The combination of experience, resources, and research that is unique to Microsoft puts us in a strong position to transform this vision into reality.

We are investing heavily in the future — from world-class customer support to the $3.8 billion we plan to spend in fiscal 2000 on research and development for the products of tomorrow. There is, however, no guarantee of success. Competition continues to intensify, and regulatory pressures are unlikely to ease. Although global PC sales have proved remarkably robust, some slowdown is likely in the coming year. And as Microsoft's business becomes more complex, the strategic challenges and risks we face grow exponentially.

I remain optimistic, because the new opportunities for great software products are still incredible. I appreciate the unwavering support and trust of our shareholders and customers as Microsoft enters the 21st century.

Bill Gates

INCOME STATEMENTS

msft In millions, except earnings per share

Year Ended June 30	1997	1998	1999
Revenue	$11,936	$15,262	**$19,747**
Operating expenses:			
Cost of revenue	2,170	2,460	**2,814**
Research and development	1,863	2,601	**2,970**
Acquired in-process technology	-	296	**-**
Sales and marketing	2,411	2,828	**3,231**
General and administrative	362	433	**689**
Other expenses	259	230	**115**
Total operating expenses	7,065	8,848	**9,819**
Operating income	4,871	6,414	**9,928**
Investment income	443	703	**1,803**
Gain on sale of Softimage, Inc.	-	-	**160**
Income before income taxes	5,314	7,117	**11,891**
Provision for income taxes	1,860	2,627	**4,106**
Net income	$ 3,454	$ 4,490	**$ 7,785**
Earnings per share[1]:			
Basic	$ 0.72	$ 0.92	**$ 1.54**
Diluted	$ 0.66	$ 0.84	**$ 1.42**

1 Earnings per share have been restated to reflect a two-for-one stock split in March 1999.

See accompanying notes.

MANAGEMENT'S DISCUSSION AND ANALYSIS

msft RESULTS OF OPERATIONS FOR 1997, 1998, AND 1999

> Microsoft develops, manufactures, licenses, and supports a wide range of software products for a multitude of computing devices. Microsoft software includes scalable operating systems for intelligent devices, personal computers (PCs), and servers; server applications for client/server environments; knowledge worker productivity applications; and software development tools. The Company's online efforts include the MSN network of Internet products and services; e-commerce platforms; and alliances with companies involved with broadband access and various forms of digital interactivity. Microsoft also licenses consumer software programs; sells PC input devices; trains and certifies system integrators; and researches and develops advanced technologies for future software products.

REVENUE

> The Company's revenue growth rate was 32% in fiscal 1997, 28% in fiscal 1998, and 29% in fiscal 1999. Revenue growth rates reflected the continued adoption of Windows operating systems and Microsoft Office, particularly as Microsoft software is deployed across entire corporate, academic, and governmental organizations. Software license volume increases have been the principal factor in the Company's revenue growth. The average selling price per license has decreased, primarily because of general shifts in the sales mix from retail packaged products to licensing programs, from new products to product upgrades, and from stand-alone desktop applications to integrated product suites. Average revenue per license from original equipment manufacturer (OEM) licenses and organizational license programs is lower than average revenue per license from retail versions. Likewise, product upgrades have lower prices than new products. Also, prices of integrated suites, such as Microsoft Office and BackOffice, are less than the sum of the prices for the individual programs included in these suites when such programs are licensed separately. During each of the three years, an increased percentage of products and programs included elements that were billed but unearned and recognized ratably, such as Microsoft Windows, Microsoft Office, maintenance, and other subscription models. See accompanying notes to financial statements.

As noted above, the Company's business model continues to evolve from selling packaged products to licensing organizational licenses and subscriptions. The Company's products are generally delivered to customers through a multi-tiered channel of distributors and resellers, but the distribution model is also changing for selected retail products that are now being shipped straight to resellers and other selected products that are now being shipped straight to customers. Due to these changes in channel mechanics and the business model, the risk of returns of product from distributors and resellers has declined. Accordingly, the estimate for future product returns was reduced by $250 million in the fourth quarter of fiscal 1999.

The Company changed the way it reports revenue and costs associated with product support, consulting, MSN Internet access, and training and certification of system integrators. Amounts received from customers for these activities have been classified as revenue in a manner more consistent with Microsoft's primary businesses. These amounts had been previously netted in sales and marketing expenses, except for MSN access fees, which had been netted in research and development expenses. Direct costs of these activities are classified as cost of revenue. Prior financial statements and disclosures have been reclassified for consistent presentation. Revenue from these activities was $578 million, $778 million, and $1.06 billion in 1997, 1998, and 1999.

Microsoft also made two changes related to the ratable recognition of revenue for a portion of its revenue for certain products. A new accounting rule that interprets American Institute of Certified Public Accountants (AICPA) Statement of Position (SOP) 97-2, *Software Revenue Recognition,* requires companies to use the average sales price of each undelivered element of software arrangements. Prior authoritative guidance allowed a comparison of the total price differential between a licensed product sold through different channels of distribution to derive the value of undelivered elements offered to customers acquiring product from one channel but not the other. Upon adoption of this new rule in the fourth quarter of fiscal 1999, the percentages of the total arrangement treated as unearned decreased. This change in the timing of revenue recognition reduced the amount of Microsoft Windows and Microsoft Office sales treated as unearned and increased the amount of revenue recognized upon shipment. Additionally, as part of the Company's long range planning process and a review of product shipment cycles, it was determined that the life cycle of Windows should be extended from two years to three years. The net impact of these changes was to increase reported revenue $80 million in the fourth quarter of 1999.

BUSINESS DIVISIONS > Microsoft has three major segments: Windows Platforms; Productivity Applications and Developer; and Consumer, Commerce, and Other.

> WINDOWS PLATFORMS revenue was $4.92 billion, $6.28 billion, and $8.50 billion in 1997, 1998, and 1999. Platform revenue is primarily licenses of PC operating systems and business and enterprise server systems with client/server, Internet, and intranet architectures.

The Company's principal PC operating systems are Windows 95, Windows 98, and Windows NT® Workstation. Windows 95 was released in August 1995, while its successor, Windows 98, became available at the end of fiscal 1998. Windows NT Workstation version 4.0 was released in fiscal 1997. Although the growth rate of new PC shipments slowed, PC operating systems contributed to revenue growth as shipments of new PCs preinstalled with such systems increased during the three-year period. Additionally, increased penetration of the higher value Windows NT Workstation led to growth in all three years.

WINDOWS PLATFORMS REVENUE

In billions

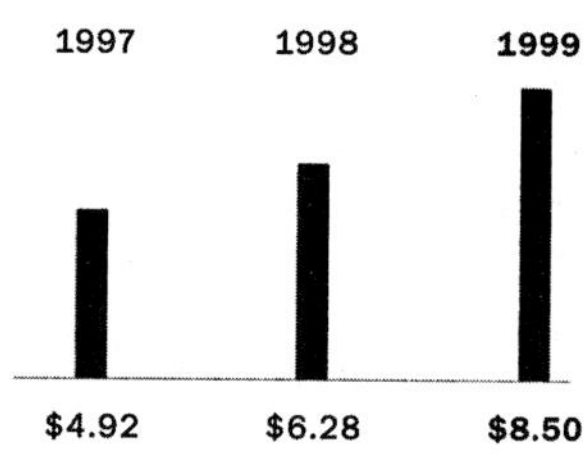

Windows NT Server is a comprehensive business and enterprise server operating system, combining application, file and print, communication, and Web services. Windows NT Server version 4.0 was released in fiscal 1997. Revenue from Windows NT Server increased strongly during each of the three years due to greater corporate demand, particularly for intranet computing solutions.

> PRODUCTIVITY APPLICATIONS AND DEVELOPER revenue was $5.62 billion, $7.04 billion, and $8.82 billion in 1997, 1998, and 1999. Products include primarily desktop applications, server applications, and software developer tools.

Microsoft Office integrated suites, including the Standard, Small Business, Professional, and Premium Editions, are the Company's principal desktop applications and a key driver of revenue growth. Microsoft Office 97 was released in fiscal 1997 and Microsoft Office 2000 was released at the end of fiscal 1999. The primary programs in Microsoft Office are the word processor Microsoft Word, Microsoft Excel spreadsheet, and Microsoft Outlook® messaging and collaboration client. Various versions of Office, which are available for the Windows and Macintosh operating systems, also include Microsoft Access database management program, Microsoft PowerPoint® presentation graphics program, Microsoft FrontPage® Web site creation and management program, or other programs. Revenue from stand-alone versions of Microsoft Excel, Word, and PowerPoint continued to decrease as the sales mix shifted to integrated product suites.

PRODUCTIVITY APPLICATIONS AND DEVELOPER REVENUE

In billions

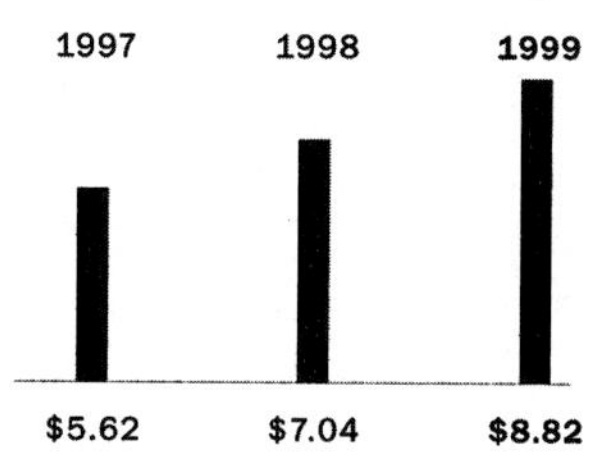

Server applications, based on Microsoft Windows NT Server, offer an enterprise-wide distributed client/server, Internet, and intranet environment. Products include Microsoft Exchange Server, Microsoft SQL Server, and other server applications in the Microsoft BackOffice family of products. Microsoft Exchange is an enterprise messaging and collaboration server while Microsoft SQL Server is a scalable database and data warehouse platform. Revenue from these products increased strongly over the three-year period, albeit with slowing growth rates in 1998 and 1999.

Independent software vendors, corporate developers, and solutions developers license tools such as the Microsoft Visual Studio® development system, which includes the Microsoft Visual Basic® development system, to develop software for the Windows operating systems and the Internet. Revenue from developer products increased moderately in 1997, was flat in 1998, and increased strongly in 1999.

Although revenue was not significant, preinstallations of Windows CE by OEMs on intelligent devices were strong in 1998 and 1999.

> CONSUMER, COMMERCE, AND OTHER revenue was $1.40 billion, $1.94 billion, and $2.43 billion in 1997, 1998, and 1999. This category of product revenue includes learning and entertainment software; PC input devices; training and certification fees; consulting; and the online services. The Company's Internet services include the MSN portal, MSN access, WebTV®, and vertical properties such as MSN Hotmail Web-based e-mail service, Expedia.com™ travel site, CarPoint car buying site, and MoneyCentral personal finance site.

CONSUMER, COMMERCE, AND OTHER REVENUE

In billions

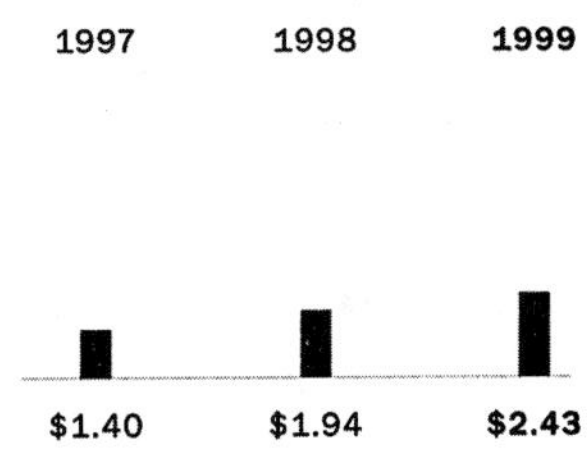

Learning and entertainment revenue was relatively flat in all three years. Mouse, gaming device, and keyboard sales increased in 1997 and 1998, but were steady in 1999. Training and certification fees from system integrators, along with consulting services to large enterprise customers and technology solution providers, increased strongly in all three years. Revenue from MSN Internet access fees and WebTV services increased due to higher subscriber levels. Advertising revenue, although relatively small in amount, increased exceptionally well in 1999 for the online portal and vertical properties.

SALES CHANNELS > Microsoft distributes its products primarily through OEM licenses, organizational licenses, and retail packaged products. OEM channel revenue represents license fees from original equipment manufacturers who preinstall Microsoft products, primarily on PCs. Microsoft has three major geographic sales and marketing organizations: the South Pacific and Americas Region; the Europe, Middle East, and Africa Region; and the Asia Region. Sales of organizational licenses and packaged products via these channels are primarily to and through distributors and resellers.

OEM channel revenue was $3.49 billion in 1997, $4.72 billion in 1998, and $6.40 billion in 1999. The primary source of OEM revenue is the licensing of desktop operating systems, and OEM revenue is highly dependent on PC shipment volume. Growth was also enhanced by increased penetration of higher-value Windows NT Workstation licenses.

Revenue in the South Pacific and Americas Region was $4.39 billion, $5.57 billion, and $7.25 billion in 1997, 1998, and 1999. Revenue in the Europe, Middle East, and Africa Region was $2.77 billion, $3.50 billion, and $4.33 billion for the three years. Growth rates have been lower in Europe than in other geographic areas due to higher existing market shares and a faster shift to licensing programs. Asia Region revenue was $1.29 billion in 1997, $1.48 billion in 1998, and $1.78 billion in 1999. After strong growth in prior years, revenue was relatively flat in Japan and Southeast Asia in 1998 and the first half of fiscal 1999 due to economic issues and weak currencies.

The Company's operating results are affected by foreign exchange rates. Approximately 32%, 32%, and 29% of the Company's revenue was collected in foreign currencies during 1997, 1998, and 1999. Since a portion of local currency revenue is hedged and much of the Company's international manufacturing costs and operating expenses are also incurred in local currencies, the impact of exchange rates is partially mitigated.

OPERATING EXPENSES

> Microsoft encourages broad-based employee ownership of Microsoft stock through an employee stock option (ESO) program in which most employees are eligible to participate. Historically, exercise prices of grants of ESOs were struck at the lowest price in the 30 days following July 1 for annual grants and the 30 days after the start date for new employees. In connection with this practice, which is no longer employed, a charge of $217 million was recorded in the fourth quarter for fiscal 1999 compensation expense, calculated under the provisions of Accounting Principles Board Opinion 25 (APB 25). Charges related to ESO compensation were reflected in 1999 operating expenses as follows (in millions):

Cost of revenue	**$ 44**
Research and development	**105**
Sales and marketing	**46**
General and administrative	**22**
Total	**$217**

> COST OF REVENUE Cost of revenue as a percent of revenue was 18.2% in 1997, 16.1% in 1998, and 14.3% in 1999. The percentage decreases resulted primarily from the trend in mix shift to OEM and organizational licenses. The decrease was also due to the shifts in mix to CD-ROMs (which carry lower cost of goods than disks) and higher-margin Windows NT Server, other servers, and client access licenses in the BackOffice product family. Additionally, cost of revenue in 1999 was positively impacted by a reduction in estimates of obsolete inventory and other manufacturing costs of $67 million. As discussed above, the Company's business model continues to evolve toward licensing from sales of packaged products through distribution channels. Consequently, risks associated with manufacturing and holding physical product have declined.

> RESEARCH AND DEVELOPMENT Microsoft continued to invest heavily in the future by funding research and development (R&D). Expense increases in 1997, 1998, and 1999 resulted primarily from development staff headcount growth in many areas, particularly Windows platforms, including PC operating systems, servers, and Internet and intranet technologies. R&D costs also increased for productivity applications, development tools, and online services.

In 1998, the Company acquired WebTV Networks, Inc., an online service that enables consumers to experience the Internet through their televisions via set-top terminals. Microsoft paid $425 million in stock and cash. The accompanying income statement reflects a one-time write-off of in-process technologies under development by WebTV Networks of $296 million.

> SALES AND MARKETING The increase in the absolute dollar amount of sales and marketing expenses in the three-year period was due primarily to expanded product-specific marketing programs, such as Office 97 in 1997, Windows 98 in 1998, and Office 2000 in 1999. Sales and marketing costs as a percentage of revenue decreased primarily due to moderate headcount growth. Microsoft brand advertising expenses rose slightly in 1998, but declined in 1999.

> GENERAL AND ADMINISTRATIVE Increases in general and administrative expenses were attributable to higher legal fees, litigation costs, and growth in the number of people and computer systems necessary to support overall increases in the scope of the Company's operations.

> OTHER EXPENSES Other expenses include the recognition of Microsoft's share of joint venture activities, including DreamWorks Interactive and the MSNBC entities.

INVESTMENT INCOME, GAIN ON SALE, AND INCOME TAXES

> Investment income increased primarily as a result of a larger investment portfolio generated by cash from operations in 1997, 1998, and 1999, coupled with realized gains from the sale of certain bond and equity securities in 1999.

In fiscal 1999, Microsoft sold its Softimage, Inc. subsidiary to Avid Technology, Inc. for a pretax gain of $160 million.

The effective income tax rate was 35.0% in 1997. The effective income tax rate increased to 36.9% in 1998 due to the nondeductible write-off of WebTV in-process technologies. Excluding the impact of the gain on the sale of Softimage, Inc., the effective tax rate for fiscal 1999 was 35.0%.

NET INCOME

> Net income as a percent of revenue increased in 1997, 1998, and 1999 due primarily to the lower relative cost of revenue and sales and marketing expenses, combined with greater investment income.

FINANCIAL CONDITION

> The Company's cash and short-term investment portfolio totaled $17.24 billion at June 30, 1999. The portfolio is diversified among security types, industries, and individual issuers. Microsoft's investments are generally liquid and investment grade. The portfolio is invested predominantly in U.S. dollar denominated securities, but also includes foreign currency positions in anticipation of continued international expansion. The portfolio is primarily invested in short-term securities to minimize interest rate risk and facilitate rapid deployment in the event of immediate cash needs.

Microsoft also invests in equities, primarily strategic technology companies. The Company has made large-scale investments in access providers, including cable, telephony, and wireless communications companies. During 1999, the Company purchased $5.0 billion of AT&T convertible preferred securities and warrants, $600 million of Nextel Communications, Inc. common stock, $500 million of NTL, Inc. convertible preferred stock, $330 million of United Pan-Europe Communications common stock, and $200 million of Qwest Communications International Inc. common stock. In connection with AT&T's proposed merger with MediaOne Group, Inc., the Company agreed to acquire MediaOne's interest in Telewest Communications plc, a leading provider of cable television and residential and business cable telephony services in the United Kingdom, subject to certain regulatory approvals and other conditions. During 1997, Microsoft purchased $1.0 billion of Special Class A common stock and convertible preferred stock of Comcast Corporation. Microsoft also owns an interest in MCI WorldCom, Inc.

Microsoft and National Broadcasting Company (NBC) operate two MSNBC joint ventures: a 24-hour cable news and information channel, and an interactive online news service. Microsoft is paying $220 million over a five-year period that ends in 2001 for its interest in the cable venture and one-half of the operational funding of both joint ventures. Microsoft guarantees a portion of MSNBC debt.

Microsoft has no material long-term debt and has $100 million of standby multicurrency lines of credit to support foreign currency hedging and cash management. Stockholders' equity at June 30, 1999 was $28.44 billion.

Microsoft will continue to invest in sales, marketing, and product support infrastructure. Additionally, research and development activities will include investments in existing and advanced areas of technology, including using cash to acquire technology. Additions to property and equipment will continue, including new facilities and computer systems for R&D, sales and marketing, support, and administrative staff. Commitments for constructing new buildings were $275 million on June 30, 1999. Cash will also be used to fund ventures and other strategic opportunities.

In addition, cash will be used to repurchase common stock to provide shares for employee stock option and purchase plans. The buyback program has not kept pace with employee stock option grants or exercises. Beginning in fiscal 1990, Microsoft has repurchased 710 million common shares while 1.79 billion shares were issued under the Company's employee stock option and purchase plans. The market value of all outstanding stock options was $69 billion as of June 30, 1999. Microsoft enhances its repurchase program by selling put warrants. During December 1996, Microsoft issued 12.5 million shares of 2.75% convertible exchangeable preferred stock. Net proceeds of $980 million were used to repurchase common shares. In December 1999, each preferred share is convertible into common shares or an equivalent amount of cash determined by a formula that provides a floor price of $79.875 and a cap of $102.24 per preferred share, equivalent to $19.97 and $25.56 per common share.

Management believes existing cash and short-term investments together with funds generated from operations will be sufficient to meet operating requirements for the next 12 months. The Company's cash and short-term investments are available for strategic investments, mergers and acquisitions, other potential large-scale cash needs that may arise, and to fund an increased stock buyback program over historical levels to reduce the dilutive impact of the Company's employee stock option and purchase programs.

Microsoft has not paid cash dividends on its common stock. The preferred stock pays $2.196 per annum per share.

ISSUES AND UNCERTAINTIES

> While Microsoft management is optimistic about the Company's long-term prospects, the following issues and uncertainties, among others, should be considered in evaluating its growth outlook.

> RAPID TECHNOLOGICAL CHANGE AND COMPETITION   Rapid change, uncertainty due to new and emerging technologies, and fierce competition characterize the PC software industry. The pace of change continues to accelerate, including "open source" software, new computing devices, new microprocessor architectures, the Internet, and Web-based computing models.

> FUTURE INITIATIVES   The Company continues to expand its efforts to provide and support mission-critical systems to large enterprises. Microsoft is also developing a Windows Web-centric platform and simpler and new natural interfaces for PC users. Additionally, Microsoft is committed to providing technologies, operating systems, and online services for all types of computing devices, including PCs, televisions, and intelligent appliances. Future revenue from these initiatives may not duplicate historical revenue growth rates.

> PC GROWTH RATES   The underlying PC unit growth rate and percentage of new PCs acquired as replacement units directly impact the Company's software revenue growth. Additionally, inexpensive PCs and specialty devices create less demand for Microsoft software than traditional PCs. The PC shipment growth rate may continue to decrease, the replacement rate may continue to increase, and limited-use PC growth may increase, reducing future software revenue opportunity.

> PRODUCT SHIP SCHEDULES Potential delays in new product releases, including seminal products such as Windows 2000, could dampen revenue growth rates and cause operational inefficiencies that impact manufacturing and distribution logistics and relationships with customers, OEMs, and independent software vendors.

> CUSTOMER ACCEPTANCE While the Company performs extensive usability and beta testing of new products, user acceptance and corporate penetration rates ultimately dictate the success of development and marketing efforts.

> PRICES Future product prices may decrease from historical levels, depending on competitive market and cost factors. European and Asian software prices vary by country and are generally higher than in the United States to cover localization costs and higher costs of distribution. Increased global license agreements, European monetary unification, or other factors could erode such price uplifts in the future.

> SATURATION Product upgrades, which enable users to upgrade from earlier versions of the Company's products or from competitors' products, have lower prices and margins than new products. Also, penetration of the Company's desktop applications into large organizations is becoming saturated. These factors are likely to depress future desktop applications revenue growth.

> ORGANIZATIONAL LICENSES Average revenue per unit from organizational license programs is lower than average revenue per unit from retail versions shipped through the finished goods channels. Unit sales under licensing programs may continue to increase.

> EARNINGS PROCESS An increasingly higher percentage of the Company's revenue is subject to ratable recognition, which impacts the timing of revenue and earnings recognition. This policy may be required for additional products, depending on specific license terms and conditions. Also, maintenance and other subscription programs may continue to increase in popularity, particularly with organizations.

> CHANNEL MIX Average revenue per license is lower from OEM licenses than from retail versions, reflecting the relatively lower direct costs of operations in the OEM channel. An increasingly higher percentage of revenue was achieved through the OEM channel during 1998 and 1999.

> COST OF REVENUE Decreases in cost of revenue as a percentage of revenue in 1998 and 1999 were due to general shifts from packaged products to OEM and organizational licenses, from lower-margin products to higher-margin products, and from disks to CD-ROMs. These shifts may not continue. Direct costs of product support; services such as consulting and training and certification of system integrators; and online operations comprise the majority of cost of revenue and are not likely to decrease. The trend of declining cost of revenue as a percentage of revenue is unlikely to continue in 2000.

> EMPLOYEE COMPENSATION Microsoft employees currently receive salaries, incentive bonuses, other benefits, and stock options. Fiscal 2000 salaries will be enhanced, with the mid-point salary range raised from the 50th to the 65th percentile of competitive positions. Additionally, new government regulations, poor stock price performance, or other factors could diminish the value of the option program to current and prospective employees and force the Company into more of a cash compensation model. Had the Company paid employees in cash the equivalent of the Black-Scholes value of options vested in 1997, 1998, and 1999, the incremental pretax expense would have been approximately $620 million, $850 million, and $1.10 billion.

> LONG-TERM R&D INVESTMENT CYCLE Developing and localizing software is expensive, and the investment in product development often involves a long payback cycle. The Company plans to continue significant investments in software research and development, including online initiatives. Significant revenue from these product opportunities is not anticipated for a number of years. Total spending for R&D in 2000 will increase over spending in 1999.

> SALES AND MARKETING INVESTMENTS The Company's plans for 2000 include accelerated investments in its sales groups, customer satisfaction, and marketing activities.

> INTERNATIONAL OPERATIONS Much of the Company's operations are conducted outside of the United States, and a large percentage of sales, costs of manufacturing, and marketing is transacted in local currencies. As a result, the Company's international results of operations are subject to local economic environments and foreign exchange rate fluctuations.

> MARKET RISK The Company is exposed to foreign currency, interest rate, and equity price risks. A portion of these risks is hedged, but fluctuations could impact the Company's results of operations and financial position. The Company hedges the exposure of accounts receivable and a portion of anticipated revenue to foreign currency fluctuations, primarily with option contracts. The Company monitors its foreign currency exposures daily to ensure the overall effectiveness of its foreign currency hedge positions. Principal currencies hedged include the Japanese yen, British pound, German mark, French franc, and Canadian dollar. Fixed income securities are subject to interest rate risk. The portfolio is diversified and consists primarily of investment grade securities to minimize credit risk. The Company routinely hedges its exposure to interest rate risk with options in the event of a catastrophic increase in interest rates. Many securities held in the Company's equity and other investments portfolio are subject to equity price risk. The Company hedges its equity price risk on certain highly volatile equity securities with options.

The Company used a value-at-risk (VAR) model to estimate and quantify its market risks. The VAR model is not intended to represent actual losses in fair value, but is used as a risk estimation and management tool. Assumptions applied to the VAR model at June 30, 1999 include the following: normal market conditions; Monte Carlo modeling with 10,000 simulated market price paths; a 97.5% confidence interval; and a 20-day estimated loss in fair value for each market risk category. Accordingly, 97.5% of the time the estimated 20-day loss in fair value would be nominal for foreign currency denominated investments and accounts receivable, and would not exceed $95 million for interest-sensitive investments or $1.38 billion for equity securities.

Previously, the Company used a sensitivity analysis to estimate interest rate and equity price risk. A 10% increase in interest rates would have reduced the carrying value of interest-sensitive securities by $128 million and $101 million at June 30, 1998 and 1999. A 10% decrease in market values would have reduced the carrying value of the Company's equity securities by $300 million and $1.37 billion at June 30, 1998 and 1999.

> INTELLECTUAL PROPERTY RIGHTS Microsoft diligently defends its intellectual property rights, but unlicensed copying of software represents a loss of revenue to the Company. While this adversely affects U.S. revenue, revenue loss is even more significant outside of the United States, particularly in countries where laws are less protective of intellectual property rights. Throughout the world, Microsoft actively educates consumers on the benefits of licensing genuine products and educates lawmakers on the advantages of a business climate where intellectual property rights are protected. However, continued efforts may not affect revenue positively.

> LITIGATION Litigation regarding intellectual property rights, patents, and copyrights occurs in the PC software industry. In addition, there are government regulation and investigation risks along with other general corporate legal risks.

> YEAR 2000 The Year 2000 presents potential concerns for business and consumer computing. In addition to the well-known calculation problems with the use of 2-digit date formats as the year changes from 1999 to 2000, the Year 2000 is a special case leap year and in many organizations using older technology, dates were used for special programmatic functions. The problem exists for many kinds of software and hardware, including mainframes, mini computers, PCs, and embedded systems. The consequences of this issue may include systems failures and business process interruption.

Microsoft has tested more than 3,000 versions/languages of its products. The vast majority of these tested products are Year 2000 compliant, as defined by Microsoft. There are a small number of older products that are identified as being non-compliant, and Microsoft will provide recommendations regarding these products. Not all versions of products or all products will be tested. All Year 2000 software updates, resources, and tools are available to customers at no charge from the Microsoft Year 2000 Portal Page or Microsoft Year 2000 Resource CD.

Current information needed to evaluate the impact of the Year 2000 on organizational and home computing environments is available at the Microsoft Year 2000 Portal Page (www.microsoft.com/year2000) and the Microsoft Year 2000 Resource CD, which is released on a quarterly basis. The Web site and Microsoft Year 2000 Resource CD detail specific Year 2000 information concerning Microsoft products and technologies for large organizations. The detailed information available on the Web site and Microsoft Year 2000 Resource CD is presented to assist information technology (IT) professionals in planning their transition to the Year 2000. The Microsoft Year 2000 Portal Page also contains information for small business and home PC users, including in-depth product information, answers to frequently asked questions, and links to the other Year 2000 sites.

Variability of definitions of "compliance" with the Year 2000 and of different combinations of software, firmware, and hardware will likely lead to lawsuits against the Company. The outcome of such lawsuits and the impact on the Company are not estimable at this time.

The Year 2000 issue also affects the Company's internal systems, including IT and non-IT systems. Microsoft has assessed the readiness of its mission-critical systems for handling the Year 2000. Although testing and remediation of all systems have not been completed, management currently believes that all mission-critical systems will be compliant by the Year 2000 and that the cost to address the issues is not material. Nevertheless, Microsoft is creating contingency plans for certain internal systems.

Microsoft is addressing the effect this issue will have on its third-party supply chain and has undertaken steps to formulate a system of working with key third parties to understand their ability to continue providing services and products through the change to 2000. Microsoft is working directly with its key vendors, distributors, and resellers to avoid material business interruptions in 2000. Contingency plans are being developed where practicable for these key third parties.

Resolving Year 2000 issues is a worldwide phenomenon that is absorbing a substantial portion of IT budgets and attention. Certain industry analysts believe the Year 2000 issue will accelerate the trend toward distributed PC-based systems from mainframe systems, while others believe a majority of IT resources will be devoted to fixing older mainframe software in lieu of large-scale transitions to systems based on software such as that developed by Microsoft. The impact of the Year 2000 on future Microsoft revenue is difficult to discern, but it is a risk to be considered in evaluating the future growth of the Company.

> FUTURE GROWTH RATE The revenue growth rate in 2000 may not approach the level attained in prior years. As discussed previously, operating expenses are expected to increase in 2000. Because of the fixed nature of a significant portion of such expenses, coupled with the possibility of slower revenue growth, operating margins in 2000 may decrease from those in 1999.

CASH FLOWS STATEMENTS

msft In millions

Year Ended June 30	1997	1998	1999
Operations			
Net income	$ 3,454	$ 4,490	$ 7,785
Depreciation and amortization	557	1,024	1,010
Write-off of acquired in-process technology	-	296	-
Gain on sale of Softimage, Inc.	-	-	(160)
Unearned revenue	1,601	3,268	5,877
Recognition of unearned revenue from prior periods	(743)	(1,798)	(4,526)
Other current liabilities	321	208	966
Accounts receivable	(336)	(520)	(687)
Other current assets	(165)	(88)	(235)
Net cash from operations	4,689	6,880	10,030
Financing			
Common stock issued	744	959	1,350
Common stock repurchased	(3,101)	(2,468)	(2,950)
Put warrant proceeds	95	538	766
Preferred stock issued	980	-	-
Preferred stock dividends	(15)	(28)	(28)
Stock option income tax benefits	796	1,553	3,107
Net cash from (used for) financing	(501)	554	2,245
Investing			
Additions to property and equipment	(499)	(656)	(583)
Cash portion of WebTV purchase price	-	(190)	-
Cash proceeds from sale of Softimage, Inc.	-	-	79
Purchases of investments	(18,216)	(19,114)	(36,441)
Maturities of investments	1,874	1,890	4,674
Sales of investments	13,752	10,798	21,080
Net cash used for investing	(3,089)	(7,272)	(11,191)
Net change in cash and equivalents	1,099	162	1,084
Effect of exchange rates on cash and equivalents	6	(29)	52
Cash and equivalents, beginning of year	2,601	3,706	3,839
Cash and equivalents, end of year	3,706	3,839	4,975
Short-term investments	5,260	10,088	12,261
Cash and short-term investments	$ 8,966	$ 13,927	$ 17,236

See accompanying notes.

BALANCE SHEETS

msft In millions

June 30	1998	1999
Assets		
Current assets:		
Cash and short-term investments	$13,927	**$17,236**
Accounts receivable	1,460	**2,245**
Other	502	**752**
Total current assets	15,889	**20,233**
Property and equipment	1,505	**1,611**
Equity and other investments	4,703	**14,372**
Other assets	260	**940**
Total assets	$22,357	**$37,156**
Liabilities and stockholders' equity		
Current liabilities:		
Accounts payable	$ 759	**$ 874**
Accrued compensation	359	**396**
Income taxes payable	915	**1,607**
Unearned revenue	2,888	**4,239**
Other	809	**1,602**
Total current liabilities	5,730	**8,718**
Commitments and contingencies		
Stockholders' equity:		
Convertible preferred stock – shares authorized 100; shares issued and outstanding 13	980	**980**
Common stock and paid-in capital – shares authorized 12,000; shares issued and outstanding 4,940 and 5,109	8,025	**13,844**
Retained earnings, including other comprehensive income of $666 and $1,787	7,622	**13,614**
Total stockholders' equity	16,627	**28,438**
Total liabilities and stockholders' equity	$22,357	**$37,156**

See accompanying notes.

STOCKHOLDERS' EQUITY STATEMENTS

msft In millions

Year Ended June 30	1997	1998	1999
Convertible preferred stock			
Balance, beginning of year	-	$ 980	$ 980
Convertible preferred stock issued	$ 980	-	-
Balance, end of year	980	980	980
Common stock and paid-in capital			
Balance, beginning of year	2,924	4,509	8,025
Common stock issued	744	1,262	2,338
Common stock repurchased	(91)	(165)	(64)
Structured repurchases price differential	-	328	(328)
Proceeds from sale of put warrants	95	538	766
Reclassification of put warrant obligation	45	-	-
Stock option income tax benefits	792	1,553	3,107
Balance, end of year	4,509	8,025	13,844
Retained earnings			
Balance, beginning of year	3,984	5,288	7,622
Net income	3,454	4,490	7,785
Other comprehensive income:			
Net unrealized investment gains	280	627	1,052
Translation adjustments and other	5	(124)	69
Comprehensive income	3,739	4,993	8,906
Preferred stock dividends	(15)	(28)	(28)
Common stock repurchased	(3,010)	(2,631)	(2,886)
Reclassification of put warrant obligation	590	-	-
Balance, end of year	5,288	7,622	13,614
Total stockholders' equity	$10,777	$16,627	$28,438

See accompanying notes.

NOTES TO FINANCIAL STATEMENTS

msft ACCOUNTING POLICIES

> ACCOUNTING PRINCIPLES   The financial statements and accompanying notes are prepared in accordance with generally accepted accounting principles.

> PRINCIPLES OF CONSOLIDATION   The financial statements include the accounts of Microsoft and its subsidiaries. Significant intercompany transactions and balances have been eliminated. Investments in 50% owned joint ventures are accounted for using the equity method; the Company's share of joint ventures' activities is reflected in other expenses.

> ESTIMATES AND ASSUMPTIONS   Preparing financial statements requires management to make estimates and assumptions that affect the reported amounts of assets, liabilities, revenue, and expenses. Examples include provisions for returns and bad debts and the length of product life cycles and buildings' lives. Actual results may differ from these estimates.

> FOREIGN CURRENCIES   Assets and liabilities recorded in foreign currencies are translated at the exchange rate on the balance sheet date. Translation adjustments resulting from this process are charged or credited to other comprehensive income. Revenue and expenses are translated at average rates of exchange prevailing during the year. Gains and losses on foreign currency transactions are included in other expenses.

> REVENUE RECOGNITION   Revenue is recognized when earned. The Company's revenue recognition policies are in compliance with all applicable accounting regulations, including American Institute of Certified Public Accountants (AICPA) Statement of Position (SOP) 97-2, *Software Revenue Recognition,* and SOP 98-9, *Modification of SOP 97-2, With Respect to Certain Transactions.* Revenue from products licensed to original equipment manufacturers is recorded when OEMs ship licensed products while revenue from certain license programs is recorded when the software has been delivered and the customer is invoiced. Revenue from packaged product sales to and through distributors and resellers is recorded when related products are shipped. Maintenance and subscription revenue is recognized ratably over the contract period. Revenue attributable to undelivered elements, including technical support and Internet browser technologies, is based on the average sales price of those elements and is recognized ratably on a straight-line basis over the product's life cycle. When the revenue recognition criteria required for distributor and reseller arrangements are not met, revenue is recognized as payments are received. Costs related to insignificant obligations, which include telephone support for certain products, are accrued. Provisions are recorded for returns and bad debts.

> COST OF REVENUE   Cost of revenue includes direct costs to produce and distribute product and direct costs to provide online services, consulting, product support, and training and certification of system integrators.

> RESEARCH AND DEVELOPMENT   Research and development costs are expensed as incurred. Statement of Financial Accounting Standards (SFAS) 86, *Accounting for the Costs of Computer Software to Be Sold, Leased, or Otherwise Marketed,* does not materially affect the Company.

> INCOME TAXES   Income tax expense includes U.S. and international income taxes, plus the provision for U.S. taxes on undistributed earnings of international subsidiaries. Certain items of income and expense are not reported in tax returns and financial statements in the same year. The tax effect of this difference is reported as deferred income taxes. Tax credits are accounted for as a reduction of tax expense in the year in which the credits reduce taxes payable.

NOTES continued

> STOCK SPLIT During March 1999, outstanding shares of common stock were split two-for-one. All share and per share amounts have been restated.

> FINANCIAL INSTRUMENTS The Company considers all liquid interest-earning investments with a maturity of three months or less at the date of purchase to be cash equivalents. Short-term investments generally mature between three months and six years from the purchase date. All cash and short-term investments are classified as available for sale and are recorded at market using the specific identification method; unrealized gains and losses are reflected in other comprehensive income. Cost approximates market for all classifications of cash and short-term investments; realized and unrealized gains and losses were not material.

Equity and other investments include debt and equity instruments. Debt securities and publicly traded equity securities are classified as available for sale and are recorded at market using the specific identification method. Unrealized gains and losses are reflected in other comprehensive income. All other investments, excluding joint venture arrangements, are recorded at cost.

Derivative financial instruments are used to hedge certain investments, international revenue, accounts receivable, and interest rate risks, and are, therefore, held primarily for purposes other than trading. These instruments may involve elements of credit and market risk in excess of the amounts recognized in the financial statements. The Company monitors its positions and the credit quality of counter parties, consisting primarily of major financial institutions, and does not anticipate nonperformance by any counter party.

During June 1999, the Financial Accounting Standards Board (FASB) issued SFAS 137, *Accounting for Derivative Instruments and Hedging Activities - Deferral of the Effective Date of FASB Statement 133*. The Statement defers the effective date of SFAS 133 to fiscal 2001. Management is evaluating SFAS 133 and does not believe that adoption of the Statement will have a material impact on its financial statements.

> PROPERTY AND EQUIPMENT Property and equipment is stated at cost and depreciated using the straight-line method over the shorter of the estimated life of the asset or the lease term, ranging from one to 15 years.

> RECLASSIFICATIONS The Company changed the way it reports revenue and costs associated with product support, consulting, MSN Internet access, and certification and training of system integrators. Amounts received from customers for these activities have been classified as revenue in a manner more consistent with Microsoft's primary businesses. Direct costs of these activities are classified as cost of revenue. Prior financial statements have been reclassified for consistent presentation. Certain other reclassifications have also been made for consistent presentation.

UNEARNED REVENUE

> A portion of Microsoft's revenue is earned ratably over the product life cycle or, in the case of subscriptions, over the period of the license agreement.

End users receive certain elements of the Company's products over a period of time. These elements include browser technologies and technical support. Consequently, Microsoft's earned revenue reflects the recognition of the fair value of these elements over the product's life cycle. Upon adoption of SOP 98-9 during the fourth quarter of fiscal 1999, the Company was required to change the methodology

NOTES continued

of attributing the fair value to undelivered elements. The percentages of undelivered elements in relation to the total arrangement decreased, reducing the amount of Windows and Office revenue treated as unearned, and increasing the amount of revenue recognized upon shipment. The percentage of revenue recognized ratably decreased from a range of 20% to 35% to a range of approximately 15% to 25% of Windows desktop operating systems. For desktop applications, the percentage decreased from approximately 20% to a range of approximately 10% to 20%. The ranges depend on the terms and conditions of the license and prices of the elements. The impact on fiscal 1999 was to increase reported revenue $170 million. In addition, the Company extended the life cycle of Windows from two to three years based upon management's review of product shipment cycles. The impact on fiscal 1999 was to decrease reported revenue $90 million. Product life cycles are currently estimated at 18 months for desktop applications. The Company also sells subscriptions to certain products via maintenance and certain organizational license agreements. At June 30, 1999, Windows platforms products unearned revenue was $2.17 billion and unearned revenue associated with productivity applications and developer products totaled $1.96 billion. Unearned revenue for other miscellaneous programs totaled $116 million at June 30, 1999.

FINANCIAL RISKS

> The Company's cash and short-term investment portfolio is diversified and consists primarily of investment grade securities. Investments are held with high-quality financial institutions, government and government agencies, and corporations, thereby reducing credit risk concentrations. Interest rate fluctuations impact the carrying value of the portfolio. The Company routinely hedges the portfolio's return with options in the event of a catastrophic increase in interest rates. At June 30, 1999, the notional amount of the options outstanding was $4.0 billion. The fair value and premiums paid for the options were not material. Much of the Company's equity security portfolio is highly volatile, so certain positions are hedged.

Finished goods sales to international customers in Europe, Japan, Canada, and Australia are primarily billed in local currencies. Payment cycles are relatively short, generally less than 90 days. Certain international manufacturing and operational costs are disbursed in local currencies. Local currency cash balances in excess of short-term operating needs are generally converted into U.S. dollar cash and short-term investments on receipt. Although foreign exchange rate fluctuations generally do not create a risk of material balance sheet gains or losses, the Company hedges a portion of accounts receivable balances denominated in local currencies, primarily with purchased options. At June 30, 1999, the notional amount of options outstanding was $662 million. The fair value and premiums paid for the options were not material.

Foreign exchange rates affect the translated results of operations of the Company's foreign subsidiaries. The Company hedges a portion of planned international revenue with purchased options. The notional amount of the options outstanding at June 30, 1999 was $2.25 billion. The fair value and premiums paid for the options were not material.

At June 30, 1998 and 1999, approximately 40% and 50% of accounts receivable represented amounts due from 10 customers. One customer accounted for approximately 12%, 8%, and 11% of revenue in 1997, 1998, and 1999.

Microsoft lends certain fixed income and equity securities to enhance investment income. Adequate collateral and/or security interest is determined based upon the underlying security and the credit worthiness of the borrower.

NOTES continued (in millions)

CASH AND SHORT-TERM INVESTMENTS

June 30	1998	1999
Cash and equivalents:		
Cash	$ 195	$ 635
Commercial paper	2,771	3,805
Certificates of deposit	419	522
Money market preferreds	454	13
Cash and equivalents	3,839	4,975
Short-term investments:		
Commercial paper	868	1,026
U.S. government and agency securities	3,511	3,592
Corporate notes and bonds	3,998	6,996
Municipal securities	1,361	247
Certificates of deposit	350	400
Short-term investments	10,088	12,261
Cash and short-term investments	$13,927	$17,236

PROPERTY AND EQUIPMENT

June 30	1998	1999
Land	$ 183	$ 158
Buildings	1,259	1,347
Computer equipment	1,182	1,433
Other	428	578
Property and equipment - at cost	3,052	3,516
Accumulated depreciation	(1,547)	(1,905)
Property and equipment - net	$ 1,505	$ 1,611

During 1997, 1998, and 1999, depreciation expense, of which the majority related to computer equipment, was $353 million, $528 million, and $483 million; disposals were not material.

NOTES continued (in millions)

EQUITY AND OTHER INVESTMENTS

June 30, 1999	Cost Basis	Net Unrealized Gains	Recorded Basis
Debt securities recorded at market, maturing:			
Within one year	$ 682	$ 8	$ 690
Between 10 and 15 years	533	(3)	530
Beyond 15 years (AT&T)	4,731	347	5,078
Debt securities recorded at market	5,946	352	6,298
Equity securities recorded at market:			
Comcast Corporation common stock	500	1,394	1,894
MCI Worldcom, Inc. common stock	14	1,088	1,102
Other	849	1,102	1,951
Unrealized hedge loss	-	(785)	(785)
Equity securities recorded at market	1,363	2,799	4,162
Equity securities and instruments recorded at cost:			
Nextel Communications, Inc. common stock	600	-	600
Comcast Corporation convertible preferred stock	555	-	555
NTL, Inc. convertible preferred stock	511	-	511
Other	2,179	-	2,179
Equity securities and instruments recorded at cost	3,845	-	3,845
Other investments	67	-	67
Equity and other investments	$11,221	$3,151	$14,372

Debt securities include corporate and government notes and bonds and derivative securities. Debt securities maturing beyond 15 years are composed entirely of AT&T 5% convertible preferred debt with a contractual maturity of 30 years. The debt is convertible into AT&T common stock on or after December 1, 2000, or may be redeemed by AT&T upon satisfaction of certain conditions on or after June 1, 2002. Unrealized gains on equity securities recorded at market were $1.4 billion on June 30, 1998. Equity securities and instruments recorded at cost include primarily preferred stock, common stock, and warrants that are restricted or not publicly traded. At June 30, 1998 and 1999, the estimated fair value of these investments was $2.4 billion and $6.1 billion, based on publicly available market information or other estimates determined by management. The Company hedges the risk of significant market declines on certain highly volatile equity securities with options. The options are recorded at market, consistent with the underlying equity securities. At June 30, 1999, the notional amount of the options outstanding was $2.1 billion; the fair value was $1.0 billion; and premiums paid for the options were not material. Realized gains and losses of equity and other investments in 1997 and 1998 were not material; realized gains were $623 million and losses were not material in 1999.

NOTES continued (in millions)

INCOME TAXES

> The provision for income taxes consisted of:

Year Ended June 30	1997	1998	1999
Current taxes:			
U.S. and state	$1,710	$2,518	**$4,027**
International	412	526	**281**
Current taxes	2,122	3,044	**4,308**
Deferred taxes	(262)	(417)	**(202)**
Provision for income taxes	$1,860	$2,627	**$4,106**

U.S. and international components of income before income taxes were:

Year Ended June 30	1997	1998	1999
U.S.	$3,775	$5,072	**$10,649**
International	1,539	2,045	**1,242**
Income before income taxes	$5,314	$7,117	**$11,891**

The effective income tax rate was 35.0% in 1997 and increased to 36.9% in 1998 due to the non-deductible write-off of WebTV in-process technologies. In 1999, the effective tax rate was 35.0%, excluding the impact of the gain on the sale of Softimage, Inc. The components of the differences between the U.S. statutory tax rate and the Company's effective tax rate were not significant.

Income taxes payable were:

June 30	1998	1999
Deferred income tax assets:		
Revenue items	$ 713	**$ 1,145**
Expense items	613	**648**
Deferred income tax assets	1,326	**1,793**
Deferred income tax liabilities:		
Unrealized gain on investments	(479)	**(1,046)**
International earnings	(373)	**(647)**
Other	(26)	**(16)**
Deferred income tax liabilities	(878)	**(1,709)**
Current income tax liabilities	(1,363)	**(1,691)**
Income taxes payable	$ (915)	**$(1,607)**

Income taxes have been settled with the Internal Revenue Service (IRS) for all years through 1989. The IRS has assessed taxes for 1990 and 1991, which the Company is contesting in U.S. Tax Court. The IRS is examining the Company's U.S. income tax returns for 1992 through 1994. Management believes any related adjustments that might be required will not be material to the financial statements. Income taxes paid were $1.1 billion in 1997, $1.1 billion in 1998, and $874 million in 1999.

NOTES continued (in millions)

CONVERTIBLE PREFERRED STOCK

> During 1996, Microsoft issued 12.5 million shares of 2.75% convertible exchangeable principal-protected preferred stock. Dividends are payable quarterly in arrears. Preferred stockholders have preference over common stockholders in dividends and liquidation rights. In December 1999, each preferred share is convertible into common shares or an equivalent amount of cash determined by a formula that provides a floor price of $79.875 and a cap of $102.24 per preferred share, equivalent to $19.97 and $25.56 per common share. Net proceeds of $980 million were used to repurchase common shares.

COMMON STOCK

> ISSUED AND OUTSTANDING Shares of common stock outstanding were as follows:

Year Ended June 30	1997	1998	**1999**
Balance, beginning of year	4,776	4,816	**4,940**
Issued	188	202	**213**
Repurchased	(148)	(78)	**(44)**
Balance, end of year	4,816	4,940	**5,109**

> REPURCHASE PROGRAM The Company repurchases its common stock in the open market to provide shares for issuing to employees under stock option and stock purchase plans. The Company's Board of Directors authorized continuation of this program in 2000.

During 1998, the Company executed two forward settlement structured repurchase agreements with an independent third party totaling 42 million shares of stock and paid cash for a portion of the purchase price. In 1999, the Company settled the agreements by returning 28 million shares of stock, based upon the stock price on the date of settlement. The timing and method of settlement were at the discretion of the Company. The differential between the cash paid and the price of Microsoft common stock on the date of the agreement was originally reflected in common stock and paid-in capital.

PUT WARRANTS

> To enhance its stock repurchase program, Microsoft sells put warrants to independent third parties. These put warrants entitle the holders to sell shares of Microsoft common stock to the Company on certain dates at specified prices. On June 30, 1999, 163 million warrants were outstanding with strike prices ranging from $59 to $65 per share. The put warrants expire between September 1999 and March 2002. The outstanding put warrants permit a net-share settlement at the Company's option and do not result in a put warrant liability on the balance sheet.

EMPLOYEE STOCK AND SAVINGS PLANS

> EMPLOYEE STOCK PURCHASE PLAN The Company has an employee stock purchase plan for all eligible employees. Under the plan, shares of the Company's common stock may be purchased at six-month intervals at 85% of the lower of the fair market value on the first or the last day of each six-month period. Employees may purchase shares having a value not exceeding 10% of their gross compensation during an offering period. During 1997, 1998, and 1999, employees purchased

NOTES continued (in millions, except per share amounts)

5.6 million, 4.4 million, and 2.7 million shares at average prices of $14.91, $27.21, and $52.59 per share. At June 30, 1999, 70.9 million shares were reserved for future issuance.

> SAVINGS PLAN The Company has a savings plan, which qualifies under Section 401(k) of the Internal Revenue Code. Participating employees may contribute up to 15% of their pretax salary, but not more than statutory limits. The Company contributes fifty cents for each dollar a participant contributes, with a maximum contribution of 3% of a participant's earnings. Matching contributions were $28 million, $39 million, and $49 million in 1997, 1998, and 1999.

> STOCK OPTION PLANS The Company has stock option plans for directors, officers, and employees, which provide for nonqualified and incentive stock options. Options granted prior to 1995 generally vest over four and one-half years and expire 10 years from the date of grant. Options granted during and after 1995 generally vest over four and one-half years and expire seven years from the date of grant, while certain options vest over seven and one-half years and expire after 10 years. At June 30, 1999, options for 406 million shares were vested and 998 million shares were available for future grants under the plans.

Stock options outstanding were as follows:

		Price per Share	
	Shares	Range	Weighted Average
Balance, June 30, 1996	952	$ 0.28 - $14.74	$ 5.52
Granted	220	13.83 - 29.80	14.58
Exercised	(180)	0.28 - 14.74	3.32
Canceled	(36)	4.25 - 24.29	9.71
Balance, June 30, 1997	956	0.56 - 29.80	7.86
Granted	138	16.56 - 43.63	31.28
Exercised	(176)	0.56 - 31.24	4.64
Canceled	(25)	4.25 - 41.94	14.69
Balance, June 30, 1998	893	0.56 - 43.63	11.94
Granted	**78**	**45.59 - 83.28**	**54.62**
Exercised	**(175)**	**0.56 - 53.63**	**6.29**
Canceled	**(30)**	**4.25 - 74.28**	**21.06**
Balance, June 30, 1999	**766**	**0.56 - 83.28**	**17.28**

For various price ranges, weighted average characteristics of outstanding stock options at June 30, 1999 were as follows:

	Outstanding Options			Exercisable Options	
Range of Exercise Prices	Shares	Remaining Life (Years)	Weighted Average Price	Shares	Weighted Average Price
$ 0.56 - $ 5.97	**242**	**2.9**	**$ 4.31**	**230**	**$ 4.24**
5.98 - 13.62	**158**	**3.9**	**10.85**	**89**	**10.62**
13.63 - 29.80	**173**	**4.7**	**14.92**	**66**	**14.67**
29.81 - 43.62	**117**	**5.5**	**32.06**	**21**	**31.83**
43.63 - 83.28	**76**	**6.2**	**55.04**	**-**	**-**

NOTES continued (in millions, except per share amounts)

The Company follows Accounting Principles Board Opinion 25, *Accounting for Stock Issued to Employees,* to account for stock option and employee stock purchase plans. Historically, exercise prices of grants of ESOs were struck at the lowest price in the 30 days following July 1 for annual grants and the 30 days after the start date for new employees. In connection with this practice, which is no longer employed, a charge of $217 million was recorded in the fourth quarter for fiscal 1999 compensation expense.

An alternative method of accounting for stock options is SFAS 123, *Accounting for Stock-Based Compensation.* Under SFAS 123, employee stock options are valued at grant date using the Black-Scholes valuation model, and compensation cost is recognized ratably over the vesting period. Had compensation cost for the Company's stock option and employee stock purchase plans been determined based on the Black-Scholes value at the grant dates for awards, pro forma income statements for 1997, 1998, and 1999 would have been as follows:

Year Ended June 30	1997		1998		**1999**	
	Reported	Pro forma	Reported	Pro forma	**Reported**	**Pro forma**
Revenue	$11,936	$11,936	$15,262	$15,262	**$19,747**	**$19,747**
Operating expenses:						
Cost of revenue	2,170	2,290	2,460	2,628	**2,814**	**3,024**
Research and development	1,863	2,168	2,601	3,023	**2,970**	**3,504**
Acquired in-process technology	–	–	296	296	**–**	**–**
Sales and marketing	2,411	2,539	2,828	3,003	**3,231**	**3,448**
General and administrative	362	424	433	520	**689**	**822**
Other expenses	259	259	230	230	**115**	**115**
Total operating expenses	7,065	7,680	8,848	9,700	**9,819**	**10,913**
Operating income	4,871	4,256	6,414	5,562	**9,928**	**8,834**
Investment income	443	443	703	703	**1,803**	**1,803**
Gain on sale of Softimage, Inc.	–	–	–	–	**160**	**160**
Income before income taxes	5,314	4,699	7,117	6,265	**11,891**	**10,797**
Provision for income taxes	1,860	1,646	2,627	2,325	**4,106**	**3,723**
Net income	3,454	3,053	4,490	3,940	**7,785**	**7,074**
Preferred stock dividends	15	15	28	28	**28**	**28**
Net income available for common shareholders	$ 3,439	$ 3,038	$ 4,462	$ 3,912	**$ 7,757**	**$ 7,046**
Diluted earnings per share	$ 0.66	$ 0.58	$ 0.84	$ 0.73	**$ 1.42**	**$ 1.29**

The pro forma disclosures in the previous table include the amortization of the fair value of all options vested during 1997, 1998, and 1999, regardless of the grant date. If only options granted after 1996 were valued, as prescribed by SFAS 123, pro forma net income would have been $3,179 million, $4,019 million, and $7,109 million, and earnings per share would have been $0.61, $0.75, and $1.30 for 1997, 1998, and 1999.

The weighted average Black-Scholes value of options granted under the stock option plans during 1997, 1998, and 1999 was $5.86, $11.81, and $20.90. Value was estimated using an expected life of five years, no dividends, volatility of .32 in 1999 and 1998 and .30 in 1997, and risk-free interest rates of 6.5%, 5.7%, and 4.9% in 1997, 1998, and 1999.

NOTES continued (in millions, except per share amounts)

EARNINGS PER SHARE

> Basic earnings per share is computed on the basis of the weighted average number of common shares outstanding. Diluted earnings per share is computed on the basis of the weighted average number of common shares outstanding plus the effect of outstanding preferred shares using the "if-converted" method, assumed net-share settlement of common stock structured repurchases, and outstanding stock options using the "treasury stock" method.

The components of basic and diluted earnings per share were as follows:

Year Ended June 30	1997	1998	**1999**
Net income	$3,454	$4,490	**$7,785**
Preferred stock dividends	15	28	**28**
Net income available for common shareholders	$3,439	$4,462	**$7,757**
Weighted average outstanding shares of common stock	4,782	4,864	**5,028**
Dilutive effect of:			
Common stock under structured repurchases	–	6	**13**
Preferred stock	26	34	**16**
Employee stock options	436	458	**425**
Common stock and common stock equivalents	5,244	5,362	**5,482**
Earnings per share:			
Basic	$ 0.72	$ 0.92	**$ 1.54**
Diluted	$ 0.66	$ 0.84	**$ 1.42**

OPERATIONAL TRANSACTIONS

> In August 1997, Microsoft acquired WebTV Networks, Inc., an online service that enables consumers to experience the Internet through their televisions via set-top terminals based on proprietary technologies. A director of the Company owned 10% of WebTV. Microsoft paid $425 million in stock and cash for WebTV. The Company recorded an in-process technologies write-off of $296 million in the first quarter of fiscal 1998.

In August 1998, the Company sold a wholly-owned subsidiary, Softimage, Inc. to Avid Technology, Inc. and recorded a pretax gain of $160 million. As part of a transitional service agreement, Microsoft agreed to make certain development tools and management systems available to Avid for use in the Softimage, Inc. business.

In November 1998, Microsoft acquired LinkExchange, Inc., a leading provider of online marketing services to Web site owners and small and medium-sized businesses. Microsoft paid $265 million in stock. During fiscal 1999, Microsoft also acquired several other entities primarily providing online technologies and services. The Company did not record significant in-process technology write-offs in connection with these transactions.

In July 1999, Ticketmaster Online CitySearch, Inc. agreed to purchase certain online properties of Sidewalk in exchange for stock and warrants at a price to be determined upon closing.

NOTES continued

COMMITMENTS

> The Company has operating leases for most U.S. and international sales and support offices and certain equipment. Rental expense for operating leases was $92 million, $95 million, and $135 million in 1997, 1998, and 1999. Future minimum rental commitments under noncancelable leases, in millions of dollars, are: 2000, $133; 2001, $121; 2002, $97; 2003, $83; 2004, $75; and thereafter, $194.

In connection with the Company's communications infrastructure and the operation of online services, Microsoft has certain communication usage commitments. Future related minimum commitments, in millions of dollars, are: 2000, $125 and 2001, $22. Also, Microsoft has committed to certain volumes of outsourced telephone support and manufacturing of packaged product and has committed $275 million for constructing new buildings.

During 1996, Microsoft and National Broadcasting Company (NBC) established two MSNBC joint ventures: a 24-hour cable news and information channel and an interactive online news service. Microsoft agreed to pay $220 million over a five-year period for its interest in the cable venture, to pay one-half of operational funding of both joint ventures for a multiyear period, and to guarantee a portion of MSNBC debt.

CONTINGENCIES

> On October 7, 1997, Sun Microsystems, Inc. brought suit against Microsoft in the U.S. District Court for the Northern District of California. Sun's complaint alleges several claims against Microsoft, all related to the parties' relationship under a March 11, 1996 Technology License and Distribution Agreement (Agreement) concerning certain Java programming language technology. The Complaint seeks: a preliminary and permanent injunction against Microsoft distributing certain products with the Java Compatibility logo, and against distributing Internet Explorer 4.0 browser technology unless certain alleged obligations are met; an order compelling Microsoft to perform certain alleged obligations; an accounting; termination of the Agreement; and an award of damages, including compensatory, exemplary, and punitive damages, and liquidated damages of $35 million for the alleged source code disclosure.

On March 24, 1998, the court entered an order enjoining Microsoft from using the Java Compatibility logo on Internet Explorer 4.0 and the Microsoft Software Developers Kit (SDK) for Java 2.0. Microsoft has taken steps to fully comply with the order.

On November 17, 1998, the court entered an order granting Sun's request for a preliminary injunction, holding that Sun had established a likelihood of success on its copyright infringement claims, because Microsoft's use of Sun's technology in its products was beyond the scope of the parties' license agreement. The court ordered Microsoft to make certain changes in its products that include Sun's Java technology and to make certain changes in its Java software development tools. The court also enjoined Microsoft from entering into any licensing agreements that were conditioned on exclusive use of Microsoft's Java Virtual Machine. Microsoft appealed that ruling to the 9th Circuit on December 16, 1998. Oral argument on that appeal was held on June 16, 1999. In the interim, Microsoft is complying with the ruling and has not sought a stay of the injunction pending appeal. On December 18, 1998, Microsoft filed a motion requesting an extension of the 90-day compliance period for certain Microsoft products, which was granted in part in January 1999. Microsoft filed a motion on February 5, 1999, seeking clarification of the court's order that Microsoft would not be prevented from engaging in independent development of Java technology under the order. The court granted that motion. On July 23, 1999 the court also granted Microsoft's motion to increase the bond on the preliminary injunction from $15 million to $35 million.

NOTES continued

On January 22, 1999, Microsoft and Sun filed a series of summary judgment motions regarding the interpretation of the contract and other issues. On May 20, 1999, the court issued tentative rulings on three of the motions. In the preliminary rulings, the court (1) granted Sun's motion for summary judgment that prior versions of Internet Explorer 4.0, Windows 98, Windows NT, Visual J++® 6.0 development system, and the SDK for Java infringe Sun's copyrights, because they contain Sun's program code but do not pass Sun's compatibility tests and, therefore, Microsoft's use of Sun's technology is outside the scope of the Agreement and unlicensed; (2) granted Microsoft's motion that the Agreement authorizes Microsoft to distribute independently developed Java technology that is not subject to the compatibility obligations in the Agreement; and (3) denied Sun's motion for summary judgment on the meaning of certain provisions of the Agreement, tentatively adopting Microsoft's interpretation that Sun is required to deliver certain new Java technology, called "Supplemental Java Classes," in working order on Microsoft's then existing and commercially distributed virtual machine. On June 24, 1999, the court heard oral argument on the three tentative rulings. No final orders have been issued. At the hearing, the court also directed the parties to identify other pending summary judgment motions that the court should next consider. There are no other hearing or trial dates set.

On May 18, 1998, the Antitrust Division of the U.S. Department of Justice (DOJ) and a group of 20 state Attorneys General filed two antitrust cases against Microsoft in the U.S. District Court for the District of Columbia. The DOJ complaint alleges violations of Sections 1 and 2 of the Sherman Act. The DOJ complaint seeks declaratory relief as to the violations it asserts and preliminary and permanent injunctive relief regarding: the inclusion of Internet browsing software (or other software products) as part of Windows; the terms of agreements regarding non-Microsoft Internet browsing software (or other software products); taking or threatening "action adverse" in consequence of a person's failure to license or distribute Microsoft Internet browsing software (or other software product) or distributing competing products or cooperating with the government; and restrictions on the screens, boot-up sequence, or functions of Microsoft's operating system products. The state Attorneys General allege largely the same claims and various pendent state claims. The states seek declaratory relief and preliminary and permanent injunctive relief similar to that sought by the DOJ, together with statutory penalties under the state law claims. The foregoing description is qualified in its entirety by reference to the full text of the complaints and other papers on file in those actions, case numbers 98-1232 and 98-1233.

On May 22, 1998, Judge Jackson consolidated the two actions. The judge granted Microsoft's motion for summary judgment as to the states' monopoly leverage claim and permitted the remaining claims to proceed to trial. Trial began on October 19, 1998. Microsoft believes the claims are without merit and is defending against them vigorously. In other ongoing investigations, the DOJ and several state Attorneys General have requested information from Microsoft concerning various issues.

Caldera, Inc. filed a lawsuit against Microsoft in July 1996. It alleges Sherman Act violations relating to Microsoft licensing practices of the MS-DOS® operating system and Windows in the late 80s and early 90s – essentially the same complaints that resulted in the 1994 DOJ consent decree. Caldera claims to own the rights of Novell, Inc. and Digital Research, Inc. relating to DR-DOS and Novell DOS products. It also asserts a claim that Windows 95 is a technological tie of Windows and MS-DOS. Trial is scheduled for January 2000. Some partial summary judgment motions are pending. Microsoft believes the claims are without merit and is vigorously defending the case.

The Securities and Exchange Commission is conducting a non-public investigation into the Company's accounting reserve practices. Microsoft is also subject to various legal proceedings and claims that arise in the ordinary course of business.

Management currently believes that resolving these matters will not have a material adverse impact on the Company's financial position or its results of operations.

NOTES continued (in millions)

SEGMENT INFORMATION

Year Ended June 30	Windows Platforms	Productivity Applications and Developer	Consumer, Commerce, and Other	Reconciling Amounts	Consolidated
1997					
Revenue	$5,213	$5,992	$ 1,129	$ (398)	$11,936
1998					
Revenue	$6,236	$7,458	$ 1,765	$ (197)	$15,262
Operating income	3,661	4,824	(1,050)	(1,021)	6,414
1999					
Revenue	**$8,590**	**$8,686**	**$ 1,784**	**$ 687**	**$ 19,747**
Operating income	**6,007**	**5,568**	**(1,072)**	**(575)**	**9,928**

The Company's organizational structure and fundamental approach to business reflect the needs of its customers. As such, Microsoft has three major segments: Windows Platforms; Productivity Applications and Developer; and Consumer, Commerce, and Other. Windows Platforms includes the Business and Enterprise Division, which is primarily responsible for Windows NT and developing Windows 2000. Windows Platforms also includes the Consumer Windows Division, which oversees Windows 98 and Windows 95. Productivity Applications and Developer includes the Business Productivity Division, which is responsible for developing and marketing desktop applications, server applications, and developer tools. Consumer, Commerce, and Other products and services include primarily learning, entertainment, and PC input device products; WebTV and PC online access; and portal and other Internet services. Assets of the segment groups are not relevant for management of the businesses nor for disclosure. In addition, it is not practicable to discern operating income for 1997 for the above segments due to previous internal reorganizations.

Segment information is presented in accordance with SFAS 131, *Disclosures about Segments of an Enterprise and Related Information.* This standard is based on a management approach, which requires segmentation based upon the Company's internal organization and disclosure of revenue and operating income based upon internal accounting methods. The Company's financial reporting systems present various data for management to run the business, including profit and loss statements (P&Ls) prepared on a basis not consistent with generally accepted accounting principles. Reconciling items include certain elements of unearned revenue, the treatment of certain channel inventory amounts and estimates, and revenue from product support, consulting, and training and certification of system integrators. Additionally, the internal P&Ls use accelerated methods of depreciation and amortization, but do not reflect the charge for the ESO exercise price methodology previously employed by the Company.

Revenue attributable to U.S. operations includes shipments to customers in the United States, licensing to OEMs and certain multinational organizations, and exports of finished goods primarily to Asia, Latin America, and Canada. Revenue from U.S. operations totaled $7.8 billion, $10.1 billion, and $13.7 billion in 1997, 1998, and 1999. Revenue from outside the United States, excluding licensing to OEMs and certain multinational organizations and U.S. exports, totaled $4.1 billion, $5.2 billion, and $6.0 billion in 1997, 1998, and 1999.

Long-lived assets totaled $1.2 billion and $1.5 billion in the United States in 1998 and 1999 and $287 million and $154 million in other countries in 1998 and 1999.

QUARTERLY INFORMATION (in millions, except per share amounts, unaudited)

	Quarter Ended				
	Sept. 30	Dec. 31	Mar. 31	June 30	Year
1997					
Revenue	$2,405	$2,808	$3,365	$3,358	$11,936
Gross profit	1,923	2,250	2,782	2,811	9,766
Net income	614	741	1,042	1,057	3,454
Basic earnings per share	0.13	0.15	0.22	0.22	0.72
Diluted earnings per share	0.12	0.14	0.20	0.20	0.66
Common stock price per share:					
High	17.33	21.54	25.88	33.74	33.74
Low	13.44	16.36	20.19	22.44	13.44
1998					
Revenue	$3,334	$3,792	$3,984	$4,152	$15,262
Gross profit	2,800	3,179	3,344	3,479	12,802
Net income	663	1,133	1,337	1,357	4,490
Basic earnings per share	0.14	0.24	0.27	0.27	0.92
Diluted earnings per share	0.13	0.21	0.25	0.25	0.84
Common stock price per share:					
High	37.69	36.66	45.47	54.28	54.28
Low	30.82	29.50	31.10	40.94	29.50
1999					
Revenue	**$4,193**	**$5,195**	**$4,595**	**$5,764**	**$19,747**
Gross profit	**3,544**	**4,407**	**3,887**	**5,095**	**16,933**
Net income	**1,683**	**1,983**	**1,917**	**2,202**	**7,785**
Basic earnings per share	**0.34**	**0.40**	**0.38**	**0.43**	**1.54**
Diluted earnings per share	**0.31**	**0.36**	**0.35**	**0.40**	**1.42**
Common stock price per share:					
High	**59.81**	**72.00**	**94.63**	**95.63**	**95.63**
Low	**47.25**	**48.13**	**68.00**	**75.50**	**47.25**

The Company's common stock is traded on The Nasdaq Stock Market under the symbol MSFT. On July 31, 1999, there were 92,169 registered holders of record of the Company's common stock. The Company has not paid cash dividends on its common stock.

REPORTS OF MANAGEMENT AND INDEPENDENT AUDITORS

Management is responsible for preparing the Company's financial statements and the other information that appears in this annual report. Management believes that the financial statements fairly reflect the form and substance of transactions and reasonably present the Company's financial condition and results of operations in conformity with generally accepted accounting principles. Management has included in the Company's financial statements amounts that are based on estimates and judgments, which it believes are reasonable under the circumstances.

The Company maintains a system of internal accounting policies, procedures, and controls intended to provide reasonable assurance, at appropriate cost, that transactions are executed in accordance with Company authorization and are properly recorded and reported in the financial statements, and that assets are adequately safeguarded.

Deloitte & Touche LLP audits the Company's financial statements in accordance with generally accepted auditing standards and provides an objective, independent review of the Company's internal controls and the fairness of its reported financial condition and results of operations.

The Microsoft Board of Directors has an Audit Committee composed of nonmanagement Directors. The Committee meets with financial management, internal auditors, and the independent auditors to review internal accounting controls and accounting, auditing, and financial reporting matters.

Gregory B. Maffei
Senior Vice President, Finance and Administration; Chief Financial Officer

To the Board of Directors and Stockholders of Microsoft Corporation:

We have audited the accompanying balance sheets of Microsoft Corporation and subsidiaries as of June 30, 1998 and 1999, and the related statements of income, cash flows, and stockholders' equity for each of the three years ended June 30, 1999, appearing on pages 17 and 27 through 42. These financial statements are the responsibility of the Company's management. Our responsibility is to express an opinion on these financial statements based on our audits.

We conducted our audits in accordance with generally accepted auditing standards. Those standards require that we plan and perform the audit to obtain reasonable assurance about whether the financial statements are free of material misstatement. An audit includes examining, on a test basis, evidence supporting the amounts and disclosures in the financial statements. An audit also includes assessing the accounting principles used and significant estimates made by management, as well as evaluating the overall financial statement presentation. We believe that our audits provide a reasonable basis for our opinion.

In our opinion, such financial statements present fairly, in all material respects, the financial position of Microsoft Corporation and subsidiaries as of June 30, 1998 and 1999, and the results of their operations and their cash flows for each of the three years ended June 30, 1999 in conformity with generally accepted accounting principles.

Deloitte & Touche LLP
Seattle, Washington
July 19, 1999

DIRECTORS AND OFFICERS

DIRECTORS

William H. Gates, III
Chairman of the Board;
Chief Executive Officer,
Microsoft Corporation

Paul G. Allen
Chairman of the Board,
Vulcan Northwest Inc.

Jill Barad
President and
Chief Executive Officer,
Mattel, Inc.

Richard A. Hackborn
Chairman-Elect of the Board,
Hewlett-Packard Company

David F. Marquardt
General Partner,
August Capital and
Technology Venture Investors

Wm. G. Reed, Jr.
Chairman of the Board,
Simpson Investment
Company (retired)

Jon A. Shirley
President and
Chief Operating Officer,
Microsoft Corporation
(retired)

EXECUTIVE OFFICERS

William H. Gates, III
Chairman of the Board;
Chief Executive Officer

Steven A. Ballmer
President

Robert J. Herbold
Executive Vice President;
Chief Operating Officer

Frank M. (Pete) Higgins
Group Vice President
(on leave)

Paul A. Maritz
Group Vice President,
Developer

Jeffrey S. Raikes
Group Vice President,
Sales and Support

James E. Allchin
Senior Vice President,
Platforms

Orlando Ayala Lozano
Senior Vice President,
South Pacific and Americas

Joachim Kempin
Senior Vice President,
OEM Sales

Michel Lacombe
Senior Vice President;
President, Microsoft
Europe, Middle East,
and Africa

Gregory B. Maffei
Senior Vice President,
Finance and Administration;
Chief Financial Officer

Robert L. Muglia
Senior Vice President,
Business Productivity

Craig Mundie
Senior Vice President,
Consumer Strategy

William H. Neukom
Senior Vice President,
Law and Corporate
Affairs; Secretary

Bernard P. Vergnes
Senior Vice President;
Chairman, Microsoft
Europe, Middle East,
and Africa

VICE PRESIDENTS

Robert J. Bach
Home and Retail

Dick Brass
eMerging Technologies

Brad Chase
Consumer and Commerce

Frank M. Clegg
Central United States
and Canada

David Cole
Consumer Windows

John G. Connors
Enterprise

Jean-Philippe Courtois
Customer Marketing

Jon DeVaan
Consumer and Commerce

Richard R. Devenuti
Information Technology;
Chief Information Officer

Richard W. Fade
OEM Multinational Accounts

Dianne Gregg
Eastern United States

Paul H. Gross
Server Applications

William V. Henningsgaard
Western United States
and South Pacific

Laura Jennings
Planning

Kevin Johnson
Product Support Services

Pieter Knook
Asia

Harel Kodesh
Productivity Appliances

Thomas Koll
Network Solutions

Bruce A. Leak
WebTV

John Leftwich
Europe, Middle East,
and Africa Marketing

Lewis Levin
TransPoint

Moshe Lichtman
Consumer and Commerce,
International

Nick N. MacPhee
Operations

Mich Mathews
Corporate Communications

Robert L. McDowell
Enterprise Business
Relationships

Tod Nielsen
Developer Marketing

Umberto Paolucci
Europe, Middle East,
and Africa

Richard F. Rashid
Research

Darryl E. Rubin
Software Strategy

Stephen A. Schiro
Home and Retail Sales

Steven J. Sinofsky
Office

Charles Stevens
Business Solutions

Rick Thompson
Hardware

Rich Tong
Business Audience
Management

Brian Valentine
Business and Enterprise

David Vaskevitch
Distributed Applications
Platform

Henry P. Vigil
Consumer Strategy
and Partnerships

Christopher L. Williams
Human Resources

Deborah N. Willingham
Business and
Enterprise Marketing

glossary

A

Activity-based costing (ABC). A method of attributing costs to products based on first assigning costs of resources to activities and then costs of activities to products.

Activity-based management (ABM). The identification and use of cost drivers and performance measures to manage the costs, quality, and timeliness of activities.

Appraisal costs. Costs of quality that specifically relate to the effort of inspecting, testing, and sampling activities performed in order to identify and remove low-quality products and services from the system.

Asset turnover ratio. An overall measure of how effectively assets are used during a period; computed by dividing revenue by total assets.

B

Balanced Scorecard. A new management model designed to link together performance measures for financial, customer, internal process, and learning/growth perspectives that are unique to an organization's particular strategy.

Batch-level activities. Activities that take place in order to support a batch or production run, regardless of the size.

Benchmarking. A performance evaluation process used by companies to target areas for improvement by comparing the company's financial and operating performance against the performance of other companies or the performance of internal departments against each other.

Break-even point. The amount of sales at which total costs of the number of units sold equal total revenues; the point at which there is no profit or loss.

Budget. A quantitative expression of a plan of action that shows how a firm or an organization will acquire and use resources over some specified period of time.

Budget committee. A management group responsible for establishing budgeting policy and for coordinating the preparation of budgets.

C

Capability costs. Costs necessary to have the capability to produce a particular product or to provide a particular service. Capability costs are also known as the costs of product line activities.

Capital. The total amount of money or other resources owned or used to acquire future income or benefits.

Capital budgeting. Systematic planning for long-term investments in operating assets.

Capital rationing. Allocating limited resources among ranked acceptable investments.

Cash budget. A schedule of expected cash receipts and disbursements during the budget period.

Cash inflows. Any current or expected revenues or savings directly associated with an investment.

Cash outflows. The initial cost and other expected outlays associated with an investment.

Centralized company. An organization in which top management makes most of the major decisions for the entire company rather than delegating them to managers at lower levels.

Channel. The distribution line that a product travels from the original manufacturer to the eventual end-user customer. The channel is typically composed of a manufacturer, a wholesaler, a retailer, and the end-user customer.

Common costs. Manufacturing overhead costs, such as executive salaries or property taxes, that cannot be attributed to products. Costs of facility support activities are common costs.

Contribution margin. The difference between total sales and variable costs; the portion of sales revenue available to cover fixed costs and provide a profit.

Contribution-margin ratio. The percentage of net sales revenue left after variable costs are deducted; the contribution margin divided by net sales revenue.

Controlling. Implementing management plans and identifying how plans compare with actual performance.

Conversion costs. The costs of converting raw materials to finished products; include direct labor and manufacturing overhead costs.

Cost behavior. The way in which a cost is affected by changes in activity levels.

Cost center. An organizational unit in which a manager has control over and is held accountable for costs.

Cost driver. A factor that determines an activity cost. An activity can have more than one cost driver.

Cost of capital. The average cost of a firm's debt and equity capital; equals the rate of return that a company must earn in order to satisfy the demands of its owners and creditors.

Cost of goods manufactured schedule. A schedule supporting the income statement; summarizes the total cost of goods manufactured during a period, including direct materials, direct labor, and manufacturing overhead

Costs of quality (COQ). Costs spent to achieve high quality of products and services, as well as costs spent when products fail to have high quality. The four types of costs of quality are prevention costs, appraisal costs, internal failure costs, and external failure costs.

Cost-volume-profit (CVP) analysis. Techniques for determining how changes in revenues, costs, and level of activity affect the profitability of an organization.

Critical resource factor. The resource that limits operating capacity by its availability.

Cross-subsidization. A distortion of costs that occurs when costs of one product are erroneously assigned to another product.

Curvilinear costs. Variable costs that do not vary in direct proportion to changes in activity level but at decreasing or increasing rates due to economies of scale, productivity changes, and so on.

Cycle time. The total time a product spends moving through a particular process or cycle within the organization, such as the product design cycle, the production cycle, or the order and delivery cycle.

D

Days in inventory. Average number of days of sales that can be made using only the supply of inventory on hand.

Death spiral. A series of management decisions based on bad information that results in reducing or removing the activities or segments from the organization that are actually profitable.

Decentralized company. An organization in which managers at all levels have the authority to make decisions concerning the operations for which they are responsible.

Deregulation. The term used to describe the process of removing restrictions on competition in the marketplace for a particular industry.

Differential costs. Future costs that change as a result of a decision; also called incremental or relevant costs.

Direct costs. Costs that are specifically traceable to a unit of business or segment being analyzed.

Direct labor. Wages that are paid to those who physically work on the direct materials to transform them into a finished product and are traceable to specific products.

Direct labor budget. A schedule of direct labor requirements for the budget period.

Direct materials. Materials that become part of the product and are traceable to it.

Direct materials budget. A schedule of direct materials to be used during the budget period and direct materials to be purchased during that period.

Discounted cash flow methods. Capital budgeting techniques that take into account the time value of money by comparing discounted cash flows.

Disposable income. Income left after withholdings and fixed expenses have been subtracted from gross salary; the amount left to cover variable expenditures.

E

Economic order quantity (EOQ). A specific calculation used to determine the most cost-effective size of a purchase order. The EOQ balances the costs of placing an order against the costs of carrying inventory in the organization.

Economic profit. The difference between net operating profit and holding costs of inventory and other asset investments. Note that generally accepted accounting principles (GAAP) do not formally recognize opportunity costs such as holding costs.

Economic Value Added (EVA™). A commercialized performance measurement system that emphasizes the incremental profits an organization creates over and above the profit required to cover its costs of capital.

Equivalent units of production. A method used in a process costing system to measure the production output during a period. Equivalent units of production essentially measures the "work done" by the center or department in terms of units of output.

Estimated manufacturing overhead. Budgeted manufacturing overhead costs that are used to establish the predetermined overhead rate.

Evaluating. Analyzing results, rewarding performance, and identifying problems.

Exception report. A report that highlights variances from, or exceptions to, the budget.

External failure costs. Costs of quality that specifically relate to the costs that occur when low-quality products and services fail after production and delivery to customers.

F

Facility support activities. Activities necessary to have a facility in place in order to participate in the development and production of products or services. However, these activities are not related to any particular line of products or services. Costs of facility support activities are often called common costs.

Finished goods inventory. Inventory that has completed the production process and is ready for sale to customers.

Fixed costs. Costs that remain constant in total, regardless of activity level, at least over a certain range of activity.

Flexible budget. A quantified plan that projects revenues and costs for varying levels of activity.

G

Goal congruence. The selection of goals for responsibility centers that are consistent, or congruent, with those of the company as a whole.

H

Hierarchical Product Cost Model. A method of categorizing costs based on types of activities. Activity types include unit-level activities, batch-level activities, product line activities, and facility support activities.

High-low method. A method of segregating the fixed and variable components of a mixed cost by analyzing the costs at the highest and the lowest activity levels within a relevant range.

Holding costs. The financial opportunity costs that result from investing money in an asset such as inventory. Whatever income the money could generate in an alternative investment is the holding cost of the current investment.

Hurdle rate. The minimum rate of return that an investment must provide in order to be acceptable.

I

Indirect costs. Costs normally incurred for the benefit of several segments within the organization; sometimes called common costs or joint costs.

Indirect labor. Labor that is necessary to a manufacturing or service business but is not directly related to the actual production of the manufactured or service product.

Indirect materials. Materials that are necessary to a manufacturing or service business but are not directly included in or are not a significant part of the actual product.

Industry volume variance. The part of the sales volume variance that accounts for the difference between the expected market share of the total market and the expected or standard quantity of goods sold.

Interest. The payment (cost) for the use of money.

Internal failure costs. Costs of quality that specifically relate to the expenses that occur when low-quality products and services fail before production and delivery to customers.

Internal rate of return. The "true" discount rate that will produce a net present value of zero when applied to the cash flows of investment inventory goods held for resale.

Internal rate of return method. A capital budgeting technique that uses discounted cash flows to find the "true" discount rate of an investment; this true rate produces a net present value of zero.

Interpolation. A method of determining the internal rate of return when the factor for that rate lies between the factors given in the present value table.

Inventory shrinkage. The disorder, spoilage, and theft that result when a company chooses to maintain inventory on site, resulting in additional out-of-pockets costs to replace inventory.

Inventory turnover (stockturns). The number of times the inventory in the organization "turns over" during a period of time. It is often easier to think of inventory turnover as the number of times a dollar invested is sold during a period of time. Inventory turnover is computed as Cost of goods sold ÷ Average inventory value.

Investment center. An organizational unit in which a manager has control over and is held accountable for costs, revenues, and assets.

J

Job order costing. A method of product costing whereby each job, product, or batch of products is costed separately.

Just-in-time (JIT). A management philosophy that emphasizes removing all waste of effort, time, and inventory costs from the organization. One obvious result of JIT is the reduction or removal of needless inventory in a production system.

L

Labor efficiency variance. The extent to which the actual labor used varies from the standard quantity; computed by multiplying the difference between the actual quantity and the standard quantity of labor by the standard rate.

Labor rate variance. The extent to which the actual labor rate varies from the standard rate for the quantity of labor used; computed by multiplying the difference between the actual rate and the standard rate by the quantity of labor used.

Lagging indicators. Measures that indicate the success of past business activities. Lagging indicators are related to the concept "outcome measures."

Lead time. Generally, the time interval between initiating a request and finally fulfilling the request.

Leading indicators. Measures that indicate the potential success of future business activities. Leading indicators are related to the concept "leading measures."

Leading measures. Measures that, if successfully implemented, will support desired performance in other business activities. Note that some leading measures can also serve as outcome measures.

Least-cost decision. A decision to undertake the project with the smallest negative net present value.

Least squares method. A method of segregating the fixed and variable portions of a mixed cost; the regression line, a line of averages, is statistically fitted through all cost points.

Life cycle costing. The process of measuring all costs involved in creating, producing, and using a product or service. Life cycle costing is not limited to costs incurred by the organization measuring these costs but also includes all costs incurred by the suppliers and the customers of the product or service.

Line of credit. An arrangement whereby a bank agrees to loan an amount of money (up to a certain limit) on demand for short periods of time, usually less than a year.

Logistics. The management process involved in obtaining, managing, and transporting inventory and other assets in organizations.

M

Management by exception. The strategy of focusing attention on significant deviations from a standard.

Manufacturing organizations. Organizations that focus on using labor and/or machinery to convert raw materials into marketable products.

Manufacturing overhead. All costs incurred in the manufacturing process other than direct materials and direct labor.

Manufacturing overhead budget. A schedule of production costs other than those for direct labor and direct materials.

Manufacturing overhead rate. The rate at which manufacturing overhead is assigned to products; equals estimated manufacturing overhead for the period divided by the number of units of the activity base being used.

Market share. The percentage share one company receives of the total sales revenue in the economy for a particular product or service.

Market share variance. The part of the sales volume variance that accounts for the difference between the actual market share of each product sold and the expected market share of each product sold.

Materials price variance. The extent to which the actual price varies from the standard price for the quantity of materials purchased or used; computed by multiplying the difference between the actual and standard prices by the quantity purchased or used.

Materials quantity variance. The extent to which the actual quantity of materials varies from the standard quantity; computed by multiplying the difference between the actual quantity and the standard quantity of materials used by the standard price.

Merchandising organizations. Organizations that focus on procuring tangible products, then distributing them to customers. These customers may include individuals or other business organizations such as manufacturing organizations.

Mixed costs. Costs that contain both variable and fixed cost components.

N

Net operating profit. The difference between normal business sales and normal business expenses.

Net present value. The difference between the present values of an investment's expected cash inflows and outflows.

Net present value method. A capital budgeting technique that uses discounted cash flows to compare the present values of an investment's expected cash inflows and outflows.

Non-value-added activities. Unnecessary activities in a production or service process that customers typically do not see or care about and for which they are unwilling to pay.

O

Operating (master) budget. A network of many separate schedules and budgets that together constitute the overall operating and financing plan for the coming period.

Operating leverage. The extent to which fixed costs are part of a company's cost structure; the higher the proportion of fixed costs to variable costs, the faster income increases or decreases with sales volume.

Operational budgeting. Managerial planning decisions regarding current operations and those of the immediate future (typically one year or less) that are characterized by regularity and frequency.

Opportunity costs. The benefits lost or forfeited as a result of selecting one alternative course of action over another.

Outcome measures. Measures of desired outcome performance in activities critical to an organization's strategic goals. Note that some outcome measures are also leading measures to support desired performance in other business activities.

Out-of-pocket costs. Costs that require an outlay of cash or other resources.

Overapplied manufacturing overhead. The excess of applied manufacturing overhead (based on a predetermined application rate) over the actual manufacturing overhead costs for a period.

Overhead cost allocation. A system of assigning the indirect costs of the manufacturing or service process to the actual product being created for the customer.

P

Payback method. A capital budgeting technique that determines the amount of time it takes the net cash inflows of an investment to repay the investment cost.

Performance measures. A general term used to describe all measures designed to capture information about performance related to a particular activity or process.

Period costs. Costs not directly related to a product, service, or asset that are charged as expenses to the income statement in the period in which they are incurred.

Per-unit contribution margin. The excess of the sales price of one unit over its variable costs.

Planning. Outlining the activities that need to be performed for an organization to achieve its objectives.

Predetermined overhead rate. A rate at which estimated manufacturing overhead costs are assigned to products throughout the year; equals total estimated manufacturing overhead costs divided by a suitable allocation base, such as number of units produced, direct labor hours, direct materials used, or direct labor costs.

Prevention costs. Costs of quality that specifically relate to the effort to ensure that processes are performed correctly the first time and that products and services meet customers' expectations.

Prime costs. The direct costs that are "primarily seen" in the product (i.e., direct materials and direct labor).

Process costing. A method of product costing whereby costs are accumulated by process or work centers and averaged over all products manufactured in a center or department during a particular production period.

Product costs. Costs associated with products or services offered.

Product line activities. Activities that take place in order to support a product line, regardless of the number of batches or individual units actually produced. Costs of product line activities are also known as capability costs.

Production budget. A schedule of production requirements for the budget period.

Production cost report. A document that compiles all the costs of a manufacturing center for a particular production period. The information on this report is used to control and evaluate production costs, as well as transfer costs and units of output from one manufacturing center to another.

Production prioritizing. Management's continual evaluation of the profitability of the various product lines and divisions within an organization so that products or divisions that are performing below expectations can be analyzed to identify problems and potential solutions.

Profit center. An organizational unit in which a manager has control over and is held accountable for both costs and revenues.

Profit graph. A graph that shows how profits vary with changes in volume.

Profit margin. An overall measure of the profitability of operations during a period; computed by dividing profit by revenue.

Profit margin (operating performance) ratio. An overall measure of the profitability of operations during a period; computed by dividing net income by revenue.

Profitability index. The present value of net cash inflows divided by the cost of an investment.

Purchases budget. A schedule of projected purchases over the budget period.

R

Ranking. The ordering of acceptable investment alternatives from most to least desirable.

Raw materials inventory. The inventory of raw materials that have not yet begun the production process.

Regression line. On a scattergraph, the straight line that most closely expresses the relationship between the variables.

Relevant range. The range of operating level, or volume of activity, over which the relationship between total costs (variable plus fixed) and activity level is approximately linear.

Reorder point. The point at which the inventory level in the organization drops low enough to trigger a new purchase order.

Residual income. The amount of net income earned above a specified minimum rate of return on assets; used to evaluate investment centers.

Responsibility accounting. A system of evaluating performance; managers are held accountable for the costs, revenues, assets, or other elements over which they have control.

Responsibility center. An organizational unit in which a manager has control over and is held accountable for performance.

Retailers. Second-tier merchants who typically purchase products from wholesalers to distribute to end-user customers. Many large retailers, however, will often bypass wholesalers to purchase products directly from original manufacturers.

Return on investment (ROI). A measure of operating performance and efficiency in utilizing assets; computed in its simplest form by dividing net income by average total assets.

Return on sales revenue. A measure of operating performance; computed by dividing net income by total sales revenue. Similar to profit margin.

Revenue budget. A service entity's budget that identifies how much revenue (and often cash) will be generated during a period.

Robust quality. The capability of a product to perform according to customer expectations regardless of surroundings and circumstances.

S

Safety stock. The minimal level of inventory required to ensure against the organization running out of inventory in the case of unforeseen problems in receiving its next purchase order.

Sales budget. A schedule of projected sales over the budget period.

Sales mix. The relative proportion of total units sold (or total sales dollars) that is represented by each of a company's products.

Sales mix variance. The part of the sales volume variance that accounts for the difference between the actual quantity of each product sold and the percentage of the actual total products sold that was expected to be represented by each product based on expected market share of the products.

Sales price variance. The difference between the actual price and the expected or standard price multiplied by the actual quantity; measures the part of the difference between expected and actual sales revenue that is due to differences between expected and actual prices of goods.

Sales volume variance. The difference between the actual quantity and the expected quantity multiplied by the expected or standard price; measures the part of the difference between expected and actual sales revenue that is due to the difference between expected and actual volume of goods sold.

Sales yield variance. On a combined product basis, that part of the sales volume variance that is not explained by the mix of products sold. The sales yield variance is the amount of sales volume variance explained by differences between actual and expected market share and total industry sales. The sales yield variance is further broken down into the industry volume variance and market share variance and is also referred to as the "final volume variance."

Scattergraph (visual-fit) method. A method of segregating the fixed and variable components of a mixed cost by plotting on a graph total costs at several activity levels and drawing a regression line through the points.

Screening. Determining whether a capital investment meets a minimum standard of financial acceptability.

Segment. Any part of an organization requiring separate reports for evaluation by management.

Segment margin. The difference between segment revenue and direct segment costs; a measure of the segment's contribution to cover indirect fixed costs and provide profits.

Segment-margin income statement. An income statement that identifies costs directly chargeable to a segment and further divides them into variable and fixed cost behavior patterns.

Segment-margin ratio. The segment margin divided by the segment's net sales revenue; a measure of the efficiency of the segment's operating performance, and therefore of its profitability.

Selling and administrative expense budget. A schedule of all nonproduction spending expected to occur during the budget period.

Sensitivity analysis. A method of assessing the reasonableness of a decision that was based upon estimates; involves calculating how far reality can differ from an estimate without invalidating the decision.

Service organizations. Organizations that focus on delivery of marketable services, such as legal advice or education, to individuals or other organizations.

Service overhead budget. The budget, prepared by service entities, that identifies projected costs associated with providing the service.

Six sigma quality. A measure of quality based on statistical analysis. Products or services with six sigma quality have no more than 3.4 defects per million opportunities (e.g., parts or events).

Special order. An order that may be priced below the normal selling price in order to utilize excess capacity and thereby contribute to company profits.

Standard cost card. An itemization of the components of the standard cost of a product.

Standard cost system. A cost-accumulation system in which standard costs are used as product costs instead of actual costs.

Static budget. A quantified plan that projects revenues and costs for only one level of activity.

Statistical process control (SPC). A statistical technique for identifying and measuring the quality status of a process by evaluating its output to determine if serious problems exist in the process.

Stepped costs. Costs that change in total in a stair-step fashion (in large amounts) with changes in volume of activity.

Strategic planning. Broad, long-range planning, usually conducted by top management.

Sunk costs. Costs, such as depreciation, that are past costs and do not change as the result of a future decision.

Supplies budget. The budget, prepared by service entities, that identifies projected supplies expenses over the budget period.

T

Taguchi quality loss function. A method developed by Genichi Taguchi for measuring the actual size of all external failure costs, particularly the opportunity costs of lost customer sales that result from dissatisfied customers.

Target costing. A costing approach that designs a product to meet specific cost objectives based on target market prices less the target margin.

Target income. A profit level desired by management.

Target market price. The price that consumers will pay for a product or service.

Theory of constraints (TOC). A management philosophy that focuses on constraint resources and holds that they should operate at full capacity.

Total cost. The total variable and fixed costs incurred in making a product or providing a service.

Total quality management (TQM). A management philosophy focused on increasing profitability by improving the quality of products and processes and increasing customer satisfaction, while promoting the well-being and growth of employees.

Total variable manufacturing overhead variance. The extent to which actual manufacturing overhead varies from the amount included in work-in-process inventory; the difference between actual and applied variable manufacturing overhead.

U

Unadjusted rate of return method. A capital budgeting technique in which a rate of return is calculated by dividing the increase in the average annual net income a project will generate by the initial investment cost.

Underapplied manufacturing overhead. The excess of actual manufacturing overhead costs over the applied overhead costs for a period (based on a predetermined application rate).

Unit-based costing (UBC). The traditional method of allocating manufacturing overhead using an approach that is essentially based on the number of units produced.

Unit-level activities. Activities that take place each time a unit of product is produced.

V

Value-added activities. Necessary activities in a production or service process that customers identify as valuable and for which they are willing to pay.

Variable cost rate. The change in cost divided by the change in activity; the slope of the regression line.

Variable costs. Costs that change in total in direct proportion to changes in activity level.

Variable manufacturing overhead efficiency variance. The difference between manufacturing overhead costs expected at actual hours and manufacturing overhead costs expected at standard hours.

Variable manufacturing overhead spending variance. The difference between actual manufacturing overhead incurred and the standard manufacturing overhead for the actual activity level.

Variance. Any deviation from standard.

W

Wages and salaries budget. The budget, prepared by service entities, that identifies projected labor costs involved directly in providing the service over the budget period.

Wholesalers. Top-tier merchants who typically deal directly with the original manufacturers to distribute products to retailers.

Work-in-process inventory. Inventory that is partly completed in the production process, yet not ready for sale to customers.

appendix c

CHECK FIGURES*

CHAPTER 1

Exercises

1-2 N/A
1-4 N/A
1-6 N/A
1-8 N/A
1-10 100 baby chairs
1-12 (1) Total manufacturing cost per bat = $51.80
1-14 (1) X-96 segment profit = $11,300

CHAPTER 2

Exercises

2-2 (3) $500 per unit
2-4 (3) $30.25
2-6 (2) Total cost = $60,000
2-8 (1) Profit = $17
2-10 (4) Additional fixed costs = $100,000
2-12 (1) (c) 25,000 units
2-14 (4) Loss of approximately $7,500
2-16 N/A
2-18 (7) Profit = $141,750
2-20 (2) $19.69
2-22 (1) Break-even units = 17,857 units

Problems

2-2 (1) Variable cost = $4 per unit
2-4 (1) Contribution margin = $110,000
2-6 (1) Loss = ($18,400)
2-8 (3) (b) $4,500,000
2-10 (1) Y = 900 bags
2-12 (7) Profit = $850,000
2-14 (1) Profit = $18,750
2-16 (4) 153,033 units
2-18 (2) Total sales = $500,000

CHAPTER 3

Exercises

3-2 (1) Predetermined manufacturing overhead rate = $5
3-4 (1) (b) 2002 Predetermined overhead rate = 26%
3-6 N/A
3-8 (3) Applied manufacturing overhead = $66,500
3-10 (3) Cost per unit = $194
3-12 (1) Overhead rate = $81.82 per direct labor hour
3-14 (1) (c) 2003 = $2.01 per mile
3-16 (1) Overhead rate = $41.33 per consulting hour
3-18 (1) Equivalent units of production for conversion costs = 582 units

Problems

3-2 (1) (g) Credit to Manufacturing Overhead = $400
3-4 (3) Underapplied manufacturing overhead = $12,500
3-6 (3) Total cost of Job #29 = $78,304
3-8 (5) Operating income = $28,003
3-10 (4) Debit to Work-in-Process Services = $21,000
3-12 (3) Overhead = $3,000 debit balance
3-14 (3) Total costs transferred out = $108,760
3-16 Equivalent units of production for direct materials costs = 2,750 units

CHAPTER 4

Exercises

4-2 (2) Present value = $247,314
4-4 Unadjusted rate of return = 22.5%
4-6 Alternative 2 net present value = ($86,024)
4-8 Average cost of capital = 16.7%
4-10 (1) Net persent value = ($100,811)
4-12 N/A
4-14 N/A
4-16 Investment B profitability index = 1.075

Problems

4-2 Net present value = $12,060
4-4 (1) IRR = 10.55%
4-6 Internal rate on return = 4.5 factor
4-8 Alternative 2 = $32,104
4-10 (1) Net present value to rent = $308,174
4-12 (2) Net present value = $380

*Note: Check figures are provided for even-numbered exercises and problems, where applicable.

4-14 (1) Project E net present value = $9,000
4-16 (1) Payback period = 5.2 years
4-18 (2) Net present value at 10 percent = $3,345

CHAPTER 5

Exercises

5-2 (1) Net income = $270
5-4 Quarter 4 EGA units to be produced = 2,175
5-6 VHS total direct materials cost = $170,000
5-8 March total direct labor cost = $18,740
5-10 Projected cash balance July 31, 2003 = $470,000
5-12 (1) Deficiency of cash = ($42,900)
5-14 Income before income taxes = $165,000
5-16 (2) Net increase in cash = $41,650
5-18 (1) Budgeted salary expense = $180,000

Problems

5-2 (2) 34 months
5-4 Total cost of material used = $4,050
5-6 (2) Direct materials costs, bolts = $168.75
5-8 (3) June budgeted purchases (units) = 3,450
5-10 January excess cash = $45,100
5-12 (1) Net operating profit = $140,050
5-14 (2) Additional net income = $16,714
5-16 Expected income per doctor at 34,000 visits = $158,333

CHAPTER 6

Exercises

6-2 (3) Cost of goods sold = $460,000
6-4 Asset turnover = 4.44
6-6 Profitability percentage = 37.9%
6-8 Financial holding costs = $16,250
6-10 EOQ = 872 tires
6-12 559 backpacks

Problems

6-2 (2) Cost of goods manufactured = $1,138,050
6-4 (1) (a) Direct labor cost = $310,000
6-6 (2) Profitability percentage = 74.3%

CHAPTER 7

Exercises

7-2 N/A
7-4 (1) Product A manufacturing overhead = $45,000
7-6 (1) Product Z gross margin = $50,000
7-8 Low quality total expected cost of quality = $86,000
7-10 N/A

Problems

7-2 (1) Agricultural products gross margin = $150,000
7-4 (2) Product J gross margin = ($50,000)
7-6 (3) Machine setups cost per activity = $2,500
7-8 (2) Product 1 manufacturing overhead costs = $147,720
7-10 (2) Lawn Pipe total overhead costs = $151,220
7-12 (1) Opportunity costs at an error rate of 1 percent = $21,600

CHAPTER 8

Exercises

8-2 New machine total relevant costs = $930,000
8-4 (2) Expected increase in profit if order is accepted = $40,000
8-6 (1) Total cost using total-cost analysis to buy the monitor = $1,380,000
8-8 Alternative 3 net expected benefit = $340,000
8-10 Product line contribution = $120,000
8-12 (2) Far Out maximum production = 18,000 units
8-14 (2) 10 engines per month

Problems

8-2 (2) Total cost per unit to make = $2.10
8-4 (2) Alternative 1 differential costs = $565,000
8-6 (1) Skis and ski boots net income = $60,000
8-8 Net cost of closing = ($142,000)
8-10 (1) Y-707 contribution margin = $17.25
8-12 (2) Charger lost contribution = ($150,000)
8-14 N/A

CHAPTER 9

Exercises

9-2 (1) Price variance = $250U
9-4 N/A
9-6 (1) Price variance = $9,000F
9-8 (3) Efficiency variance = $10,200F
9-10 N/A

9-12 N/A
9-14 N/A
9-16 (1) North's segment margin = $10,000
9-18 Caramel Wafers' sales price variance = $10,000U
9-20 Sales mix variance = $1,820U
9-22 (1) South Division asset turnover ratio = 4.0
9-24 (1) Proposal 1 residual income = $1,000
9-26 (2) Overapplied by $900

Problems

9-2 (1) (b) Quantity variance = $800U
9-4 (d) Standard cost per direct labor hour = $3.50 per hour
9-6 (2) Manufacturing rate variance = $420U
9-8 (4) Actual labor rate per hour = $6.20
9-10 Grocery department total margin = $70,000
9-12 (2) Product Y sales price variance = $760F
9-14 (1) Atlantic Division ROI = 17.5%
9-16 (1) (a) ROI without investment = 19.4%
9-18 (d) Residual income = $3,950
9-20 (1) (a) Total residual income = $25,000
9-22 (1) August spending variance = $83,000U

CHAPTER 10

Not Applicable

indexes

SUBJECT INDEX

D

O

P

T

U

V

W

indexes

REAL WORLD COMPANY INDEX

indexes

INTERNET INDEX*

*Note: These Web site addresses may also be accessed at **http://albrecht.swcollege.com**